World Faiths

WORLD FAITHS

SECOND EDITION

S. A. Nigosian

Victoria College, University of Toronto

St. Martin's Press
New York

Executive editor: Don Reisman
Development editor: Kristin Bowen
Managing editor: Patricia Mansfield-Phelan
Project editor: Diana Puglisi
Production supervisor: Alan Fischer
Art director: Sheree Goodman
Photo research: Gene Crofts
Cover art and design: Rod Hernandez

Library of Congress Catalog Card Number: 92-62755

Manufactured in the United States of America.

8 7   ⁻
f

For information, write:
St. Martin's Press, Inc.
175 Fifth Avenue
New York, NY 10010

ISBN: 0-312-08414-5 (paperback)
        0-312-10274-7 (cloth)

Published and distributed outside North America by
THE MACMILLAN PRESS LTD
Houndmills, Basingstoke, Hampshire RG21 2XS and London Companies
and representatives throughout the world.

ISBN 0-333-61696-0

A catalogue record for this book is available from the British Library.

Acknowledgments: Appreciation is expressed to the following publisher and
author for permission to quote from copyrighted material: *Tao Te Ching* by Lao Tsu,
trans. Feng/English. Copyright © 1972 by Gia-Fu Feng and Jane English. Reprinted
by permission of Alfred A. Knopf, Inc. Published in the U.K. by Gower Publishing,
Ltd.

To
Henaz
Leo and Donna
Diana and Mike
Kevin, Rafi, Alex, and Natalie

Foreword

Of the writing of introductions to the world's religions there is no end. The importance of the subject assures that. But *World Faiths* is different. As you read you find yourself watching the moving stage of the human drama through the great systems of faith, thought, and action that have won the allegiance of millions. You see religious traditions in their interplay with historical forces, shaping history and being shaped by it. You see them alive and changing—sometimes dying from inner atrophy or outer pressures. You see common features in similar stages of development as though different actors used the same stage props. Then the old becomes new as, responding to thought, intuition, or inspiration, some actor calls for a new scene or a new act.

You see different groups on the stage at the same time, overhearing each other and unconsciously incorporating something of what they hear. Finally, there is a tantalizing glimpse of the moving stage bringing on players asking one another if, in fact, they are acting in the same play. If so, are there to be dominant themes? Major and minor characters? Optional garments and dialects, music and stories? Is it still to be a historical drama, influencing and influenced by individuals and nations, or is it to become a specialized drama of the occult? Meanwhile, it is seen to be very much alive as little groups practice new parts they believe should be worked into the pattern, and large groups respond to new challenges.

One of the strengths of this text is the absence of generalizations. For instance, instead of listing the characteristics of "animism" or "primitive religion," *World Faiths* describes actual societies and their religious customs. Also notable is the near-absence of value judgments. The history of a whole spectrum of faith, ancient and modern, is presented succinctly and with a genuine attempt at fairness. Readers are left to do their own judging, if judge they must. One conviction does emerge: The moving stage has brought us to a new act in which we must all be players—players who have learned enough to respect the "lines" of others and to work with them so that humanity will survive to continue its high drama.

Kingsley J. Joblin
Emeritus Professor of Religious Studies
University of Toronto, Canada

Preface

World Faiths is a general introduction to the study of world religions. As such, it is deliberately limited and selective in concept. It presents a modern and concise picture of the more influential living religions, with special emphasis on their historical context. And in doing so, *World Faiths* provides essential information of the sort that few beginners have either the time or ability to piece together out of the enormous mass of published material on each religious tradition. The book is not, however, a definitive treatise nor a comprehensive study of all the religions of the world. It omits massive infusions of encyclopedic data and avoids esoteric points of doctrine. *World Faiths* is a balanced presentation, covering the historical, ideological, and cultural aspects of several religions.

Several instructors who used the first edition were invited to submit their suggestions for improving the text. Their comments were very positive and encouraging, and wherever possible a serious effort was made to incorporate their suggestions. Thus, this second edition of *World Faiths* differs from the previous edition in several respects. Chapters that represent either Western or Eastern traditions have been grouped together. Also an attempt has been made to reproduce a more parallel organization between chapters. As in the first edition, each chapter deals with the traditional viewpoint as well as the latest scholarly opinion on the subject under discussion. Content now includes more detail, additional scriptural quotations, and improved time lines and maps in addition to discussions of all or some of the following: background history and historical development, important characteristics, life and teachings of a founder (if any), scriptures, teachings, mythologies, roles of women, sectarian groups, practices, rituals, and observances. A glossary and bibliography are provided as aids for further study, and numerous new photographs evoke the richness of humanity's religious experiences and practices.

A quick glance at the table of contents will indicate the changes included in this second edition. The first chapter describes learning strategies appropriate to the study of religion. This is followed by chapters surveying religion in prehistory (new to this edition), African religion, American Indian traditions, Hinduism, Buddhism, Jainism and Sikhism, Taoism and Confucianism, Shinto, the roots of Western religions (Mesopotamian, Egyptian, Greek, and Roman religions), Zoroastrianism, Judaism, Christianity, Islam, and, in a newly expanded discussion, Baha'i. The new concluding chapter offers a conceptual framework for comparing the central categories of religious thought in an emerging global culture and a religiously pluralistic society.

Also new to the second edition is an Instructor's Manual that offers for each chapter in *World Faiths* a synopsis, key terms, assignments, and multiple-choice and true-false questions. (To order, see the note at the end of this preface.)

No project of this magnitude can be accomplished without the help of others. A word of thanks is therefore in order. I want to acknowledge once again my debt of gratitude to all those who were involved with the success of the first edition, especially the reviewers of the book: Virginia Black, Pace University; Nancy Falk, Western Michigan University; George Kim, Manchester Community College; Harry Partin, Duke University; Franklin Proano, Ohio State University; Lynda Sexson, Montana State University; William Shealy, Virginia Wesleyan College; Donald Smith, Lakeland Community College; Maurine Stein, Prairie

State College; Victor Wan-Tatah, Youngstown State University; and Kenneth Zysk, Eastern Michigan University at Ypsilanti.

Although their names are mentioned there, I again want to offer my thanks to all those who helped in the preparation of the first edition: the members of the University of Toronto Advisory Committee on Educational Development, who provided a grant; Grant Bracewell and Lynda Hayes, who graciously helped in obtaining and loaning some hard-to-find books; Steve Jaunzems, who carefully prepared the photographs; Patrick Trant, who has the ability to make "the rough places plain"; and Deborah van Eeken, a faithful friend and superb typist.

Next, I want to offer special thanks to all those who were directly concerned with this second edition. To the following reviewers for their helpful suggestions: Mattie Hart, Flagler College; Scott Lowe, University of North Dakota; Judith Martin, University of Dayton; and Ronald Spores, Vanderbilt University; to the staff of St. Martin's Press, in particular Don Reisman, Kristin Bowen, and Diana Puglisi, for their confidence and support in seeing this edition into production. I am also deeply grateful to June Hewitt, Eleanor Murphy, and Bernadette McNary for their tireless stenographic labors. My wife and family, who lived with the preparation of the manuscript for several years (and more recently, with its revision), need to be told publicly, even though they already know it, that I am grateful to them.

S. A. Nigosian

Note to Instructors

An Instructor's Manual containing approximately 460 test questions is available. For more information, please write St. Martin's Press, College Desk, 175 Fifth Avenue, New York, NY 10010, or call (1–800–446–8923), or contact your local St. Martin's sales representative.

Contents

Foreword   vii

Preface   ix

1   UNDERSTANDING RELIGION   1

What Is Religion?   1
Etymological Definitions   1   Subjective
Definitions   2   Objective Definitions   2
A Proposed Definition   4

The Study of Religion   6
Why Study Religion?   6   Approaches to
the Study of Religion   7   Approaches and
Goals   8   Specific Structure   12
Proper Point of View   14

Notes   15

2   RELIGION IN PREHISTORY   17

Archeological Discoveries   17
Human Skulls   17   Bear Skulls   19
Corpses   20   Works of Art   22
Massive Stone Structures   24

Prehistoric Civilization   26

3   AFRICAN RELIGION   27

The Study of African Religion   27
  Meaning of African Religion   27
  From Cultural Prejudices to Scholarly Studies   28
African Religion in Historical Perspective   29
  Beginnings   29   Precolonial Period   30
  European Impact   31
Religious Interactions:
Christian, Muslim, African   32
  Spread of Christianity and Islam   32
  Impact of Christianity and Islam   33
  New Syncretistic Movements   34
African Traditional Religions   35
  Dinka Religion   35   Yoruba Religion   37
  Patterns of Belief   39
  Manifestations of Religious Activity   45
Notes   50

4   AMERICAN INDIAN TRADITIONS   53

Traditional Characteristics   53
Origins   54
Mayans   55
  Sources of Mayan Religion   56   Mayan
  Beliefs   56   Mayan Practices   58
Aztecs   59
  Sources of Aztec Religion   60   Aztec
  Beliefs   60   Aztec Practices   61
Modern American Indians   62
  American Indian Creation Myths   64
  American Indian Ceremonials   65   American
  Indian Values   69   Modern Trends   72
Notes   73

5   HINDUISM   75

Hindu Characteristics   75
Historical Background   75
Hindu Scriptures   76
Hindu Mythology   79

Development of Hinduism 79
Vedic Deities 79   The One 81
Brahman-Atman 83   Reincarnation 86
Caste 88   Stages of Life 90

Paths to Emancipation 91
Karma Marga 91   Jnana Marga 93
Bhakti Marga 96

Forms of Hinduism 98
The Trimurti 98   Shaktism and
Tantrism 100   Folk Hinduism 100
Cow Veneration 103

Hindu Observances 104
Ritual Purification 104   Devotional
Ritual 104   Pilgrimages 106
Religious Festivals 106

Evolution of Modern Hinduism 109
Hindu-Muslim Encounters 112
Hindu-Christian Encounters 112
Women and Modernity 115

Notes 117

6 BUDDHISM   119

Historical Background 119

Gautama Buddha 120
Early Life 120   Four Sights 121   Quest
for Truth 121   Temptations of Buddha 123
The Great Enlightenment 123   First
Discourse 124   Founding of the
Sangha 124   Buddha's Teachings 126

Development of Buddhism 132
Early Councils 132   Establishment of
Monastic Orders 133   Spread of
Buddhism 134   Strength of Buddhism 140
Women in Buddhist History 140
Modern Trends 141

Buddhist Scriptures 142

Buddhist Groups 143
Theravada Buddhism 143
Mahayana Buddhism 144   Tantrism 148

Buddhist Observances 149
Relics 149 Image Worship 150
Precepts 151 Pilgrimages 151
Devotional Rites 151
Memorials and Festivals 152
Notes 153

7 JAINISM AND SIKHISM 157

Jainism 157
Historical Background 157
Mahavira 157 Mahavira and
Hindu Tradition 159 The Five Great
Vows 160 Jain Groups 160 Jain
Scriptures 162 Jain Teachings 162
Jain Practices and Institutions 164

Sikhism 166
Historical Background 166 Guru Nanak 167
Succession of *Gurus* 168
Khalsa 170 Militant Sikhism 170
Sikh Scripture 171 Sikh Teachings 171
Sikh Groups 172 Sikh Ceremonies
and Observances 173 Modern Trends 175
Notes 176

8 TAOISM AND CONFUCIANISM 177

Early Chinese Religion 178
Historical Background 178
Five Classics 179 Deities and Spirits 180
Yin-Yang 181 Divination 182 Emperor
Rites 182 Ancestor Rites 183
Rival Philosophical Schools 184

Taoism 185
Lao Tzu 185 Taoist Scriptures 186 Taoist
Concepts 188 Taoism through the Ages 191

Confucianism 194
Historical Background 194 Confucius 196
Teachings of Confucius 199
Confucian Canon 202
Confucianism through the Ages 203
Women and Changing Traditions 208

Chinese Observances 210
Devotional Functions 211   Ceremonies
and Festivals 212
Notes 214

9 **SHINTO** 217

Characteristics 217
Concept of *Kami* 218   Gods, Nature,
and Human Beings 218
Scriptures 219
Mythology 220
Shinto through the Ages 220
Early Shinto 220   Shinto, Confucianism,
and Buddhism 223   Shinto and
Christianity 225   State Shinto 227
Women in Shinto Tradition 230
Shinto Groups 231
Shrine Shinto 231   Sectarian Shinto 233
Folk (Popular) Shinto 237   New Religions 238
Shinto Observances 239
Festivals 240
Notes 243

10 **ROOTS OF WESTERN RELIGIONS** 245

The Middle East 245
Mesopotamian Religion 246
Historical Background 246   Mesopotamian
Pantheon 248   Cult Practices 250
Religious Festivals 250   The Ziggurat 251
Mythologies 251
Egyptian Religion 253
Historical Background 253   Pharaoh
Worship 255   Animal Cult 255   Egyptian
Deities 256   Death and Resurrection
of Osiris 258   Monotheism: Worship of
Aton 259   Death, Heaven, and Hell 260
Temples, Sphinxes, and Pyramids 261
Religious Festivals 262   Occult Practices 263
Mythologies 264

Greek Religion   264
Historical Background   264   Early Greek
Religion   265   Greek Pantheon   267
Intellectual Views   269
Popular Religion   271   Mystery Religions   275
Greek Mythology   277
Hellenistic Religions   278
Roman Religion   278
Historical Background   278   *Numina*   280
Deities   281   Priests, Diviners, and Cultic
Functionaries   282   Roman Religious
Festivals   283   Foreign Accretions   285
Emperor Worship   291
Themes and Foreshadowings   292
Notes   294

11   ZOROASTRIANISM   297

Historical Background   298
Zoroaster   299
Revelation and Mission   301   Teachings   302
Historical Development of Zoroastrianism   304
Achaemenid Period   304   Seleucid
Period   305   Parthian Period   305
Sassanid Period   306
Exile and Survival   307
Zoroastrian Scriptures   308
Zoroastrian Teachings   309
Human Choice   309   Cosmic Dualism: Ahura
Mazda versus Ahriman   310   Judgment,
Resurrection, Eternal Life   310   Creation,
Time, Eschatology   311
Zoroastrian Observances   313
Naojote   313   Purification   315   Death   315
Fire   315   Ceremonies   316
Festivals   317
Sects   318
Modern Trends   318
Notes   320

12 JUDAISM 323

Historical Background 323
Canaanites 324 Philistines 325
The Patriarchs 325
Moses 327
Biblical Religion 330
Judges and Monarchs 330
Prophets 332 Exile 333
Rise of Judaism 334
Scribes and Priests 334 Jewish-Persian
Contact 335 Jewish-Hellenistic Contact 337
The Bible 340
Torah 341 Prophets 344 Writings 346
Talmud and Midrash 348
Noncanonical Material 350
Jewish Teachings 351
Jewish Groups 353
Jewish Observances 356
Holy Days 358 Festivals 358
Modern Judaism 360
The Diaspora 360 State of Israel 362
Status of Women 365
Notes 367

13 CHRISTIANITY 369

Historical Background 369
Christian Scriptures 371
Jesus Christ 372
Primary Sources 372 Early Life of
Jesus 373 Baptism and Temptation 374
Mission and Crucifixion 375 Resurrection
and Ascension 376 Teachings 377
Paul 382
Early Christianity 385
Christianity and Medieval Society 390
Spread of Christianity 390 Rivalries and
Persecutions 392 Reformation and Counter-
Reformation 395 The Enlightenment 397

Modern Christianity   400
   Religious Movements   400   Ecumenism   401
   Religious Pluralism   402   Emancipation
   of Women   406
Christian Teachings   408
Christian Sacraments   410
Christian Observances   412
   Veneration of Saints   412
   Liturgical Calendar   412
Notes   414

14   **ISLAM**   417

Misrepresentations of Islam   417
Historical Background   419
Muhammad the Prophet   419
   Divine Call and Revelation   420
   Establishment of Islamic Community   421
Islamic Empires   424
   Establishment of the Caliphate   424
   Conquest and Settlement   425
   Mongol Empire (c. 1200–1368)   428
   Ottoman Empire (c. 1300–1922)   429
   Mughal Empire (1526–1857)   430
   Persecution and Decline   431
   Abolishment of the Caliphate   433
Modern Trends   434
   Role of Women   434   Conflict of Values   436
Qur'an   437
Hadith   441
Islamic Teachings   442
   Articles of Faith   442   The Five Pillars of
   Islam   445   *Jihad* (Holy War)   448   *Shari'ah*
   (Divine Law)   449
Islamic Groups   450
   Khariji   450   Sunni and Shi'ite   451
   Sufi   452
Islamic Observances   453
   Friday Prayer   454

Festivals 454   Muharram 455
Other Memorials 456
Notes 456

15 BAHA'I 459

Beginnings 459
The Bab (1819–1850) 460
Baha'u'llah (1817–1892) 460
Abdul Baha (1844–1921) 462
Shoghi Effendi (1896–1957) 463
Baha'i Scriptures 463
Baha'i Teachings 463
Baha'i Worship 466
Baha'i Obligations 468
Spread of Baha'i Faith 468
Baha'i Festivals 469
Notes 470

16 RELIGION IN GLOBAL PERSPECTIVE 471

Global Awareness 471
New Religious Movements 472
Comparison of Religions 473
Obedience, Belief, or Submission? 475
Similarities and Differences in
Ultimate Goals 477   Comparing Eastern
Religions 478
Notes 480

Glossary 481
Bibliography 491
Index 521

Maps and Time Lines

Maps

Distribution of the Major Faiths of the World   10
African Peoples   40
Traditional Locations of Native American Peoples   66
Native American Peoples   70
Hinduism   110
Life of Buddha   122
Spread of Buddhism   134
China and Japan   195
Japan   226
Egypt–Mesopotamia   254
Greece–Rome   273
Traditional Route of the Exodus   327
Cities of the Diaspora   361
Palestine at the Time of Jesus   374
Cities Visited by Paul   383
Christianity at the Time of the Schism, 1054   393
Christianity at the Treaty of Westphalia, 1648   398
Early Islam   422
Islam in 750 CE   426

Time Lines

Evolution of Humans   18
Hinduism   76
Buddhism   136
Jainism and Sikhism   166
Taoism and Confucianism   204
Shinto   228
Mesopotamia and Egypt   246
Greece and Rome   266
Zoroastrianism   306
Judaism   338
Christianity   400
Islam   432
Baha'i   461

World Faiths

1

Understanding Religion

What Is Religion?

The Christian theologian Augustine (354–430) once said, "If you do not ask me what time is, I know; if you ask me, I do not know."[1] The same point applies to the terms *religion* and *religious*. At first sight these words appear to be self-explanatory, yet they defy precise definition because they carry different meanings for different people.

Etymological Definitions

Religion is derived from the Latin term *religio*, the etymology of which is disputed. Some scholars have tried to connect *religio* with other Latin terms, such as *relegere* (to reread), *relinquere* (to relinquish), and *religare* (to relegate, to unite, to bind together). This last root word, particularly when applied in the sense of persons being bound to God or to superior powers, has been the most common, or classical, understanding. The explanation of religion in such a narrow sense is a mistake, however.

A most important point is that the term *religion* has little, if any, significance to non-Western people. The national Japanese religion (to use the Western label) is Shinto, meaning the "way of the gods";

1

Buddhism is described as the "Noble Eightfold Path"; Confucius called his teaching "the Way"; and the term *Taoism* derives from *Tao*, meaning "the Way."

The terms *religion* and *the Way* thus can be considered as two different explanations of a worldwide phenomenon. To non-Western people "the Way" means a process, a concept that implies direction and therefore relation to a goal or purpose. Western people, on the other hand, are more concerned with the concept of a person, which implies a relationship between (let us say) God and human beings.[2]

Subjective Definitions

Another way to describe religion is through the attitudes and/or habits of "religious" people. Ultimately, however, all such attempts at subjective definitions prove either too narrow or too broad. To say, for example, that one is religious only through *belief* in God is to err by restricting the meaning to intellectual activity—as well as by excluding all those who like the Buddhists act and behave very much like conventional religious believers although they do not believe in a god. Similarly, to say that one is religious only when one *feels* an experience is to restrict the meaning to emotional activity. Human beings possess multiple capacities: we think, feel, and act by responding inwardly as well as outwardly. Hence, the concept of religion cannot be tied solely to either the concept of God or that of feeling.

Equally fallacious is any definition of *religion* and *religious* in terms of participation in a particular faith, which thereby excludes all those outside the one faith. It is also misleading to define religion as a code of ethics or of morals, since people can reject all religions yet maintain high moral and ethical standards. Belief in a religion or loyalty to a particular faith is no guarantee against immoral or unethical behavior. The pages of human history are filled with accounts of "religious" people who have committed "immoral" acts in the name of religion.

But if defining religion very narrowly is a mistake, an equally dangerous practice is to define it so broadly that the term loses all significance. To say, for instance, that religion is awe or wonder or love is to say nothing at all, because a flash of lightning or a flight of birds can inspire awe or wonder and because love is as often equated with self-indulgence or self-gratification as it is with self-sacrifice. Awe, wonder, and love are only aspects of religion.

Objective Definitions

At the beginning of the modern era, several attempts were made to define religion in terms of its origin or its (supposedly) universal characteristics. Chief among these "objective" analyses were philological, sociological, and psychological theories proposed in the late nineteenth and early twentieth centuries.

Perhaps the most influential philologically based theory was proposed by Friedrich Max Müller (1823–1900), who suggested that religion arose out of the myths and cults based upon an original personification of natural phenomena. Rejecting this view in favor of a sociological perspective, Herbert L. Spencer (1820–1903) located the origin of religion in early experiences of ghosts (later to be identified as spirits, and later yet as gods), who were thought to be the heroic ancestors of a particular tribe or group. Since a person's first reaction to the experience of ghosts is one of fear, that emotion, said Spencer, is the fundamental cause of all religion. Enlarging on Spencer's views, Edward B. Tylor (1832–1917) suggested belief in souls as the origin of religion, whereas James G. Frazer (1854–1941) pointed to totemic rites that were designed to promote the social solidarity or well-being of a group or tribe. It remained for Karl Marx (1818–1883) to offer the most sweeping sociological theory—that religion was "the opium of the people . . . the sigh of the oppressed creature."

Psychologically motivated theories of the origin of religion as a definition for religion took their departure from the works of Sigmund Freud (1856–1939). In Freud's estimation, religion arose from humanity's infantile wish to defend itself from the forces and terrors of life. In this sense, religion represents the rationalization of human delusions and deceptions—the insistent, but unrealistic, wishes of humanity. Following Freud, others suggested that religion arose as a result of the appearance in dreams of deceased members of the tribe, which led to the belief in the existence of spirits.

Although all these theorists made significant contributions in other ways to the study of religion, their attempts to define religion in terms of its origin have long been discredited. Among other weaknesses of such theories is the fact that they are based on speculation about prehistoric times and are therefore impossible to verify. The origins of religion, like those of many other human activities, are lost in humanity's unrecorded past.

Other seekers after an objective definition took a different route, attempting to define religion by discovering a basic element or essence (such as an activity, an experience, a belief) common to all religions. Unfortunately, the task of identifying a common feature in terms of which all religious phenomena are to be understood has been more or less abandoned.[3] As knowledge of religions increased, it became apparent that beyond superficial similarities exist profound differences among the religions of the world.

A Proposed Definition

· The preceding attempts at definition generally fall into one of two categories: those that seek to define religion in terms of human attitudes and relationships, and those that seek to do so in terms of the human motivation underlying these attitudes. In other words, one category of definition seeks to explain *what* religion is by analyzing human attitudes and behavior, whereas the other seeks to explain *why* religion is a factor in human affairs by analyzing the motives behind human attitudes and behavior.

What is needed is a definition of religion that both combines the two categories and provides a workable hypothesis for a study of East–West religious traditions. These requirements are met by the following statement: religion is an invention or creation of the human mind for regulating all human activity, and this creative activity is a human necessity that satisfies the spiritual desires and needs inherent in human nature. This statement demands close analysis.

To put it another way, religion is a specialized activity of the imaginative mind. Certain individuals—prophets, priests, mystics, visionaries, sages, gurus, imams, and other religious masters—possess a unique, uncommon, or rarefied quality of this imaginative mind. They see and hear in the "mind's eye and ear" that which is hidden from the sight and hearing of ordinary people. Their imagination takes the shape of an extraordinary revelation (a Western notion) or a profound insight (an Eastern notion). So powerful is this mode of imaginative thinking that the thinker's mind soars in time and space, moves beyond reason, visualizes and generates ideas, alters the course of events, and creates or invents another order of existence or reality beyond this life.

Creative religious individuals are possessed and haunted by fixed and besetting images that are ascribed either to an internal source known as insight, awareness, or consciousness (an Eastern notion) or to an external source known as revelation (a Western notion). This imaginative experience is immediately translated as Ultimate Reality or Absolute Truth. Finally, through the labor of the individual and, usually, of several supporters or disciples, the image takes organic form and body; is realized in actions, customs, and laws; and imposes itself on millions of people.

In this way, organized religion—with its elaborate temples, shrines, mosques, and churches; its complex system of rituals related to the stages of life; its sacred festivals and solemn observances; its hymns, prayers, and occult activities; its formulations of moral and ethical codes; its legacy of holy books, sacred narratives, and basic beliefs—originates in the imaginative projection of a religious innovator. And faith—the unquestioning belief, trust, or confidence in someone or something—can be seen as the product of a privileged imagination.

Often, it is very difficult to fully understand and appreciate the nature or behavior of these religious innovators. Statements made by their disciples affirm the paradoxical character (i.e., natural–supernatural or human–divine) of these religious masters. Some have regarded them as incarnations of a divine being or a cosmic principle; others have considered them to be infallible individuals, possessing the power of dissimulation, transmigration, or resurrection.

Whatever ambiguities they exhibit in behavior or character, religious geniuses initiate radical and massive changes in civilization because their religious imagination appeals to large segments of society. Such geniuses help shape the course of human history, instituting actions by which whole governments and societies are organized. They break with custom, with accepted norms and values, with tribal and societal loyalties, with time-honored traditions, with fixed patterns. They strongly react against established religious systems, openly challenge ancient beliefs, courageously threaten prescribed rituals. They set their own norms and lead people to yet another vision of truth or reality. They express their experiences in terms of the inconceivable. They make demands that are difficult, and at times unintelligible. Their influence begins at once—during their lifetimes—because they actively proclaim their religious imaginations as eternal truths.

How do religious geniuses exert an incalculable and enduring influence? How does their mode of imaginative thinking differ from that of others? According to T. A. Ribot:

> For reasons of which we are ignorant, analogous to those that produce a great poet or a great painter, there arise moral geniuses who feel strongly what others do not feel at all, just as does a great poet, in comparison with the crowd. But it is not enough that they feel: they must create, they must realize their ideal in a belief and in rules of conduct accepted by other men.[4]

Indeed, the imaginative projections of religious geniuses deal with moral issues and ideal situations arising from needs and desires that stimulate action, habit, and law, with the additional promise of an ultimate bliss or happiness after death. The imaginative thinking of others arises from reflections that are at least amusing or entertaining, at most speculative and theoretical. For instance, music, ranging from pop songs to operas, from musical comedies to symphonies, might be categorized as the imaginative creation of the musical/entertaining mind. So, too, might works of art, ranging from basket weaving to dancing, from painting to sculpturing. Poems, novels, and plays, among other literary works, are the creations or inventions of what may be characterized as the speculative/theoretical mind.

Religion, then, may be viewed as that creative activity of the human mind that satisfies our inherent spiritual needs and desires. This proposition will become intelligible only in the light of knowledge about the history of religions and an understanding of how different people act when they are religious.

The Study of Religion

What rewards does the study of religion yield? What is the best approach to the study of religion? What is the proper point of view to adopt in studying world religions? These important questions must be answered before we explore the many facets of the various major world religions.

Why Study Religion?

The justification for a systematic investigation of religion varies according to the investigator. Some consider religion an integral part of human life and, therefore, an appropriate subject for scientific analysis. Others are motivated by a sincere interest in some specific information about or insight into other people's religious activities. Still others study religion in order to examine its relation to other cultural forms. Possibly, some study religion in order to establish patterns and characteristics of humanity's religious life and activity that seem to have universal application. Whatever the reasons, the challenge of this complex field of inquiry has exercised the talents and energies of some of the greatest thinkers, past and present.

Interest in understanding religions is not peculiar to the twentieth century, though it has been evident primarily in Western rather than Eastern cultures. On the whole, approaches to understanding religion grew out of attempts to defend, to criticize, or to interpret religious faiths in harmony with the development of knowledge.

The rise and spread of Christianity provided the early Church Fathers with a standard by which to understand and assess the various religious movements and philosophical systems that flourished in the vast Greco-Roman world. This standard not only helped them to confirm the overall skeptical attitude of ancient Greek and Roman philosophers toward religion, but it also provided them with a rationale for dismissing divergent beliefs as irrelevant to the worship of the one true God.

In the thirteenth century European travelers (such as the Italian Marco Polo) came in contact with Asiatic peoples and returned with knowledge of Asian religions. Their reports opened the way for an inductive (fact-based) treatment of these religions. The ongoing interest in the systematic documentation of religions around the world, made possible by the explorations of hitherto unknown lands in the sixteenth, seventeenth, and eighteenth centuries, prepared the way for the development of modern analytical methods for the study of religion.

Approaches to the Study of Religion

The growth of various academic disciplines (such as history, archeology, philology, philosophy, anthropology, sociology, and psychology) in the latter half of the nineteenth century compelled scholars to develop improved scientific procedures for and objective, analytical approaches to the study of world religions. At least five basic methodological approaches can be distinguished: (1) the historical, (2) the philosophical, (3) the sociological, (4) the psychological, and (5) the phenomenological.

History of Religion. Historians of religion study religious behavior through the sequences of events, or series of transformations, that characterize the evolution of various religious traditions into their present forms or up to the points at which they vanished. Historians consider religions as specific traditions encompassing fundamental beliefs, important practices, and institutionalized systems, all of which have gone through a complex course of development and transformation. To unravel the process of religious development requires special skill and scientific knowledge. The contributions made in the last few centuries by historians, archeologists, philologists, classicists, and Orientalists, among other scholars, are invaluable to those who apply the historical method in order to understand religion.

Philosophy of Religion. For many years the study of religion was principally the province of theologians and philosophers. Consequently, matters of faith and belief, of truth and falsehood, and of revelation and reason often served both as the starting point and the principal focus of inquiry. Three main trends are discernible in the present scope of the philosophy of religion: (1) an analysis of religious language, (2) an analysis of the nature of religion in the general framework of a world view, and (3) a philosophical justification or rejection of various religious positions. Thus, theological argumentations, metaphysical systems, moral and ethical issues, and many similar matters arising from philosophical discussions have come under critical examination by all those who apply the tools of philosophy.

Sociology of Religion. The basic unit of study among sociologists is not the individual personality, but the network of relationships that bind people together in cohesive groups called societies. Somewhat related to sociologists are social anthropologists, who have made important contributions to the study of religion, particularly through studies of primitive or tribal peoples. The sociological method is applied to crucial issues such as how religion contributes to social integration and what function religion serves in the social complex of which it is a part. Thus, both sociologists and anthropologists emphasize the importance of religion through its cultural symbols and expressions.

Psychology of Religion. The study of religious psychology involves, among other things, the collection and classification of psychological data, the investigation of religious responses as correlated with various personality types, the testing of various psychological explanations, the examination of the religious symbols and practices that aid or impede individuals in working out personal problems, and the bearing of religious issues on the integration of one's personality. Some researchers have also conducted empirical investigations into the effects of mystical and meditative experiences and drug-induced states of consciousness.

Phenomenology of Religion. Phenomenologists believe that every human activity is relevant to the study of whatever "phenomenon" they focus on. To the phenomenologist who focuses on religion, then, music, painting, sculpture, labor, and/or any other product of human endeavor must be observed and analyzed in terms of its potential for illuminating and explaining the phenomenon of religious faith. Thus, the phenomenological approach to religion is to identify a general pattern and to define its essential elements. Significant contributions have been made by this method, especially in the comparison of one religious form with another.

Approaches and Goals

The five approaches outlined above represent the application of modern scientific techniques to the study of religion, and each of the five is in some way invaluable to the study and understanding of religion. The profound impact of religion on the course of human civilization is best examined in the context of an appropriate historical setting. The relationships among religion and cultural values, social customs, and political developments, along with the effects of religion on art, architecture, literature, music, theater, and dance, are brought into sharp focus through the application of several of these methods. The reaction of human beings to the enigmas represented by conception, birth, life, and death is uniquely analyzed within historical, social, psychological, and philosophical contexts.

The goal of this text, however, is to introduce the reader to the study of world religions, for which purpose the historical model offers the most advantages. Consequently, we will examine certain basic religious features from the point of view of history and the historical interactions of religions. This choice of method, in turn, dictates the structure for grouping world religions. At least three important models deserve to be briefly sketched: (1) the evolutionary, (2) the phenomenological, and (3) the geographical.

Evolutionary Model. The underlying principle of this scheme is that a religion, over the course of time, passes through a series of definable stages of development that represent progressively advanced levels of religious sophistication. Although the division of religions into evolutionary levels or categories has been subjected to severe criticism, religious scholars still recognize the appeal of three evolutionary categories: (1) from a low (or primitive) level to a higher level; (2) from tribal or national to universal; and (3) from religions of nature to ethical religions. Such evolutionary divisions of religion have provoked wide dissension among scholars, and especially among social scientists. The reason is not hard to find. The guiding principle of any evolutionary scheme is to explore how religion has developed in world history, rather than to trace the historical development of each tradition. As long as the main lines or stages of religious evolution are disputed, however, this method is inherently flawed.

Phenomenological Model. In this scheme of classification, religions are categorized according to characteristics that correspond to the essential and typical elements or forms of the religious life, no matter where (geographically) or when (historically) they occur. Some practitioners of this method group religions according to three distinguishable affinities: (1) religions of the past (Mesopotamian, Egyptian, Canaanite-Phoenician, Greater Syrian, Grecian and Roman, Shamanism, and American Indian); (2) ethnic religions of the present (African, Hinduism, Jainism, Sikhism, Confucianism and Taoism, Shinto, Zoroastrianism, and Judaism); and (3) universal religions of the present (Buddhism, Christianity, and Islam). Others group religions according to the same structure but in terms of the characteristics of prophecy and wisdom. Religions characterized as prophetic include Judaism, Christianity, Islam, and Zoroastrianism; those described as religions of wisdom include Hinduism, Jainism, Buddhism, Shinto, Confucianism, and Taoism. This scheme is of little practical use, since it falls short of satisfying the aim of the whole exercise: to reduce the complexity and diversity of world religions by a system of classification.

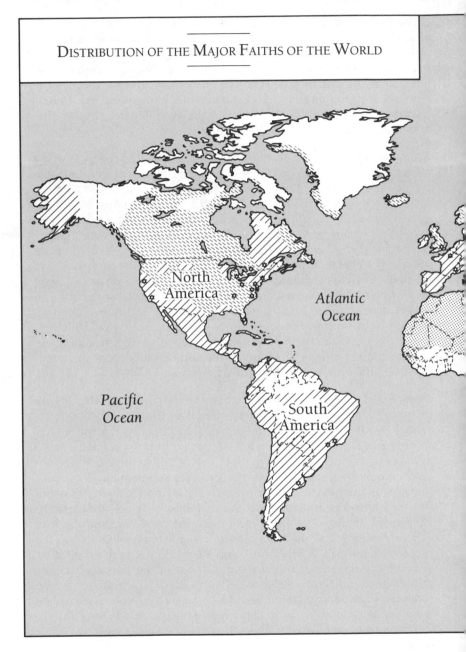

DISTRIBUTION OF THE MAJOR FAITHS OF THE WORLD

North
America

Atlantic
Ocean

Pacific
Ocean

South
America

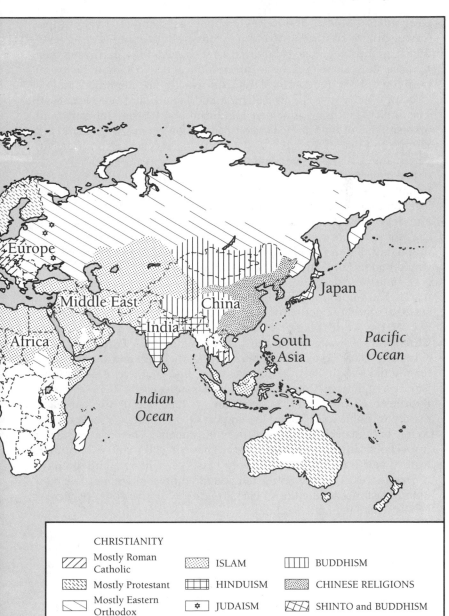

CHRISTIANITY

	Mostly Roman Catholic		ISLAM		BUDDHISM
	Mostly Protestant		HINDUISM		CHINESE RELIGIONS
	Mostly Eastern Orthodox		JUDAISM		SHINTO and BUDDHISM

Geographical Model. The most commonly used and relatively simple framework for classifying world religions is the geographical scheme, which groups together religions that emerged in a particular area because they share a genetic connection and a common historical tradition. Three geographical regions usually are identified in this structure: India, the Far East (China and Japan), and the Near East. The Indian grouping includes Hinduism, Buddhism, Jainism, and Sikhism; that of the Far East encompasses Confucianism, Taoism, and Shinto; and that of the Near East comprises Zoroastrianism, Judaism, Christianity, Islam, and Baha'i.

The geographical scheme of classification, like any other universal model, suffers from some basic difficulties. For one thing, the physical location of a religion reveals little, if anything, of the specific growth and development of that religion or of its constituent elements. Then, too, some religions are most widespread away from their regions of origin (e.g, Buddhism, Christianity), and others are not confined to a single region (e.g., Judaism, Zoroastrianism).

Despite these drawbacks the geographical scheme provides the most useful and appropriate framework for a historical approach to the study of world religions. In addition, the geographical distribution of five of the world religions presents an interesting global pattern. Christianity prevails in the West, predominantly in Europe and the Americas. Islam occupies an area between the West and the Far East, mainly the Middle East, Africa, Pakistan, and southern Asia. Hinduism is a significant force in India and southeastern Asia, whereas Buddhism and Taoism-Confucianism predominate in the Far East, mainly in China and Japan. The impact of these five religions on the course of human civilization has been inestimable. They command the respect of a large segment of society. They direct the course of human history and lead to a wide variety of social, cultural, and political consequences. The remaining religious traditions maintain their own unique historical and cultural backgrounds, with their own particular beliefs, customs, and practices.

Specific Structure

Our attempt, then, is to describe within a historical/geographical context the religions categorized as follows:

- Religion of early humans: Religion in Prehistory
- Religion of Africa: African Religion
- Religion of the Americas: American Indian Traditions
- Religions of India: Hinduism, Buddhism, Jainism and Sikhism
- Religions of the Far East: Taoism and Confucianism, Shinto

TABLE 1.1 Religions of the World

Name of Religion	Country of Origin	Name and Date of Founder	Distribution in the Modern World
Hinduism	India		India and throughout the world
Buddhism	India	Gautama (Buddha) (c. 563–483 Before the Common Era [BCE])	Adherents found all over the world
Jainism	India	Mahavira (c. 599–527 BCE)	India
Sikhism	India	Nanak (1469–1539 Common Era [CE])	India. Adherents also found throughout the world
Taoism	China	Li-Poh Yang/ Lao-Tzu (?) (? 6th cent. BCE)	Far East, including China and Japan
Confucianism	China	K'ung-Fu-Tzu (c. 551–479 BCE)	Far East, including China and Japan
Shinto	Japan		Japan
Zoroastrianism	Persia (Iran)	Zarathustra (c. 628–551)	Iran, India. Adherents also found in Britain, Europe, USA, and Canada
Judaism	Palestine (Israel)	Moses (? 13th cent. BCE)	Israel and throughout the world
Christianity	Palestine (Israel)	Jesus (Christ) (4 BCE–29 CE)	Adherents found all over the world
Islam	Arabia	Muhammad (c. 571–632 CE)	Adherents found all over the world
Baha'i	Iran	Baha'u'llah (1817–1892 CE)	Adherents found all over the world

- Roots of Western Religions: Mesopotamian, Egyptian, Greek and Roman religion
- Religions of the Near East: Zoroastrianism, Judaism, Christianity, Islam, Baha'i

Each chapter deals with the traditional viewpoint as well as the latest scholarly opinion on the subject under discussion. The discussion includes all or part of the following:

- a background setting
- a description of the founder or teacher (if any)
- an indication of the various sects and institutions
- a review of the sacred texts or literature
- a discussion of the central concepts and philosophical views
- a description of the more important practices and ceremonies
- an insight into the cultural conventions conferred on women
- a survey of the historical development, including modern trends

Maps, time lines, photographs, a glossary, and a bibliography are also provided in the text as aids for further study.

Proper Point of View

The structure of a study is inextricably tied to its philosophy or point of view, which may be explicit or implicit. Readers and writers bring their own beliefs, values, and points of view to bear in interpreting what they read and write—and the author of this text is no exception to this general rule. However, the structure of this book represents a conscious attempt to apply discipline and impartiality to the manner in which disparate religious traditions are introduced and studied.

Many people, of course, do not make a conscious choice of a religion. By virtue of parentage, culture, or geographical location, a religious tradition embraces and enfolds them. They, in turn, accept it and by inference or by overt word and action come to disparage everyone else's religious beliefs as incomplete, false, or somehow inferior. This attitude must be vigorously refuted and dispelled. My concern is to promote objectivity and understanding, and to discourage the influence of preconceived notions, invidious comparisons, bias, prejudice, and partiality.

As a consequence, this book will have limited appeal to people who are either indifferent to any kind of religion or so totally committed to one religious tradition that they perceive all other religions as perversions at worst and inconsequential at best. The point of view taken in this work is that different religions and sectarian branches within them satisfy different people for different reasons. Thus, the study of world religions requires an appreciation of the values that each individual religion gives to its followers and an understanding of how people in different times and under different circumstances thought, felt, and acted.

Notes

1. Saint Augustine, *The Confessions of St Augustine,* trans. E. B. Pusey (London: J. M. Dent & Sons Ltd., 1957), p. 262.
2. Summarized from A. C. Bouquet, *Comparative Religion* (New York: Penguin, 1956), p. 12.
3. Among those who continue the search for an essence is F. Schuon, *The Transcendent Unity of Religions* (New York: Harper & Row, 1975).
4. T. A. Ribot, *Essay on the Creative Imagination,* trans. A. H. N. Baron (Chicago: Open Court, 1906), p. 301.

p.14 tolerence.

2

Religion in Prehistory

Archeological Discoveries

Religion is virtually as old as the human scene itself. And yet, precisely when, where, or how religion originally emerged are matters of conjecture. Discoveries by archeologists are the principal source of data, but the difficulty here lies in the fact that for the most part these data are strictly confined to discoveries or finds that have escaped the destructive forces of time. These consist of human skeletal remains, stone tools, animal bones, cult objects, sculptures, paintings, and engravings. However, the best type of archeological evidence relating to prehistoric religion is skeletal remains. The treatment of the human corpse—its disposal, its position, the objects placed by it, and the types of graves used—provides the most valuable information for reconstructing the religion of early human beings.

Human Skulls

Several reliable finds dating from the prehistoric period at various sites in Germany (Mauer and Steinheim), England (Swanscombe), France (Fontéchevade), Italy (Monte Circeo), Yugoslavia (Croatia), China (Dragon-bone Hill near Choukoutien), and elsewhere, seem to offer some proof of cultic or religious customs. From these sites, skeletal remains of several human beings, quantities of animal bones, a few hearths, human skull fragments, and heaps of cherry pits have been identified. No matter how one tries to explain these discoveries, two elements are worth noting. First, the skeletal remains appear to have been scattered about indiscriminately, just like the animal bones. And second, the human skulls, as well as a number of animal bones, show signs of injuries or are split open. In fact, most of the human and animal bones are greatly damaged and partially burned.

These facts have led many scientists to conclude one or more of the following theories about early human beings:

- They practiced cannibalism and had a preference for the human brain and marrow as particular delicacies.

- They practiced cannibalism of a ritual nature connected with some belief in the magic properties of the human brain and marrow.

- They preserved human skulls or scalps as trophies, family relics, or souvenirs.

- They assigned human skulls and other bones some special role within human settlements, though what that role was cannot be established with any degree of certainty.

- They carried about skulls of dead persons as an expression of fidelity and pious remembrance.

- They venerated human skulls and bones as the indestructible relics

Evolution of Humans

Human Types	*Homo erectus*					*Homo sapiens*	Modern huma
Glacial Chronology		First interglacial		Mindel glaciation	Second interglacial	Riss glaciation	Third interglaci
	BCE 1,000,000			600,000		100,000	
Culture Stages					Paleolithic		
						Stone Age	
						Prehistoric Period	
Cult Practices			Cult of human skulls			Cult of bear skulls	
						Cult of the dea	

of the dead and as possessing magico-religious powers and potency.

No matter how ingenious or intriguing these theories are, one thing is certain: the ideas and religious conceptions bound up with the cult of the skulls was not immediately discernible.

Bear Skulls

Animal remains from the prehistoric period are available from numerous sites and illuminate an interesting aspect of the religious sphere of early humans. One of the most contended possessions of early humans was the skull of the enormous cave bear, and Alpine caves present the most fascinating bear cult practices.

The richest finds come from the Swiss Alps (Drachenloch and Wildenmannlishloch caves), the southern German Alps (Petershohle cave), and the Austrian Alps (Salzofen cave). Partly intact, partly broken, bear skulls from these places were arranged in groups, and in most cases the first of two cervical vertebrae were distinguishable. According to scientists, only human hands could have performed this decapitation. At any rate, the two most remarkable finds in the caves of the Swiss Alps were the seven well-preserved cave-bear skulls in a stone-made chest and fifteen cave-bear skulls set in niches on the wall of the cave. The latter skulls lay on stone slabs bordered by other slabs and covered by a protective slab.

As for the finds in the foothills of the southern German Alps, excavators discovered a tremendous collection of bear skulls and bones in niches or on stone platforms along the walls of the remotest

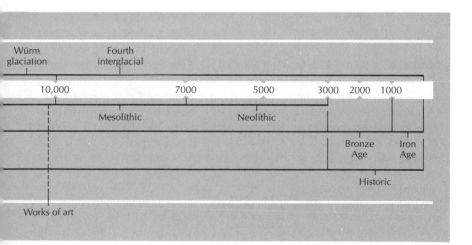

part of Petershohle cave. The cave was also rich with charcoal deposits. In the Austrian Alps as well, the cave-bear skulls were deposited in niche-like hollows in the innermost cave wall and covered with thick charcoal. Near each skull lay in orderly arrangement some bear limb bones orientated from east to west.

Remarkable finds like these are by no means confined to the Alps. In Mornova cave in Slovenia, Yugoslavia, a bear skull with its lower jaw missing was found in a niche. Directly above the skull and across it lay several unimpaired limb bones. In Furtins cave in France, seven cave-bear skulls arranged in a distinctive concentric pattern on a stone slab were discovered. Thus, cave-bear skulls and limb bones were displayed with unmistakably pious care in the remotest and darkest parts of caves by early humans. But what were the religious concepts underlying this ritual?

Interpretations vary from the purely secular to the highly religious. According to one theory, these finds are evidence of an ancient supply depot, or a kind of storage cellar. According to another theory, these discoveries point to the practice of storing brains and marrow either as delicacies or as tanning agents for skin treatment. Still another theory explains these discoveries as hunting trophies. A theory that favors a religious interpretation explains these remains partly in terms of an animal cult and magic, and partly in terms of sacrifice to a superior power.

Undoubtedly, there is here something more than mere disposal of bear skulls. It seems that those who placed them in the caves sought, for one reason or another, to guard them from damage and desecration. While it may be impossible to know the precise rubrics connected with the skull ceremonies or the beliefs associated with them, it must be admitted that some sort of cave-bear skull ritual was performed by early humans.

Corpses

More important than the cult of bear or human skulls is the cult of corpses. Numerous prehistoric graves discovered in Asia, Europe, and other areas indicate the attitude of early humans toward death. For instance, the two skeletons found in the Kiik-Koba cave on the Crimean Peninsula were those of a man and a male baby. The man lay on his right side, with the legs slightly contracted, in a trench dug in the cave floor. The infant lay on his left side, with his left hand placed under the left knee, only a few feet away from the man. The skeleton of a woman lying on its back, with the lower jaw of a man nearby, was found in Et-Tabun cave in Israel. Ten skeletal remains—five males, two females, and three children—were discovered in Es-Sukhul cave in Israel. In all cases, the legs were completely contracted, but the positions and the directions they faced varied considerably. In Teshik-Tash cave in Uzbekistan, the damaged skeleton of a child with a circle of ibex horns around the corpse was found.

Excavations in Europe have yielded various interesting burial sites too. In France, the skeleton of a youth lying on its right side, with legs slightly bent and head supported by a pillow of flint flakes resting on the right arm, was discovered at Le Moustier. Next to the skeleton were animal bones, a flint scraper, and a hand axe. In a cave at La Chapelle-aux-Saints, a male skeleton was found lying in a trench with animal bones, flint tools, and lumps of ochre beside it. At the entrance of the cave was a hearth containing charred bones and their ashes. In a cave at La Ferrassie, the skeletal remains of a female, a male, and four children were discovered. Much like the other sites, near the corpses were flint tools, quantities of animal bones and ashes, and a limestone slab marked with cup-shaped depressions. All the bodies, with the exception of the female, were oriented east to west in the direction of the setting sun.

All these finds clearly indicate concern over and special treatment of human corpses. But what were the beliefs underlying such attitudes?

Many scholars consider the care bestowed on the disposal and ornamentation of human corpses as evidence of a cult of the dead with a belief in an afterlife. This inference is based on several evidences.

First, the implements left next to the corpses seem intentional and indicate the equipment necessary for the departed to provide provisions in the world beyond. If this assumption is correct, then life in the world beyond was conceived to be virtually identical to life on earth. Yet there is no way of knowing whether the world beyond was in any way associated with the idea of a god or divine being, or with the idea of just rewards and punishments.

Second, the tightly or semiflexed positions of the skeletons are assumed either to be an imitation of sleep and rest, a symbolic form of the fetal position of the embryo (presupposing prehistoric humans' knowledge of the prenatal embryo!), or an attempt to shackle or prevent the dead from returning and molesting the living survivors. The ashes are also regarded as a magical covering that no corpse could breach, keeping it confined to its grave.

Third, the deposits of red ochre are thought to be associated with a life-giving principle and therefore a security for a renewal of life in the hereafter. As for the vast numbers of animal bones, it is generally assumed that the survivors held funerary feasts, either in memory of the deceased ancestors, or as sacrificial meals. In the latter case, it is impossible to determine whether the offerings were made to solicit good fortune or protection or any other favors.

Of course, these theories are quite hypothetical. Yet the positioning of the corpses, the implements placed beside them, the numerous animal bones, the ashes, and the red ochre all seem to describe some sort of religious practice or cult of the dead.

Works of Art

One of the most remarkable achievements of early humans is their artwork. Precisely where and when humans started to create works of art and what prompted them to do so, are, admittedly, difficult to discern. Nevertheless, numerous paintings and sculptures indicate the use of artwork as part of magical rituals.

Some of the earliest works of art date earlier than 10,000 BCE* and are found on the rock surfaces inside the darkest recesses of caves in Europe. They consist of images of animals, such as bison, deer, horses, wild boars, reindeer, cave bears, and mammoths, which are incised, painted, or sculpted on the walls and ceilings of caves and rock-shelters. Since these images are hidden away in almost inaccessible places as if to protect them from the casual intruder, it is often supposed that they served a purpose far more serious than public display or mere decoration. In fact, there can be little doubt that they were produced as part of a magic ritual to ensure a successful hunt.

The magical use of the works of art of early humans is also suggested in several other clear examples. A vivid mural in the cave of Les Trois Frères at Ariège, France, shows an image that is part human, part animal. The image has the antlers of a reindeer, the ears of a stag, the eyes of an owl, the beard and feet of a man, the front paws of a bear, and the tail of a horse. Modern experts believe the representation to be that of a "sorcerer" or shaman engaged in a magical hunting ritual.

Similarly, the cave of Niaux at Ariège has the image of an engraved and painted bison whose body is punctured with spears and darts indicating one magical assumption of early humans: like produces like. The walls of the caves of Addaura in Sicily have incised drawings of animal and human figures in dancelike poses, representing some sort of a magical ritual.

Sculptures or carvings in stone, bone, or horn comprise another category of prehistoric artwork. Here too, early humans saw in these materials certain representational qualities that rendered them magical. Numerous tiny sculptures of nude, female figures dating before 10,000 BCE have been discovered all over Europe and Asia. In most of these figurines, like the famous "Venus" found at Willendorf, Austria, the head and hair are generally blank and represented as mere knobs,

---

*Throughout this text, the terms BCE (Before the Common Era) and CE (Common Era) are used in place of the traditional BC and AD. See p. 373.

Prehistoric painting of the "Dancing Sorcerer" from a cave of Les Trois Frères at Ariège, France. The image depicts a shaman (or possibly a "spirit" engaged in a hunting dance) wearing a costume made of reindeer antlers, the ears of a stag, the eyes of an owl, the beard and feet of a man, the paws of a bear, the tail of a horse, and a patchwork of animal skins. Courtesy of the American Museum of Natural History.

while the breasts, abdomen, and buttocks are extremely large. It is believed that such figurines were symbols of maternity or female fertility and may have been used as charms or in fertility rituals. A mural painting in the rock shelter of Cogul, Spain also attests to the existence of prehistoric fertility rituals. Nine women are depicted surrounding a nude male, who seems to be the leader in a ritual connected with fertility magic.

Carved and modeled animal figurines have also been discovered in central Europe and southern Russia. Carved ivory representations of mammoths and lions and clay models of rhinoceroses, tigers, wolves, reindeer, and other animals all seem to indicate that the religion of early humans was based on magic—whether for hunting or for reproductive processes.

The discoveries of a group of sculpted human skulls in Jericho, Jordan, dating from 10,000 to 7000 BCE also indicate the use of magic rituals. Faces modeled in plaster with seashells for eyes were added to existing skulls. In the view of some scholars, these heads were not intended to "create" life but to perpetuate it beyond death. In fact, these sculpted faces were, apparently, "spirit traps" designed to keep the spirit or soul of the departed in its original place (the head) in order to insure its beneficent presence over the fortunes of later generations. This theory is based on the circumstances in which these sculpted skulls were discovered. They were displayed above the ground, while the rest of the corpse was buried beneath the floor of the house.

The Great Goddess, or the so-called Venus of Willendorf. The exaggerated breasts, hips, and abdomen suggest that this image was connected with fertility or mother-goddess rituals. Courtesy of the American Museum of Natural History.

Massive Stone Structures

Other discoveries dating from 7000 to 3000 BCE include various collective tombs and sacred monuments in Europe. Structurally, the tombs consist of two types: those in which the grave room or chamber is approached by a long passage, and those in which there is a single chamber, sometimes with a small antechamber. The tombs with long passages have walls made from dry stone or large rocks, or are walled and roofed by megalithic (i.e., large stone) slabs.

Although these tombs are quite impressive, there are other structures which are in some respects of greater interest. These are the remarkable "sacred" monuments of megalithic construction found in France and Great Britain. These monumental structures consist of huge blocks or boulders placed upon each other without mortar. Some, known as *menhirs*, are single stones on end. Others known as *dolmens*, are two upright stones bridged by a single giant slab for a roof. Still others, known as *cromlechs*, form a circular structure. Then, there are the alignments, or rows of stones that extend over several miles like the one in Carnac, France.

The function of these megalithic monuments has often been de-

A close view of Stonehenge, Britain's prehistoric monument dating from about 2200–1300 BCE, situated on Salisbury Plain in the county of Wiltshire in southern England. Stonehenge consists of a circular earthwork about 200 feet in diameter, within which is a ring of fifty-six small pits, at the center of which is the circle of standing stones seen in this photograph. The heaviest stone on the site weighs fifty tons.   Courtesy of The British Travel Association, British Consulate-General, Toronto, Canada.

bated, but many scholars insist that these impressive structures were in some way connected with religious observances. For instance, the structures at Stonehenge in England consist of a huge circular enclosure, spaced evenly by upright stones supporting horizontal slabs. Two inner circles are similarly formed, with an altar-like stone at the center. The entire closure is apparently oriented toward the exact point of sunrise on the day of the summer solstice (June 21). Some have therefore concluded that Stonehenge was a sacred spot for sun-worshiping rituals.

Prehistoric Civilization

Thus, our knowledge of prehistoric religion is very limited. The scattered skeletal and material remains found in different parts of the world indicate that in remote ages representatives of the human race existed in Asia, Africa, Europe, and the Americas. They took refuge in caves, depended on stone implements for tools and weapons, and gathered or hunted food for existence. Soon, they devised the bow and arrow, invented fine bone needles, and made clothes from the skins of animals. Later, they improved their stone implements and were able to carve embellishments and useful objects. Their artistic skill was also expressed in drawings and paintings. Gradually, they developed the cultivation of plants and the domestication of animals, which in turn led to the rise of villages and the emergence of civilizations.

3

African Religion

The Study of African Religion

The study of African religion has recently become a special field of inquiry with a sizable body of literature containing a wide variety of perspectives. It is necessary, therefore, to discuss at the outset the important questions of perspective as a proper framework for understanding African religion.

Meaning of African Religion

African religions encompass a variety of indigenous religions of Africa south of the Sahara Desert. Christianity and Islam, long confined to Africa north of the Sahara and east of the Nile River, have in recent centuries expanded into sub-Saharan Africa and today are the dominant faiths of the continent. Then there are the "new religious movements," the product of syntheses drawn from Christianity, Islam, and African religions. Customarily, however, the presentation of African religion is strictly confined to the indigenous religions of sub-Saharan African peoples, distinguished from churches, missions, mosques, or any other religious bodies that have recently taken root in parts of Africa.

From Cultural Prejudices to Scholarly Studies

For the past five hundred years, European merchants, travelers, explorers, soldiers, and missionaries traveled throughout the world, including Africa, to extend Western culture and civilization. The earliest accounts of African religion, therefore, derive from such European agents, whose works are considered to be generally unreliable because they are usually based on random observations, inaccurate information, and cultural prejudices.[1] To these early Europeans, African religion appeared to be a "morass of bizarre beliefs and practices" at best, or a "degraded form of mental and moral character" at worst.[2] Some learned people in modern times still harbor such prejudices and thus characterize African culture and religion from an uncomplimentary perspective.[3]

The next stage of studying African religion started about two hundred years ago and consisted of a group of trained anthropologists, whose interest lay primarily in proposing their "evolutionary" theories for the origin and development of religion.[4] The advent of social anthropology at the turn of this century successfully challenged and overturned these evolutionary theories based on the superiority of European culture and the inferiority of African, or "primitive," culture. Soon, anthropological studies became divided between two schools of thought: British and French. Consequently, fieldwork studies of African social and religious systems were interpreted according to the nationality of the anthropologist.[5]

The persistent emphasis on fieldwork, however, led anthropologists to make a shift in their analysis from function to meaning. This new viewpoint, called the phenomenological approach, attempted to understand African ideas, concepts, beliefs, and practices through an analysis of their own mode of thought, or logical patterns.[6] Today, anthropologists attempt to integrate the social-functional and phenomenological approaches within a unified perspective.

Modern anthropological studies of African religion, however, have resulted in a timeless "ethnographic present." Little attention has been paid to the historical dimensions of African religion. Three important reasons are usually cited for this neglect: the lack of archeological data, the absence of historical information, and the highly mixed tribes and peoples that exist in sub-Saharan Africa. Nevertheless, attempts have been made by cultural historians. For a while, these scholars held to the popular "Hamitic-Negro" theory. According to this theory, the Hamites (alleged to be a branch of the Caucasian race) arrived in Africa in successive waves and imposed upon the indigenous Negro races in Africa their higher elements of language, culture, and civilization.[7] Hence, scholars tried to sort out the "earlier, primitive" Negro from the "later, advanced" Hamitic layers of culture. This European notion of "racial superiority" is gradually being abandoned as scholars are more and more recognizing that race, language, and culture are independent elements.

In addition to anthropologists and historians, modern theologians and philosophers have also attempted to interpret African religious concepts according to Western philosophical and theological categories.[8] Basically, such works concentrate on religious beliefs and systems, thus reducing African religions to a set of doctrines or philosophical categories analogous in structure to Western faiths.

These, then, are the various modern approaches to the study of African religion, which allow different levels of interpretation. And since the purpose of this chapter is to facilitate the understanding of African religion rather than to solve problems of interpretation, the adoption of alternate approaches certainly seems preferable to rigid adherence to one.

African Religion in Historical Perspective

Beginnings

Africa has been the home of human beings long before the dawn of history. Scientists believe that humanlike creatures roamed the plateaus of eastern Africa at least 3 million years ago. Today, archeologists are increasingly convinced that it was in Africa that humans became differentiated from other primates. And yet, little is known of the beginnings of African religion, particularly the area south of the Sahara Desert.

Historians know a lot about the religion of the ancient Egyptians living in northern Africa because they developed a system of writing by 3000 BCE and left a rich legacy of written records. But no such written material is available for sub-Saharan Africa before the arrival of Europeans in the fifteenth century of this era. Archeological evidence provides the only source of information for reconstructing the beginnings of religion in sub-Saharan Africa.

Archeological evidence based on several sites dating from 30,000 BCE indicates premeditation in the treatment and burial of human corpses. There are also rock paintings, depicting masked figures or serpentlike creatures, associated with some sort of religious activity. And finally, the discoveries of a variety of artifacts, particularly objects related to divination, also indicate the presence of religious activity. Naturally, religious objects—like shrines, stools, masks, and dress, from which a certain amount of historical study can be derived—do not survive long on account of the tropical climate of Africa. Consequently, these

Hidden in remote valleys of the mountains are some three thousand galleries of rock paintings.   Courtesy of South African Tourism Board, Toronto, Canada.

archeological finds are limited in terms of what they reveal about the beginnings of African religion. Nonetheless, they provide valuable evidence of a link between past and present.

Precolonial Period

The dearth of written records prevents scholars from reconstructing clearly the history of sub-Saharan Africa before the colonial period, that is, the period before the European explorations, which started in the 1400s. Nevertheless, the available information provides some significant episodes in the long development of African culture and civilization.

Long before the discovery of Africa by Europeans, Africans had developed their languages, cultures, political structures, social institutions, and religious systems. African religious systems consisted of Christianity (mainly concentrated in Egypt and Ethiopia), Islam (predominantly in northern Africa), Judaism (scattered communities throughout the continent), and a variety of indigenous religions. The contact of African culture with these other cultures, particularly with

Islam, resulted in the creation of several great kingdoms. The best known were those of Ghana in the interior of western Africa along the Niger River from the eighth to the eleventh centuries, and its successor Mali, which controlled trade across the desert until about 1500, when it was overthrown by the Songhay. Smaller kingdoms also flourished in other parts of Africa. In Nigeria and to the west were the kingdoms of Benin, Oyo, and Akan; to the east were the Baganda; and the territory of Sudan was occupied by the Funj. Other African societies were scattered throughout central and southern Africa. But all these developments were arrested by the arrival of Europeans into Africa.

European Impact

The first European nation to become seriously interested in sub-Saharan Africa was Portugal. Prince Henry the Navigator sent Portuguese sailors to explore the west coast of Africa in the early 1400s. Their expeditions brought them as far south as Sierra Leone. Subsequent Portuguese expeditions led to the discovery of an all-sea travel route to the Far East by sailing around the Cape. Soon, the Dutch, the French, and the British followed the Portuguese in establishing trade routes and settlements serving as supply stations for ships traveling to the Far East. The presence of these European nations disrupted age-old African social patterns and traditional powers.

Before the arrival of Europeans, Arab slave traders dealt in the profitable business of buying and selling human beings. Under the Europeans, the African slave trade became the most lucrative business in supplying cheap labor for plantations in the newly discovered lands of the Americas (south, central, and north) and the Caribbean. The first African slaves arrived in Haiti in 1502. African tribes and kingdoms waged wars against each other to take captives and sell them to European agents—the British, Dutch, French, and Portuguese. The king of Dahomey, for instance, sent his armies against neighboring tribes each year to capture slaves. By the mid-1800s, most European nations considered slave trafficking an illegal enterprise. In the meantime, millions of Africans were sold, the effects of which are still being felt in Africa, Europe, and the Americas.

During all these years, Europeans made little effort to explore the interior of Africa. They lived along the shores of western and southern Africa, while African traders brought them slaves, ivory, gold, and other valuables from the interior. The two most famous African explorers were David Livingstone (1813–1873) and Henry M. Stanley (1841–1904). Livingstone, a Scottish medical missionary, came to Africa in 1841 and lived there for several long periods, during which he explored the interior. In 1869, Stanley, who was then a reporter for the *New York Herald*, was sent to search for Livingstone, who had not been heard from for over five years. When they finally met, Stanley greeted Livingstone with the now famous words, "Dr. Livingstone, I presume?"

Others followed suit. European governments, private companies, scientific institutions, and missionary societies all entered the race of exploring inland Africa. This European advance spurred national rivalries among British, French, German, and Belgian powers. In 1884–1885, the major European powers held a conference in Berlin to decide territorial rights in equatorial Africa. The decision of the conference stipulated that any nation had the right to claim any African territory it could occupy and develop. Consequently, most of Africa, with the exception of Ethiopia, the Union of South Africa (comprising four British colonies), and Egypt, was under colonial rule from 1900 until the end of World War II in 1945.

This massive advance of European civilization into Africa had two far-reaching effects: the disappearance of many, though not all, African tribes, and the modification of traditional African patterns of life as a compromise required for life in a European society. But after World War II, resistance to compromises developed as Africans increasingly demanded self-rule. European powers soon found themselves caught between pro- and anti-independence movements. Before long, the majority of Africans were chanting the slogan "Africa for Africans." One by one, African societies gained their freedom from colonial rulers. But the struggle for independence is by no means over, especially in South Africa, where colonial heritage is still a haunting problem.

Religious Interactions: Christian, Muslim, African

Spread of Christianity and Islam

Undoubtedly, African religion was most affected by its contact with Christianity and Islam, although the interaction of these religions did not mean a total abandonment of African religious traditions. Christianity reached Egypt, Ethiopia, Sudan, and northern Africa within the first five centuries of its history, but then suffered serious setbacks when Islam conquered and occupied northern Africa immediately after its inception in the seventh century CE. From then on, Islam's expansion in other parts of Africa was relatively slow until the colonial period, when it spread once again south of the Sahara, establishing various important centers both inland and along the entire coast of Africa. During the colonial period European Christians were also very active in spreading their form of Christianity.

Impact of Christianity and Islam

The relationship of colonial Christians to the peoples of Africa was based on the following assumption: Africans were "savages" with an inferior culture who needed the Christian faith and European civilization before they could take their place proudly with the Western world. The two most effective means to achieve this end were conversion and education. Consequently, the Christian scriptures were translated into hundreds of vernacular languages, and modern institutions of learning were established in virtually all of Africa.

By contrast, cultured Muslims held a certain degree of disdain for the "ignorant" masses of African tribes, and Islamic scriptures remained untranslatable in principle. True, the steps to become a Muslim were easier than those necessary for Christian conversion and baptism. Moreover, Muslim converts had more freedom to achieve religious status, or leadership roles, than their Christian counterparts, who had to acquiesce to the demanding requirements of ordination and strong moral discipline. Again, Islam was able to accommodate readily to a wide range of African practices, such as polygamy, certain

A mass in a stadium in Maputo, Mozambique marks the start of a meeting of southern African Catholic bishops.   Alfredo Mueche/AIM Impact Visuals.

forms of magic and divination, and traditional male dominance. And yet, at certain points Islam rejected African traditions, particularly the representation of divinities by images and the secret societies that challenged the prerogatives of the Islamic *umma,* or unitary community.

In spite of these restrictive features, both Christianity and Islam took root and expanded in sub-Saharan Africa. Today, these two religions are the dominant faiths of the continent. But the most dynamic modern phenomenon has been the emergence of a wide range of new religious movements that draw on local African religious traditions and one or both of the introduced faiths. These new movements represent the creative attempts of African peoples to adapt religion to African conditions and needs by synthesizing in varying degrees all available religious and cultural resources.

New Syncretistic Movements

Syncretism involving African, Christian, and Muslim religious traditions has resulted in thousands of new movements among hundreds of African peoples.[9] Some movements are more concerned with practical, relevant social issues than with African traditions or Christian and Muslim orthodoxies. Some tend to emphasize the indigenous religious tradition but have also adopted some important features from one or both of the other faiths. A few groups have added to their traditional spirit-possession cults the Muslim *jinn* (spirits) and claim that this spirit power is present in human embodiment rather than in a cultic object. Others endeavor to minimize African traditions by adopting Christian or Muslim features in a reshaped form. For instance, the movement founded by Hamallah in 1925 regarded Nioro, Mali, as a holy city and more important than Mecca or Jerusalem; Yakouba Sylla, who in the 1930s claimed to have received a new revelation from Fatima, the daughter of Muhammad, rejected the authority of the Qur'an and the centrality of Islamic prayer, and made fasting optional; the God's Kingdom Society has replaced the festivity of Christmas with the Jewish Feast of Tabernacles.

Some of these syncretistic attempts are very flexible in matters of belief and practice. They usually lack the elements inherent in an established tradition or the characteristics of an organized institution. Essentially, such movements do not represent anti-Western protests. Rather, they seek positive spiritual goals. And most of these new movements offer religious identity and status based on what they consider to be African values. Today, such religious movements are increasing and represent a distinctive part of African religion that cannot be readily ignored.

African Traditional Religions

The conversion of African peoples to Christianity, Islam, or the new movements has in no way eclipsed African traditional religions.[10] In terms of the entire population of Africa, followers of African traditional religions have declined since the beginning of the twentieth century. But in specific areas of Africa today, there is a resurgence of traditional religions. Thousands of self-contained tribes, with their distinct languages and cultures, live on the continent of Africa and constantly shift from territory to territory. The size and complexity of these scattered tribes create an enormous problem in identifying common beliefs and practices. Nonetheless, an analysis of concepts and practices shared by African tribes is offered after a brief description of two African tribes: the Dinka and the Yoruba. These two examples suffice for grasping the general in terms of the particular.

Dinka Religion

The Dinka are a tribal group, numbering nearly 4 million people, who speak different dialects of a common language and live in the southern Sudan region. Their way of life is simple, rural, and centers on cattle herding. Some of the Dinka grow crops of grain and vegetables. Others are poor, have no cattle, and do not cultivate, but depend for subsistence on hunting and fishing.

The Dinka believe in superhuman forces in the world, called *Jok* or *Nhialic*, that transcend ordinary human ability. They are powerful, unseen, and affect human lives for good or ill. Some Dinka tribes believe that their "first" ancestor was one of these powers. Other tribes use the word *Nhialic* to identify the greatest of these powers. Nhialic is, in this context, referred to as creator, father, and bestower of rain. Prayers and sacrifices are offered to both Nhialic and Jok.

Clan divinities form part of this pantheon of occult powers. They are associated with a great number of symbols that represent birds, insects, animals, trees, rivers, and forests. Clan divinities are treated with great respect. For instance, a portion of whatever hunters and gatherers take for themselves they return as sacrificial offerings that are left for the animals or thrown into rivers, since these are the totems or the personifications of different clan divinities.

Other Dinka divinities have general rather than specific tribal associations and are known by name though they are not endowed with human forms. They operate as natural but invisible and immaterial agents of unusual and unexplainable events, such as dreams, sickness, and sudden rain or thunder.

Dinkas believe that every individual has a *tiep*, a ghost, shadow, or spirit. At death, though the individual's *tiep* escapes from the body, it is thought to hover or linger near the corpse at the place of burial. Survivors offer sacrifices to the *tiep* of relatives that have died recently as propitiatory gestures to safeguard the living against any possible disaffection from the lingering *tiep* of the dead. In time, each *tiep's* presence or influence fades and weakens so that, with the passage of several generations, ancient *tieps* may be safely ignored.

Among other rituals and ceremonies, prayers and sacrifices play a major role among the Dinka. Animal sacrifices are offered to divine powers as well as to the dead. For instance, life and health are thought of as gifts attributable to Nhialic and Jok. In return, gifts of prayer and sacrifice to them form part of regular rather than seasonal or sporadic observances, such as votive offerings in thanksgiving for recovery from illness, relief from famine, and success in hunting.

Those who lead the prayers are known as "spear masters." It is their function to intone prayer phrases, often with spear in hand and sometimes thrusting it toward the sacrificial offering in order to emphasize a particular phrase. Observers and participants repeat these prayer phrases in chorus, but usually with more fervor than is generally characteristic of worship in a temple, church, or mosque. This pattern of invocation and response, especially on occasions of particular significance or crisis, may continue for several hours and may induce in the spear master a condition of deep ecstasy.

The vitality and well-being of the Dinka tribe depend on these prayer leaders or spear masters. They preside over all affairs of life, including petitions made to divine powers. They settle quarrels, plead for rain, make peace between enemies, and ask protection for their tribe and herds. They are the most important men in the tribe.

The office of a spear master is hereditary. Sometimes, however, an individual may be recognized to be possessed by a divine power. The signs of such possession are trembling fits followed by a trance. In this state, the possessed is capable of answering questions and solving problems.

The Dinka build small shrines to "house" the *tieps* of important people. These shrines, however, are nothing more than clay mounds where relatives may place their offerings. Equally simple but more elaborate sanctuaries resembling small cattle barns shelter divine powers. They also house sacred spears and other objects of ritual and veneration.

The term *myth* has been denigrated by its association with the supernatural and merely fanciful. It also refers to an allegory or a traditional narrative embodying ideas on natural and social phenomena, including topics of a sacred or religious nature. The Dinka have an interesting myth about the origin of the human condition. In the beginning the sky, domain of the divine, and the earth, home of mortals, were joined or connected by a rope that made a concept like death quite meaningless since humans could climb up and down at will. The divinity granted one grain of millet per day to the first human couple in order to satisfy their needs until, one day, the woman decided to plant the grain of millet and, in raising her hoe, struck the divinity. Offended, the divinity retaliated by sending a small blue bird to sever the rope that gave humans access to the sky. Ever since then, humans have had to labor for food; have become subject to famine, sickness, and death; and are denied free access to the divinity.

This story represents only one of many Dinka myths. Another myth rationalizes human dependence on fire, especially for cooking. And another myth illustrates the life-supporting role of rivers. Yet another explains the origin of the priestly function of the spear masters. All Dinka myths represent expressions of their ethos or life-style. The universe, for the Dinka people, contains an intermixture of benign and dangerous elements, or powers. These powers must be properly and respectfully treated in order to maintain a consistent equilibrium between tribal society on the one hand and the entire cosmos on the other.

Yoruba Religion

Unlike the pastoralist society of the Dinka, the Yoruba are a highly urbanized society organized around large city-state kingdoms, numbering between 12 and 15 million people. Presently, they occupy portions of southwestern Nigeria and the neighboring areas of Dahomey and Togo, in western Africa.

Yoruba religion is centered on the worship of a variety of *orisha* (divinities), each having its own priests, shrines, cultic functions, and a special section in town. At the head of this extensive *orisha* pantheon is Olorun (whose name means Lord Owner of the Sky), the supreme being in Yoruba religion, who is regarded to have partly transcendent and partly immanent features.

Olorun is said to have created the world by delegating this task to one of his sons, Obatala. One version relates how Olorun gave Obatala the necessary supplies, some dry soil, and a five-toed hen to scratch and spread the soil over the primordial waters covering the earth. After this performance, Obatala fashioned human beings from clay. Another version, however, has Oduduwa, Olorun's younger son, being entrusted to complete the task, because Obatala's drunkenness while performing the work of creation resulted in misshapen people. Oduduwa then fashioned people, built a town, and became its first king. Whatever the political implications behind these two versions, Olorun clearly retains his supreme position. In fact, Olorun is regarded as the supreme determiner of human destiny. Every individual's guardian soul receives a destiny and a fixed span of life from Olorun. If a person has led a good life, Olorun will consider him or her worthy of reincarnation. If, however, a person has led an evil life, Olorun will consign him or her to a hot place of punishment and destruction.

The numerous *orisha* worshiped in Yoruba religion differ from region to region and from group to group. Generally, however, an individual worships the *orisha* of his or her father. This desire for a close association with *orisha* at times verges upon personal identification with them. If the individual encounters some misfortune, then it is time to change one's devotion to another *orisha*. Thus, to the Yoruba devotee, the *orisha* symbolize certain unconscious aspects of the self and also act as guardian spirits.

The most popular and widely accepted *orisha* is Ogun, the divinity of war, hunting, iron, and steel. Dogs, who help in hunting and war, are uniquely appropriate therefore to be sacrificed to Ogun. This ritual of sacrifice is an annual festival celebrated by the entire people of the town or, more often, by family compounds. The feast consists of several phases. First, the most appropriate date to celebrate the ritual is determined by divinatory acts. Next, the officiating family heads prepare themselves by abstaining from cursing, fighting, eating certain foods, and sexual intercourse. Then, the men go on a hunting expedition to gather fresh game. In the evening, an all-night vigil is kept near Ogun's shrine, which consists of a simple stone column set before a tree. Throughout the night, songs are chanted in honor of Ogun and quantities of beer and palm wine are consumed by the family members. The ceremony of sacrifices begins on the day following the vigil, with offerings made to Ogun. These offerings consist of kola nuts, snails, pigeons, palm oil, and dogs. Following the immolation and consecration of the victims, participants share the consecrated flesh of the dogs, and a general carnival atmosphere prevails, particularly if the festival involves a whole town.

These offerings are appropriate mediating symbols that control Ogun's relations with his people. Conceived in this way, rituals of sacrifice have special power to evoke the spirits and channel them according to the wishes of the worshiper. Other rituals consist of mythic celebrations, such as the reenactment of the battle between Oduduwa and Obatala. In fact, feasts play a significant role in Yoruba religion. The annual feast of male ancestors consists of a masked stately procession; the feast of mothers celebrates female powers; and the feast of kings and ritual functionaries deals with dialectical relations.

Patterns of Belief

African religious concepts and practices differ from tribe to tribe, but several basic patterns are common to most of them. Many Africans believe that the essence of life lies in the perception that the chief god, lesser gods, ancestors, spirits, sky, earth, vegetation, water, climate, animals, and persons all form an integral part and are inextricably bound to the rhythms and patterns of the universe.

Chief God. The concept of a chief god or supreme being as creator, preserver, and sustainer of the universe is self-evident to most Africans. This chief god, called by a hundred different names varying from tribe to tribe, is conceived of as self-existent, eternal, maker of the world, master of human destiny, omnipotent, omnipresent, kind, just, good, father, mother, and friend.

Several questions, however, have puzzled Western observers. Is the chief god a personal being, an impersonal spirit, a sort of creative energy, or an abstract idea? Does the chief god exist apart from or pervade the universe? Is the chief god indifferent to or actively involved in human affairs? The answers to these questions differ from group to group. To the Bantu and Sudanese, for instance, the chief god Mulungu is both a personal being and an impersonal spirit. As such, Mulungu is ruler, judge, omnipotent, and omnipresent, whose voice is heard in thunder and whose power appears in lightning. Similarly, to the Dogon, the chief god Amma created the heavens and the earth, and then united himself with the earth to produce a series of mortal twins. In other instances, such as with the Shona and the Kimbu, the chief god is clearly and exclusively personalized as a creator and life giver. Thus, sometimes the chief god is spoken of personally, often with a wife and family; and sometimes the chief god is associated with nature, represented by sun, rain, lightning, mountains, rivers, and so on.

Lesser Gods, Ancestors, and Other Spirits. In addition to a chief god, many Africans believe in the existence of lesser gods, ancestor spirits, nature spirits, various powers, and impersonal forces. These lesser divinities, who derive their power from the chief god, govern all human activities and natural phenomena. Sometimes they act directly as messengers of the chief god; sometimes they appear as personifications of natural phenomena, such as wind, rain, thunder, and death; and sometimes they manifest themselves in an object or place, such as a rock, a tree, or a lake. No matter how they appear, these lesser spirits and forces are regarded by many Africans as the most immediate link between themselves and the chief god. Although generally beneficent, they can also be dangerous, causing harm and

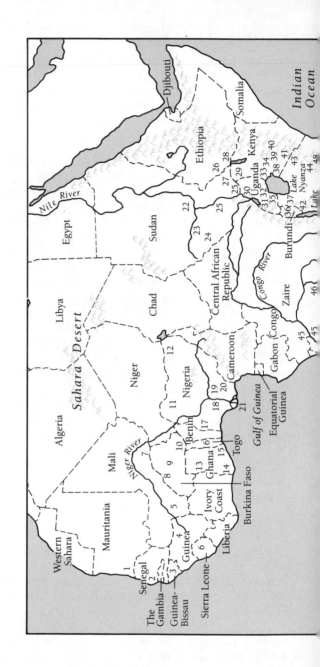

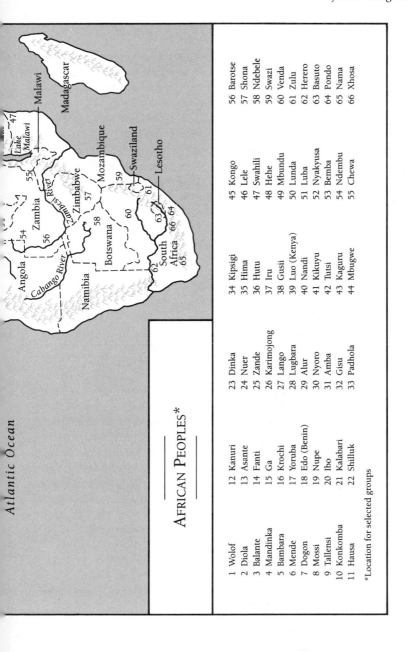

AFRICAN PEOPLES*

1 Wolof
2 Diola
3 Balante
4 Mandinka
5 Bambara
6 Mende
7 Dogon
8 Mossi
9 Tallensi
10 Konkomba
11 Hausa
12 Kanuri
13 Asante
14 Fanti
15 Ga
16 Krochi
17 Yoruba
18 Edo (Benin)
19 Nupe
20 Ibo
21 Kalabari
22 Shilluk

23 Dinka
24 Nuer
25 Zande
26 Karimojong
27 Lango
28 Lugbara
29 Alur
30 Nyoro
31 Amba
32 Gisu
33 Padhola

34 Kipsigi
35 Hima
36 Hutu
37 Iru
38 Gusii
39 Luo (Kenya)
40 Nandi
41 Kikuyu
42 Tutsi
43 Kaguru
44 Mbugwe

45 Kongo
46 Lele
47 Swahili
48 Hehe
49 Mbundu
50 Lunda
51 Luba
52 Nyakyusa
53 Bemba
54 Ndembu
55 Chewa

56 Barotse
57 Shona
58 Ndebele
59 Swazi
60 Venda
61 Zulu
62 Herero
63 Basuto
64 Pondo
65 Nama
66 Xhosa

*Location for selected groups

damage. Consequently, most Africans attach great importance to these lesser divinities and try to live at peace with them.

The belief in spirits and powers is so widespread throughout Africa that it is often difficult to distinguish their role and function. Generally, however, Africans recognize different levels of spirits. Totemic spirits are invoked as the guardians of clans and lineages. Territorial spirits (i.e., ancestor spirits of chiefs or eminent personalities) are invoked on behalf of larger social groupings. Ancestor spirits, who are the most important members of a community, offer protection to living relatives. Hence, each group, family, or individual maintains a special relationship with ancestors. Much of traditional morality is therefore based on pleasing the ancestor spirits and living in harmony with them. The method of contact with ancestor spirits varies from tribe to tribe but generally involves the use of libation, prayers, sacrifices, and offerings.

Then, there are gods created in the form of various disembodied spirits, and still other spirits are enshrined in nature. Storm spirits are most popular in areas where tropical tornadoes, torrential rains, lightning, and thunderbolts cause severe damage. Water spirits are revered by fishermen and by those dwelling close to rivers or lakes. Earth spirits include mountains, hills, forests, trees, and rocks. Hunters, soldiers, and rainmakers, among others, call upon earth spirits by placing their offerings at the foot of a hill, tree, or stone.

Many African peoples claim to see, hear, or be possessed by spirits, often for purposes of divination. Some societies perform masquerades both to renew human contact with the spirits and to maintain a friendly relationship between the spiritual and material worlds. These two worlds are inseparable and represent a dynamic, unified universe. Any evil or disorder, either among humans or in the material world, is commonly traced to those who possess special powers to bring harm secretly. Consequently, people appeal to these various sources of power for help. Many houses and villages have images or symbols of guardian divinities, whose powers are turned against intruders and in favor of the householders.

Mythical Views. African myths are extremely popular and are told at all levels of society. They include animal fables, creation stories, heroic feats, divine intrigues, folk tales, and countless numbers of legends. Collections of such myths have been made from various parts of Africa, but there are still peoples whose mythology is hardly known. These collected myths, however, throw light on the religious dimension of African peoples.

Most African peoples have their own version of creation. The Dogon, for instance, believe that the chief god created the sun and the moon like pots—the sun with red copper rings and the moon with white copper rings. Next, he created the stars and the earth—the former from pellets of clay that were flung into space and the latter from a lump of clay. Next, the union of the chief god and earth resulted in a series of twins, four males and four females, who were the ancestors of the tribe.

Another creation account is found among the Luyia of Kenya. They believe that the chief god created his own dwelling place in heaven all by himself but then required the help of two assistants to place the pillars that support heaven. Next, he created the moon and its younger brother, the sun. Because the moon was bigger and brighter than the sun, jealousy stirred the sun to wrestle with the moon. But the moon easily defeated the sun. A second round of wrestling, however, resulted in the victory of the sun. The moon was thrown down and splashed with dirt. At this point, the chief god intervened and determined their boundaries: the sun was to shine brightly during the day, and the moon was to glow through its muddy face at night.

Other myths depict the withdrawal of the chief god from earth after completing his work of creation. Such myths describe how in ancient times the chief god lived on earth among human beings but eventually was forced to leave the world because of some human misdeed. The Mende, for instance, believe that the chief god quietly left this world while people slept, because they bothered him with their requests. A more common theme, however, depicts the departure of the chief god from this world by means of a rope or spider's web hanging from heaven to earth.

A number of myths related to the origin of human beings suggest that humankind was lowered from the sky to the earth as husband and wife. Other myths tell that men and women emerged out of the ground, out of a tree, or out of a reed bed. The Zulu and Thonga, for instance, believe that the first man and woman burst out of the explosion of the reed. The Ashanti hold to the view that several men and women, a dog, and a leopard all emerged together from the earth at night. According to a Pygmy story, the first man and woman came out of a tree when the chameleon split the tree with an axe because it heard a noise within the tree. Other myths tell that the chief god pulled the first man and woman out of the marshes or waters.

A number of other myths deal with the origin of death. One myth explains death as the result of sleep. The story goes that primordial ancestors were told to stay awake until the chief god came back from a trip. But these ancestors were so overcome by sleep that they failed to receive from the chief god their reward of immortality. Another myth suggests that at one time human beings lived together with the chief god in the same village in heaven. But human beings quarreled so much with each other that the chief god finally exiled them in disgust to a place below, where they experienced hunger, sickness, and death. Longing for their earlier heavenly place, they quickly built a tower, whose top reached heaven. Overtaken with joy over this accomplishment, they beat their drums and played their flutes so loudly that the noise angered the chief god, who quickly flattened the tower.

Many African myths depict the original state of human beings as one of childlike ignorance, happiness, immortality, and eternal bliss. The loss of this original state of bliss differs in detail from one group to another. According to some, human beings disobeyed one or another divine law; according to others, a mischievous divine creature interfered. For some, people pestered the chief god until he withdrew from them; for others, the loss of the original state was a consequence of unforeseen circumstances. No matter how these stories depict the original state and present condition of African peoples, they all attempt to establish a divine-human link, which in turn provides a framework for self-identity.

Individuals, Morals, and Society. African people are conscious of themselves in terms of kinship or relationships. This means that each individual is inextricably bound to three interrelated entities:

1. A group, community, or society, including its social, economic, religious, and political obligations
2. The universe, with all its rhythms and patterns, and its animate and inanimate objects
3. The chief god, his divine assistants, ancestors, and all other spirits, who provide the immediate context in which life must be lived

In addition, each person is believed to possess two components: the material body, inherited from one's parents, and the animating principle, received from either the chief god or some other divine being. The harmony and interdependence of these two components define one's personality and character. Hence individual qualities, facial character, tone of voice, and physical stature all belong to an individual and cannot be acquired by another person. Any physical abnormality suggests that the person is possessed by the spirit of disease. Children born with such bodily marks are either burdened with protective charms, neglected for fear of bad luck, or exposed to die.

A person's happiness or misery is usually attributed to the activity of the chief god or to any one of the lesser divinities, powers, or forces. People believe that illness and death do not happen naturally but because of the maleficence of some person or power. This wicked person may be a witch or a sorcerer who lives among wild beasts and acts by night, plotting against a person or a group. By contrast, the person who knows how to harness and use power for the happiness of a person or for the benefit of a group is greatly respected.

Moral virtues and offenses naturally vary from place to place and group to group, but their presence is always recognized. The ethical teachings and moral responsibilities of most African traditional religions are not codified, since there is no writing. And yet proper and improper human behavior is delineated in the customs, laws, taboos, and traditions of each African people. Custom regulates what ought not to be done. Stealing, lying, disrespecting elders, adultery, murder, causing deliberate injury to persons or property, and practicing witchcraft are, among others, considered great social offenses. African traditional religions are generally silent about rewards and punishments in eternity. Rather, society rewards the good person and punishes the evildoer. If an offender is not detected immediately by the community, then the chief god, the ancestor spirit, or some other divine power will sooner or later punish that person by means of a misfortune.

Thus, the primacy of society over the individual is so important that any offense against the laws, customs, and rules that govern a particular society is considered to diminish the value of that society. Ethics and morality are therefore conceived in terms of kinship or relationships. And it is precisely this sense of kinship that guides an individual's action and generates a wide range of social expectations.

Manifestations of Religious Activity

African religion is a communal affair, and certain individuals within the community are responsible for the religious activities of the group or community. These include kings, royal personages, chiefs, rulers, priests, priestesses, prophetic figures, spiritual intermediaries, diviners, elders, holy men and women, shamans, shamanesses, keepers of sacred places, musicians, drummers, and so on. Some of these individuals inherit their role by virtue of birth, some require long training before a formal commissioning is publicly declared, and some are self-made specialists who claim to have received divine power, knowledge, or insight to assist an individual or a group at times of crisis. Regardless of the role they play, these individuals are highly respected within the community, because the community relies on them for the performance of important rituals.

Sacrifice. The most important ritual among African religious practices is sacrifice. This may be in the form of offering libations, foodstuffs, first fruits, first portions of harvested grain, nonedible goods, and living animals such as cows, goats, sheep, or fowl. Sacrifices are made for various purposes, either individually or communally. Some sacri-

African Bantu (Swazi) tribe en route to the queen's kraal *(homestead) to celebrate a special ceremony.*   Courtesy of South African Tourism Board, Toronto, Canada.

fices are preventive in character and serve to avert dangers or misfortunes that threaten a person, a family, or the whole community. Others are expiatory in nature and are intended to remove guilt or offense. Still others are periodic offerings made to ancestors at their graves. And, finally, special occasions, such as an annual festival, call for a great sacrifice offered to honor and propitiate the chief god, his divine assistants, ancestors, and other spirits.

Prayer. Many Africans offer prayers daily to the guardian spirit or other deities enshrined in the home or hut. In many families, the oldest person, male or female, performs daily devotions on behalf of the rest of the family, while the other members stand in devotional respect or join in a simple prayer. Naturally the words of the prayer vary, but generally petitions are made for the health and welfare of the family. A simple offering of a libation and a tiny portion of some foodstuff is customarily placed in front of the shrine.

Rites of Passage. To African peoples, practically every element of life, from birth to final entry into the ancestral community after death, has a religious aspect that is marked with a specific ritual. Four stages in the life of an individual, however, represent significant transitional moments that require appropriate ritual acts. These four transitional stages are: (1) birth, (2) initiation, (3) marriage, and (4) death.

Birth ceremonies vary from group to group, but almost all African peoples observe this happy occasion by naming the child, by introducing him or her to relatives and neighbors, and by offering sacrifices and prayers to the ancestors for the cleansing of the mother and child from birth impurities.

Initiation rites are usually very elaborate, lasting from a few days to more than two years. They are performed often in seclusion with the aim of introducing the youth into adult membership. In some societies initiates submit to physical hardships and emotional strains, symbolizing their transition from a childhood condition to a stage of adult responsibility. Widely practiced are the rites of circumcision for boys and clitoridectomy (incision of the clitoris) for girls. But the whole purpose of the initiation rite is to ensure that boys and girls receive basic knowledge of tribal history, social duties, and ancestral customs before they assume their proper role in society.

Marriage is a festive communal event involving the entire extended family—that is, the bride and groom, their families, clans, ancestors, and the unborn. Customs vary from group to group, but generally speaking, the ritual associated with marriage includes the preparation and arrangement of the ceremony to cement family alliances and to sustain the sanctity of life. With few exceptions, everyone is expected to get married, whether the marriage partners choose each other or are matched by parents or relatives. Failure to do so constitutes an offense against society. Hence, the concept of renunciation or asceticism is foreign to African peoples. Rather, marriage and procreation are the proper duties of a person; and the more children one has, the greater the blessings both in this life and hereafter. Consequently, polygamy is accepted and respected in most societies. In cases of sterility or barrenness, custom dictates the following options: if the wife is barren, the husband marries another woman; if the husband is sterile, the wife produces children through the brother of her husband; and in a few cases, divorce is permitted. In some societies, if a man dies before being married, his parents or close relatives arrange for his marriage *in absentia,* so that children born on his behalf may perform the necessary ancestral rites.

Death is considered to provide the passage from this world to the world of spirits and the company of departed ancestors. Funeral rites thus are observed very carefully so as not to offend the departed. These rites vary from society to society and last from several months to several years. The corpse may be kept for a while in a special hut before it is buried in a grave. Some societies bury the dead with

African Zulu chief with his wives, in their ceremonial dresses, in front of his kraal
(village compound).   Courtesy of South African Tourism Board, Toronto, Canada.

foodstuffs, personal belongings, weapons, and money to ensure the
sustenance and safety of the departed during the journey to the next
world. In most cases, a shrine near the household or village of the
departed acts as a contact point between the living and the "living
dead."

Occultism.   Another important category of religious activity in African
traditional religions is occultism. At the popular level, this involves
either manipulating or counteracting the forces or powers of evil.
Witches, sorcerers, diviners, and medicine men, among others, thus
render an important service by providing a protective or retaliatory
course of action. Seeking omens, consulting magicians, and appealing
to diviners to discover or influence the will of the spirits is, of course, a
common practice among most Africans. Moreover, symbolism and
ritual are common to occult activity. Objects that may be ordinary in a

daily situation may be endowed with magical significance. Similarly, the forces symbolized in rituals frequently function as external representations of the supernatural or spiritual world.

The art of magic, as practiced in most African traditional religions, is always for the attainment of practical aims or specific goals. In case of failure, stronger magic is used, or a substitute magic is called on to offset the countermagic of enemies. The techniques to attain such goals are quite diverse and vary not only in form but also in motivation and significance. Some persons, for instance, wear protective amulets, whose efficacy has been proven to protect against evil powers and influences. Some groups impose various restrictions and prohibitions not so much to please deities, but to protect themselves from the dangers and harms of evil influences and hostile spirits. Among pastoral and agricultural peoples, magical acts are performed in the belief that departed spirits are able to grant or withhold fertility to the soil. And finally, imitative magic (also referred as mimetic or sympathetic magic) is employed for numerous purposes: banishing evil and misfortune, such as sickness, guilt, and uncleanness; casting or averting curses or spells; gaining victory in war; and so on.

Incredible as the alleged phenomenon may appear to modern, scientifically oriented people, most Africans sincerely believe that certain individuals have the power to evoke, and to communicate with, the "living dead" or other spirits. These possessors of extrasensory powers claim to be able to act upon the course of events and obtain any required information. Their art, commonly known as *divination*, is very popular, and their message varies from discovering the past to revealing future events or interpreting dreams. Because they are in constant contact with spirits, they respond to seekers of guidance and information either by direct intuition or through spirit-possessed trances.

Sacred Sites and Objects. Natural objects and places are focal points for African peoples to interact with the world of the spirits and deities. Hence, trees, caves, springs, ponds, stones, hills, and mountain peaks are regarded as possessed by spirits or as the places of abode of spirits and deities. Such spots thus acquire a sacred character and are recognized as sites of worship. Each region has its sacred sites, some of which are used for saying prayers, making vows, offering sacrifices, or holding ceremonial meetings.

Sacred objects include, among others, drums, masks, headdresses, amulets, hunting trophies, divination objects such as rainmaking stones, fires, carvings, certain animals, colors, and numbers. Masks and body painting often reflect ritual possession. Such colors as black or white have a potent effect for certain groups, so that during certain ceremonies animals bearing these colors only are offered for sacrifice.

African Xhosa women prepare ochre and paint it on children's faces.   Courtesy of South African Tourism Board, Toronto, Canada.

Among other groups, the number nine is so significant that certain ceremonies require the use of nine items. Many taboos are associated with these objects, the misuse of which entails misfortune or even death.

Sacred sites and objects thus represent the presence of a spirit or a deity. This deep affinity with natural objects and places reflects not a form of nature worship but the African understanding of the inseparable link between the visible and invisible worlds.

Notes

1. For a brief survey of perspectives on African religions, see Benjamin C. Ray, *African Religions* (Englewood Cliffs, N.J.: Prentice-Hall, 1976), pp. 2–22.
2. Among others, see the works of Samuel Baker, Richard F. Burton, T. J. Bowen, and David Livingstone.

3. Kenneth Clark, *Civilization* (New York: Harper & Row, 1969), p. 2.

4. See, for instance, the works of August Comte, Edward Burnett Tylor, James G. Frazer, and Wilhelm Schmidt.

5. For British anthropologists, see, for instance, the works of A. R. Radcliffe-Brown and Max Gluckman; for French anthropologists, see, for instance, Marcel Griaule and Germaine Dieterlen.

6. Among others, see the works of E. E. Evans-Pritchard, Joachim Wach, John Middleton, Godfrey Lienhardt, Clifford Greetz, and Victor Turner.

7. See, for instance, C. G. Seligman, *Races of Africa* (London: Oxford University Press, 1930); and E. R. Sanders, "The Hamitic Hypothesis: Its Origins and Functions in Time Perspective," *Journal of African History* 10, 4 (1969):521–532.

8. See, for instance, the works of Robin Horton, Geoffrey Parrinder, John S. Mbiti, Joseph B. Danquah, Idowu E. Bolaji, Ali A. Mazrui, Chinua Achebe, and Wole Soyinka.

9. Estimates of the number of new religious movements vary, but probably there are about ten thousand spread over eastern, southern, western, and central Africa.

10. Estimates of the number of Africans belonging to African traditional religions vary from 30 to 50 percent of the total population of Africa.

4

American Indian Traditions

Traditional Characteristics

American Indians (also referred to as Natives, Native Americans, or Amerindians) live in various parts of Canada, the United States, and Central and South America. Their existence on the American continents is estimated to date from as early as 40,000 to 20,000 BCE. Some groups, such as the Sioux, Crow, and Comanche, were primarily nomadic, hunting societies; others, such as the Hopi and Algonquin, developed advanced agricultural societies. Each of these societies spoke a different language and evolved a different way of life. Even tribes living in close proximity to each other differed significantly in linguistic dialects, beliefs, and ceremonies.

Because of their contact with white, Western cultures, few American Indians live today as their ancestors did. Many tribes have been virtually annihilated, either by European expansion since the sixteenth century or through intertribal warfare. Contact with Christianity over four centuries resulted in bloody conflict with settlers and pioneers, in defeat when resistance provoked military intervention, and in survival in restricted areas in North America and on "reservations" in various locations all over the continent. Inevitably, these events brought irremediable changes, although a few American Indian tribes were able to retain certain aspects of their ancient life-styles and religious tradition.[1]

Unfortunately these traditional aspects are sometimes taken out of context by the writers of westerns and by film or television program producers more intent on provoking an exotic thrill or a shudder of horror in their audiences than on ascertaining authenticity. The temptation to speculate about the heritage of American Indians is further heightened by the dearth of evidence. Certain constraints are involved in the study of Native American cultures. First, the American Indians kept no written records. Much of the information that survives derives from oral traditions passed on from generation to generation. Second, anyone who does not belong to the tribe is considered an outsider. This means that a certain amount of information is withheld, so that even the most scholarly study or close observation is ultimately doomed to be somewhat restricted or deficient. Third, many tribal members are never fully initiated into a particular rite, for various reasons—one of which is the constraint imposed by long, involved ceremonies. Hence, it is difficult, if not impossible, to obtain any clear definition of doctrine or of religious systems. Finally, American Indians have developed diverse religious traditions involving the beliefs and practices of particular tribes in particular geographical locations.

In spite of these points of contrast, the beliefs of Native Americans are distinguished by some common characteristics. For instance, they all seem to share a belief in the existence of a high god or vital force, along with lesser gods and spirits. Again, they all hold to the idea that certain individuals possess sacred power and therefore can act as intermediaries between the tribe and the deities. In ceremonies associated with ritual and initiation, they all engage in certain traditional rites that are designed to perpetuate the smooth operation of the natural order, including human society, and they all believe that by repeating stories or by storytelling they literally keep the world alive. What follows is a summary of the rituals and traditions of a few extinct and surviving groups of Native Americans, illustrating both the characteristics they share and their points of contrast.

Origins

Recent excavations conducted by Mexican archeologists indicate that about 10,000 to 12,000 years ago nomadic hunters and food gatherers wandered in the valley of Mexico (the region around present-day Mexico City). It is not known precisely when the earliest settlements were established in the valley of Mexico, but radiocarbon techniques reveal dates between 1500 and 900 BCE.

Among the early civilizations in present-day Mexico and surround-

These gigantic figures once supported the roof of the temple of Quetzalcoatl (ket-säl-kwat-əl), lord of life, death, and the wind. The Toltecs who built them considered themselves to be the descendants of Quetzalcoatl. In the fifteenth century CE, *Aztec chiefs married the Toltec princesses in order to inherit the divine right to rule.* Courtesy of Mexican Government Tourism Office, Toronto, Canada.

ing areas were those of the Olmec and Toltec peoples, who built ceremonial centers, erected carved monoliths and altars, developed the art of architecture, and devised a system of hieroglyphic writing. The Toltecs worshiped earth, water, and astral deities. Archeologists have discovered in Teotihuacán (in central Mexico) monuments that date from 200 to 700 CE. The site, which is teeming with small pyramids and buildings, is dominated by two huge pyramids, popularly known as the Pyramid of the Sun and the Pyramid of the Moon.

Mayans

Mayan civilization was at its height between 300 and 900 CE. But little is known of the formative period (starting perhaps as early as 1200 BCE), except that several groups, such as the Zapotec, the Olmec, and the Teotihuacán, existed from early times. Just when the Mayan civilization assumed its distinctive role and character is difficult to determine. What is known is that the Mayan civilization spread over what is now Mexico, Guatemala, Honduras, and Belize. The Mayans developed the highest civilization in the so-called New World before the arrival of the Spaniards, who conquered the area in the years 1520–1545, leaving the entire region in an uninhabitable condition.

During the classic period (c. 350–800 CE), Mayan cities were composed of many pyramidlike structures. Impressive flights of steps led to the temples and palaces that were situated within the pyramids. People also lived in scattered settlements over the surrounding countryside. All important events, such as religious ceremonies and judicial proceedings, took place in the cities.

Some time between the ninth and tenth centuries CE, these cities, or centers, were abandoned. No conclusive evidence is available to explain this shift, although several conjectures have been offered. One hypothesis is that the peasants revolted and overthrew (or massacred) the ruling theocratic class. Others hinge on natural causes: soil exhaustion or pestilence. Whatever the reason, the area was invaded by native "foreigners" who ruled for a brief period of time (c. 1000–1200). Then followed a period of stability (c. 1200–1450), during which the power of control passed from the priesthood to the warrior chiefs. Soon, however, warfare between petty chiefs led to independent chiefdoms (c. 1450–1545). This disunited period accelerated a cultural decline and helped the Spanish, who easily won allies among discontented Mayans. Although the Spaniards ended the chaotic situation brought about by the warring states, they also put an end to what is considered to be the most brilliant pre-Columbian civilization.

Sources of Mayan Religion

Four main sources provide valuable knowledge of Mayan religion: (1) archeological remains, such as temples, tombs, sculpture, pottery, and other artifacts; (2) three books written in Mayan hieroglyphics (possibly copies of early originals), although, unfortunately, modern scholars are still unable to decipher most of these inscriptions; (3) several books, written by European-instructed Indians in native languages transliterated into Latin, that provide historical chronicles mixed with mythology, divination, and prophecy; and (4) accounts of Mayan life and history written in Spanish by conquerors or priests. To these sources may be added the observations recorded by modern anthropologists about the few existing Mayan people who have resisted conversion to Christianity.

Mayan Beliefs

Mayans believed that before the existence of the present world, several worlds had been successively created and destroyed. Humans were made at first from earth, but since they possessed no minds, they were destroyed. Next, humans were made of wood; but again, lack of intelligence and absence of souls made them ungrateful to the deities, and they were drowned in a flood (or, according to another version, devoured by demons). Finally, humans were made of maize gruel, and this time they survived to become the ancestors of the Mayans.

Humanity and the universe were, in the beginning, in darkness. The deities created the sun (god) and the moon (goddess), both of whom at first inhabited this world. However, they were both taken up to the sky as a result of the moon's sexual license. As a punishment for her

Temple of Kukulkan (also known as El Castillo) in Chichen Itza, Mexico. The pyramid structure is seventy-five feet high, and the Temple of Kukulkan, situated on top of the pyramid, is another fifteen feet high. The number of steps on the four sides, plus the summit platform, add up to 365, the number of days in a year. During the fall and spring equinox, the afternoon sun creates the image, in light and shade, of a serpent descending the northwest stairway. The Mayans considered this the descent of Kukulkan. Courtesy of Mexican Government Tourism Office, Toronto, Canada.

infidelity, the sun pulled out one of the moon's eyes—hence, lunar light is less bright than that of the sun.

Mayan deities were thought of as being simultaneously one and four as with the one-and-four gods who sustained the sky, the one-and-four deities who were assigned to each direction of the universe, and the one-and-four rain gods. Then there were the sun god and his wife, the moon goddess; the young maize god; the snake god; the feathered serpent; the nine gods of darkness, who ruled the nine subterranean worlds; and Itzamna, the lord of heavens, a benevolent god. To these deities must be added divinized stars or planets and the gods of the months, the days, and the numerals.

The Mayans also believed that their dead descended to the nine underworlds. There is no evidence of a belief in paradise. As to the universe, the Mayans believed it was doomed to come to a sudden end, just as the previous worlds had ended. But a new world would be created, so that the eternal succession of cycles would remain unbroken. Time was believed to be divine and accordingly was worshiped. Time periods were considered as gods, and priest-astronomers viewed time as a succession of cycles, with no beginning and no end.

Mayan Practices

Religion was woven into the entire social and political fabric of Mayan culture. Prayers and sacrifices were used to placate the deities. Sacrifices were made of animals, birds, fish, insects, food, drink, incense, gold, jade, and human blood drawn from the tongue, ears, arms, legs, or genitals. Prayers, fasting, sacrifices, dancing, and drawing blood from one's body often preceded important ceremonies.

To these practices were added human sacrifices. The victims were killed by arrows, beheading, or, more commonly, splitting the breast to remove the heart. As with the Aztecs, most victims were males.

Specialized priests dominated all of Mayan life, especially as sun worship and human sacrifice gained more and more importance. These priests acted as state administrators, architects, scholars, and astronomers. In fact, an extraordinary refinement of mathematical and astronomical knowledge, inextricably mixed with mythological concepts, may be deemed one of the most brilliant achievements of the Mayan priesthood.

Among the priests, some used hallucinatory drugs to induce prophetic and divinatory messages. Others made use of magical formulas or medicinal herbs in their roles as sorcerers and occult practitioners. Witchcraft was widespread, and because of their occult knowledge, priests were thought to inflict or heal diseases and to determine favorable or unfavorable days for undertakings. Even when the nobility acquired increased power in the postclassical period, the priesthood remained the most influential group in Mayan society until the Spanish conquest.

Aztecs

The Aztec Indians were one of a number of small nomadic tribes that moved southward from the present-day western United States, troubling the civilized people of central Mexico—most notably, the Toltecs. Shortly before 1200, the Aztecs occupied the valley of Mexico and its surrounding areas. Then, as they became numerous and warlike, they

Stone sculpture at San Agustin, Colombia. Note the elaborate headdress, the feline teeth, and the wide nostrils. The feline cult is an ancient element in American Indian culture. The jaguar personifies fertility as well as an ambivalent force capable of good and evil. From the private collection of E. Neglia.

formed allies with other powerful groups, conquered much of central Mexico, and expanded their territory into a large empire that included most of central and southern Mexico. Much of Aztec culture was borrowed from the people of the region that they conquered.

The capital of the Aztec Empire was Tenochtitlán (modern-day Mexico City), which had an estimated population of 100,000. Thousands of artisans worked to build and to maintain numerous flat-topped pyramids, temples, and palaces. In 1519, Cortés and his Spanish troops invaded the Aztec capital; within two years, they had conquered the Aztec Empire with the aid of thousands of Indian allies. The Spanish troops leveled the ceremonial center in Tenochtitlán and converted the buildings for public use.

Sources of Aztec Religion

Aztec religion is known through a large number of primary and secondary sources, usually divided into five groups: (1) the archeological materials, which include clay statuettes and vases, mural paintings and bas-reliefs, and statues of deities; (2) painted Aztec works (known as codices) on deerskins or agave-fiber paper, done by priests who used a combination of ideograms, pictography, and phonetic symbols; (3) Aztec works written in Latin script by European-instructed native Indians, who used ancient pictographic manuscripts as their basis; (4) the early accounts of the *conquistadores* (conquerors), notably the letters sent by Hernan de Cortés to his emperor, Charles V (which are usually treated with utmost caution, because of the deep hostility they harbor against the Aztecs); and (5) the accounts of Roman Catholic missionaries, who described the observances of Aztec life from a Christian cultural perspective.

Aztec Beliefs

Religion was a central element of Aztec life. Many deities, rites, and myths were inherited from the earlier inhabitants of the Mexican plateau. In fact, their religion was a synthesis that combined many features from different cultures. They shared with the Mayans the belief that the world had been created five times and destroyed four times—by floods, earthquakes, hurricanes, and jaguars. The present creation, they believed, was to be destroyed by fire.

The Aztecs also believed that there were thirteen heavens and nine underworlds, all arranged in layers. In the highest heaven resided the deities (male and female) of creation. In the lowest underworld resided the deities (male and female) of death. Those who died went to the underworld—except for warriors, traveling merchants, women dying

View of the stairs of temple of Quetzalcoatl, lord of life, death, and wind. The Bettman Archive.

in childbirth, and those who were offered as sacrifices, all of whom went to be with the sun god.

The inhabitants of central and southern Mexico worshiped numerous deities for centuries before the arrival of the Aztecs. These deities were adopted by the Aztecs. The concept of a supreme divine couple took the form of Mother Earth and Father Sun. There were also the deities of rain, of fertility, of crops, of plants, of running waters, of drunkenness, and so on. But the Aztecs brought with them the cult of their tribal warrior sun god, Huitzilopochtli. In fact, the Aztecs thought of themselves as the "people of the sun." Consequently, they considered it their duty to wage war in order to provide the sun god with nourishment. As a result, human sacrifice became the most important feature of Aztec religion. The very survival and welfare of the people depended on the human offerings to the sun god—a notion that was later extended to all sorts of deities.

Aztec Practices

The practice of human sacrifice was not unique to the Aztecs—the Toltecs also performed this ritual—but the sheer number of sacrifices performed by the Aztecs was singular. Most of the victims were either slaves or prisoners of war, although in some cases small children (five or six years old) and women were chosen. The Aztecs fought many wars in order to get a supply of prisoners to sacrifice. The priests forced the victim backward onto a sacrificial stone, opened the breast with a stroke of a flint knife, and tore out the heart to be sacrificially burned. Some ceremonies required decapitation, drowning, or burning. This practice reached incredible extremes: according to Aztec sources, some 20,000 prisoners were sacrificed at the dedication of the great pyramid and temple of Tenochtitlán.

Other offerings to the deities consisted of blood drawn from various parts of the body (the tongue or ears), birds, animals, produce, and incense. Sacrificial rites were presided over by priests, who were ranked in categories. A special category of priests interpreted magical formulas to predict the future. Others were in charge of ritual, and yet others were in charge of education. Each deity had his or her own group of priests and priestesses. Priests of high rank were members of the electoral body; although they did not intervene directly in affairs of state, they certainly designated rulers and greatly influenced their policies.

Witchcraft and sorcery were widespread among the Aztecs. It was believed that the sorcerers possessed the power of transforming themselves into animals, such as owls and dogs. Moreover, sorcerers could cause great harm by practicing magic. They also could prepare love potions or poisonous drinks.

The Spanish conquest and mass conversion to Christianity did not prevent the Aztecs from retaining some of their magical rites and religious beliefs, which survived to the present. Many descendants of the Aztecs still live in small villages around Mexico City, speak their ancestral language, and often combine their Christian faith with ancient traditions to form a distinctive style of Mexican Catholicism.

Modern American Indians

American Indians of North America believe in the existence of a variety of natural and supernatural forces, at the center of which is a primary force or high god. For the Sioux, this primary holy force is *wakan;* for the Algonquin, *orenda;* for other tribes, a mystery that can never be fully comprehended. Life, for American Indians, evolves around this holy force that holds all things together. The basic goal in life, then, is to be in harmony with all natural and supernatural powers. In fact, the key to success in hunting or war, as well as in the maintenance of good health, high fertility, and bountiful crops, is behavior calculated to maintain harmony between human beings and the powers that populate the environment. In contrast, disharmony leads to individual and communal disaster, to ill health, and to the ruin of crops.

The ways in which this primary force is recognized in rituals and ceremonies vary from group to group. By and large, however, American Indians believe that the aid of the high god may be propitiated by ritual action. Alternatively, the pleasure or displeasure of the high god—or, for that matter, of all the other powers—is communicated through special messengers, or shamans. For instance, the shamans among the Zuñi of New Mexico (a subgroup of the Pueblo of the southwestern United States) are believed to possess special powers that enable them to predict future events, to explain unusual experiences, and to deal with religious and sociopolitical affairs, including tribal relationships with the United States government.

Some Native American tribes associate the supreme power with either the sky or the sun, with an animal or a bird, or with a particular creator spirit. Thus, the Maidu of California believe that a turtle collaborated with a heavenly spirit to bring the earth up out of the water. The Yavelmani Yokuts of California have a slightly different version, in which a duck and an eagle replace the turtle and the heavenly spirit.

Then there is the "culture hero," whose function is to socialize the tribe. In contrast to this figure is the "antihero," often called the trickster, whose dualistic role sets him aside from all others. The trickster is considered to be the founder of convention and yet its chief defier. He brings order and disorder; he is shrewd and yet stupid; he makes jokes and mocks jokers. He has an insatiable appetite, an enlarged intestine, an incontinent bladder, and an enormous, uncontrolled penis that travels on its own for fun and adventure.

Despite seeming disparities among regions, the majority of American Indians believe in the active role of both protective and evil spirits. Among the protective spirits are mythical creatures such as thunderbirds, as well as mountains, rivers, minerals, flint, and arrowheads. Opposing these protective spirits are giant monsters, water serpents, tiny creatures that haunt woods and ponds, and the spirits of the dead that come to inflict pain, sorrow, or death.

All supernatural beings and protective or evil spirits possess ambivalent powers, but in general, creator gods and protective spirits reside on mountaintops or in celestial worlds, whereas monsters and evil spirits inhabit the depths of the sea or underground worlds. The universe is regarded as a series of worlds set one above the other, at the center of which is the world inhabited by human beings.

This series of ascending worlds (or cosmic sectors) is thought to be linked and to be characterized by six points of space or direction: north, south, east, west, zenith (top), and nadir (bottom). Each cosmic sector is, in turn, associated with a sacred mountain, animal, plant, and color. For instance, several Pueblo societies think of the north as yellow, the south as red, the east as white, the west as blue, the zenith as multicolored, and the nadir as black.

All such views can in no way be considered abstract inferences or philosophical conclusions; rather, they provide the substance of song, dance, and storytelling—that is to say, of mythical and ceremonial matters. Such views express the particular ways in which American Indians understand their relationship to each other and to the world in which they live. Hence, an instinctive reverence for supernatural powers, spirits, land, nature, creatures, and human beings—both living and departed—is strikingly evident in their ancestral traditions.

American Indian Creation Myths

Creation myths, or myths that are associated with the beginnings of the universe, are a common feature of American Indian traditions. In these imaginative stories, no distinctions are made among gods, spirits, the universe, nature, animals, and human beings. On the contrary, the stories imply a close mystical relationship binding each element. The following creation story[2] illustrates this quite clearly.

Once, the Osage Indians lived in the sky, way beyond. Wanting to know their origin—the source from which they had come into existence—they went to the sun, who told them that they were his children. Then they wandered about until they came to the moon. She told them that she had given birth to them and that the sun was their father. Moreover, she told them that they were to leave their present abode and go and settle on earth.

When they came to the earth, they found it covered with water. So they wept, because no one would answer them, nor could they return to their former place. Floating in midair, they sought help from a god but found none. The animals were with them, too, and of all these the finest and most stately was the elk, who inspired them with confidence. So they appealed to the elk for help.

He dropped into the water and began to sink; but then he called to the winds, who came blowing from all quarters and lifted up the water like a mist. First, rocks were exposed and people moved from rock to rock, but there was nothing to eat. Soon, however, the water subsided and the soft earth was exposed. So overjoyed was the elk at this that he rolled over and over on the soft earth until all his loose hair clung to the soil. From this hair sprang grass, trees, corn, beans, potatoes, and wild turnips.

Although the American Indians have several types of creation stories, the two most common themes are those of creation emerging out of chaos and creation resulting from a conflict between good and evil forces.[3] The creation account of the Osage of Oklahoma, recounted above, is representative of the first type. An example of the second type can be seen in the story of the Seneca. According to this story, the earth emerged from the fall of the bride of the Sky Chief from heaven. After first landing on the back of a turtle, she was impregnated by the wind and finally gave birth to twins. These twins created whatever exists today. One of them caused the good things to come into being — such as the sun, moon, stars, fruit, vegetables, and domestic animals. The other created all evil things and creatures of darkness on earth — such as snakes, monsters, owls, worms, flies, bats, and carnivorous animals. No matter how hard the evil brother tried, he was unable to overcome the good created by his twin. Consequently, there is more good than evil in the present world.[4]

The imaginative language and the graphic imagery of these stories establish bonds between present and past, among nature, humans, creatures, and divine beings, and between the natural and supernatural forces that cause things to come into existence. And to ensure a harmonious relationship among spirits, humans, animals, trees, rivers, birds, and the earth, American Indians developed intriguing religious songs, dances, and ceremonies.

American Indian Ceremonials

Traditionally, Native Americans express their close, mystical unity with all forms of existence in a variety of ways, including visual representations, songs, dances, games, and ceremonies. Visual representations of gods, spirits, animals, birds, fish, and humans are widespread and diverse. Some groups, such as the Nootka and Tlingit tribes of the Pacific coast of Canada, use totem poles to produce naturalistic images of animals or of human beings, historical or mythical. Others, such as the Pueblo, express the unity between all forms of existence in their artistic, geometric pottery designs. Still others express the coherence of the physical and spiritual world in costumes, paintings, craftsmanship, textiles, weaving, and decorated weapons.

Of all the symbols used to express the oneness of all existence among some American Indians of North America, the sacred pipe is accorded the highest place of honor. No artifact is more endowed with mystery and reverence among some tribes than is the ceremonial pipe, whose role in all ceremonies cannot be overemphasized. It is used for numerous purposes, including the ratification of contracts and treaties, the reception of important guests, the declaring of war and peace, the invocation of the spirits for a safe journey, and for all activities that require the bond of sincerity and brotherhood.

The origin of the ceremonial pipe among Native Americans is as mysterious as its role and function. Among the Sioux it is believed that

TRADITIONAL LOCATIONS OF NATIVE AMERICAN PEOPLES

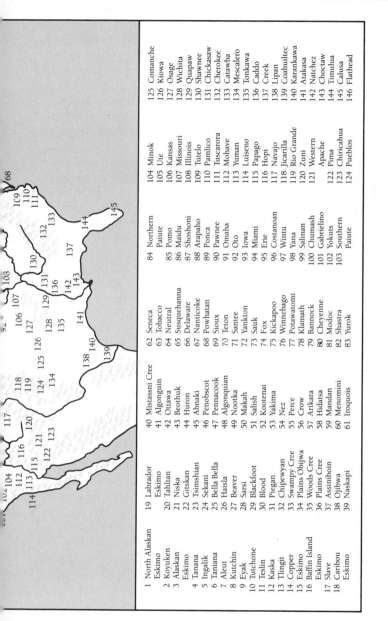

1 North Alaskan Eskimo
2 Koyuken
3 Alaskan Eskimo
4 Tanana
5 Ingalik
6 Taniana
7 Aleut
8 Kutchin
9 Eyak
10 Tutchone
11 Teslin
12 Kaska
13 Tlingit
14 Copper
15 Eskimo
16 Baffin Island Eskimo
17 Slave
18 Caribou Eskimo
19 Labrador Eskimo
20 Tahltan
21 Niska
22 Gitskan
23 Tsimshian
24 Sekani
25 Bella Bella
26 Haisla
27 Beaver
28 Sarsi
29 Blackfoot
30 Blood
31 Piegan
32 Chipewyan
33 Swampy Cree
34 Plains Objiwa
35 Woods Cree
36 Plains Cree
37 Assiniboin
38 Ojibwa
39 Naskapi
40 Mistassni Cree
41 Algonguin
42 Ottawa
43 Beothuk
44 Huron
45 Abnaki
46 Penobscot
47 Pennacook
48 Algonquian
49 Nootka
50 Makah
51 Salish
52 Kootenai
53 Yakima
54 Nez Perce
55 Nez Perce
56 Crow
57 Arikara
58 Hidatsa
59 Mandan
60 Menomini
61 Iroquois
62 Seneca
63 Tobacco
64 Neutral
65 Susquehanna
66 Delaware
67 Nanticoke
68 Powhatan
69 Sioux
70 Teton
71 Santee
72 Yankton
73 Sauk
74 Fox
75 Kickapoo
76 Winnebago
77 Potawatomi
78 Klamath
79 Bannock
80 Cheyenne
81 Modoc
82 Shasta
83 Yurok
84 Northern Paiute
85 Pomo
86 Maidu
87 Shoshoni
88 Arapaho
89 Ponca
90 Pawnee
91 Omaha
92 Oto
93 Iowa
94 Miami
95 Erie
96 Costanoan
97 Wintu
98 Yana
99 Salinan
100 Chumash
101 Gabrielino
102 Yokuts
103 Southern Paiute
104 Minok
105 Ute
106 Kansas
107 Missouri
108 Illinois
109 Tutelo
110 Pamlico
111 Tuscarora
112 Mohave
113 Yuman
114 Luiseno
115 Papago
116 Hopi
117 Navajo
118 Jicarilla
119 Rio Grande
120 Zuni
121 Western Apache
122 Pima
123 Chiricahua
124 Pueblos
125 Comanche
126 Kiowa
127 Osage
128 Wichita
129 Quapaw
130 Shawnee
131 Chickasaw
132 Cherokee
133 Catawba
134 Mescalero
135 Tonkawa
136 Caddo
137 Creek
138 Lipan
139 Coahuiltec
140 Karankawa
141 Atakasa
142 Natchez
143 Choctaw
144 Timulua
145 Calusa
146 Flathead

in ancient times two hunters met a woman who said that she was sent from the high god to deliver the sacred pipe to their village as a gift to be used in all future ceremonies. The Pawnee, however, claim to have received the sacred pipe as a gift directly from the sun. Whatever the explanation of the origin of the sacred pipe, its importance is enormous. It is made in different shapes and sizes, with distinct, elaborate decorations of human figures, animals, birds, beads, and feathers. Almost every activity is bound up with the ritual of the ceremonial pipe.

Next in importance among symbols is the masked costume worn by performers assuming various roles in sacred dancing ceremonies. Elaborate preparations ensure that every color and part of the costume, every gesture and every utterance of the performer are faultless. Some of these dancing ceremonies are performed by shamans in private, for the purpose of healing individual members of the tribe. Other dancing ceremonies are public displays designed to taunt supernatural forces into granting a request. In the event of failure, recourse is made to a sequence of magical rites until all avenues are exhausted.

Many of the rituals and ceremonies of the American Indians are associated with the celebration or recognition of stages in the cycle of human life, such as birth, puberty, marriage, old age, and death. Other rites and ceremonies have to do with activities such as hunting, fishing, rainmaking, planting, harvesting, and healing. American Indians believe that through their songs, dances, and ceremonies, it is possible to join with the forces of nature to produce rain and good crops. Corn, beans, and other vegetables are as much the gifts of Mother Earth as are their own lives. Naturally, specific rituals used in connection with planting and harvesting vary greatly from one tribe to another and from region to region. Also, these rituals range from singing simple songs (a characteristic of the Papago of Arizona) to the very elaborate ceremonies of the Pueblo. No matter how simple or complex these rituals are, their goal is the same: to promote the sustenance and welfare of the tribe.

Some chants, prayers, and dances are the perquisites of specialists, who are equipped to confer added benefits, including fertility and healing. Traditionally, the American Indian medicine man is expected to perform a wider variety of services than is the modern medical doctor. In addition to his knowledge of medicine, he is expected to communicate with gods and to perform religious ceremonies; accordingly, his role combines the functions of healer, shaman, and priest. Medicine, magic, and religion are all combined in treating illness. Prophecy, clairvoyance, spiritualism, demonology, herbs, roots, pollen, leaves, and religious practices all harmoniously blend for curing both physical and mental illness. Many such ceremonies deal with the evil forces that have invaded the body of a patient. Only the medicine man possesses the power to exorcise the evil forces that consume body and mind with sickness and to restore individuals as productive members of society through appropriate rituals.

Another important ritual among most Native Americans is the vision quest—the seeking of a vision from a guiding spirit. Traditionally, no tribal undertaking, such as war or hunting, was begun without invoking or soliciting a vision. Today, the vision quest serves several purposes, including preparing brave warriors, healing sick relatives, asking favors from gods, and offering thanksgiving to spirits and forces.

Every young male (and female, in some tribes) is expected to submit to the vision quest ritual, which determines his role and status among his people, his place in hunting or war parties, and his assigned duties in performing religious functions. If a young man's vision quest fails, he is barred from participating in various roles and is often considered a marginal tribal member. Although a shaman serves as a spiritual guide and conducts certain secondary rites connected with the vision quest, the onus is on the postulant, or candidate, to complete six rituals, as follows:

1. Preparation and withdrawal from other members of the tribe for a brief period of fasting
2. Taking a steam bath to exclude all worldly thoughts
3. Ascending the most commanding summit or hilltop
4. Stripping down to moccasins and breechcloth
5. Standing erect and motionless for several days
6. Cutting off the little finger or offering strips of flesh from the arm as a sign of sincerity

In order to qualify, the candidate's vision should include a glimpse of a tutelary animal, a promise for the tribe, a token (which is valued as the holder's most prized possession), and a song (which is reserved for important occasions only). If additional visions occur in the future, the individual may accumulate a "medicine bundle" for treating or healing illness. As a result, many Native American shamans function as medicine men, healers, prophets, and diviners.

American Indian Values

In keeping with their belief in maintaining equilibrium between themselves and nature, the moral principles of American Indians represent a harmonious, patterned system that promotes social equilibrium, community well-being, and an orderly universe. There is no concept

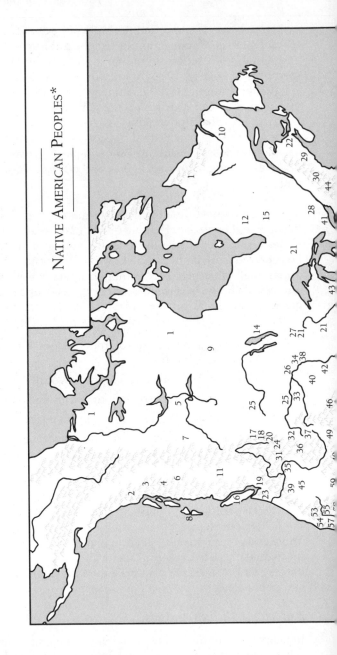

NATIVE AMERICAN PEOPLES*

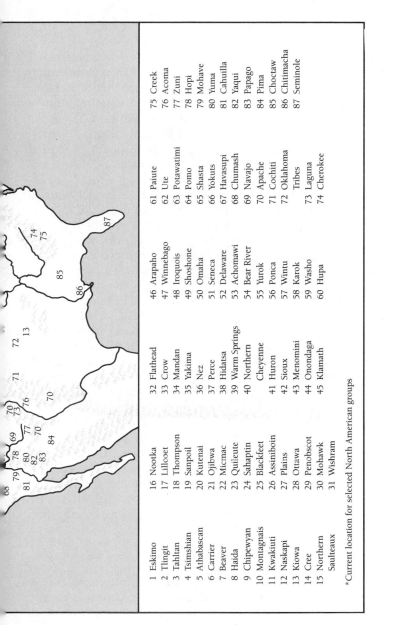

1 Eskimo
2 Tlingit
3 Tahltan
4 Tsimshian
5 Athabascan
6 Carrier
7 Beaver
8 Haida
9 Chipewyan
10 Montagnais
11 Kwakiutl
12 Naskapi
13 Kiowa
14 Cree
15 Northern
   Saulteaux

16 Nootka
17 Lillooet
18 Thompson
19 Sanpoil
20 Kutenai
21 Ojibwa
22 Micmac
23 Quileute
24 Sahaptin
25 Blackfeet
26 Assiniboin
27 Plains
28 Ottawa
29 Penobscot
30 Mohawk
31 Wishram

32 Flathead
33 Crow
34 Mandan
35 Yakima
36 Nez
37 Perce
38 Hidatsa
39 Warm Springs
40 Northern
   Cheyenne
41 Huron
42 Sioux
43 Menomini
44 Onondaga
45 Klamath

46 Arapaho
47 Winnebago
48 Iroquois
49 Shoshone
50 Omaha
51 Seneca
52 Delaware
53 Achomawi
54 Bear River
55 Yurok
56 Ponca
57 Wintu
58 Karok
59 Washo
60 Hupa

61 Paiute
62 Ute
63 Potawatimi
64 Pomo
65 Shasta
66 Yokuts
67 Havasupi
68 Chumash
69 Navajo
70 Apache
71 Cochiti
72 Oklahoma
   Tribes
73 Laguna
74 Cherokee

75 Creek
76 Acoma
77 Zuni
78 Hopi
79 Mohave
80 Yuma
81 Cahuilla
82 Yaqui
83 Papago
84 Pima
85 Choctaw
86 Chitimacha
87 Seminole

*Current location for selected North American groups

of individual sin and salvation. Rather, the good of the tribe is always more important than the interests of the individual. As a result, there are lists, or specific rules, of appropriate and inappropriate behavior. Any person who violates these rules or acts irresponsibly is brought before the tribal council and judged. Commonly, it is assumed that the offender is sick, insane, or possessed; seldom is anyone found guilty. A ritual then is performed by a medicine man to heal the sickness of the offender, and thereby to ensure the stability of the group. If such ritual fails, alternative measures may include banishment or death either at the hand of a tribal elder or through starvation, freezing, or animal attack.

Rules governing the conduct of members within a society deal with a wide range of matters, including property belonging to the group, sexual abuses, behavior toward relatives and other members of the society, lying, stealing, fighting, gambling, laziness, drinking of alcohol, and killing. Naturally, the enforcement of appropriate behavior varies from tribe to tribe and from region to region.

As to the concept of self or soul, most American Indians believe that they have several souls, one or more of which may live on after death. The notion of reincarnation seems to be a common belief, although the conception of what that continuing existence is like varies from tribe to tribe. Some, such as the Pueblo, believe that the dead either join a *kachina* (masked dancer) or become rain clouds. Others, such as the Hopi (a Pueblo subgroup), believe that the soul leaves the body at death to travel to the "next world," where an earthlike existence awaits.

Regardless of differences in beliefs held by American Indians in North America regarding death or the human soul, they seem to be less concerned with life in the hereafter than they are in a good life here and now. To know the spirits intimately, to enjoy the gifts of Mother Earth, and to have many children are for the American Indian far more important than a future heaven. Happiness and success in this existence far outweigh the promise of bliss to come beyond the grave.

Modern Trends

Recent developments among American Indians indicate considerable changes in terms of religious belief and practice. A pantribal movement called the Ghost Dance was inaugurated in 1886 by Wowoka, a Paiute from Nevada. This movement spread rapidly across the United States, because it promised deliverance from the oppression of the white people and the return of the dead and the buffalo simply through the ritual of dancing for periods of up to five days without stopping. In 1890 the United States cavalry and support troops surrounded a large group at Wounded Knee and slaughtered unarmed men, women, and children. This tragedy, along with further suppression by the United States government, put an end to the Ghost Dance movement. Instead, new religious movements emerged that combined old tribal traditions with certain features of Christianity. The Native American church, the members of which were once known as Peyotists because of their belief in peyote as a sacramental food, is one such interesting movement whose membership is growing in both the United States and Canada.

Today, American Indians of one or more tribes drive long distances to be together for a day or a week, to greet old friends, and to eat and dance together. Such events, known as *powwows*, commonly occur throughout the summer months and provide a good opportunity to renew tribal identification. For these people, religion is not something nurtured by books, doctrines, scholars, or monks. Rather, it is an aspect of human activity that is linked to the orderly system of the universe.

Notes

1. This is what Robert Coles concluded after extensive contacts with Pueblo and Hopi children of New Mexico. See R. Coles, *Children of Crisis*, vol. 4, *Eskimos, Chicanos, Indians* (Boston: Little, Brown, 1977).
2. Adapted from F. Laflesche, *The Osage Tribe: The Rite of Vigil*, Thirty-Ninth Annual Report of the Bureau of American Ethnology (Washington, D.C.: 1925), pp. 123–24.
3. See, for instance, the stories recounted in W. E. Coffer, *Spirits of the Sacred Mountain: Creation Stories of the American Indians* (New York: Van Nostrand Reinhold, 1978).
4. Ibid., p. 85.

5

Hinduism

Hindu Characteristics

The chief concern of those of Hindu religious conviction is not the existence or nonexistence of God, or whether there is one God or many gods. Hindus can choose to be monotheists, polytheists, pantheists, atheists, agnostics, dualists, monists, or pluralists. They may or may not follow strict standards of moral conduct, spend much time on everyday religious rituals, or attend a temple. Magic, fetishism, animal worship, and belief in demons _(asuras)_ coexist, supplement, or accompany profound theological doctrines, asceticism, mysticism, and esoteric beliefs. Religious truth, according to Hinduism, is not conceived in dogmatic terms, since truth transcends all verbal definitions. In consequence, Hinduism represents an astonishingly complex conglomeration of doctrines, cults, rituals, practices, observances, and institutions.[1]

Historical Background

The term _Hindu_ derives from the Persian word _Hind,_ the name given to the Indus River region in northern India. Although it may once have identified the people of Hind, the word _Hindu_ came to refer to anyone from India. Today, it is usually applied only to members of the Hindu religion.

Any positive correlation between the ancient people of the Hind and the Hindus is tenuous. Excavations from two ancient sites, Harappa and Mohenjo-daro, indicate that a civilization flourished there in the area of the Indus River, in what is now western Pakistan, dating to approximately 2500 BCE. However, scholars are as yet unable to explain who the original inhabitants were, how or when they arrived in India, and what, if any, relation they bore to the "dark-skinned, curly haired, snub-nosed people" described in later Aryan hymns.

Around 1500 BCE, migrating bands of "fair-skinned" people invaded India from the great plains of central Asia through the mountain passes of the Himalaya. These wandering, warlike invaders called themselves Aryans, meaning noblemen or landlords, and for the next thousand years they extended their influence all over India. They perfected the Sanskrit language and developed a socioreligious hierarchy, known as *varna*, a social-class system also known as *caste*. They established a network of village communities, each governed by either a ruler or a council of respected elders. In addition, India's new masters were free to develop during this period, with little or no opposition, the basic patterns of the Hindu religion, including religious concepts, socioreligious institutions, forms of worship, and spiritual practices. Eventually, many of their hymns, prayers, epics, and traditions came to be considered sacred writings.

Hindu Scriptures

The Hindu attitude toward Hinduism's sacred writings is eclectic. Although hundreds of sacred texts are considered authoritative, there is no equivalent of the Christian Bible or the Muslim Qur'an—no

Hinduism

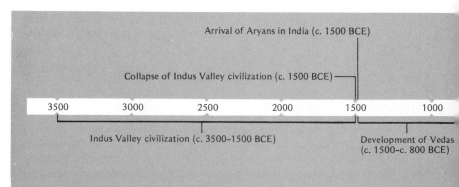

Arrival of Aryans in India (c. 1500 BCE)

Collapse of Indus Valley civilization (c. 1500 BCE)

| 3500 | 3000 | 2500 | 2000 | 1500 | 1000 |

Indus Valley civilization (c. 3500–1500 BCE)

Development of Vedas
(c. 1500–c. 800 BCE)

single, definitive text. Instead, Hindu scriptures are classified in two categories: *sruti* and *smriti*. *Sruti* means hearing and applies to a group of writings that represent eternal, sacred knowledge. They were revealed to *rishis,* or seers, and transmitted orally for generations by *brahmins* (one of the castes, made up of priests). *Smriti* means memory and identifies writings that represent tradition: knowledge remembered and transmitted from generation to generation.[2] The Vedas, the Brahmanas, the Aranyakas, and the Upanishads are among the most important of the *sruti*. The Epics, the Code of Manu, and the Puranas are significant examples of *smriti*.

The *Vedas* (bodies of knowledge),[3] composed between 1500 and 800 BCE, consist of four collections, known as the Rig-Veda, the Sama-Veda, the Yajur-Veda and the Atharva-Veda. The Rig-Veda is a collection of about one thousand hymns, mostly prayer and praise, to either a single deity or a group of deities. The Sama-Veda consists mainly of rhythmic chants borrowed from the Rig-Veda. The Yajur-Veda contains, in addition to verses taken from the Rig-Veda, many original prose passages dealing with sacrificial ritual. The Atharva-Veda, a special class of texts, deals with charms, magical spells, incantations, and kingly duties.

The *Brahmanas* are a voluminous body of writings that describe in exhaustive detail ritual observances and sacrifices and discuss the mystical meanings of various rites. Each of the four Vedas is supplemented by its own Brahmana or Brahmanas, which probably were written between 800 and 300 BCE.

The *Aranyakas,* or Forest Books, which supplement the Brahmanas, were written mainly for the religious aesthete who chooses to retire to the isolation of the forest and thus is unable to perform ritual sacrifices. They are esoteric in content and are concerned with the innermost nature of humankind and the universe.

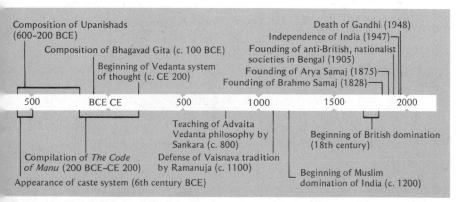

Composition of Upanishads (600–200 BCE)
Composition of Bhagavad Gita (c. 100 BCE)
Beginning of Vedanta system of thought (c. CE 200)

Death of Gandhi (1948)
Independence of India (1947)
Founding of anti-British, nationalist societies in Bengal (1905)
Founding of Arya Samaj (1875)
Founding of Brahmo Samaj (1828)

500   BCE CE   500   1000   1500   2000

Compilation of *The Code of Manu* (200 BCE–CE 200)
Appearance of caste system (6th century BCE)

Teaching of Advaita Vedanta philosophy by Sankara (c. 800)
Defense of Vaisnava tradition by Ramanuja (c. 1100)

Beginning of British domination (18th century)
Beginning of Muslim domination of India (c. 1200)

The *Upanishads,* a large group of writings attached to the end of the Aranyakas, contain the basic philosophic framework of Hinduism. They are viewed as the "culmination of sacred knowledge" *(Vedanta),* and their importance to those who seek a nonritualistic type of religion and insight into the oneness of things through self-consciousness can scarcely be exaggerated. As a collection of speculative texts composed by many authors, the Upanishads do not attempt to present a logical, coherent view of reality. They probably were composed over a period of three to four centuries, from 800 to 500 BCE.

The Epics (the first of the sacred writings in the *smriti* category) consist of two great literary works known as the *Mahabharata* and the *Ramayana.* The Mahabharata, the longer of the two, is the longest epic in world literature—over seven times the combined length of the Iliad and the Odyssey (although, strictly speaking, it is not entirely epic, since more than half of it consists of material dealing with politics, law, religion, and other topics). The entire work was probably completed by the second or third century CE. Within the Mahabharata are three famous stories greatly loved by Hindus, including the *Bhagavad-Gita* (Song of the Lord). This immortal poem, produced about the second century BCE, is written in the form of a dialogue between a warrior and the Blessed Lord Krishna, disguised as the warrior's charioteer, and emphasizes the Path of Devotion as the way of liberation from "rebirth." A number of Hindu movements base their teachings on the Bhagavad-Gita.

The Ramayana recounts the story of a prince called Rama who is exiled to the forest for fourteen years because of a rival half-brother and the intrigues of a jealous mother. In the meantime, Sita, Rama's ever-faithful wife, is abducted by a wicked demon. Unable to find her, Rama is aided by his friend Hanuman, the monkey, who succeeds in restoring Sita to her husband. Rama, Sita, and Hanuman have long since been deified, and they remain objects of worship for millions of Hindus.

The Code of Manu, compiled some time before the second century CE, is accepted by most branches of Hinduism as the most complete expression of Hindu sacred law. Manu is traditionally acknowledged as the father of humankind (somewhat like Adam) and of the social and moral orders. The book includes marriage laws, dietary regulations, the duties of various castes, civil and criminal laws, and daily rites and sacrifices, as well as statements on a variety of ethical subjects. Although many practices and rules are no longer rigidly followed in detail, these laws still exert an enormous cultural influence on Hindus.

The Puranas are a collection of ancient lore, mythological data (on the genealogy of gods, sages, and kings) and descriptions of the creation, destruction, and re-creation of the universe. These texts, eighteen of which are generally held to be authoritative, represent the product of theistic developments during the fourth to the eighth centuries CE. Closely linked with the Epics in origin, the Puranas are the scriptures of the common folk, since they are accessible to everybody—including women (whose status in Hinduism is lower than that of men) and the lowest members of the society.

Hindu Mythology

Hindu mythology is incredibly complex. The stories of gods, demons, demigods, goddesses, sages, and heroes overlap and form a tangled web. Scholars find it almost impossible to isolate one story from the other. Millions of deities, each bearing a different name and a variety of functions, represent the chief protagonists in the mythology of Hindu traditions. The Indologist Norman Brown believed that Hindu mythologies have been a vehicle to explore "science, philosophy, religion, history, sex, love, psychology, literary entertainment and edification, and the creation of art."[4]

The major sources of Hindu mythology are the scriptures discussed earlier, beginning with the Rig-Veda and ending with the Puranas. Other important myths are found in the Mahabharata and the Ramayana.

It is impossible to describe, even in broad outlines, the immense wealth of Hindu mythology. Suffice it to say that two categories of Indian religious mythology are distinguishable. One strain incorporates the mythology of preliterate tribes who were never absorbed into Hinduism or who remain in early states of acculturation. These people are unaware of the "great" Hindu gods and their mythology and recognize their own local deities with their related mythologies. The second category includes the mythologies that are recognized by different Hindus in various parts of the subcontinent. For Hinduism is not a single or unified, coherent religion, but a system of many religions that are tolerated within the social framework of Hindu society. Hindus have thus incorporated in their mythologies the customs, beliefs, practices, and institutions that have developed throughout the centuries.

Development of Hinduism

Vedic Deities

The characteristics of early Hinduism—or, as it is more popularly known, Vedic religion—can be derived from the Vedas. In that work numerous deities, called *devas*, are identified with powers and func-

Carvings and decorative details of Hindu temples are superb examples of ancient Indian art. Reliefs such as those depicted at Meenakshi Temple in Madurai show scenes from the lives of gods and goddesses.   Courtesy of Government of India Tourist Office, Toronto, Canada.

tions associated with natural phenomena: celestial, atmospheric, and terrestrial.

The most important celestial deities are Varuna, Mitra, and Vishnu. Varuna, the sky god, maintains cosmic order and protects moral action. Conceived of as the creator of the universe, he rules by the standard of rite—an ordered form of procedure, or the proper course of things. Mitra, the sun god (corresponding to the Iranian god Mithra), stimulates life and brings prosperity to humans, animals, and vegetation. He is infinitely benevolent and omnipresent, the chief assistant to Varuna, and the benefactor of humanity. Vishnu, the third in this triumvirate of celestial divinities, is distinguished by his "three strides," which encompass earth, atmosphere, and paradise. Another of Vishnu's distinguishing attributes is his ability to appear in this world in various incarnations, or *avatars*, the most famous of which is his avatar as the divine-human Lord Krishna.

The most important of the atmospheric deities is Indra, the thunder god. As the model and champion of the Aryan warrior, he is appealed to for help in waging successful warfare against the human enemies of the Aryans. Other deities in the atmospheric pantheon are Vayu, the wind god; Parjanya, the rain cloud god; a troop of storm gods called Maruts; and Rudra, the father of the Maruts. As the god of violence, destruction, disease, and death, Rudra is able to define and control the limits of these catastrophes. Those who invoke his name do so in the expectation that he will prescribe healing remedies that will protect them from his anger and destruction.

Among the terrestrial group of deities are Agni, the fire god, and Soma, the god of libation. Agni is identified with the sacrificial fire (called *agni*) the most important symbol of Hindu worship. Consequently, he is the progenitor of humankind, the lord of good fortune, and the first *hotar* (sacrificial priest). Agni is viewed as the divine agent who acts on behalf of humanity and mediates between the universe and, on the one hand, the public, official cult of the temple and, on the other, everyday life and the private, domestic cult of the home. He is the primordial element sustaining all of creation and is omnipresent—even in water, since rain accompanies lightning, which is another manifestation of fire.

The list of major deities is filled out by numerous female divinities, including Surya, the sun goddess; Dhishana, the fertility goddess; and Sarasvati, the patron goddess of language, literature, and knowledge.

Supplementing the functions of these major figures are "helper" deities, responsible for, among other things, creating prosperity and happiness, healing sickness, contracting marriages, protecting roads and pastures, and getting people out of bed each morning. Among these, the god whose importance and popularity has survived to the present day is Shiva, thought of as the "lord of creatures" and depicted as the great ascetic, with an erect penis—his symbol. Shiva's animal companion is Nandi, the bull on which he rides.

No less popular than Shiva are his numerous consorts. One among them, Kali (also called Durga), is particularly revered. A more terrible divinity than Shiva, Kali is frequently depicted as drinking blood, as tearing away the flesh of sacrificial animals, and as wearing a necklace of human skulls. Hindu mythology also connects her with the founding of Calcutta.

The One

The Vedic religion evolved over time a ritualistic cult, a complex system of sacrifices, an elaborate class of priests to officiate at a host of esoteric rites, and ecstatic ascetics who became known for transcending the limits of the physical body. Various ceremonies, in which spells, incantations, and occult practices were emphasized, occupied the center of the Hindu religious stage. Eventually, the ritual of sacrifice by fire increasingly came to dominate Hindu religious life. Agni, the god of fire, became the sacrificial fire itself, the medium by which Hindus related to the other deities. In fact, the deities themselves were said to have performed sacrifices in order to attain divine status. Sacrifice was (and is) not regarded merely as a ceremony offered to the deities, or as a symbolic gesture representing reality—but as reality itself. Through sacrifice, the adherent learns of reality, or truth.

As the various sacrificial rites developed, spoken formulas, called *mantras*, came to be considered as formulations of truth in sound: in other words, mantras were thought to embody *in their sounds* truth or reality. Mantras were not viewed as the only means of expressing truth, however. Thought, which was defined as internalized speech, offered yet another aspect of truth. And if words and thoughts designated different aspects of truth, or reality, then there had to be an underlying unity behind all phenomena. This unity, or the One, constituted hidden and unmanifested reality. Belief in the One meant that the deities could no longer be considered "creators" of the universe, but only components of it—a divine expression of the entire cosmic order. Who or what, then, was the creator or origin of the multiple forms and appearances of truth?

One answer to this question was that the universe originated in a cosmic human sacrifice. In this view, Purusha, the original cosmic Man, produced gods from himself, who in turn made a sacrifice of Purusha:

> Purusha alone is all this universe, what has been, and what is yet to be. . . . All creatures are one-fourth of Him; three-quarters are the immortal heaven. . . . When the gods performed the sacrifice with Purusha, Spring was melted butter, Summer the fuel, and Autumn the oblation. The gods, the celestial beings, and the seers performed the sacrifice with Him. (Rig-Veda X.90)*

The basic significance of this quotation is clear: creation is a sacrifice, and all celestial beings, as well as the universe and everything in it, are Purusha. This conclusion had such an impact that eventually sacrifices came to be regarded as a cosmic ritual. In other words, the sacrificial ritual performed by the priests came to be regarded as a creative act. But this view was only one among several that were being shaped.

Other profound thinkers were questioning the nature of the universe and the role of the deities vis-à-vis the universe and human

---

*Throughout this chapter, the numbers in parentheses are section-subsection citations from Hindu scriptures.

beings. Their search for a unity in the totality of things led them to belief in a nameless, all-originative One.

> They call it Indra, Mitra, Varuna, Agni; or it is the heavenly Sun-bird. That which is One, the seers speak of in various terms. (Rig-Veda I.164)

Most arresting was the emergence of the view that before anything was created, before the universe existed or the deities had come into being, there was a great, unnamed cosmic reality—a neutral principle or activity, simply referred to as *Tad Ekam,* or That One:

> Then was not nonexistent nor existent; there was no realm of air, no sky beyond it. What covered in, where and what gave shelter? Was water there, unfathomed depth of water? Death was not then, nor was there aught immortal; no sign was there, the day's and night's divider. That One breathed without breath by its own nature; apart from it was nothing else whatsoever. Darkness there was; at first hidden by darkness, this All was indiscriminate chaos. All that existed then was void and formless: by the great power of warmth That One was born. Who truly knows and who can here declare it, whence it was born and whence came this creation? The gods are later than this world's production. Who knows, then, whence it first came into being? He, the first origin of this creation, whether he formed it all or did not form it, Whose eye controls this world in highest heaven. He verily knows it, or perhaps he knows not. (Rig-Veda X.129)

The imagery is unambiguous. Before anything existed or did not exist, before there was any realm of air or sky, before there was any death or deathlessness, before there was light or darkness, day or night—there was only That One. From the void, formless, and indiscriminate chaos emanated That One, the generative principle and impelling force behind all creation.

Out of such philosophical speculations grew the idea that knowledge alone, without recourse to ritual observances, might reveal cosmic unity—the unmanifested reality, the ultimate truth. In other words, it was believed that ritual sounds and actions could all be performed in the mind and that this mental performance would yield the same results as external ritualistic performance. An individual, then, could meditate on and search for the hidden meaning of sacrifice, or reality. In their search for inner connections between the cosmic principle of creation, the universe, and human beings, Hindu thinkers discovered equivalents or identities everywhere.

Brahman–Atman

Thus did the ancient, ritualistic Vedic religion, with its elaborate sacrifices, gradually give way to the doctrine of Brahman-Atman—a doctrine that is difficult to grasp, since it attempts to define the undefinable and transcendent. *Brahman* is Absolute Reality, which transcends time, space, and causality. Brahman pervades the entire universe and yet remains beyond it. Moreover, Brahman is all that is objective as well as subjective: in other words, Brahman is the whole external world, as well as the whole inner being—self, or soul—of an individual, a beast, a bird, a fish, or a rock. This innermost and unseen force, or self, of a human, animate, or inanimate object is called *Atman*. And Atman is Brahman.

These concepts are expressed most fully, and most beautifully, in the Upanishads. Consider this verse:

> Verily in the beginning this was Brahman; that Brahman knew its Atman only, saying, "I am Brahman." From it all this sprang. . . . Now also he who thus knows that he is Brahman becomes all this. (Brihadaranyaka Upanishad I.iv.1)

The most significant contribution of the Upanishads to the Hindu religion is this idea of the utter oneness of Brahman-Atman. The identification of the individual "self" with the universal "Self" in a mystical experience establishes the existence of a reality which is infinite, unlimited, directly perceived, and spiritual. Neither philosophical speculation nor any kind of reasoning can penetrate deeper than this metaphysical reality: the nonduality of existence. Hence, Hindus do not believe that a person is "created in the image of God"; rather, a person *is* God, or divine. The universe, with everything in it, including human beings, is not to be considered as something apart and distinct from the Absolute Being; it *is* the Absolute Being! There is no subject-object, no "I" and no "you." The Absolute is not "up there" or "beyond," but within. The First Principle of things must not be sought in the external, but rather in one's innermost self. Thus, the true "self" of a person and the Absolute Universal "Self" are one; they are identical. This identity is most emphatically expressed in a famous formula: *tat tvam asi,* which means, "That art thou!"

Hindu religious literature attempts to explain this concept of identity by analogy and illustration. For example, just as honey is the nectar of different flowers, so Brahman is the Atman of every living and nonliving being.

> "As bees, my dear," explains the father to his son, "make honey by collecting the juices of trees located at different places, and reduce them to one form; and as these juices have no discrimination (so as to be able to say): 'I am the juice of this tree,' or 'I am the juice of that tree'—even so, indeed, my dear, all these creatures, though they reach Pure Being, do not know they have reached Pure Being. . . . Now that which is the subtle essence—in it all that exists has its self. That is the True. That is the Self. That art thou." (Chandogya Upanishad VI.9.1–2)

Again, just as a river originates from the sea as moisture and precipitation, only to merge once more with the sea, so does the individual Atman emerge from Brahman and return to a source or origin that is substantially one.

> "Please, venerable Sir, give me further instruction," says the son.
>
> "So be it, my dear," Uddalaka replies. "These rivers, my dear, flow — the eastern towards the east, and the western towards the west. They arise from the sea and flow into the sea. Just as these rivers, while they are in the sea, do not know: 'I am this river' or 'I am that river', even so, my dear, all these creatures even though they have come from Pure Being, do not know that they have come from Pure Being. . . . Now, that which is subtle essence — in it all that exists has its self. That is the True. That is the Self. That art thou." (Chandogya Upanishad VI.10.1–3)

Brahman-Atman is, therefore, Absolute Reality. There is no subject-object, no creator and creature, no "I" and "you," no "I" and the universe — there is simply the identity of everything. This Absolute Reality pervades everything.

> "Place this salt in water and then come to me in the morning." The son does as he is told. Uddalaka says to him: "My son, bring me the salt which you placed in the water last night." Looking for it, the son does not find it, for it is completely dissolved. The father says: "My son, take a sip of water from the surface. How is it?"
>
> "It is salt."
>
> "Take a sip from the middle. How is it?"
>
> "It is salt."
>
> "Take a sip from the bottom. How is it?"
>
> "It is salt."
>
> "Throw it away and come to me."
>
> The son does as he is told, saying, "The salt was there all the time."
>
> Then the father says, "Here also, my dear, in this body, verily, you do not perceive Being; but It is indeed there." (Chandogya Upanishad VI.13.2)

It is interesting to note that the analogies of the bees and of the rivers stress the loss of individuality, the merging of the individual self into the universal Self. The analogy of the salt on the other hand illustrates the pervasive quality of Being. The Absolute Being — That One, Brahman, God, whatever the appropriate label may be — is present in everything that exists. In other words, there is in the Hindu religion no Creator above and creatures below; no duality; only One. Brahman-Atman is ultimately one; the human soul or self *is* the Absolute. Ignorance of this truth — or rather, the inability to grasp Absolute Reality — leads to a continuous chain of rebirths or reincarnations.

Reincarnation

What is known about the origin and development of the concepts of *samsara* (rebirth or reincarnation) and *karma* (action or work) basically is limited to teachings in Hindu literature that are attributed to two sages: Uddalaka Aruni for *samsara,* and Yajnavalka for *karma.* Both doctrines may predate the sages, who may simply have recorded beliefs and ideas originated among small groups of ascetics. They probably kept them secret from the public, fearing the orthodox priests. Whatever its precise origins, *samsara* and *karma* eventually became parts of established belief associated with the concept of Brahman-Atman.

Samsara, the whole process of rebirth, or reincarnation, is based on the assumption that every living form is subject to an indefinite series of lives or existences that culminates when the form becomes at death indistinguishable from Brahman. *Samsara* is beginningless and, in most cases, endless. It is neither a process of purification nor a cycle of progress, but a perpetual sequence of rebirth in one form or another. This endless series of births and deaths may occur on earth in any of the forms of life—human, animal, or vegetable—or in any of the series of heavens or hells. What determines the outcome of each successive birth?

One's future existence is determined by the law of *karma,* which literally means action in general—whether it be good or bad, religious or secular. Under the law of *karma,* everything one does in this life—in thought, word, or deed—ordains one's destiny in future existences. Hindus believe that because actions invariably produce their own good and evil fruits, their future lives will be determined by their *karma* in the present; or, to put it differently, a Hindu's present life is the result of accrued past karma. Consequently, pain, suffering, and any sort of misfortune are regarded by Hindus not as afflictions imposed externally by a divine being or by the actions of the individuals, but as the result of people's evil *karma* in a past existence or existences.

Thus, Hindus, in common with adherents of many other religions, do not think of life as an end in itself. The end of one life on earth simply signals the beginning of another, which will represent the inevitable consequences of *karma.* In this chain or cycle of rebirths, to which all living things are inescapably bound, reincarnation may occur at either a higher or a lower level than the status of life in the present or in any past existence. What determines the nature of the next rebirth is the law of *karma*—a law considered as implacable and impersonal as a law of nature. Inequalities of birth are accordingly explained and even justified by the theory of *karma* and *samsara.*

This central concept of *karma-samsara* evolved from a question that has preoccupied the human mind from time immemorial: what happens after death? Not only do different religions offer different answers, but within each religion these answers seem to change into new ideas with the passage of time. Why is this so? Perhaps because what happens after death is, to the rational mind, a mere matter of conjecture; each successive age develops a more plausible theory. This evolution of ideas is true of Hinduism.

The early scriptures, such as the Rig-Veda, describe how the "soul" of the dead is carried up on high by Agni (the fire-god who consumes the body at cremation). When the soul arrives on high there is eating and drinking, various other enjoyments, reunion with loved ones, and perfect, carefree bliss. In that heavenly world there are neither rich nor poor, neither powerful nor oppressed; no sickness or old age detract from joys that are a hundred times greater than the greatest bliss on earth. For evildoers there is an "abyss," a place which is "black-darkness."

This idea of a post-mortem judgment evolved during the later Brahmanic period. It was an idea that, during the same period, was prominent in the Iranian tradition of Zoroastrianism. One's deeds, it was thought, were weighed in the balance after death and rewarded or punished according to their good or evil nature. But to certain profound thinkers these theories seemed questionable and difficult to accept, so once again the element of doubt played a significant role in shaping a new concept.

"Who can demonstrate the experiences of the hereafter?" ask Upanishadic thinkers. "There is doubt about a man when he is dead," says an inquirer to Yama (the Death-deity), "some say that he exists; others, that he does not. This I should like to know, taught by you . . ." (Katha Upanishad I.I.20). Yama, the God of Death, replies by first illustrating the indestructibility of the "Soul."

> The knowing Self [or Soul] is not born; It does not die. It has not sprung from anything; nothing has sprung from It. Birthless, eternal, everlasting, and ancient, It is not killed when the body is killed.
>
> If the killer thinks he kills and if the killed man thinks he is killed, neither of these apprehends aright. The Self kills not, nor is It killed. (Katha Upanishad I.2.18–19)

Then Yama goes on to state the doctrine of rebirth:

> Well then . . . I shall tell you about this profound and eternal Brahman, and also about what happens to the Atman [soul] after meeting death.
>
> Some [souls] enter the womb for the purpose of re-embodiment, and some enter into stationary objects—according to their work [*karma*] and according to their knowledge.
>
> If a man is able to realize Brahman here, before the falling asunder of

his body, then he is liberated; if not, he is embodied again in the created worlds. (Katha Upanishad II.2.6–7; 3.4)

Two similes vividly describe the cycle of rebirth:

> Just as a leech moving on a blade of grass reaches its end, takes hold of another, and draws itself together towards it, so does the "self," after throwing off this body, that is to say, after making it unconscious, take hold of another support and draw itself together towards it.
> Just as a goldsmith takes a small quantity of gold and fashions [out of it] another—a newer and better form—so does the self, after throwing off this body, that is to say, after making it unconscious, fashion another—a newer and better form—suited to the *manes* [dead and deified ancestors] or the *gandharvas* [demigods] or the gods, . . . or other beings. (Brihadarenyaka Upanishad IV.4.3–4)

The concept of *karma-samsara* finally became the central concept in all Hindu thought. If living souls are subject to an indefinite series of lives or existences, how can one be released or liberated (*moksha* is the Indian word for this liberation) from this cycle of rebirths? True, if one could only reach the point at which one experienced a total identification of one's individual self with the universal Self (Brahman-Atman) then one would attain *moksha*. But how could one attain this transcendent experience? The Hindu masses, with their socioreligious caste system, were far from attaining such a blissful state.

Caste

The characteristic that most distinguishes the Hindu religion from other religions is its system of social stratification, called *varna* (literally, color). This Hindu system of caste, or *jati* (literally, birth), has had no historical counterpart in terms of persistence, continuity, and pervasive consequences long after the circumstances that gave it credence in tradition had been forgotten. Scholars can only speculate as to its origins. Some have maintained that the caste system developed out of the multiracial nature of Indian society, although it is not clear whether this development predated or postdated the arrival of the Aryans. Others have explained caste as a discriminatory system of color differentiation imposed by the lighter-skinned Aryan conquerors on the darker-skinned Dravidians. For whatever reasons, the class system grew and expanded, eventually evolving into a highly complex system comprising some 3000 distinct groups.

In theory, there are four major classes: the *brahmana* or *brahmin*, the *kshatriya*, the *vaisya*, and the *sudra*. This classification system in all probability has always been theoretical, since references to a much more complicated structure date back to the earliest times. Nevertheless, analysis of the four main social classes will adequately serve to describe the caste system, which represented a division of labor based on accidents of birth and justified by moral and religious concepts.

The traditional duties or obligations of the four groups were ranked as follows. In the first rank are the *brahmins*, who occupied the central place of power in Hindu society. The *brahmins* were priests, the spiritual and intellectual leaders of society. They devoted their time to studying, teaching, performing sacrifices, and officiating at religious services. Second came the *kshatriyas*, who as rulers, warriors, and nobles protected, administered, and promoted the material welfare of society. Third in rank were the *vaisyas*, who as farmers, merchants, or traders contributed to the economic well-being of the society. And fourth were the *sudras*, who as laborers or servants supplied the manual labor or service needed by the first three groups.

Eventually, a fifth category emerged—the *chandalas*, "untouchables," whose status was so low that they belonged to no class at all and were excluded from communal ritual and, in some parts of India, were forbidden access to certain public roads and bazaars. They often were required to identify themselves as untouchables as they walked, so that members of higher castes could avoid them. They were not allowed entrance to certain temples and were not permitted to draw water from public wells, except from those designated for their use.

Linked with and justifying this social stratification was the religious justification of *karma* and *samsara:* social status as determined by birth. Each individual's birth into a particular class was considered to be determined by the past *karma* of that person. Birth into a *brahmin* class, for example, would be a consequence of good *karma* accumulated in previous existences. Status as a *sudra* or as any lower form of life (i.e., an animal or a plant) would imply *karma* in previous existences that merited no better status.

> Those whose conduct here [on earth] has been good will quickly attain some good birth—birth as a *brahmin*, birth as a *kshatriya*, or birth as a *vaisya*. But those whose conduct here has been evil will quickly attain some evil birth—birth as a dog, birth as a pig, or birth as a *chandala*. (Chandogya Upanishad V.10.7)

In this view, birth determines class, which in turn defines an individual's social and religious status, the duties and obligations that such status requires, and the restrictions that apply to all aspects of everyday life (food, clothing, occupation, marriage, social intercourse, civil rights, and religious duties).

In time, each class made its own rules and established its own customs and values. Although some of these traditions have been modified or discarded, they remain potent forces in Indian culture today.

A sadhu *(wandering holy man) who has broken ties with the world and its ordinary social duties to enter the fourth stage of life as the* sannyasin *(renouncer). A* sadhu *typically wears rags and carries a begging-bowl, a water pot, a staff, and a few other meager possessions.*   Malcolm S. Kirk/ Peter Arnold, Inc.

Stages of Life

The Hindu doctrine of *ashrama* (stage of life) dates from about 500 BCE. Just as birth determines a Hindu's status, *ashrama* prescribes a specific set of duties and responsibilities for each of four stages in the lives of upper-caste male Hindus—those in the three upper castes, who often are known as "twice-born." These four stages, corresponding to youth, adulthood, middle age, and old age, are termed *brahmacarin, grihashta, vanaprastha,* and *sannyasin.*

The stage of the *brahmacarin,* or student, starts after a boy undergoes a ceremony between the ages of eight and twelve in which he becomes a full-fledged member of his caste. From this point until the boy reaches the age of twenty to twenty-four, he is disciplined and instructed by his *guru* (teacher), whom he obeys and serves with absolute humility.

The second stage, that of the *grihashta,* or householder, is the longest of the *ashramas,* lasting until middle age. During this period the Hindu is supposed to lead an active married life and apply with particular rigor the three ideals of social living associated with this stage in life: the observance of accepted religious duties, the accumulation of wealth, and the enjoyment of pleasure—including sensual pleasures.

The stage of the *vanaprastha,* or forest dweller, starts when the householder's hair begins to turn gray or when his first grandson is born. He—accompanied by his wife, if she so wishes—leaves home and retires into the forest in order to lead a life of reflection and meditation. Here, as a hermit, he is expected to concentrate on developing a complete detachment from everything in the world to which he was previously attached.

In the fourth and last stage, a pious Hindu becomes the *sannyasin,* or renouncer. This begins when the forest dweller feels spiritually ready to leave the forest life and begin the life of a wandering ascetic. Renouncing all former ties—including his wife, if she had been with him in the forest—the *sannyasin* becomes a homeless nomad released from material desires, attachments, and possessions. His goal is to attain liberation or the self-realization of Brahman-Atman.

The four stages of life largely remain doctrine rather than practice. The last two stages are honored more in spirit than in observance, except among a few *brahmins,* who often live apart in a small cottage or in a room in their home compound.

Paths to Emancipation

From a very early period Hinduism recognized four basic needs of human life, or lives. The first two, pleasure and wealth, are referred to as the "path of desire;" the last two, moral duty and liberation, as "path of renunciation." Hindus do not criticize those who pursue personal pleasure, nor blame those who wish to accumulate great possessions. Nevertheless, it is thoroughly understood that neither of these needs represents the highest goals and that sooner or later in this or in some future existence (as a member of a lower caste, as an animal, or as a thing) the individual must come to terms with this fact. Hindus recognize the satisfaction of performing their duty, but ultimate satisfaction can only be found in liberation from the cycle of rebirth.

Although there is a difference of opinion among the Hindus about the path *(marga)* to final emancipation *(moksha),* three paths are now recognized by orthodox Hindus. These paths are valued differently by different adherents, but all three are respected.

Karma Marga

The path of duties, or *karma marga,* represents the methodical fulfillment of rites, ceremonies, and social obligations. These include sacrificing to the deities and to one's ancestors; reverencing and saluting the sun; keeping the hearth fire alight; performing the appropriate rites and ceremonies that mark the important events in life, such as birth, naming, the first ingestion of solid food, the first haircut, initiation, marriage, and death; and observing strictly all the social regulations and dietary laws of one's caste.

The Code of Manu prescribes for each separate caste a list of dietary laws, social regulations, domestic rites, public ceremonies, and religious duties. Another part of the Code stipulates the honors due to the guardian deities of the household. For example, the head of the house must see to it that such deities are properly worshiped each day and that portions of prepared food are presented to them before each meal. An important domestic rite is the *shraddha* rite—the rite to ancestral spirits. The *shraddha* rite consists of periodic offerings of portions of food and memorial prayers. The most important food offering is the *pinda*—little balls of rice pressed into a firm cake.

The role of the women within the "code" can be stated very simply: to humbly serve their men. A virtuous woman occupies herself with household duties. She respects, obeys, and worships her husband, even if he is unfaithful, virtueless, and devoid of good qualities. After her husband's death, a woman may not remarry but must remain quiet, patient, and chaste until her death. Should she violate this code of behavior, she brings disgrace to herself in this world and, instead of joining her husband in the next existence, will "enter the womb of a jackal."

Many other rites and ceremonies are associated with the practice of the *karma marga*. High ethical values are also a characteristic feature of those who follow this path:

> Against an angry man let him not in return show anger; let him bless when he is cursed; and let him not utter speech devoid of truth. (Manu VI.48)

Although it is true that many Hindus observe the "code" in minute detail even to the present day, modern conditions have forced certain changes in its ancient customs and rites. To an outsider, the path of duties may seem to be an exacting way of life, but to the faithful Hindu, it is an action-filled way of fulfillment and ultimately a means to liberation.

> He who thus recognizes the Self through the self in all created beings, becomes equal minded towards all, and enters the highest state, Brahman. (Manu XII.125)

Jnana Marga

For those spiritual aspirants who have a strong intellectual bent, Hinduism prescribes *jnana marga,* or the path of knowledge. Its purpose is to enable the aspirant to attain ultimate bliss through the perception of the illusory nature of names and forms and the realization of the sole reality of Brahman-Atman. Naturally, only those who are of a philosophical temperament can develop a keen power of reasoning by which they can distinguish the real from the unreal, the changing from the changeless. These aspirants must cultivate control over their mind and their senses, which leads to inner calm, forebearance, and concentration. By reasoning and uninterrupted contemplation, their ignorance gives way to the realization that the entire universe and all beings are one and the same Brahman. But to reach this ultimate realization requires long preparation and self-discipline.

Through the centuries (from about 500 BCE to CE 1500) a great number of "systems of philosophy" or *darshana* developed. Hindus have pointed out that most of them cover the same ground as any of six recognized systems. Thus, Hindu scholars have arranged the six systems in their logical rather than their chronological order.

The Nyaya System. Based upon a text ascribed to a philosopher called Gautama (not Gautama the Buddha), a complete analysis of correct reasoning is attempted. The Nyaya system asserts that true or real knowledge is based upon four processes of knowing: sense-perception, inference, comparison of fact, and trustworthy testimony. False notions give rise to activities that have evil consequences in successive rebirths. Hence, all misery arises from false notions. Liberation, therefore, depends upon sound or true knowledge.

The Vaisheshika System. This system, founded by Kanada, applies logical methods to the study of the external world. The external world is regarded as a self-existent reality, formed by eternal and indivisible atoms eternally combining and recombining. Later thinkers, however, declared that this process is not purely mechanistic but takes place by the power of Advishta, the divine "unseen force." All agree that alongside the eternal atoms and individual selves is an eternal Self, the source of all selves. Hence, both atoms and selves are eternally indestructible.

The Sankhya System. The Sankhya system is dualistic, in sharp contrast to the doctrine that only one Being exists (Brahman-Atman) expressed in the Upanishads. It maintains that there are only two real eternal categories of being: *prakriti* ("matter"), and *purusha* ("self"). Individual selves are not the product of an eternal Self but are regarded as eternal, independent and infinite. Why these selves *(purushas)* are associated with a body and a mind *(prakriti)* in one existence or life after another is an insoluble mystery associated, in some way, with *karma*. The self needs to be liberated from its association with matter. But the self cannot achieve this. It is in the realm of matter that the "higher intelligence" *(budhi)* realizes in its moment of insights the true character, or being, of the *purusha*. The insight destroys not only ignorance or illusion, but also matter. Hence, it enables the self to realize its freedom of eternal and unearthly existence.

The Yoga System. The term *yoga* ("discipline") is used in two distinct senses. The meaning most familiar to the West is the physical, mental, and psychic discipline, or technique, practiced for either purely spiritual purposes or to attain maximum physical and mental, as well as spiritual, well-being. The second sense in which the word is used is to denote one of the six philosophical systems.

The greatest appeal of the Yoga system lies in its physiological and psychological measures to control the mind in an effort to concentrate. It consists largely of special postures, controlled breathing, and rhythmical repetition of the proper thought-formulas. The claim of this system is that through controlled breathing one may control the senses. By controlling the senses one may gradually control mental processes. By controlling the activity of the mind, one may pass through a succession of stages in which the activities of the mind become more and more restricted: first to an area of concentration, then to a restricted concentration on a single object of thought, and finally to a state of uninterrupted contemplation in which there is no distinction between the mind and its object of thought. Devoid of all mental activity, there is only pure undistracted consciousness in this final state.

Mentioned first in the Upanishads, Yoga was given its classical form by Patanjali—a yogin who probably dates from the second century CE. Influenced partly by the Sankhya system, Patanjali defined the Yoga system as "the suppression of the modifications of the mind." Its goal is the attainment of a state of pure consciousness, undisturbed by psychic or mental processes, or by any object of awareness. This state is known as *samadhi*—a state of trance in which the mind, "emptied of all content and no longer aware of either object or subject, is absorbed into the Ultimate and is one with the One."

The means of this goal is the eightfold yoga, or discipline, described in the Yoga Sutras. The first two deal mainly with ethical disciplines, such as nonviolence, truthfulness, study, and prayer. The next two describe the correct postures and controlled breathing, which, in turn, help in the practice of the next four steps associated with concentration or meditation.

The characteristic feature of yoga in any of its forms is the discipline of the whole body in order to aid the suppression of the activities of the mind. The result is a state of pure ecstasy, of complete freedom of the "true self" from earthly bonds.

The Purva-Mimansa System. Founded by Jaimini, this system is considered to be the least philosophical of the six systems. Followers of this system are known as literalists because they cling to the literal inspiration of the Vedas. So highly did Jaimini regard the truth of the Vedas that he asserted that they never had an author, that they were uncreated and eternal, and written in the language of Being Itself. Hence, the Vedas have a magical power which prevails even over the deities.

The Vedas, and for that matter, the Brahmanas, prescribe the whole duty of a person. By determining the literal meaning of the Vedas and Brahmanas and carrying out their rites and ceremonies, one could attain liberation.

Although this position was not essentially altered, followers of this system declare that the duties of a person prescribed in the Vedas and Brahmanas should be studied and practiced as an offering to a "Supreme God," who waits to liberate his followers as a reward for their faithfulness.

The Vedanta System. The name of this system derives from the Upanishads, also commonly called Vedanta, which means "the concluding portions of the Vedas." Although an attempt was first made in the first century BCE by Badarayana to set forth the monistic teaching (the doctrine that only one being exists) of the Upanishads in a systematic philosophical structure, it was not until centuries later that three different systems of Vedanta philosophy were founded by Sankara (ninth century CE), Ramanuja (twelfth century CE), and Madhva (thirteenth century CE).

Sankara's system of thought (called *advaita,* or nondualism) holds that the world, the individual self, and Brahman, while not absolutely one, do not really exist separately and are in reality "not different." Brahman is eternal, undecaying, indescribable, and impersonal. Besides Brahman, all else is transient, impure, and unsubstantial; in short, a product of "illusion" *(maya).* To regard the physical world and the individual self as "realities" (as is the common experience) is to exist in the world of "illusion." There is only one reality, which is spaceless, timeless, and solely existent; in short, Brahman-Atman. Liberation from the cycle of rebirths comes when the "veil of ignorance" is lifted and one realizes the identity of Brahman-Atman.

Three hundred years later, a diametrically opposed interpretation of the Upanishads (Vedanta) was suggested by Ramanuja. He asserted that the physical world, individual selves, and Ultimate Reality are not illusions but each real, though nondivisible, because the physical world and individual selves make up the "body" of the Ultimate Reality. In other words, the physical world and individual selves are the forms through which the Ultimate Reality is manifested. However, this Ultimate Reality is a personal being and not, as Sankara stated, an impersonal being. His name is Vishnu. He is endowed with every desirable quality; he is all-knowing, all-powerful, all-loving, and manifests himself in many ways. The ideal goal of humans is not absorption in an impersonal reality, but going to "heaven to enjoy Vishnu's presence in full consciousness."

A third interpretative version of the Upanishads came through Madhva. He maintained that the individual self is neither to be identified with, nor one with, the Ultimate Reality. Furthermore, liberated selves will enjoy bliss in the presence of the Supreme Self, Vishnu. Nonliberated selves are doomed to spend eternity in hell or in endless rebirths. The self is liberated through Vayu, the Wind-god, son of Vishnu. He is the "vehicle of the grace of God," a sort of "holy spirit," who "breathes his life-giving power into those whom he liberates." The echo of Christian or Muslim views, which were known in India by Madhva's time, is quite apparent in this version.

Bhakti Marga

Many people cannot be inspired by pure reasoning or rationality, but can rise to heights of spiritual elevation through the path of devotion, *bhakti marga*. Often, such experiences assume the form of a passionate love of a deity, whether a god or a goddess. The most characteristic features, however, of such experiences are the surrender of self to the deity or divine being, private acts of devotion, and temple worship.

The first important literary record of *bhakti marga* as a true way of liberation is found in one of the great classics of religious literature, the Bhagavad-Gita, which means *Song of the Blessed One*. Its author is unknown and the date of its composition may fall anywhere from 200 BCE to 200 CE.

This poem is in the form of a dialogue between the warrior Arjuna and his charioteer Krishna, who is none other than the manifestation of the Supreme Deity, Vishnu, in human form. Their conversation takes place just before a battle. Arjuna sees in the ranks of the opposing army a large number of his friends and kinsmen. Horror-stricken at the thought of fighting against them, he quickly lays down his weapons, preferring to be killed than to kill. Krishna, however, justifies the fight on the grounds that a person's "real soul" is immortal and independent of the body; it neither kills nor is killed.

> These bodies come to an end.
> It is declared, of the eternal embodied [soul],
> Which is indestructible and unfathomable.
> Therefore fight, son of Bharata!
>
> Who believes him a slayer,
> And who thinks him slain,
> Both these understand not:
> He slays not, is not slain.
>
> He is not born, nor does he ever die;
> Nor, having come to be, will he ever come not to be.
> Unborn, eternal, everlasting, this ancient one
> Is not slain when the body is slain. (Bhagavad-Gita II.18–20)

In the course of eighteen chapters, the Bhagavad-Gita sets forth many religious viewpoints. While it expounds *karma marga* and *jnana marga*, its preeminent emphasis is on *bhakti marga,* the path of devotion. It grants that both the path of knowledge and the path of duties lead to liberation:

> In this world, aspirants may find enlightenment by two different paths:
> for the contemplative, the path of knowledge; for the active, the path of
> duties. (Bhagavad-Gita III.3)

Nevertheless, the highest secret of all and the supreme message of the Bhagavad-Gita is devotion:

> I am the same to all beings;
> no one is hateful or dear to me;
> those who revere me with devotion
> are in me and I in them. . . .
>
> No devotee of mine perishes.
> for those who take refuge in me,
> though they may be born of base origin—
> women, *vaisyas* or *sudras*—
> all attain the highest goal.
>
> Fix your mind on me,
> be devoted to me,

worship me, adore me,
and to me you will come. (Bhagavad-Gita IX.29–34)

Thus, the path of devotion assumes passionate devotion of and absolute surrender to a particular deity, either a god or a goddess. Neither the path of duties, which is largely traditional, nor the path of knowledge, which is highly intellectual, can satisfy the profound religious need of millions of Hindus to the same degree as the path of devotion does. For most Hindus, unconditional, selfless love and faith in a deity are the highest ideals in attaining emancipation. To adore a personal god or goddess with every element of one's being is the ultimate goal of this path. Devotees are expected to adore the deity not out of a sense of fear or punishment, and much less from expectations of reward, but for love's sake alone. Needless to say, *bhakti marga* is the most popular of the three paths.

Forms of Hinduism

The Trimurti

Among the thousands of deities worshiped to a greater or lesser extent by some Hindus, three command the respect of millions: Shiva, Vish-

Devotees of Shiva worship the lingam *and* yoni *emblems (the male and female sex organs), representing Shiva's universal male energy in everlasting union with his female counterpart.*   Courtesy of John Campana.

nu, and Brahma. These divinities make up the *trimurti*, the three figures who represent Absolute Reality.

Shiva. The most popular of the three gods is Shiva, who is known as the Destroyer. His followers, called Shaivites, give him the title *Mahadeva*, which means "Great God." His character is a complex amalgam of contrasting attributes. He is the god of death, destruction, and disease, but he is also the god of the dance and reproduction. He is both terrible and mild, "ceaselessly active and eternally restful." This seemingly contradictory aspect of his character is generally accepted as representing two sides of one nature.

The origins of Shaivites and the cult of Shiva may lie in pre-Aryan times. Most, though not all, groups associated with them represent manifestations of local folk worship combined with various pan-Hindu religious ideologies. The reproductive and sexual energy identified with Shiva is represented by one group of his worshipers as the human reproductive organs—the erect penis *(lingam)* and the vagina *(yoni)*. To another group, the mystery of Shiva's creative force is mainly characterized by a miniature phallic symbol worn around the neck. To yet another group, Shiva is worshiped as the Skull Bearer, an image represented by a necklace of beads shaped like miniature human skulls.

Vishnu. In contrast to Shiva, Vishnu is known as the Preserver. He is the god of love and benevolence and the preserver of values associated with such attributes. His chief characteristic is his concern for humanity, which he expresses by appearing on earth at different times and in various forms, or *avatars*. According to tradition, Vishnu has so far made nine appearances on earth as various animals and creatures, which are associated with functions that help to preserve and restore humanity, and has also appeared in human form as Krishna and as Gautama, the Buddha. He is expected to appear on earth once more to close this era and bring the world to an end.

Faith in Vishnu is essentially monotheistic, whether the object of worship is Vishnu himself or one of his alternative forms, and the doctrine of corporeal appearances or *avatars* is a powerful integrating force in Hinduism. It is based on the belief that whenever the world degenerates, Vishnu, the Protector and Preserver, manifests himself by assuming an earthly form to destroy evil and guard goodness.[5]

Brahma. Of the three gods with mass appeal in the contemporary era, Brahma, the Creator, is perhaps the oldest and least worshiped. Even though he is accorded deep respect as one of the *trimurti*, his importance is gradually declining. Few Hindus describe themselves as devotees of Brahma, and there are very few temples dedicated to him. Both nature and society derive from Brahma. In art, he is represented with four faces and is often shown riding on a white swan or goose.

Shaktism and Tantrism

Generally speaking, Tantrism is based upon mystic speculations concerning divine *shakti*—that is, creative feminine energy. Opinions differ as to what Tantrism is, however. Followers of Tantrism assume that the macrocosm (the universe) and the microcosm (the individual) are closely connected. The initiate has to perform certain physical rites in order to transform the chaotic state of the "body" into a normal "cosmos." Thus, by yoga and ritual means, in part magical and in part orgiastic, adherents attempt to master transcendent powers in order to realize oneness with the highest Principle. They describe physiological processes with cosmological terminology and define states of consciousness with sensual or erotic language.

Some followers of Tantrism seek emancipation from rebirth by awakening the "female nature-energy" (representing the *shakti*), which is said to be dormant and coiled like a serpent, or *kundalini*. This energy is awakened and made to rise through the six centers of the body. Other followers, like the Hatha Yoga and Mantra Yoga, apply yoga practices of abstinence, bodily postures, breath control, concentration, contemplation, and muscular contractions. Hatha Yoga involves some form of self-torture and internal purification, such as an emetic flushing of the bowels. The entire process is intended to control the "gross" body in order to free the "subtle" body.

Among some *shakti* cults, the experience of transcending space and time and of realizing the identity and unity of the divine in all things is also expressed through the ritual satisfaction of lust as means of release from the cycle of rebirth. In this context, ritual copulation becomes (for males only) a sacred rite in experiencing and participating in cosmic and divine processes. The very mystery of shakti cults (Shaktism) is the realization of the identity of God and his creative energy. Sexual relationships, therefore, help to transcend all opposites—but only among initiates, since participation in such rites is conditional on the capacity of merging one's mind with the Supreme Being.

Folk Hinduism

The main motive of religious practices for millions of Hindus is the fear of malevolent and benevolent deities, because these deities are omniscient and perpetual observers of day-to-day events in every person's life. Each god must be appropriately propitiated to forestall

Pilgrims purify themselves by bathing in the holy Ganges River. Temples, rivers, and junctions of rivers are important sites for pilgrimage. George Bellerose/Stock, Boston.

disaster or guarantee security. The lower castes often confine themselves to manipulating the deities or spirits that dwell in trees, stones, water, and other natural elements. To counteract plagues, diseases, curses, witchcraft, and evil, most villagers—which is to say, most Hindus—and millions of urban workers resort to divination, astrology, and various occult practices. To millions of Hindus, ritual purifications, time-honored rites and customs, charms, and amulets are of greater importance than the doctrine of Brahman-Atman.

Scholars generally find it difficult to distinguish popular folk Hinduism from Indian tribal religion, since such beliefs and practices are closely allied. Practices based on ritual nudity, black magic, and the worship of snakes are as prevalent as ever. Exorcists and mediums claim to be possessed by divine powers and submit themselves to self-torture. One of the striking features of folk Hinduism is the propitiation of female deities associated with local village communities. These goddesses, like the tutelary deities of ancient Near Eastern cities, have no relation to the universe nor any jurisdiction beyond the life of a particular village. They are usually represented by sticks, stone pillars, clay figurines, or, on occasion, a small shrine.

Lord Ganesha, the popular Hindu god, is regarded as the son of the god Shiva and the goddess Parvati (Kali). As the god of good luck, prosperity, and wisdom, Lord Ganesha is venerated as the remover of all obstacles. Hence, he is highly popular among Hindu worshipers, who offer prayers to him before undertaking any sort of enterprise. He is usually represented as a fat, elephant-headed being riding on the back of a rat. From the private collection of John A. Campana.

The beliefs and customs of the masses are much the same today as they were in the past. To obtain rain, fertility, or children, many Hindu women worship stone figures of snakes. The snake goddess Manasa is believed to live in a plant or a stone carving bearing her name, and a special day is devoted to her worship.

Many Hindus adopt and enshrine a single god or goddess as their household patron. The number of these deities is, according to Hindu tradition, "thirty-three *cores*"—some 330 million! Hindus also go from temple to temple as need arises. For good fortune and luck, they may worship Ganesha, the elephant-headed son of Shiva. For physical health and bodily strength, they may turn to Hanuman, the monkey god. In times of sorrow and anguish, they may call on Rama. Above all, the average Hindu villager has two spiritual or religious ambitions: to go to some holy place of pilgrimage, and to attend temple festivals.

Sacred places for pilgrims are plentiful throughout India. Mountains, caverns, rivers, and the sites of mythological occurrences (such as theophanies) have become sacred or holy spots. Temples or shrines are erected on or beside these locations, and pilgrims long to go to one or more of them. Sites such as Harwar in the Himalayas, the Bay of Bengal, or Varanasi (Benares) are considered hallowed territories, and pilgrims who come from all over India are often overcome with joy at the sight of the temples that identify the significance of these holy places. The Ganges is the holiest river of all; also sacred are the Jumna and Saraswati rivers, to which millions of pilgrims go for religious festivals.

Cow Veneration

Another widespread feature of Hinduism is the veneration of cows, which receive the same honor as deities. Garlands are placed around their necks, and water is poured at their feet and oil on their fore-heads. The deep and sincere feelings of Hindus toward cows (also oxen and bulls) were best expressed by M. Monier-Williams:

> The cow is of all animals the most sacred. Every part of its body is inhabited by some deity or other. Every hair on its body is inviolable. All its excreta are hallowed. Not a particle ought to be thrown away as impure. On the contrary, the water it ejects ought to be preserved as the best of all holy waters—a sin-destroying liquid which sanctifies every-thing it touches, while nothing purifies like cow-dung. Any spot which

Funeral procession for a sacred cow in Veranasi (Benares), India. Bernard Pierre Wolff/Photo Researchers, Inc.

a cow has condescended to honor with the sacred deposit of her excrement is forever afterwards consecrated ground.[6]

In most villages today, Hindus use cow dung as fuel, as a disinfectant, and as medicine. In the words of Mahatma Gandhi, the cow "is the mother to millions of Indian mankind. Protection of the cow means protection of the whole dumb creation of God."

Hindu Observances

According to ancient Hindu philosophy, knowledge is fruitless, good deeds vain, and true happiness impossible without proper ritual observance. Consequently, Hindu religion lays great emphasis on the performance of numerous rituals, all observed during any of the successive stages of a Hindu's life. These rituals at one time numbered more than three hundred, but they have been gradually reduced over a period of time to less than twenty. Today, most Hindus observe one or more devotional obligations, which may be performed either privately in daily rituals in a home or communally in a temple.

Ritual Purification

Ritual purification plays a vital part in Hindu religious observances and is closely related to the concepts of cleanliness and contamination. Hindu scriptures declare that only those who practice cleanliness are qualified to witness Brahman.

Purity is of several kinds and can be achieved by various means. Physical purity has two aspects, external and internal, and can be achieved either through the natural functions of the body or through external cleansing, including washing and bathing. Internal purity is accomplished by esoteric techniques that include the intoning of prescribed formulas, yogic postures, and certain purificatory acts. These acts or rites are designed to remove all traces of contamination that may have come from infringing some caste regulation or neglecting to discharge certain obligatory acts.

Devotional Ritual

There are countless forms of devotional service. Ideally, a Hindu should make five offerings daily: (1) to gods, (2) to ancestors, (3) to seers, (4) to animals, and (5) to the poor. Many, however, perform their ritual once a day or, at most, three times daily. Private devotions consist also of the tending of the sacred household fire, the recitation of texts, the repetition of mantras, meditation, and yoga exercises.

Temple of Lord Krishna in Mathura, Uttar Pradesh, considered to be the birthplace of the Lord Krishna. Large temples, rivers, and the junctions of rivers attract huge numbers of pilgrims. Hindu temples have developed rest houses for travelers and provisions for feeding pilgrims who travel great distances from one part of the country to another in order to arrive at renowned sacred sites. Hindu pilgrims consider bathing in sacred waters, especially at specific times, as a most auspicious act. Courtesy of Government of India Tourist Office, Toronto.

In modern times, and especially in Westernized cities, many Hindus find it difficult, if not impossible, to give the necessary time for these private traditional religious requirements. Hence they tend to go at least once a week to their temples, where there is usually an image of a deity in whose honor regular ceremonies are conducted. These rites include the ceremonial awakening and bathing of the deity, and an invocation of the name of the deity, followed by a formal adoration and salutation in which the deity is presented with garlands and water. As an act of homage, worshipers circumambulate the image and then offer a gift, generally consisting of rice, grain, *ghee* (melted butter), spices, incense, and aromatic vapors. Next, a lighted lamp is waved before the deity as *mantras* are chanted. Then follows supplication for personal requests. Finally, the deity is dismissed, and the ceremonies close with the chanting of appropriate *mantras*.

On special occasions, such as festive days, the deity is entertained by dancing girls and fanned by a retinue of farmers, as well as bathed, garlanded, and robed. Wherever possible, the deity is taken into procession around the temple or even around the streets.

Pilgrimages

Visiting holy places is one of the main sacred duties of all Hindu devotees desirous of pleasing the deity, accumulating religious merit, and securing bliss in the hereafter. There are thousands of holy places in India, some especially sacred to followers of Shiva, others to followers of Vishnu; but a Hindu need not be limited to a sectarian shrine for purposes of pilgrimage.

All pious Hindus, in or outside India, attempt to visit one of the holy places at least once in their lifetimes. Many devout Hindus hope to die within the precincts of Varanasi (Benares), since this ensures advancement at the time of rebirth. The merit of a pilgrimage is further enhanced if pilgrims add self-inflicted hardships to the normal rigors of the journey (by, for example, performing the journey by hopping on one foot, or going on their knees). Today, of course, the time spent on pilgrimage has been considerably shortened by the conveniences of modern travel.

Religious Festivals

No religion has a longer calendar of holy days than does Hinduism. Hundreds of sacred occasions are celebrated by festive observances. Many festivals are seasonal. Others commemorate the birth, inauguration, or victory of a god or a hero. A number are celebrated in honor of deities: Krishna, Vishnu, Shiva, Parvati, Kama, Devi, Ganesha, Rama, Gayatri, Lakshmi, Saravati, Chitragupta, and so on. Many festivals are held in honor of snakes, cows, buffaloes, rivers, hills, plants, coconuts, ancestors, and spirits. Still other festivals are dedicated to important days, to famous incidents in mythology, to phases of the moon, and to eclipses, solstices, equinoxes, and the stars.

A festival may be observed in different ways: with acts of worship, fasting vigils, bathing, recitation of chants, taking of vows, lighting of lamps, fairs, games, drinking, gambling, and the offering of gifts to *brahmins*. Certain days are considered more auspicious than others.

The local deities at a festival in Kulu (Valley of the Gods), high in the Himalayas. The festival is the Dussehra, *ten days of merriment and feasting. Observed throughout India each fall, the celebration honors the triumph of good over evil, and each region of the country has its own special way of marking the holiday.* Courtesy of Government of India Tourist Office, Toronto.

The merit resulting from virtuous deeds is believed to be augmented and intensified if they are performed on a particularly auspicious day.

To provide a complete list of all Hindu festivals would be difficult, since many are linked to local legends and myths. Thus, only the most important festivals are discussed below.

Divali or Dipavali (Cluster of Lights) is celebrated in October or November. In northern India, Divali lasts for four days and is a New Year festival. In other parts of the country, however, Divali comprises many festivals in one and lasts for five days.

In general, the first day is dedicated to Parvati and Lakshmi, the goddesses of wealth and prosperity. Homes are lighted with clay oil lamps, and windows are kept open to welcome these goddesses into the house. The second day is devoted to gambling, especially with dice, to celebrate the reconciliation of the deity Shiva with the consort Parvati. The third day commemorates the victory of the deity Vishnu over the demon king Bali (or Naraka). Also on this day, which is called Lakshmi-puja, the goddess Lakshmi is worshiped in the evening, after an all-day fast. (Among Bengali Hindus, however, the goddess Kali is the object of worship.) The fourth day is Divali proper, when little earthen bowls filled with oil are lighted and set up in extended rows both inside and outside homes. The fifth day commemorates an occasion when the deity Yama dined with his sister Yamuna and commanded everyone to do likewise. Consequently, every Hindu male must dine in the house of a sister, cousin, or other female relative and give her presents.

Another major Hindu festival is that of Holi (also referred to as Hutashani), which starts about ten days before the full moon of the month of either February or March but is generally observed only during the last three or four days before the full moon. The Holi festival commemorates either the frolics of the youthful deity Krishna, the death of the female demon Puthana, the burning of the female demoness Holika, or the destruction of Kama by Shiva. The ceremonies are somewhat like a carnival. Bonfires are lit and evil influences (represented by effigies of demons) are symbolically burned. A pole is erected, and people walk around it in ritual fashion, while a great din from horns, drums, and cymbals accompanies dancing and shouting. The distinguishing feature of this festival is the throwing of colored powders on and the sprinkling of colored liquids over people.

The thirteenth day in the dark half of each month is sacred to Shiva. The celebrations occurring during the months of January–February and February–March are regarded as exceedingly auspicious. A day of strict fasting precedes the days of festival, and a vigil is kept all night, during which the phallic symbol of Shiva is worshiped and various rites performed.

The birthday of Ganesha, the elephant-headed god of good luck, is celebrated in August or September. On this occasion clay figures of Ganesha are made and worshiped for a period ranging from two to ten days. Lights are waved before the image, *mantras* are chanted, and coconuts are broken. At the end of the festival the image is thrown into water and left to sink.

Numerous celebrations revolve around Krishna. The festival that commemorates the birth of Krishna (called Janmashtami or Gokulashtami) is celebrated in the month of August–September. Preceding the festival is a day of fasting that terminates at midnight, the time Krishna is said to have been born. Another popular festival commemorates the occasion on which Krishna lifted a hill of cow dung called Govardhana. Krishna taught the cowherds to pay homage to this hill instead of to the god Indra, his rival. Angered by this act, Indra sent a deluge to wash away the hill and its inhabitants. Krishna reacted by lifting the

Govardhana hill on his little finger and holding it like a canopy for seven days, until Indra was thwarted in his design and departed in frustration.

In addition to the above festivals, Hindus celebrate the anniversaries of their religious leaders or founders. For instance, the birthday of Swami Vivekananda is celebrated in January, the birthday of Sri Ramakrishna in February, and the birthday of Swami Prabhupada in September. Such occasions are marked by elaborate preparations, devotional worship, and rejoicing.

Hindu religious ceremonies and festivals represent nothing more than imaginative symbols of the infinite aspects of Cosmic Reality. In fact, the festive occasion itself, rather than the deity who is honored, takes precedence. The most important attribute of a festivity is that it be celebrated.

Evolution of Modern Hinduism

The Hindu masses continue to practice their traditional religious beliefs today as they did centuries ago, even as the religion continues to evolve and form new branches or systems. Not only are there millions of people who worship in the method they best understand, but there are also numerous individuals who try to interpret the complexities of particular religious doctrines according to a modern way of thinking. Like most religions, then, Hinduism evolved slowly from remote beginnings and reached its present shape through the rise and growth of new religious movements. The following passages detail a few of the more important influences on the Hindu faith through the history of India.

Great changes occurred in the religious life of India when, shortly after 600 BCE, several ascetics challenged the authority of the *brahmins* and the scriptures after claiming to have discovered the secrets of life and of release from the cycles of existence. The most important of these innovators were Siddhartha Gautama, the *Buddha* and founder of Buddhism; and Nataputta Vardhamana, called Mahavira. Other heterodox teachers organized bands of ascetic followers and developed specific codes of conduct. The established Hindu priests and teachers reacted by devising the doctrine of *ashrama.*

In 326 BCE, Alexander the Great invaded India at the head of his army and conquered the northwestern region. However, the establishment of the Maurya Empire, founded by the Indian Chandragupta (c. 317–293 BCE), forced the governing satraps (who were Greek generals) to leave, and the Maurya Empire eventually came to embrace all India and part of central Asia. Most of the Mauryan rulers were heterodox, and King Asoka (c. 265–238 BCE), the most famous of Mauryan rulers,

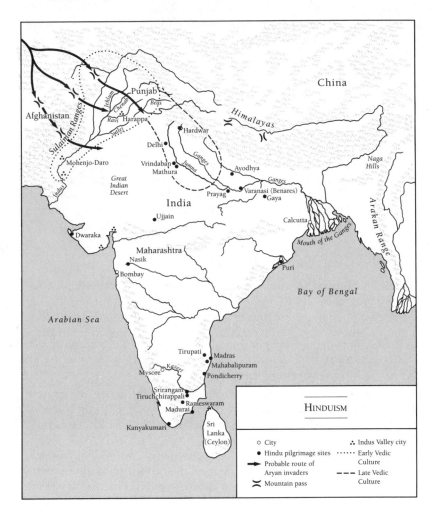

was a professed Buddhist who favored nonviolence and vegetarianism.[7] Although he respected the Hindu priesthood, his patronage of Buddhism did much to spread that religion from Greece to China. In the meantime, the Hindu religion was developing tendencies toward *theism*, or belief in the existence of gods, centered around the gods Vishnu and Shiva.

The period between the fall of the Mauryan Empire in the second century BCE and the rise of the Gupta Empire in the fourth century CE was characterized by a succession of invaders and by great disruption, but it was also the era in which Hinduism spread beyond tribal, regional, and purely Indian limits. These six centuries were distinguished by the emergence of religious characteristics in Hinduism that had widespread, rather than merely local, influence. Three sects in particular—the Vaishnavites, Shaivites, and Shaktiites—established subcontinent-wide presence and status, and several goddesses, such as Lakshmi and Durga, became objects of mass rather than local or sectarian devotion. At the same time, the status and wealth of the *brahmins* rose steadily. Finally, the custom of child marriage and the rite of *sati* or *suttee* (the voluntary immolation of a widow on her husband's pyre), though probably in existence earlier, assumed the authority of established tradition.

The Gupta period (fourth to sixth centuries) was marked by the rapid development of temple architecture and the spread of Hinduism (and Buddhism) beyond the Indian continent into southeastern Asia and Indonesia. Chinese chronicles attest to the existence of an Indianized kingdom in Vietnam at this time, and the people of Bali, in Indonesia, still follow a form of Hinduism overlaid with distinctive local features that dates back to the Gupta period. The Hindu epics of Ramayana, the stories of the Mahabharata, and the Code of Manu were translated and modified to relate them to non-Indian cultures, to the point that they lost most of their original content. Hindu ascetics even visited Europe occasionally; as a result, several Greek and Latin writers show considerable knowledge of Hinduism. The most striking literary evidence of this cross-cultural exchange is the resemblance between the Yoga-sutras, attributed to the Indian teacher Patanjali, and the *Enneads* of the Roman philosopher Plotinus (205–270 CE). The Yoga-sutras set forth the spiritual discipline of *yoga*—methods of self-control and meditation directed toward identification or union with Brahman.

Toward the end of the fifth century, devotion to an active creative principle, personified as the Divine Mother (the female manifestation of Brahman), began to achieve a significant place in Hinduism, and the period between the fourth and eighth centuries was notable for the rise of Tantrism (or Tantricism), Darshanas, and Puranas. We have already noted what the Puranas are (see pp. 78–79). *Tantrism* is the belief in the search for spiritual power and ultimate release from the cycle of rebirth by means of the repetition of *mantras* (sacred phrases or syllables) and other secret rites (see p. 100). Like Tantrism, the purpose of the *Darshanas* (the six Systems of Philosophy) is liberation from the repetitive cycles of rebirth and death through the use of intuition to dispel ignorance.

The rise and growth of new devotional religious movements continued through the eleventh century. These devotional cults helped to weaken the influence of Buddhism in India, which was already in decline. Two Hindu rulers, Mihirakula (sixth century) and Shashanka (seventh century) are reported to have persecuted Buddhist monks and destroyed their monasteries. Opposition from Hindu philosophers, such as Shankara (c. 788–840), also weakened the strength of Buddhism.

Hindu-Muslim Encounters

Meanwhile, a new and vital religion had sprung unheralded, with the force of a coiled spring suddenly released, from the deserts of Arabia in the seventh century. This new religion, under the name of Islam, spread rapidly across the entire Middle East and, a century later, penetrated into India. Northwestern India was conquered by the Muslim Mahmud al-Ghazni in 1021, and during the twelfth and thirteenth centuries, all of northern and central India came under Islamic rule from a single administrative center at Delhi. Several centuries later the Islamic conquest of India was completed by the Mughals (Mongol rulers). The advent of Islam meant the end of universal royal patronage of Hinduism in India. The attitude of Muslim rulers toward Hinduism varied. Some persecuted their Hindu subjects, whereas others were tolerant. Numerous Hindu temples were destroyed by the more fanatical rulers.

Muslim occupation of India, though it brought Hinduism into close contact with a different, more aggressive religion, did little to inhibit the continued development of new forms of Hindu devotional sects, popular folk religion, and philosophical systems. Hindu-Muslim syncretic influences also inspired spiritual leaders such as Kabir (1440–1518), whose teaching was essentially a simplified form of Hinduism blended with Islamic mysticism. Later, Nanak (1469–1539), one of Kabir's disciples, became the founder of a new religion, Sikhism, which in its final form represented elements from both Hinduism and Islam (see Chapter 7).

Hindu-Muslim syncretism reached its zenith in the reign of Akbar (1556–1605), who tried to establish a single, all-embracing religion for his empire. Although his efforts failed, his influence persisted for half a century, until, during the reign of Aurangzeb (1659–1707), orthodox Muslim teachers did all in their power to discourage the growth of syncretic tendencies. The advent of British domination in the nineteenth century virtually brought Hindu-Muslim syncretic movements to an end.

Hindu-Christian Encounters

Although, according to tradition, Christianity came to southern India in the first century CE, its impact on Hinduism was minimal until the arrival of the Portuguese in the sixteenth century, followed by the

Dutch, the British, and the French. Both Catholic and Protestant missionaries made converts, although the masses were, and still are, largely unaffected.

The spread of Christian ideas by missionaries influenced a number of Hindus who, in turn, launched Hindu reform movements. One such movement was the Brahmo Samaj, founded in 1828 by Ram Mohun Roy. From his perspective, the precepts of Jesus were "the guide to peace and happiness." He denounced all forms of polytheism and advocated a purge of Hinduism, to strip from it all elements of idolatry and polytheism. In religious services, the worship of the Brahmo Samaj was patterned after Protestantism: hymns, scripture readings, and sermons. Another reformer was Dayananda Sarasvati, who founded the Arya Samaj group in 1875. Sarasvati believed that the religion documented in the Vedas was the oldest and purest of all faiths, because the Vedas represented a direct revelation from the one God.

The most important, because it was the most widespread, Hindu adaptation of the Christian tradition was proposed by Sri Ramakrishna (1836–1886), founder of the Ramakrishna movement. A mystic and a devotee of the goddess Kali, he came to the conclusion that "all religions were different paths to God; nevertheless, the religion of a person's own time and place is the best expression of God." After Ramakrishna's death, his successor, Vivekananda, established Ramakrishna centers in India, Europe, and the Americas.

Many other Hindu teachers and thinkers were attracted to the Western intellectual tradition and Christian ideals. Among them were the Bengali poet Rabindranath Tagore (1861–1941); Swami Sivananda (1862–1902), who organized the Divine Life Society; Sri Aurobindo Ghose (1872–1950); Sarvepalli Radhakrishnan (1888–1975); and Mahatma Gandhi (1869–1948), who preached the doctrine of *satyagraha*, or passive resistance to British rule.[8]

Mahatma Gandhi. Mohandas Gandhi, popularly known as Mahatma Gandhi (1869–1948), represents an outstanding figure in modern India and a famous religious personality who was loved throughout the world. Born on October 2, 1869, in Porbandar, a small coastal town in Gujarat in Western India, Gandhi (usually called "Gandhiji" or "Bapu" by Indians) was the son of an important minister of a princely state. Having completed his primary and secondary education in India, he left for England at the age of nineteen to study law and soon became a barrister.

A legal case sent him to South Africa at the age of twenty-four. He lived there for the next twenty years and experienced firsthand the prejudice of "white-skinned" European settlers against "dark-skinned" people (Africans and Indians). It was this attitude and the treatment that accompanied it that persuaded Gandhi to stay in South Africa and fight for the rights of Africans and Indians. But the method he used for fighting prejudice and discrimination was novel and significant.

Gandhi believed that violence was too great a price to pay even for fair treatment and justice. Violence, he said, always led to more violence. There was only one way to fight injustice: through nonviolence. Hence, if Ghandi decided that a certain law was unfair or unjust, he considered it his duty to disregard it, cheerfully accepting the consequences without hatred and without retaliation. *Truth* and *nonviolence* were the two basic values of life to which Gandhi always adhered.

Gandhi returned to India during World War I, only to find that the same situation and attitudes he had resisted in South Africa existed between the ruling British officials and the Indian public. After the war, Gandhi and a few Indian national leaders challenged Indians to oppose British rule and what they considered was British injustice. Hundreds of thousands of men and women accepted Gandhi's call; among them was a future prime minister of India, Jawaharlal Nehru.

Gandhi wanted Indians to fight for their freedom, but he wanted them to achieve their goals in such a way that Britons and Indians could reach new levels of understanding and become better people. To him, achieving the goals was far less important than the way they were achieved. In a world full of violence and hatred, he was profoundly convinced all national and international problems could be solved through nonviolence.

At midnight on August 14, 1947, India (excluding Pakistan) finally won freedom by virtue of Gandhi's two principles. Less than six months later, this "apostle of nonviolence and angel of peace" died at the hands of an assassin. Three pistol shots struck Gandhi as he knelt for prayers on the evening of January 30, 1948. With his hands folded in prayer, he uttered the words, *"Ram, Ram,"* (the name of God) and fell.

Gandhi was murdered before he could achieve all of his objectives. He preached religious tolerance in an attempt to alleviate frictions between India's warring Hindu and Muslim factions. In addition, in his fight against all practices that he thought unjust, Gandhi attempted to reform India's socioreligious tradition of caste, even going so far as to champion the rights of the *chandalas,* or untouchables.

In a world of hatred, injustice, and violence, Gandhi's timeless message still rings out:

My message and methods are, indeed in their essentials for the whole world. . . . I feel in the inmost recesses of my heart. . . . that the world is sick unto death of blood-spilling. The world is seeking a way out. I believe that true democracy can only be the outcome of nonviolence.

Other Hindus resisted—and still resist—Christian missionary teaching as inimical to their time-honored institutions. Since India achieved independence in 1947, in fact, conversion to Christianity has been viewed with disfavor by many influential Hindus, who advocate in Hinduism the same characteristics that prompted other Hindus to accept Christianity (e.g., incantation, faith in and devotion to one deity, the pursuit of ultimate bliss). Serious efforts are being made to reconvert Indian Christians to Hinduism. Some Indian Christians have even formed groups analogous to castes, but these are exceptions rather than the rule. In general, the Hindu masses tolerate Christian converts, even though the latter ignore time-honored Hindu customs and traditions.

The most recent manifestation of the Hindu-Christian encounter is the Hare Krishna movement (officially known as the International Society of Krishna Consciousness), founded by Swami Prabhupada in 1965. Its purpose is to spread Hindu religious beliefs in the Western world, a process that began in the eighteenth century with the first English translation of the Bhagavad-Gita. Although modern forms of Hinduism barely seem to maintain a tenuous existence in Christian lands, new manifestations are more than likely to develop in the future.

Women and Modernity

Generally speaking, Hindu theology represents Absolute Reality as male-female. The female aspect is represented as the more energetic, violent, emotional, and potentially destructive; the male aspect as cool, dispassionate, and serene. The goddess Kali (see p. 81) is one of the most dramatic representations of this feminine aspect of Absolute Reality, but Hindu theology often juxtaposes opposites in order to heighten the transcendent quality of male-female reality. Inconsistency or contradiction is not an issue in Hindu theology, so long as one understands the ineffability of infinity. Hindu epics blend theology, romance, poetry, dramatic stories, and models of human behavior to suggest the oneness of all opposites, including divine-human and male-female. Texts such as the Code of Manu, however, identify and regulate the daily duties of the different castes and the two sexes.

The ideal couple in Hindu thought is represented by the epic story of Rama and his wife, Sita, in the Ramayana. Rama represents the concern, sensitivity, and tenderness of a male lover, whereas Sita's pleas, tears, and utter devotion reflect the behavior appropriate to women. Although Rama boasts that none can guard Sita better than he in the perilous forest, she is stolen away by the demon Ravana, only to be rescued by Rama's friend, the monkey god Hanuman. Even so, the onus is on Sita, the victim, to prove her fidelity.

The various Hindu codes of law that developed over the centuries prescribed the different duties of castes and defined the role of women in society. The views proposed in the Code of Manu concerning women are quite explicit. From birth to death, women are to be protected by—that is, under the control of—their father, husband, or son. Here is how it is stated:

> In childhood a female must be subject to her father; in youth, to her husband; when her lord [husband] is dead, to her sons. A woman must never be independent. She must not seek to separate from her father, husband or sons. (Manu 5.148–149).

In no way, then, are women considered to be equal to men, or even to be free members of the family or caste. The Code lists the various disciplines to be imposed by males upon women in order to guarantee proper behavior by the latter. The assumption is that uncontrolled women tend to be emotional, sensual, violent, and potentially destructive to social order.

"Proper behavior" for a woman means an arranged marriage by her father at the proper time—usually soon after puberty, although in some localities child marriage is still a common practice. Monogamy has been the rule, but polygamy is customary in many communities. The next proper duty of a woman is to respect, obey, and worship her husband, even if he is unfaithful, virtueless, and devoid of good qualities.

> Him to whom her father may give her, or her brother with the father's permission, she shall obey as long as she lives. Though destitute of virtue, or seeking pleasure elsewhere, or devoid of good qualities, a husband must be constantly worshiped as a god by a faithful wife. (Manu 5.151–154)

A husband's duty is to protect his wife from threats inherent in both society and in a woman's nature. This ensures the purity and virtue of their offspring. Besides fulfilling the proper obligations to a husband and occupying herself with household duties, a bride is expected to become a member of her husband's family. This means, as a rule, the subjugation of every wife to the will of her mother-in-law.

After her husband's death, a woman of whatever age, be it fifteen or sixty-five, may not remarry. She is to live quietly, patiently, and chastely until death:

> She must never mention the name of another man after her husband has died. Until death let her be patient, self-controlled, chaste and strive to fulfill that most excellent duty which is prescribed for wives who have one husband only. (Manu 5.157–158)

If she lacks sons to protect her, she is expected to fast, to sleep on floors, and to live as an ascetic dressed in "widow's weeds." Should she violate this duty, she "brings on herself disgrace in this world, and loses her place with her husband in heaven." (Manu 5.160–161).

Traditionally, as we noted above, a widow was expected to accompany the corpse of her husband to the funeral pyre and be burned alive by his side *(sati)* on the assumption that a woman who outlived her husband had caused his death by her evil *karma.* How widespread the practice of *sati* was and is in India is uncertain, but attempts have been made to eradicate it in modern times.

Although the role and status of women in Hindu society are, from the point of view of Western life, unenviable, conditions are gradually improving since Prime Minister Indira Gandhi's tenure in office. Exemptions from caste and other social constraints are being worked out. Women are able to pursue certain careers, and religious restraints on their civil liberties are being reevaluated. Despite opposition to the introduction of Western influences, ancient traditions are slowly changing, particularly among upper-class and well-educated Hindus.

Other far-reaching changes in Hindu culture have been made in modern times. Attempts to abolish stratified class distinctions, and especially the restrictions imposed upon untouchables, are gradually succeeding, although the process is still far from complete. In 1948, India's Constituent Assembly abolished untouchability, and although social integration has lagged far behind legislation, the process of modern industrialization is gradually eroding the justification for time-honored traditions of class. In addition, various Hindu religious leaders have formed new sects in which all converts are regarded as equals, no matter what their previous castes, and are free to visit, eat, mix, and intermarry with other members of their sect.

The nationalistic desire to preserve Hindu unity and to prevent the development of national minority religious groups has led to a struggle for self-determination. Leading minds of India have established two important objectives: national self-determination for Hindu India, and unyielding ideals in matters of religious principles. Many orthodox Hindus advocate making India officially a Hindu state.

Notes

1. For helpful guides to understanding the complexity of Hinduism, see T. M. P. Mahadevan, *Outlines of Hinduism* (Bombay: Chetana, 1956); and K. Morgan, ed., *The Religion of the Hindus* (New York: Ronald Press, 1953).
2. Anthologies of Hindu sacred writings can be found in A. T. Embree, *The Hindu Tradition* (New York: Vintage Paperbacks, 1972); and W. T.

de Bary et al., eds., *Sources of Indian Tradition* (New York: Columbia University Press, 1958).

3. Translations of the Vedas are listed in C. J. Adams, ed., *A Reader's Guide to the Great Religions,* 2nd ed. (New York: Free Press, 1977), pp. 110–11.

4. N. W. Brown, "The Creation Myth of the Rig Veda," *Journal of the American Oriental Society* 62 (1942): 85–98.

5. For bibliographical material on Vishnu and Vaishnavites, see Adams, *A Reader's Guide,* pp. 131–37.

6. M. Monier-Williams, *Brahmanism and Hinduism* (London: Murray, 1891), p. 381.

7. For the achievements of King Asoka, see pp. 134–135.

8. There are extensive writings on each of these thinkers. For bibliographical material, see Adams, *A Reader's Guide,* pp. 147–52.

6

Buddhism

Historical Background

In India, the sixth century BCE was a time of doubt about, challenge to, and rejection of traditional religious patterns. By this point, many Hindus had become disenchanted with a religion that emphasized class, sacrifice, and ritual, and some religious leaders surrendered their status in society in favor of the life of the wandering ascetic. Small religious movements formed about these ascetics, whose spiritual qualities appealed to many discontented Hindus.

Chief among these dissident leaders was a man named Siddhartha Gautama (in Sanskrit, the classical Indic literary language) or Gotama (in Pali, an Indic dialect no longer in use except in Buddhist religious works),[1] later known as Buddha. The term *Buddha*, which means awakened one or enlightened one, is a title, such as Christ or Messiah, rather than a name.

The traditional story of the life and teachings of Buddha was transmitted orally for over four centuries before being documented some time between the first century BCE and the first century CE. The Pali texts of the *Tripitaka* (i.e., the Triple Canon, or Three Baskets) are considered to be the earliest extant records of Buddha's discourses, although it is almost impossible to distinguish historical fact from legendary material. The following biography of Buddha is based on the Pali texts.[2]

Gautama Buddha

Early Life

Siddhartha (c. 563–483 BCE)[3] was born in the ancient kingdom of the Sakyas (modern Nepal). His father was an Indian chieftain of the Sakya clan, and thus a member of the Hindu *kshatriya* (warrior) caste. According to the traditional account of the life of Siddhartha, one night before he was born his mother dreamed that a white elephant entered her womb through her side. Hindu priests, called in to interpret this dream, predicted the birth of a son who would become either a universal monarch or a universal teacher.

Ten lunar months after conception, the mother set out to visit her parents in a neighboring village. On her way she passed through a park called Lumbini, where she went into labor and gave birth to a son. The site, now called Rummindei, lies within Nepal, and a pillar raised by King Asoka in the third century BCE stands there still in commemoration of the event.

Details associated with the infancy of Siddhartha are fragmentary. According to tradition, the Hindu sage Asita (also called Kala Devala) recognized auspicious signs on the child's body at the time of his birth.[4] His conclusion was that the child would be a universal teacher, or Buddha—an augury that was partly confirmed five days after the child's birth when Hindu priests predicted, during the name-giving ceremony, that if the child remained at home, he would become a universal monarch and that if he did not, he would become a Buddha.[5] On the seventh day after the child's birth, his mother died and he was placed in the care of his mother's sister.

Accounts of Siddhartha's boyhood are no better documented than are details concerning his infancy. Part of the traditional record refers to an incident during this period that presaged the young boy's eventual career. One day, the little boy Siddhartha was taken to a local public festival, in which both his father and the local farmers took part. The nurses attending Siddhartha were so attracted by the festivities that they left the boy alone in the tent. When they returned, they found him seated cross-legged in the posture of a *yogin* (one who practices a self-controlled, meditative position prescribed by yoga—see pp. 94–95), absorbed in a trance.[6]

Siddhartha was brought up in great luxury and comfort. At the age of sixteen (or according to another account, nineteen), he married a cousin, who was also sixteen years old. Although the birth of a son followed this union, Siddhartha was dissatisfied with a life limited to family and social obligations. His concerns transcended such limitations.

Four Sights

Tradition states that the turning point in Siddhartha's life came at the age of twenty-nine, when his awareness of human suffering became the source or motivating force of his quest for truth. Four sights, or perceptions, are usually cited as the instigation of his religious crisis.

The first image associated with Siddhartha's heightened perception was that of a decrepit old man leaning on his staff as he walked. The second was that of a sick man, suffering in pain and soiled by incontinence brought on by his enfeebled condition. The third was that of a human corpse being carried to a funeral pyre; and the fourth, that of a calm, ascetic monk with a clean, shaven head, wearing a yellow robe. The sum of these images struck Siddhartha with the force of a revelation: all humans are subject to suffering. Transformed by this insight, he decided to leave home in search of a solution to the problem of human suffering. Thus began what is known as the "great renunciation": Siddhartha's abdication of a princely life in favor of one of selfless denial of material possessions as a wandering ascetic.

Quest for Truth

For the next six years, Siddhartha struggled to find an answer to human misery. His first recourse was to Alara Kalama, a famous Hindu sage, who gladly taught him to achieve the "realm of nothingness." Though Siddhartha quickly matched his teacher's mastery of the mystical state of nothingness, he found the consequences to be disappointing and consulted another great Hindu teacher, who taught him to attain the "realm of neither perception nor nonperception." This higher mystical state, however, proved no more satisfying than had previous solutions that Siddhartha had tested and rejected. He thereupon turned from Hindu philosophic meditation to severe bodily austerity in his search for absolute truth.

After a short period of wandering, Siddhartha reached a village near Uruvela (modern Gaya in India), where he was joined by a group of five ascetics—one of whom, according to tradition, was the Hindu priest who had predicted during the name-giving ceremony that the child Siddhartha would one day become a Buddha. In the company of this group, Siddhartha subjected himself to a regimen of extreme austerity that is vividly described in sacred texts (Buddhacarita XII.90– 106). It is said that, among other things, he sat on a couch of thorns,

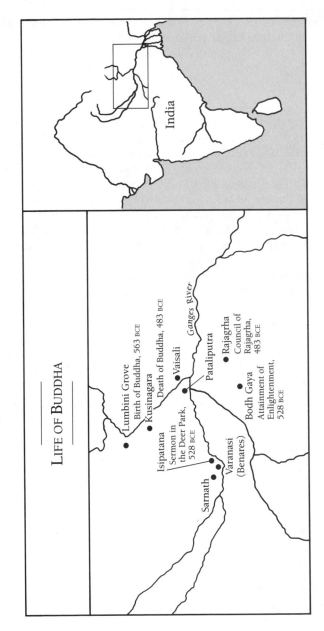

LIFE OF BUDDHA

India

Ganges River

Lumbini Grove
Birth of Buddha, 563 BCE

Kusinagara
Death of Buddha, 483 BCE

Vaisali

Pataliputra

Rajagrha
Council of
Rajagrha,
483 BCE

Isipatana
Sermon in
the Deer Park,
528 BCE

Bodh Gaya
Attainment of
Enlightenment,
528 BCE

Varanasi
(Benares)

Sarnath

ate all sorts of nauseous foods, and let filth accumulate on his body. As a result of such self-mortification, Siddhartha's health deteriorated to the point where his friends thought that he had died. In the course of a slow recuperation, Siddhartha came to the conclusion that a regimen of austerity and self-mortification was no more effective a path to the identification of absolute truth than asceticism and philosophic meditation had been. As a prerequisite to a new approach, he decided to restore his health by eating and drinking properly once again. His five Hindu companions, outraged by what they interpreted as his surrender to self-indulgence, left him in disgust.

Temptations of Buddha

Having regained his health, Siddhartha set out once more by himself to follow his own quest for truth. At some point he turned off the road to sit cross-legged at the foot of a tree (now known as a *bodhi* tree, or tree of knowledge), determined not to rise before he had attained enlightenment. According to the earliest canonical texts, Siddhartha's first encounter or experience was with the personification of evil, the tempter Mara, whose mission it was to confound and frustrate Siddhartha's search.

Mara's three temptations are graphically described in the texts (Buddhacarita XIII.1–6, 71–72). First, Mara tried to convince Siddhartha that a cousin and a former archenemy had revolted at home, taken his wife, and imprisoned his father. Siddhartha sat unmoved. Next, Mara paraded three voluptuous "daughters," or goddesses, accompanied by a group of sensuous dancers, around Siddhartha's tree with instructions to seduce him by any means they might devise. Siddhartha ignored them. Finally, Mara summoned a host of demons to terrify Siddhartha with their deadly missiles. Siddhartha reacted by touching the ground with his right-hand fingers. This contact produced a great thundering sound, at which Mara and his host of demons fled in confusion.[7]

The Great Enlightenment

Having defeated Mara, Siddhartha spent the night under the tree in deep meditation. As he passed through deeper and deeper states of consciousness, he was transported by visions of his former existences, and with the insights born of this knowledge, he suddenly understood the cause and the cycle of rebirths. He had solved the riddle of human suffering and discovered a way of eliminating it. Thus, at the age of thirty-five, Siddhartha attained enlightenment and became the supreme Buddha (Buddhacarita XIV.1–9, 47–51, 83–108).

Buddhist texts describe the cosmic portents that accompanied Buddha's enlightenment: the earth swelled, fruit and blossoms fell, and the sky shone bright. Buddha, however, spent the next several weeks (five or seven, according to different accounts) meditating on the various aspects of the truth he had realized and debating with himself the wisdom of communicating his discovery to others. He resolved this conflict by means of an analogy to a lotus pond, in which some lotuses remain under water, some float on the surface, and some rise above it. In a similar way, Buddha decided, humans differ in their capacity to comprehend the cosmic truth, or *dharma,* that he had discovered. To those to whom it was given to understand, he would communicate his discovery.

First Discourse

Buddha's next concern was to identify those capable of receiving *dharma.* His two former Hindu teachers were dead, and his five ascetic Hindu companions had deserted him. Nevertheless, since he had been close to them, Buddha decided to find these five companions, who were now in Benares (modern Varanasi, a city halfway between Delhi and Calcutta). When he met them, Buddha described his "awakened" state and offered to share his new-found insight into *dharma* with them, but to no avail. His former companions accused him again of abandoning austerity in favor of self-indulgence and of forfeiting any prospect of enlightenment. When Buddha asked them only for a fair hearing, they reiterated their disappointment and disgust. Buddha appealed to them yet once more, and when, for the third time, they demonstrated their bitterness and resentment, he is said to have challenged them with this brief question: "Do you admit, O monks, that I have never spoken like this before?" Struck by his sincerity and persistence, Buddha's five former friends answered, "Lord, you have not." Buddha then delivered his first discourse, now known as "Setting in Motion the Wheel of Truth"[8] (see pp. 127–130).

Founding of the Sangha

At the end of the discourse, Buddha's five ascetic companions became his first disciples and founding members of the *sangha,* or monastic order. Buddha now devoted his time in preaching his new doctrine. His father, stepmother, and former wife were converted, followed by many others. Some converts, as might be expected, were from either his own societal caste (the *kshatriya*) or from lower castes; but many Hindu priests of the *brahmin* caste also joined the *sangha.* Hindu caste distinctions, so sharply defined in Indian society, ceased to apply once an individual joined the *sangha.*

So compelling was the attraction of this new movement that soon

Gautama Buddha delivering his first discourse. Beneath him, his disciples are shown surrounding a wheel, a symbol of early Buddhist iconography. This sculpted sandstone, Gupta style, dates from the fifth century BCE *and is presently at Sarnath Museum.* Courtesy of Government of India Tourist Office, Toronto.

Buddha had sixty *arhats*, or "perfected" disciples who had attained liberation and enlightenment. Buddha commissioned them to travel all over India and into the world beyond to spread his message of peace, truth, and compassion. He remained in India, converting leading ascetics and leaders of influence, including several rulers. As the number of his followers increased, monasteries were built for Buddha and his *sangha* in virtually every important city in India, including monasteries in Savatthi and Jetanana.

These were institutions dominated by men. Ananda, Buddha's cousin and later his chief and constant disciple, pleaded with him on behalf of women. After some hesitation, Buddha agreed to the institu-

self/nothing

tion of an order of nuns. His aunt and some of her friends were the first women to enter the order.

Devadatta, another cousin of Buddha, was a convert with ulterior motives. First, Devadatta plotted to succeed the aging Buddha as leader of the *sangha*. When no one would take him seriously, he made three unsuccessful attempts on the life of Buddha. Finally, he tried to induce a schism in the *sangha* by establishing a separate order; this was short-lived, however, and Devadatta's supporters soon returned to Buddha. Nine months after he had seen his hopes dashed for the third time, Devadatta sickened and died.

Buddha's mission, never seriously threatened by rivals such as Devadatta, lasted for forty-five years. He taught and trained a large group of well-disciplined followers until, at the age of eighty, he succumbed to a serious illness. His last words to his disciples were, "And now, O monks, I take leave of you; transient are all conditioned things; try to accomplish your aim with diligence." A week later his body was cremated by his clansmen in Kusinara (modern Kasia).[9] In spite of Buddha's dying injunction to be aware of the transience of "conditioned things" (actions, thoughts, and the like, dictated by societal norms or natural instinct), his family and followers quarreled over the disposition of his relics. Finally, by common consent they were divided into eight portions, satisfying the wishes of all disputants.

The portrait of Buddha that emerges from ancient texts is one of great wisdom and great compassion. The spectacle of human suffering made him seek a rational system of thought that would free humanity from its fetters. His unique reputation rests less on his intellectual power and his abilities as a leader than it does on his record as a great teacher.

Buddha's Teachings

Buddha wrote nothing. Like most religious leaders, he talked with his disciples on various topics and on many different occasions. The teachings attributed to him were transmitted orally for centuries by his disciples before they were finally committed to writing by several different Buddhist groups. Allowing for factors such as oral distortions and differences of opinions and interpretation, scholars more or less agree on the following essentials of Buddha's teachings.

Buddha challenged several of the religious tenets of Hinduism and rejected the two most fundamental Hindu paths to liberation from cycles of rebirths: the philosophical path and the ascetic path. He also rejected the Hindu concept of religious devotion as a path to liberation. Liberation from rebirths, for Buddha and for Buddhists, meant cessation of *tanha*, or selfish craving for sentient existence, not the Hindu concept of the union of Brahman-Atman (see pp. 83–85).

Buddha maintained that *Atman*—in the sense of an individual soul or ego—does not exist. Nothing within a person, Buddha claimed, is metaphysically real. The Human beings are made up of five *skandhas*, or components: (1) body, (2) feelings, (3) perceptions, (4) dispositions, and (5) consciousness. Humans are caught in a cycle of rebirth because of the mechanism by which human beings evolve—the chain of causation called the law of dependent origination. According to this law, every mode of being is caused by another immediately preceding mode and in turn causes a subsequent mode. Stated differently, one condition arises out of another, which, in turn, had arisen out of prior conditions.

The original condition in this chain of causes and effects is ignorance, which, in turn, gives rise to the following series of causes and effects: predispositions, or karmic agents; consciousness; name and form (or individuality); the five sense organs and the mind; other objects (selves or things); sensation; self-desire *(tanha)*; attachment to existence; the process of becoming; progressive states of being (each unlike preceding states); and human suffering *(dukkha)*.

Buddha placed no credence or value in Hindu scriptures, because he challenged the Hindu belief in gods and goddesses. He argued that the so-called deities of Hinduism were no more immortal than were the people who worshiped them and that to offer sacrifices, rituals, and prayers to deities was a useless exercise. If deities, sacrifices, rituals, and prayers were all unnecessary, what need was there for Hindu priests? Buddha's challenge called into question the traditional superiority of the *brahmin* caste, the belief in Brahman-Atman, the Hindu law of *karma* and *samsara,* and the whole structure of the caste system. He rejected the Hindu hierarchy of caste because, in his view, no individual, permanent entity passed from one existence to another.

Buddha reduced the many ideas that Hindus associated with rebirth to one concept: the flow of becoming. This is the *dharma* (the cosmic truth) summed up in the Four Noble Truths propounded in Buddha's first discourse, "Setting in Motion the Wheel of Truth." Ever since that epochal address, the wheel has become the symbol of Buddhism, and the Four Noble Truths have become the foundation of Buddhist teaching.

Here is how Buddha's first discourse is recorded:

There are two extremes, O monks, that should not be practiced by one who has assumed that homeless life.

And what are these two?

That devoted to passions and luxury—which is low, vulgar, unworthy and useless; and that devoted to self-mortification—which is painful, unworthy and useless.

By avoiding these two extremes, the *Tathagata* ["one who has discovered the truth," referring to the Buddha] has gained the enlightenment of that Middle Path, which gives insight of knowledge; which leads to calmness, to higher knowledge and enlightenment—*Nirvana.*

And what, O monks, is the Middle Path, which gives insight of knowledge, which leads to calmness, to higher knowledge and enlightenment—*Nirvana?*

Truly it is the Noble Eightfold Way: right understanding, right intention, right speech, right conduct, right occupation, right endeavor, right contemplation, and right concentration.

This, O monks, is the Middle Path, which gives insight and knowledge, which leads to calmness, to higher knowledge and enlightenment—*Nirvana.*

Now this, O monks, is the noble truth of *dukkha* ["suffering"]: birth is *dukkha;* old age is *dukkha;* sickness is *dukkha;* death is *dukkha;* sorrow, lamentation, anguish, and despair are *dukkha;* contact with unpleasant factors is *dukkha;* not acquiring what one desires is *dukkha.* In short, the five *skandhas* ["one's constituents"] are *dukkha.*

Now this, O monks, is the noble truth of the cause of *dukkha; tanha* ["selfish, craving, desire"] which leads to rebirth . . . *tanha* for passions; *tanha* for existence; *tanha* for nonexistence.

Now this, O monks, is the noble truth for the cessation of *dukkha;* the cessation without a residue of *tanha:* abandonment, forsaking; release; nonattachment.

Now this, O monks, is the noble truth of the way that leads to the cessation of *dukkha:*

The Noble Eightfold Way: right understanding, right intention, right speech, right conduct, right occupation, right endeavor, right contemplation, and right concentration. (Vinayana Pitaka)

The Middle Way. The content of this landmark of religious history can be summarized as follows. Anyone searching for truth should avoid the two extremes of self-indulgence and self-mortification. Self-indulgence is degrading, sensual, vulgar, unworthy, and useless. Self-mortification is painful, degrading, and useless. By avoiding these extremes, one gains the enlightenment of the Middle Way, which leads to insight, to knowledge, to calmness, to awakening, and finally, to *nirvana* (literally, extinction).

The Four Noble Truths. The First Truth is that all composite things (existing phenomena) are, by their very nature, in a state of *dukkha.* There is no precise English equivalent for this term, which encompasses dissatisfaction, anxiety, frustration, suffering, pain, and misery. All events or features in life are characterized by *dukkha:* birth, sickness, old age, death, failure to fulfill ambitions or desires, separation from loved ones, marriage, association with people one dislikes, and so on. Such experiences as happiness and enjoyment, which are characteristic of most lives, merely presuppose their opposites. Consequently, life, or existence, is characterized not only by *dukkha,* but also by *anicca* (impermanence) and *anatta* (no self). Everything in the universe is in an endless process of impermanence, change, and decay. Life is transitory; nothing about it is permanent. And if there is no permanent reality inside or outside the individual (except the reality of the ceaseless state of becoming), and all forms are ever-changing, then there is no permanent self or ego, let alone an immortal soul.

The Second Truth is that this unsatisfactory state of affairs is a consequence of *tanha.* This term means a desire or craving for sentient material possessions or intellectual gratification induced by clinging to things without realizing their impermanent, insubstantial, and unsatisfactory nature. Most people delude themselves into thinking that possessions, attachments, and relationships represent the essence of a happy, civilized life, whereas in reality they are simply the cause of *dukkha.*

The Third Truth is self-evident: escape from *tanha* is a prerequisite to inner peace and tranquility. By eliminating all desire and selfish craving, one eliminates *dukkha.* To put it differently, freedom from *dukkha* is possible only by severing the chain of *tanha.*

The Fourth Truth concerns the path, or way, that leads to this freedom, or Middle Way, the life of calm detachment through which the wise person avoids the extremes of asceticism and self-indulgence. The practical techniques to be followed in the Middle Way fall into eight categories, known collectively as the Noble Eightfold Path. These categories do not represent successive stages or steps to be followed in sequence; rather, they are characteristics of day-to-day living that must be practiced and realized simultaneously. The Noble Eightfold Path consists of right knowledge, right intention, right speech, right conduct, right means of livelihood, right effort, right mindfulness, and right concentration.

The Noble Eightfold Path. The key to this concept is the word "right" and consists of the following eight points:

- Right Understanding. Having a right understanding means perceiving and believing the Four Noble Truths.

- Right Intention. Once one has perceived and believed the Four Noble Truths, one must renounce worldly life, accept the "homeless" state, and follow the Noble Eightfold Path.

- Right Speech. One must act with compassion and consideration of others, abstaining from lies, slander, abuse, and idle talk.

- Right Conduct. Right conduct or behavior means abstaining from killing, stealing, lying, committing adultery, and using intoxicants.

- Right Occupation. One must never accept an occupation that may be considered questionable.
- Right Endeavor. One must always strive after all that is good and make a strong effort to keep away from all that is evil or wicked.
- Right Contemplation. One must always learn to control the mind in peaceful contemplation so that neither joy nor sorrow nor any other emotion is allowed to disturb one's calm.
- Right Concentration. When all the other principles have been followed, then one can reach the stage where the mind is completely subject to one's will. One can develop the mind to heights beyond reasoning, indeed, to *nirvana.*

A short but interesting narrative recorded in the Buddhist scripture illustrates the significance of these important principles.

Once, Gotami, an Indian woman, came to the Buddha crying, "O Exalted One, my only son has died. I went to everyone and asked, 'Is there no medicine to bring my son back to life?' And they replied, 'There is no medicine; but go to the Exalted One, he may be able to help you.' Can you, O Exalted One, give me medicine to bring my only son back to life?"

Looking at her compassionately, the Buddha replied, "You did well, Gotami, in coming here for medicine. Go, and bring me for medicine some tiny grains of mustard seed from every house where no one— neither parent, child, relative, nor servant—has died."

Gotami, delighted in her heart, went away to fetch as many tiny grains of mustard seed as she could find. From one house to the other, she moved frantically all day long, as each time she was told, "Alas! Gotami, great is the count of the dead in this house."

Overcome with exhaustion, she finally went to the burning-ground outside the city with her dead son in her arms. "My dear little boy," said she, "I thought you alone had been overtaken by this thing which men call *death.* But now I see that you are not the only one, for *this is a law common to all mankind.*" And so saying, she cast the little corpse into the fire.

Then she sang:

> No village law, no law of market town,
> No law of a single house is *this,* [death]
> Of all the world, and all the worlds of gods,
> This only is law: *All things are anicca.*

When she returned to the Buddha, she was greeted by him. "Gotami, did you get the tiny grains of mustard seed for medicine?"

"Done, O Exalted One, is the business of the mustard seed! Only give me refuge."

All that exists is *anicca* and is subject to the changes which occur through the cycle of birth, growth, decay, and death. To crave or desire life (*tanha*) is to go through this process, and this process is *dukkha*. Even death, the Buddhists believe, is only one point in the cycle of change: it does not mark the end of existence. *Nothing* is permanent, unchanging, eternal, or immortal.

Nirvana. Those who follow the Noble Eightfold Path, Buddha taught, will ultimately break the bonds that tie them to life and to their craving for existence. They will alone achieve release from the cycle of rebirth. Only the extinction of *tanha*, like the extinction of a candle flame after it has passed from candle to candle, can free a person from the cycle of rebirth, and consequently, from *dukkha* or misery. This extinction, or "going out," is the state of *nirvana*.

Nirvana is difficult, if not impossible, to define, since it is not an intellectual goal.[10] The term literally means "extinction," as the flame of a candle is said to be extinguished. Hence, *nirvana* means the extinction of all *tanha*. However, *nirvana* is not a state of total annihilation; on the contrary, it is a state in which a person, having been freed from all *tanha*, is liberated from the cycle of rebirth and, hence,

The reclining Buddhas are the principal attraction at Gal Vihara, near Polonnaruva, Sri Lanka. The Buddhas recline, heads propped up, like monuments to relaxation. They are forty-four feet long.   From the private collection of Mr. and Mrs. G. Brooks.

from *dukkha*. In the words of Buddha, "There is, O monks, a condition where there is neither earth, nor water, nor fire, nor air, nor the sphere of infinite consciousness, nor the sphere of the void. . . . That condition, O monks, do I call . . . nirvana."[11] *Nirvana*, accordingly, is the end of all transitory states; the final, peaceful bliss; the ultimate goal of each individual.

To put his imaginative vision in its simplest form, Buddha saw life as a stream of countless individuals going through an endless cycle of rebirth, within which the form of every new life is dictated by former lives and every fate is the effect of former good or evil deeds. Within this cycle of rebirth, suffering is inevitable. Liberation from suffering is conditional on a break from this cycle and the attainment of *nirvana*, an inscrutable state of absolute transcendence.

Buddha's final message to his disciples was:

> Be ye lamps unto yourselves; rely on yourselves; and do not rely on any external help! Hold fast to the Truth [The Four Noble Truths] as a lamp! Seek salvation alone in the Truth. Look not for assistance to any one besides yourselves!
>
> Be earnest then . . . be steadfast in resolve. Keep watch over your own hearts. Who wearies not, but holds fast to his Truth, shall cross this ocean of life—shall cease *dukkha!* (Mahaparinibbana Suttanta)

Development of Buddhism

Early Councils

All Buddhist traditions maintain that a council was called immediately after the death of Buddha, though many scholars have questioned whether or not such a council was ever convened.[12] At this council, according to tradition, five hundred monks formulated an authorized canon and rules governing early Buddhist monasteries (see below).

That a second council was held a century later has more or less been accepted by scholars. This council resulted in a schism over doctrinal issues and disciplinary rules, principally between a group called the Mahasanghika (Great Sangha), which interpreted doctrine and discipline liberally, and a group called the Theravadins (Adherents of the Teaching of the Elders), which represented orthodoxy and conservatism. Other groups, or schools (the traditional number is eighteen), also emerged from this council.

Tradition refers to a third council, held in the third century BCE. At this gathering, according to some accounts, the Buddhist canon, the Tripitaka, was completed and longstanding sectarian controversies led to additional splits and divisions.

A fourth council, dealing with the composition of commentaries, is believed to have been held some time during the first century CE, although the absence of several Buddhist groups from this council has led scholars to conclude that it was simply a sectarian synod, not an ecumenical council. This conclusion is partly based on subsequent events within the Buddhist community, which eventually split formally into several sects (see pp. 143–149).

Establishment of Monastic Orders

Several scholars have argued that monasticism originated with Buddhism and that later, primarily Christian, monastic traditions which spread from the Middle East to Europe and elsewhere represented adaptations of ancient Buddhist models. During Buddha's lifetime, he and his followers gathered annually during the rainy season. After his death, his followers continued these yearly "rain retreats," which gradually turned into permanent monastic settlements. These, in turn, developed into great monasteries serving as centers of Buddhist learning and missionary enterprise. From these monasteries, Buddhist missionaries were sent to propagate the faith in China, Japan, Tibet, and southeastern Asia.

Naturally, monks who lived closely together in permanent monasteries required disciplinary rules and a degree of hierarchical organization. The first such rules, according to tradition, were handed down by the first council. Soon the abbot became the head of this administrative hierarchy and was vested with almost unlimited powers over monastic affairs.

Eventually, Buddhist monastic orders developed different characteristics according to which country and branch of Buddhism they belonged to. Today, some permit lay participation in monastic affairs, whereas others are strictly authoritarian. Entry to monastic orders, however, has always been an individual affair, dependent upon the commitment of either the applicant or the applicant's family.

The life of a Buddhist monk was originally one of poverty, celibacy, and wandering mendicancy. Over time, however, these early features were modified or changed. For instance, begging has become merely a symbolic gesture to teach humility, and the growth of large monasteries, made possible through large endowments from wealthy donors, has often led to compromises on the rule of poverty. In Japan during the tenth to thirteenth centuries, Buddhist monasteries even recruited large armies of mercenaries and monks to fight rival religious groups as well as temporal wars. Celibacy and strict sexual abstinence, once the rule in all Buddhist monastic orders, have been relaxed. The Shin sect of Japan encouraged the abolition of monastic celibacy, and some groups have allowed sexual intercourse as symbolic of enlightenment.

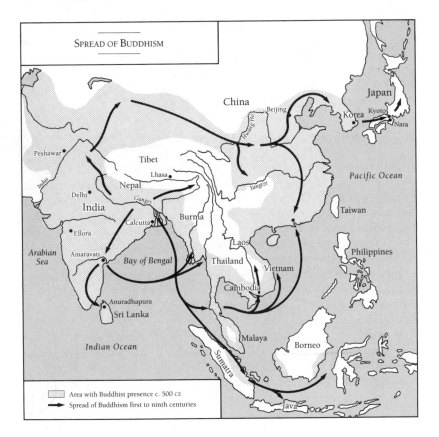

SPREAD OF BUDDHISM

Area with Buddhist presence c. 500 CE
Spread of Buddhism first to ninth centuries

Spread of Buddhism

Asoka. Little is known about the spread of Buddhism immediately after the death of Buddha until the advent, sometime during the third century BCE, of Asoka, a king of India who ranks among the most remarkable figures in Indian history.

Asoka was the grandson of an army officer who defeated the forces of Alexander the Great. Like his father and grandfather, Asoka continued to expand his imperial territory through conquest until he was attracted to the teachings of Buddhism. Upon publicly accepting Buddhism, he forswore warfare and sought to foster the spread of Buddhism throughout his empire. Archeologists are still finding traces of the temples he built and other legacies of his conversion. Asoka is best remembered, however, for the missionary work he sponsored. He sent Buddhist missionaries not only to all parts of India, but also westward, to the Hellenized kingdoms of Asia, Africa, and Europe;

Inner courtyard of Wat Phra Keo Temple in Bangkok, Thailand. Built in 1784 by Rama I, the first king of Bangkok, it is also known as the Temple of the Emerald Buddha. The outer walls and columns are covered with porcelain mosaics, the doors are resplendent with inlays of mother-of-pearl, and the spires are covered with gold leaf. Towering masked figures, standing about 20 feet high, guard the entrance gates. Courtesy of Trans World Airlines.

southward, to Sri Lanka (Ceylon); and eastward, to Burma. The last-named two countries—along with Laos, Thailand, and Cambodia, which accepted Buddhism between the fifth and seventh centuries—have preserved the essential teachings of Buddha to the present.

China. By the beginning of the first century CE, the two main branches of Buddhism, Theravada and Mahayana, were moving through central Asia into China. Ruling China at that time was the Han dynasty (206 BCE–220 CE), a power in the East that matched the Roman Empire in the West. The Han regime dominated eastern Asia from Korea to Turkistan and from the Gobi Desert to Vietnam. At the time Buddhist missionaries arrived, the national creed was Confucianism (see Chapter 8), which emphasized social rankings according to intellectual status, a rigid family structure, and a moral code based on humanity and the practice of perfect virtue for its own sake.

Tradition has it that the White Horse Temple, reputedly the first Chinese Buddhist monastery, was founded as a consequence of a manifestation of Buddha, in the form of a golden deity, in a dream of Emperor Ming (58–76 CE). The earliest historical reference to a Chinese Buddhist community dates from 65 CE, and by the middle of the second century, Buddha was being worshiped in the imperial palace, along with other deities.

Incursions by Turkish and Tibetan tribes into northern China produced a social climate ripe for Buddhism, for by becoming Buddhist monks, Chinese adherents could avoid military and labor service, as well as taxation. Also, the invaders of the northern territories came to embrace the Buddhist faith in order to consolidate their conquests and ensure continued prosperity. Meanwhile, social uncertainty and frustration in southern China favored the growth of metaphysical speculation. Taoists (see Chapter 8), predecessors of Confucians, considered "inactivity" as virtue and "nonbeing" as the origin of all things. These beliefs seemed to mirror the basic Buddhist ideal of *nirvana*, and a sympathetic dialogue developed between Buddhist monks and the Taoist literati, whose influence enabled Buddhism to gain converts among royalty and the rich.

The philosophical foundation of Chinese Buddhism was laid by a few eminent monks during the fourth century, a period in which cave

Buddhism

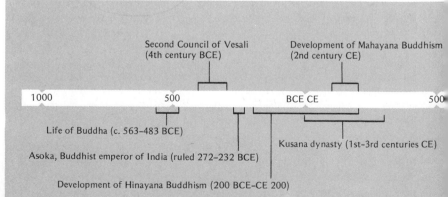

temples were carved out of hills to serve Buddhist traveling monks and native believers. These cave temples served as centers of devotion and pilgrimage for the next thousand years, and as repositories of Buddhist art to this day.

Two great events marked the turn of the fifth century. In 399, Fa-hsien became the first Chinese Buddhist monk to complete his pilgrimage to India, during which he survived great hardships to reach sacred Buddhist sites along the Ganges and to study Buddhist teachings at the source. After visiting Sri Lanka, he returned to China in 414. And in 401, the Buddhist monk Kumarajiva, captured by a Chinese raiding force, traveled from Kucha in northwestern India to the Chinese capital of Ch'ang-an, where he remained for the rest of his life. Under his direction, approximately three hundred scholars rendered into Chinese some of the most important of the Mahayana scriptures.

By that time, northern China was unified by a Turkic tribe whose emperors identified themselves with Buddha. These emperors encouraged the erection of Buddhist images and temples and invited Buddhist monks to be their advisors. In 446, however, one of these potentates issued a draconian edict calling for the destruction of all Buddhist temples, shrines, paintings, and scriptures and the summary execution of all monks. The storm was brief: eight years later, the destroyer's successor pronounced himself to be the reincarnation of Buddha and restored Buddhism to his realm.

A second persecution of Buddhists occurred in 574, when Emperor Wu sought to advance Confucianism by charging Buddhism with fostering disloyalty and breaking down filial piety. Before Emperor Wu died in 578, tens of thousands of temples were appropriated by the imperial family and the aristocracy and more than 1 million monks and nuns were defrocked.

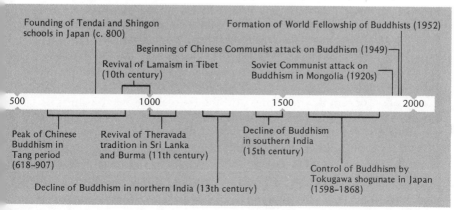

Founding of Tendai and Shingon schools in Japan (c. 800)

Formation of World Fellowship of Buddhists (1952)

Beginning of Chinese Communist attack on Buddhism (1949)

Revival of Lamaism in Tibet (10th century)

Soviet Communist attack on Buddhism in Mongolia (1920s)

500   1000   1500   2000

Peak of Chinese Buddhism in Tang period (618–907)

Revival of Theravada tradition in Sri Lanka and Burma (11th century)

Decline of Buddhism in southern India (15th century)

Control of Buddhism by Tokugawa shogunate in Japan (1598–1868)

Decline of Buddhism in northern India (13th century)

These reverses in China were mirrored to an aggravated degree in India, where numerous Buddhist monasteries were destroyed by invading Huns, a nomadic Asian people. This invasion presaged the decline of Buddhism in India. Scholars are not satisfied that they have yet established all the factors that contributed to the disappearance of Buddhism from India, though some maintain that the tolerance of Buddhism for other faiths doomed it to reabsorption by the dominant Hindu tradition.

Buddhism survived sporadic pogroms in China until the founding of the Sui dynasty by Emperor Wen in 581 ushered in the golden age of Chinese Buddhism. Calling himself a disciple of Buddha, Emperor Wen used Buddhism as a binding influence in the reunification of northern and southern China. His fame attracted envoys from Japan and Korea, who came to receive Buddhist teaching. For the next two and a half centuries Buddhism spread throughout China, Korea, and Japan. Then, in 845, Buddhist hegemony in China came to an abrupt end amid a third great wave of persecution. Thousands of temples and shrines were demolished, hundreds of thousands of monks and nuns were defrocked, hundreds of acres of temple land were confiscated, and an untold number of gold, silver, bronze, and iron images were melted down. Although the emperor responsible for these punitive measures died only one year after implementing them, and with his death Buddhism was restored, this wave of persecution marked the end of the golden age of Chinese Buddhism.

Japan. Buddhism was introduced to Japan in the sixth century, from Korea. At first, this new religion was regarded only as a talisman for the protection of the country. During the Nara period (710–794), however, Buddhism became a state religion, and a great statue of Buddha, called Daibutsu, was erected in the capital city of Nara, which became a national cult center. In time various Buddhist groups found acceptance among the Japanese people, who in turn developed their own sectarian variants.

Buddhism proved no less vulnerable to sporadic persecution in Japan than it had in China. The most recent pogrom occurred during the Meiji period (1868–1912), when Japan's ruling class sought to promote Shinto (see Chapter 9) as the state religion. The result was the confiscation of temple properties and the defrocking of thousands of Buddhist priests. In spite of these comparatively recent depredations, no other Buddhist country in the world can match the number and diversity of Buddhist sects that characterize Japan in modern times.

Tibet. Though Buddhism had spread into Tibet as early as the seventh century, it was not until the eighth century that Buddhism overshadowed Bon, the native shamanistic cult. The Tibetans followed

Pilgrims and worshipers visit and pay homage to the revered image of Buddha (Daibutsu) in Kamakura, Japan. The statue is fifty feet tall, made of bronze, and was crafted in 1252.
Courtesy of British Airways (BOAC), Toronto, Canada.

Indian, rather than Chinese, forms of Buddhism and eventually formulated the curious mixture of Bon, Indian Buddhism, and Tantrism (an esoteric practice and doctrine; see pp. 148–149) presently known as *Lamaism*. After initially receiving active encouragement from Tibetan rulers, Buddhism was subjected in the ninth century to persecution so severe and protracted that it took two centuries for it to become reestablished. By this time, two distinctive groups of Lamaists, the Dalai Lamas and the Panchen Lamas, along with numerous Buddhist sects based mainly on Indian teachings, had evolved.

By the fourteenth century, the Tibetans had translated all the Buddhist literature they could obtain and had produced their own canon. Separate orders of Buddhist monks also developed, and as the various monasteries acquired power, rivalries grew intense. The political struggle for dominance was ultimately resolved in the seventeenth century by the Mongol chieftain Guuhri Khan, who awarded Tibet to the Dalai Lama, who became both spiritual and temporal leader.

The history of Tibetan Buddhism is characterized by political intrigue motivated by a lust for power. Rivalry between Buddhist factions was exacerbated by the territorial claims of various military forces and, in this century, of various governments, including the Nationalist

Chinese, the British, and the Chinese Communists. The latter finally took over Tibet in 1959 and sent the Dalai Lama into exile.

Other Areas. Buddhism still survives in Nepal, where its founder was born. It also flourishes in Bhutan, Burma, Thailand, Laos, Vietnam, and Indonesia. The Indian heritage is clearly evident in most of these places.

Strength of Buddhism

The strength of Buddhism in Asian cultures is difficult to assess, because religion cannot be measured solely in terms of numbers of members or institutions. Buddhist virtues and ideals still play a dominant role in Asia, and new Buddhist movements serve to give lay people a deeper sense of commitment to religious activities and goals. In addition, several Buddhist groups have shown a new interest in Buddhist missions in Europe and the Americas. Some scholars have maintained, in fact, that the increasing interest in Buddhist teachings shown by Western societies represents more than academic curiosity—that it may represent a sincere acceptance of the teachings of Buddha and an application of spiritual energy. For many Western people, the Buddhist faith meets the challenge of present needs and contributes to peace on earth.[13]

Women in Buddhist History

The role of women in Buddhist history has been characterized by tension between their perceived roles as seductresses and domestic paragons. On the one hand, women have been associated with sensual indulgence of lust, carnal desire, and seduction. Buddhist monks have perceived women as bestial and evil purveyors of sexuality, and hence as a potential threat to their spiritual welfare. Pain, suffering, mental anguish, and ritual impurity, according to the monks, result from attachment to women. Consequently, women have been viewed as biologically and mentally weaker than men, more vulnerable to ignorance, somewhat defective, and spiritually handicapped. On the other hand, married women have been respected as paragons of motherhood through their procreative role and function.

This tension, or inconsistency, has remained the basic Buddhist attitude to this day. Even the idealized domestic function is seen as preventing women from active involvement in religious institutions in that it keeps them from pursuing the Buddhist goal of detachment.

And when women do decide to leave their homes and familial responsibilities to join monastic orders, they are accused of causing the disintegration of the family structure, which in turn is viewed as potentially disruptive to the stability of society.

Nonetheless, Buddhist nuns have lived and worked in their separate convents from the time of the death of Buddha. A large number of female disciples, particularly among the Theravada group, have pioneered much of what is now known in the West as social service; they are also noted for their learning, piety, and austere life-style. They either live in separate convents or share the same monastic settlement with male monks but live in their own quarters. Female monks shave their heads and wear precisely the same clothing as their male counterparts do. In each principal convent or monastery is an abbess, whose tutorial, leadership, and meditative abilities are considered to be unmatched, even though each differs in her techniques for achieving the common Buddhist goal.

Modern Trends

An ancient Buddhist prophecy foretold that after 2500 years, Buddhism would either fade away or enjoy a renaissance. Some Buddhist historians speculate that the critical period anticipated by the ancient prophecy began with the triumph of the Chinese Communist Party (CCP) in 1949, which was accompanied by draconian measures against Buddhists reminiscent of those of the early emperors.

The Communist government promptly deprived monasteries of their lands and revenues, forced monks and nuns to work in fields and factories, and shipped young men off as "volunteers" in the Korean War. Chinese Buddhist scholars were carefully screened for political "reliability." U Nu, prime minister of neighboring Burma, convinced that it was futile to challenge the Chinese government with arms alone, sponsored a meeting of the Sixth World Buddhist Council in Rangoon in 1954–1956—the first meeting of its kind in more than five hundred years. Thousands of monks and devout Buddhists from all over southeastern Asia gathered in an attempt to build a Buddhist ideological front. Many, however, knew that Communism had won the day, in China at least, and that no strategy was likely to modify the attitude of the Communist regime in China to Buddhism. The Communists themselves were quick to point out any apparent similarity between Buddhism and Marxism, such as a commitment in both ideologies to a classless society.

Buddhism has in the past survived greater and more sustained depradation than has been its lot in China since 1949, and it still maintains its prominence in Japan and in southeastern Asia. In fact, some observers have seen a Buddhist renaissance and a vindication of positive prophetic vision in the active growth of popular expressions of Mahayana Buddhism. These observers have pointed out that Buddhist religious life is still practiced in many temples and homes, and that Buddhism is highly compatible with modern science and psychological studies.

Whatever the future may hold, it is undeniable that in the twentieth century Buddhism has become a global religion. Buddhist groups and temples can be found not only in Asian countries, but also in most of the major cities of Africa, Europe, and the Americas. Asian Buddhists are sending missionaries to the West to win their allegiance, and Western converts are proclaiming Buddha's teachings through books, pamphlets, films, and meditation centers. The Indian Buddha is now honored by millions of adherents all over the world.

Buddhist Scriptures

Buddhism does not require orthodoxy of belief. Consequently, though Buddhist texts include canonical treatises, there is no closed canon of sacred writings. As Buddhism developed through the centuries, numerous important works attained the status of scripture. Today different groups and subgroups emphasize one or more of these works, according to how they understand and interpret Buddha's teaching. Of the hundreds of Buddhist texts in Pali, Sanskrit, Chinese, and Tibetan considered to be sacred, only a few of the most important can be mentioned here.[14]

The most basic and possibly the earliest body of sacred writings is the Tripitaka (the Three Baskets), so-called because it consists of three "baskets," or collections, of disciplines:

1. The Vinayana Pitaka, consisting of the rules of the Buddhist order
2. The Sutta Pitaka, containing dialogues between Buddha and his disciples on Buddhist teachings
3. The Abhidhamma Pitaka, consisting of metaphysical instruction

Besides the Tripitaka, texts written in Pali that are considered to be reliable sources of early Buddhism include the Dhammapada, the Intivuttaka, the Udana, the Sutta Nipata, the Theratherigatha, and a few others.

Sacred collections written in Sanskrit and used primarily by Mahayanists include the Mahavastu, the Lalita Vistara (in which Buddha's divinity is emphasized), the Prajnaparamitas, the Samadhiraja, the Lankavatara, the Saddharmapundarika, and the Amitayurdhyana.

Tibetan and Chinese sources retain their independent value and are too numerous to be listed here. There is, for instance, a collection of stories, known as the *Jataka* (Birth Tales), that relates popular beliefs about the 550 previous births of Buddha.

Buddhist Groups

From the time of the second council (see p. 132), Buddhism has been divided into two main branches: Theravada (also called Hinayana) and Mahayana. During the first centuries after the death of Buddha, the Buddhist community, according to the ancient records, consisted of eighteen different groups. In actual fact, the number of Buddhist sects was probably legion, but scholars tend to group them under one or the other of the two main branches. Only a few of the more important and popular groups are briefly examined here.

Theravada Buddhism

Theravada Buddhism has already been identified as the "orthodox" wing of the movement.[15] The central figure in Theravada Buddhism is the monk, whose ideal is to attain *nirvana*. Hence, monastic discipline and solitary meditation are the rule. With shaven head and yellow robe, a monk rises at daybreak, washes himself, lights a candle before the image of Buddha, and chants and meditates before leaving the monastery. Outside, his begging bowl in hand, he makes his silent rounds, stopping quietly at every door to receive whatever food is offered. He returns to the monastery to eat breakfast, after which he joins other monks at the assembly hall for prayers, instruction, and meditation. The main and last meal of the day follows between 11:00 and 11:30 A.M. in a communal dining room. The afternoon is devoted to scripture reading and meditation. Before retiring to bed, monks gather at one final assembly at sunset. By following this daily routine, they acquire merit toward their liberation.

All Buddhists revere Buddha as the great Master and living embodiment of the religious ideal they seek to realize. But when Theravada Buddhists speak of their Master, they refer to the "human" Buddha of flesh and blood — not the manifestation in human form of an eternal essence, the abstraction that represents the way in which Mahayana Buddhists think of their Master. In other words, Theravada Buddhists regard Buddha as the great enlightened man — but still, only a man. By practicing detachment, Buddha simply pioneered and fulfilled his quest for *nirvana*, and anyone may follow his lead. By accepting the "homeless" state, each individual can attain the same liberation through effort and self-discipline.

Naturally, not everyone can justify setting aside the obligations and responsibilities of everyday life in favor of the homeless state, but it is the Theravadin's only recourse. To attain *nirvana*, every individual must, sooner or later, renounce worldly pursuits and join the homeless state of a monk. The alternative is consignment to an eternal cycle of rebirth. Not surprisingly, Theravada Buddhism is referred to as *Hinayana*, or the Small Vehicle.

The scriptures of Theravada Buddhism consist of the three collections written in Pali that are known as the Tripitaka. In contrast, Mahayana Buddhism (see the following section) acknowledges numerous canonical texts in various local dialects. The Pali texts of Theravada Buddhism contain some early ideas that were later elaborated by the Mahayanists: for instance, that other Buddhas had preceded Gautama and that the latter was a divine being who, through countless rebirths, lived a perfect life.

Over the centuries various divisions developed within Theravada Buddhism on the basis of doctrinal matters, the acceptance or rejection of certain canonical texts, and disputes over disciplinary rules and the observance of ethical precepts. Basically, though, Theravada Buddhism was, and remains, restricted to monastic orders.

Mahayana Buddhism

Although the character and nature of Mahayana Buddhism vary a great deal from sect to sect, most, if not all, Mahayana Buddhists regard Buddha as an incarnation of an eternal Buddha essence that existed in all ages and in innumerable worlds for the liberation of all sentient beings. His manifestation on earth in human form, they believe, came about out of compassion for others. Buddha, they claim, willingly postponed his entrance into *nirvana* in order to help others attain it too.

Mahayana Buddhists, in contrast to Theravadins, believe that an individual may aspire to *nirvana* without accepting the homeless state of a monk. This liberal attitude contributed to the gradual development of many sects and many versions of Buddhist belief. For instance, the idea that the eternal Buddha essence was incarnate in Siddhartha prompted some Mahayana Buddhists to deify and worship Siddhartha. Similarly, the special significance of the *bodhisattva* (one who, out of compassion for the welfare of others, vows and delays his entry into *nirvana*) created a vast number of "saviors" who became objects of faith, worship, and devotion. In turn, images were introduced to help many Buddhists worship *bodhisattvas;* and vivid portrayals of heaven and hell, which appealed to the public at large because they gave substance to vague abstractions, were invented. Of the innumerable schools of thought and independent sects in

Mahayana Buddhism, only a few of the more important can be described here.

Madhyamika. This important philosophical school of Buddhism was founded by the Indian Nagarjuna in about the second or third century CE and later spread to China and Japan. Nagarjuna taught the necessity of taking the "middle position" between two opposites: being and nonbeing, existence and nonexistence, affirmation and negation, and so forth. With rigorous logic, he demonstrated the absurdity of philosophical positions that advocated or were postulated on extremes. To Nagarjuna, any opposites or contradictions were proof of error. In his words:

> Nothing comes into being, nor does anything disappear.
> Nothing is eternal, nor has anything an end.
> Nothing is identical, nor is anything differentiated.
> Nothing moves here, nor does anything move there.[16]

Such pairs of opposites, Nagarjuna argued, are empty of meaning, or at best relative; the truth lies somewhere in the middle or, more correctly, "above opposites." This middle position is beyond thought and words and devoid of name and character.

Madhyamika never gained wide appeal. Rather, it has provided the basis of logical or philosophical thought among groups of intellectuals whose numbers never justified the formation of an independent sect.

T'ien-t'ai/Tendai. T'ien-t'ai is associated with Chinese Buddhism; Tendai is its Japanese counterpart. Tradition states that Chih-i (538–597 CE) established a monastery on Mount T'ien-t'ai in China and became the founder of the school identified by the same name. His teachings were markedly syncretistic, incorporating various forms of Buddhism. Central to his doctrine was the "threefold truth":

1. Emptiness: All things being void, without substantial reality
2. Temporary Existence: All things having only a passing life
3. Middle State: All things being empty and temporary at the same time, thus constituting the mean or middle state

These three truths are mutually inclusive and exist in harmonious unity, with the middle state being equivalent to Absolute Reality.

This religious philosophy never became widely acceptable to the masses. A few Buddhists still adhere to its tenets, however.

Pure Land. The Pure Land sect is one of the most popular Buddhist groups in China and Japan. Its enchanting picture of a Pure and Happy Land that is presided over by *Amitabha* (the Buddha of Infinite Light), who responds to anyone meditating or calling upon his name

Buddhist monks playing horns during prayer near Thangboche, Nepal. Bill O'Connor/Peter Arnold, Inc.

in good faith, has been particularly appealing to ordinary working people. The main proponents of this view were Tao-cho (562–645 CE) and his disciple Shan-tao (613–681). These teachers promoted various devotional practices, including uttering the name of Amitabha with an undivided mind, to ensure rebirth in the "Western Paradise"; chanting *sutras* (scriptural texts); worshiping images; and meditating on and singing praises to the Buddha. They also painted vivid images of heaven and hell, the latter replete with horrors of torture and violence.

A Japanese convert introduced this sect to Japan in the twelfth century CE, where it is now known as the Jodo school. The emphasis of this school is on salvation by faith in *Amitabha* (O-mi-to in Chinese, and Amida in Japanese). Traditionally, O-mi-to was once a king who renounced his title, became a monk, and later took the vow of a *bodhisattva.* Out of his infinite compassion and by the power of his accumulated merit, he called into existence the domain called Sukhavati, the "Western Paradise," or, as it is generally known, "the Pure Land." According to the Pure Land sect, all who are ensnared by desire (*tanha*) or ignorance, but who sincerely invoke the name of O-mi-to, are reborn in the Western Paradise, where they can continue the process of liberation under happier and more encouraging conditions than they can in this existence. The Pure Land, then, is not the goal, but a stepping-stone to the goal; it is simply a place where one can receive, under favorable conditions, liberation from the cycle of bodily existence.

A devotee who merely repeats the sacred name of O-mi-to unceasingly is assured of reaching the Pure Land:

- Namu O-mi-to Fo (Chinese version)
- Namu Amida Butsu (Japanese version)
- Hail Amitabha Buddha (English version)

Ch'an/Zen. The most important Buddhist sect originating in China is the Ch'an group, whose Japanese parallel is called Zen.[17] *Ch'an* (or *Zen*) represents intuitive meditation accompanied by strict discipline, through which one's Buddha nature can be revealed.

According to tradition, this school was introduced by Bodhidharma (470–543), an Indian Buddhist who came to China by crossing the Yangtze River on a reed branch. Legend also has it that the Chinese emperor sent for Bodhidharma and, during their interview, asked him, "How much merit would I accumulate if I were to donate to the Buddhist Order and encourage the translation of the sacred books?"

"No merit at all!" was the blunt reply. "No merit is accumulated from good works; reading scriptures is useless and worthless; only inward meditation is the path to enlightenment." To demonstrate to the skeptical emperor what he meant, Bodhidharma is said to have gone to Mount Su and to have sat in meditation, facing a wall, for the next nine years.

Whatever its origin and historicity, this story illustrates the emphasis placed by Ch'an or Zen on inner enlightenment, to the exclusion of words, images, temples, or scriptures. Ch'an Buddhism has no set pattern and no institutions. Its adherents absolutely reject deification of Buddha. A frequently quoted expression of this sect is, "If you meet the Buddha, kill him." The quotation implies that the Buddha was a man, not a god, and that he never wished to be worshiped; it also implies that a meditative awareness is greater than Buddhahood.

An argument among adherents over how enlightenment can be gained split Ch'an into northern and southern subschools in the seventh century. The southern group championed the idea that intuitive wisdom and enlightenment came suddenly; the northern group insisted on gradual enlightenment. Eventually, the southern group prevailed.

Ch'an masters differ in their approaches to teaching. Some enjoin meditation and silence; others advocate instruction in a question-and-answer format; still others apply enigmatic sounds, gestures, or acts, which may include such extreme measures as scolding and beating.[18] Whatever their techniques, they all consider words a poor medium and logic self-defeating. Everyone, they believe, possesses a Buddha nature; one has simply to awaken it. The result is a sudden flash of insight encompassing enlightenment and the unity of all existence.

In order to achieve *satori* (enlightenment), one must practice *zazen* (sitting in meditation). To promote the experience of *satori*, the technique of the *koan* is employed. The *koan* is a riddle or problem that cannot be solved by the intellect. Zen masters propose *koans* to students in an effort to heighten and develop the students' intuitive faculty, thus forcing them to reach beyond reasoning and attain *satori*.

There are hundreds of different *koans*, each designed to probe beyond the grasp of reasoning. One of the favorite *koans* introduced to a new disciple is, "What was your original face before your parents begot you?" Others include "All things return to the one; what does the one return to?" and "If clapping two hands produces a sound, what is the sound of one hand clapping?"

Obviously, there is no logical answer to any of these *koans*. The purpose of the exercise is to realize one's own Buddha nature, to accept the limitations of human reasoning, and to probe beyond the barriers of rational thinking to insight. If a learner persists on reasoning by asking further questions, then the Zen Master may kick him, slap him, or even throw him down. This treatment is justified by the necessity of breaking the learner's hold on reason.

Tantrism

The precise origin and development of Tantrism are difficult to ascertain, since its doctrine is mysterious and/or esoteric and its practices are unorthodox. Yet this school of Buddhism has gained prominence in India, China, Tibet, and Japan. Tantrism is fundamentally nonspeculative: aspirants must experience numerous yoga stages before achieving enlightenment. *Nirvana* is seen as one side of a polarity. The other side is *karuna* (compassion) emanating from the *bodhisattvas*, whose help is solicited through appropriate rituals. These fall under the three *M* groups:

1. *Mudra:* Various symbolic gestures made by the hands and fingers
2. *Mantra:* Formulas of an esoteric nature based on scientific knowledge of the occult power of sound
3. *Mandala:* Visual aids, such as picture charts, diagrams, and magical circles, designed to help the devotee acquire a mystical union with the particular *bodhisattva*

Before they are allowed to share the more important secrets of the sect, devotees go through a preliminary training period. This consists of thousands of prostrations, breathing exercises, repetitions of mystical formulas in precise sound patterns, and preparations of symbolic sacrifices. Each *bodhisattva* is represented by certain symbols and formulas peculiar to himself or herself. By performing these rituals, the devotee is gradually able to identify and become one with a particular *bodhisattva*. Some of the mystical rites consist of elaborate rituals performed to the accompaniment of music. Secret formulas, symbols, and visualizations are all interpreted gradually to the disciples as their insight into the mystical nature of the *bodhisattva* grows deeper.

Enlightenment is achieved when one realizes experientially, not cognitively, that seeming opposites are in truth one and the same. In other words, Tantrism maintains that all things are in fact of one nature: *sunyata* (emptiness or void). Physical and mental processes are, therefore, equal means for enlightenment.

Experts in Tantrism teach that an individual's body is the entire cosmos, and in this age of degeneration (i.e., human existence), one must achieve enlightenment through one's own body. However, only a Master who has been thoroughly initiated into the mysteries of Tantrism can teach an aspirant how to use the body's processes correctly in order to achieve identification with the void, which is enlightenment.

After undertaking several yogic exercises that help to produce mental and physical experiences, the Master leads the initiate to further stages of spiritual growth. This process of advancement involves leading the initiate to identify with deities that represent various cosmic forces. The purpose of this procedure is to help the initiate discover that each identification is *sunyata,* or void; the outcome is to endow the initiate with a "diamondlike" body representing a condition beyond all duality.

Buddhist Observances

Relics

Since the death of Buddha, relics of his body, including his teeth, hair, and collar bone, have been preserved and enshrined in *stupas* or *pagodas* (domed or towerlike shrines), both in major cities and in the countryside throughout the Far East. Every temple has a *stupa,* some small and some enormous. When devotees enter the temple precincts, they first walk around the *stupa* three times and then worship it, either kneeling, prostrate, or standing. This observance is believed to bring

Two monks standing in front of the temple of the Sacred Tooth in Kandy, Sri Lanka (Ceylon). This temple houses a tooth of the Buddha, honored every August with a colorful festival.   Courtesy of Trans World Airlines, Toronto, Canada.

great merit. Laypersons as well as monks flock to these shrines to make offerings of food and flowers and to meditate on Buddha's teachings. Such acts also acquire merit that leads to rebirth in a better life. In fact, building a *stupa* or contributing to building one in itself brings great merit.

Image Worship

Image worship occupies a central place in the devotional life of Buddhists. In earlier ages there were no images of Buddha, who was represented by symbols: his footprint, the seat on which he sat, or the eight-spoked wheel. Later, Buddha was represented by images carved on rocks or made of stone or metal. Most Buddhist temples and private homes possess images of Buddha. Usually a corner in a home is set aside as a shrine for images, which are believed to be a source of "magical" protection or blessing. Images of Buddha show him in one of three postures: standing, seated, or reclining.

Buddhist worshipers offer flowers, incense, food, and drink. Offerings of light, such as candlelight or the light of oil lamps, are believed to bring rich stores of merit that last endlessly. Prayers accompany these offerings, since any sort of offering is considered meritorious.

Precepts

Every act of worship begins with the recital of the following homage formula: "Homage to Him, the Blessed One, the Exalted One, the fully Enlightened One." Next comes the recitation of the Three Refuges:

> I go to the Buddha as my Refuge:
> I go to the Dharma [Law, Doctrine] as my Refuge:
> I go to the Sangha [Brotherhood of Monks] as my Refuge.[19]

Immediately after this recitation the following resolutions—or Five Precepts, as they are commonly known—are renewed:

1. I undertake to abstain from destroying life.
2. I undertake to abstain from taking things not given.
3. I undertake to abstain from sexual misconduct.
4. I undertake to abstain from false speech.
5. I undertake to abstain from intoxicants.

Monks, who renounce the world, repeat an additional Five Precepts:

1. I undertake to abstain from eating at forbidden times.
2. I undertake to abstain from dancing, singing, and shows.
3. I undertake to abstain from adorning or beautifying myself by the use of garlands, scents, unguents, ornaments, and finery.
4. I undertake to abstain from using a high or large couch or bed.
5. I undertake to abstain from accepting gold or silver.

Pilgrimages

Pilgrimages to sacred sites (holy places) are considered to be meritorious deeds, and the more pilgrimages an individual completes, the greater the merit. The birthplace of Buddha, the site of his enlightenment, the park where he preached his first discourse, and the place where he died are the four most sacred destinations of any Buddhist pilgrimage. Millions of pilgrims through the ages—monks, nuns, and laypeople from all over the Far East—have made, and continue to make, the long journey to these four remote places, often on foot, frequently braving many dangers, and seldom undergoing this experience without hardship.

Devotional Rites

Many Buddhists have in their homes pictures and images of the Buddha in front of which candles and incense are burnt, and other spirits may be venerated as well. Other Buddhists have a household *butsudan* (Buddha shelf, or altar). This is often an elaborate shrine in which the central figure of Buddha is surrounded by decorations, utensils, flowers, and oil lamps.

Several times daily a devout Buddhist recites the Three Refuges invocation. Rosaries are widely used—small ones by the laity, larger ones by the monks. The larger ones have 108 beads, with one large bead in the middle representing Buddha. Generally, the rosary is carried on the left wrist in daily life and encircles the two hands when clasped together for prayer. Worshipers perform individual or congregational acts of devotion.

In modern times, and especially in Western societies, worshipers gather every Sunday for congregational meetings (since it is the most convenient day), and *dharma* schools are provided for children, after the Western model (Sunday schools). Other groups prefer to hold regular sessions one or more evenings during the week.

Memorials and Festivals

Many festivals and ceremonies observed in Buddhism commemorate historical and religious events in the life of Buddha, as well as in the lives of numerous *bodhisattvas* and founders of various groups. In addition, there are seasonal festivals and regional festivals that are celebrated differently by Japanese and Chinese Buddhists.

The major festivals may be divided into two types: (1) festivals observed by all Buddhists, whether Theravada or Mahayana, although the dates may differ according to each tradition; and (2) festivals observed by either Japanese Buddhists or Chinese Buddhists only. But here, too, there are two types: those observed by all sects and those observed only by some groups.

Three important festivals are observed by all Buddhists the world over: Hanamatsuri/Vesak, Bodhi Day, and Nirvana Day. Two festivals observed by all Japanese Buddhist sects are Ohigan and Obon. A brief description of these five and a few other ceremonies observed by different groups follows.

Hanamatsuri (Flower Festival) is observed on April 8 by Mahayana Buddhists to celebrate the birthday of the Buddha. According to Mahayana tradition, he was born on this day in 563 BCE in Lumbini Gardens (present-day Nepal) in the midst of flower blossoms. On this occasion a flower shrine is set up in front of the main shrine in the worship hall of Buddhist temples; enshrined in the flowers is a statuette of the infant Buddha. According to Theravada tradition, however, Buddha was born on Vesak (Wesak), or Full Moon Day (corresponding to April–May), in 623 BCE. Theravada Buddhists celebrate this day not simply as the birthday of Buddha, but in memory of the triple events in his life: his birth, his enlightenment, and his entry into *nirvana*.

Mahayana Buddhists celebrate the historic event of Buddha's enlightenment on Bodhi Day, December 8. To them, this event took place as the first faint light of day began to glow in the eastern sky while Buddha was sitting in meditation under a tree. As for Nirvana Day, Mahayana Buddhists commemorate Buddha's death and entry into *nirvana* on February 15. Some Buddhists also reserve this day for a memorial service for the deceased members of the family.

Ohigan or Higan (other shore) is observed by all Japanese Buddhists twice a year: during the spring and autumn equinoxes. The celebrations generally last for a week, during which faithful Buddhists gather in their temples to express to Buddha their thankfulness for his great compassion and to offer flowers and various foods of the season to Buddha. More important, on those occasions Buddhists recall and devote themselves to the fulfillment of the Six Perfections—charity, morality, endurance, endeavor, meditation, and wisdom—which are considered to be the gates through which one enters and crosses to the "other shore," or the Pure Land of the Amitabha Buddha.

The Obon or Bon festival is essentially an ancestral memorial rite held either on July 15 (according to the solar calendar) or August 15 (according to the lunar calendar). A festive mood pervades the entire gathering, even though there is a solemn sense of loss of loved ones. Buddhists celebrate this traditional festival by lighting candles or lanterns to guide the spirits of the departed ancestors on their annual visit to the family home. Delicacies are also offered to the spirits, and the festival ends with a circular folk dance.

The festival of Dharma-chakka is celebrated by Theravada Buddhists on the day of the full moon in July to commemorate the first proclamation of the *dharma* by Buddha to the five ascetics in the Deer Park in Varanasi (Benares). The festival of Dharma-vijaya or Poson is also celebrated by Theravada Buddhists at the full moon in June. It commemorates the beginning of the preaching of the *dharma* to foreign countries, especially to Sri Lanka (Ceylon), under the reign of Emperor Asoka of India.

Besides these special days, each Buddhist group or sect observes its particular festival or ceremony. In many cases, traditional customs have been intermingled with Buddhist celebrations. Nevertheless, all these festivals bring a special religious fervor into the life of Buddhists everywhere.

Notes

1. Handy dictionaries that may be useful in clarifying the terminology of Buddhism include T. Ling, *A Dictionary of Buddhism* (New York: Scribner's, 1970); C. Humphreys, *Popular Dictionary of Buddhism* (New

York: Citadel, 1963); and M. Nyanaponika, *Buddhist Dictionary*, rev. ed. (Colombo, Sri Lanka: Frewin, 1956).

2. The classical Pali collection has been translated by E. W. Cowell et al., 6 vols., Pali Text Society (London: Luzac, 1969).

3. The dates given for Buddha's life vary from one Buddhist group to another. According to the Theravada group of Burma and Ceylon, the correct dates are 623–543 BCE; and for the same group in Cambodia, Laos, and Thailand, 624–544 BCE. The Mahayana group and most modern scholars prefer the dates c. 566–486 BCE or 563–483 BCE. Note that all these dates give a life span of eighty years. For the problem of Buddha's birth date, see E. Frauwallner, "The Historical Date We Possess on the Person and Doctrine of the Buddha," *East and West* 7, 4 (January 1957): 9–12.

4. The episode of Asita is related in Ashvaghosha's *Buddhacarita*, I.49, 60–61, 68–77, and at great length in *Lalita Vistara* (one of the most important texts of Mahayana Buddhism). Asita's prediction has been compared with the episode of Simeon and the baby Jesus in Luke 2:8–20, 25–35.

5. On the concept and symbolism of universal sovereign Buddhahood, see A. J. Prince, "The Concepts of Buddhahood in Earlier and Later Buddhism," *Journal of the Oriental Society of Australia*, 7 (1970): 87–118.

6. For an interesting study related to the changing conceptions of Buddha's status and power, see A. Bareau, "The Superhuman Personality of the Buddha," in J. M. Kitagawa and C. Long, eds., *Myths and Symbols: Studies in Honor of Mircea Eliade* (Chicago: University of Chicago Press, 1969).

7. It is revealing to compare Buddha's temptation to that of Jesus (Luke 4:1–13). For an analysis, see J. W. Boyd, *Satan and Mara: Christian and Buddhist Symbols of Evil* (Leiden, Netherlands: Brill, 1975).

8. The "Setting in Motion the Wheel of Truth" speech is regarded as one of the four great events in Buddha's life—the other three being birth, enlightenment, and entering *nirvana* (or *paranirvana*).

9. One of the four holy sites of Buddhism, Kasia is situated in the east of the Gorakhpur district, in Uttar Pradesh, south of the Nepal border.

10. For Western interpretations of *nirvana* see G. R. Welbon, *The Buddhist Nirvana and Its Western Interpreters* (Chicago: University of Chicago Press, 1968); and T. Stcherbatsky, *The Buddhist Conception of Nirvana* (Leningrad: Academy of Science of U.S.S.R. 1927).

11. Cited in E. A. Burtt, ed., *The Teachings of the Compassionate Buddha* (New York: Mentor, 1955), pp. 113ff.

12. The number of councils accepted as authentic in Buddhist tradition varies from country to country. For instance, Ceylon and Burma acknowledge six councils, whereas Thailand acknowledges ten. All, however, agree on the first three councils: the first held c. 483 BCE, at Rajagriha (Rājagaha); the second about a hundred years later, at Vaisali (Vesāli); and the third held c. 250 BCE at Pātaliputra (Patna). Some

modern scholars have maintained that the historicity of the first council is purely legendary; others have insisted that an assembly did take place shortly after Buddha's death. See C. Prebisch, "Review of Scholarship on the Buddhist Councils," *Journal of Asian Studies* 33, 2 (February 1974): 239–54.

13. Christian-Buddhist comparative and dialogic studies are quite extensive. For a summary listing, see C. J. Adams, ed., *A Reader's Guide to the Great Religions,* 2nd ed. (New York: Free Press, 1977), pp. 219–21.

14. Buddhism, like Christianity, is divided into numerous sects; but, unlike Christianity, each Buddhist sect possesses its own set of scriptures. The bulk of these sacred books is truly enormous, amounting to hundreds of volumes. For instance, one sect adheres to the Pali canon of 45 volumes, exclusive of commentaries, whereas the Tibetans include no fewer than 325 volumes. Only a small portion of this vast collection has been translated into English.

15. For works dealing with the Theravada tradition, see Adams, *A Reader's Guide,* pp. 179–83.

16. From "Examination of Causality," cited in Burtt, *Teachings of the Compassionate Buddha,* pp. 170–172.

17. The bibliographical resources on Ch'an/Zen are legion. For a selective list, see Adams, *A Reader's Guide,* pp. 202–03.

18. For unusual forms of Buddhist practices, see C. Luk, *The Secrets of Chinese Meditation* (London: Rider, 1964); and J. Yun-Hua, "Buddhist Self-Immolation in Medieval China," *History of Religions Journal* 4, 2 (1965): 243–68.

19. Reference to the devotional practice of taking refuge in these "three gems" *(tri-ratna)* is found in the Pali canon, in Samyutta Nikaya. See the English translation by C. A. F. Rhys Davids, *The Book of Kindred Sayings,* vol. I, (London: Luzac & Co., 1950), p. 283.

7

Jainism and Sikhism

Jainism

Historical Background

Jainism[1] originated in India in the sixth century BCE, during a period of reaction against the prevailing Hindu priestly class, which was seeking to extend its dominant power through prescribed rituals, sacrifices, and yoga exercises, as well as in other ways. Dissatisfied with this trend, several thinkers sought a more coherent and intellectual system of religion than that which was flourishing at the time. Some attempted to undermine the control of priestly power, others developed philosophical ideas, and still others sought to explore the nature of Ultimate Reality. One of the foremost of these dissident thinkers was Mahavira.

Mahavira

Mahavira, meaning Great Hero, is the accepted title of Nataputta Vardhamana, the founder of Jainism. According to Jain tradition, however, twenty-three *Tirthankaras* (makers of a *tirtha*, or ford—a crossing place) had preceded Mahavira in the present degenerating cosmic age. In the next cosmic age, which will represent an ascending order of happiness, another twenty-four *Tirthankaras* will appear. Modern scholarship credits only the last two *Tirthankaras*, Parshva and Mahavira, as historical figures.[2] The alleged dates and life spans of other *Tirthankaras* are too impractical (and incredible) to make their earthly existence plausible. Jains, however, worship all twenty-four *Tirthankaras*.

Tradition states that Mahavira was born in Vaisali (modern Bihar) in 599 BCE and died at the age of seventy-two, in 527 BCE. Scholars have debated the traditional date of his birth, suggesting a date of some sixty years later. However, the question is academic in the context of Jain tradition, which does not identify the beginning of Mahavira's life with his physical birth. Rather, Jains recognize several incarnations as god, king, and priest that antedate Mahavira's birth.

The uncertain state of the records, written by one of the Jain sects some nine hundred years after Mahavira's death, make the task of authenticating historical facts almost impossible. In spite of this difficulty, scholars have been able to reconstruct the following story.

Mahavira was the second son of a wealthy Indian ruler, or *rajah*. As members of the *kshatriya* caste, his parents most probably adhered to the established religious patterns of the Hinduism of the time, although some scholars think that they may have belonged to Parshva's group. Mahavira married and had a daughter, but he found his status and wealth a burden to endure rather than a privilege to enjoy. Conforming to tradition, however, he waited until his parents died before renouncing his family and status. At the age of thirty, he joined a band of wandering ascetics who followed the rule of Parshva.

Before long, Mahavira grew disillusioned with his companions, who did not practice extreme asceticism. In Mahavira's opinion, one had to apply two principles in order to liberate oneself from the cycles of birth or existence: extreme asceticism and *ahimsa*, or noninjury, of all living things. Consequently, he tore at his hair and beard, stripped off his loincloth, and walked nude through the villages and plains of central India during the hottest and coldest seasons. On rainy days he stayed off the roads to avoid stepping inadvertently on insects, and in dry weather he swept the road before him for the same reason. He always first strained his drinking water through a cloth in order to reduce the risk of extinguishing the life of any creature.

Tradition states that for some years Mahavira wandered about with Goshala Makkhali, another naked mendicant who was the head of an ascetic sect, the Ajivakas. Whatever the association of these two men may have been, Mahavira and Goshala apparently disagreed on the issue of *karma*, and Mahavira went off on his own. He refrained from speaking to or greeting anyone, lest he form agreeable attachments that might bind him to the world and its pleasures. As an ascetic he felt he should give up all worldly attachments, including clothes. Thus, he conquered his senses, including the sense of shame.

After twelve years of wandering from place to place and applying his principles of severe asceticism and *ahimsa*, Mahavira claimed to have attained *moksha* (release from the bonds of rebirth) and turned his attention to a search for people who might be capable of learning from him. He considered himself a *jina* (conqueror) who had achieved *kevala* (pure omniscient consciousness).

For thirty years he went about preaching and teaching his form of severe asceticism. His followers were deeply impressed by his perceptive, ethical teachings and believed that he was omniscient and an incarnation of the divine. Accounts of Mahavira's death vary greatly; one states that he died practicing self-starvation, whereas another records his peaceful death after a lecture.

Mahavira and Hindu Tradition

Mahavira challenged the traditional societal caste system of Hindu faith. As disciples and followers converted into the Jain religion, they dropped their caste distinctions. Much later, however, the pervasive and established dominance of Hindu tradition influenced Jains to resume some caste distinctions.

Mahavira also spoke out against the deities of Hinduism. In his view, it was useless to pray to or to seek the aid of any deity. He stated that an individual needed no friend or being beyond himself or herself, either on earth or anywhere else. In fact, Mahavira may be said to have been an *atheist*, for he rejected any justification for a supreme being or a creator of the universe. He insisted, further, that no special authority was vested in priestly castes; that the Hindu scriptures, the Vedas, were not sacred; and that no one should place any trust in external aids to liberation, the only path to which lay through one's self. Ironically, in spite of such teachings, his followers later considered him to be a divine incarnation.

Mahavira also modified the Hindu doctrine of *karma*. Contrary to Hindu thought of the time, Mahavira insisted that both matter and mind (or soul) are separate and eternal existences. This dualistic ultimate reality he identified as *jiva* (soul, or living things) and *ajiva* (matter, or lifeless things). The purpose of life, according to Mahavira, is to liberate the *jiva* from *ajiva*, the soul from matter. He taught that gods, prayers, worship, and rituals are profitless. Since *karma* encrusts the soul with matter, one must simply act as little as possible. The mere accumulation of *karma*, far from being a medium of liberation, is an obstacle to release from successive rebirth. The most rewarding alternative, then, is severe asceticism.

The Five Great Vows

Mahavira's asceticism is summed up in what came to be called the Five Great Vows. Some modern critics have speculated that these vows were derived from Mahavira's association with the religious movement of Parshva. Others have insisted that they represent Mahavira's independent thinking. Whatever the case, the Five Great Vows distinguish Jains from non-Jains. They concern, in order, *ahimsa*, truth, stealing, sex, and attachment. They may be stated as follows:

1. The First Vow: To renounce killing and to deny the right of others to kill

2. The Second Vow: To renounce all vices associated with lies arising from greed, fear, laughter, or anger, and to repudiate indifference to the lies of others

3. The Third Vow: To renounce all forms of stealing, whether the object is great or small, animate or inanimate, and to refuse to accept anything that is not freely given

4. The Fourth Vow: To renounce all sexual pleasures in favor of chastity and not to consent to sensuality in others (Mahavira renounced not only sexual pleasures, but also women in general. He is said to have declared that "women are the greatest temptation in the world.")

5. The Fifth Vow: To renounce all forms of attachment that cause pleasure or pain, love or hate, and to forbid consent to others to do so (It was precisely because of the Fifth Vow that Mahavira renounced his family and possessions and refused to stay in any place more than five days.)

These five vows constituted the ground rules for the ascetic followers of Mahavira. In time, a less severe moral system of twelve vows was developed for disciples unable to match the rigors of the original five.

Jain Groups

Jainism, with its emphasis on asceticism, may have been popular at one time in India, but today less than 2 million people follow its tenets. Various schisms gradually led to two principal sects: the Svetambaras, the "white-clad" group, who allowed the wearing of at least one garment and admitted women; and the Digambaras, the "sky-clad" group, who insisted on total nudity and the exclusion of women from temples and monasteries, on the assumption that women could not attain liberation until they were reborn as men. The Svetambaras are dominant in Kathiawar, Gujarat, and Rajasthan (in northwestern In-

Interior view of one of the many Jain marble temples on top of Mount Abu, Rajasthan, India. The statue of a Tirthankara sits in meditative repose surrounded by exquisite figurative carvings in marble. Built in the eleventh century CE, *these Jain temples at Mount Abu command a magnificent view of the surrounding countryside in Rajasthan.*   Courtesy of Government of India Tourist Office, Toronto.

dia, near the Pakistan border), whereas the Digambaras prevail in southern India in Hyderabad and Mysore. These two groups are further divided into subsects.

Proscriptions against clothing and veneration of the *Tirthankaras* became the two critical issues dividing the followers of Mahavira. The eminence of Mahavira was gradually reduced by the veneration accorded the twenty-three *Tirthankaras* who were thought to have preceded him. Shrines and temples were erected to honor, for instance, Rishabha, the first of the *Tirthankaras;* Nemi, the twenty-second *Tirthankara;* and Parshva, the twenty-third *Tirthankara.*

Jain Scriptures

Jain canonical scriptures do not belong to a single period, nor are the texts free from later revisions and additions.[3] Tradition states that a sacred piece of literature, the Purvas, was preserved orally for three hundred years from Mahavira's time until the death of Bhadrabahu (c. 300 BCE), the last person to have memorized it. A council was called after the death of this venerable person to reconstruct and systematize a sacred canon. However, the Svetambaras and the Digambaras could not agree on the compilation of sources. The Digambaras declared that the Purvas were hopelessly lost and began to compose new texts. Later, two more councils were called, one in the third century CE and the other in the fifth century, to commit the current oral texts to writing. By this time, some texts had been lost, some had been corrupted, and some new material had been added. Despite these difficulties, the Jain scriptures were finally formulated and, according to scholars, seem to contain some of Mahavira's basic teachings.

The Svetambara canon consists of forty-five Agamas, or texts, that deal with matters such as *cosmogony* (or account of the origin of the universe), astronomy, geography, divisions of time, doctrines, views on Hindu and Buddhist heresies, rules on ascetic life, and death by voluntary starvation. The Digambara canon consists of two major works that address the doctrines of *karma* and passions, such as attachment and aversion, that defile and bind the *jiva.* Digambaras and Svetambaras also value other works that deal with logic, epistemology, ethics, and so on.

Jain Teachings

Jainism is fundamentally an ethical religion, and its chief concern is the moral life of an individual. To be sure, Jainism has developed a set of beliefs; yet strictly speaking, these beliefs relate not to theology, but to a philosophy of life.

Time and the Universe. Time, for the Jains, is eternal and formless. The universe is infinite, beginningless, and endless. There is no god, no creator, no ultimate being. The universe operates in accordance with its own inherent principles. It was never created. Its constituent elements are soul, matter, time, space, and the principles of motion and rest. These elements change constantly, but they are indestructible and eternal. Time is conceived of as a wheel with twelve spokes, called ages, which are divided into two cycles. Six ages make an ascending cycle, during which humans progress in age, stature, knowledge, and happiness. The other six ages make a descending cycle, during which there is a gradual deterioration in the state of everything. Joined together, the two cycles make one rotation of the wheel of time.

Jiva *and* Ajiva. Jains conceive of ultimate reality as being dualistic. As we noted above, the two separate eternal entities of *jiva* and *ajiva* constitute reality.

Jiva is the life principle. Its essential characteristic is consciousness, or mental function. In its pure state, it possesses the qualities of limitless knowledge, endless perception, infinite power, and eternal bliss. It is formless and cannot be perceived by the senses. By expansion or contraction, it can occupy various proportions of space.

Ajiva is the lifeless principle, or matter. Its essential characteristic is lack of consciousness. In its pure state, it possesses the characteristics of touch, taste, smell, and color. It clusters into any shape or form, such as earth, water, wind, and sentient beings.

Jiva is divisible into five groups, depending on the number of sense organs possessed. The highest group has the five senses of touch, smell, taste, hearing, and sight; included in this group are animals, humans, deities, and demons. Next comes the group that possesses four senses, such as bees, flies, and the larger insects. The three-sense group includes the smaller insects, such as moths, and the two-sense group includes leeches, worms, and shellfish. The final, single-sense group includes vegetables, trees, seeds, and the animated four elements of earth, water, air, and fire.

Karma *and Liberation.* Jains conceive of *karma* rather materialistically, as formation of subtle matter around the soul. Because every event has a definite cause behind it, all phenomena are linked in a universal chain of cause and effect. The influx of *karma* adheres to the soul like a sticky substance and affects the course of rebirth. At the end of each substance, the soul carries with it the *karma*-matter that vitiates its purity, causing its rebirth in a form appropriate to its moral condition. If the soul has only a little *karma*-matter, it will be light enough to rise on the scale of transcendental embodiments. If, however, the soul carries a heavy *karma*-matter, it will sink into the lower levels of existence.

To release oneself from this *karma*-matter, one must be embodied in a human form and live the life of an ascetic monk (or of an ascetic nun, in some groups). All the ascetic practices designed for the monk are to be followed in order to arrest further accretion of *karma*-matter. Of the three main steps leading to the path of liberation, the first is faith in the twenty-four *Tirthankaras*. Next, one must obtain right knowledge by studying the teachings of these omniscient masters. And finally, this essential knowledge must be realized by practicing right conduct, which involves the control of thoughts, words, actions, emotions, and senses in light of the Five Great Vows.

Observance of these three principles—faith, knowledge, and right practices—prevents the formation of further *karma*. But how can one rid oneself of the *karma* already accumulated? The remedy is to practice severe asceticism, such as prolonged endurance of thirst, hunger, pain, heat, and cold. Confession, penance, the study of scriptures, and meditations are also important, but a prolonged period of severe austerity will annihilate more *karma*-matter than will meditation and scripture reading combined. When all *karma*-matter is completely annihilated, the soul attains liberation.

Since the attainment of liberation is very difficult, Jains believe that many souls will never succeed in liberating themselves but will migrate from one form to another all through eternal time. The few who attain liberation—freedom from *karma*-matter—also shed their physical bodies, and their souls ascend in a straight line to the top of the universe, where all the released souls, called *siddhas*, dwell. In this pristine, blissful state, the *siddhas* have no individuality and are invisible and intangible. Moreover, all *siddhas* are identical and possess a spiritual quality of omniscience, an absolute blissful state. Because of their spiritual feat in the conquest of *karma*, these *siddhas* are called *jinas*, or conquerors. Thus Jainism, the religion of conquerors, or victors, involves a heroic feat of self-liberation.

Jain Practices and Institutions

Mahavira's ascetic rigor for monks was too severe a doctrine for any except the most disciplined followers. Consequently, a modified rule of life, consisting of twelve vows, was prescribed for ordinary people:

1. Maintain *ahimsa* at all times. Never take the life of a sentient creature.
2. Never lie.
3. Never steal nor take what is not given.

4. Never be unchaste.

5. Check greed by limiting wealth and giving away any excess.

6. Avoid temptation by refraining from excessive travel.

7. Lead a simple life by limiting material needs.

8. Guard against evils that can be avoided.

9. Meditate at stated periods.

10. Observe special periods of self-denial.

11. Spend time occasionally as a monk, to devote all your energies to a higher order of human behavior.

12. Give alms generously, especially to monks and ascetics.

Of these twelve vows, the first has had the most important social and economic effects in India. Jain adherents have avoided all occupations—such as farming, fishing, butchering, brewing, and the sale or manufacture of arms, instruments, and intoxicants—that threaten life. Instead, they have turned to business and professional careers, such as banking, merchandising, landowning, the law, and teaching. Along with the status of Jains as professionals, their observance of the rest of the vows, which place moral restraints on their behavior, has earned them a level of social respect that has contributed to their survival in India.

Some time during the Middle Ages, several castes emerged within the Jain laity, although not among the monks. Social differentiations in Jainism are not as marked as those in Hinduism, although certain features (mainly occupational) are common to both.

The contributions of Jains to public welfare and culture in India have been extraordinary. They have founded such welfare institutions as public dispensaries, public lodging, and boarding institutions for the poor and helpless. Their cultural contributions have also been numerous—not only in religion and philosophy, but in other fields as well.

Jains observe the Hindu domestic rites of birth, marriage, and death. Hindu rites of worship such as prayers and offerings to the gods *(puja)* have also been adopted, together with Hindu gods and goddesses, although the latter occupy a position greatly subordinate to the *Tirthankaras*. Despite the fact that the *Tirthankaras* in their released state have no concern for human beings, prayers are offered to them daily by devout Jains. In the temple the central image is a *Tirthankara*. The favorites are the first Rishabha and last three *Tirthankaras*: Arishtanemi, Parshva, and Mahavira. There are also a few temples to the other *Tirthankaras*. The Digambaras' images are naked, but the Svetambaras' images are clothed and wear ornaments and crowns. Every twelve years, they stage a great celebration to bathe the image with *ghee*, or melted butter.

Their reputation for honesty and morality have made the Jains excellent businessmen. Ironically, however, as one commentator notes, "a group that began with asceticism and poverty has become, by virtue of its respect for life, one of the wealthiest classes of India."[4]

Sikhism

Historical Background

Sikhism, the religion of the Sikh community, originated in the Punjab region of India around the sixteenth century. Some scholars view Sikhism primarily as a reform movement of Hinduism; others see it as an outstanding example of religious syncretism—a blend of Hinduism and Islam.[5] The Sikhs, however, reject such interpretations of their religion as misrepresentations. To its followers, Sikhism is not simply the reworking of two older religions, but a new, divine revelation and, consequently, a genuinely independent religion.

In the seventeenth century, the Sikhs became involved in politics, with the result that they earned the displeasure of the ruling Mughal dynasty. During the reign of Emperor Aurangzeb (1658–1707) many of the Sikhs, including one of their *gurus*, were executed. They reacted with armed resistance, which fostered military characteristics that they retain to this day.

The fact that the Sikhs are an adventurous and enterprising people perhaps accounts for the numerous Sikh communities found outside India. Wherever they have gone, they have installed their Holy Book, the Guru Granth Sahib, in their homes and in their temples *(gurdwara)*. The Sikhs are mainly distinguishable by their beards, long hair, turbans, and steel bracelets, but some, especially those who live in large

Jainism and Sikhism

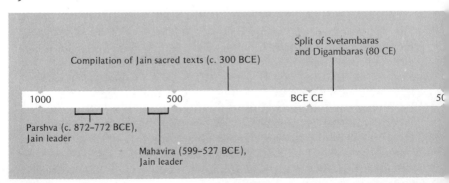

Compilation of Jain sacred texts (c. 300 BCE)

Split of Svetambaras and Digambaras (80 CE)

1000   500   BCE CE   5(

Parshva (c. 872–772 BCE), Jain leader

Mahavira (599–527 BCE), Jain leader

Western cities, have shaved off their beards, cut their hair, and discarded the turban. Whether or not they retain these external symbols of their faith, Sikhs show their devotion to God in daily prayer and similar religious observances. Equality and democracy are the two outstanding characteristics of Sikhism, and its code emphasizes truth, good behavior, and moral courage.

While Sikhs are mainly concentrated in the province of the Punjab (presently divided between Pakistan and India), a considerable number have emigrated, especially since India's independence and partition in 1947, to Great Britain, Europe, and the Americas.[6]

Guru Nanak

The founding of Sikhism is attributed to Guru Nanak (1469–1539), who was born of Hindu parents in the village of Talwandi, some sixty kilometers (forty miles) from Lahore, India. The earliest source materials on Nanak were written fifty to eighty years after his death. Most scholars, however, have rejected these sources, relying instead on the accounts of historians of the eighteenth and nineteenth centuries and on the records of Mughal court historians.

Nanak's father was the village clerk and his mother was a pious woman who was devoted to the family. Nanak was a reflective boy, and at an early age studied both the Islamic Qur'an and the Hindu Shastras (scriptures). He was also greatly influenced by Kabir (1440–1518), a Muslim poet who taught the oneness of God, the union of humankind with God, the consubstantiality between Hinduism and Islam, and the irrelevance of formal creeds and dogmas.

Tradition asserts that Nanak's marriage, which took place while he was still in his teens, was unhappy. Even though two sons resulted from this marriage, Nanak left his home and, in traditional fashion, wandered around India in search of truth and wisdom. He is also

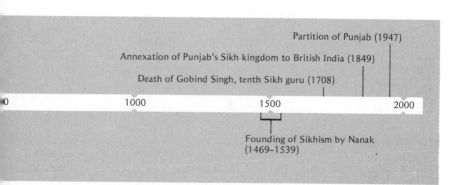

Partition of Punjab (1947)

Annexation of Punjab's Sikh kingdom to British India (1849)

Death of Gobind Singh, tenth Sikh guru (1708)

| 0 | 1000 | 1500 | 2000 |

Founding of Sikhism by Nanak
(1469–1539)

believed to have made a pilgrimage to Mecca, even though he was a Hindu.

The revelation that transformed Nanak from an obscure wanderer to a *guru* came to him as he was meditating in a forest in Sultanpur, India, when he was about thirty years old. The message of the vision was that God had singled him out to proclaim the True Name. Shortly after this, Nanak announced his message: "There is no Muslim and there is no Hindu."

Nanak and his constant companion, the Muslim minstrel Mardana, traveled widely in India over the next few decades, preaching the essential unity of Hinduism and Islam. To illustrate his absolute conviction in this unity, he dressed in a mixture of Hindu and Muslim styles. His greatest success was in the Punjab area, where groups of Hindus and Muslims began to follow him.

The story of his death perhaps best illustrates his success in attracting followers from both groups. The story goes that in his final hours his disciples began arguing about what to do with his body—whether to burn it according to Hindu custom or to bury it as Muslims do. Nanak, who had overheard them, settled the dispute by telling both groups to lay flowers at his side, adding that the group whose flowers remained fresh the following morning could have his body. Then Nanak covered himself with a sheet and died. When the sheet was lifted next morning, the disciples found, to their amazement, that there was no way of distinguishing one group of flowers from the rest. They were all fresh.

Succession of Gurus

Nanak was succeeded by nine other *gurus* during the next 150 years, as follows:

Name	Birth–Death	Leadership
Guru Angad	1504–1552	1539–1552
Guru Amar Das	1479–1574	1552–1574
Guru Ram Das Sodhi	1534–1581	1574–1581
Guru Arjun Dev	1563–1606	1581–1606
Guru Har Gobind	1595–1644	1606–1644
Guru Har Rai	1630–1661	1644–1661
Guru Har Kishan	1656–1664	1661–1664
Guru Tegh Bahadur	1621–1675	1664–1675
Guru Gobind Singh	1666–1708	1675–1708

These nine *gurus*, in turn, shaped the religion of Sikhism by consolidating, institutionalizing, and contributing significantly to its social, political, and religious life. A few of these leaders merit special mention.

Gurdwara *Hari-Mandir Sahib in Amritsar, the state of Punjab in India. The most famous* gurdwara *among Sikhs, it is often called the Golden Temple because its dome is covered with gold leaf. The temple, built above the huge watertank, was completed in the sixteenth century* CE *by Guru Arjun Dev, the fifth Guru.* Courtesy of Government of India Tourist Office, Toronto.

Guru Angad, whom Nanak appointed as his successor, distinguished himself particularly by devising a Punjabi script—the script in which Sikh scriptures are written. Significant changes also occurred under the administration of the fifth *guru,* Arjun Dev, who completed his father's project of building the Golden Temple at Amritsar, which today is the holy city of the Sikhs, and pioneered the practice of making pilgrimages there. His greatest contribution, however, was the compilation of the Granth Sahib (Holy Book)—the Sikh scripture.

When Guru Arjun was killed by the Mughal emperor Jahāngir in 1606, he was succeeded by his son, Har Gobind, who was responsible for the development among Sikhs of a more militant and aggressive attitude toward their enemies. Under Guru Gobind, Sikhs were forced for the first time to resort to the sword and to assume a national character—factors that contributed considerably to their persecution at the hands of Mughal rulers.

Khalsa

One of the worst persecutions came during the leadership of Tegh Bahadur, the ninth *guru*. The Mughal emperor Aurangzeb, who was then on the throne, was a religious fanatic who was determined to convert all his subjects to Islam, by force if necessary. Guru Tegh Bahadur was beheaded because he advocated freedom of religious worship.

The "sword of leadership" was conferred on Gobind Singh, the tenth and last *guru,* who, after Nanak himself, is considered by Sikhs to have been their most outstanding leader. In his thirty-three years of leadership, he concentrated on strengthening the political, social, and religious aspects of the Sikh religion. Men and women were trained in the use of arms, and Guru Gobind Singh led them in the struggle against the Mughal emperor. He organized a defense group modeled along military lines to ward off punitive attacks on the Sikh community. This group, known as the Khalsa (the Brotherhood of the Pure), survives today as a vital force in the life of the Sikh community, as do several religious observances initiated by Guru Gobind Singh.

Militant Sikhism

Before his death, Guru Gobind Singh declared the succession of *gurus* at an end. Henceforth the Adi Granth, more commonly known as the Granth Sahib, represented the final, definitive statement of Sikhism for all Sikhs and the authority by which they were to be governed. Military leadership of the Sikhs, however, now devolved upon Banda Singh Bahadur (1670–1716).

At first, Banda Singh was successful in defying the Mughals, but his military career ended in disaster when he and seven hundred of his followers were captured and executed in Delhi in 1716 and the Sikh community was forced to disperse into the neighboring hills. Shortly after this incident, however, the Mughal Empire was completely disrupted by a series of Iranian and Afghan invasions. The Sikhs acted swiftly. Ranjit Singh (1780–1839) exploited the occasion to bring under his suzerainty a territory extending from the Jamuna River to the Indus River. After Ranjit Singh's death, however, his Sikh kingdom disintegrated rapidly, as a consequence of the disruptive influence of internal squabbles over his succession and of the advance of British forces. In a series of bitterly contested battles between 1845 and 1849, the Sikhs were defeated and the Sikh kingdom was annexed to Great Britain.

Sikh loyalty to the British in World War I was rewarded by grants of land in and around the Punjab, but the depression that followed the war led to widespread disturbances. Ultimately the Sikhs, disillusioned by their treatment at the hands of the British, joined Gandhi's freedom movement, only to find that after the division of the subcontinent into India and Pakistan in 1947, their communities had been split in half by the partition. The bloody, brutal riots between Sikhs and Muslims preceding partition forced millions of Sikhs to leave Pakistan. Today, the majority of Sikhs are settled in the Indian Punjab region and maintain their separate identity, as encouraged by state legislatures and the Indian Parliament.

Sikh Scripture

The Holy Book of the Sikhs, Guru Granth Sahib (or Adi Granth), is in general a devotional book similar to the book of Psalms and is divided into three main sections. The first section, called the Japji, is considered by Sikhs to be the epitome of their teaching because it was written by Guru Nanak. After the Japji come the Ragas (tunes), consisting of four books. The following twenty-six minor books, which form the third section, are elaborations on the Ragas.

The Guru Granth Sahib is the focal point of *gurdwaras* (temples) and homes. It is always ceremoniously installed and treated with the utmost reverence. For instance, when the Guru Granth Sahib is installed in a *gurdwara,* all stand and bow their heads. The Guru Granth Sahib is placed on cushions on a dais covered in rich hangings below a canopy. The officiating reader, who sits on a lower cushion, occasionally waves a long-haired, ceremonial whisk over it in imitation of an ancient custom once reserved for monarchs. All who enter the area hallowed by the Guru Granth Sahib must remove their shoes and cover their heads. Worshipers circle the temple clockwise and come to bow before the Guru Granth Sahib with folded hands. Prayers are addressed to the Guru Granth Sahib, an appropriate sermon accompanies the service, and the congregation joins in chanting various hymns and in eating a communal meal, commonly known as a "free kitchen."

Every Sikh is expected to set aside a room in the home to house a copy of the Guru Granth Sahib. Ceremonial rituals and daily readings chosen at random form part of obligatory observances within every household. Many Sikhs recite verses from the Guru Granth Sahib during their day-to-day activities.

Sikh Teachings

Sikhism, in keeping with the teachings of Nanak, asserts that there is only one God, called Sat Nam (the True Name, or the True One). Sat Nam is an unborn, uncreated, and immortal deity, through whom all things are created. Although Sat Nam is a personal God, he is formless, omniscient, omnipotent, omnipresent, and infinite—characteristics that are stated quite clearly in the Guru Granth Sahib:

When God was himself self-created, there was none else. He took counsel and advice with Himself. What he did came to pass. Then there was no heaven or hell or the three regional world. There was only the Formless One Himself! (Guru Granth Sahib, 1)

Although everything is created by Sat Nam, he nevertheless is the "in-dweller of nature," filling all things and contained in everything. Thus, the immanent and transcendent qualities of Sat Nam are combined: the universe and everything within it are rooted in Sat Nam, at once containing him and being contained by him. Since he is indivisibly One and pervades everything, he is both within all else and above all else.

Moreover, Sat Nam is the God not only of a chosen group of people, but of all humanity. He cannot be reached through the mere accumulation of knowledge or on a merely theoretical plane, but only through love and faith. Humanity's duty is to repeat the True Name, Sat Nam, while living a life of dedicated and active service. Devotion to Sat Nam manifests itself in right conduct and correct attitudes. Honesty, compassion, patience, and contentment distinguish the righteous, who are committed to denounce such vices as greed, slander, murder, robbery, and falsehood.

Every individual inherits a legacy represented by his or her performance in past existences, because Sikhs believe that each individual is successively reborn in human form as he or she strives to attain the ultimate goal of existence. This goal is described as the union of the individual's spirit or soul, which is an immortal, divine spark, with its source, Sat Nam. An individual's family and racial inheritance as well as acquired characteristics also influence his or her conduct. Those who behave selfishly or cruelly, disregarding the rights and needs of others, suffer the consequences not in any future hell, but in the next existence. Consequently, Sikhism, unlike many other religions, is not predicated on a Day of Judgment and its aftermath—on an alternative between reward or punishment. Instead, the individual spirit, or soul, develops through countless births until it is absorbed by the infinite One.

In the last analysis, Sikhism is based on character training—on a discipline of spiritual purification designed to control five specific vices: anger, greed, false pride, lust, and an attachment to material or worldly things. The philosophy implicit in Sikhism is best expressed in its motto: "He who conquers his mind conquers the world!"

Sikh Groups

All Sikhs, no matter what sect they belong to, accept the following three precepts: the oneness of God, the leadership of the ten *gurus*, and the divine revelation of the Guru Granth Sahib. Each of a number of divisions within the main body of Sikhism places a particular emphasis on one or more aspects of the religion.

A group known as the Nirankari seeks to restore the worship of the formless and invisible God to its pristine purity. Another group, commonly known as Singh Sabha, fosters education in order to help Sikhs play a more significant role in the modern world. Still another group, the Sahajdharis, rejects the militant aspects of Sikhism, and its adherents are always clean-shaven. The Udasis, basically an order of holy men, follow many of the principles that govern Indian ascetics. With a begging bowl as their sole possession, they vow celibacy and go about either naked, like Jain monks, or dressed in yellow garments, like Buddhist monks. Unlike most other Sikhs, they frequently cut their hair and shave their heads. Then there are the Singhs, the group with which the West has become the most familiar and therefore the one that merits closer scrutiny.

The Singhs take their lead from the tenth and last *guru*, Gobind Singh, who assumed leadership of the Sikhs when he was nine years old, at the beginning of a period of particularly harsh persecution heralded by the execution of his father, Tegh Bahadur, the ninth *guru*. The Singhs represent the soldier-saints of the Brotherhood of the Pure, the Khalsa, founded by Guru Gobind Singh in order to ensure the survival of his followers in the face of persecution. To this day the Singhs live by the code formulated by Gobind Singh. All members are baptized in a special ceremony and assume a common surname— Singh (Lion) for males and Kaur (Princess) for females—to symbolize their equality in the brotherhood and their repudiation of caste. All of them carry five distinguishing marks, the names of which begin with the letter k: *keshas*, uncut hair; *kangha*, a comb; *kara*, a steel bangle or bracelet worn on the right wrist; *kuchka*, a pair of shorts; and *kirpan*, a short sword or dagger. Singhs are also committed to avoid tobacco and intoxicants, the meat of animals that have not been killed by one stroke of the sword but have been bled slowly to death, and adultery.

Sikh Ceremonies and Observances

Four principal ceremonies mark the life of a Sikh: naming, initiation, marriage, and death. Soon after birth, a child is taken to the *gurdwara* for a ceremony that culminates in the naming of the child. During the service and in the presence of the congregation, the Guru Granth Sahib is opened at random for a reading. The first letter of the first verse on the left-hand page becomes the initial of the child's name.

In the initiation ceremony, the adherent acquires full membership in the Sikh community. This ritual consists of a baptismal ceremony initiated by Guru Gobind Singh, who stipulated that it must be per-

A couple singing during their wedding ceremony, the third of the four principal ceremonies in the life of a Sikh, in Eugene, Oregon. Michael Mathers/Peter Arnold, Inc.

formed by five baptized Sikhs. It is their duty to prepare the ceremonial agent of baptism, the Amrita (nectar of immortality)—a measure of water and sweetmeats mixed with a double-edged sword in a steel bowl. While they stir the liquid, they recite five prayers over the ceremonial bowl. Candidates, who are between the ages of eight and fifteen, first bathe and present themselves carrying the five marks of the Khalsa. Next they kneel and, cupping their hands, receive five handfuls of the Amrita, which they drink. Their eyes and hair are also sprinkled five times with Amrita. Now they are ready to assume the responsibilities dictated by the religion and to accept the obligations implied by the five marks of the Khalsa.

Marriage, the third event in a Sikh's life that is celebrated with special ceremony, symbolizes the transcending and eternal union. It is celebrated in Sikh hymns that describe the human spirit as the bride of the eternal husband, God. During the marriage ceremony, the couple circle the Guru Granth Sahib four times to the accompaniment of four verses of the marriage hymn composed by Guru Ram Das.

The fourth and last ceremony that marks stages of the Sikh's life occurs at death. The body is cremated, and a brief service is conducted for the relatives with the reading of appropriate hymns. Later, a religious ceremony is generally conducted either at home or at the *gurdwara*, during which a relay of readers maintains a continuous reading of the Guru Granth Sahib.

In addition to these observances, Sikhs follow a number of daily rituals. They begin the day with a ritual bath, followed by meditation on the name of God and the recitation of certain hymns and prayers. Other rituals of hymns and prayers follow in the evening and before bedtime.

Sikhs also commemorate the anniversaries of the birth and death of their ten *gurus*. The dates of these celebrations, however, vary from year to year, since Sikhs base their calculations on a combination of two factors: the Indian calendar and the lunar cycle.

There are three other important festivals. Two of them commemorate the martyrdom of the four sons of Guru Gobind Singh: Ajit Singh and Jujhar Singh, who were slain in battle; and Zorawar Singh and Fateh Singh, who were executed by order of the Mughal emperor for refusing to accept Islam. The third festival commemorates the anniversary of the Baisakhi, the birthday of the Khalsa.

Local *gurdwara* committees may authorize other celebrations from time to time, but of all the Sikh festivals, only five rate as major observances: Guru Nanak's birthday, Guru Gobind Singh's birthday, Guru Arjun Dev's martyrdom, Guru Tegh Bahadur's martyrdom, and the anniversary of the Baisakhi. These special occasions are preceded by a forty-eight-hour continuous reading of the Guru Granth Sahib from beginning to end and are concluded by the customary distribution of *karah parshad* (sweet food) to everyone present.

Modern Trends

Two of the most pressing issues facing the Sikhs today are the establishment of a Sikh state and the status of Sikh-Hindu relations in India.

Sikh religion and politics have always been intimately connected. In fact, the belief in a Sikh state is an article of faith that is chanted at the conclusion of every service: "The Khalsa shall rule." In 1970 a Sikh-dominated state was established in the area of Punjab, with Chandigarh as its capital.

The matter of Sikh-Hindu relations is a sensitive one. The tendency of the modern generation of Sikhs is to abandon their distinguishing characteristics and socially to affiliate with Hindus. Efforts to combat this tendency have not yielded great results.

Nonetheless, the main body of Sikhs has gradually broken away from Hindu social structure and asserted Sikh separatism. For instance, Sikh insistence on commensality—that is, on eating together at the kitchen of the *gurdwara*—destroyed among Sikhs the traditional, rigid Hindu class or caste system. However, Sikh social structure imposed an alternative, three-level system, based on ethnic differences: *jats,* made up of agricultural people; *non-jats,* comprising priests, warriors, and professionals; and *mazahabis,* converts from Hindu outcastes. But this three-tiered structure is at present in a state of flux, especially among the educated, urban classes. Thus, the political, social, and religious role of Sikhism, like those of most other religions, needs reassessment in the light of modern influences and changes.

Notes

1. *Jain* or *Jaina* is derived from *jina,* an Indian term meaning "conqueror"; it is applied as an honorific title to the ascetic teachers of the Jain tradition.
2. Parshva is said to have lived around the eighth century BCE (some two centuries before Mahavira) and is often depicted in iconography in the posture of meditation, with hooded serpents over his head.
3. For a bibliographical listing of Jain sacred literature, see C. J. Adams, ed., *A Reader's Guide to the Great Religions,* 2nd ed. (New York: Free Press, 1977), pp. 238–44.
4. L. Hopfe, *Religions of the World* (New York: Macmillan, 1983), p. 139.
5. For an understanding of the Hindu and Muslim scene of Guru Nanak's time (fifteenth to sixteenth centuries), see the essay on Sikhism by W. H. McLeod, in A. L. Basham, ed., *A Cultural History of India* (Clarendon, Eng.: Oxford University Press, 1975).
6. Of the estimated 9 million Sikhs throughout the world, 85 percent live in the state of Punjab. On Sikh dispersion, see A. G. James, *Sikh Children in Britain* (Clarendon, Eng.: Oxford University Press, 1974).

8

Taoism and Confucianism

THE SYSTEMATIC, SCHOLARLY STUDY OF CHINESE RELIGION (excepting Buddhism) is in its infancy. Much of what has been written in the West in the past has been colored by attempts to find parallels between Chinese and Christian traditions. Christian apologists, often ill informed and rarely objective, arrived at rash conclusions regarding the religious elements of the Chinese.[1] Largely unappreciated by these early Western scholars were the many facets of Chinese religious thought and feeling, as expressed in social, political, and economic organizations as well as in philosophical systems.[2]

Chinese attitudes toward religion are eclectic. They choose either to adhere to one particular religious group or to actively participate in several. The following story illustrates this syncretistic tendency. Around the sixth century, a famous Chinese scholar was asked by the emperor if he were a Buddhist. The scholar pointed to his Taoist cap. Asked if he were a Taoist, he raised the skirt of his robe to reveal his Confucian shoes. "Are you then a Confucian?" asked the puzzled emperor—whereupon the scholar tugged at the Buddhist scarf he wore.

It is possible for Chinese people to belong to any or all of three religions—Taoism, Confucianism, and Buddhism—without feeling guilty or confused about priorities. Many Buddhist priests are often in charge of Taoist temples, and many Taoists worship Confucius as their ancestral deity. The three great Chinese religions are mutually inclusive and fulfill complementary needs in the lives of the Chinese. Confucianism teaches the social rules of good order and right behavior for everyday living. Taoism stresses the cultural elements of beauty, mystery, romance, and color. Buddhism presents an organized religious system of worship, devotion, temples, and monastic orders. And all three blend into Chinese daily activities as a single aspect of Chinese religiosity.

Early Chinese Religion

Historical Background

Ideograms scratched on bones, together with human remains and cultural artifacts excavated in the valley of the Hwang River, place the beginnings of Chinese history with the rule of the Shang dynasty, some time around 1500 BCE. (Early Chinese writers refer to an earlier kingdom, the Hsia dynasty, but no archeological evidence supporting the historicity of this dynasty has yet been discovered.) During the

A mother and daughter praying at a Confucian shrine in Seoul, South Korea. Martha Cooper/ Peter Arnold, Inc.

Shang dynasty (c. 1500–1125 BCE), the cult of the royal ancestor was practiced and a priestly calendar was adopted for religious and agricultural activities. This period was also characterized by two particularly significant inventions: ideographic writing and the two-wheeled chariot.

The Shang dynasty fell to the Chou warriors, whose dynasty ruled for almost a thousand years (1125–221 BCE). The founders of the Chou dynasty introduced the concept of the virtuous ruler, whose chief duty was the welfare of his subjects. During this period appeared the first Chinese literary records, providing the earliest evidence of Chinese ethical ideas and religious beliefs, practices, and observances. Toward the end of the Chou dynasty, Confucius and Lao Tzu are said to have lived and taught. Meanwhile, the earlier humanitarian tradition began to disintegrate as feudal lords competed for hegemony, and the old moral concepts were redefined with the rise of several philosophical schools.

Five Classics

The classical literature of Chinese religion consists of a set of texts called the Five Classics. A sixth text, the Book of Music, has been lost, but its existence is implied in Confucian tradition. The texts of the Five Classics were edited during the Chou dynasty to conform to the official philosophy of the period, destroyed in the Ch'in era (221–206 BCE), and reconstructed during the Han dynasty (206 BCE–220 CE). The authenticity of these reconstructed texts has been a subject of dispute, but it is generally agreed that although much of the material is of late derivation, it preserves the outlines of older religious ideas.

The Five Classics are:

1. Shu Ching (Book of History or Historical Documents)
2. Shih Ching (Book of Poems)
3. I Ching (Book of Changes)
4. Chun Chiu (Spring and Autumn Annals)
5. Li Chi (Records of Ceremonies or Ritual)

The Shu Ching is the primary source for the "legendary" history of China. It also contains moralizing speeches by emperors and noblemen.

The Shih Ching is a collection of 305 folk songs covering a period of more than one thousand years, beginning with the Shang dynasty. According to tradition, at one time it consisted of 3000 poems, of which Confucius selected the best 305 dealing with love, piety, and war.

The I Ching, perhaps the most important of the five texts, presents a system of divination based on the symbolic interpretation of trigrams and hexagrams. The system of hexagrams, traditionally attributed to an ancient hero, Fu Hsi, is composed of varying combinations of unbroken lines *(yang)* and broken lines *(yin)*. This complicated method of combining broken and unbroken lines gave diviners the evidence or data or signs that they needed to fulfill a petitioner's request for prophesy or advice. Later, it provided the basis for much philosophical and mystical speculation.

The Chun Chiu, traditionally ascribed to Confucius, is a history of the kingdom of Lu (722–484 BCE), Confucius's native country. This work is considered to be one of the first accurate historical texts of China.

The Li Chi contains rules for dancing, music, ancestor worship, and imperial sacrifices. In its present form, it represents the work of later Confucian generations.

Deities and Spirits

The character of folk religion in early Chinese history is obscure. The available evidence indicates that the following important deities and spirits were worshiped.

The highest of all deities was Shang Ti, the Supreme Ruler. His status in heaven was analogous to that of the emperor on earth, although his petitioners were occult practitioners rather than court officials continuously intent on anticipating his demands. Later, during the Chou dynasty, a deity appeared called *T'ien.* This impersonal designation meant "the abode of the great spirits"—that is, the sky or heaven. T'ien was identified with Ti and was worshiped as the reigning universal power—the ultimate regulator of human affairs.

Also worshiped were the messengers of Ti, known as the deities of wind, cloud, sun, and moon; the gods of the four cardinal points of the compass; and deities of the mountains and the rivers. In different regions different deities were the objects of consistent worship. Every village had a mound of soil called *She,* symbolizing fertility. This mound was the focal point of an agricultural cult, the purpose of which was to ensure the growth of crops. In addition to deities related to agriculture, each home was guarded by a group of household deities, including those of the outer and inner doors, the hearth, the well, and the cupboard, who were propitiated to guarantee the prosperity and security of the family.

From the earliest times, then, the Chinese believed that the universe was alive with spirits, in heaven as well as on earth. Not all deities or spirits were considered beneficent. One category of spirits, the *kuei,* was associated with malevolent agents of destruction. A second category, the *shen,* came to represent benevolent forces.

Shen spirits were believed to animate seas, mountains, rivers, trees, and stones, as well as the sun, moon, stars, wind, and thunder. Whereas *shen* spirits animated nature, *kuei* spirits lurked in its shadows. They haunted the lonely places—the desolation of mountain rock and desert, the dark forest path, the uninhabited stretch of road—and infested crops. There were also demons, gigantic devils, and vampires. Fear of *kuei* spirits and demons so dominated the lives of Chinese villagers that they spent much of their time keeping them at a distance with bonfires, torches, candles, and lanterns. Conversely, all *shen* spirits were kept firmly on the villagers' side with appropriate talismans, taboos, gestures, and gifts.

Yin-Yang

Perhaps as early as 1000 BCE, Chinese thinkers established a distinction between two interacting cosmic forces that they attributed to every natural phenomenon. These forces they identified by an ideogram: *yin-yang.*

Yin represented the passive, cold, wet, feminine, evil, and negative principle or force; *yang* represented the active, warm, dry, masculine, good, and positive principle. The two concepts were viewed not as mutually exclusive, implying a cosmos of diametrically conflicting opposites, but as complementary and necessary opposites, implying a cosmos in equilibrium.

According to this philosophical theory, *yin-yang* is an attribute of

The yin-yang symbol surrounded by the Pa Kua (Eight Trigrams), arranged within an octagon. A black spot appears within the light-colored yang, symbolic of the embryonic yin; and a light spot appears within the dark-colored yin, symbolic of the embryonic yang.

everything and every person. Although *yin* is the higher principle and *yang* the lower, *yin-yang* represents a union of elemental principles essential to creative interaction in the ceaseless, dynamic movement of the universe. Nature and humanity operate through the interplay of *yin-yang* until death, at which time an individual's *yang* component is received into heaven, where it influences surviving descendants for good. The *yin* component of a person accompanies a corpse to the grave and must be propitiated through sacrifices performed by surviving relatives and succeeding generations, in order to inhibit unwelcome metamorphoses of *yin* into hostile spirits. Thus, gods were essentially *yang* spirits (*shen* in Chinese) and demons or malignant beings were *yin* spirits (*kuei* in Chinese).

Divination

One of the major practices of Chinese religion during the classical period was divination: determination of the most auspicious period for any undertaking and of the predilection of the appropriate deity. The media for these messages—apart from Fu Hsi's closed and broken lines—were ox bones and tortoise shells, although occasionally sheep bones were used. Tortoise shells were preferred as sources of information, since their structure was thought to resemble the shape of the universe. Other methods of divination included signs and portents revealed by the seasons, astrology, dreams, coins, and the *pa kua*, or eight trigrams. Eventually, the I Ching became the principal manual for providing clues concerning one's actions.

The status of diviners, popularly known as *wu*, was sometimes second only to that of the emperor. The *wu* were charged not only with divination, but also with rainmaking, ridding the community or an individual of pestilence and plague and securing them against disaster, offering sacrifices, fortune telling, and performing exorcisms and various forms of magic.

Emperor Rites

Chinese religion stressed the importance of imperial authority and the grave responsibilities attached to it. The growth of crops in the fields and the maintenance of law and order in society were dependent, according to Chinese religion, on the sacrifices the emperor performed. As a monarch, he surpassed all others in *te*, an attribute of inherent power and virtue invested in his office; accordingly, he was the only individual capable of reaping the greatest advantage from any sacrifice. In other words, the emperor's unique contribution to society, aside from the day-to-day administration of the country, lay in the performance of appropriate rituals dedicated to each of a pantheon of cosmic powers and spirits.

Those emperors who regularly worshiped the spirits and took seriously the welfare of the society, for which they acted as supreme advocates of last resort, were highly revered and thought of as fulfilling the duty of the mandate of heaven. Any failure to live by this celestial mandate represented a threat to cosmic prosperity and might result in crop failure and social revolt. Thus, the emperor played a pivotal role in maintaining harmony in the cosmic process.

At no time were the emperors considered divine; on the contrary, it was their duty to pay the utmost reverence to the spirit *tablets* of heaven and earth, the great powers of the universe. To the subsidiary powers of nature—such as the sun, moon, heavenly bodies, mountains, and rivers—emperors sacrificed without humbling themselves. Emperors also owed imperial ancestors their due: burial rites appropriate to their stations in life and spirit tablets raised in their memory in the ancestral hall alongside the spirit tablets of heaven and earth. This association of imperial ancestral tablets with spirit tablets of heaven and earth was the symbolic expression of the belief that the ancestors of the emperors dwelt with the Supreme Ruler in heaven, where they presumably could exert influence. Consequently, emperors often consulted their ancestors and offered sacrifices to them.

According to surviving bone inscriptions, some emperors of the Shang and Chou dynasties were buried with bronze vessels, hunting weapons, animals, and human victims—all provided to accommodate the emperor in the next world. This practice of animal and human sacrifice (replicated in Egypt and other cultures) continued late into Chou times, when funerary substitutes—first pottery, later paper— gradually displaced live victims in imperial tombs.

Ancestor Rites

Although it was introduced by members of the royal family during the Shang period, the cult of ancestor worship soon spread to court officials, and beyond them to the general populace. Every family reserved a special spot in the homes for an ancestral shrine, which became a repository of wooden tablets inscribed with the names of family ancestors. Later, local clans maintained family temples, often elaborately furnished, containing the spirit tablets of their ancestors.

Both the clan temple and the domestic shrine became focal points for propitiatory offerings of food and drink and the performance of religious rituals. Here, in the presence of their ancestors, family members announced plans for enterprises such as business ventures, journeys, and marriages and delivered formal decisions of all kinds, in order to receive ancestral endorsement. Spring and autumn were occasions for special pilgrimages to ancestral graves, where sacrifices and offerings were performed. According to this cult tradition, anyone who abandoned or betrayed the ancestral rites was doomed to suffer the vengeance of ancestral spirits and, in death, to wander as an unlucky, lonely, hungry ghost lacking a living soul to sustain memorial rites and sacrifices.

Similarly, the absence of a male heir was a heinous offense against ancestral spirits, because without him the ancestral rites could not be continued. In such cases a substitute son was found, either by adopting one or by making the son of a concubine the heir. In families in which there was more than one son, the eldest assumed the responsibility for performing ancestral rites at the death of his father.

Ancestral rites, therefore, played an indispensable role in Chinese religion from the beginning. They implied continuous contact between the dead and the living and an affirmation of life after death, in some form or other. By virtue of their close association with the Supreme Ruler in heaven, which gave them the power to intercede on behalf of their living descendants, ancestors were seen as possessing influence that was denied the living. Ancestors were thus, in a sense, deified. Their relationship with their living descendants was one of mutual dependence: protection in exchange for filial sacrifices.

Aside from religious rites, the frequent recall of names and accomplishments recorded in genealogical accounts gave people a sense of being rooted in established traditions. Some lineages stretched in unbroken succession through many generations, often to the remotest past. The presence of ancestors thus was a pervasive and comforting element of daily family activity.[3]

Rival Philosophical Schools

The Classic period (722–221 BCE) was also one of gradual decay and feudal conflict that resulted in the impoverishment of many of the old noble families and the enrichment and political ascendancy of a new middle class of farmers and merchants. In addition, the inability of the Chou emperors of this era to protect the country from invading Asian hordes encouraged local warlords to raise private armies to defend their own territory. Agricultural serfs seized the opportunity offered by the declining power of landlords to free themselves from the system that had denied them possession of property and to become owners of their own fields. The decay of the feudal system culminated in violent civil disorders, called the Warring States period (481–221

BCE), that lasted for some two hundred years. The result was the disappearance of feudal states and kingdoms, the collapse of royal families, and the reunification of China in 221 BCE under Emperor Shih Huang Ti.

This period of conflict, transition, and change stimulated a search for political and philosophical solutions and alternatives to chaos. Some schools of thought, such as the Legalists, attacked the feudal system and did what they could to discredit and demolish it. A few, such as the Mohists (or Motseans), advocated the return of "old-time religion" and universal benevolence. Yet others, such as the Confucians, wanted the feudal system to be restored, but in a more rationalized or idealized form. Still others, such as the Taoists, refused to have anything to do with a political system that required structure and conformity. According to Chinese tradition, the age witnessed the flowering of a "hundred philosophers." From among the host of contenders, Taoism and Confucianism overshadowed all others. These two, along with Buddhism, shaped and maintained the structure of a durable society.

The following sections examine the lives and thought of Lao Tzu and Confucius, and the consequences of their teachings for the religion and history of eastern Asian people. Lao Tzu lived in the Yangtze River region, which was characterized by a population that opposed the thousand-year feudal stranglehold of the Chou dynasty. Confucius lived in the Yellow River region, which was dominated by Chou culture.

Taoism

Lao Tzu

The question of whether Lao Tzu was a legendary figure or a historical individual has not been answered with certainty.[4] The first mention of Lao Tzu (meaning Old Master) was made in an early Chinese classic book called Chuang Tzu, written probably around the fourth or the third century BCE, in which Lao Tzu is described as the teacher of Chuang Tzu, the author of the book. Parts of the text are even attributed to Lao Tzu, who is represented as a renowned Taoist Master who earned his living working as a curator of the archives at the courts of the Chou dynasty. The book also asserts that Lao Tzu met Confucius and, as the senior of the two, confounded Confucius with his Taoist teachings. The sole account of Lao Tzu's death occurs in this book.

A biographical account of Lao Tzu written after the Classic period is incorporated into the Shih-chi (Historical Records), China's first historical record, authored around the second century BCE by Ssu-ma Ch'ien. According to Shih-chi, Lao Tzu's given name was Erh, and his family name was Li. The biography also records that Lao Tzu worked at the Chou court as an archivist and that he left the court as the result of disenchantment with the declining Chou dynasty. He is said to have written, at the request of the guardian of the frontier gate where he made his exit from China, his treatise on *Tao and its Power*, better known as *Tao Te Ching*. The biography also states that Lao Tzu instructed Confucius on points of ceremony before he left China for good. It does not say what became of him.

Most modern scholars have questioned the credibility of these two accounts and attributed references concerning Lao Tzu to legend. Some even have argued that the Lao Tzu of tradition is nothing more than a fictitious figure invented by Taoists to establish their historical primacy over Confucianism. A few scholars have dissented from this assessment by the majority. Based on certain Confucian evidence, they have accepted the traditions associated with Lao Tzu as historical, although disagreeing among themselves on the precise dates of Lao Tzu's life. According to some, the midpoint of his career came around 570 BCE; according to others, it may have fallen closer to 604 BCE. All scholars are agreed that nothing for certain is known about Lao Tzu, including authorship of the Tao Te Ching.[5]

Taoist Scriptures

Tao Te Ching. The Tao Te Ching is at once a short anthology of paradoxical statements on the nature of Tao (the Way), and a handbook of maxims for the ruler-sage. Nothing is known for certain about its date of origin, which scholars have placed some time between the sixth and fourth centuries BCE, or about its originator(s). Tradition holds that Lao Tzu was its author, but modern critics have speculated that it represents an anthology of works from a variety of sources that were collected in an effort to preserve them for posterity.

The Tao Te Ching is written so cryptically that understanding may escape the casual reader of this deceptively short book. Behind its brevity, ambiguity, and paradoxical style is a mystical philosophy centered on five fundamental principles: Tao, Relativity, Nonaction, Return, and Government. In spite of its enigmatic language the Tao Te Ching remains the fundamental text for both philosophical and religious Taoism.

Chuang Tzu. The Chuang Tzu, named after its author, was probably written in the fourth to third centuries BCE. Along with valuable documentary material and passages that reflect the philosophical trends and religious practices of the Warring States period (481–221 BCE), it includes descriptions of "spirit journeys"; practices of ecstatic

A worshipful moment at a Taoist temple in Taichung, Taiwan.   Bruno P. Zehnder/
Peter Arnold, Inc.

religion; accounts of Taoist Masters and disciples; and techniques of
meditation, breath control, sexual activity, gymnastics, and diets.

Tao is represented as indescribable. One can only attain identity
with Tao—complete identification or fusion with the "rhythm" of the
forces of nature. This identity is totally indistinguishable from the
rhythm of nature and shares its infinity, beyond the cycle of life and
death. In other words, identity with Tao is identity with the power or
rhythm behind the forces of all nature, existence, and the universe.

Other Scriptures. There is a vast body of Taoist sacred texts of special
significance to popular Taoism, in contrast to philosophical-mystical
Taoism. These sacred texts are reserved for and restricted to priests
alone, in order to help them to communicate with the deities, to ward
off demons, to learn esoteric secrets, to perform liturgies for burial, to
chart spiritual maps, and to check the lists or names of spirits. The use
or even the perusal of one of these proscribed texts by the un-
initiated—and therefore, the unauthorized—is regarded as sacrile-
gious.

The 1120 volumes of the Tao Tsang (Storehouse of Tao) were not
published in their entirety until some time during the Ming dynasty
(1368–1644). The collection consists of several sections representing
the teachings of each separate Taoist sect, in addition to the teachings
of other groups. Each section includes basic doctrines, vows, and

rituals for initiates; collections of magical rites; hymns and melodies; cures and incantations; memorials and biographies of famous Taoists; and miscellaneous documents.

Two other important texts associated with Taoism are the T'ai-p'ing Ching (Classic of the Great Peace), and the Pao P'u Tzu (Master Embracing Simplicity), both written between the third and fourth centuries CE. The latter work includes Confucian teachings, but its main theme is the quest for immortality through alchemic elixirs, special diets, and certain sexual activities. In fact, the major concern of most Taoist sacred texts is with gaining superhuman, immortal power by engaging in special exercises.

Taoist Concepts

Tao. One of the most fundamental concepts in Chinese thought is Tao. In common usage it means "the way," and by extension, a code of behavior. Tao also means *the Way*, the cosmic force behind all phenomena. In religious Taoism, Tao identifies the magical feat of bringing supernatural powers into communication with humans. In philosophical Taoism, Tao is understood as the ecstatic integral fusion of a person with the Principle behind cosmic order and disorder.

The Tao Te Ching defines, or attempts to define, the undefinable: the various meanings of Tao, which is imperceptible, indiscernible, formless, and nameless. All categories in heaven and earth arise from Tao, but Tao lies outside all categories. Nothing can be predicated about Tao, yet it latently embodies the forms, categories, entities, and forces behind and within all phenomena. Tao even defies description as nonbeing. Tao and nonbeing are not identical. Being and nonbeing, which grow out of one another and are interdependent, are two aspects of Tao. Nonbeing does not mean nothingness, but emptiness—the void, the absence of perceptible qualities. Tao, then, is the primordial, undivided state underlying both being and nonbeing. In short, Tao is the inherent, purposeless, impersonal, amoral Cosmic Principle. Here is how it is stated in the Tao Te Ching:

> Look, it cannot be seen—it is beyond form.
> Listen, it cannot be heard—it is beyond sound.
> Grasp, it cannot be held—it is intangible.
> From above it is not bright;
> From below it is not dark:
> An unbroken thread beyond description.
> It returns to nothingness.
> The form of the formless,
> The image of the imageless,
> It is called indefinable and beyond imagination.

Stand before it and there is no beginning.
Follow it and there is no end.
Stay with the ancient Tao,
Move with the present.
Knowing the ancient beginning is the essence of Tao.
(Tao Te Ching. 14)[6]

Nonaction. Tao is usually expressed by its aspects, one of which is *wu-wei*, or nonaction. This term does not imply anti-action or deliberate intervention (such as passive resistance). On the contrary, nonaction is nonstriving; it represents the natural course of things, the harmonious, cyclical order of change and reversal, of active-passive (i.e., *yang–yin*) complementary energies. One need only look at nature to understand natural action or nonaction. Nature functions quietly, and through nonaction (or the natural course of things) accomplishes its purposes of creating, sustaining, or destroying. The concept of nonaction excludes efforts to fight for or against the course of events. Nature does not support or resist the cosmic rhythm; it simply lets things happen naturally. According to the Tao Te Ching:

The Tao of heaven does not strive, and yet it overcomes.
It does not speak, and yet is answered.
It does not ask, yet is supplied with all its needs.
(Tao Te Ching. 73)

In the pursuit of Tao, every day something is dropped.
Less and less is done until non-action is achieved.
When nothing is done, nothing is left undone.
The world is ruled by non-action, not by action.
(Tao Te Ching. 48)

Relativity. Another aspect of Tao is *chiao*, or the relativity of everything. According to this concept, good and evil, right and wrong, beauty and ugliness, strength and weakness, glory and humiliation are not polar opposites, but standards of value that are relative to time and place.[7]

Judgments of what is right or wrong are relative to one's personal stance, situation, and needs. What is considered cold weather for people living in the southern regions, for example, is welcomed as warm by those living in the northern territories. Water is precious for travelers in the desert but a constant hazard for people in lowlands.

Neither water nor climate nor morality nor anything else has any intrinsic or absolute value or specific purpose. Value and purpose arise only in relation to something else. The Tao Te Ching expresses it this way:

> Under heaven all can see beauty as beauty only because
>   there is ugliness.
> All can know good as good only because there is evil.
> Therefore having and not having arise together.
> Difficult and easy complement each other.
>   (Tao Te Ching. 2)

Identity of Opposites. This concept of relativity was further developed by Chuang Tzu, who argued that since truth or knowledge is relative to one's need and situation, then opposites are identical. All dualities—like and dislike, large and small, short and long, life and death, beginning and end, knowledge and ignorance, finite and infinite—are not really opposites but are identical aspects of one and the same reality. Tao transcends distinction.

Chuang Tzu's view is best expressed by his "wake-dream" reality. After dreaming that he was a butterfly, Chuang Tzu woke and pondered: "I do not know whether I dreamt that I was a butterfly, or I am a butterfly now dreaming that I am Chuang Tzu!" The reality (or Tao) that characterizes waking and dreaming has no opposites, only identical aspects. A prerequisite to the attainment of a real state of identity is to discard all concepts of opposites and distinctions. When the duality of aspects is dissolved, all things become the One, or Tao.

Return. The invariable law of nature is *fu*, or return. This phenomenon of reversal, the process by which all things are ordained to return to their original state, is yet another aspect of Tao. The law of Tao, as it relates to natural order, means the continuous reversion of everything to its starting point. Anything that develops a certain quality will invariably revert to the opposite quality. Since everything issues out of Tao, everything inevitably returns to Tao. The One becomes the all, and the all returns to the One. From nonbeing comes being, from which comes nonbeing. This is the eternal or endless law of Tao.

> The ten thousand things rise and fall while the Self
>   watches their return.
> They grow and flourish and then return to the
>   source.
> Returning to the source is stillness, which is the way
>   of nature. (Tao Te Ching. 16)

Transformation. Chuang Tzu saw this invariable law of nature not as *fu*, or return, but as *hua*, or transformation. For him, life was an eternal transformation from one form to another. This does not mean that Chuang Tzu believed in a "soul" that transmigrated from one form to another, nor did he understand this transformation as a moral cause-and-effect relationship. On the contrary, Chuang Tzu conceived of life in terms of an infinite process of change or transformation that involved ceaseless mutations with no absolute end. It is precisely this process, which is the function of the Tao, that makes humans, like the universe, immortal.

To let oneself follow this natural process of transformation results, according to Chuang Tzu, in a sense of peace and tranquility that transcends description. Only those who experience it are aware of the reality beyond duality. This reality is nothing less than an identity with Tao.

Taoism through the Ages

Philosophical and Religious Taoism. Both Chinese scholars and Western sinologists distinguish between philosophical (mystical) and religious (popular) Taoism.[8] The former is viewed as a philosophy of life or a form of mysticism, the first evidence of which is found in texts dating from the sixth to the third centuries BCE. In this form, Taoism has represented, throughout Chinese history, the spiritual goal of the educated few. Religious Taoism, on the other hand, is a highly organized system with ceremonials, temples, and a hereditary priesthood, the earliest evidence of which dates from the second century CE. As such it is a popular folk religion that attracts all ranks and classes of Chinese people.

Although in theory these two views of Taoism are distinct, in actual fact they are interrelated, sharing many linguistic and conceptual features. A Taoist may participate in both the ceremonial aspects of organized religion and the realm of solitary, mystical abstraction. An earlier view that religious Taoism represents a debasement of philosophical Taoism is no longer considered valid by some modern scholars, who have argued that any distinction between the two types of Taoism should be made simply for the sake of descriptive convenience.

Philosophical Taoism has attracted much attention among Western scholars, but investigation of religious Taoism is still in its infancy. Western scholars have generally restricted their studies of religious Taoism to aspects that particularly interested them: breath control, the quest for immortality, alchemy, dietetics, and so on.[9] An adequate investigation would require close critical study of the history and development of religious Taoism, especially in its interaction with Confucianism, Buddhism, and shamanistic religion. The effects of modern technology and outside—particularly Western—cultures lend urgency to this research task. Traditional Taoist practices must be closely observed and critically assessed before they are modified or erased by the pressures of modernization.

Origins and Development. Behind all forms of Taoism stands the figure of Lao Tzu, who, as we have seen, is traditionally considered to be the founder of Taoism and the author of the Tao Te Ching. Modern scholarship has discredited both claims, although it is generally agreed that the first evidence of philosophical Taoism occurs in the Tao Te Ching.

Taoism in the Ch'in (221–206 BCE) and Han (206 BCE–220 CE) periods is associated, at least among scholars, with official or imperial patronage. Representatives of different religious traditions met at the imperial court not only to exchange ideas, but also to compete for official favor. Their activities were recorded by court officials, who often were active participants in the events they described. Taoists were among the various thaumaturgic (wonder-working) individuals who visited the courts of the Ch'in and Han dynasties.

By the third century BCE, Taoist Masters were expounding the teachings of Lao Tzu, which spread from court officials to various learned individuals throughout the country. Their teachings about ideal government and immortality evoked considerable interest, especially among Han statesmen. These officials applied Taoist principles of nonaction to the function of government—an early example of laissez-faire statesmanship.

During the first and second centuries CE, several Messianic revolts broke out, some of them led by *charismatic* (gifted, or divinely empowered) Taoist leaders, one of whom claimed to be the reincarnation of Lao Tzu. Other would-be Messiahs included Taoist ideological elements in revolutionary religious movements that somehow reconciled action and nonaction as two elements of the same indivisible concept. These sporadic revolutionary manifestations of Messianism were eventually defeated by imperial forces.

Official Recognition of Religious Taoism. It is generally thought that religious Taoism was developed in the province of Szechwan by a certain Chang Ling (Chang Tao-Ling) in 142 CE. Chang Ling is said to have received a revelation from the Most High Lord Lao Tzu, who instructed him to replace the degenerated and demonic religious practices of the people with Lao Tzu's "orthodox and sole doctrine of the authority of the covenant." Later, according to tradition, Chang Ling ascended to heaven and received the title of Heavenly Master. His successors, also called Heavenly Masters, established an independent organization to continue his work and to instruct the faithful in the revealed work of the Most High Lord Lao Tzu. Their fundamental teachings concerned right actions and good works, which, in turn, ensured immunity from disease.

In 215, Chang Lu, grandson of Chang Ling, pledged himself to the

Lu Tung-Pin, known in English as the Immortal Lui, is one of the Taoist Eight Immortals, familiar figures in Chinese art, theater, and literature. The Eight Immortals became the most popular figures in China, and their legends have survived to this day. Many temples are built in honor of Lu Tung-Pin, since from time to time he is believed to reappear on earth to guide people into a righteous way of life.

Wei dynasty of northern China. This act of submission or fealty resulted in official imperial recognition of the group as an organized religion. The Heavenly Masters were authorized to act as intermediaries between the responsible ruler and the public, and, as their influence grew, they sometimes assumed secular power when a ruler proved weak or ineffective.

This Taoist group was so readily accepted that in less than a century it counted among its adherents most of the powerful families in northern China. By the beginning of the fourth century, the religious Taoism of the Heavenly Masters had penetrated into southeastern China, where nonaction was complemented by coercion. After war had been waged against indigenous cults, sorcerers, and mediums, the entire region was converted to the religion of the Heavenly Masters.

In time, each Heavenly Master represented a different aspect of religious Taoism. Detailed liturgies replaced the older, simpler rites of the earlier Heavenly Masters. Certain observances, featuring countless formulas and practices, were developed in the expectation that they would restore vital life forces and thus increase longevity. Various hygienic and respiratory techniques were also developed to maintain a continuous circulatory process of all energies in the body. Some Taoist priests performed exorcisms and increasingly complex rituals. Other eminent Taoists searched, edited, or annotated revealed texts. Some were recipients of revelations from the heavenly immortals.

The founders of the T'ang (618–907) and Ming (1368–1644) dynasties routinely resorted to Taoist prophecies and occult practices in order to ensure and maintain public support. The most spectacular success of religious Taoism came during the Tang dynasty, whose founder, Li Yuan, claimed to be a descendant of Lao Tzu. Taoists accepted him as the long-awaited fulfillment of messianic prophecy, and this conviction became the ideology of the state. The wide diffusion of Taoism throughout the vast T'ang Empire is evident from contacts of Taoists with Buddhists, Christians, Eastern Nestorians, and Manicheans. In the seventh century, Taoism reached Japan, where adherents can be found to this day.

This wide dissemination encouraged the development, to impressive dimensions, of a number of new Taoist sects, some of which have survived to the present. Other Taoist sects formed religious communities and established monasteries to facilitate the daily observance of Taoist meditation, liturgy, hygiene, and other characteristics of the contemplative life. It must be emphasized, however, that religious Taoism never established a permanent central authority. No institutional cohesion existed among the sects. Each sect looked back to its founder, adhered independently to its scriptures, and observed its ritualistic ceremonies.

The essential and distinctive element of philosophical Taoism, in contrast, was to gain and preserve the vital force through a realization of Tao. The quest to be in harmony with Tao—with the universal rhythm or mechanism behind all perceptible and imperceptible existence—was the essential preoccupation with one's vital force. In this regard, Taoist mystics were neither theologians in the Christian sense nor philosophers in the Buddhist sense, but poets who expressed the individual need of harmony with Tao.

Confucianism

Historical Background

The world into which Confucius was born is considered by scholars to have been one of the most intellectually creative periods in Chinese history, and yet it was characterized by political and cultural anarchy. Petty rulers attempted to extend their authority at the expense of the royal house of the Chou dynasty, then in decline. Boundaries between

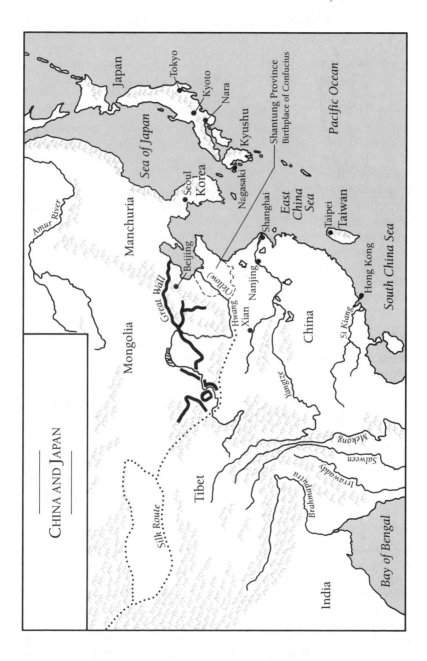

states were in a constant state of flux. Feudal rulers, who reigned by virtue of their noble ancestry, were so corrupt that society suffered economic and moral deterioration. Nevertheless, the Eastern Chou period (771–255 BCE) was one of intense social, political, and intellectual activity that provoked fundamental changes in most established conventions and institutions.

This is the age commonly referred to as the Classical period, but also as the Age of a Hundred Philosophers. Contending vigorously for solutions to the pressing social and political problems of the period, these "hundred philosophers" were eventually classified into six schools: Confucianism, Taoism, Mohism, the School of Yin-Yang, the Dialecticians, and Legalism. In the second century BCE, Confucianism was elevated to the status of a state cult at the expense of the other schools.

Debate on the question of whether or not Confucianism is a religion or a philosophical system implies a characteristic ambiguity. Those who tend to see Confucianism as a system of philosophy argue that it has no religious structure or sanction; rather, it represents a body of noble ethical teachings and important political ideologies. They point out, moreover, that exponents of the claim that Confucianism is a religion have difficulty explaining the absence of any reference to immortality or life beyond death—a concept fundamental to most, if not all, religions. Those who are inclined to see Confucianism as a religion justify their views in terms of the religious characteristics embraced by Confucianism: reverence toward heaven, ancestor worship, ceremonial and sacrificial practices, and temples. True, Confucian temples are memorial monuments rather than religious institutions. Nevertheless, the Chinese consider Confucianism more than a creed to be professed or rejected. To them, Confucianism is Chinese life in all its political, social, moral, and religious aspects. After all, Confucius taught the principle of morality that should govern political and social relations.

Confucius

No accurate account of the life of Confucius is likely to be found, because his biographies were written centuries after his death, by which time he had been elevated to a semidivine status. His given name was Chiu, meaning small hill—a reference to a noticeable bulge on his head. His family name was Kung. The name Confucius is a Latinized form of K'ung Fu Tzu, meaning Master Kung.

Confucius was born in 551 BCE in the state of Lu, the present Ch'u Fu, in the northern province of Shantung. His father, Shu Ho (Shu-

Liang Ho) was a distinguished soldier, and his mother was from the Yen family. Both of his parents died when he was a child.

He married at the age of nineteen, although nothing is known about his wife, and had a son and a daughter. His son, Po-Yu, later became one of his early disciples but died before his father. Nothing is known of his daughter.

Government Service. Confucius's first occupation was as a clerk in the Memorial Temple of the Duke Chou, where he was expected to attend and participate in all ceremonies. Later, he was a leader of ceremonies in a village temple. His love for learning prompted him to study the ceremonial rituals of the local community from the well-informed elders of the village school. He became the local prodigy—a boy wonder who went on to read the Shu Ching (Book of History or Historical Documents) and the Shih Ching (Book of Poems) with the village music master and so, even in his callow youth, to acquire a reputation as an expert in ancient ritual.

According to tradition, Confucius attempted to pass the qualifying examination for a government post several times, failing each time. Frustrated but not embittered, he withdrew from the competitive scramble for prestigious government preferment and began to teach— not as a tutor for aristocrats' children, but as a mentor of anyone, poor and rich alike, who matched his capacity and will to learn. In short, he was very demanding; he selected only the cream of the crop.

Tradition states that after countless attempts, Confucius finally passed the civil service examination at the age of fifty. Accordingly, he became the chief magistrate of Cheng-tu, an outlying town west of the Lu capital, where he was able to apply his political ideologies in practice. The following year he was a delegate in the retinue of the imperial ambassador appointed to head a peace conference in Outer Mongolia. An assignment as deputy minister of justice, one of the six highest-ranking imperial offices achieved by commoners, followed. Yet, his wisdom, though widely praised, was not always heeded. Disillusioned with this state of affairs, he resigned his post.

That is the traditional account. Western scholars have found little, if any, historical evidence to confirm it. They have argued that if ever Confucius had occupied a commanding position of authority in imperial service, it would surely be mentioned in the definitive collection of Confucian quotations, the Analects. Far from documenting any such record in the corridors of power, the Analects reflects concern, self-doubt, and speculation about whether or not he possessed the qualities that would enable him to hold important office. Perhaps, critics have said, Confucius may have held office in minor roles in the court of Lu in later life, but his resignation may have been prompted by boredom or by the inconsequential nature of the work or simply by the fact that the court was corrupt, weak, and increasingly impotent.

In Search of a Ruler. Accompanied by a few disciples, Confucius spent the next ten or more years traveling and visiting vassals of the imperial court, regional governors, and warlords in the hope of putting his philosophy into practice. He first went north to the state of Chi and almost immediately became a victim of the lawlessness that prevailed outside bastions of government authority: he was mistaken for someone else and almost lost his life. This setback did not dampen his enthusiasm for recommending his vision of government to those in power. After completing his mission in the north, he traveled south to the state of Sung, then to the state of Wei, and then to the rest of the states in China.

Traditional accounts of this odyssey imply that Confucius was well received, especially when he advised rulers on government policy, but the effect of such encouragement must have been tempered by the reluctance of any potentate to take him on staff. Confucius offered to justify his teachings and policies in terms of concrete results within a year, and to apply his total program of governmental reform within three years, but no one ever took him up on this offer. Disappointed and disheartened, Confucius returned to his hometown in the state of Lu.

For the next five years, Confucius devoted himself to teaching and editing the Five Classics while his disciples reaped the benefits of their teacher's former proselytizing zeal. Some were appointed to important posts in different states. Others established schools and taught Confucius's ideas. Confucius himself died in 479 BCE, at the age of seventy-two, with the conviction that he had failed to achieve his mission.

Master Kung. What kind of man was Confucius? Invariably, his manner is described in traditional accounts as informal and cheerful. The keystone of his teaching was sincerity—a characteristic that bordered on uncompromising frankness and, although he had many friends and admirers, that may have weakened his prospects of achieving his political ambitions. He also had a sense of humor and approved of pleasure in moderation.

Although he may have viewed himself as a failed politician, Confucius never lost his keen appetite for learning and teaching, which may have been his primary vocation. He demanded two qualities from his students: intelligence and willingness to work hard. This earned him the well-deserved title of Master. His humility was always evident in his capacity to listen to his disciples and to compromise or admit error. He was totally dedicated to the improvement of government in the interest and to the advantage of the governed—a goal that escaped him, at least during his lifetime.

Teachings of Confucius

The Analects. The aphorisms, discourses, and sayings attributed to Confucius provide the subject matter of Lun Yu, meaning Conversations—though it is more commonly identified in the Western world as the Analects, a term derived from the Greek word *analekta* (things gathered). The text, consisting of some twenty sections (12,700 Chinese characters), is a collection of notes and journals of the Master's discourses, conversations, and travels, ostensibly recorded for posterity by his disciples. Although rival versions existed at one time, the present form dates from about the first century CE.

The Analects is considered to be the earliest and most reliable single source on the life and teachings of Confucius, and it is the most widely read of all the Chinese classics. Even though it is unsystematic, repetitive, and sometimes historically inaccurate, it contains practically all the basic concepts of Confucius and Confucianism.

Government Principles Challenged. Confucius has often been accused of merely seeking to revive the past or the ways of antiquity. Actually, he was a "selective traditionalist"[10]—that is, he affirmed certain traditional concepts and rituals that were significant to him, but he was also an innovator. Two of his fundamental principles were revolutionary in the Chinese culture of the time. They are (1) that those who govern should be chosen not on the basis of heredity, but on demonstrable characteristics of virtue and ability; and (2) that the true end of government is the total welfare and happiness of the people.

In accord with these ideas, Confucius maintained that the state should be a totally cooperative enterprise. This view was in direct opposition to those of the existing regime. Confucius openly challenged the idea that aristocrats were descended from divine ancestors and ruled by virtue of the latter's authority. In his view, the right to govern depended on the individual ruler's moral character and ability to make his subjects happy.

Good government could only be established, Confucius argued, by governors schooled in virtue and cultivated in character as well as in competence. The essence of Confucian doctrine was the negation of punishment and rigid law in favor of a positive example of virtue based on *li*, or proper conduct exemplified by the criterion of *shu* (reciprocity)—that is, the capacity to deal with others as we would have them deal with us. In the famous words of Confucius, "Do not do to others what you would not desire yourself" (Analects XV.24; see also XII.2 and V.11).[11] Putting the case more positively, he said, "You yourself desire rank and standing; then help others attain rank and standing" (Analects VII.28).

Confucius did not advocate revolution, but he challenged established principles of government based on feudal states parceled out like private properties among those wealthy or ruthless enough to exercise the power of life and death over those they ruled. Whereas these nobles and aristocratic families waged war, levied ruinous taxes, and oppressed their subjects with forced labor, Confucius disparaged warfare as a solution to any problem, urged that taxes be reduced, and pleaded for measures to mitigate the severity of punishment for even minor infractions of the law. He challenged the very foundations of authoritarian government by insisting on the right of all individuals to make basic decisions for themselves, and he did what he could to mitigate the monopoly on education that the aristocracy enjoyed by accepting the poorest students, provided that they were intelligent, hardworking, and unpretentious.

The Superior Man. According to Confucius the characteristics that distinguish the superior man (*chun-tzu,* literally prince-son) from the inferior man are qualities such as *li* (the code of moral, social conduct), *jen* (virtue, compassion, human heartedness, love), *yi* (righteousness), and *te* (virtue). In the words of Confucius, "The superior man is concerned with virtue, the inferior man with land; the superior man understands what is right, the inferior man what is profitable" (Analects IV.11).

Confucius acknowledged that individuals vary in inherent virtues and abilities, but he believed that an appropriate education could nurture and cultivate the inherent moral characteristics that are prerequisites for the creation of the superior man. His curriculum for developing ability, skill, and strength of character stressed music, poetry, and ritual. Poetry, in his view, stimulated the emotions, heightened powers of observation, increased sympathy, and moderated resentment of injustice. Music, Confucius claimed, expressed the inward, heavenly aspect of the universe; and rituals expressed the outward, earthly aspect. A harmonious relationship among all three was necessary for perfect order: "All three arts—music, poetry and ritual—rise from the human soul and are integral in understanding proper human conduct" (Analects VIII.8).

With the components of art and nature blended in harmony, the superior man feels neither fear nor anxiety, but is always calm and at peace. The inferior man, in contrast, is always worried and full of anxiety.

A consequence of this inner harmony is *li,* an outward manifestation of moral and social conduct that affects every contact with fellow beings, both within the family and within society. From a practical point of view, this means that a husband is considerate of his wife and a wife subservient to her husband; that a father is kind to his son and a son obedient to his father; that an elder brother is helpful to his younger brother and a younger brother respectful of his elder brother. Extending this principle to society, Confucius urged that a senior friend help a junior friend and a junior friend respect his senior, and that a ruler act beneficently to his subjects and the subjects obey their ruler. These obligations and duties came to be known as the Five Relationships that characterize Confucian teaching.[12]

Thus, an individual's conduct should reflect in private, social, or government life the obligations of the role he plays. Confucius identified this correspondence between conduct and role as the true "meaning of names," or in the Master's words, *cheng ming*. That is to say, one must fulfill the proper functions of a father (an elder brother, a senior friend, or a ruler) before one can be truly called a father.

Religion and Religious Conduct. In terms of religion, Confucius was concerned with honesty and conduct rather than with theological speculation. He himself prayed, fasted, attended sacrifices offered to ancestors, and respected those who venerated heaven and performed religious ritual aesthetically; but at the same time, he severely condemned a large part of the religious activities of his day as sheer superstition (Analects VI.22). Confucius remained silent about spirits and supernatural forces. The closest he came to expressing an opinion on the topic was his statement that it was more productive to establish the purpose of life on earth than to waste energy on fruitless speculation about life after death. In his opinion, no one was qualified to speak of serving the spirits without first learning how to serve humanity (Analects XI.11).

Obedience and trust in heaven (*T'ien*) gave Confucius courage and a sense of mission, and he recommended the "way of heaven" as the model by which sages, rulers, and nobles should conduct their lives (Analects XV.28; XVI.2). A ruler, according to Confucius, rules by the authority vested in *T'ien*, or the Mandate of Heaven; but if he is unworthy, that authority should be transferred to others. "There are three things of which the superior man stands in awe," Confucius is reported to have told his disciples. "He stands in awe of the ordinances of Heaven. He stands in awe of noblemen. He stands in awe of the words of the sages" (Analects XVI.8).

Confucius accepted the importance of ritual, but he stressed that the inner attitude of the worshiper, not the outward display, made a ritual meaningful. He therefore condemned pompous ceremony and was

Every year a memorial celebration of the birthday of Confucius is held on September 28 in the Confucian temple in Taipei, Taiwan. This celebration is a family affair because the man without the head-covering (extreme right) is a descendant of Confucius.   Courtesy of Jordan Paper.

critical of those who took part in rituals and sacrifices without reverence or inner feeling. For Confucius, sincerity and reverence in ritual were absolutely essential; otherwise, ritual was meaningless. What determined the value of ritual, in other words, was the motive of the worshiper.

Confucian Canon

The heart of the Confucian canonical texts, or scriptures, is a massive, heterogeneous collection of material that occupied the minds of all educated Chinese from the second century BCE to the mid-twentieth century. Those who mastered the contents of the Confucian canon became the literati—the elite, or learned, who by virtue of their learning were eligible to be appointed as officials in the imperial government.

An imperial university was founded in the capital around 124 BCE, during the early Han period (206 BCE–9 CE) for the teaching of the Confucian canon. The importance of this institution may be judged from its enrollment, which is said to have reached some 30,000 students.[13]

The contents of the Confucian canon were never fixed permanently. During the early Han period the Confucian canon included nine works: the Five Classics (Shu Ching, Shih Ching, I Ching, Chun Chiu, and Li Chi); and the Four Books, consisting of Lun-Yü, Meng Tzu (Mencius), Hsiao Ching, and Erh Ya.[14] In T'ang times (618–907) the Confucian canon was comprised of thirteen works: the Five Classics and the Four Books plus the Chung Yung, Ta Hsüeh, I Li, and Chou Li. In the Sung period (960–1280), Confucian philosophers edited a revised version of the canon consisting of the Five Classics and the Four Books. The Five Classics included the five items described above; but the Four Books now consisted of Lun-Yü, Chung Yung, Ta Hsüeh, and Meng Tzu. This Sung version has remained to this day the "orthodox" Confucian canon.

The antiquity of these works and the traditional claim that Confucius himself compiled or edited them give them a status unequaled by other sacred literature. But modern Western scholars have seriously questioned the authorship and authenticity of these works. The burning of the Five Classics during the short-lived Ch'in dynasty (221–206 BCE) is known to have created immense problems for the Han scholars, who tried to restore the original texts from the different versions that they were able to retrieve. Modern research indicates that these restored originals not only show evidence of editorial liberties assumed by Han scholars, but also of outright forgery. In addition, four of the Five Classics antedate Confucius, even though tradition credits Confucius with having collected or edited all of them. Nevertheless, all five constitute the common literary heritage of all educated Chinese, both ancient and modern.

Confucianism through the Ages

Perhaps because Confucius lived in an era of great political and social unrest dominated by warlords more interested in their own comfort than anyone else's, his ideas of reform had little, if any, impact during his lifetime. Nevertheless, a select number of enthusiastic disciples combined forces in what they called the Ju school to maintain Confucian ideals in the face of competition from rival ideologies all during the Warring States period (481–221 BCE). They perpetuated the study of the ancient classics, which their Master had esteemed so highly, and preserved and transmitted the many oral traditions that were associated with Confucius.

Meng Tzu (Mencius). The next major Confucian thinker, Meng Tzu or Mencius (390–305 BCE), appeared at the end of the fourth century BCE. The book that bears his name describes how he, like Confucius before him, traveled all over China and beyond in order to persuade rulers

Taoism and Confucianism

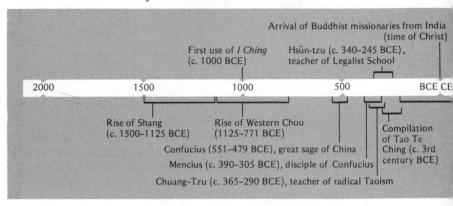

Arrival of Buddhist missionaries from India
(time of Christ)

First use of *I Ching*   Hsün-tzu (c. 340–245 BCE),
(c. 1000 BCE)   teacher of Legalist School

| 2000 | 1500 | 1000 | 500 | BCE CE |

Rise of Shang   Rise of Western Chou
(c. 1500–1125 BCE)   (1125–771 BCE)   Compilation
                                                                of Tao Te
Confucius (551–479 BCE), great sage of China   Ching (c. 3rd
Mencius (c. 390–305 BCE), disciple of Confucius   century BCE)
Chuang-Tzu (c. 365–290 BCE), teacher of radical Taoism

that he had an alternative to the endless wars between states. Two of his theories are worth noting. First, he emphasized government by compassion and virtue instead of by guile and reliance on force. He maintained that if a ruler was sincere and righteous, he would so win the hearts of neighboring populations, as well as his own, that people would flock to his standard, abandoning leaders who suffered by comparison. Second, Meng Tzu insisted on the innate goodness of human nature—an issue that has occupied Confucian thinkers for centuries. He based his view on personal observations, which had persuaded him that humans were naturally disposed to sympathetic responses. Evil, he believed, was a consequence of the corruption of this innate sympathetic disposition.

Hsün Tzu. Hsün Tzu (340–245 BCE), who followed Meng Tzu, strongly opposed the latter's doctrine of the innate goodness of human nature. In Hsün Tzu's view, humans were born with desires, and since the means of satisfying these desires were limited, conflicts were inevitable unless some kind of order or conformity could be imposed on society from above. Like an orthodox Confucian, he propagated the concept of a universal moral order, embodied in the teachings and institutions of the ancient sages.

From Persecution to State Recognition. The Classical period of intellectual creativity came to an end with the rise and establishment of the Ch'in dynasty. During this short-lived but important political period, writing was standardized, the Great Wall of China was built, and the totalitarian principles of the Legalists (who believed that people should be nothing more than organs of the state, having no personal thoughts or feelings) were adopted. The Confucian school

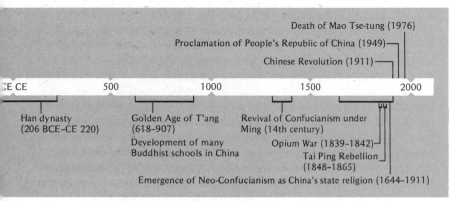

opposed many of these principles and consequently suffered. In 213 BCE a deliberate attempt was made to kill all Confucian scholars, and orders were given for the burning of the Classics.

Fortunately the Ch'in dynasty did not last long. Under its successor, the Han dynasty (206 BCE–220 CE), there was a resurgence of Confucianism heralded, according to tradition, by the first Han emperor, who demonstrated his respect for Confucius by attending the family's ancestral temple in Shantung in 195 BCE. However, imperial patronage did not entirely shield Confucianism from competition with other doctrines, such as Taoism and Legalism. Confucianism did not supplant competing ideologies until, in the reign of Emperor Wu (140–87 BCE), it became the orthodox ideology of the state and the basis of education for official positions. As a result, posthumous titles were conferred on Confucius, special honors were accorded to his descendants, and sacrifices at the ancestral temple of the Kung family were officially sponsored.

Eclipse of Confucianism. The second century was a time of deepening crisis, as power passed from the Han court into the hands of military leaders. During this period of disunity, which lasted for over three and a half centuries (221–589), Confucianism fell somewhat into disrepute. Although Confucianism remained as the foundation of all literate culture and the model for political life, various brands of Taoism and the new, foreign religion of Buddhism pushed Confucianism into the background.

This period of unrest ended with the rise of the Sui dynasty (589–618), which was followed by the T'ang dynasty. During these three centuries, Confucianism regained some measure of influence, but it never approached its former status as the leading intellectual force.

The Great Wall of China, symbol of the unification of China during the Ch'in dynasty. From the private collection of the author.

Buddhism provided the unifying element in the Sui dynasty and reached the zenith of its power and prestige during the T'ang dynasty. Taoism also had a particular appeal to the T'ang emperors, who claimed to be the descendants of Lao Tzu.

Thus, the arrival and spread of Buddhism in China put Confucianism to a severe test. Many intellectuals were attracted by the novelty and freshness of Buddhism, which they compared unfavorably to the formal, traditional, lifeless, and prescriptive character that Confucianism had assumed as the ideology of an educated elite. Taoists scoffed at Confucianists and circulated derogatory stories about Confucius and his movement. Nevertheless, Confucians maintained their distinctive character. And as long as the Imperial Academy and several other educational institutions drilled their students in the Analects and the Five Classics, Confucians felt themselves safe from rival religions. Indeed, their persistence finally gave rise to another Confucian revival.

Neo-Confucianism. From the time of the Sung dynasty (960–1127) until the establishment of the Republic of China in 1912, Confucianism

Temple of Heaven in Beijing (Peking), an Imperial Temple in which Chinese priests and the Emperor performed sacrificial rites. From the private collection of the author.

was the dominant intellectual force in Chinese history. This revived Confucianism, or Neo-Confucianism, absorbed certain metaphysical and mystical elements from Taoism and Buddhism in response to the needs of the age. Throughout this long period, no radically new school of thought or rival religion threatened Confucian hegemony in China, except for minor incursions by Islam and Christianity, neither of which were ever fully accepted into Chinese life and culture.

In promoting traditional Confucian morality, which emphasized loyalty, filial piety, self-cultivation, and involvement in society, Confucians succeeded in turning the public's view outward, toward relations with others and away from the inner contemplative or mystical life advocated by Buddhists and Taoists. Not that Confucian thinkers neglected human nature; on the contrary, self-cultivation meant for some not the study of texts, but introspection designed to bring out what was present in one's own inner world. In accord with this line of thought, Wang Yang-ming (or Wang Shou-jen, 1472–1529) identified the individual mind with the Universal Mind and maintained that the way to moral perfection lay in discovering one's innate "good knowledge." This innate principle, he insisted, was constantly in danger of being obscured by rationalizations and selfish desires.

Neo-Confucianism also spread to Japan and Korea, where it evolved into a peculiarly rigid form and nearly extinguished Buddhism. In

China, during the rule of the Mongols (1279–1368), the Confucian curriculum was at first proscribed but then reinstated as a means of recruiting officials.

The disruptive influences of Western culture since the nineteenth century have had only a superficial impact on Chinese scholars, who remain immersed in the Confucian tradition. In fact, Confucian tradition has for centuries provided the thread that has linked all Chinese together, despite the many changes Chinese culture has undergone.

Women and Changing Traditions

In 1905, the examination system for civil service, based on Confucianism, was abolished. Even more important, the Nationalist Revolution in 1911 swept away the imperial system and, with it, the institutional Confucianism. Confucian traditionalists' efforts to perpetuate the state's former commitment to sponsor sacrifices to Confucius were nullified or countered after 1916 with the emergence of the New Culture Movement, whose proponents saw Confucianism as an obstacle in the path of modernization. Although many traditional characteristics of Chinese civilization survived these ideological pogroms, the currents of social change gradually eroded Confucian ideology.

The victory of Communism in 1949 and the impact of the Cultural Revolution in 1966 may have rung down the final curtain on Confucianism. According to the Communists, Confucianism had divided society into two basic classes: the aristocrats, who possessed wealth, enjoyed leisure, were the privileged recipients of education, and were the undeserving beneficiaries of hereditary status; and the masses, who lived in utter ignorance and squalor. Communists justified their point of view, for instance, by arguing that one legacy of Confucianism was the subjugation of women, a conclusion implied by a direct quote from the Analects: "Women and small people [those who are not gentlemen] are difficult to keep" (Analects XVII.23).

Confucian teaching, Communist detractors pointed out, gave no credence to the concept that women were individuals. The code of conduct for women was defined in terms of three stages of dependence: when a female is young, she is dependent on her father; when she marries, she is dependent on her husband; and when she is old, she is dependent on her son. Each stage represented a link in an unbroken chain of dependence in the life of women. And along with acknowledging their dependent status, women were obliged to accept four Confucian criteria for virtuous female conduct: (1) a woman has to know her proper place in the home; (2) she must not speak unless she is spoken to; (3) she has to be pretty; and (4) she must be able to fulfill traditional female tasks, such as taking care of the family, cooking, and sewing.

Confucian teachings on the subject of correct behavior and ritual protocol *(li)*, which largely shaped the status of women in China through the centuries, was based on five superior/inferior relationships: (1) ruler/subject, (2) elders/juniors, (3) father/son, (4) husband/wife, and (5) eldest son/younger sons. The relationship of husband and wife established or codified the inferior role and position of women and girls. No daughter could perform ancestral rites for her parents; only sons had that right. The dire poverty of many periods in Chinese history forced many poor couples to get rid of their baby daughters, either by selling them to wealthy people or by infanticide. An alternative method of disposal was the "rearing marriage"—a custom that allowed parents to place the custody and care of a baby daughter in the hands of her future in-laws. In the last resort, females were expendable.

Moreover, to ensure family stability and purity of lineage, Confucianism demanded premarital chastity and marital fidelity for females. At times this rule was applied so rigidly that it led to absolute sexual segregation until couples were formally married. Because women were regarded primarily as sources of sons, few females were ever educated. All land inheritance was divided solely among sons. Daughters were simply "possessions," first of the father, then of their husbands and mothers-in-law.

In spite of these cultural denials of any sense of female autonomy, many women managed to transcend cultural limitations by force of character, but they were the exception rather than the rule. Others sought refuge in the Buddhist female order of the *sangha* as an alternative to marriage. Overall, Confucian ethics hardened social norms that forced women into greater seclusion than had been common in the past.

The revolution headed by Mao Tse-tung and the establishment of a Communist regime in China in 1949 brought about a radical change in the position of women. The old Confucian system of clan oppression, male dominance, bigamy, concubinage, child bethrothal, and dowries was swept aside in favor of free choice of a marital partner, monogamy, equal divorce rights for both sexes, equal rights to child custody, the right for widows to remarry, and the right to own land regardless of sex. Also in line with Communist ideology, the new regime established regulations associated with paid maternity leave, day-care centers, assignments to nursing mothers, and assistance to older women. Nonetheless, disparities persist between women in urban and rural communities and among old and new generations. But if some old stereotypes and ancient prejudices remain, the age-old Confucian order is dead.

The cultural influence of Confucianism remains potent, however. Communist vilification of Confucianism as an outdated, repressive, and retrograde ideology irrelevant to a modern, progressive, proletarian society may have compromised the status of Confucianism as a uniquely Chinese ideology, but not as a wellspring of Chinese culture.

The same may be said of Taoism and Buddhism in mainland China, because Marxist categories and Communist policies discourage religious affiliations of any kind. Drastic changes and suppressive measures have certainly changed the forms of Chinese religion, but whether such measures will permanently extinguish the religious aspirations of the Chinese people remains highly doubtful.

Chinese Observances

Millions of rural Chinese, as well as emigrants residing in other parts of Asia, have preserved the major currents of Chinese religion. The most obvious religious activities are the construction of new temples, birthday celebrations of gods and goddesses, reenactment of ancient

A funeral ceremony performed by Taoist priests at the home of the deceased. Mourners wear hemp cloth and prostrate themselves during the ceremony. From the private collection of Julian Pas.

rituals, and a series of annual festivals. An almanac, or religious calendar for festivals, lists the festival days for each year. Tradition prescribes how these festivals are to be celebrated, but customs vary from region to region.

Devotional Functions

Most Chinese cities and towns enshrine a tutelary god, who protects and watches over all municipal projects and businesses. The same function is fulfilled in homes by the guardian hearth or kitchen god, Tsao Chün or Tsai Wang, who is dispatched to heaven on New Year's Eve to report on the behavior of each family to the Jade Emperor Yü Huang, the deified personification of Tao. Women pray to various goddesses for conception, for a safe delivery at childbirth, and for the resolution of family problems. Farmers invoke the agricultural god, carpenters call on the god of carpentry, and each trade has a patron deity.

The services of a particular deity are dictated by the need of the moment. To seek the blessings of a certain god or goddess on one day and the aid of another deity the next day is quite appropriate in Chinese religion. This does not mean that the other gods and goddesses are dishonored or rejected—only that some deities are better equipped or more effective than others in responding to specific requests.

Worshipers make offerings to the temple if the resident god or goddess has answered their request, so that the maintenance of a temple is a measure of the deity's performance. A public crisis such as crop failure, famine, plague, or a similar disaster may revive interest or renew confidence or inspire hope in the power of long-neglected deities. Their temples are then quickly restored, and worshipers return to submit their prayers and offerings.

Among the numerous gods and goddesses invoked by Chinese worshipers, two have gained popular respect and devotion: the god Kuan Kung (also called Kuan Yü), and the goddess Matsu T'ien Hou. Kuan Kung is a mighty warrior and a god of war, but he is also worshiped by the common people as a beneficent healer. Merchants, professionals, and businessmen worship him as a god of avowal in sealing or affirming business contracts and as a god of wealth. Soldiers recognize him as their patron god. Local communities, social organizations, fraternities, and secret societies look to him for protection, and to supervise the operation of mutual interest and justice among fraternal ties.

Matsu, the Queen of Heaven, is particularly revered in Taiwan, and pilgrims come from all over the island to her central shrine at Peikang. Here, devotees worship Matsu with warm and enthusiastic devotion, often parading for hours in the streets in her honor.

Ceremonies and Festivals

A series of annual ceremonies and festivals is celebrated by the entire Chinese people, regardless of social group or religious orientation. No festival is more popular throughout the Chinese world than the celebration of the autumn Harvest Moon. This festival is celebrated in China on the fifteenth night of the eighth month, and people feast out of doors late at night to enjoy the glorious moon. Gifts are exchanged, and the traditional gift is a circular "moon cake."

The second major popular celebration is the Dragon Boat Festival, celebrated on the fifth day of the fifth month. This festival may represent the search for the drowned poet Ch'ü Yüan, who committed suicide because his advice was spurned by his lord, although its theme is a traditional Chinese one—the fighting of dragons in the skies. Whatever its true origin, the festival is nowadays a purely secular observance.

The third of the most popular and universally celebrated Chinese festivals is the Ch'ing Ming (Clear and Bright Festival), observed on the third day of the third month in memory of ancestors. On this date, people visit ancestral tombs, renovate them if necessary, and offer sacrifices to their ancestors. This remembrance is the most important of the three special occasions of the year reserved for visiting ancestral tombs. The second observance takes place during the entire seventh month, when special measures are taken by family members to placate and avert the harm brought about by ghosts and spirits upon the souls of departed ancestors. These measures include elaborate ceremonies and generous offerings to temples and shrines. The third annual ancestral observance is held on the first of the tenth month. It differs from similar visits to ancestral tombs in that families leave mock paper money and paper effigies of clothes and articles that are thought to be necessary in life beyond the grave.

The celebration of the New Year is undoubtedly the most important and, at the same time, the most elaborate of all Chinese festivals. In the past, all government offices throughout China remained closed for a whole month, starting ten days before the end of the old year. Nowadays, the period of celebration varies from region to region. Nevertheless, a week before the New Year—that is, on the twenty-third day of the twelfth month—every home sends off Tsao Chün (the guardian kitchen god) on his annual duty to report to the Jade Emperor. Tsao Chün is ordinarily represented by a printed image pasted on the wall above the stove—a strategic location from which to hear and keep a daily record of the words and deeds of the family before he is sent to the ethereal realm by burning. On New Year's Eve, a new picture of Tsao Chün is pasted up over the stove as a sign of his return to the home.

Offerings at the graveside by all the members of the family during the Ch'ing Ming Festival. Food offered to the deceased is later taken back home to be eaten by the family members. From the private collection of Jordan Paper.

The rituals connected with New Year's Eve include the worship of the tutelary deities of the home, of Heaven and Earth, and of ancestors. Then comes the family feast, which is attended by as many family members as possible, but not by "foreign" guests. At midnight, all attending family members approach the eldest family couple and in order of precedence prostrate themselves by touching the floor with their foreheads. The next few days of the New Year (in some places as long as a week) are spent visiting family members and friends. Several other symbolic observances mark the hope for a healthy and prosperous year.

There are numerous other observances and celebrations marking agricultural occasions, natural forces, and the birthdays of hundreds of deities. All such traditional forms of Chinese ceremonies vary from region to region, depending on the social and political climate. Nevertheless, an indestructible element in the Chinese psyche inevitably operates to permit society to adapt to any new developments with a slight effort of adjustment. The evidence lies in the demonstrated ability of the Chinese to handle the incredible diversity of beliefs and practices that surround them.

Notes

1. As, for instance, in P. A. Cohen, "The Anti-Christian Tradition in China," *Journal of Asian Studies* 20, 2 (1961): 169–80.

2. To compare the Western missionary view with that of the Chinese, see W. E. Soothill, *The Three Religions of China* (Oxford, Eng.: Milford, 1923); and C. K. Yang, *Religion in Chinese Society* (Berkeley, Calif.: University of California Press, 1961).

3. The Chinese cult of the dead (ancestral rite) is still prevalent in parts of Asia. See, for instance, E. M. Ahern, *The Cult of the Dead in a Chinese Village* (Stanford, Calif.: Stanford University Press, 1973); and M. Freedman, ed., *Family and Kinship in Chinese Society* (Stanford, Calif.: Stanford University Press, 1970).

4. On the question of the historicity of Lao Tzu, see M. Kaltenmark, *Lao Tzu and Taoism* (Stanford, Calif.: Stanford University Press, 1969), pp. 5–18.

5. For the different, and at times contradictory, positions held by scholars regarding Lao Tzu and the Tao Te Ching, see M. Eliade, *A History of Religious Ideas*, vol. 2 (Chicago: University of Chicago Press, 1982), pp. 25–33 (see esp. p. 26, n. 59).

6. From a translation by Gia-Fu Feng and Jane English (New York: Vintage Books, 1972).

7. For a detailed explanation, see M. Saso, *Taoism and the Rite of Cosmic Renewal* (Pullman, Wash.: Washington State University Press, 1972); and P. Rawson and L. Legeza, *Tao: The Eastern Philosophy of Time and Change* (New York: Avon Books, 1973).

8. The matter is still under dispute. Some experts have insisted on the differences that separate philosophical from religious Taoism. Others have maintained that there is a structural likeness between the two. For a discussion that illustrates these two approaches, see the article of N. Girardot and N. Sivin, "On the Word 'Taoist' as a Source of Perplexity. With Special Reference to the Relations of Science and Religion in Traditional China," *History of Religions* 17, No. 3 and 4 (1978): 303–30.

9. A good list of bibliographical material on Taoist techniques of immortality, magic, alchemy, and other esoteric issues can be found in Eliade, *A History*, vol. 2, pp. 428–33. For a modern popular rendering of Taoist techniques, see Da Liu, *The Tao of Health and Longevity* (New York: Schocken Books, 1978).

10. So called by Ch'u Chai and Winberg Chai, in *Confucianism* (Woodbury, N.Y.: Barron's Educational Series, 1973), p. 46.

11. Compare with Matthew 7:12 and Luke 6:31.

12. The scheme of the Five Relationships is found in the Li Chi (Canon of Ritual and Protocol). It is very doubtful that Confucius ever developed such a systematic framework, but it follows logically from his teaching of *shu*.

13. L. G. Thompson, *Chinese Religion*, 3rd ed. (Belmont, Calif.: Wadsworth, 1979), p. 136.

14. An additional Book of Music is said to have been lost in Han times.

9

Shinto

SHINTO IS THE JAPANESE NATIONAL RELIGION, and because it is closely associated with the Japanese value system, it is better assessed in terms of the social behavior and personal motivation of the Japanese people than in terms of formal beliefs or codified doctrine. Ancient religious practices, concepts of patriotism, and social attitudes that have been established by long historical precedent are all equated with the term *Shinto*.

Characteristics

To put the matter differently, Shinto represents various indigenous Japanese religious beliefs and practices, as well as a Japanese pattern of social conventions, that have persisted for centuries without necessarily being consciously regarded as a religion. Shinto is a collective term referring to a multitude of varying Japanese religious and national practices, including folklore, magic, ancestral spirits, ritualism, and nationalism. As a result, the word *Shinto,* unless it is qualified in some way, may refer to an animistic cult, a healing group, or a political ideology.

Concept of Kami

The term *Shinto* was not officially coined until the sixth century CE, and then only to distinguish the native Japanese religious systems from those introduced from abroad, such as Buddhism and Confucianism. The word derives from the Chinese term *Shen-tao,* which, roughly translated, means "the way *(tao)* of the gods/spirits *(shen).*" The Japanese prefer the Japanese term *kami-no-michi,* which also means "the way *(no-michi)* of the gods/spirits *(kami).*"

Though *kami* is usually translated as "gods" or "spirits," the term is more inclusive. Certainly, *kami* refers to the deities of heaven and earth; but it also refers to the spirit of human beings and to spirits in the universe—in animals, plants, seas, mountains, and so on. Anyone, anything, or any force that possesses "superior power" is considered a *kami.*

As a religion, then, Shinto is concerned with a variety of *kami,* from heavenly gods, deified ancestors, heroes, or emperors, to the forces or spirits of trees, rocks, mountains, rivers, foxes, and other animals. In other words, the concept of *kami* does not refer to an Absolute Being who stands apart from the world, but rather to a quality in the universe, in persons, in animals, in things, and in forces, that evokes a sense of awe, wonder, fear, attraction, or repulsion. Ceremonies and festivals centered around these *kami* are closely related to community and national traditions that are rooted in the indigenous beliefs and practices of the ancient Japanese. This peculiar awareness of *kami* is one basis of Shinto belief.

Gods, Nature, and Human Beings

The second basis of Shinto belief is awareness of the productive goodness of nature. This awareness, which is implicit in the Shinto interpretation of life, has significant philosophical and ethical implications. Central to the ethical outlook of Shinto is the recognition of *on,* the obligation individuals have to their benefactors and the gratitude that expresses it. Concepts of purity and pollution are closely related to this awareness of productivity and life.

Another important theme in Shinto is the principle of *saisei-itchi,* according to which the religious and political dimensions of life are essentially one. This concept forms the basis of national consciousness. Commitment to the nation is the ultimate commitment, because the emperor is the leader of the nation and the priest who serves the nation's *kami.* Though this principle was set aside after World War II as a result of the separation of church and state, many Japanese remain convinced that the ideal human society can only be realized when both mundane and divine activities are completely and harmoniously integrated.

It is worth reiterating that according to Shinto, the most important determinant of life here and in the hereafter is the observance of rituals and taboos, not ethical conduct. Keeping out of trouble by fulfilling obligations is more important than doing good to others. One's thoughts, words, and actions should demonstrate loyalty to, and fulfill the duties and expectations of, one's family, ancestors, emperor, country, and Shinto rites. No Shinto tradition better illustrates this preoccupation with conduct than the ritual of *hara-kiri* (literally, belly cutting), the act of honorable self-execution or ritual suicide. When an individual believes that he has failed the standard of conduct prescribed for him by tradition and wishes to prove his continuing loyalty and to redeem whatever honor has been lost, he performs *hara-kiri*.[1] Disloyalty, not disbelief, is therefore the greatest shortcoming for a Shinto adherent.

Scriptures

Shinto has no accepted or official scriptures and no fixed system of doctrine or ethics. Consequently, no binding moral code or list of commandments has ever evolved from Shinto. In fact, Shinto adherents are not at home with ethical codes or moral laws, believing that the actions of individuals are dependent on the circumstances and situations by which they are conditioned. The realm of human experience is more important to Shintoists than is the sphere of ethical codes. Nonetheless, a number of valuable records exist, two of which are considered to be the most ancient and important of all surviving documents: the Kojiki (Records of Ancient Matters) and the Nihongi or Nihon-shoki (Chronicles of Japan), both written in Chinese script and completed in 712 and 720 CE, respectively. Two other works produced in the eighth century are the Kogoshui (a historical account of early Japan) and the Manyoshu (a collection of ancient poems). Finally, two valuable documents for understanding early Shinto are the Shinsen Shojiroku (a compilation of the register of families), dating from 815; and the Engishiki or Yangi-shiki (Codes of the Engi Era), written around 927 but containing materials predating the era.

All these works contain legends, chronicles, ballads, and poems thematically centered on the divine origin and the early history of the islands of Japan. They also prescribe prayers for various ceremonial occasions, as well as patterns of behavior and action. In general, however, the concept of major catastrophes or tragic themes as well as the idea of fear-inducing divinities are absent. Ritual is mainly devoted to acts of praise: if the need arises, it may also serve to placate or reconcile the *kami*.

Mythology

The main sources of information for the beginnings of the world are the two ancient books of history, the Kojiki and the Nihongi. According to tradition, three self-created *kami* created a series of male and female *kami*. One day, two of these *kami*, Izanagi (male) and Izanami (female), were on the bridge of heaven when Izanagi lowered his celestial spear into the ocean of chaos beneath. As he raised his spear, the drops of water that fell from the shaft coagulated in the sea and formed the Japanese islands. Descending next upon the islands, these two *kami* married and gave birth to numerous *kami* offspring that are popularly worshiped in Shinto.

Besides these natural offspring, Izanagi produced the sun goddess Amaterasu and the moon god Tsukiyomi-no-Mikoto by an act of purification. Years later, Amaterasu, who was dissatisfied with the disorder prevalent among the islands, commissioned her grandson Ninigi to descend and rule them. Ninigi obeyed, and later his great-grandson, the first human emperor, succeeded as ruler. Meanwhile, the leading families of Japan (the *samurai)* and the entire Japanese people were sired by other *kami* who had settled on the islands.

The implication of this story is obvious: the islands of Japan, as well as the Japanese people, have a divine origin. Every emperor from that day until after World War II was considered a direct descendant, in an unbroken line, of the sun goddess Amaterasu.

Shinto through the Ages

Early Shinto

The little that is known about early Japanese history and religion is the fruit of speculation based on archeological discoveries, racial characteristics, and ancient legends. "The deity who originally founded this country," says one legend, "is the deity who descended from heaven and established this state in the period when heaven and earth became separated, and when the trees and herbs could speak" (Nihongi i.64 and ii.77).

The historical evidence suggests a human presence on the Japanese islands after, rather than during or before, the Paleolithic Age. Whenever they came, there is no doubt that many autonomous clans, each competing for the control of territory, lived in prehistoric Japan. In the opinion of some historians, these settlers represented three racial strains: one indigenous and the other two from the Chinese mainland and the islands of southeastern Asia.[2] The cultural, linguistic, and religious fusion of these different strands resulted in what is generally referred to today as early Shinto.

The religion of the early Japanese was an unorganized, animist worship of various *kami* that included all natural phenomena. Their reaction to the strange, the unknown, and the inexplicable was characterized by a mysterious feeling of awe and by a keen sense of the presence of superior forces. Such traits encouraged the development of occult practices carried out by males or females who were thought to possess the requisite powers to perform various religious rites— usually in the form of ceremonial purification or lustration to guard against evil, pollution, and decay by means of magic and divination.

Adherents of early Shinto made little or no distinction between the superior forces of heaven and those of earth, the world of the living and that of the dead, or animate and inanimate objects. Gods, animals, and all natural and unnatural objects were believed to be in communion with humans. As a result, the roles of the deities in the Shinto pantheon were so ill defined, and their powers so nebulous, that religion and social conventions, magic and politics, and other aspects of daily life were combined in the early Shinto religion. Two major harvest festivals, one in the spring and the other in the autumn, were held to celebrate and honor the appropriate *kami*. This tradition led, in turn, to the erection of appropriate *kami* shrines.

These patterns of belief and worship were rooted in the life of an agricultural people settled in tightly knit communities with local legends and customs. Eventually, local beliefs with universal appeal coalesced into acceptance of the supremacy of Amaterasu, the sun goddess, who was adored as the protectress of agriculture and revered as the ancestress of the ruling family. How did this come about?

As we stated earlier, ancient Japan was divided among numerous autonomous clans. Religious rites, which basically consisted of ceremonial purifications and agricultural rituals, were performed either by clan chieftains or by members of the community who were respected agents of occult powers—a magical attribute that is recognized as so-called folk Shinto in modern Japan. These autonomous clans dominated their own territory and prescribed the *kami* that should serve as local gods. Religious observances in each autonomous enclave gradually centered around the local clan's tribal site, where the tutelary *kami* of the clan resided and eventually was enshrined.

Some time around the third or fourth century, one dominant group, the Yamato clan, established its authority over the other clans through conquest and consolidation. Although regional traditions and prac-

The Miyajima Itsukushima Shrine, situated off the shore of Miyajima Island, is dedicated to the goddess Itsukushima-Hima, daughter of the storm god Susanowo. Except for the tame deer and for unpreventable events, no person or animal is allowed to be born or to die on the sacred island. In the background is the Torii (the sacred gateway), extending into the sea with the rest of the sacred buildings. Courtesy of Japan Information Centre, Consulate General of Japan, Toronto.

tices at local shrines continued with little or no change, the Yamatos imposed their traditions and their tutelary *kami*, Amaterasu, the sun goddess, on the other clans and established the authority of their chieftain to perform certain religious rites on behalf of all the people. Successive chieftains of the Yamato clan gradually came to be recognized as the rulers and chief priests of the nation. In time, their legends and deities dominated popular belief, which included dogmas associated with the divine origin of the chief national leader and the country of Japan and the superiority of the Japanese race.

As it evolved, the Shinto pantheon of gods came to encompass both human and nonhuman personalities and elements. For instance, early Shinto characterized both human beings and animals as gods and attributed the power of speech to plants and rocks, among other objects—a belief that persists among some modern adherents. Shinto always has recognized no firm dividing line between the mortal and immortal, the human and divine, the spiritual and material worlds. Gods, spirits, humans, animals, principalities, and powers operate on both sides of the line separating the spiritual from the material, moving across it at will depending on the force of the influence they command.

Shinto, Confucianism, and Buddhism

The history of modern Shinto can be summed up as a course of contact and change in a series of ebbs and flows between the sociopolitical creed of popular and national Shinto and the Chinese systems of Confucianism and Buddhism. Shinto, Confucianism, and Buddhism have combined, through the force of circumstances, to mold the Japanese nation's composite religious and cultural life by a process of gradual accretion. The elements of confrontation, conflict, and persecution that characterize the religious lives of so many other cultures proved the exception rather than the rule in Japan. By and large, tolerance prevailed among all three religious systems throughout Japanese history, although their interaction never resulted either in full harmony or in complete absorption of one by another.

Between the third and sixth centuries the Japanese, through minor expeditions associated with war and trade, came into contact with Chinese culture and religion, which, compared with Japanese standards, seemed far superior. The ruling Yamato dynasty therefore sent envoys to China to study Chinese civilization as a prerequisite to social and cultural reform at home. One effect of this admiration of Chinese models was that Yamato chieftains, although retaining their role as high priests, assumed the title of emperor in the Chinese sense and tradition. The aristocratic governing elite learned to read and write China's monosyllabic language, and soon efforts were made to use Chinese script to express the Japanese polysyllabic language. Inevitably, many Japanese were particularly attracted to Confucian ethics and/or to the Buddhist religion.

In a very short time, elements of Chinese superstition, the cult of ancestor worship, and Taoist philosophical concepts were incorporated into Shinto. It was Confucianism, however, that gave the Japanese the model that they were looking for to further their religious and national development. Although Confucian ethics came to govern Japanese morality, Confucianism's greatest influence was on the development of Japanese legal and educational institutions. Confucianism, unlike Buddhism, was a pragmatic religion—a system of practical ethics, with little or no room for creed and dogma. In the spheres of family and ruler-subject relationships, Confucian concepts quickly took hold in Japanese life.

The syncretistic character of Shinto also facilitated the introduction of Buddhism into Japan in the sixth century. Buddhism was particularly influential in promoting higher ideals and in encouraging the arts, the sciences, and literature. Within a century, Buddhism had become the religion of the upper classes, since its artistic and ceremonial forms, its organizational structures, and its highly developed doctrine or philosophical outlook had few if any counterparts in the Shinto customs and traditions that prevailed among the common people.

Surprisingly, the advent of Chinese culture and religion in Japan did not eclipse the old forms. Although Buddhism and Confucianism prospered under the patronage of the imperial court and dominated the intellectual outlook of government officials, Shinto's solar deity, Amaterasu, proved a convenient vehicle through which to assert the divine origin of the imperial ruler of the people and of the land. In this way, Shinto remained part of the political machinery of the court. Amaterasu was elevated to the status of a national deity, and a great national shrine to honor her was established at Ise, where virgin imperial princesses conducted appropriate ceremonies. Meanwhile, large Buddhist temples were built and dedicated under the auspices of priests conducting Shinto ceremonies. Many Buddhist temples in Japan still include within their precincts protective Shinto shrines erected to house guardian spirits.

Buddhism and Shinto became most closely integrated during the classical Heian period (794–1192), which was characterized by peaceful coexistence and the intermingling of the two religions.[3] Even as Buddhism gradually attained an overpowering dominance, Shinto's oral traditions, legends, and myths were documented for the first time in the form of Shinto "scriptures." Buddhism was modified or adapted to accommodate the numerous *kami* of Shinto as manifestations of the Buddhist pantheon of preexistent Buddhas; and, in turn, Shinto added to its pantheon the Buddhist deities introduced from China.

The merging of Shinto deities with those of the Buddhist pantheon resulted in the rapid spread of Buddhism among the general population.[4] Buddhist priests took charge of Shinto shrines, Shinto priests were relegated to minor roles in the officiating of ceremonies, and Shinto shrines and celebrations took on a decidedly Buddhist flavor. Amalgamation or eradication did not ensue, however. What developed was a division of labor. Ecclesiastical organization, preaching, dogma, and funeral services became the responsibility of Buddhist priests; births, marriages, and the celebration of seasonal festivals and national victories were assumed by Shinto priests. Exorcism and divination were shared responsibilities, as were rituals associated with ancestor worship, which, under Confucian influence, had become a national practice.

Gradually, Shinto became, to ordinary people at least, almost indistinguishable from Buddhism. Between the twelfth and thirteenth centuries, the new cults of Amida, Zen, and Nichiren, which represented Japanese adaptations of Buddhism, enlisted such a groundswell of popular support that despite official government persecution, they eventually became the most important Buddhist groups in Japan. Attempts by Shinto priests to reverse the order of primacy in Japanese religious life were of no avail, as Buddhism continued to dominate the political and religious life of the nation.

Confucianism, which never achieved the status of an independent religion in Japan, provided the ideological framework of the governing feudal regime, complementing in secular affairs Shinto's role as the official religion of government. Ancestor worship was a key Confucian contribution to Japanese society, as was a system of ethics that became the basis for Japanese social conduct. During the eighteenth and nineteenth centuries, Confucianism abetted the rise of the loyalist movement, the restoration of imperial rule, and the reestablishment of Shinto as a national cult preeminent over all other religions.

Of course, efforts to revive Shinto had never been abandoned. Successive Shinto apologists, imbued with a fervent nationalistic spirit, had attempted to purge Shinto of all "foreign" influences. For these thinkers, the simplicity and unsophisticated traditions of Shinto represented the apex of religious thought and the ideal for which they should strive. They considered Buddhist philosophy and metaphysics as corrupting and irrelevant influences on a people of divine origin who were descended from the *kami*. Not surprisingly, advocates of a return to Shinto basics cited the prerogative of the divine emperor to rule the country to justify their arguments. Over the centuries, various local Shinto sects developed around certain personalities, particular traditions, and specific shrines. Finally, in the nineteenth century a political upheaval enabled Shinto nationalism to triumph. Meanwhile, another foreign religion, Christianity, sought to establish roots in Japanese soil.

Shinto and Christianity

Japanese contact with the West dates from 1542, when Portuguese explorers landed in Japan. Seven years later, Francis Xavier and two other Spanish Jesuits came to spread Christianity among the Japanese. Soon they were followed by other Catholic missionaries, both Jesuits and Franciscans, whose efforts met with considerable success, especially in southern Japan. No doubt, because of the tolerant attitude

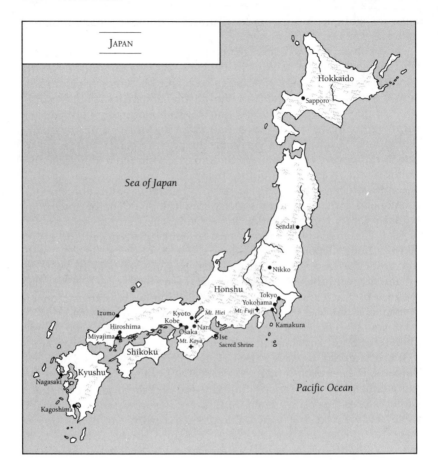

of Buddhist and Shinto leaders, Christianity at first enjoyed the favor of the political authorities as well as the public.

It was not long, however, before the imperial court, as well as Shinto and Buddhist leaders, recognized in Christianity a dangerous rival. What provoked their enmity and contributed to a rising tide of anti-Christian sentiment was the arrogant assumption of Christian missionaries that all religions but their own were inferior and that their mission was to convert the nation. Another contributing cause of irritation was the Christian doctrine that all converts owed allegiance to the pope in Rome. In addition, the rivalry for converts and control between the Jesuits and the Franciscans convinced the imperial court that Christian missionaries were the harbingers of Western political intrigue and aggression.

As a result, Japanese authorities undertook a series of campaigns, mounted between 1587 and 1638, to suppress Christianity. First, all Christian missionaries were banned from Japan. Next, warnings and mild persecutions were directed against Japanese Christian converts. Initially, only those who clung to the Christian faith with tenacity were put to death. The disclosure of pockets of resolute Christian resistance, where even missionaries might find shelter, soon led to wholesale persecution, however. As the wave of persecution gathered force, leading to the torture, imprisonment, and death of Christian converts and missionaries, Japanese authorities severed all relationships with the West and, eventually, eradicated all overt signs of Christianity in Japan. For the next two hundred years Japan remained isolated from the West, and Christianity survived only among clandestine groups operating underground in certain parts of the country.

The propagation of Christianity continued covertly until the 1880s, when Japanese authorities realized that their nation's isolation had caused it to lag behind Western civilization. A renewal of contact with Western nations and a government policy calculated to exploit international trade and technology eased the strictures imposed on Christians in Japan. Meanwhile, the government officially sponsored a national Shinto cult for the purpose of inculcating loyalty and obedience. No efforts were spared to establish a theocratic state based on Shinto.

State Shinto

An immediate effort was made by the young Emperor Meiji, who ascended to the throne in 1868, to dissociate Shinto from Buddhism. Under his rule, Shinto was designated the national religion, and most shrines and priests were brought under government control. Persecution of Buddhists inevitably followed: temples were closed, estates appropriated, and priests dispossessed and dispersed. Buddhism proved too deeply rooted in the culture and tradition of the people to be easily exterminated, however. Despite official disfavor and occasional periods of suppression, Buddhism gradually recovered much of its lost prestige, although it never regained its former stature.

In 1882, the Meiji government recognized three religious organizations: Buddhist, Christian, and Shinto. All religious institutions and organizations that were not associated with Buddhism or Christianity were classified as Shinto, which itself was divided into two categories or groups: Jinja, or Shrine Shinto; and Kyoha, or Sectarian Shinto. As a national obligation, the government required all Japanese, whatever their religious inclinations, to participate in the rites conducted at the State Shinto shrines. Such rituals were considered patriotic expressions and sentiments of respect owed to the divine imperial personage. In addition, the government promoted Shinto ancestral traditions through systematic instruction in all schools and assumed responsibility for the administration and supervision of religious organizations, the priesthood, and religious ceremonies.

From 1868 to 1945, the government promoted Shinto as the national religion of Japan. The test of loyalty to the government was acceptance of State Shinto. Other religions, such as Buddhism and Christianity, were able to maintain a presence in Japan so long as they were willing to accommodate themselves to the government's views on State Shinto, which included beliefs in a land divinely created, in a succession of emperors descended in unbroken line from Amaterasu, and in a people of divine origin. Under the sanction of religious belief, the government maintained absolute political and military power.[5]

Belief in the emperor as the living incarnation of the sun goddess Amaterasu was based on longstanding traditions predating the twelfth century, but in the nineteenth century this belief was enshrined in dogma. Accordingly, the emperor was considered sacred, inviolable, and a manifestation of the Absolute. At its most extreme, the dogma incorporated the belief that the emperor was a god in human form who deserved the worship and devotion of his people. In addition, some believed that the emperor was not only the head of the Japanese nation, but also the ruler of the entire universe. By extension and another leap of faith, they also believed that the Japanese nation was destined to rule the world.

This edifice of state religion endured until December 15, 1945, when the supreme commander of the Allied forces of occupation ordered the emperor and the Japanese government to disestablish State Shinto, to

Shinto

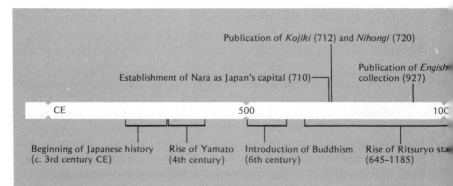

Publication of *Kojiki* (712) and *Nihongi* (720)

Establishment of Nara as Japan's capital (710)

Publication of *Engish* collection (927)

CE   500   100

Beginning of Japanese history (c. 3rd century CE)

Rise of Yamato (4th century)

Introduction of Buddhism (6th century)

Rise of Ritsuryo sta (645–1185)

relegate rites performed by the imperial family to the status of private religious ceremonies, and to place all existing religions, including Shrine Shinto and Sectarian Shinto, on the same footing, with equal entitlement to support and protection. On January 1, 1946, the emperor publicly denounced the "false conception that the emperor is divine and that the Japanese people are superior to other races and fated to rule the world."

The impact, in both practical and theoretical terms, of this sudden reversal of Shinto hegemony was too widespread to document here.[6] A few examples will have to suffice. Imperial portraits, which had been kept in sacred repositories in schools, were removed. The imperial chrysanthemum crest that had identified all court buildings was obliterated and banned from future issues of postage stamps and currency. Some 110,000 State Shinto shrines, which had been dependent on and supported by the national government, suddenly found themselves thrown back on their own resources and on the generosity of voluntary contributors. Fundamental Shinto doctrines and ideologies that had advocated ritual suicide as an honorable act of expiation were suddenly declared "myths, legends, and false conceptions." The emperor, who had been venerated as divine, was now regarded as a mere mortal.

Today, religion and state in Japan are completely separate. There is no compulsory national religion, religious instruction in public schools is prohibited, and freedom of religion is guaranteed to all. According to the postwar constitution, the emperor is considered "the symbol of the state and of the unity of the people." His function as the high priest of Shinto is restricted to officiating at traditional ceremonies in one of three shrines within the imperial palace grounds. State Shinto is—at least for the present—dead.

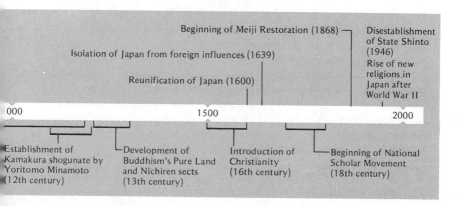

Women in Shinto Tradition

There is some evidence that early Japan was politically matriarchal, and priestesses and shamanesses played an important role in early Shinto. All this changed when Japan came into contact with China and wholeheartedly adopted Confucian ethics. By the eighth century, women were no longer permitted to rule, and by the fifteenth century they had lost virtually all civil rights. Only during periods of severe crisis were some women politically influential, but only briefly.

Contact with the West during the nineteenth and twentieth centuries has done little to change the rights of women. Modern Japanese males have simply shifted their allegiance from feudal lords to the presidents of corporations and businesses. Husbands still consider their wives to be functional creatures essential to the fulfillment of family life: as mothers of their children and managers of their households. In traditional Confucian style, the ideal Japanese family consists of three generations living under one roof. Marriage provides a line of

The Grand Shrine of Ise on the Shima peninsula of Nagoya, dedicated to the worship of the sun goddess Amaterasu. The sacred precincts are secluded behind one outer and two inner fences. The buildings, which conform to ancient Japanese architecture, are made of unpainted cypress wood. The shrine (at left) has been rebuilt every twenty years since the day of Emperor Temmu in the seventh century CE.   Courtesy of Japan Information Centre, Consulate General of Japan, Toronto.

heirs for the "ancestral house." Marriages are still arranged by parents and a barren woman is promptly returned to her home.

Another role that is symptomatic of the status of women in urban Japan is that of *geisha* girls. Though a *geisha* is principally an accomplished entertainer, a sympathetic listener, and a graceful hostess, not simply a lover or prostitute, hers is a secondary—never a primary—role. Large firms subsidize all-male gatherings at *geisha* houses, where business is often conducted and ties among coworkers strengthened. Female employees, numerous as they are in the Japanese business world, have few opportunities beyond jobs as clerks or secretaries.

In rural areas the impact of women that function as mediums and diviners is still quite strong. Their practices involve fortunetelling, praying for and healing the sick, and contacting the *kami*—the spirits of the dead. Many of these women are charismatic leaders who have received a vision and possess the power of healing. A few have been social reformers; others have founded "new religions."

There are relatively few Japanese feminist leaders. On the whole, Japanese women tend to accept male dominance. Confucian tradition by and large prevails, and society expects women to settle down to marriage and a family life. Women's rights and full equality seem to be a distant dream.

Shinto Groups

Shrine Shinto

Shrine Shinto is Japan's indigenous religion. The perpetuation of its religious practices is centered in rites related to numerous shrines found in every locality of Japan. Like all other Shinto groups, Shrine Shinto originated in the worship of nature and spirit. Though shrines were rare in early prehistoric times, when trees, mountains, rivers, rocks, lightning, and so forth were all worshiped directly, in the course of time worshipers built shrines to house the gods or the objects of worship. Today these shrines include a variety of structures, from simple, modest shelters to elaborate buildings. Many are nothing more than worship halls; others are sacred enclosures identified by a fence or even a straw rope hung with paper cutouts surrounding the object to be worshiped. Currently, there are about 110,000 shrines throughout the islands of Japan.

As we noted above, the Meiji government, in its attempt to make Shinto the official national or state religion, had sponsored and partly supported Shrine Shinto. Nationalistic sentiment was particularly associated with certain shrines—especially those that were closely

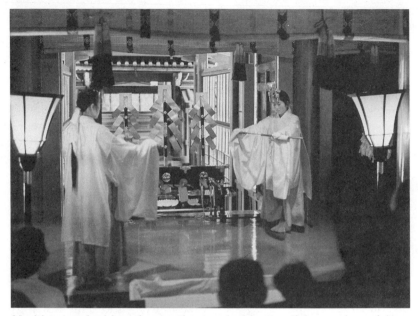

Novitiate temple girls performing the annual celebration of the sacred sword dance during the Yayoi festival in March in the Futaarasan shrine, in Nikko, Japan.
Courtesy of British Airways (BOAC), Toronto, Canada.

linked to emperor worship. The shrine at Ise, for example, came to be known as the Grand Shrine of the sun goddess Amaterasu.

Under State Shinto, the government administered the shrines and designated some of them as centers for the worship of Amaterasu and the emperor. In this way, shrines, which for centuries had been identified with and maintained by particular families, became subject to bureaucratic control. Political or military friends of government officials often were made priests. All rites, ceremonies, and festivals were prepared by government and centered around loyalty to and worship of the emperor and Amaterasu.

Today, Shinto shrines are entirely dependent on public contributions. The priests, no longer government officials, are not bound to invoke the aid of particular deities. Some shrines are devoted exclusively to historical emperors, such as Meiji, Omi, and Hideyoshi, whereas others are dedicated to deities. The most common objects of worship are mirrors, swords, stones, trees, mountains, caves, pigeons, snakes, and foxes.

No clear distinction is made between the *kami* of human beings and those of natural phenomena. Humans have the potential to become *kami*. Human defilements and impurities can easily be purified by very simple ceremonies, since human nature is regarded as essentially good.

Shrine Shinto is characterized by ritual rather than by doctrine and by the absence of any legalistic code of ethics, systematic statement of creed, or collection of sacred writings. Instead of indulging in speculative abstractions about another world, Shrine Shinto emphasizes this physical, material world and respect and veneration for traditional values and forms. Its primary aim is to promote human health and happiness—not in a future blissful realm, but here and now, in this world.

Sectarian Shinto

Sectarian Shinto encompasses thirteen heterogeneous Shinto sects that were grouped arbitrarily by the Meiji government in 1882 as an administrative convenience designed to foster government control. As a condition of government approval to function as religious sects, they were required to fulfill certain obligations. Any group not specifically identified under government regulations had no choice except to seek affiliation with a group that was.

For a while, the Meiji government managed to maintain administrative control over all these religious sects, but gradually a few were permitted to become independent. Since the end of World War II and the disestablishment of State Shinto, all restrictions have been removed, and many Shinto groups that were nominally affiliated with the thirteen established sects have become independent. However, the purely arbitrary classification of thirteen Shinto sects that was established by government fiat still survives. The classification contains five groups:

1. Pure Shinto (3 sects)
2. Confucian Shinto (2 sects)
3. Mountain Shinto (3 sects)
4. Purification Shinto (2 sects)
5. Redemptive Shinto (3 sects)

Estimates of the number of subsects range as high as six hundred, although the exact total is not known. Unlike Shrine Shinto, Sectarian Shinto is characterized by large congregations that meet regularly for religious services and that incorporate elaborate rituals and modern sermons. Some of these sects lay claim to a historical founder, an organized membership, a canonized scripture, a codified doctrine, and a prescribed ritual. Others are centered around ancient traditional practices and imperialistic loyalism. Many actively promote and publicize their doctrines and practices with missionary fervor.

Pure Shinto Sects. The three groups in this category are Tai-kyo, Shinri-kyo, and Taisha-kyo. In the tradition of early Shinto, none acknowledges an authentic historical founder, and all three claim to represent the authentic embodiment of "pure" Shinto as practiced in prehistoric times and seek to perpetuate ancient beliefs and practices, and to foster national patriotism. The group's name implies purification from all contaminating foreign influences. Its teachings are based on the classical myths, with special emphasis on gratitude to ancestors and loyalty to emperors. The predominant deities in all three sects are the two parent deities of the Japanese people and the sun goddess Amaterasu. Loyalty to the state, anonymous charity, moral virtue, and purification through appropriate rites are among the basic aims of these sects.

Confucian Shinto Sects. This group comprises two sects: Shusei-ha and Taisei-kyo. Their main purpose is to emphasize the ethical principles of Confucianism along with the fundamentals of Shinto; accordingly, they exalt patriotism and are considered to be the most nationalistic of the Shinto sects. They embrace divination, fortunetelling, and astrology, and adherents rely on prayer and meditation to gain inner tranquillity.

Mountain Shinto Sects. The three sects that associate mountains with the dwelling place of the *kami* are Jikko-kyo, Fuso-kyo, and Mitake-kyo. Mountain worship is an ancient tradition whose origins are lost in Japanese antiquity. The custom is to erect small shrines on every mountain peak, at which the indwelling *kami* are invoked and honored with a combination of occult practices, purification rites, and elaborate ceremonies. Organized bands of pious pilgrims climb to the top of these sacred mountains to exalt the holy dwelling places of the deities. Although all mountains are believed to harbor *kamis,* Mount Fuji and Mount Ontake are the most sacred (and popular). Believers strive for simplicity and purity in their everyday lives and for universal brotherhood, or love of humankind.

Purification Shinto Sects. Almost all Shinto sects perform some form of purification rites; but two sects, Shinshu-kyo and Misogi-kyo, place a special emphasis on ceremonial purity. Their performances of ritualistic purification are perpetuations of age-old ceremonies associated with purity of soul, mind, and body from evil. Followers of these two sects worship ancient Shinto deities, accept the Kojiki and the Nihongi as scriptures, and uphold filial piety, moral living, dutiful citizenship, and emperor loyalty. The Shinshu-kyo purification rites

A shugendo *priest (wandering mountain ascetic) in traditional costume blows the* horagai, *or trumpet shell.* Courtesy of Japan Information Centre, Consulate General of Japan, Toronto, Canada.

include a fire-subduing ceremony, a hot water ritual, the twanging of bowstrings, and a rice-cooking ceremony, all performed together with the recitation of prayers. The rites of Misogi-kyo consist of several rituals; the most important is the act of proper breathing, by which one can commit the direction of one's life to the divine will. Proper breathing is also considered to contribute to physical and mental well-being, because breathing is the source of life.

Redemptive Shinto Sects. This group of three sects represents a radical departure from traditional Shinto. Kurozumi-kyo, Konko-kyo, and Tenri-kyo sects were founded by modern individuals whose revelatory experiences are characterized by a message of redemption. Though the labels are misleading, they are also known as "faith healing" sects or sects of "peasant origin," because faith healing does play a part in all three sects and because two of the three founders were of peasant origin and, at first, drew their strongest support from peasant folk. The popularity of these sects can be attributed, at least in part, to the magnetic personalities of the founders.

All three sects are theistic and attribute the source of all existence to a divine power, and the achievement of a happy and healthy life to "pure" faith in the divine source. The question of who or what is divine is not considered important, provided that the individual recognizes his or her inner divine qualities and strives to actualize this divine power in everyday life. A vital missionary spirit that may account for the very successful and extensive influence of these sects pervades each of them.

Kurozumi-kyo was founded by Kurozumi Munetada (1780–1850), the son of a chief priest of a sun goddess shrine. Three religious crises, or revelations, marked the beginning of Kurozumi's mission in 1814. He received his sacred commission in his third experience, which took place while he was praying to the rising sun goddess. In obedience to her will, he set out to convert the world to the belief that the sun goddess was the source of all happiness and health. Although numbering other Shinto deities in his sectarian pantheon, Kurozumi believed that the sun goddess was the all-inclusive, universal parent spirit, the source of all things, and the sustaining guide of all believers. Followers were enjoined to keep the Seven Rules of the Divine Law, which consisted of faith, humility, self-possession, compassion, sincerity, gratitude, and industry.

After Kurozumi's death, his poems, letters, and written observations were all recognized as sacred scriptures by his followers. Kurozumi himself was deified and is now worshiped along with Shinto deities and the sun goddess not only in Japan, but also in Korea and Manchuria, where proselytizing activity has won converts.

One of the chief attractions of this sect is faith healing—achieved sometimes by faith and the recitation of purification ritual, sometimes by rubbing affected parts of the body in order to transfer therapeutic energy from the healer to the patient, sometimes by hypnosis, and sometimes through the agency of consecrated water drunk by the patient or sprayed over the patient from the priest's mouth, or even sprinkled on a piece of paper bearing the patient's name.

Konko-kyo was founded by the peasant Kawade (1814–1883), who, in a vision in 1859, was assigned to mediate between Tenche-kane-no-kami (Great Father of the Universe) and humanity. Tenche-kane-no-kami is a modern accretion to Shinto who is described as the source and eternal spirit of everything, the *kami* of infinite love and mercy. Believing that all human suffering and calamity result from two basic defects—ignorance of Tenche-kane-no-kami's love and violation of his laws—adherents of Konko-kyo hold that all people should have faith in this Great Father of the Universe, love each other, fulfill their respective responsibilities, and pray for peace, happiness, and prosperity in the world.

Since Kawade left no writings, his teachings and ideas were compiled by his followers and are now considered the sacred scriptures of the sect. Adherents pay special reverence to Kawade as the founder of their religion, but he is not considered a deity. They reject all occult activities, ascetic practices, and religious austerities. Believers are enjoined to rely for strength on their inner creative spiritual powers, the gift of the Great Father of the Universe. Although it is strongest in southeastern Japan, the missionary efforts have extended this sect to northern and central China, Taiwan, Singapore, Hong Kong, and Hawaii.

Tenri-kyo was founded by Nakayama Miki (1798–1887), a peasant woman and a former Buddhist of the Pure Land sect who claimed to have been possessed during a trance in 1838 by a god calling himself Tenri-o-no-mikito (the God of Divine Reason). He commanded her and her whole family to dedicate everything to his cause for the sake of humankind. In keeping with these directions, Nakayama gave away all her property and devoted herself to the teaching of the true God, Tenri, supplemented by mental cures and faith healing.

Nakayama taught that human life is based on reason and that ultimate reality is Divine Reason, Tenri. Those who live according to reason prosper; those who violate it perish. According to Nakayama, happiness and prosperity in this life are the will of Divine Reason, which human beings oppose by substituting misfortune and suffering in pursuit of their own selfish ends. Original purity can be restored if one can get rid of the accumulated "dust" of the inner vices. Through faith in Tenri, or Divine Reason, one can gain mastery over vices, sweep off the "dust," attain divine favor, and reach ultimate contentment.

The activities and institutions of Tenri-kyo are nationwide, and its missionary efforts have extended to various countries in Asia. To this date, Nakayama's direct descendants hold the office of chief priest. A strong, organized, central administrative system, public services, and faith healing, among other factors, account for the rapid growth of Tenri-kyo.

Folk (Popular) Shinto

Various Shinto beliefs and practices are not generally included in Sectarian or Shrine Shinto because they are so diversified and so disorganized. For the lack of a more descriptive label, these religious tendencies are usually referred to as Folk (or Popular) Shinto.[7] Generally speaking, Folk Shinto emphasizes aspects of Shinto worship that are common but peripheral elements of other sects. Superstition, occult practices, and devotion accorded to innumerable deities whose images or symbols dot the countryside are its most common features.

As would be expected, household rituals and ceremonies are of primary importance to Folk Shinto, especially in celebration or remembrance of family on such occasions as births, marriages, business ventures, deaths, and anniversaries associated with relatives and ancestors. Rituals are centered on the *kami-dana* (*kami* shelf), a miniature shrine that serves as a family altar and is usually mounted in a small alcove above a closet door in the main room. Well-to-do families maintain small shrines in gardens. The devout Shinto steps in front of the *kami-dana* early in the morning, after washing or bathing, to pay homage to the deity. First, he or she bows, then claps the hands twice (to get the attention of the deity), then bows again for a moment before going to work or beginning the day's chores.

On special occasions, worshipers first purify themselves by bathing and then by waving a small branch of the sacred *sakaki* tree (or an imitation made of hemp and paper) at each of the shoulders while standing in front of the *kami-dana*. It is also customary to announce special occasions (such as visits to the tutelary shrine) before the *kami-dana*.

Similar rituals are associated with the thousands of popular deities whose images and symbols are found throughout the land. Prominent among such deities are Daikoku-ten, the god of luck and good fortune; Ryu-jin, the serpent deity who controls the rain and the wind and who acts as the guardian god; Doso-jin, the guardian deity of the crossroads; and Kamado-no-kami, the deity who presides over the kitchen fires.

Simple rituals express the devotion of a devout Shinto worshiper. A passerby usually stops before any symbol or image of a deity, claps the hands twice, and bows in silence before going on. A tossed stone that happens to land on the image is considered to be a sign of good fortune.

Slightly different are the ceremonies and rituals connected with the purification of land used for construction. Ceremonies in such cases are usually performed before the earth is broken, in order to appease the particular *kami* of the land. Appropriate rituals are also performed to guard against accidents on bad corners, broken or shaky bridges, sagging roofs, unlucky days, and so on.

Generally speaking, Folk Shinto acknowledges or gives credence to people—usually women distinguished by wild appearance and behavior—who claim to possess the power to communicate with the spirits of the dead or to invoke any of the deities. That people still consult these "spirit-possessed" authorities for advice on queer feelings, strange behavior, unusual events, or physical disabilities testifies to a widespread and popular reliance on black magic, witchcraft, and numerous other occult practices.

New Religions

Although hundreds of religious sects that have emerged since World War II have categorized themselves as "new religions," many of them were in existence prior to World War II as involuntary affiliates of officially recognized Sectarian Shinto sects. Some sects are of such recent origin, however, that their founders are still living—a circumstance that does not make an analysis of their teachings any simpler, since these leaders guide their followers by means of oracles or revelations. Similarly, there are no reliable estimates as to the number of these new sects and no satisfactory criterion for classification. Consequently, only a general characterization of these new Shinto sects can be offered.

Frequently a magnetic, or charismatic, personality who has had an unusual experience and possesses an extraordinary ability becomes the central figure of a new movement. Next, an organizational figure is required to ensure the continuity of this new sect. Innovations combined with ancient traditions, uncomplicated rituals, and promises of physical and material benefits accruing from purposeful daily activity form the core features of these new sects.

The teachings of most of these sects represent a reconstitution of traditional values and a reformulation of the general metaphysical outlook derived largely from one or more of the following backgrounds: Shinto, Buddhist, Confucian, Taoist, Christian. The characteristic function of such groups is to provide the individual with a stable basis for coping with pressing contemporary problems. Unfortunately, no reliable evidence exists of their strength or influence, although undoubtedly, like so many other religious groups, they will leave their mark upon Shinto character as a whole.

Shinto Observances

Shinto observances involve religious and cultural practices that include folklore, magic, pilgrimage, ritual, worship, and nationalism. The complexity of Shinto practices emerged from the vigorous flow of Japanese religious and social history. The result has been a phenomenal growth of ritual evolving from diverse origins and reflecting a wide variety of influences. Elements of animism, fertility rites, ancestor and hero rites, and nature worship are only a few ingredients.

At the birth of a child, the usual custom is to register the baby at the Shinto shrine where the family normally worships. Children are also taken to the shrine during their third, fifth, and seventh years. Marriages usually take place at a Shinto shrine with a Shinto priest officiating. Funerals, however, are frequently conducted by a Buddhist priest, and on these occasions the mourning family visits the local Buddhist temple.

Ceremonial rites are performed daily by the priests in Shinto shrines. Individuals visit these shrines at any time for personal devotion or to obtain charms or talismans. On entering the shrine, devotees bow toward the *honden* (*kami* altar), make a special offering, and clap their hands as a symbol of communication with the *kami* before advancing farther.

In addition to visiting local shrines, many Shintos maintain a *kami-dana* in their homes, business places, and workshops (see p. 238). On it are placed memorial tablets made of wood or paper, each inscribed with the name of an ancestor or a patron *kami*. In most cases, a miniature shrine containing a sacred mirror, strips of paper inscribed with sacred texts, and charms or talismans occupies the center of the *kami-dana*. On special family occasions, such as births, weddings, or anniversaries, candles are lit at the *kami-dana* and flowers, food, and *sake* (an alcoholic beverage made from rice) are offered by the family head, while the remaining members sit on the floor with bowed heads. The more important the occasion, the more elaborate the ceremony.

Festivals

Great preparations and special family observances take place in anticipation of the New Year festival. Houses are cleansed of the evil influences of the past and the *kami-dana* is renewed with fresh memorial tablets, strips of sacred texts, charms, flowers, and so on. Both actions invite good fortune for the future. Bills are paid as well, and

The annual Jidai Matsuri festival performed on October 23 by Shinto devotees. The ark represents the presence of the kami and is carried through the streets.   Courtesy of Japan Information Center, Toronto, Canada.

special food is prepared to obviate the necessity of cooking during the first three days of the New Year. Pounded rice, prepared with special care and ritual, is the appropriate New Year's dish. Homes are decorated with special arrangements of flowers, pine branches, bamboo sticks, straw, and white paper (to indicate purification). Where possible, 108 peals of bells are rung at Shinto shrines on New Year's Eve, marking the banishment of evil in preparation for the New Year.

The Girls' Festival (also called the Dolls' Festival), a fête emphasizing family and national life, is celebrated annually on March 3. Fifteen or more dolls are arrayed on ascending ceremonial shelves. The highest shelf is occupied by a brilliantly costumed emperor and empress, followed, in descending order, by ladies-in-waiting, ministers of the court, musicians, and footmen. At the lowest level are the dolls' furniture and utensils.

The Boys' Festival, which is celebrated on May 5, provides each family with an opportunity for proclaiming to the community its good fortune in begetting sons. Colored paper carp, each representing one boy in order of age, are suspended one below the other. Inside the house are *samurai* dolls and weapons, symbolizing courage, loyalty, and patriotism.

A great festival of the dead, called Bon, is held some time during the middle of the year. The souls of the departed are believed to return to their homes, where they are entertained and fed by their families. When the feast is over, farewell fires, adapted to the local environment, light the souls on their return journey. In coastal communities, for instance, tiny paper or wood boats bearing lanterns and food are launched on the waters and set adrift.

Numerous other festivals commemorate either important dates in the long annals of Japanese imperial history or seasonal events. For instance, an especially elaborate ceremony, Nihi-namé, occurs in October–November and celebrates the offering of the first fruits of harvest. Singing, dancing, and feasting are the main events of this festival. Strict Shintos do not eat the new season's rice until the entire ceremony is performed and the rice *kami* is honored. There are also seasonal flower festivals to celebrate the blossoming of peach trees and irises. Flowers, dolls, and lanterns are carried about in celebration.

Regional festivals are conducted to honor particular aspects of a local shrine. Artisans of most kinds venerate their own patron *kamis* and observe special days in their honor. Shinto *kamis* are recognized by their own special festivals, when flowers and other gifts are brought to the shrines. Most Shinto sects celebrate the birth and death of their founders in public services.

During the Boys' Festival, streamers of carp are suspended for each boy, represent-ing strength, perseverance, and courage. Note the miniature samurai with his weapons.   Courtesy of Japan Information Centre, Consulate General of Japan, Toronto, Canada.

Shinto has also adopted numerous Buddhist festivals, and new festivals, such as Christmas, have begun to infiltrate Shinto obser-vances. This is especially true in large urban centers and among merchants and advertisers. In the final analysis, all festivals express Japanese sentiments of patriotism and national pride.

Notes

1. *Hara-kiri* was not mere suicide. It was a legal and ceremonial institution invented about the twelfth century and carried out with great ceremony by warriors and nobles, usually in the presence of witnesses and with a relative or special friend in attendance. The ritual was still practiced in World War II.

2. The identity of the earliest inhabitants of Japan has been the subject of scholarly debate, particularly over a group called the Ainu, who have no written language of their own but have preserved their oral tradition for centuries. For bibliographical material on the Ainus and early clans of Japan, see C. J. Adams, ed., *A Reader's Guide to the Great Religions*, 2nd ed. (New York: Free Press, 1977), pp. 262–64.

3. During the Heian period, two new Buddhist movements, the Tendai and the Shingon, were introduced from China. The Shingon school stressed ritual and the use of art objects. These aspects are discussed in M. Anesaki, *Buddhist Art in Its Relation to Buddhist Ideals, with Special Reference to Buddhism in Japan* (Boston: Houghton Mifflin, 1915); and E. D. Saunders, *Mudra: A Study of Symbolic Gestures in Japanese Buddhist Sculpture* (New York: Pantheon Books, 1960).

4. For an understanding of everyday court life and the religious and cultural atmosphere during the Heian period, see I. I. Morris, *The World of the Shining Prince: Court Life in Ancient Japan* (New York: Knopf, 1964); A. Waley, *The Tale of Genji*, 2 vols. (London: Allen & Unwin, 1935); and S. P. Brower and E. R. Miner, *Japanese Court Poetry* (Stanford, Calif.: Stanford University Press, 1961).

5. These ideological, social, political, and religious principles are best stated in R. K. Hall, ed., *Kokutai no Hongi: Cardinal Principles of the National Entity of Japan*, trans. J. O. Gauntlet (Cambridge, Mass.: Harvard University Press, 1949).

6. For a brief bibliography on the features of postwar Japan, see Adams, *A Reader's Guide*, pp. 277–79.

7. Folk religion is a complex matter of study. Among other works, see I. Hori, *Folk Religion in Japan: Continuity and Change*, ed. J. M. Kitagawa and A. L. Miller (Chicago: University of Chicago Press, 1968); and T. Otto, *Folklore in Japanese Life and Customs* (Tokyo: Kokusai Bunka Shinkokai, 1963).

10

Roots of
Western Religions

The Middle East

No area in the world has played a more important role in human affairs, or has been as often and as bitterly contested, as has the Middle East. Because it straddles a vital corridor of trade and conquest, the area has formed a perpetual arena for violent conflict among nomadic tribes, agricultural city-states, empires, and colonial powers. Hurrians, Hittites, Kassites, Midianites, Amorites, Edomites, Moabites, Ammonites, Canaanites, Phoenicians, Arameans, Greeks, Romans, Arabs, and Jews are among the peoples who occupied the area at one time or another.

Excavations have produced evidence of flint stones dating from the Paleolithic period (any time before 12,000 BCE) and of settlements from the Mesolithic period (about 10,000 BCE). The oldest remains of village life, unearthed at Jericho, date from about 5000 BCE. The earliest recorded history of Israel (from Egyptian sources), supplemented by archeological discoveries, dates from about 3000 BCE. From that point on, the region was subject to successive waves of invasion and occupation by migrating tribes and nations.

Even before these random invasions began, overlordship of the area

Mesopotamia and Egypt

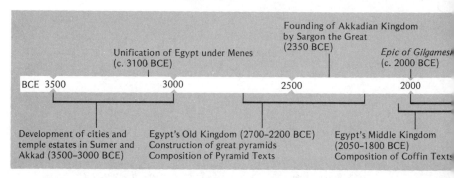

had oscillated between two great civilizations: the Egyptian and the Mesopotamian. Ancient Egypt controlled key cities, such as Lachish and Megiddo, whereas Mesopotamian empires ruled a large part of the region. Throughout the second millennium BCE, nomadic tribes kept interrupting the even tenor of garrison life in Egyptian and Mesopotamian outposts.

Of the various ancient civilizations that once dominated the arena of history, only to succumb to internal and external forces, four left records extensive enough to permit an understanding of the religious beliefs and practices that died with them. The religious traditions of the Mesopotamian, Egyptian, Greek, and Roman civilizations[1] merit inclusion in a survey of world religions because of the incalculable influence that they have exerted on the Western religious traditions of Judaism, Christianity, and Islam. In these ancient and "pagan" beliefs lay the roots of Western culture and religion.

Mesopotamian Religion

Historical Background

Archeological evidence suggests that during the third millennium BCE the Sumerians emerged as an established people in the area of Mesopotamia, in the southern part of modern Iraq. This was not their true starting point, however. The Sumerians (named after their city of Sumer) were a non-Semitic, non–Indo-European people* of unknown origin who invaded the Tigris-Euphrates valley either from the south

---

*The terms *Semitic* and *Indo-European* refer to language families, not cultural groups. The Indo-European family includes the vast majority of the extinct and living languages spoken from India to Ireland. The Semitic family, a much smaller grouping that includes Arabic and Hebrew, has been disproportionately influential in world history through its associations with Judaism, Christianity, and Islam.

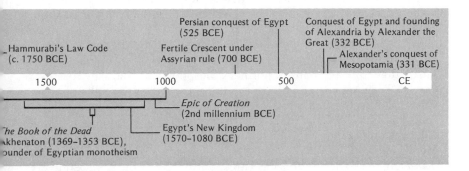

Hammurabi's Law Code (c. 1750 BCE)

Fertile Crescent under Assyrian rule (700 BCE)

Persian conquest of Egypt (525 BCE)

Conquest of Egypt and founding of Alexandria by Alexander the Great (332 BCE)

Alexander's conquest of Mesopotamia (331 BCE)

1500   1000   500   CE

Epic of Creation (2nd millennium BCE)

The Book of the Dead Akhenaton (1369–1353 BCE), founder of Egyptian monotheism

Egypt's New Kingdom (1570–1080 BCE)

by sea or from the east across the mountains, some time in the fourth millennium BCE. The ensuing struggle between the indigenous population and the Sumerians lasted for almost two thousand years, until Sargon the Great (a Semitic king) united Mesopotamia under his rule around 2350 BCE and pressed northward and westward into what is presently Syria and Turkey.

The story of King Sargon's success and of the dynasty that he founded is intriguing, particularly in that the theme of the "exposed child" rescued by chance would recur in the stories of Moses, Perseus, Oedipus, Romulus and Remus, and others. Briefly, the baby Sargon was abandoned by his mother, set adrift in a reed basket on the river. But the baby was rescued by the king's gardener, and through the love goddess Ishtar, Sargon eventually triumphed. As the chronicler records:

> Sargon, the mighty king, king of Agade, am I.
> My mother was a changeling (?), my father I knew not.
> My changeling mother conceived me, in secret she bore me.
> She set me in a basket of rushes, with bitumen she sealed my lid.
> She cast me into the river which rose not over me.
> The river bore me up and carried me to Akki, the drawer of water.
> Akki, the drawer of water, lifted me up. . . .
> Akki, the drawer of water, took me as his son and reared me.[2]

King Sargon's dynasty survived for some two centuries, until a group called the Gutians arrived around 2150 BCE to ravage and rule the area. They, in turn, were succeeded a century later by a Semitic group called the Amorites, who united all of Mesopotamia under one of their rulers shortly after 1800 BCE. He was the great and powerful King Hammurabi of Babylon, whose fame derives from an impressive legal code or juridical document attributed to his administration. The Code of Hammurabi stipulated that in his kingdom, among other things, the weak were to be protected, justice was to extend even to the orphan and widow, inheritance was to be based on legitimate succession, and judicial proceedings were to take place before judges.

Around 1530 BCE, an invasion of Kassites from the Iranian mountains brought Hammurabi's Babylonian dynasty to an abrupt end. Meanwhile, the Assyrians in northern Mesopotamia gradually rose to power. Their expansion followed paths spearheaded by military advances and reached its zenith around the seventh century BCE, under King Esarhaddon. The entire area from the Tigris-Euphrates to the Nile was united in a single but short-lived Assyrian Empire. Then the Medes, followed by the Persians, swept down from the Iranian plateau in the sixth century BCE. Three centuries after the sixth century BCE, Alexander the Great conquered the area and brought the history of the Mesopotamian empires to an end.

Mesopotamian Pantheon

Mesopotamian religion was a "naturalistic polytheism": the natural forces of the universe—the forces that govern rivers, vegetation, climate, astral laws, birth, death, and so on—were all regarded as laws instituted by gods and goddesses who needed to be evoked or worshiped. An overlapping function of many deities was supervision of the destiny of particular cities. In other words, a cosmic god was also the tutelary god (guardian) of a city, even though other gods were worshiped in that city. Thus, An (Anu),* the sky god, was considered the king and ruler of all the other gods, but also the tutelary god of the city of Uruk. Similarly, Enlil (Bel), the air god, lord of the wind and storm, was the chief deity of the city of Nippur; Nanna (Sin), the moon god, reigned over Ur (the city of the biblical Abraham); Utu (Shamash), the sun god, ruled Larsa until it was destroyed and then became the tutelary god of Sippar; and Enki (Ea), the god of water and wisdom, reigned over Eridu.

The list of Mesopotamian deities is incredibly long—about two thousand names! More interesting than the sheer number of gods, however, are the characteristics of and the relationship between the deities. Although the deities represented natural forces and cosmic elements, they assumed or were invested with the likenesses of human beings. Thus, the deities were robed like sovereigns but in vestments more dazzling. Like human beings, the deities represented both sexes, had families, made love, hated and fought among themselves—

---

*Names that appear within parentheses are Semitic/Akkadian forms of original Sumerian counterparts.

but on a much grander and more terrible scale. The deities were immortal models of perfect humans.

Though the population of each city might recognize and worship subsidiary gods, there was one supreme god or absolute lord of the city who manifested his or her will through various portents. The human ruler or sovereign of the city was the earthly representative of this absolute lord. It was the ruler's task to interpret the mandates of this god and to honor the divine metropolitan mentor by erecting temples and building canals in the city so that prosperity might follow. The social and political fortunes of the city were hung in a balance that was determined by its tutelary god. Drought and famine resulted from mortals' neglect of the god's temple. Human sovereignty was determined by divine decree; victory or defeat in war was the result of divine favor. For instance, a surviving Sumerian inscription dating from the time of Lugalzaggisi, the ruler of Umma in about 2350 BCE, indicates how Enlil, the supreme tutelary god of the city, supported the sovereign's political ambitions.

> When Enlil, king of the countries, presented to Lugalzaggisi the kingship of the country, when he established full justice before the land, when his might had overthrown the countries, from the sunrise to sunset, he imposed tribute upon them. At that time, from the lower sea, the Tigris and the Euphrates, to the upper sea, Enlil took for him as a possession.[3]

Every human endeavor or activity, therefore, depended on the city god, so that every social and political enterprise was performed for the benefit of the city god. The temple of the city god was centrally located and surrounded by other temples belonging to the god's spouse, children, and related deities. In this way, the greatest landowner of the city became the city god because most, if not all, of the land in the city was temple land. The inhabitants of the city, accordingly, earned their livelihoods as servants of the city god and of other deities. As a matter of fact, Mesopotamians held the view that humans were created to relieve the deities from the labor of maintaining their estates.

As different groups of people ruled the area, new local divinities succeeded established deities. For instance, the ascendancy of the god Marduk and his authority over all the other deities resulted from the political ascendancy of the Babylonian dynasty, whereas the honor accorded to the god Ashur was characteristic of succeeding Assyrian rulers. Each major political change catapulted the victor's supreme home town deity to "national" prominence as the true creator and orderer of the universe.

Cult Practices

The worship of deities in Mesopotamian religion took the form of a complex and highly developed system of rites and rituals, temple celebrations, sacrificial festivals, and occult practices. Whereas gods and goddesses protected human beings and provided them with material blessings, demons and demonesses brought terror and torment. For the most part, demons were wicked, restless spirits of the dead who lived in tombs, in darkness, and in desolate places. They were insatiable in their greed and relentless in their pursuits, but they could be exorcised and their intent frustrated by incantations and occult practices.

Confronted by such forces, Mesopotamians divided religious functions among both males and females in order to meet the conflicting demands of service to one class of gods and vigorous offensive action against the others. Religious officials were classified according to the function they performed: magic, sorcery, divination, wailing, singing, sacrificing, and so on. Animals, birds, fish, vegetation, cooked food, milk, wine and beer, as well as clothing and perfumes, were either sacrificed or offered to deities.

The most widespread cultic practice was divination based on scrutiny of animal livers. An entire class of occult practitioners was qualified to read omens and to draw conclusions for practically every event in life through a detailed analysis of the liver of a sacrificial animal. Another divinatory practice was based on astronomy. Because the position, movement, and conjunction of the stars were believed to pronounce omens, observatories were established at the top of temples to record accurately the courses of the stars and to predict eclipses—a scientific bonus at least as significant as the guidance that this celestial research provided. Divination was also practiced by oracles (divine communication transmitted through a priest or priestess). Kings consulted the oracles before setting out for war and regulated their plans in accordance with the answer. For instance, the following message encouraged King Esarhaddon to go to war:

> Fear not, Esarhaddon!
> I, the god Bel, speak to you. . . .
> Sixty great gods stand round about you, ranged for battle.[4]

Religious Festivals

Festivals seem to have played a central role in Mesopotamian religion. There were two kinds of festival: the fixed feasts of the New Year and the new moon; and the movable feasts dedicated either to particular deities or to special occasions, such as temple dedications, royal coronations, wars, and victories.

The New Year's festival, celebrated in the spring, was the central point of the Mesopotamian religious year. For twelve successive days, purificatory rites, prayers, and sacrifices were offered, while the king paid special homage to the national god and the other deities. The main feature of the ceremony, however, was the celebration of the death and resurrection of the god Marduk. Although the mythical texts and consequently the rites connected with the feast are still matters of dispute among scholars, the celebration probably involved reenacting the story of Marduk's captivity in the underworld (indicating his death) and his triumph in returning to life (indicating his resurrection). This celebration was an expression of faith in the earth's cycle—in the renewal of nature. Just as life followed death and order followed chaos, so the seasonal vegetation that had died in the winter would emerge anew in the spring.

The Ziggurat

Mesopotamian religious activity centered around the city temples and their sacred precincts or courtyards. These temples contained altars with offering tables and images of gods, rooms for priests, storerooms, and rooms for various other purposes. The largest and most splendid of Mesopotamian temples was that of Marduk, the tutelary god of Babylon. Situated on the eastern bank of the Euphrates River and surrounded by high, turreted walls, Marduk's temple complex included a great rectangular temple tower, known as a *ziggurat* (the biblical Tower of Babel). A succession of stairways or ramps led to the sanctuary at its summit.

Apart from the conclusion that ziggurats played an important part in Mesopotamian religion, modern scholars are uncertain of their function. Were they, like Egyptian pyramids, tombs for deified kings? Were they the abodes of the gods? Were they simply outward expressions of an inner need to approach the deities? Did they symbolize the link between heaven and earth, between gods and mortals? Were they astronomical observatories for astrological prophesy? They may have fulfilled any or all of these functions.

Mythologies

Among the various Mesopotamian religious literary works, those of mythology were prominent. Mesopotamian mythology featured the adventures and interrelationships of the gods, the origin of the universe, the creation of humanity, the netherworld, the cycle of vegetation, and "the flood."

The Flood. The story of the flood is of Sumerian origin and perhaps derived from grim experiences associated with the flooding of the Tigris and Euphrates rivers. The Sumerian account relates how an assembly of gods decided, for reasons that are unclear, to punish humanity by a flood. The decision is "leaked" by one of the deities to a god-fearing man called Ziusudra (the counterpart of the Babylonian Utnapishtim and the biblical Noah), who builds an ark and embarks in it with his entire family and as many animals and birds as the ship can accommodate. The well-preserved Babylonian version continues:

> After I had caused all my family and relations to go up into the ship, I caused the game of the field, the beasts of the field (and) all the craftsmen to go (into it). I viewed the appearance of the weather; the weather was frightful to behold. I entered the ship and closed my door. . . . Six days and [six] nights the wind blew, the downpour, the tempest (and) the flood overwhelmed the land. When the seventh day arrived, the tempest, the flood, which had fought like an army, subsided in (its) onslaught. The sea grew quiet, the storm abated, the flood ceased. . . . I looked upon the sea, (all) was silence, and all mankind had turned to clay. I sent forth a dove and let (her) go. The dove went away and came back to me; there was no resting-place, and so she returned. . . . (Then) I sent forth a raven and let (her) go. The raven went away . . . (and) did not return. (Then) I sent forth (everything) to the four winds and offered a sacrifice. I poured out a libation on the peak of the mountain.[5]

The relationship between the Mesopotamian and biblical flood story (Genesis 7–8) is obvious.

Gilgamesh. The adventures of the deities, life and death, the origin and destiny of the universe, and the remarkable feats of heroes also played large roles in Mesopotamian mythology. One outstanding heroic figure was Gilgamesh (considered by some scholars to be the Sumerian antecedent of Hercules), whose fate mirrors the inevitable fate of all human beings—death.

In the story, Gilgamesh, the ruler of the city of Uruk (Erech) appeals to Utu, the sun god, to allow him to undertake the long and perilous journey to "the land," home of the gods, in order to assure himself of an immortal name, since he is not on his own account eligible for immortality. Utu grants Gilgamesh's plea, whereupon the latter, accompanied by his trustworthy friend Enkidu and by fifty loyal volunteer citizens, sets off on his enterprise. After crossing several perilous mountain barriers, the companions finally look down on "the land," with its vast forest and its guardian monster Huwawa. In spite of the warnings of his friends, Gilgamesh determines to confront the unknown by seeking out and overcoming the monster, whose corpse he presents to the gods.

Another version of this story features the death of Gilgamesh as its main theme. According to this account, Enkidu, the wild but trustworthy friend of Gilgamesh, dies prematurely for offending Ishtar, the goddess of love. Forced to set out in search of immortality on his own, Gilgamesh travels to the realm of the immortals, among whom his ancestor Utnapishtim lived after having escaped the flood. Utnapishtim helps Gilgamesh to find the herb of immortality at the bottom of the sea, but fate intervenes in the shape of a serpent that swallows the herb and so robs Gilgamesh of immortality. The pathos of human disappointment in the face of imminent death is beautifully described in the following inscription:

> Gilgamesh, whither runnest thou? The life which thou seekest thou wilt not find. (For) when the gods created mankind, they alloted death to mankind; (but) life they retained in their keeping.[6]

The discovery of entire retinues interred beside their dead sovereigns in the royal tombs at Ur confirms that the Mesopotamians believed in life beyond the tomb, but the prospect as conceived by Mesopotamian religion is cheerless and uninviting, "with poor possibilities and overshadowed with gloom."[7] Mesopotamian religious beliefs represent the dead as wretched, abandoned, and restless, haunting the living and subsisting on dust and dirty water.

Egyptian Religion

Historical Background

Long before the advent of the pharaohs, the Egyptians were already an ancient people with roots in the Old Stone Age, when scattered groups of hunters wandered along the mud strip of the Nile River. Some time between 10,000 and 7000 BCE, a pastoral group settled along the fertile Nile valley. Between 7000 and 3000 BCE, these people organized themselves into independent villages constructed of wood, brick, and stone. By about 3000 BCE they had developed the art of hieroglyphic writing (picture script), an advance followed shortly afterward by the unification of many village communities into a single kingdom under one imperial ruler, called the pharaoh. This pharaonic dominion of a united kingdom of Egypt, extending at its apogee

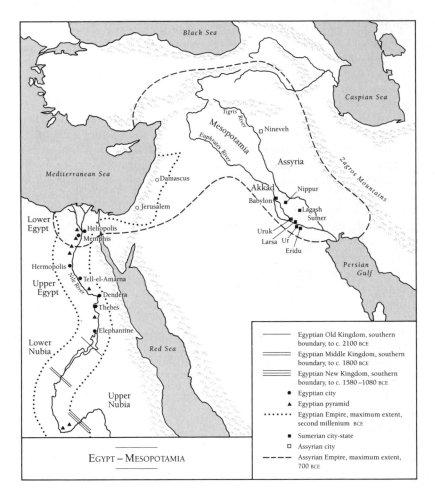

EGYPT – MESOPOTAMIA

(before 1800 BCE) to include the littorals of modern Israel and Syria, lasted until 332 BCE, with a few interruptions. One such break occurred some time around 2200 BCE, when the authority of the pharaohs was broken by the emergence of several petty states, only to be restored two hundred years later. Another interregnum of two hundred years occurred around 1800 BCE, when Egypt was ruled by the Hyksos, a group of Asiatic nomads whose origins are still a subject of controversy. Then, for over a thousand years, the royal authority of the pharaohs was supreme, until a series of incursions first by the Assyrians, then by the Persians, and finally by Alexander the Great in 332 BCE brought the Egyptian kingdom to an end.

Pharaoh Worship

The development of Egyptian religious traditions represents a long, continuous process uninterrupted and unaffected by developments in other civilizations. From about 3000 BCE the official religion recognized every pharaoh as the incarnate son-god of the sun god. It was unnecessary, then, to seek the will or mandate of the sun god, for that mandate was expressed through the pharaoh-god. Justice was based not on a code of laws, but on the pharaoh's own decisions, made in accordance with custom. Those who resisted the pharaoh's supreme authority were punished as rebels.

The cult of the pharaoh was perhaps best expressed by the immense structure of the pyramids. These divine tombs were central to the cult of the pharaoh-god, who in dying was assumed to have returned to the company of all pharaoh-gods while the next pharaoh-god succeeded to his earthly mandate. The sight of these monuments suggested to the Greek invaders, centuries later, harsh, forced labor imposed by a hateful tyrant. To take such a view is to misunderstand the religious conviction and mentality of the Egyptians, who willingly accepted the obligation to work on monumental projects as service befitting the incarnate pharaoh-god.

The political power of the pharaohs, and especially their royal conquests over subject peoples, justified the kind of divine exaltation that is attributed to one of the gods at the victory of the Pharaoh Thutmose III, as follows:

> I have come that I may cause thee to tread down the princes of Palestine; I spread them out under thy feet throughout their countries. I cause them to behold thy majesty as The Lord of Radiance; thou shinest in their faces as my similitude.[8]

Animal Cult

Along with the pharaoh cult, Egyptian religion embraced a remarkable variety of gods and goddesses: each region in Egypt had its own deity, and cities or villages within each region recognized local extensions to regional pantheons. The most striking feature of Egyptian religious tradition, however, was not its polytheistic nature or its sheer quantity of gods; rather, Egyptian religion was distinguished by the remarkable qualities of its deities. Egyptian gods and goddesses were represented as either complete animals or as semihuman and semianimal forms. Thus, Horus, the god of the Delta region, was represented with a human body and a falcon's head. The goddess Hathor had a woman's head and a cow's body. Anubis featured a man's body and an ibis's (or jackal's) head. The goddess Sekhmet was distinguished by a female's

body and a lioness's head. Tueris had a crocodile's head, a hippopotamus's body, a lion's feet, and the arms of a human. Other deities
appeared as complete animals in the form of a crocodile, a cat, a frog,
an eel, a hippopotamus, and so on.

Modern scholars are, to say the least, puzzled by this strange phenomenon. Some have speculated that these animal-shaped deities
represented vestiges of prehistoric totemism, or simply animal guardians. Others have argued that ancient Egyptian religious traditions
tended to blur distinctions and incompatibilities between gods, humans, and beasts—all of whom shared common supernatural characteristics. Still others have postulated that since the pharaoh was a god
in human form, other divinities could also appear in animal, semianimal, or semihuman form. Whatever the underlying concept, the
Egyptians saw no difficulty in the worship of powers with human or
animal characteristics.

Egyptian Deities

Besides the sun god and deities endowed with animal forms, Egyptian
religion recognized a host of other divinities. Among them were
various cosmic deities, such as the earth god Geb, the heaven goddess Nut (note the reversal of the usual order of the sexes in ancient religions—a male earth god and a female god of heaven), and
the air god Shu. Among the astral deities, the sun god Horus initially
was the most prominent. He was not the only sun god, however;
others included Kheprer, Atum, and Re (or Ra), who in time eclipsed
Horus.

Like the rising sun, Horus was symbolized by the widespread wings
of the mounting falcon. Each morning the sun god rose out of the
ocean to traverse the sky in his majestic ship; each evening he descended through the ocean to the underworld, where a great serpent
daily attempted to overturn him, to no avail. Horus's substitute Thoth,
the moon god, presided in the sky in his absence.

More unusual than the falcon imagery was the identification of the
sun god with the scarab, or dung beetle. Just as the scarab diligently
rolled its dung ball as a repository for its eggs, so also the sun god
Kheprer (or Khapri) rolled the huge sun ball across the sky.

Around 2000 BCE, the sun god acquired another characteristic by
becoming Amon-Re. Amon, originally the local god of the city of
Thebes, had become a national god and therefore was assimilated with
Re to become Amon-Re, the greatest of the gods.

Besides these deities, there were others who were represented as

The goddess Isis stretching her winged arms in a protective gesture, depicted in a fresco from the tomb of Seti I of the 19th dynasty. The Granger Collection.

entirely human or, sometimes, as abstract concepts. The list is long, so a few examples will have to suffice: Maat, the goddess of truth and world order; Safekht, the goddess of writing; Hu, the god of taste; Anubis, the guardian god of the cemetery; Neit, the goddess of hunting; and Ptah, the creator god who conceived the world in his heart and ordered it to rise from primordial mud by an utterance of his tongue.

Attempts by the priests to organize this amorphous collection of deities and beliefs into some sort of a system resulted in a variety of family groupings. Some deities, such as the creator god Ptah, the war goddess Sekhmet, and the medicine god Imhotep, were identified in a triad as father, mother, and son, as were the sun god Amon-Re, the Nile goddess Mut, and their son, the moon god Khonsu. Other deities were grouped into a four-generation family of nine: Atum, the hill god who emerged from the primordial sea; his son, the air god Shu, and his daughter, the dew goddess Tefnut; Shu and Tefnut's children, the earth god Geb and the sky goddess Nut; Geb and Nut's two sons, Seth and Osiris, and two daughters, Nephtys and Isis.

Death and Resurrection of Osiris

No grouping of deities stirred popular interest more than the family that included the Isis-Osiris-Horus group. According to the earliest Egyptian version of the story (the Pyramid Texts, assembled from fragments of funerary hymns and rituals), Osiris was a good and beneficent god-king who was killed by his evil brother, Seth. Seth made good his escape, taking Osiris's "third eye" (symbolic of kingship) with him. Meanwhile, Isis and Nephtys found their brother's body, and while Isis wept and embraced the corpse, Osiris suddenly came to life long enough to impregnate her. The result of this union was the child god Horus, who, as soon as he was old enough, was asked by Isis to avenge his father's death.

Horus first appealed to the court of deities, accusing Seth of murdering his father. Because the court was slow to act, Horus then took the law into his own hands, killing Seth and recovering his father's third eye. As soon as Horus replaced the eye in his dead father's corpse, Osiris was resurrected. From then on, Osiris presided over the underworld as judge of the dead. He bequeathed his third eye to Horus, who wore it as the ruler and sun god of Egypt.

According to a later, Greek account of the same story, attributed to Plutarch in the first century CE, the good and beneficent King Osiris was tricked by Seth and a group of fellow conspirators into stretching out in a coffin especially prepared for him. Seth had had this handsome coffin made to measure for Osiris, and at a banquet he promised to give it to anyone who could fit it exactly when he lay inside it. The attempts of various guests having failed, Osiris lay down and fit into it perfectly. Seth's fellow conspirators then closed the coffin, carried it to the water, and threw it into the Nile, which swept it out to sea. When she heard the news, Isis, overcome with grief, set out in search of her brother's corpse, which she finally found washed up on the Phoenician coast (the coastline of modern Israel and Syria). Then, taking the form of a kite, Isis hovered with wings extended over the body of Osiris until it stirred and Osiris was restored to life. The Greek account, like the early Egyptian version, relates how Osiris left the living in favor of descending to rule the realm of the dead.

Although no complete version of the story has survived, these accounts have provided modern scholars with insight into the views and ideals held by a large proportion of the adherents of Egyptian religious practices. The prevailing view is that Osiris's story represents the victory of good over evil, and that the third eye of the sun god-king brings life and resurrection to the grain in the soil.[9] As for Isis, worship of her centered at first around Memphis, then spread throughout Egypt. By about 100 BCE, it had become one of the popular mystery religions adopted by Greeks and Romans (see pp. 287–288), lasting until the fifth century CE, when Christian suppression ultimately brought it to its end.

Monotheism: Worship of Aton

A radical break from the established traditional Egyptian religion took place during the reign of the Pharaoh Amen-hotep IV (c. 1380–1362 BCE), who moved his capital from Thebes to Tell-el-Amarna, changed his name to Akh-en-Aton (or Ikhnaton), and instituted the exclusive worship of Aton, the sun disk, as the creator and sustainer of all things. Moreover, he ordered the priests to expunge the names and images of all deities other than Aton from all public records, monuments, and temples; and he created new centers throughout his empire, from Syria to Nubia, for the sole worship of Aton.

Because Akh-en-Aton was devoted to the one and only god, and because he identified this god as *exclusive* and supreme (not merely the highest god among many), some scholars have regarded him as the founder of *monotheism*.[10] His monotheistic beliefs are best expressed in the following hymn:

> Thou sole god, there is no other like thee! Thou didst create the earth according to thy will, being alone: mankind, cattle, all flocks, everything on earth which walks with (its) feet, and what are on high, flying with their wings.[11]

The entire "Hymn to Aton" is much longer than the excerpt quoted here and refers to the universality and beneficence of the Creator and Re-Creator Aton. The similarity of spirit and wording of the entire hymn to Psalm 104 has been noted and argued by scholars often. This argument was fueled by Freud's ingenious speculation, voiced in *Moses and Monotheism* (1939), that Akh-en-Aton's monotheism had an influence on Moses and on the way in which the latter interpreted his role.

Whatever links there were between Atonism and Mosaic religious traditions, the reforms instituted by Akh-en-Aton failed to survive his death. In fact, the new capital he founded was destroyed, his memory was effaced, and the name of Aton was obliterated from every public place. The succeeding pharaoh, Tut-ankh-Aton, changed his name to Tut-ankh-Amon (more popularly known today as King Tut) and yielded to the entreaties of his priests to return to traditional religious structures. Osiris, Isis, Horus, Amon-Re, and many other deities resumed their former status and survived until Christianity discredited them beyond hope of redemption.

Death, Heaven, and Hell

The erection of the pyramids and the process of mummification (embalming) are perhaps the best-known symbols of an Egyptian preoccupation with the afterlife. The Egyptians perfected the technique of mummification to such a degree that a corpse could be preserved from decomposing almost indefinitely.

Retribution for the deeds of this life pervaded the thinking behind mummification. After death, so the Egyptians thought, everyone was fated to appear before the tribunal of Osiris. There, in the presence of forty-two divine jurors and Osiris, the newly dead were expected to confess to and to exonerate themselves of various crimes, sins, and misdemeanors. To do this, the dead were provided with a guidebook or mortuary text—a collection of hymns, prayers, mythologies, and magical formulas gathered together by modern scholars under the title of *The Book of the Dead.*[12] In these mortuary texts the important experiences awaiting the deceased were described, along with a long list of "negative confessions," or protestations of guiltlessness, which the dead had to recite in order to certify themselves as worthy to enter the land of Osiris. Here is a short portion of this long confessional list, taken from Chapter 125 of *The Book of the Dead:*

> Hail to thee, great god, lord of Truth. . . .
> I have committed no sin against people. . . .
> I allowed no one to hunger.
> I caused no one to weep.
> I did not murder.
> I caused no man misery.
> I did not decrease the offerings of the gods.
> I did not commit adultery.
> I did not diminish the grain measure.
> I did not diminish the land measure.
> I did not deflect the index of the scales.
> I did not take milk from the mouth of the child.
> I did not report evil of a servant to his master.
> I did not catch the fish in their pools.
> I am purified four times.[13]

After this plea each heart was weighed on a scale against an ostrich feather—the symbol of truth. If the heart overbalanced the scale, retribution followed. One view held that the guilty were destroyed by "the Devouress," a terrifying and frightful creature. Another view was that retribution took the form of a fiery hell where the guilty writhed in nameless agony.

If, however, the scales were evenly balanced, the dead were permitted to enter the world of the blessed. Here they were free to make use of the funerary articles stored in their tombs to speed their journey and ease their transition to the netherworld: chairs, beds, chariots, boats, kitchen utensils, combs, hairpins, cosmetics, gilded and silver objects of art, foodstuffs (such as jars of water, wine, grain, dates, cakes, portions of beef and fowl), and models of women and servants. Spells and incantations were provided to vivify the models of women and servants so that they could be put to work as soon as their masters or mistresses arrived in the world of the blessed.

Temples, Sphinxes, and Pyramids

Egyptian intellectual activity, cultural life, and religion centered around the temples. These temples were independent and well-organized social, economic, and religious centers that contained statues of the deities. Various classes of specialized attendants, both male

Each pharaoh built a pyramid complex which was both a symbol of his power and his final resting place. This pyramid-sphinx complex, built at Giza, is that of King Khafre (Chephren) of the Fourth Dynasty of the Old Kingdom (c. 2613–2494 BCE). The pyramid measures 471 feet high and 708 feet to a side. An existing natural rock in a nearby valley was transformed by the king's sculptors into a guardian sphinx—the largest sculpture ever carved by human hands. The sphinx is in the form of a recumbent lion with a royal human head, in which the features of Khafre are thought to have been carved.   Courtesy of Richard Arthur Couche.

and female, were organized hierarchically to perform the necessary duties. High priests, their acolytes (attendants), scribes, readers, purifiers, sacrificers, singers, prophets, and musicians all served various functions in temple activities.

The architectural scheme of the temple reached its climax after 1600 BCE: Several associated structures surrounded the temple area, which was approached by a wide avenue flanked by rows of sphinxes (see illustration on p. 261), set up as guardians at the entrances to the temple. The gates opened onto a huge roofless courtyard surrounded by single or double rows of columns. The courtyard led up to a chamber, which in turn led to a higher level where the sanctuary of the deity was situated. Other rooms associated with the deity and the priests were also incorporated into the temple area.

Priests performed daily ceremonies in the temples. After a preliminary purification, the priest appointed for the occasion entered the sanctuary or temple and censed the entire area. Next, he broke the seals and unlocked the doors of the holy sanctuary. Standing before the statue of the deity, he offered a brief prayer, followed by the awakening, washing, perfuming, and reclothing of the statue of the deity. A meal was then offered to the deity and set alight to be burned in the deity's presence before the priest withdrew. The ceremony concluded with the priest relocking and resealing the doors of the holy sanctuary.

The pyramids offer striking evidence of royal power and confirmation of the pharaoh's continuing life after death. These massive structures were the tombs of the god-kings. To the Egyptians, it was only natural that people of divine origin should have grandiose tombs as an assurance of a full and untroubled existence in the next world. Built in conjunction with the pyramids were funerary temples or shrines, which consisted of either simple chapel constructions or elaborate rock hollows arcaded by several terraces.

Religious Festivals

In addition to daily worship in the temple, great seasonal, agricultural, and fertility festivals were held that varied from center to center and from one local deity to another. During these festivals, the statue of the deity was brought out of its holy sanctuary and carried in procession through the town or city. At times, devotees enacted some episode in the life of the deity—the conflict between Osiris and Seth, for instance. Devotees reenacted the murder of Osiris by Seth, the mourning of Isis, and the resurrection of Osiris by Horus. Undoubtedly, these solemn performances drew large crowds of pilgrims from all over Egypt. Centuries later, the Greek historian Herodotus described the celebration of the festival of the cat goddess Bast in the city of Bubastis:

> When they congregate at Bubastis, they go by river, men and women together, many of both in every boat; some of the women have rattles and rattle with them and some of the men play the flute all the way; the rest, both sexes alike, sing and clap their hands. At every city they find in their passage, they bring their boats close to the bank, and some of the women continue with their music while others shout opprobrious language at the women of the place, some dance and some stand up and pull up their garments. And this they do at every town that stands by the shore. When they come to Bubastis, they celebrate the festival with great sacrifices, and more wine is drunk at this feast than in all the rest of the year. For the people of the place say that seven hundred thousand men and women, apart from children, assemble there.[14]

Ceremonials on behalf of deities and pharaohs were detailed and very elaborate. Egyptian religion was characterized by a high degree of ritual, ceremony, and festival.

Occult Practices

Another characteristic feature of Egyptian religion among the general population was its magical element: charms, curses, and threats. Magical curses were leveled against anyone who violated royal decrees or even defamed the name of a dead pharaoh. Similarly, threatening magic was invoked against anyone who violated a tomb. Here, for instance, is the inscription on the tomb of the Egyptian vizier (royal executive) Ankh-ma-Hor:

> May it go well with you, my successors; may it prosper you, my predecessors! As for anything ye may do against this tomb of the necropolis, the like shall be done against your property.[15]

Another inscription, found on the tomb of the Egyptian official Meni, invokes vengeance and retribution against violators of the tomb:

> The crocodile be against him in the water, the snake be against him on land—against him who may do a thing to this tomb.[16]

However, even vandals had some recourse in ancient Egypt. Those anathematized by the most terrible imprecations or even threatened by real or potential enemies could exorcise the threat by inscribing the names of their foes on bowls or figurines and then smashing them, so as to shatter or break the power of their enemies.

Mythologies

Egyptian mythologies are largely embodied in the mortuary texts and cover the most disparate themes. Creation and the origin of all things, rivalry among the gods (such as Seth's enmity with Horus), family life among the gods, the good fortune of those who have passed from the tomb to life everlasting, the fields of paradise, a legend about seven years of famine, and a story about a princess possessed by spirits are themes that represent the rich variety of Egyptian mythologies— several of them common to many religions. But unlike some religions, the mythology of Egypt does not reflect one uniform pattern or explanation for various phenomena. On the contrary, several mutually exclusive, and sometimes contradictory, conceptions coexisted. Instead of a single account of the origin of things, for example, there are several creation myths. Creation is attributed to the creator god Atum (or Atum-Kheprer), who created air, moisture, earth, sky, and the deities, and who put his own vital force into the first creatures. But the Egyptians also conceived of the god Ptah as the First Principle, taking precedence over other creator deities. Or alternately, they viewed the origin of everything as the work of Kheprer, the morning-sun god conceived of as a scarab beetle.

Attribution of creation to at least three divine agents is only one example of many apparent contradictions implicit in Egyptian mythology. Another involves the notion of the sky being supported. The sky was variously thought of as being supported on posts, on walls, on a cow, by a goddess whose arms and feet touched the earth, or by a god. It is very difficult, if not impossible, to establish which of these mythologies most appealed to the Egyptians. Possibly they represented regional or local variations on common themes or were all current but at different times.

Greek Religion

Historical Background

The ancient Greeks called their land Hellas and referred to as Hellenes anyone whose native tongue was Greek, whether or not that person lived in Greece. Anyone who did not speak Greek was identified as a barbarian.

The origins of the earliest inhabitants of mainland Greece and the adjacent islands are far from clear. What is certain is that by 2000 BCE, Crete, the largest adjacent island, had developed the first flourishing Hellene culture. The Cretan culture, also called Minoan culture (after the legendary King Minos of Crete[17]), extended its influence northward to the cultural center of Mycenae in southern mainland Greece.

Agamemnon, the legendary king of Mycenae, was regarded as the most powerful and the richest ruler on the mainland.

From 1200 to 1000 BCE, groups of migrating tribes invaded Greece from the north and destroyed the existing Minoan-Mycenaean cultures. At the end of these migrations, three cultural groups dominated: the Aeolic in northern Greece, the Ionic in central Greece, and the Doric in southern Greece.

From 800 to 600 BCE, the Greeks expanded their culture by colonization. The Ionians moved northeastward to the Black Sea, the Aeolians westward to France and Spain, the Dorians to Sicily and southern Italy. Several centuries later, the Greeks were forced to contend with the Persians. After several attempts, the Persian army crossed the Hellespont (the modern Dardanelles) in 480 BCE and marched into Greece. They captured Athens and burned the Acropolis before their fleet was routed by the Athenians and their allies in the naval battle of Salamis.

There followed a period of great cultural and intellectual achievement, before power politics between Greek city-states led to political decay and warfare. In the fourth century BCE, Greece was conquered by King Philip II of Macedon. Philip's son, Alexander the Great, gathered an army composed of Greeks and Macedonians and crossed the Hellespont to attack the Persians. In ten years he conquered western Asia as far as modern India and overran Egypt in northwestern Africa. Over time, Greek cities were established everywhere throughout western Asia and in Egypt, and Greek civilization and language predominated in the vast area in spite of Alexander's untimely death in 323 BCE.

The period that followed Alexander is called the Hellenistic Age. As the power of Macedon declined, many Greek city-states formed independent leagues. Then, in 197 BCE, the Romans arrived and conquered Macedon and Greece, an event that precipitated a struggle between the Romans and the Greeks for the next fifty years. Finally, the Romans destroyed Macedon in 148 BCE and a year later made Greece a Roman province. The Romans gradually completed their conquest of most of the Hellenistic world between 146 and 127 BCE.

Early Greek Religion

The roots of Greek religion go as far back as Neolithic times, when the Indo-European sky god, variously known as Zeus, Jupiter, and Dyaus, was believed to control the weather. As waves of Greek-speaking tribes moved into mainland Greece, they absorbed Pelasgian (pre-Greek) cults, such as the horse-headed Demeter and the oracles of Zeus centered at Dodona. Each Greek deity possessed its familiar

Greece and Rome

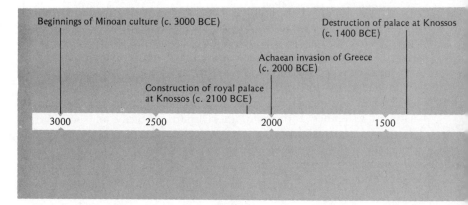

Beginnings of Minoan culture (c. 3000 BCE)

Destruction of palace at Knossos (c. 1400 BCE)

Achaean invasion of Greece (c. 2000 BCE)

Construction of royal palace at Knossos (c. 2100 BCE)

3000   2500   2000   1500

beast or bird, although it is uncertain whether these deities were ever visualized in animal forms. Some deities, such as the hearth goddess Hestia, were only vaguely personified. Others, such as Apollo, Hermes, and Dionysus, were often represented as posts, columns, or stones.

In Crete, the cult of the Mother Goddess seems to have played an important part. The Mother Goddess combined a number of different functions. She was associated with vegetation, depicted as a mountain deity, worshiped as ruler of the netherworld, and thought of as mistress of all beasts. She was sometimes shown as a female figure holding snakes in each outstretched hand; sometimes she was accompanied by a male deity. Her cult was later submerged by that of the Olympian gods, but her importance survived in the mystery religions of occult practitioners, discussed at greater length at the end of this section.

All of life's major events, such as birth, marriage, and death, required the invocation of a deity. No occupation or journey was undertaken without a deity's prior approval. In fact, the ancient Greeks invoked the gods for help or guidance on any occasion. Between them and their deities was a natural, everyday, down-to-earth interaction, free of any sense of servitude or fear.[18]

Such was the religious climate of ancient Greece prior to the invasions from the north of the twelfth century BCE. Thereafter, religious traditions were amalgamated, and local deities were identified with the gods and goddesses of the invading groups. At this point, and for a long time afterward, up to the Hellenistic Age, the chief religious developments occurred in the city-states, each of which had its own

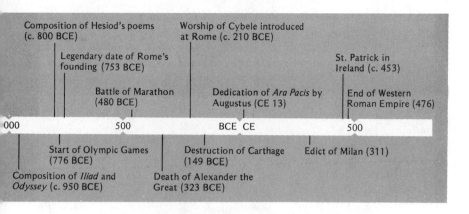

cult and its own calendar of religious ceremonies and festivals. Some of the most important developments are characterized below.

Greek Pantheon

The deities in Greek religion were regarded as the immortal controllers of natural forces. Zeus was the weather god, known also as Zeus Maemactes (Storm) or Zeus Cataebates (Striker). His shrines, sited on mountaintops, were visited in times of drought. Apollo was the god of plagues and herdsmen; alternately, he sanctioned purification rites. Hades (or Pluto) was the god of the underworld. Poseidon was the god of the sea and of horses. Themis personified justice; Aphrodite and Eros aroused love and sexual passion. The list could go on and on.[19]

Homer. The Greek poet Homer, whose birthplace and birth date are unknown (although it is conjectured that he lived some time between 1000 and 800 BCE), left an artistic and intellectual picture of the Greek deities. To serve the purposes of his epic poetry, Homer assembled all the major deities on Mount Olympus and portrayed them as fair in form and of superhuman size, yet capable of moving with the lightness of birds. The Homeric pantheon was a divine aristocracy ruled by Zeus, a splendid sky god who held dominion over clouds, thunderbolts, and rain. As father of the gods, Zeus was involved in numerous generative relationships, though his permanent consort was Hera. Other important deities in the Homeric pantheon were Apollo, Poseidon, Aphrodite, and Athena. Apollo was identified as the god of light and had a wide range of interests, including the care of animals, music, and medicine. In addition, the oracle at Delphi was identified with his voice.

Athena, patron goddess of Athens, who was also worshiped in other parts of Greece. A virgin goddess, Athena personified wisdom, and she was the patron of arts and crafts and closely connected with war. According to Greek mythology, her birth occurred when she leapt, fully armed, from the head of Zeus, which had been split open by an axe. Her most famous shrine is the Parthenon, on the Acropolis of Athens. From the private collection of Tom G. Elliott.

On the whole, the Homeric deities were stripped of their primitive characteristics. Earlier views of the deities in animal form, of the Mother Goddess, and of the Minoan and the Pelasgian cults were either absent or modified. Although immortal, those deities were attractive, charming, and amusing; indeed, they were like humans—moody, passionate, jealous, and prone to indulge their own whims. Homer's deities, in contrast, exercised great power over human lives. Cities rose or fell, armies triumphed or failed, individuals lived or died according to the will of the deities. And the gods showed little, if any, concern for justice in the modern sense. Rather than justice, tribute—a due regard for their divine status or power and sacrificial rituals—governed the relationship of the gods toward humans and the manner in which they bestowed or withheld their favors.

The influence of the Homeric pantheon in guiding the imagination of Greek artists was considerable. Humans could now gaze with awe and wonder at bronze and marble likenesses or embodiments of the gods while standing in temples, acropolises (city citadels), and marketplaces. But transcending even Zeus was a power that Zeus might change by force of will but to which he also submitted. This power was identified as Moira (fate) and Ker (doom)—the destiny allotted to each individual. Sometimes Zeus was the instrument of fate, but he was powerless to control it. So although the Homeric deities were represented as superhuman beings, their powers were not boundless.

Hesiod. Hesiod, a poet thought to have lived in the eighth century BCE, also attempted to present a detailed and systematic genealogy of the Greek deities and the order of the universe. His treatment, contained in a work titled *Theogony,* is considered to be entirely mythical and, perhaps, influenced by Near Eastern religious traditions. His theory or interpretation was that pristine Chaos gave way by a process of cosmic evolution to Love (Eros), the Pit (Tartarus), and then the Earth (Gaea or Ge). In its turn, the Earth self-generated the Mountains, the Ocean, and the Sky. Then followed the mating of Earth with the Ocean and the Sky in an attempt to bring order out of chaos.

Intellectual Views

To an extent unknown in Egypt or Mesopotamia, the Greeks intellectualized religious beliefs and concepts. Dramatists and philosophers, not content with chronicling the activities of the gods or explaining religious concepts, continually examined the bases of religious beliefs, searching for fundamental intellectual and moral values. Their rationalistic, even skeptical, attitude toward traditional religion was to exert a profound influence on the future course of Western religions.

Dramatists. Human destiny was a recurrent theme of the great dramatists of the sixth and fifth centuries BCE—especially Aeschylus, Sophocles, and Euripides. The question to which they addressed themselves was whether the gods or fate controlled human destiny. Both Aeschylus and Sophocles exalted Zeus as the administrator of cosmic justice. They took the position that all other deities yielded to Zeus's will when he overruled them in the name of justice. Aeschylus portrayed Zeus in command of fate and in control of human destiny. Sophocles, however, softened this implacable image by attributing to Zeus a judgment tempered by mercy, although he acknowledged that Zeus's favor was not easily gained without purity in word and deed. In contrast, Euripides, who was influenced by humanist sentiments, expressed skepticism about the justice and integrity of the gods. He pitied human beings, whose destiny lay at the mercy of uncaring, unfeeling, and unseeing deities. The following excerpt reflects his sentiments:

> Ah pain, pain! O unrighteous curse . . .
> Thou Zeus, doest see me?
> Yea, it is I; the proud and pure, the server of god;

The white and shining in sanctity!
To a visible death, to an open sod, I walk my ways;
And all the labor of saintly days lost, lost without meaning![20]

Philosophers. Greek philosophers of the fifth century BCE also attempted to come to terms with contemporary beliefs in the gods. On the whole they maintained a reserved, if not skeptical, attitude toward traditional views. Xenophanes, born in Colophon around 540 BCE, favored the concept of a divine, creative power—one god who was the greatest among deities and human beings, who thought all, saw all, and heard all. He ridiculed the human proclivity to represent such a god in the likeness of another human, thus perpetuating what he saw as an anthropomorphic fallacy. If animals, argued Xenophanes, were able to think and act, they too would represent the deities in their own likeness or form:

> Mortals think that the gods are begotten, and wear clothes like their own, and have a voice and a form. If oxen or horses or lions had hands and could draw with them and make works of art as men do, horses would draw the shapes of gods like horses, oxen like oxen; each kind would represent their bodies just like their own forms.[21]

Plato, born in Athens in 429 BCE, criticized the traditional piety expressed by earlier thinkers. For him, the immoralities of the Olympian deities were far from inspiring or edifying to the youth of his day. He was severely critical of the Homeric pantheon and advocated a revision of traditional tales of the gods in order to censor passages to which he objected. Plato did not deny the existence of the deities so much as he rejected the Homeric representation of them as wayward and fallible. Plato also disagreed with mystery religions for representing the deities as easily swayed from impartial justice.

For Plato, the highest of all values was the Good, the beginning of the realm of ideal forms, the "creator" above and behind all other things. Gods, humans, animals, mountains, plains, and seas all embodied the Good in various degrees. Consequently, the gods required none of the magical or superstitious rituals that contemporary human beings considered to be their rightful due. Each human being, Plato argued, was a soul encased in a body, and all that the gods required was that each soul should seek to grow toward the highest good in order to move into a timeless, eternal realm where the soul would see and enjoy ideal forms in all their truth, beauty, and goodness.

Plato's conception of a timeless realm lying beyond the reach of the senses and culminating in the form of the Good impressed students and fellow philosophers alike. Aristotle, born in Stagira, Macedon, in 384 BCE and a student in Plato's school of philosophy for twenty years, postulated a pattern of thought that affected all subsequent philosophers, scientists, and theologians. In his philosophy Aristotle dispensed with the traditional Greek deities. Instead, he posited as the highest type of being the Prime Mover, a motionless being who caused all the movements of celestial and terrestrial bodies by attracting them toward himself.

Popular Religion

Even as the philosophers seriously challenged traditional religious beliefs, however, Greek popular religion flourished along with the various civic cults. People worshiped all sorts of nature spirits and local deities. Magic, spells, and witchcraft were widespread. Religious civic festivals attracted large gatherings and punctuated daily life, and the oracles, with their claim to reveal the future, were eagerly consulted by individuals as well as states.

Daemons, Nymphs, and Heroes. The most persistent form of Greek religion was that of simple and unlettered peasants. Gods were often overthrown and forgotten, but nature spirits, daemons, nymphs, and heroes persisted in the memories and in the day-to-day activities of ordinary people.

Daemons seem to have been of two types: the *centaurs* and the *seilenoi*. The *centaurs*, inhabiting bodies that were half-human and half-horse, were believed to have originated as spirits of the precipitous mountain torrents. They represented the nature spirits of wood and wilderness—that is, the rough and violent aspect of nature. *Seilenoi* were daemons distinguished by the body of a man with the hindquarters (legs, tail, and testicles) of a horse. In Greek mythology, the *seilenoi* (and their Roman counterparts, the satyrs) have sexual intercourse with nymphs, the female spirits of nature. Nymphs were always thought of as human in shape. They were beautiful, omnipresent, and benevolent, although at times capable of anger and threatening behavior. Their usual habitats were groves, caves, meadows, and mountains, but there were also sea and tree nymphs. Artemis, the great and most popular goddess of Greece, was associated with trees, rivers, and springs, and haunted mountains and meadows; she was viewed as the leader of the nymphs. She protected women in childbirth and watched over children, but she was also the goddess preferred by hunters and was considered the virgin twin sister of Apollo.

Heroes in ancient Greece were regarded as inferior to gods, even though some, such as Heracles, Asclepius, and the Dioscuri, were not far removed from divinity. Not necessarily heroic figures in the mod-

Detail of the head of Heracles (Hercules) in the Pitti Palace, Florence. Heracles was the most popular and widely worshiped of Greek heroes. Of his celebrated twelve endeavors, three had to do with the conquest of death, giving Heracles the character of a savior. (It is possible that he thus affected the development of Christology.) As the Roman god of victory and traders, an ancient altar was built in his honor in the Forum Boarium (Cattle Market). His emblems are the lion skin, the club, and the poplar tree.
The Granger Collection.

ern sense, the Greek heroes were people who in death transcended the admiration that they had earned in life and continued to walk the earth in corporeal form. The cult of heroes was centered on tombs or on the relics buried in the tombs of heroes. For this reason the bones of heroes were sometimes dug up and transferred to another place during wartime. The Lacedaemonians, for instance, with some difficulty recovered the bones of Orestes at Tega and transferred them to Sparta to help the Spartans fight the Arcadians. And in the battle of Marathon (490 BCE), King Theseus was said to have risen from his tomb to fight with the Athenians against the Persians. Be that as it may, heroes and heroines in ancient Greece were so numerous that their tombs and shrines dotted the countryside. They were believed to appear in concrete form, and any individual could call on them for help in all matters of life. The similarity of Greek heroes and heroines to Christian saints is striking enough to have provoked frequent comment by historians of comparative religion.[22]

Oracles. Another aspect of Greek religion that was of great importance was that of the oracle—an answer to a specific question vouchsafed by a deity to a human inquirer, usually through a priest or priestess. Other methods of inquiry included the casting of lots; incubation, a process by which an inquirer sleeping in a holy precinct would receive a response from the deity in a dream; and an oracular

GREECE – ROME

pronouncement in response to a question delivered orally by a human agent. Thus, responses were supposed to emanate by supernatural inspiration either through a human agent or through some object. In either case, the idea was that a power took possession of a person or thing and made the person or thing a medium of response.

Among the famous oracular shrines were those of Zeus at Dodona and Olympia, of Apollo at Delphi and Delos, and of Asclepius at Epidaurus. The most ancient oracular shrine was at Dodona, where priests (later priestesses) revealed the responses of Zeus from the rustling of oak trees, from a sacred spring, and from the striking of a gong. The most popular oracular shrine, however, was that of Apollo at Delphi, where the medium was a woman known as Pythia. After certain introductory rituals, she became possessed by the god while she sat on a sacred tripod, and her ecstatic utterances were passed on by priests to the inquirer. These inquirers were either private citizens who consulted the oracle for personal matters, or kings who sought the advice of the deity in matters of war or politics. At times, priests had difficulty in understanding the oracle and consequently passed on the response in the form of ambiguous verse. For instance, Croesus, king of Lydia, consulted the oracle before he invaded Cappadocia. The answer he received stated that if he invaded the country he would "bring ruin to the empire." Croesus jumped to the conclusion that the oracle referred to Cappadocia. He was wrong—but he did not realize his mistake until he had lost his empire.

The influence of the Delphic oracle gradually waned during Roman times, and ultimately the sanctuary was closed by the Christian Roman Emperor Theodosius in 390 CE.

Festivals. These large gatherings expressed the social aspect of religion. Basically agrarian in origin, festivals were seasonal, were held often at the full moon, and always included animal sacrifices. They were not always strictly religious in nature. Some served as occasions for official functions, such as honoring citizens or receiving foreign embassies. Others, such as the Pan-Hellenic Pythian and Olympic festivals, expressed the unity of the Greek peoples and included dramas, poetry recitals, music, and athletic contests. Thus, no rigid distinction was drawn between the artistic expression, the political life, and the religious concern of the populace.

The precise details of many festivals are obscure. In Athens, some seventy festivals were celebrated in a year. The Athenians honored their deities by seasons of the year: Apollo, Athena, and Demeter in the summer and fall; Dionysus and Artemis in the spring. The manifold functions of Zeus made him an exception, in that he received honors all year round.

Among the more elaborate Athenian festivals was the Panathenaea, honoring Athena, the patron goddess of the city. This festival was held annually in midsummer, and, on a more splendid scale, every fourth year. Its purpose, besides the offering of sacrifices, was to provide the image of Athena, housed in the temple on the Acropolis, with a newly embroidered mantle woven by Athenian women. Every fourth year, the celebration included, in addition to the procession, a torch race, bardic recitations, mock fights, and athletic contests.

Another important festival celebrated in Athens in the spring was the Dionysia, honoring the god Dionysus. At the end of this six-day ritual, the image of Dionysus was escorted to the theater, where he presided over the dramatic performances of Aeschylus, Sophocles, Euripides, and Aristophanes.

The Pan-Hellenic festivals were the most famous: the Olympic, held at Olympia in honor of Zeus; the Pythian, held at Delphi in honor of Apollo; the Isthmian, held at the Isthmus of Corinth in honor of Poseidon; and the Nemean, held at Nemea in honor of Zeus. All travelers to the Pan-Hellenic festivals were guaranteed safe passage, even in wartime.

The Olympic festivals, which were celebrated every fourth summer in Zeus's sacred precinct in the western Peloponnesus, attracted large numbers of athletes from all parts of the Greek world. A nationwide truce was proclaimed, to allow warring Greeks to compete, and the celebrations lasted five days. After sacrifice and libation were offered at the altars of Zeus and Hestia and at the tomb of Pelops, the judges and competitors took the oath to observe the rules. Then followed the processions, the bardic recitations, and the honoring of the winners at state banquets. In all this, women were banned, although they competed at the festival of the goddess Hera. The festivals in honor of Apollo at Delphi and of Poseidon at Isthmus followed the Olympian pattern.

Mystery Religions

The third major component of Greek religious life addressed a human need largely untouched by the intellectual speculations of the philosophers and the formulaic prescriptions of traditional religious forms. Those seeking an intensely personal, emotionally satisfying religious experience turned to the mystery religions, or cults. Initiates of these religious movements underwent purification rites, received instruction in mystical knowledge, viewed sacred objects, watched the enactment of a divine story, and were crowned as full-fledged members. The initiation was spread over several days and included various celebrations and processions. These experiences were referred to as "mysterious" rather than "mystical" because the rites were kept absolutely secret from all except the initiates. Individuals who wished to join any of these religious movements were initiated to the secret rites by a *hierophant*—a revealer of sacred mysteries and esoteric principles. Initiates were sworn to secrecy and put to death if they broke their vows.

So passionately devoted were the members of the mystery religions that they carried on with their rites even during public crises. According to the historian Herodotus, even while Attica was being ravaged by the Persians and the Greek fleet at Salamis was in danger, thousands of devotees of the Eleusinian mysteries marched in a procession from Eleusis to Athens, chanting their mystical hymn to Dionysus.[23] The mystery religions, then, provided not only a personal religious satisfaction, but a deep sense of a mystic reality—the reality of sharing the immortal nature of the gods.

Eleusinian Mysteries. The Eleusinian mysteries were by far the greatest of all Greek mystery religions. The three deities involved were the grain goddess Demeter, her daughter Kore, and the underworld god Hades. The story underlying the Eleusinian mysteries went as follows. After Kore was carried off to the underworld by Hades to be his bride, the sorrowing mother searched for her everywhere with a lighted torch, until finally she arrived at Eleusis exhausted and in utter despair. During this state, she refused to make the grain grow, and so terrible was the resultant famine that the deities persuaded Zeus to ask Hades to return Kore to her mother. Hades agreed to let Kore return to earth, but only after he had cunningly persuaded her to eat a pomegranate (the fruit that symbolized marriage), thus ensuring her return to the underworld. Zeus then effected a compromise, whereby Kore had to return to the underworld for only one-third of each year. Consequently, Kore was identified in Greek mythology with Persephone, queen of Hades.

Some time later—precisely when is not clear—the god Dionysus was also incorporated into the Eleusinian mysteries. The content and nature of the mysteries were kept secret, though the public could witness the procession of candidates going down to the sea for ritual purification. Several days later, after the candidates had gone through their initiation rites, the public could witness the procession of the *mystae* (initiates) from Athens to Eleusis and back. As to the initiates, they could claim knowledge to the secret of happiness after death.

The main ceremonies of the Eleusinian mysteries eventually became common knowledge throughout the Hellenic world and, later, the Roman Empire. (Several Roman emperors became *mystae*.) Only the destruction of the temple at Eleusis following the invasion of Greece by Alaric the Goth in the fourth century CE put an end to the Eleusinian mysteries.

Dionysian Mysteries. Dionysus, a god from Phrygia, in Asia Minor, who came to Greece through Thrace, became the central figure of yet another extravagant mystery religion. The practices of the Dionysian mysteries were normally held in remote places, such as mountainsides, where devotees, predominantly women, gathered to express their religious excitement in eating, drinking, music, and dancing. The ritual culminated in tearing apart and eating the raw flesh, and drinking the blood, of a bull or kid, which was identified with Dionysus. The blood, the raw flesh, the wail of music, the whirling dance, and the glow of torches all heightened the consciousness of the devotees to a state of divine possession. They felt themselves identified with Bacchus, one of Dionysus's aspects as god of the vine. These devotees were, therefore, known as bacchants or maenads (mad ones).

Some time around the sixth to fifth centuries BCE, the wildness and frenzy of Dionysian mysteries aroused criticism and hostility among those who respected tradition. Nevertheless, the ecstatic practices continued up to Roman times.

Orphic Mysteries. The Orphic movement was said to have been founded in the fifth century BCE by Orpheus, legendary poet and musician of Greek mythology, a victim of *sparagmos* (tearing to pieces) by the maenads in Thrace. According to Orphic tradition, Dionysus, under the name of Zagreus, was the offspring of Zeus and Persephone. The Titans, an ancient race of giant gods, killed the infant Zagreus and ate his flesh. In retaliation, Zeus burned the Titans with his thunderbolts and formed the human race from the ashes. Humans, then, were conceived as a combination of good and evil—the ashes of the Titans (evil) containing the substance of Zagreus (good). However, Zagreus, as it turned out, had not been entirely swallowed by the Titans. The goddess Athena had managed to rescue the infant's heart, which was swallowed by Zeus. Zagreus was then reborn as the son of the earth goddess Semele. And through *ascetic* (not, as in the Dionysian mysteries, ecstatic) practices, such as food restrictions, self-denying practices, and purification rites, devotees of the Orphic mysteries attempted to liberate themselves from bodily entanglements in order to achieve immortal life.

Strangely enough, Orphic ideas were incorporated into the philosophies of both Pythagoras (c. 582–507 BCE) and Plato. In fact, the Pythagoreans insisted on the need for purity, food *taboos* (forbidden food), and a belief in reincarnation. Their studies in mathematics, medicine, music, astronomy, and philosophy were designed to awaken the divine elements in humans so that they could regain the state of purity and end their earthly transmigration.

Greek Mythology

Greek religion in all its manifestations—intellectual, popular, and mysterious—was so rich in myths that even the barest outline would require more space than is available here. The origins of many Greek myths are lost. What remains is the creation of the poets, starting no earlier than 1000 BCE with Homer and his epic poem the *Iliad*. Greek mythology does not portray prehistoric humankind, but it clearly reveals what early Greeks thought and imagined. The Greeks, unlike the Egyptians and Mesopotamians, made their gods in their own image. Greek deities were real, normal, and natural: they ate, drank, feasted, made love, and amused themselves as human beings did. Naturally, these deities were very powerful and dangerous when they were angry, so they were to be feared. Yet with proper care, a person could be at ease with them, sometimes even laugh at them. In fact, these gods were not only exceedingly human but also very attractive.

The terrifying, irrational world of spooky monsters was lacking in Greek mythology, and demonic creatures were few. Thus, the world of Greek mythology was, by and large, far from a place of terror. What stood out predominantly in Greek mythology were the stories and adventures of gods, goddesses, heroes, and heroines: the mighty Zeus, who was all too human; Hera, his wife, the prototype of the jealous woman; the love affairs of Cupid and Psyche or Pygmalion and Galatea; the adventures of Jason and the quest for the Golden Fleece; the superhuman achievements of Odysseus and Heracles; the tragic fate of Oedipus and the heroic Antigone—all these contributed to the texture of the Greek mythological tapestry.

Hellenistic Religions

Because of the conquests of Alexander the Great, the Greeks and the Macedonians came into contact with a number of impressive Oriental religious cults. The international associations and racial mixture that resulted from Greek contact with Asiatic peoples created opportunities for cultural and religious diffusion. This did not mean that traditional Greek religion and cults disappeared, but rather that an ever-increasing number of people came in contact with "foreign" beliefs and practices. Thus, the assimilation of various deities led to unification. Greek and, later, Roman monarchs, like Oriental monarchs, were considered emanations of gods. Indeed, the deities of Greece, Egypt, Asia Minor, and Persia attracted all Greeks.

The Roman conquest in the second century BCE ultimately absorbed Greece into a wider political world. Greek religion, like most other aspects of Greek life, had a considerable impact on Roman religion. Greek and Roman deities mingled, and a process of syncretism took place. Greek religion survived in this form until 529 CE, when the Christian Roman Emperor Justinian dealt a death blow by closing the Athenian schools of philosophy.

Roman Religion

Historical Background

No one knows how or when Rome was founded. One story, popularized in Vergil's *Aeneid*, held that the Trojan warrior Aeneas set up a kingdom in Italy after the fall of Troy around 1100 BCE. Another legend described how Romulus and Remus, twin brothers, founded Rome around 753 BCE. According to this story, the twin infants were placed in a basket and set adrift on the Tiber River, which carried them to the foot of the Palatine Hill. There a she-wolf cared for the boys until the shepherd Faustulus found them and took them to his house. (Up to this point the story bears a striking resemblance to stories about the Mesopotamian King Sargon and the biblical Moses.) Faustulus reared the boys with his own children. Later, the two brothers decided to build a new city at the spot where their lives had been saved, but an argument that came to blows about the exact site of their deliverance culminated in the death of Remus at the hand of Romulus. The building of the city of Rome followed, and Romulus became its founder and leader.

Archeological study has offered no evidence to support the legendary claims of either Aeneas or Romulus as founders of Rome. Excavations show that the city of Rome was the site of a small farming village of Latin inhabitants as early as the eighth century BCE. This simple community later became the capital of a huge empire, whose boundaries at its height, during the reign of Emperor Trajan in the second century CE, included most of Europe, part of the Middle East, and the northern coastal area of Africa. Its millions of people, speaking many languages and worshiping different deities, were united by the military power and imperial administration of the Romans.

According to tradition, seven kings ruled early Rome, though their power was limited by a council of advisors, called the Senate, and by an assembly of citizens. In 509 BCE the Romans rose against the ruling Etruscan king and established a republic. Rome remained a republic until 27 BCE, when Augustus named himself emperor and vested himself with supreme authority. The establishment of an empire, however, did not at first radically alter forms of republican government; as time went on, however, the Senate lost its power and the emperor became an absolute monarch.

During the republican period, the Romans gradually defeated and subjugated their rivals, expanding their territory until Rome became one of the most powerful nations on the Mediterranean littoral. In 149 BCE the Roman forces destroyed Carthage (in modern Tunisia), and in 146 BCE they completed their conquest of Greece by destroying Corinth. This victory paved the way for a Roman penetration of western Asia and an extension of their dominion over a large portion of the Middle East.

Peace and prosperity prevailed in the Roman Empire for the greater part of its course. For two centuries, no country was strong enough to pose a serious threat to or to launch a major war on Rome. This period of successful administrative stability, however, gave way to a century of military and economic crises that presaged a series of internal rivalries and struggles. The consequence of the social instability and disorder that ensued was the division of the Roman state into an eastern and western empire in the fourth century CE. Constantine, the first Christian emperor, created the new eastern capital and named it Constantinople (modern Istanbul in Turkey). In 410 Rome was sacked by the Goths, and in 476 the last western Roman emperor was deposed by invading Germanic tribes. Meanwhile, the eastern Roman Empire, which came to be known as Byzantium, survived as a beleaguered bastion of Christianity until 1453, when Constantinople finally fell into the hands of the Muslim Turks.

The expansion of Roman power during the republican period favored Greek religious influences, especially the adoption of Greek deities; at this time many Roman gods became identified with Greek ones. Similarly, Greek education and philosophy penetrated Roman life and culture. During the period of the empire, many Romans were attracted to western Asian religions, such as the worship of Cybele (Phrygian), Isis (Egyptian), Serapis (Egyptian), and Mithras (Persian). Converts to Christianity challenged conventional religious orthodoxies and perceptions to such an extent that they were at first opposed and persecuted. In 313 CE, however, the Emperor Constantine gave Christianity a legal status that was further confirmed around 380 by Emperor Theodosius I, who established it as the state religion.

Numina

Roman religion involved belief in the potency of a supernatural quality called *numen* (pl., *numina*), from which the term *numinous* is derived. The numina were thought of in a personal way and were associated with deities, humans, and particular places, functions (such as procreation, healing, and fighting), and things (such as homes, kitchen utensils, trees, rivers, and boundary stones). The deities derived their power and greatness in proportion to the strength of their numina. Jupiter, as the chief deity, had more numen than the rest of the deities. Appropriate sacrifices performed by humans enhanced the numen of the deities to whom they were offered. Humans also possessed numen—particularly in groups or tribes. Numen was transferable and was conferred by a deity upon a person, a tribe, a farm, a tool, and other elements.

The importance of the concept of numen in Roman religion led to a rather ambiguous definition of divine characteristics. There was a lack of distinct personality, and even sometimes of sex, among the various deities. No anthropomorphic images, no divine genealogies, and no mythical histories seemed to have intrigued the imaginative faculty of the Romans. Roman religion focused on the diverse functions of numina, not on the characteristics and personal histories of the deities.

To ensure success in any endeavor, the Romans invoked the relevant numina. In the cultivation of grain, for example, Saturnus represented the best source of numen in sowing, Ceres in growing, Consus in harvesting, and Ops in storing. Pales was the numen in pasture, Faunus in woods and forests, and Lares in sown fields, family estates, and crossroads. In the home, Janus was the numen in the door, Vesta in the hearth. Penates were the numina in the cupboard or storeroom; Lar Familiaris, the numina in the whole household.

The list of Roman numinous functions is as diverse and as interesting as a weekend grocery list. However, a few important numina are hard to define. Genius was the numen in every male, representing the energy, vitality, and essence of manhood. Juno was the numen in every female, representing the energy, vitality, and essence of womanhood. The Manes were the numina of the dead, which had to be propitiated with appropriate burial rites in order to secure entrance to the underworld. To do less was to risk the haunting presence of Lemures—unhappy spirits denied entrance to the underworld, spreading misfortune among the living.

The Roman numina were propitiated and honored by a variety of magical acts, ceremonial rituals, and festivals, each of which was regulated by certain principles that were carried out with formal exactness. Any deviation from appropriate formulas rendered the whole exercise ineffective.

Deities

It has been said that the Roman deities were as alike as peas in a pod, and there is some justification for such a conclusion. Many survived in name only, having lost their following or appeal or having been superseded or incorporated by new systems of worship or belief, so that little or nothing is known about them. Some, however, retained their prominence through the centuries by virtue of art or literature and merit some comment.

Jupiter was the ancient Indo-European Dyaus Pitar (or Diovis Pater, Zeus Pater), whose exalted title was Optimus Maximus. He was the god of light, lightning, thunder, rain, and storm. He prescribed and ordered human affairs, which augurs or soothsayers could predict by signs in the heavens or by the flight of birds, and he was the guardian of laws and oaths. His sanctuary, or temple, was on the Capitoline Hill, called Jupiter Capitolinus. In later years, he was associated with the imperial glories of Rome and acquired various titles: the Victor,

Invictus, Imperator. His consort was Juno, whom the Greeks identified with Hera.

Mars, originally the protector of fields and herds, was best known as a war god whose sacred symbols were the lance and shield and whose sacred animal was the wolf. He was honored in the first month (later changed to the third month) of the Roman calendar. March (from *Martius*) was named after him, and the priests of Mars *(salii)* celebrated the festival with dancing in the street. Quirinus was another war god, of whom little is known. He was served by a *flamen,* a priest assigned to a particular god, and an annual festival called Quirinalia was dedicated to him.

Janus was the god of beginnings and was invoked at the opening or threshold of almost any event or structure: the New Year (January, derived from Janus), the first day of every month, the first hour of the day, or the entrance (door) of a home, or a city gate. His symbol was an opening or entrance; in Rome it was the gateway to the Forum.

Minerva was the goddess of wisdom and the patroness of the arts and trades. Later, she was associated with war and was therefore represented as wearing a helmet and carrying a shield and a spear.

Priests, Diviners, and Cultic Functionaries

The Romans believed that the health, safety, and welfare of the family, as well as of the state, depended on the protection and goodwill of the deities. Thus the performance of all religious rituals was assumed by the state, and the emperor was vested with priestly in addition to secular power.

During the republic the administrative responsibility for state religious affairs was held by an official with the title *Pontifex Maximus,* who had the power to appoint high-level priests from a well-defined hierarchy divided into colleges or guilds or according to specific functions. The *sacerdos,* for instance, was a priest whose function was to officiate at sacrificial rites, especially animal sacrifices, which were central to worship in public temples. In addition, each deity had his own *flamen,* or priest, whose duty was to light the altar fires. Then there was the board of augurs (consisting originally of three members but later increased to sixteen), who specialized in interpreting any unusual event or phenomenon by the flight of birds and the movements of fowl. Important decisions about state matters were often delayed until a propitious augury was obtained from the board of augurs.

The Romans also solicited omens, portents, and divine messages beyond their own borders. The Etruscan *haruspex,* an expert diviner, was consulted for important matters. Messengers were sent to the renowned Greek temple of Apollo to receive his oracles. Later, both methods were imported into Rome.

Magic, on the whole, was a discredited practice and a disreputable occupation in Rome, though fortunetelling by magical means was common enough. An ancient Roman code of law indicates that two forms of sorcery were forbidden—the use of a noxious charm and the practice of making a neighbor's crops magically leap over to a sorcerer. Expert sorcerers were believed to have the power to bring themselves into contact with a deity, or to induce a deity to exercise his numen in a specific way to achieve a particular objective. By performing the proper rites—that is, by applying magical arts—a powerful sorcerer could achieve the desired results. However, the evidence indicates that the Romans did not rely on magic to the same degree that many of their neighbors did.

Almost a corollary of magic was astrology. Several philosophical schools insisted that the stars were divine and that celestial motions, especially solar or lunar, had a religious significance far beyond their surface appearance as natural phenomena. The position of the heavenly bodies at the time of someone's birth was believed to determine the destiny of that individual. Predictions did not always satisfy expectations raised by complicated astrological rules and formulas, yet forecasts gained considerable credence among the public—so much so that astrologers were often opposed by state officials.

More numerous than public congregations of worshipers were private associations that had religious purposes. Members of such associations described themselves as *cultores*, or cult devotees. A decree of the Roman Senate stipulated the maximum number of meetings these associations could hold annually and the limitations placed on their activities. These private associations, however, did not seem to be really more than burial cult clubs. Members paid a subscription and in return received a respectable funeral at the time of their death, which included the rite of a funeral feast. Although very little is known about these private cults, it seems that they provided their members with an assurance or hope of a better life in another world.

Roman Religious Festivals

The Roman religious festivals, especially those celebrations connected with the deities, were of two kinds—fixed feasts and movable feasts. The first type, like similar festivals in modern religions, occurred on the same, fixed date or dates each year. The second type of festival was celebrated on dates that might vary and were determined from year to year. The nature of some Roman religious festivals is known; the record of others is limited to a list of names and dates, indicating the time of year at which festivals were held.

Religious public festivals, as prescribed and set down on the state calendar, occupied 104 days each year. Priests of the various deities or cults performed a long order of ceremonies and sacrifices. Their performances were meticulously enacted, whether or not anyone attended apart from themselves. A description of some of the best-known festivals indicates the importance and seriousness of these religious ceremonies.

The festival of Equirria was conducted by the *salii*, or the priests of Mars, twice a year—on the first day of March and on the last day of October. The centerpieces of both festivals were races of war-horses; in October the winning horse was solemnly sacrificed to Mars, as a way of contributing to the deity's numen. On March 19 and October 19 these same priests performed a lustration, or purification, ceremony of the weapons of the Roman legions. This ceremony consisted of a dance, in which the legionnaires brandished their spears and clashed their shields in an act of war magic. Again on March 23 and May 23 the *salii* performed a lustration of the war trumpets, the magical effects of which were associated not with war but with farmers and herders.

The festival of Fordicidia was observed on April 15 by sacrificing pregnant cows to the goddess Tellus in the hope that the fields would yield good crops. The fetus of each animal was carefully removed and burnt, and its ashes were buried by vestal virgins (virgins consecrated to the goddess Vesta, goddess of the hearth), as an effective means of ensuring the fertility of sheep. These vestal virgins, who were chosen from patrician families, were priestesses who had taken a vow of chastity, violation of which was punishable by death. There were only six of them at a time, each serving for thirty years; their chief function was to tend the holy fire of Vesta (the hearth fire) in the national shrine in Rome. An annual festival, called Vestalia, was held for nine days, June 7 to 15. During this period women came barefooted to Vesta's shrine with their offerings, which were burned in Vesta's fire in preparation for the approaching harvest.

At the festival of Parilia (April 21), sheep were made to jump through a ring of burning straw or laurel, as a magical act of purifying the animals. The festival of Cerealia was held on April 19 by the priests of Ceres to promote the growth of grain sown in the fields. The festival of Robigalia was held on April 25 in a grove, where a red dog was sacrificed to prevent red rust from endangering the grain crops.

At least six festivals observed in August were devoted to the various phases of the harvest. There were also six festivals in December, including the festival of Saturnalia, when friends and relatives exchanged gifts. Perhaps the most famous of the festivals was that of Lupercalia, which started with the sacrifice of several goats and a dog and concluded with the priests running in two bands around the walls of the Palatine settlement, striking women who suffered from sterility with thongs cut from the skins of the sacrificed animals.

Foreign Accretions

From about the sixth century BCE onward, the Romans came in contact with the Greeks and then with the peoples of the Middle East. The result was a progressive identification of the deities within and between the various religions and the reinforcement of the anthropomorphic strain in Roman piety. Thus, the Roman god Jupiter was equated with the Greek god Zeus, Juno with Hera, Mars with Ares, Minerva

Temple of the goddess Hera at Paestum, Italy, dated c. 450 BCE. Hera (Juno to the Romans), queen of the gods and the sister and wife of Zeus, was associated with marriage and the sexual life of women. Her temples at Olympia, Argos, and Samos are renowned.   From the private collection of Tom G. Elliott.

with Athena, Neptune with Poseidon, Venus with Aphrodite, and so on. More important, however, and of far-reaching ramification, was the importation of a collection of Greek oracles—the famous Sibylline Books. These books were stored in the basement of the Capitoline temple, and two priests were appointed to take charge of consulting the oracles. Later the number of priests was increased to ten and, later still, to fifteen. The introduction of the Greek oracles helped the Romans to add an entirely new dimension to their religion—personalized deities.

Soon temples were erected to Apollo, the god of healing; to Mercury, the god of commerce; to Fortuna, the goddess of luck and good fortune; and to many other deities who were represented as wooden figures, elegantly dressed and reclining on couches beside a table laid for a sacramental meal. Along with this adoption of personalized deities, the Romans also showed a keen interest in Greek myths and epics. Some Greek mythologies were recast in a Roman context, whereas other stories were adopted with little change.

The influence of Greeks on Romans was felt not only in religious matters but also in philosophical systems. Starting from the first century BCE onward, the teachings and ideals of Epicurus (342–270 BCE), Zeno (335–263 BCE), and Plato (427–347 BCE), among others, attracted the attention of many educated Romans. However, the masses were far less interested in Greek philosophical systems than they were in various Greek and Middle Eastern mystery cults, which provided them with a more personal, as opposed to a formal, religious experience.

Cybele and Attis. The first Middle Eastern mystery cult adopted by the Romans as a result of an oracular command was the worship of Cybele, the goddess of the Phrygians.[24] In 204 BCE, a black meteorite stone, representing this foreign goddess, was solemnly installed on the summit of the Palatine amid the cheers of the public and the fumes of incense. Next, a temple was erected on the spot and an annual celebration was held from April 4 to 10 in commemoration of the arrival of the goddess, now named the Great Mother Goddess of Idaea (or Ida) by the Romans. In a short time, however, the cult of Cybele encountered resistance from both the civil administration and the public, because of the orgiastic acts of its priests during the annual festival.

The annual festival of Cybele-Attis was held on the spring equinox and lasted four days, from March 22 to 25. On the first day the trunk of a pine tree wreathed with violets and swathed with woolen cloth was carried ceremonially into the temple. Then, an effigy of the god Attis, who was Cybele's lover and was reputed to have died by emasculating himself under a pine tree, was fastened to the decorated tree trunk. On the second day, a procession of mourners followed the statue of the goddess Cybele through the streets. They screamed, whirled, and leaped, and in their frenzy slashed themselves with knives or swords. On the third day, the bloody passion-drama reached its climax. Like Attis, the novitiates sacrificed their virility by emasculation, so that they could share Attis's resurrection. The severed organs were offered on the altar of the goddess Cybele. The effigy was then removed and laid in a tomb, while the castrated initiates watched and fasted until the next morning. Early at dawn on the fourth day, the tomb was opened and the crowds of worshipers shouted in joy, because the god Attis was resurrected and the tomb was empty. The festival ended with a huge and joyous procession carrying the black meteorite stone (representing Cybele) to the river, where it was ceremonially bathed, after which it was returned to its sacred place within the temple.

In addition to this festival were some rituals performed only by the emasculated initiates. These ceremonies consisted of an initiatory rite, known as the *taurobolium,* and a sacramental meal. The *taurobolium* was a baptismal font in the form of a pit into which the newly inducted members descended, to stand under a grating that supported a sacred bull. The sacrificial bull was ceremonially slain on the grating so that its blood ran over the inductees below, who, by this ritual, were considered to be purified. This ritual of purification was followed by a sacramental meal at which the inductees shared a sense of oneness or of unity as they ate from a common drum and drank from a common cymbal.

The similarity between some aspects of the rites associated with Cybele-Attis and the Christian celebration of the resurrection of Christ are striking. Two coincidences stand out: first, the very site of Cybele's temple is where the basilica of St. Peter's stands today; and second, the annual spring celebration of the death, burial, resurrection, and discovery of an empty tomb are features of the ancient rites of Cybele-Attis and of the annual spring celebration of Easter, or Pascha, commemorating the death, burial, resurrection, and discovery of the empty tomb of Jesus Christ.

Isis and Serapis. The worship of the Egyptian goddess Isis was introduced to Italy in about the second century BCE, but long before that the popularity of her cult had spread far and wide. Her statues and temples adorned Syria around the seventh century BCE, and three centuries later a great temple was built for Isis at the foot of the Acropolis in Greece. Soon every Greek city and village had a temple and a statue of Isis. The statue of Isis, which represented the Mother Goddess with her suckling infant son, Horus, became an object of veneration in the Greco-Roman world. Some scholars are of the opinion that the Christian image or statue of the Madonna and child (Mary and the infant Jesus) resembles that of Isis and her son.

The goddess Isis was regarded as the symbol of maternal love, protection, creative life, and chastity, and she was regarded as the queen of heaven. Because she encompassed such virtues, her cult attracted a large number of followers. Two festivals, one in spring and the other in autumn, were celebrated in her honor. The spring festival coincided with the Egyptian harvest. The autumn celebration, however, consisted of a four-day dramatic festival. On the first day, actors impersonated several Egyptian deities, including Isis and Horus, who wept, wailed, and searched for the body of Osiris. On the next two days, portions of the body of Osiris were found, reconstituted, and resurrected by Isis. On the fourth day a great rejoicing took place, because Osiris had been resurrected and became immortal. All devotees of Isis could also celebrate her assurance of life after death and immortality by drinking the milk of Isis from a chalice formed in the shape of a woman's breast. Those who put their trust in Isis did so in the conviction that she would intercede on their behalf with Osiris when they appeared before his throne of judgment and that Osiris would in no way deny immortality to those for whom Isis interceded.

The Egyptian god Serapis was also closely associated with the mythology surrounding Osiris. The name was a Hellenized combination of Osiris and Apis, the Egyptian bull god. His cult originated in Alexandria, Egypt, and from the beginning was identified with Osiris, the god that ruled the dead and shared immortality with them. Its adoption by the Romans began around the second century BCE, although a century later strict measures were taken by the Roman Senate to stop its diffusion.

Yet the worship of Serapis, like the cult of Isis, invaded Italy and every imperial province. Not until five centuries after they had been adopted by the Romans were the cults of Isis and Serapis finally suppressed. In 390 CE the Patriarch Theophilus, with the aid of the Roman Emperor Theodosius, consigned the temple of Serapis in Alexandria to the flames. Between the reigns of the emperors Theodosius and Justinian, an interval of about two hundred years, the worship of Isis, Serapis, Cybele, Attis, and all other Greek, Roman, and foreign deities was extirpated in favor of Christianity.

Mithra. Of all the foreign religions adopted by the Romans, the worship of the Iranian (Persian) god Mithra became the most popular and the most widespread. Introduced into the Roman Empire in the first century BCE, Mithraism spread so rapidly that in a very short time hundreds of Mithraeums (temples) had been established from India to

Scotland through the agency of zealous Mithraic proselytes who communicated their convictions with missionary fervor along the ancient trade routes of Africa, Italy, Germany, Spain, France, and Britain. Roman emperors, senators, soldiers, and civil servants were among the most ardent supporters of Mithra. This was not surprising, since he was the invincible god of war, the protector of stable government, and the upholder of social justice and brotherhood.

Mithra was a very ancient Indo-Aryan god that appeared in the religion and mythologies of the Iranians (Persians) and Indians. As the lord of heavenly light, he was identified with the sun, but he was also the god of cattle, agriculture, war, and truth. In addition, he was one of the judges who welcomed the souls of humans after death and, as the god of immortality, conferred everlasting life upon his faithful followers.

No documents or scriptures are extant on Mithra, but scholars have been able to make an analysis of the cult based on fragmentary refer-

A Mithraeum at Carrawburgh on Hadrian's Wall, the Roman line of defense across northern England. Built in the early third century CE, *it was destroyed in the fourth century. Three altars, side benches, and the statue of the torchbearer Cantes remain.* Courtesy of Roger Beck.

ences, inscriptions, bas-reliefs, and sculptures. By gathering together all this material, one can reconstruct the following story about Mithra.

According to the story, the god Mithra was born miraculously in a cave on December 25. This event was witnessed only by some shepherds that came to worship the newborn god with their gifts. From infancy, Mithra's mission was to become master of the earth. To this end he made the sun subject to his will and consequently was identified with it. Next he considered it his duty to sacrifice a bull, the pristine creation of the Iranian god Ahura Mazda.* This sacrifice was imperative, because the Persians believed that the soul of the bull was the generative source of all celestial elements, and its body of human life and all life on earth: all useful herbs from its carcass; wheat from its spinal marrow; all useful animals from its semen; and grapes, which produced the sacramental wine that was consumed during Mithraic rituals, from its blood. Mithra, therefore, was identified with the slain bull as the creator of all beneficent creatures and herbage. Above all, Mithra was the savior god who protected his devotees in this world and granted them salvation in the next.

Mithraic congregations consisted of male communicants only who gathered in small numbers of perhaps a hundred or so in underground or subterranean meeting places, because Mithra was born in a cave. Members passed through seven orders or degrees, including an initiation ritual, in which the outline of a cross was branded on the foreheads of initiates. Newly inducted members, like their counterparts in Cybelian *tauroboliums*, stood under a grating on which a sacred bull was ceremonially slain, drenching them in the bull's blood. They also took an oath never to reveal the secrets of the order or the mysteries of Mithra. Induction into the higher order involved purification; baptism by fire, in a ceremony that required postulants to submit to a sign marked on their foreheads with a hot iron; and the sacraments of bread and wine, representing mystical union with the god Mithra.

Sunday was holy to the followers of Mithra, as was December 25. Sunday was hallowed because it glorified the sun god Mithra; December 25 was the birthday of Mithra, and devotees kept a vigil on the preceding night.

The striking parallels between Mithraism and Christianity need hardly be stressed. Both taught that their founders were mediator savior gods, through whom the salvation of mankind was possible and through whom the world would be judged. Both taught the doctrines of heaven and hell, the last judgment, and the immortality of the soul. Both taught that the forces of good and evil were in a state of perpetual

*See Chapter 11, "Zoroastrianism."

conflict. Both taught self-control and abstinence as requisites to acceptance. Both offered the same sacraments, of baptism and communion. Both observed Sundays and December 25 as holy days.

For five centuries followers of Mithraism enjoyed complete freedom of worship throughout the Roman Empire. However, the accession of Emperor Constantine in 311 CE and his encouragement and support of Christianity drastically changed this situation. The hatred that Christians exhibited toward Mithraism and the terrible persecution they perpetrated against its adherents ultimately destroyed it. The most extreme measures against Mithraism came during the reign of Emperor Theodosius in the fourth century, when this once widespread mystery cult of Mithra was completely extirpated by the followers of Christianity.[25]

Emperor Worship

One of the main features and last manifestations of Roman religion was the deification of the emperors, which first took hold in the first century CE, at the end of the republican period and the beginning of the empire. At this time, many native Roman gods were losing popularity and their temples were being deserted. Patriotic statesmen and influential poets started to endow emperors with divine qualities, elevating them beside the old Roman gods as objects of worship. Thus, upon their deaths, if not during their lives, the emperors were raised to the status of Roman deities.

Some scholars have considered the deification of the emperors to have been rooted in the ancient Roman view of the quality or attribute that Romans identified as *genius* (a family or ancestral spirit, derived from the numen Genius) that was bequeathed or transmuted from the dead as a divine force to the clan. (The *clan* is a social unit smaller than a tribe but larger than a family.) Others have speculated that this practice was borrowed from Egyptian pharaoh worship. Whatever its ultimate origins, emperor worship was initiated with Julius Caesar, who was declared a god by the Senate in 44 BCE, before his death. Then Emperor Augustus, the adopted son and successor of Julius Caesar, further honored his father with a temple erected and dedicated in his name (Divus Julius). Henceforth, it became customary to add the divine epithet *divus* to the emperor's name after his death.

Emperor Augustus himself permitted the erection of shrines in which his *genius* was worshiped. In fact, to pay reverence to the emperor's *genius* (and sometimes to the emperor himself) became a sign of loyalty to the Roman Imperium. In due time, this aura of divinity was accorded to every emperor as a matter of course during his lifetime. Emperors Nero, Caligula, Domitian, and Trajan were among those who demanded the status of gods during their lifetime. Emperor Nero is said to have enjoyed being equated with Apollo.

As an expression of patriotism, emperor worship perhaps attained a degree of success, but it failed as a unifying element to give various religious faiths one inclusive meaning or purpose as a focus for Roman citizens and society. In the final analysis, ancient Roman deities, rival religions of foreign origin, and the national cult of emperor worship all yielded to the pressing force of yet another western Asian cult, one that arose from the heart of Judaism: the cult of Jesus, later identified as Christianity.

Themes and Foreshadowings

The religions of the four peoples of the ancient world surveyed in this chapter—Mesopotamian, Egyptian, Greek, and Roman—are unique testaments in the history of humanity's religious experience. The religions of the two other great centers of early civilization, India and China, acquired considerable unity over a long period of time. The world of the ancient Near East and the Mediterranean littoral, however, was forged by a series of different and overlapping peoples, whose religious traditions helped shape the forms of the three Semitic religions—Judaism, Christianity, and Islam.

Religion in the ancient world permeated the whole life both of the individual and the society, and found expression in a rich variety of forms. Almost every form of religious faith and practice was found in the religion of the ancient world:

- *Animism:* The belief that every object, like every human being, harbors an individual spirit, or soul

- *Polytheism:* The belief that numerous supernatural beings, usually endowed with anthropomorphic (humanlike) characteristics, govern various aspects of the natural world

- *Henotheism:* The worship of a single god, without denying the existence of other gods

- *Monotheism:* The belief that only one God exists

- *Dualism:* The belief that two cosmic principles, generally characterized as good and evil, or spirit and matter, are in constant conflict

- *Skepticism:* The inclination to doubt, or to suspend judgment of, religious theories (doctrine) and practices

- *Mythologies:* The fanciful and imaginative stories that picture the operations of natural and/or supernatural phenomena in terms of anthropomorphic beings; also, the relation between humans and gods explained in terms of cosmic and creative forces; and the attempt to interpret human activities, personal belongings, purpose in life, and humankind's relation to gods and goddesses who appear to rule the universe

- *Mystery Cults:* Bodies of initiates inducted through secret rites, and the secret knowledge acquired by the initiates, which ensures advantages in present life and in life after death

- *Oracles:* The utterances or responses of a god or goddess, often ambiguous and obscure, through the medium of a priest or priestess attached to the deity's temple

- *Magic and Divination:* The art of being able to influence the course of events through influencing the supernatural forces, or the means to obtain the required information from the supernatural order

The religion of the four peoples of the ancient world also embraced conceptions of judgment after death, the underworld (hell), resurrection, and immortality. Temples and tombs provided vivid scenes and depictions of the world beyond death. The gods, the dead, and the living all had their needs, which were ministered to by both the kings and the public to ensure the order of things at all levels of the universe.

People of the ancient world believed that gods and goddesses constantly intervened in human affairs. Mystery religions promised to the initiates the secrets of life, particularly immortal life. Philosophical ideas became more and more prominent. Plato, for instance, strove to develop an adequate moral and spiritual system. Other thinkers, such as Ikhnaton, Xenophanes, and Aristotle, moved toward some form of monotheism. The analytical treatment of religious questions led the Greek philosophers to raise several fundamental questions: How did the world come into being? Does God exist? If he does, what is he like and, more importantly, what is his moral attitude toward human beings and the world?

The application of such abstract thinking—in contrast to mythical thinking—to religious concepts ultimately became the legacy of Western culture and civilization. But besides these four religious traditions of the ancient world, now extinct, two surviving religions—Zoroastrianism and Judaism—that originated in the ancient world made significant contributions in shaping the religious character of Western civilization.

Notes

1. The materials on Canaanite, Hittite, Hurrian, Phoenician, Celtic, Germanic, and other ancient religions are too scanty to be discussed. For a bibliographical listing, see C. J. Adams, ed., *A Reader's Guide to the Great Religions,* 2nd ed. (New York: Free Press, 1977), pp. 47–50, 73–77; and M. Eliade, *A History of Religious Ideas,* vol. 1 (Chicago: University of Chicago Press, 1978), pp. 415–23; vol. 2 (1982), pp. 462–82.

2. L. W. King, *Chronicles Concerning Early Babylonian Kings,* vol. 2 (London: Luzac 1907), pp. 87–96; see also E. A. Speiser in *Ancient Near Eastern Texts,* ed. J. B. Pritchard (Princeton, N.J.: Princeton University Press, 1955), p. 119 (hereafter abbreviated as *ANET*).

3. G. A. Barton, *The Royal Inscription of Sumer and Akkad* (New Haven, Conn.: Yale University Press, 1929), pp. 98–99.

4. *ANET*, p. 450.

5. A. Heidel, *The Gilgamesh Epic and Old Testament Parallels* (Chicago: University of Chicago Press, 1951), pp. 84–87.

6. Ibid., p. 70. The story of Gilgamesh being robbed of immortality by an act of the serpent is somewhat parallel to the story in Genesis 3.

7. S. Moscati, *The Face of the Ancient Orient* (Garden City, N.Y.: Doubleday, 1962), p. 29.

8. A. Erman, ed., *The Ancient Egyptians* (New York: Harper & Row, 1966), p. 256.

9. In terms of the phenomenology of religion, Osiris anticipates Christ as dying-rising savior-god, though Osiris's death was not interpreted soteriologically (i.e., as a "salvation" motif).

10. The critical arguments on this point are surveyed in J. A. Wilson, *The Culture of Ancient Egypt,* 5th ed. (Chicago: University of Chicago Press, 1958), pp. 206–35.

11. D. W. Thomas, ed., *Documents from Old Testament Times* (New York: Harper & Row, 1961), p. 147.

12. There are several translations of *The Book of the Dead;* see T. C. Allen, trans., *The Book of the Dead, or Going Forth by Day* (Chicago: University of Chicago Press, 1974).

13. Ibid., p. 97.

14. *Herodotus,* II. 60, trans. by H. Carter (Oxford, Eng.: Oxford University Press, 1962), p. 117.

15. *ANET*, p. 327.

16. Ibid., p. 327.

17. The name Minos is suspiciously similar to the names of other legendary founder-kings: Manu of India, Menes of Egypt, and Mannus of Germany. See L. Cottrell, *The Bull of Minos,* rev. ed. (London: Grosset & Dunlop, 1956).

18. See W. K. C. Guthrie, *The Greeks and Their Gods* (London: Methuen, 1962).

19. See Guthrie, *Ibid.*, for a more extensive listing.

20. G. Murray, trans., *The Plays of Euripides* (Newton, Wales: Gregynog Press, 1931), p. 1347.

21. Cited in F. M. Cornford, *Greek Religious Thought from Homer to the Age of Alexander* (London: Dent, 1923), p. 85.

22. See, for instance, the discussion in M. Eliade, *A History of Religious Ideas*, vol. 1, pp. 284–89.

23. *Herodotus*, VIII. 40–68, trans. by H. Carter (Oxford, Eng: Oxford University Press, 1962), pp. 506–515.

24. On the relations between the Phrygian mysteries and Christianity, see H. Rahner, *Greek Myths and Christian Mystery* (London: Burns & Oates, 1963).

25. The famous words of Ernest Renan (1823–1892), French historian and religious scholar, are quite apropos: "If Christianity had been checked in its growth by some deadly disease, the world would have been Mithraic." Cited in W. W. Hyde, *Paganism to Christianity in the Roman Empire* (New York: Octagon Books, 1970), pp. 59–60.

11

Zoroastrianism

IF THE ROOTS OF WESTERN RELIGIONS lay in the extinct religious traditions of the Near East and the Mediterranean littoral, their content and ultimate form owe much to another ancient—yet still living—faith. During their exile in Babylon in the sixth century BCE,* the Jewish people came into close contact with a religion known as Zoroastrianism, whose ideas and tenets were to influence greatly not only Judaism, but Christianity and Islam as well.

Evidence of the influence of Zoroastrianism on the great religions of the West is provided by the following list of concepts and beliefs:

- God and Satan (or the Devil)
- Angels and demons
- Heaven and hell (and purgatory in Christianity)
- Resurrection of the body and life everlasting
- Individual judgment at death and cosmic last judgment
- Arrival of the Messiah

*For the history of the Jewish exile (commonly known as the "Babylonian Exile"), see pp. 333–334.

- Cosmic events during the end of the world
- The Armageddon battle followed by a millennium period

On all these topics Zoroastrian ideas helped to shape Jewish, Christian, and Islamic thought.

Historical Background

Zoroastrianism emerged in ancient Persia (modern Iran and Iraq) from the Indo-Iranian, or Aryan, faith.* Although the subject is still a matter of scholarly dispute, it seems likely that the Medes and the Persians, two groups of Aryans (from whom the term *Aryana,* or *Iran,* derives) arrived and settled in the territory of modern Iran in subsequent waves between 1400 and 1000 BCE. Some time around the eighth century BCE, the Medes conquered the native peoples (the Urartu in the north, the Hittites in the west, and the Assyrians in the south) and became the greatest power in western Asia. Two centuries later, the Medes were overthrown by the Persians.

The Persians traced their history back to a ruler called Achaemenes. But it was Cyrus, a young prince of Fars (from which the terms *Parsee* and *Persian* derive), who overthrew the Medes in 550 BCE and established the Achaemenid dynasty (550–330 BCE). In a short time, Cyrus invaded and conquered the entire territory from the borders of India to Greece. This extensive empire, comprising widely differing peoples, cultures, and religious traditions, was held together by Cyrus's enlightened and innovative policy of accepting existing institutions almost without modification, respecting local traditions, and honoring the gods of all the people within his domain.

The religion of ancient Persia was similar in many respects to the Vedic religion in India. Many of the gods worshiped in Persia were similar to the gods of India. Prominent among the deities were nature gods such as the god of the sky, Vivahvant (the Vedic Vavasvant); the wind god, Vayu (the Vedic Vayu); the sun god, Mithra (the Vedic Mitra); the water god, Haurvatat (the Vedic Sarvatat); the fire god, Atar (the Vedic Agni), and so on. Along with these gods there were innumerable good and evil spirits that were invoked and worshiped. They included Yima, the god of death (the Vedic Yama), Asha, the god of truth (the Vedic Rta), Ameretat, the god of immortality (the Vedic Amrta), and other comparable deities.

The central ritual of the Persian religion consisted of at least three

---

*Because the ancient Persian language is closely akin to the language spoken in northern India, it is assumed that the people of Persia and India have as common ancestors the Indo-Iranians, or Aryans.

forms of sacrifices: the animal sacrifice, the libation (drink) sacrifice, and the fire sacrifice. The animal and libation sacrifices seem to have been combined into one ritual, and the available evidence suggests this ritual was something of a drunken orgy. The traditional ritual consisted of slaughtering a bull or ox while the attending priests shouted and danced. During the ceremony, priests also performed the libation rite, in which they squeezed the juice from the *haoma* plant[1] and formally drank it, sometimes sharing the drink with worshipers. This juice must have been fermented and was certainly intoxicating, for, as we shall see later, the prophet Zoroaster condemned the priests for what he described as their filthy drunkenness and for their attempts to deceive people.

The fire sacrifice of the ancient Persians is of particular interest, not only because of its similarity to the Vedic fire ceremony, but also because of its historical significance in Zoroastrianism. It remains the most important ritual in the religion to the present day. Although the details of the ancient ceremony are not clear, it was generally a ritual to consecrate the ground upon which the sacrificial fire was to be lit. Part of the consecration ritual consisted of sprinkling the ground with *haoma* juice, and then laying out the animal to be sacrificed. Worshipers who stood by had to cover their faces in adoration of the sacred fire.

Priests performed these ceremonies, claimed to influence divine powers in order to control everyday events, and were experts in the occult sciences. They interpreted dreams, received and delivered omens, foretold future events, read signs through the movements of stars or the flight of birds, and practiced various kinds of divination.

Such, then, were the religious practices on the Iranian plateau when the prophet Zoroaster appeared on the scene. His monotheistic tendency (his tendency to favor a belief in one god) and his teaching of ethical dualism (the struggle between good and evil) affected contemporary religious practices. The impact of Zoroaster was so forceful that the reformed religion which he left has ever since borne his name.

Who, then, was Zoroaster? When and where was he born? What was his message and how did it affect the religion of ancient Persia?

Zoroaster

Zoroastrians trace the origin of their religion back to the coming of the prophet Zardusht, or Zarathustra, who is known in the West (through the Greeks) as Zoroaster. Zoroaster's place and date of birth cannot be fixed with any certainty. Modern scholars have tried to reconcile evidence from a variety of sources, such as the traditional *Gathas* (Zoroaster's writings),[2] ancient Greek sources, and Islamic sources dating from the ninth century CE,[3] but their efforts add up to no more than speculation. The dates proposed for his birth vary from 1400 BCE to 500 BCE, and prevailing ideas about his birthplace range from eastern to western Iran, because of the ambiguous nature of the linguistic and historical evidence. Despite painstaking research in the field of Zoroastrian (or Iranian) archeology, ethnology, philology, religious literature, and history, little concrete evidence exists yet to document Zoroaster's life. As a result, some scholars have even doubted the existence of Zoroaster and have argued that he may have only been invented to match prophets in other religions, although such speculation seems unwarranted in light of available evidence.

Conflicting evidence from available sources is responsible for the uncertainty and the differences of opinion displayed by scholars, but few have gone so far as to deny the existence of a historical figure identified as Zoroaster. Some have attempted to reconcile these differences by suggesting that Zoroaster was born in one area (either northeastern or northwestern Iran) and later lived and worked in another, but no specific birthplace or birth date for him has been deemed acceptable so far by the majority of scholars.

Zoroastrian tradition maintains that Zoroaster lived in the seventh to sixth centuries BCE after being born in Azerbaijan, northwest of Media, in what until recently was the Soviet Union. According to tradition, his father, Pourushaspa, was from the family of Spitama, whose genealogy can be traced back through forty-five generations to Gayomart, the first man (like Adam); and his mother, Drughdhova, was from the clan of Hvogva. Of his mother it is said that at the age of fifteen she conceived and gave virgin birth to Zoroaster.

The accounts of Zoroaster's infancy and later life abound with miracles. He is said to have been born laughing instead of weeping and, as an infant, to have escaped numerous attempts on his life through the intervention of animals. First a bull stood over him to protect him from the hooves of cattle, then a stallion saved him in the same way from being trampled by horses, and finally, a she-wolf accepted him among her cubs, instead of devouring him.

Whatever his father's own career may have been, Zoroaster was trained to be a *zaotar* (priest). According to tradition, Zoroaster left home at the age of twenty against the wishes of his parents. He married three times and had three sons and three daughters—three daughters and a son from his first marriage, and two sons from the second. Ten years after leaving home his quest for truth culminated in a vision or revelation.

Revelation and Mission

This first vision occurred, it is said, while Zoroaster was attending the celebration of the spring festival and, according to ancient custom, was fetching water at dawn from a nearby river for the *haoma* ritual. As he was returning to the bank from midstream, he saw the shining figure of the archangel Vohu Mana (Good Intention), who led Zoroaster into the presence of Ahura Mazda (Lord Mazda, an ancient Iranian god) and the five Immortals, where he was taught the cardinal principles of the "true religion." This vision was repeated a number of times, and on each occasion Zoroaster saw, heard, or felt conscious of Ahura Mazda.

This traditional account of Zoroaster's vision has persuaded some scholars to speculate that Zoroaster "was a priest, very likely of an ecstatic kind, reminiscent of the shamans of Siberian tribes: by means of the smoke of hemp or other drugs he got himself into a state of ecstasy under which his soul made a journey to heaven, having visions of divine secrets."[4] At any rate, tradition states that Zoroaster's religious experience led him to believe that he was commissioned by Ahura Mazda to preach the "true religion."

His mission, therefore, started at the age of thirty. During the next ten years he was successful in converting only one person, his cousin Maidhyoimah. These long, discouraging years brought Zoroaster into sharp conflict with the priests of his day. Bitterly disappointed by their obduracy, he cried in despair to Ahura Mazda:

> To what land shall I flee? Where shall I go to flee? I am thrust out from family and tribe; I have no favor from the village to which I belong, nor from the wicked rulers of the country. How then, O Lord, shall I obtain Thy favor? (Yasna 46.1)*

It was a despair tempered by rays of hope as he triumphed in his own faith. "So long as Thou rulest over my destiny," said Zoroaster to Ahura Mazda, "I shall be a crying suppliant of Thy Holy wisdom" (Yasna 50.9). Passionate concern for Ahura Mazda, outrage at the shameless perversion of religious rites, utter despair at being deserted by kindred and fellow workers, and inner doubts and questionings deeply moved Zoroaster. Like the words of the Jewish prophets Joshua and Micah, Zoroaster's words echoed triumphantly to haunt the imagination ever after: "As for me, O Ahura, I choose Thee alone as Master" (Yasna 46.3).[5]

---

*Yasna is one of the four principal groupings within the Avesta—the Zoroastrian scripture (see pp. 308–309).

According to the best-known and the most current tradition among Zoroastrians today, Zoroaster's eventual triumph began with his conversion of King Vishtaspah and the royal court in Bactria (in northwestern Iran). As the story goes, three days of debate at a great assembly convened at the royal palace confirmed the hostility of the *kavis* (priests) and *karapans* (religious leaders?) to Zoroaster. These functionaries were instrumental in getting Zoroaster thrown into prison, where he remained until he won the willing ear of King Vishtaspah by curing the king's favorite horse of paralysis. This event, which, according to Zoroastrian tradition, took place when the prophet was forty-two years old, marked a turning point in Zoroaster's career. So impressed were King Vishtaspah, his queen, and the entire royal court that they all accepted Zoroaster's teachings wholeheartedly. Such recognition helped to spread his doctrines as far as China.

Practically nothing is known of the way in which Zoroaster's teaching spread. Some evidence suggests that Zoroaster organized, perhaps in an informal way, a fellowship or brotherhood of his followers and that this brotherhood was characterized by at least three divisions: (1) the Xvaetu (strong in spirit), (2) the Verezena (fellow workers), and (3) the Airyamna (friends).

Zoroaster seems to have recognized an established, contemporary group called the Maga brotherhood. Most authorities consider the Maga group to be the Magi (from which the word *magic* is derived), a powerful, hereditary priestly class probably of Median origin. Their role, which entitled them to religious and political privileges, was very important. They performed the coronation of the king, accompanied the army to celebrate all religious duties, interpreted dreams, and educated the young men. Matthew, the gospel writer, states that the Magi—the "wise men from the east"—traveled to Jerusalem to worship Jesus by following the course of a star (Matthew 2:1–12).

Teachings

In what way did Zoroaster's message differ from those delivered by ancient Iranian beliefs and customs? Zoroaster tried to reform the traditional pantheistic religion into which he was born by promoting the supremacy of Ahura Mazda. With Ahura Mazda as the only God, traditions hitherto associated in the Indo-Iranian cosmology with many gods and devils became subordinate to the one God. And perhaps without losing all their primitive meaning, these traditions were incorporated by Zoroaster into the powers and characteristics that he attributed to Ahura Mazda. Furthermore, Zoroaster welded the elements of tension that lay dispersed in the ancient myths of gods, demons, and monsters into a single universal conflict: good versus evil, in which God and humans took part together.

Moreover, witnessing the religious corruption of his day, Zoroaster was deeply offended by the practices of the priests, whom he condemned as followers of the *daevas* (malevolent gods), obstructors of the "Good Mind," and frustrators of the divine purpose of Ahura Mazda. Knowing that his challenge of the priests would provoke hostility and invite persecution, he still spoke courageously against them, calling them willfully blind and deaf and accusing them of hindering "cultivation, peace and perfection of creation through their own deeds and doctrines" (Yasna 51.14).

Perhaps to everyone's astonishment, Zoroaster denounced the *haoma* ritual, at which the priests often became intoxicated through excessive use of the juice of the plant of *haoma*. His vigorous, radical preaching earned him the enmity of many, since his reform would mean, for the priests, the loss of their income and their lifework.

Ahura Mazda. Against a pantheon of deities, some benevolent, others malevolent, Zoroaster maintained the supremacy of Ahura Mazda. For Zoroaster, Ahura Mazda, the lord of life and wisdom, was "the first and also the last" (Yasna 31.8). Believing his God to be holy, eternal, just, and omniscient, the primeval being, the creator of all, and the origin of all goodness, Zoroaster chose Ahura Mazda as his sole master. Thus, from his predecessors Zoroaster took over the belief in the *ahuras* (benevolent gods), transformed that belief to a sole *ahura* (lord) whom he saw as the *mazda* (wisdom), and therefore called his God Ahura Mazda, meaning Wise Lord.

The relationship of Ahura Mazda to the other *yazata* (or *yazad*, meaning divine power or entity) is not so easy to define. He is spoken of as the father of Vohu Mana, as well as of Asha and Aramaiti. Through the Spenta Mainyu (Good Spirit) and the Vohu Mana (Good Mind), Ahura Mazda grants Haurvatat (Perfection) and Ameretat (Immortality) to those whose words and deeds are in harmony with Asha (Truth), with Xshathra (Kingdom or Majesty), and with Aramaiti (Right Mind). Are these *yazata* subordinate gods or serving angels? The question remains unresolved among scholars to date.

Good and Evil. Zoroaster saw humanity as divided into two opposing parties: the *asha-vants* (truth followers), who were just and God-fearing; and the *dreg-vants* (evil followers), among whom were classed all evil rulers, evil doers, evil speakers, those of evil conscience, and evil thinkers. And what Zoroaster saw on earth as basic dualism he projected to the whole cosmos. He came to the conclusion that the fundamental tension between good and evil existed in the material as well as the spiritual sphere. Against a transcendental good mind stood an evil mind, against a good spirit stood an evil spirit, and so on. Yet, on every level a choice had to be made. This insistence on freedom of choice was a marked characteristic of Zoroaster's teaching, which was distinguished not by the ethical dualism of good versus evil, but by the importance of the individual as an arbiter between them. Each individual, he taught, was ultimately faced with making a choice between good and evil.

Side by side with the fundamental principle of freedom of choice, Zoroaster taught that goodness was its own reward and that happiness and misery were the consequences of a person's good and evil deeds. He anticipated a final consummation of creation, at which time Ahura Mazda would come with his "three powers," sinners would surrender deceit (evil, lies) into the hands of truth, and eternal joy would reign everywhere. Moreover the souls of humans were to be judged at the "bridge of the requiter," where the just would receive their eternal reward, the wicked their final doom. Hell was the abode of all evil rulers, evil doers, evil speakers, those of evil conscience, and evil thinkers. Heaven was the abode of the righteous, who would be blessed by Ahura Mazda with perfection and immortality.

Historical Development of Zoroastrianism

The paucity and varied nature of the sources make it difficult, if not impossible, to describe the historical development of Zoroastrianism, although scholars have not abandoned the search for evidence. From the existing historical records its history can be divided into five periods:

1. Achaemenid (550–330 BCE)
2. Seleucid (330–247? BCE)
3. Parthian or Arsacid (247 BCE–227 CE)
4. Sassanid (227–651)
5. Exile and Survival (651 to the present)

Achaemenid Period

The question of whether or not the kings of the Achaemenid dynasty were followers of Zoroastrianism has been a matter of controversy that scholars have yet to resolve conclusively.[6] Four divergent views have emerged: (1) that the Achaemenid kings should be regarded as true followers of Zoroaster; (2) that the religion of the Achaemenid kings was identical with ancient Indo-Aryan beliefs and views; (3) that under

King Darius (522–486 BCE) Zoroaster's teachings were embraced, but that following King Artaxerxes I (465–424 BCE) ancient Indo-Aryan religions reemerged; and, as one scholar has suggested, (4) that "at least three different forms of religion coexisted simultaneously in Achaemenid Persia: Zarathustrian, Magian and Persian."[7]

Seleucid Period

The Seleucid period was a brief interregnum between Persian dynasties during which the area was ruled by the Macedonian Alexander the Great and his generals. Although this foreign political power was quickly overthrown by the Parthian dynasty, the cultural impact of its Hellenism was not easily expunged until the first century CE. How did Zoroastrianism fare during the Seleucid period? The evidence is so scanty and so obscure that it is impossible to determine what the status of Zoroastrianism was. All that is known is that the goddess Anahita was very popular (especially under the Greek form of her name, Anaitis) and that the chief god was not Ahura Mazda (although he was worshiped) but Mithra. In fact, the cult of Anahita spread all over western Asia and Europe as far as the Rhine and Danube, while the cult of Mithra became one of the leading mystery religions of the Roman Empire (see pp. 288–291).

It seems likely that Alexander's conquest of Iran was a disaster for Zoroastrianism. Alexander is remembered in Zoroastrian tradition as "the accursed Iskander" (Iskander = Alexander) because Alexander burned the royal capital at Persepolis and destroyed the definitive copy of the Avesta (Zoroastrian scripture), which had been meticulously transcribed in gold on thousands of oxhides.

Parthian Period

The history of the Zoroastrian religion during the Parthian period is also very obscure. The Parthian kings were constantly plagued with internal disorders that caused frequent changes of the ruling family and unfavorable social conditions. Presumably, the Zoroastrian religion regained some of its strength after its eclipse in the Seleucid period. Tradition states that one king—most probably Vologasses I (51–80 CE)—was responsible for the recovery of the Avesta by collecting the dispersed manuscripts and by writing down all the oral traditions. There is also some evidence that Tiridates, the brother of Vologasses I, was a Zoroastrian priest who observed his religion so scrupulously that he traveled to Rome (to receive his crown from the hands of Nero) by land in order to avoid defiling the sea (water being one of the sacred elements in Zoroastrianism).

Zoroastrianism

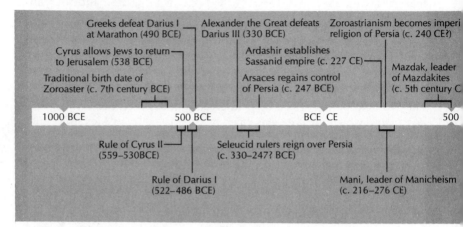

Greeks defeat Darius I at Marathon (490 BCE)

Alexander the Great defeats Darius III (330 BCE)

Zoroastrianism becomes imperi religion of Persia (c. 240 CE?)

Cyrus allows Jews to return to Jerusalem (538 BCE)

Ardashir establishes Sassanid empire (c. 227 CE)

Mazdak, leader of Mazdakites (c. 5th century C

Traditional birth date of Zoroaster (c. 7th century BCE)

Arsaces regains control of Persia (c. 247 BCE)

| 1000 BCE | 500 BCE | BCE CE | 500 |

Rule of Cyrus II (559–530BCE)

Seleucid rulers reign over Persia (c. 330–247? BCE)

Rule of Darius I (522–486 BCE)

Mani, leader of Manicheism (c. 216–276 CE)

The worship of Anahita and Mithra along with Ahura Mazda seems to have retained its hold under the Parthians. Of these three divinities, Anahita, not Ahura Mazda, occupied the most important position, since several sanctuaries were dedicated to this goddess during the reign of the Parthians. Further, the Parthian cemeteries, in which the dead were buried with their funerary furnishings, offer proof that the Zoroastrian funerary custom of exposure was not prevalent. At any rate, no evidence exists that the Zoroastrian religion was the dominant religion during the Parthian period.

Sassanid Period

During the Sassanid period divergent religions were at first in conflict with each other, and the stages through which Zoroastrianism developed into a state religion—if it did so at all—are far from clear. According to Zoroastrian tradition, Ardashir I (226–240 CE) was responsible for making Zoroastrianism the official state religion. Modern researchers, however, have discredited this account, which seems to be at variance with other texts, inscriptions, and archeological evidence. An imperial religion must have arisen, most probably during the reign of Shapur I (240–271). But it remains to be proven whether the adopted official religion was Mazdaism, the ancient Indo-Aryan Mazda worship; Zurvanism, which suggested that Good and Evil (Ahura Mazda and Ahriman) sprang as twins from a unitary world principle called Zurvan; or Zoroastrianism.

A revival of ancient Persian nationalism and intense opposition to

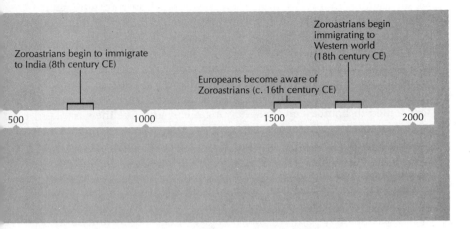

Zoroastrians begin to immigrate to India (8th century CE)

Europeans become aware of Zoroastrians (c. 16th century CE)

Zoroastrians begin immigrating to Western world (18th century CE)

500   1000   1500   2000

Judaism, Christianity, Manicheism (a sect founded by Mani, who taught cosmic dualism), Mazdakism (a sect founded by Mazdak, who advocated nonviolence and a radical communism), Brahmanism (Hindu religion), and Buddhism characterized the Sassanid period. Severe persecution occurred repeatedly. Strict laws were made against heresy, and apostasy from the official religion was punished with death—although not much is known of the nature of either orthodoxy or hereticism in this era. An authoritative canon and text known as the Avesta (the same Avesta destroyed by Alexander and reconstituted by Vologasses) was prepared from both oral and written traditions. The priesthood was organized into a powerful body, with a chief priest as the first person in the state after the king.

In 651, the last Sassanid king, Yazdagerd III, was assassinated and the entire Persian Empire, which stretched from the Indus River to Baghdad, fell to the Arab Muslims without much resistance. Little is known of the decline of Zoroastrianism under Islamic rule or of the degree to which Zoroastrianism commanded the devotion of its adherents. Doubtless, many embraced Islam, either by conversion or by coercion. The long-term effect of the Muslim invasion was not only to arrest the expansion of Zoroastrianism but to threaten the annihilation of its adherents.

Exile and Survival

A lack of evidence makes the subsequent history of Zoroastrianism as difficult to reconstruct as its early history. From time to time Zoroastrians rebelled in conquered Iran, only to bring upon themselves the persecution of the Muslims. Zoroastrian tradition speaks of "the ruin and devastation that come from the Arabs," but how and why such disasters occurred is not known. At any rate, a minority group of Zoroastrians, called by Muslims *gabar* or *gavour* (infidels), survives to this day in modern Iran.

Another small group of Zoroastrians left Iran in the eighth and ninth centuries to seek asylum in India. As descendants and survivors of the ancient Persians, they were (and still are) called Parsees (or Parsis). Most settled in Bombay and neighboring areas, and like their Iranian counterparts, they have managed to survive to this day. Unfortunately, nothing is known of the long history of Zoroastrianism in either India or Iran after the conquest of Islam. Only after the arrival of Europeans in India in the sixteenth century did Western scholars become aware of the surviving adherents of Zoroastrianism in India. For centuries this small group of followers of Zoroastrianism had resisted assimilation. Clinging tenaciously to their religion and observing many of its ancient rites and ceremonies, these Zoroastrians succeeded in their struggle to preserve their religion from near extinction.

Zoroastrian Scriptures

The collection of sacred writings of the Zoroastrian religion is known as the *Avesta*,[8] comprising four principal groups of writings:

1. The Yasna, a collection of prayers and liturgical formulas that contains the Gathas, a group of hymns believed to have been written by the prophet Zoroaster
2. The Visparat, composed in honor of and as an invocation to the celestial lords
3. The Videvdat (Vendidad), a body of writings primarily concerned with ritual purification
4. The Khorde Avesta ("Smaller Avesta"), a book of daily prayers that includes the Yashts, a collection of hymns addressed to individual deities and epic narrations concerning kings and heroes

The entire Avesta is believed to have been written over a period of a thousand years. The earliest portion was probably composed before the sixth century BCE, the most recent excerpts around the fourth century CE. According to tradition, the Avesta once comprised a vast literature, only a small part of which survives.

The Gathas fill only seventeen chapters out of the seventy-two chapters of the Yasna. They are of special interest to scholars because scholars believe that these seventeen chapters are older than the writings in the rest of the Avesta and because they have found a close link between the language and history of the Gathas and the language and history of the Rig Vedas (the collection of sacred texts of ancient India and the oldest known documents in Sanskrit). This discovery seems to support the belief of many scholars that both writings have a common cultural and linguistic origin. Although the generally accepted view is that the Gathas represent the words of Zoroaster, the opinions of experts on the Gathas differ widely. Some think that Zoroaster composed and wrote the Gathas; others think that the Gathas were composed in the main by him, but that occasional verses were later added by his disciples. Still others suggest that the Gathas, although originally composed by Zoroaster, were preserved only in memory for centuries before they were written down. Whatever theory is held about their composition, the general view is that the Gathas are the only authentic documents concerning the life and teachings of Zoroaster.

In addition to the Avesta, there is an extensive literature, probably dating from the ninth century CE, that deals with religious subjects. Of the at least fifty-five known works, the most important are the Bunda-hishn, dealing with cosmogony, mythology, and history; the Dinkard (Denkart), dealing with religious doctrines, customs, traditions, history, and literature; the Datastan-i Denik, religious opinions of the high priest Manushkihar written in response to ninety-two questions; the Zad-sparam, written by the younger brother of Manushkihar; the Shayast Na-shayast, a miscellaneous compilation of laws and customs concerning sin and impurity; and the Arday-Viraf Namak, or Book of Arday-Viraf, who describes his visit to heaven and hell while in a trance.

Zoroastrian Teachings

The essence of Zoroastrianism can be summed up in the following beliefs and concepts: the worship of one supreme God, Ahura Mazda (Ohrmazd); the veneration of *yazata* (lesser divine powers); the strong sense of personal choice to struggle against Ahriman, the embodiment of evil; individual resurrection and judgment, followed by eternal life and bliss; and the keeping of the sacred fire as the chief symbol or object of cult.

Human Choice

Zoroastrian theology asserts first and foremost that each person is genuinely free to choose his or her ultimate destiny. The whole human drama—indeed, the ultimate purpose of existence—can be reduced to the element of choice. Every person is free to pursue either of two paths: good or evil. One's choice here and now determines one's eternal destiny.

This freedom to choose between good and evil and the inevitable consequences of such a choice evolve from a moral triad: purity or impurity of thoughts, words, and deeds. This triad, in turn, is an inseparable component of three elements that constitute the greatest gifts of God to mankind: body, soul, and mind. The most precious of these three is the mind—the faculty that distinguishes right from wrong, pure from impure, truth from falsehood, good from evil. Consequently, Zoroastrianism offers no recourse to atonement or intercession. Eternal salvation rests on the efficacy of one's good thoughts, good words, and good deeds.

Cosmic Dualism: Ahura Mazda versus Ahriman

The choice between good and evil is embodied in the two supreme principles that, Zoroastrians believe, contend for control of the universe. Ahura Mazda personifies the principle and source of all good: success, glory, honor, physical health, and immortality. Ahriman is the principle and source of all evil: misfortune, disaster, war, sickness, and death. Ahura Mazda, creator of heaven, earth, and humankind, represents light, truth, justice, and life. Ahriman, the originator and initiator of all evil, represents darkness, falsehood, injustice, and the absence of life. To Zoroastrians, therefore, the universe is a battleground fought over by a pair of coexistent, but not coeternal, divine, and warring principles. In every sphere and in every situation that demands a decision between two opposites, human beings have to make a choice between these two principles. The consequences alone imply that the principle of good is more beneficent and more powerful than the principle of evil and that therefore Ahura Mazda eventually triumphs.

Judgment, Resurrection, Eternal Life

Zoroastrians maintain that every individual is judged after death. At death, the soul of an individual stays with the body for three days. On the fourth day the soul journeys to the place of judgment by crossing the Chinvat Bridge, which spans the abyss of hell and leads to paradise on the other side. If, in the balance, the record of that soul's life on earth is represented by a weighty accumulation of good thoughts, words, and deeds, then the soul crosses without difficulty to paradise. But if the reverse is the case, then the passage over the Chinvat Bridge becomes an entirely different experience for the soul. The bridge flips on its side to present a footing like the edge of a sword, from which the soul teeters and plunges into the abyss of hell.

Paradise is a place of beauty, light, pleasant scents, and eternal bliss, to be enjoyed by those who adhere in life to Zoroastrian moral and ceremonial ethics. Hell is a place of horror, misery, darkness, evil smells, and eternal suffering for those who in life violated the same ethics.

Zoroastrians also believe that the cycle of time will eventually end; that there will be a general resurrection; that a final battle between the forces of good and evil will resolve the conflict between them forever by ending in the banishment of evil; that this world will be first consumed and then restored; and finally, that there will follow an eternity of bliss, and the will of Ahura Mazda will prevail.

Creation, Time, Eschatology

The eschatological element in Zoroastrianism is combined with cosmic dualism. Time and beyond-time are of prime importance, and certain distinct periods are believed to separate the ages.

Zoroastrian literature divides time (past, present, and future) into four trimillennium periods. During the first trimillennium, the primary elements of all good creations remained motionless and dormant. At the close of this period, Ahriman, the Adversary, saw a gleam of light while wandering near the upper bounds of the dark domain. Consequently, he conceived the desire to seize the celestial realm and to control the entire universe. In order to accomplish this purpose, he created a vast army of fiends, daevas, wizards, and assorted creatures of darkness who were eternally evil.

Unprepared to withstand such an attack, Ahura Mazda concluded a treaty with Ahriman that would last for three more trimillenniums. The world would be ruled first by Ahura Mazda for three thousand years, then by Ahriman a similar period. During the last three thousand years the two antagonists would strive for mastery.

Because of his omniscience, Ahura Mazda was able to outwit Ahriman in the second trimillennium, during which he created the Primeval Ox and the Primeval Man, representing the animal kingdom and the human race, respectively. Further, to ensure his own ultimate victory he created the spiritual body of Zoroaster, who was eventually to be incarnated as the instrument by which Ahriman ultimately would be destroyed.

When it was Ahriman's turn to rule, he proceeded to disrupt all of creation. He corrupted the earth by mixing smoke with fire, sowing thorns, destroying vegetation, and creating billions of noxious creatures and destructive beasts. Nature itself served his evil purpose by generating storms, droughts, and earthquakes.

Ahriman also dug a great hole in the earth to serve as the infernal region of hell. He debased all humanity by filling people with corrupt words, wicked thoughts, and evil desires. He sought to doom the human race to suffering, misery, and total annihilation in the everlasting fires of hell. Fortunately, however, his period of rule ended before he could implement his entire plan.

Thirty years before the final trimillennium phase—that is, in the Zoroastrian year 8970 (660 BCE)—Ahura Mazda sent Zoroaster into the world. The last trimillennium began with the ministry of this prophet, beginning in 630 BCE. His mission was to teach mankind the benefits of following Ahura Mazda's doctrine of goodness and to warn them of the great events that lay in store during this last period.

Among the events that Zoroaster predicted was the appearance, at the close of each millennium, of a great savior commissioned to reconstitute the good religion. Each of these three saviors—Hushedar, Aushedar-Mah, and Saoshyant—would be a direct descendant of Zoroaster and born to a virgin. The appearance of Hushedar would be preceded by successively degenerating regimes.

In the following two millenniums, all men will become deceivers, and affection will depart from the world. Father and son, brother and brother, will hate each other. All the sacred rites and ceremonies will be treated with contempt. Wrath and avarice will precede total apostasy. In those terrible days, the sun and the moon will show signs; there will be devastating earthquakes and destructive storms. Wars and battles will greatly increase, and so many soldiers will be killed that "a thousand women will seek to kiss one man."

In the meantime, Ahriman will be able to mobilize a vast army for the great and final battle of Armageddon, during which so much slaughter will ensue that rivers of blood will reach the girths of horses. The result will be the ultimate triumph of Ahura Mazda. Then there will be a general resurrection, at which all the dead, righteous and wicked alike, will arise on the spot where they died, and all will be gathered before the great judgment seat. The wicked will be separated from the righteous and cast into the depths of hell, where frightful punishments, torture, filth, and darkness will be their eternal lot. The righteous, on the other hand, will enter heaven and enjoy every imaginable bliss in the realm of endless light. An intermediate place, called *hamestagna* (the purgatory of Christianity), is reserved for all those whose good or evil words, thoughts, and deeds balance. In *hamestagna,* souls exist in considerable discomfort but without intense torture.

Finally, there will come the great conflagration in which the world will burn in a fantastic holocaust. Ahriman and all his followers, including the pit of hell and its inhabitants, will be burned and annihilated. Everything will be totally destroyed, a new universe will come into being, and Ahura Mazda will reign supreme.[9]

Zoroastrian Observances

Naojote

All young Zoroastrians between the ages of seven and ten go through a special ceremony known as *naojote*—a term combining the words *nao* (new) and *jote*, or rather *zote* (to offer prayers). Hence, *naojote* means a new initiate to offer (Zoroastrian) prayers. In this ceremony, the young

The naojote *ceremony, in which a youth is made responsible for honoring the Zoroastrian faith. The rite of investiture with the* sudreh *and* kusti *is performed by the Zoroastrian priest.* Courtesy of Yazdi Antia.

boy or girl is invested with a sacred shirt (*sudreh*, or *sadre*) and a sacred thread (*kusti*), which he or she is to wear throughout life. Although the ceremony is often regarded by non-Zoroastrians as an initiation ceremony, its significance is greater than a mere initiation. *Naojote* makes the young person responsible for honoring Zoroastrian rites and duties.

Prior to the investiture a child is given a ceremonial bath in sacred or holy water by the officiating priests. Then follows the recital of a prayer by the priest and the child, after which the following declaration of faith is spoken by the child:

> Praised be the most righteous, the wisest, the most holy and the best Mazdaean Law which is the gift of Mazda. The good, true, and perfect religion, which God has sent to this world, is that which Prophet Zoroaster has brought. That religion is the religion of Zoroaster, the religion of Ahura Mazda communicated to holy Zoroaster.

After this declaration, the rite of investiture with the *sudreh* and *kusti* is performed by the priest. Then follows the recital of the articles of faith, spoken by the child and priest in unison:

> O Almighty! Come to my help.
> I am a worshipper of God.
> I am a Zoroastrian worshipper of God.
> I agree to praise the Zoroastrian religion and to believe in
>   that religion.
> I praise good thoughts, good words, and good deeds.
> I praise the good Mazdaean religion, which curtails discus-
>   sions and quarrels, which brings about kinship or
>   brotherhood, which is holy, which, of all the religions
>   that have yet flourished and are likely to flourish in
>   the future is the greatest, the best and the most excellent,
>   and which is the religion given by God to Zoroaster.
> I believe that all good things proceed from God.
> May the Mazdaean religion be thus praised.

The naojote ceremony ends with the recital of a benediction by the officiating priest. Nevertheless, the most significant part is the recitation of the articles of faith by which the initiate confirms his or her belief in the efficacy of his or her own good thoughts, good words, and good deeds. The Zoroastrian looks to no one but himself or herself for the salvation of his or her soul. The whole structure of the Zoroastrian religion rests on this moral triad: purity of thoughts, words, and deeds.

Purification

Zoroastrianism prescribes several types of purification rites to be observed by the faithful. Four of these, in order of increasing importance, are *padyab, nahn, riman,* and *bareshnum.* The *padyab* is a simple form of absolution performed several times a day. *Nahn* is a ritualistic bath of purification observed only on special occasions, such as after childbirth, *naojote,* marriage, and holy days. The *riman* is strictly confined to those who have come in contact with corpses. Finally, the *bareshnum* is a complicated ritual performed only at special places and lasting for several days; nowadays, this rite is restricted almost always to priests or priesthood candidates.

Death

Zoroastrian observances associated with death follow a sequence of solemn ritual. First, the corpse is placed on slabs of stone in a room in the house. Next, a "four-eyed" dog (i.e., one with a spot over each eye) is brought before the corpse; such dogs are thought to act as living intermediaries between the seen and the unseen. This ritual is repeated five times a day for three days. Then the corpse is removed to the *dakhma,* or Tower of Silence, a massive, towerlike building constructed in concentric circles, one each for males, females, and children (see figure on p. 316). Here the corpse is stripped of its clothing and exposed to the sun and the vultures. The dry bones are then swept into a deep central well consisting of deposits of lime and phosphorus. The reason for this dramatic practice is the Zoroastrian reverence for the elements: air, earth, fire, and water. Cremation pollutes air and fire, while burial contaminates the earth and water. Exposure to vultures provides a convenient solution to this dilemma.

Fire

Fire is a central symbol in Zoroastrianism. Because no Zoroastrian religious ceremony or ritual is complete without the presence of the fire, Zoroastrians maintain a perpetual sacred fire both in their homes and in the fire temples. Devout Zoroastrians attend the fire temple daily, although many believers are satisfied with four visits a month. In the *Atash Niyayesh* (fire prayer, or litany), fire is invoked as "worthy of sacrifice, worthy of prayer, in the dwellings of human beings." From the time of the Indo-Iranians to the present, the house fire has remained a cult object. Each Zoroastrian family maintains a house fire in a pot or urn. Prayers are made regularly in the presence of the house fire, because fire, like the sun, represents divine purity, light, power, and warmth. No sin is as grave as that of "extinguishing" one's fire.

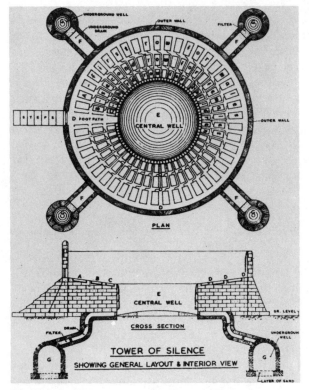

The Tower of Silence, a circular funerary platform consisting of three rows of stone slabs. Row A is for men, row B is for women, and row C is for children. The path marked D is for corpse-bearers. The corpses are placed in the tower, where the flesh and organs are consumed by vultures. The bones then dry and slip into the central well (E), where they mix with lime and phosphorus and disintegrate. The holes in the inner side of the well lead rainwater into four underground drains (F), which in turn lead into four underground wells (G) whose bottoms are covered with a thick layer of sand. A mixture of charcoal and sandstone, renewed from time to time, is placed at the end of each drain to purify the rainwater that flows over the bones. Courtesy of Illustrated Weekly of India.

Ceremonies

Zoroastrian ceremonies need not be performed in permanent buildings. Priestly rituals, religious services, prayers, and various ceremonies can be performed in a small, flat space marked as *pavi* (pure place, or sacred precinct). However, Zoroastrian ceremonies need not be confined to the *pavi*; they may be celebrated anywhere—on mountains, by streams, in the fields, or at home. Some ceremonies do not even require the offices of a priest but may be observed by an individual whenever he or she wills, for a variety of reasons—to make a vow, to offer penitence or thanksgiving, and to do other such things. The most auspicious time for religious rites is the morning.

Festivals

Besides daily ceremonies, Zoroastrians observe numerous seasonal festivals, or *gahambars*. The Naw Ruz, or Noruz (New Year), festival is the most joyous of Zoroastrian feasts. Tradition states that Zoroaster chose the six *gahambars* as celebrations for his people. At any rate, Zoroastrians also celebrate the Sada (Hundred Days feast), an ancient fire festival held nowadays close to a stream. Other Zoroastrian festivals mark the memory of the dead, the deities who preside over the Gathas and over each day and each month of the Zoroastrian year, the feast of waters, and the birthday of Zoroaster.

Worshipers offer homage and prayers at home in front of a small altar. The altar includes the image of the prophet Zoroaster and the fire urn, symbol of Ahura Mazda's power.   Courtesy of *Illustrated Weekly of India.*

Sects

Unlike in other religions, Zoroastrian sects are not divided by theological matters, but by disputes over the dates of religious observances. These disputes are centuries old, and around 1730 they caused a permanent schism. At present, three groups celebrate Zoroastrian seasonal festivals at different periods of the year, based on differences in the calendars that they recognize and in the ways that they calculate time:

1. The *Shenshahi* (Imperial), who observe the New Year in autumn (August or September, by the Gregorian calendar)
2. The *Qadimi* (Ancient), who observe the New Year in summer (July or August)
3. The *Fasli* (Seasonal), who observe the New Year at the spring equinox, (March 21)

The date of the observance of the New Year sets the dates for observing other festivals throughout the year. In spite of these differences in calendar and time reckoning, all three groups attach great religious importance to the Zoroastrian seasonal festivals.

Modern Trends

Like most religions and cultures of the Near and Far East, Zoroastrianism in India (and elsewhere, except Iran) has been irresistibly drawn into the unsettling orbit of Western technology and influence. Ancient value systems are being questioned and traditional patterns threatened. The impact of Western culture on Zoroastrianism can be discerned in several areas.

Exposure to Western ideas has led to reform movements and to vigorous attempts to uproot excessive ceremonialism and non-Zoroastrian practices. In addition, time-honored teachings and customs have been subjected to Western-style scientific methods of historical criticism. As a result, conservative and reformist forces are now in conflict, with neither side predominant. A few instances will suffice to indicate this breach within Zoroastrian communities.[10]

Under the impact of modern Western criticism, many Zoroastrian reformists insist that in spite of the evident cosmic dualism between Ahura Mazda and Ahriman, the basic teaching of Zoroaster, and hence Zoroastrianism, is monotheistic. Conservative Zoroastrians, however, continue to honor the *yazata,* thus appearing decidedly polytheistic. Heaven and hell, according to reformists, are simply mental constructions—just as Ahriman is one's own creation of evil. Conservatives, naturally, resist such rationalistic approaches.

Zoroastrian fire temple with the winged symbol of Ahura Mazda in Bombay, India. Courtesy of Yazdi Antia.

Reformists, critical of the superstitions and obscure practices embedded in Zoroastrianism, scoff at the use of bull's urine for ritual cleansing, the presence of a "four-eyed" dog to preside over a corpse before committal, and the efficacy of time-honored spells and prayers. They also question the custom of exposing corpses to the elements, on both hygienic and aesthetic grounds. They advocate cremation, arguing that modern forms of electric cremation produce no flame (the sacred symbol of Ahura Mazda) to be contaminated in the process. Conservatives despise such tampering with tradition, reject alternative methods, and cling tenaciously to the practice of *dakhma*.

Moreover, many Zoroastrians have entirely abandoned the ancient symbols of their religion: the sacred shirt and thread. Others do not feel any strong attachment to their religion and seldom visit the fire temples. Certain reformists blend their own beliefs with teachings from Hinduism or theosophy. The priesthood is declining steadily and, in all likelihood, will diminish even more.

Notes

1. This is an ancient Iranian ritual akin to the Vedic (Hindu) *soma* ritual, which involved the pressing, preparation, and drinking of the *haoma* plant (identified as the fungus *amanita muscaria*) by priests. The issue has been a matter of discussion recently. See G. Wasson, *Soma, Divine Mushroom of Immortality (Ethno-mycological Studies I)* (The Hague, Netherlands: Mouton, 1969); M. Boyce, "Haoma, Priest of the Sacrifice," in W. B. *Henning Memorial Volume* (London, Lund Humphries, 1970), pp. 62–80; and I. Gershevitch, "An Iranianist's View of Soma Controversy," in *Mémorial Jean de Ménasce*, ed. Ph. Gignoux and A. Tafazzoli (Louvain, Belgium: Fondation Culturelle Irannienne, 185, Impr. orientaliste, 1974), pp. 45–75.

2. On the basis of the linguistic evidence within Zoroastrian sacred writings, some modern scholars speculate on a date for Zoroaster some time between 1400 and 1000 BCE. Another line of inquiry, based on literary, historical, and theological evidence, puts the birth date of Zoroaster between 800 and 500 BCE. A literary study of the Zoroastrian Yashts (invocations, or collections of prayer and praise) has led some scholars to propose that Zoroaster lived between 650 and 600 BCE. An investigation of the relationship between the Achaemenid dynasty and the Zoroastrian religion, however, has led eminent historians to propose life dates of 559–522 BCE. Yet other scholars, after studying the Zoroastrian theory of world ages as given in the Bundahishn (a collection of materials dealing with creation), have suggested a date of 595 BCE for the founding of Zoroastrianism.

3. Significantly enough, the Islamic author al-Biruni gives a precise date for Zoroaster in his *Athar-ul-Bakiya* ("The Chronology of Ancient Nations," written in the year 1000 CE). Al-Biruni states that from the time of Zoroaster's "appearance till the beginning of the era of Alexander, they count 258 years." To the Iranians, the "beginning of the era of Alexander" could mean nothing other than the sack of Persepolis, the extinction of the Achaemenid Empire, and the death of the last "king of kings," Darius III, which occurred in 330 BCE. Zoroaster's date would then be 588 BCE. But, what does al-Biruni mean by Zoroaster's "appearance"? Zoroaster's birth? Or Zoroaster's first appearance to the public after his visions at the age of thirty? Zoroaster's birth date would then be 618 BCE. Or does "appearance" refer to the conversion of King Vishtaspa when Zoroaster was forty-two years old? Zoroaster's birth then would be in 630 BCE.

4. H. Ringgren and A. V. Strom, *Religions of Mankind Today and Yesterday* (Philadelphia: Fortress Press, 1967), pp. 286–287. H. S. Nyberg was the first to insist on the "shamanic" ecstasy of Zoroaster, in his *Die Religionen des alten Irans* (Leipzig, Germany: Hinrichs, 1938), pp. 177–178.

5. Compare the biblical passages in Joshua 24:15 and Micah 7:7.

6. For a discussion of this controversy, see S. A. Nigosian, "The Religions in Achaemenid Persia," *Studies in Religion* 4:4 (1974–1975):378–86.

7. Ibid.: 385.

8. The standard edition is that of K. F. Geldner, *Avesta, The Sacred Books of the Parsis*, 3 vols. (Stuttgart: W. Kohlhammer, 1885); see also J. Darmesteter and L. H. Mills's translation in *The Sacred Books of the East*, Parts I & II, vols. 4 and 23; and Part III, vol. 31, ed. M. Müller (Oxford, Eng.: Clarendon Press, 1879–1910).

9. For parallels in Christian thought, see Matthew 25 and Revelation 21–22.

10. The instances cited are the fruits of extensive research, conducted over a considerable period of time, and innumerable contacts (interviews with Zoroastrians and attendance at Zoroastrian functions).

12

Judaism

Historical Background

The early records of the religious history of Judaism date from the classical period of the "ancient Israelites," a Semitic group which roamed the northern Arabian desert. Just as other nomadic groups lived in tribes structured with a chieftain in authority over the group's members, so around the second millennium BCE the patriarch Abraham and his people lived and traveled on the fringes of the desert, seeking pasture for their animals. They normally camped beside springs and oases, but because vegetation was sparse they had to be on the move continuously. Crossing and recrossing desert wastes of pebbles and shifting sand, they traveled in search of fruit, vegetation, and water.

For centuries at a time, this group lived in perfect freedom. But some five hundred years after the time of Abraham, the Jewish people found themselves enslaved in order to provide labor for the rich and splendid civilization of the Pharaohs in Egypt. Soon, however, a dominant figure was to appear who would lead the Jewish people to the promised land.

Sometime during the thirteenth century BCE, the Jewish people, under the leadership of Moses, broke out of Egypt and made their way into the cultivated land of Canaan—the biblical name for modern Israel, the region between the Jordan River and the Mediterranean Sea. Historically, however, this area was also known as Palestine, named after the *Pelishtim*, or Philistines. This tribe of "sea peoples" from the Aegean islands (according to one account, Crete) invaded the territory in the twelfth century BCE on their way to Egypt.[1] A bloody struggle followed between the Canaanite inhabitants and the Jewish and Philistine immigrants for some three hundred years, until the Jewish King David succeeded in uniting the various groups.

Canaanites

The Canaanites were a Semitic people who moved into the area of modern Israel some time during or after 3000 BCE. Never able to form a homogeneous civilization, they remained divided into a number of independent kingdoms with specific local traditions. The Canaanite kings exercised both political and religious authority over their subjects. Each king, it was believed, was the earthly representative of El (God) and received his royal status from a pantheon of deities.[2] Consequently, it was the king's duty to build temples to the deities, to perform the prescribed religious rites, to rule righteously, and to protect the poor, the widow, and the orphan. If a king ignored or neglected to fulfill his religious and judicial duties, or was prevented from doing so by illness, he and his subjects suffered the consequences of angered deities: rain would not fall, crops would not grow, and famine would follow. When a king exercised his proper functions, however, he and his subjects could expect the favor and blessings of the deities.

Of the numerous deities in Canaanite religion, many survive merely as names, their functions and relationships unknown. The supreme god of the Canaanites was El—a great, wise, benevolent, and merciful deity, creator of all creatures and father of humankind. The next most important god was Baal (Master or Lord), often characterized as the storm and rain god and associated with thunder and lightning. Baal was also "the Prince, the Lord of the earth," whose dwelling place was Mount Saphon (in northern Syria), the site of the assembly of the gods. He was often referred to as the great fighter, the one who won a victory over Yam, the sea god. Baal's archenemy was Mot, the god of death, who threw Baal into the underworld, the land of the dead. Only through the intervention of his sister Anat did Baal return to life. Because his death and resurrection coincided with the withering and sprouting of vegetation, Baal, like Osiris and Marduk, was closely identified with fertility.

Canaanite cultic practices were performed in temples as well as in open-air places (on hilltops, near rivers, in groves). A stone pillar (symbolizing a male deity) and a wooden pole (representing a goddess) were placed next to an altar, on which sacrifices were performed regularly. These sacrifices included food offerings and, on special occasions, human victims—although the precise occasion that demanded human sacrifices is not too clear. Receiving a divine oracle or revelation through incubation (spending the night in the temple) or through dreams was a common practice. Divination by "reading" the entrails of sacrificial animals or by "interpreting" the drops of rain and dew was also popular.

Canaanite religion emphasized the mortality of humans and the immortality of gods. Humans were regarded as the "servants" of the deities, who had the power to prolong or shorten human existence. A righteous servant received material success and long life; a guilty or disobedient one deserved evil and misfortune. In other words, divine retribution occurred immediately in this life, not after death. The dead were thought "to descend into the deep of the earth to join those who had gone down."

Philistines

Shortly after 1200 BCE the Philistines invaded and occupied the territory of Canaan. Soon they had established a strong confederation of city-states and built several temples, two dedicated to the deity Dagon, one to the deity Baalzebub, and another to the goddess Ashtoreth. Little is known about them beyond the dramatic tales recorded in the Hebrew scripture (Old Testament). Typical of such episodes are the stories of Shamgar (Judges 3:31), Samson (Judges 16:23–31), and David (I Samuel 17:31–58).

The Philistine invasion and colonization of Canaan coincided with the Jewish invasion and settlement of the same territory. The ensuing struggle between the Philistines and the Jews resulted in the establishment of an independent Jewish kingdom. Of more importance, the Jewish conquest of Canaan resulted in the fusion of Canaanite and Jewish traditions. Both the Hebrew scripture and archeology reflect the profound influence of Canaanite religion and culture (particularly in language, literature, laws, and customs) on the Jews.

The Patriarchs

The consciousness of the Jews as a distinct people bound by a divine mission did not arise until their exodus from Egypt and their subsequent acceptance of a divine law, or Covenant, at Mount Sinai, around the thirteenth century BCE. Yet biblical tradition quite specifically identifies the beginnings of Jewish history with a series of *avot* (fathers or patriarchal figures): Abraham, Isaac, Jacob, and Jacob's twelve sons. Scholars have been tempted to establish a connection between the advent of Abraham and the incursion into Israel-Palestine around 1900–1800 BCE of the Amorites, a Semitic group from western Asia. But the accuracy of events attributed to the *avot*—especially the question of their relationship to each other—has often been challenged.[3] Some scholars have considered Isaac, Jacob, and the rest as the direct descendants of a single clan head, Abraham. Others have viewed the *avot* as tribal chiefs, not necessarily related, whose popular legends gradually developed into a single narrative.

Whatever the historical truth of the matter, biblical tradition holds that Abraham's god promised him and his descendants a permanent territory in an area inhabited by the Canaanites. So Abraham, along with the members of his tribe, their flocks and herds, emigrated to Canaan. After Abraham's death, his son Isaac, and then his grandson Jacob, took his place. Then a terrible famine forced Jacob and his family into a second emigration, this time to Egypt.

Tradition records that everything went well in Egypt for several centuries, until the Egyptian throne was occupied by a pharaoh whose passion for building large cities and monumental temples led him to resort to forced labor and slavery (Exodus 1–15). Among the people so enslaved were the Jews, Jacob's descendants. The Jews were delivered from bondage some time in the thirteenth century BCE by a leader called Moses, who claimed to have had a revelation from the god of the *avot*. The result was the Exodus, the departure of the Jews from Egypt, and their subsequent experience at Mount Sinai in the desert.

The precise nature of early Jewish faith is a topic of considerable debate that focuses on whether or not the *avot*, or the patriarchs, were polytheists or monotheists.[4] Certain scholars have accepted the biblical tradition that the many names of gods represent different titles for the one God, whereas other scholars have argued that the various names of gods suggest a pantheon of some sort. Names frequently encountered in biblical traditions include El Shaddai (God Almighty), El Elyon (God Most High), El Olam (God Everlasting), and El Roi (God Seeing). Then there are the designations as gods of El of Abraham, Pahad (Kinsman) of Isaac, Abir (Champion) of Jacob, Gad (possibly Fortune), Dan (Judge), Asher (perhaps the masculine counterpart of Asherah), and Elim or Elohim (plural of El).

The question of whether the early Jewish faith was polytheistic or monotheistic is still unresolved. One popular speculation, however, is that the god of the *avot* was a tribal deity who became the sole focus of worship. It does not necessarily follow that the *avot* rejected other

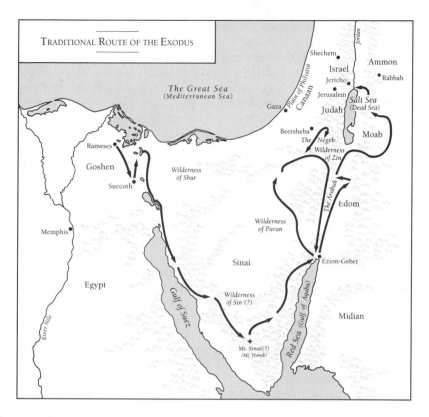

TRADITIONAL ROUTE OF THE EXODUS

gods; on the contrary, evidence that they worshiped other gods surfaces in Jacob's injunction to "put away the foreign gods that are
among you" (Genesis 35:2). There would be no reason for Jacob to
issue such an injunction to a people who followed only one God. The
conclusion that the *avot* were monotheistic is, therefore, difficult to
accept.

Moses

The story of Moses is the cornerstone of Jewish religion. Scholars—
particularly Christian scholars—have disagreed dramatically in their
views of the historicity of the traditional narrative of Moses and of
subsequent events. Some have maintained that much of the account is
a later pious fabrication. Others have argued that all the events occurred precisely as described. Still others have insisted that although
much of the account was embellished in many ways by later editors,
the memory of past experience is, in its major points, recorded correct-

ly. Even the most skeptical critic, however, has admitted that *something* happened to give the Jewish people a new sense of destiny.

Tradition states that after centuries of living in Egypt, the Jewish population had grown to such a degree that the Egyptian government feared that the Jews would become too numerous to control.[5] Consequently, the pharaoh ordered that all male babies born to Jewish families be killed. Moses, who was born during this period (perhaps the thirteenth century BCE), was hidden at home for three months, until the consequences of discovery prompted his mother to set her baby adrift in a waterproof basket in the rushes along the Nile River. There he was discovered by the pharaoh's daughter, who reared him in her palace as her adopted son.

As a young man, Moses witnessed a scene that became a turning point in his life: an Egyptian beating a Jew. Moved by a sudden outburst of anger, he killed the Egyptian on the spot; soon after Moses fled eastward and found refuge with a Midianite priest named Jethro. Eventually, he married one of Jethro's daughters, Zipporah.

A second turning point occurred while Moses was herding Jethro's flock of sheep near Mount Horeb. There he experienced the presence of a divine being amidst a burning bush—an incident that not only changed his life, but altered the destiny of his people in Egypt. The divinity charged Moses with bringing the Jews out of the land of their enslavement and taking them to the "promised land"—the land of the Canaanites, where their ancestors had lived. Moses was assured by this divine presence, or God, that he would receive all the power necessary to persuade the pharaoh to let the Jewish people go.

However, when Moses returned to Egypt, he found the pharaoh to be impervious to his pleas. Moses, directed by God, first threatened and then struck Egypt with nine terrible plagues in succession. Finally, the tenth and last plague forced the pharaoh to let the Jews go. This plague struck and killed all the first-born sons of the Egyptians, including the pharaoh's. Only the Jewish children were "passed over" (remained unharmed), and to this day this incident is commemorated as the "night of the Passover," or the Passover feast.

Moses then led the Jews miraculously through the waters of the Red (or Reed) Sea and across the desert to the foot of Mount Horeb (sometimes referred to as Mount Sinai). Though the exact location of this mountain is still debated, the events that followed are not. With Moses acting as the intermediary, a confrontation between God and the Jews resulted in a solemn pact, commonly known as the *Covenant*. Tradition relates how Moses left the people at the foot of the mountain while he went up to communicate with God. Several days later he returned with two stone tablets delivered to him by God and inscribed with the "commandments" of God.

Two lists of commandments are recorded in the Bible. One, found in Exodus 20, is the familiar formulation of an ethical code known as the Ten Commandments. The other, in Exodus 39, is largely ritualistic in character. According to most scholars, the latter represents the earlier list—although by no means the original pact made between God and Moses. Later emendations and additions are assumed to have obscured so much of the original form that the precise terms of the Mosaic Covenant are irrecoverable.[6]

The Ten Commandments

1. I am the Lord your God, who brought you out of the land of Egypt, out of the house of bondage. You shall have no other gods besides me.

2. You shall not make yourself a graven image, or any likeness of anything that is in heaven above, or that is in the earth beneath, or that is in the water under the earth; you shall not bow to them or serve them; for I the Lord your God am a jealous God, visiting the iniquity of the fathers upon the children to the third and fourth generation of those who hate me, but showing steadfast love to thousands of those who love me and keep my commandments.

3. You shall not take the name of the Lord your God in vain, for the Lord will not hold him guiltless who takes his name in vain.

4. Remember the Sabbath day, to keep it holy. Six days you shall labor, and do all your work; but the seventh day is a Sabbath to the Lord your God; in it you shall not do any work, you, or your son, or your daughter, your manservant, or your maidservant, or your cattle, or the sojourner who is within your gates; for in six days the Lord made heaven and earth, the sea, and all that is in them, and rested the seventh day, therefore the Lord blessed the Sabbath day and hallowed it.

5. Honor your father and your mother, that your days may be long in the land which the Lord your God gives you.

6. You shall not kill.

7. You shall not commit adultery.

8. You shall not steal.

9. You shall not bear false witness against your neighbor.

10. You shall not covet your neighbor's house; you shall not covet your neighbor's wife, or his manservant, or his maidservant, or his ox, or his ass, or anything that is your neighbor's. (Exodus 20:1–17 / Deuteronomy 5:6–21)

Tradition maintains that the Jews constructed a portable shrine, known as the Tabernacle of God, within which stood a box or chest containing the two stone tablets marked with the terms of the Covenant. As the Jews continued their journey, Moses was able to commune with God in the interior of this portable shrine.

During the journey, Moses led an attempt to coalesce the Jews' disparate beliefs into a conceptualized form of religion centered on a national tutelary deity called YHWH (pronounced *Yahweh*). Evidence of the people's reluctance to reject their old beliefs and practices entirely appears in their repeated complaints in the desert and, more notably, in their erection of a golden calf. The worship of graven images was obviously a custom firmly embedded in ancient Jewish society, and the people immediately reverted to images whenever it appeared to them that Moses had abandoned them or times grew hard. Had it not been for Moses' leadership, the tendency of the people may not have been to forsake the other gods, but to forsake YHWH. The fact that Moses' leadership bordered on tyranny is reflected in the people's equation of the fear of death with the worship of YHWH: "So Israel yoked himself to Baal of Peor. And Moses said to the judges of Israel: Every one of you slay his men who have yoked themselves to Baal of Peor" (Numbers 25:1–5).

When Moses finally led the Jews to the borders of Canaan, with the intention of invading it, they lost courage and rebelled against both Moses and God, bringing upon themselves years of wandering in the wilderness. Only under Joshua, Moses' successor, did the Jews cross the River Jordan into the "promised land" of Canaan.

Biblical Religion

Judges and Monarchs

The incursion into Canaan—the transition from a nomadic life to a settled, agrarian one—coincided with the adoption of Canaanite gods and practices. The traditional narrative of this period is characterized by the theme of the Jewish people in pursuit of "foreign gods" and the unhappy consequences of such misplaced devotion. Any ill that befell the Jews was interpreted as YHWH's punishment for attachment to foreign gods. That the people did indeed worship other gods is unquestionable. Numerous biblical passages attest to the willingness of the Jewish people to embrace the gods and religious practices of the Canaanites and neighboring peoples:

> The people of Israel . . . went after other gods, from among the gods of the peoples who were round about them, and bowed down to them and . . . served the Baals and the Ashtoreth. (Judges 2:11–13)

> So the people of Israel dwelt among the Canaanites, the Hittites, the Amorites, the Perizzites, the Hivites, and the Jebusites . . . and they served their gods. (Judges 3:5–7)

Eventually the Jewish people conquered the territories on the east bank of the Jordan River. Around the eleventh century BCE, under King David, they captured Jerusalem and extended their dominion over various parts of Palestine. King Solomon, David's son and successor, built a magnificent temple in Jerusalem and consolidated all religious practices, such as prayers, sacrifices, and festivals, in this center. An account of Solomon's temple is given in I Kings 5–8.

The Jewish kingdom did not last very long, however. A little over a century after its establishment, it split in two. The northern part, which was called Israel and was the larger of the two, was destroyed by the Assyrians in the eighth century BCE. The southern part, called Judah, survived until the sixth century BCE, when it was destroyed by the Babylonians (better known as the Chaldeans).

The era of the kings prior to the destruction of the Jewish kingdom did not purge Jewish religion of polytheism. On the contrary, the establishment of the monarchy gave rise to a nobility that was highly influenced by Canaanite elements. The result was an inevitable mixture of religious practices. That Solomon greatly contributed to this development is attested to in the following statement:

> I [YHWH] am about to tear the kingdom from the hand of Solomon . . . because he has forsaken me, and worshiped Ashtoreth the goddess of the Sidonians, Chemosh the god of Moab, and Milcom the god of the Ammonites. (I Kings 11:31–33)

The rulers of the split kingdoms that succeeded Solomon's reign invited an even wider acceptance of extraneous forms of worship and occult practices. In the north, King Jeroboam introduced the worship of two golden calves and established various occult rites and practices that were quickly adopted by the people and by succeeding rulers, including Jehu and Omri. The policies of these monarchs, and the willingness of the people to incorporate the religious practices of their neighbors, are well documented in the biblical record:

> The people of Israel . . . feared other gods and walked in the customs of the nations whom the Lord drove out before the people of Israel, and in

the customs which the kings of Israel had introduced. . . . They went after false idols and they followed the nations that were round about them . . . and made for themselves molten images of two calves; and they made an Asherah, and worshipped all the host of heaven, and served Baal. And they burned their sons and their daughters as offerings, and used divination and sorcery. (II Kings 17:7–18)

The kings and the people in the south were no different. Male cult prostitution, human sacrifice, idol worship, and various occult practices were features of Jewish religion at this time. Evidence of this is offered in the biblical assessment (II Kings 21:1–7) of the reign of King Manasseh, under whose leadership the people worshiped numerous idols, offered human sacrifices, and indulged in occult activities. The latter were performed by various skilled functionaries: the sorcerer, the soothsayer, the medium, the necromancer, the wizard, the charmer, the augur, the diviner, the dream expert, the seer, the prophet. The prestige that such practitioners enjoyed within Jewish society, among kings and commoners alike, is made explicit in the statements of the prophets Isaiah and Jeremiah (Isaiah 3:2–3 and 8:19; Jeremiah 27:9).

The failure of reforms attempted by both King Hezekiah and King Josiah indicates how deeply rooted was belief in the efficacy of magical practices and divinatory arts. Many feared, worshiped, and, with the help of occult practitioners, offered sacrifices with libations to numerous deities and demons in order to avert or mitigate plagues, diseases, and all other mishaps.

In the process of recruiting and retaining suppliants and devotees, an intense power struggle seems to have developed between those who practiced occultism in the name of YHWH and those who invoked it in the name of other deities. The latter were regarded as utterly "false" by the former, who anathematized the opposition. The struggle between these two groups eventually escalated into a political power struggle on a national scale. To the YHWHistic group, all occult practices that excluded YHWH were as evil or abominable as were improper intercourse, prostitution, and fornication. The chief and most articulate critics of rival cults and factions were the prophets of YHWH, whose role within Jewish society grew in importance. Their deep concern with the social systems, religious institutions, and ritual practices of their time led them to assume responsibility for the character and development of the Jewish religion.

Prophets

The Jewish prophets were a diverse group. Some were strong individualists; others were members of organized groups. Some restricted their activities to the role of experts delivering oracles; others accepted the challenge and the risk of delivering moral judgments. Some were associated with the royal courts; others openly revolted against the ruling king. Some were ecstatic; others opposed ecstasy. Some were highly regarded and respected; others were objects of suspicion or contempt.

One band of ecstatic prophets seems to have moved about the country and played various musical instruments. Another prophetic band lived together in semimonastic fashion, taking meals in common and living together. The size of these communal prophetic orders varied from one hundred to as many as four hundred. Each prophetic band was organized under a leader and was financially dependent, by and large, on the gifts of adherents or supporters.

Jewish kings retained in their courts many prophets who were qualified to interpret omens and to deliver important oracles. Among these court prophets were some staunchly independent thinkers who reacted strongly against corrupt regimes and unjust social behavior and who rebuked hypocritical attitudes and religious formalism. To these prophets, ethical principles and moral obligations related to human character and conduct were more important than methods and forms of ceremonial religiosity. They portrayed their God as a merciful, righteous, just, and holy deity who despised religious ceremonies, fasts, or prayers performed by suppliants who tolerated, condoned, or practiced social injustice, oppression, and cruelty. Stressing the inward quality of religion, these prophets defined true piety as the personal relationship of an individual to God.

Exile

Despite the denunciatory voices of the prophets and the supporters of the YHWHistic group, polytheism and occultism persisted as legitimate and accepted norms of Jewish society until the period of exile (sixth century BCE). All in all, there were three exiles, or deportations, of Jews to Babylonia. The first, in 598 BCE, included King Jehoiachin, his mother, his palace retinue, along with palace and Temple treasures, and innumerable captives. A vivid description of this Jewish-Babylonian struggle is given in II Kings 24:12–16. The second, in 587 BCE, followed an uprising against the ruling Babylonians, led by the vassal king of Judah, Zedekiah, and his nobles. This was the most catastrophic event in Jewish history: the Temple, the royal palace, and hundreds of homes were burned, the walls of the city destroyed, and thousands of people deported. Again, a description is given in II Kings 25:8–21. The third, in 582 BCE, when Gedaliah, the governor of Judah appointed by the Babylonians, was assassinated by Ishmael, leader of a band of nationalists in league with the Ammonite king. The Babylonian reprisal was swift: more deportations to Babylonia. During each of these three conflicts, many Jews fled to Egypt, lest they too become targets of Babylonian vengeance.

Gone now was the mass following of various gods, goddesses, and occult activities. Gone too was Solomon's Temple, after existing for some 350 years. Those who remained in Palestine were common people who, by and large, were accustomed to the practices that had persisted through the centuries and were now isolated from their roots by an immigrant population of colonists. Obviously, such people could not revive the worship of one God, YHWH. Instead it was left to the exiles who returned to Jerusalem in the fifth century BCE to fulfill this task. They did so with a deliberateness and exclusiveness that had been uncharacteristic of them in the past.

Rise of Judaism

Scribes and Priests

The years following the downfall of the kingdom of Judah in the sixth century BCE saw the beginning of the *diaspora*—the scattering of the Jewish people all over the world. This period is considered by many critics to mark the end of "biblical" religion and the rise of "Judaism." Far from their place of worship, the Temple in Jerusalem, the Jewish people were forced to adopt a new institution of worship—the *synagogue*, a term of Greek derivation meaning a meeting place, or an assembly. With the synagogue appeared the figure of the *rabbi*—the Jewish religious leader, teacher, or master. Unfortunately, we do not know how or when this innovation came into being. It is possible that synagogues gradually developed some time between the fifth century BCE and the first century CE.

When the Persian King Cyrus conquered Babylon in 538 BCE, he allowed those Jews that wished to do so to return to their homeland. The estimated 40,000 Jews who made their way back home, however, were soon disillusioned and disheartened by the conditions they found in Jerusalem. One of the main projects of the returning exiles was to rebuild the Temple. At first, the community proved unequal to the task; then, at the urging of the prophets Haggai and Zechariah, the project was carried through to completion in 516 BCE. Thus, seventy years after the destruction of the first temple, a second arose on its ruins.

Meanwhile, the Jews who had remained in Babylon achieved positions of wealth and influence and developed a vigorous religious life. They founded their own institutions, built up a new polity, and centered their religious life on the Torah (Law)—the first five books of the Bible, believed to have been written by Moses. From the ranks of these Babylonian Jews came Ezra the scribe and some 1700 others who arrived in Jerusalem in 458 BCE to disseminate knowledge of the Torah. Twelve years later Ezra was joined by Nehemiah, who together joined forces to bring about religious reforms. Two issues addressed by Ezra and Nehemiah had a far-reaching effect on the religion and history of the Jewish people: the status of the Torah, and the issue of foreign marriages.

The ultimate aim of these two men was to establish the Torah as the supreme, authoritative source of instruction in all facets of life. This they achieved not merely by reading from the Torah, but by applying it to their own times and by interpreting and explaining its contents to fit the circumstances and conditions of life. Ezra, for example, dramatized his disapproval of foreign marriages by begging for forgiveness from God on behalf of those who had married foreign partners, while Nehemiah resorted to the use of intimidation to encourage adherence to marriage norms that he felt were crucial to the survival of Judaism.

Ezra and Nehemiah established a new theocratic state in which power was vested in the priests. They made the people take a solemn oath to observe the Torah and to strictly fulfill the requirements of tithing, sacrifices, and festivals. Later, a demand for specialists to copy and interpret the Torah was soon filled by a class of scribes known as *sopherim*. Those who developed a special talent came to be known as *rabbis*, or masters. Others diligently applied themselves to the literary labor of writing down the Hebrew canon, or scripture.

Jewish-Persian Contact

The postexilic period, particularly the period of Jewish-Persian contact (sixth to fourth centuries BCE), was in many ways decisive for the subsequent development of Judaism. The exile forced the Jews to come to terms with certain ideas and practices. Now, special emphasis was placed on YHWH's uniqueness. He alone was God, the living Lord, king of the universe, and the sovereign of all authority. Terms such as the Almighty, the Exalted One, the Great Holy One, the Lord of Glory, the Lord of Hosts, and the King of Kings were used to stress God's transcendence—that is, that he was beyond the range of human grasp, reason, description, or experience. A tendency also developed to avoid the use of the divine name YHWH. Instead, it was replaced by *Adonay* (Lord). And God's presence and relationship with human beings came to be referred to by the word *shekinah* (literally, dwelling).

This substitute for the divine name and God's activity created another concept: the Spirit, or the Holy Spirit. This Spirit was conceived of as an ethical principle that permeates the world and holds it together—as a divine force that teaches human beings God's will. Centuries later, it was represented in rabbinic literature as a mediator of divine revelation in the scriptures. In addition, the ancient concept of God's heavenly court was transformed in the postexilic period into a highly developed doctrine of angels. These angels were holy, eternal, and immortal beings, who were made by God on the first day of creation to serve, praise, and glorify him—but most importantly, to carry out his will. These angels also received the prayers offered by the pious, intervened in perilous situations, and carried out God's punishment against the wicked. Their number and division into various ranks are not known. What is known are the names of four angels (or archangels): Uriel, Raphael, Gabriel, and Michael—the latter considered to be the guardian angel of the Jews.

Judaism's angelology may have developed under Babylonian and Persian influence. Scholars have pointed out the similarities between the Jewish angelology, on the one hand, and the astral deities of Babylonia as well as the Zoroastrian Amesha Spentas, on the other. Although the matter has not been conclusively resolved, it is hardly conceivable that Judaism's angelology came into being without Persian influence. This is even more true regarding Judaism's ideas of Satan, demons, resurrection, and the Messianic Age. One must reckon with the powerful influence of Persian ideas, no matter how difficult it is to give any particulars about the nature of this influence.

Preexilic Jews believed that everything, both good and evil, derived from God. In postexilic times this conception changed. God was conceived as exclusively good, and Satan was the author and representative of evil. The appearance of Satan as God's antagonist (called "the adversary" in the book of Job) was introduced in the postexilic period. Later developments represented Satan, along with his angels and powers, as one who constitutes the realm of evil, who seeks to lead individuals to wickedness and destruction, and who causes evil, sin, and death. He stands in complete antithesis to God, who will bind and destroy him at the end of the world.

But Judaism never maintained the thoroughgoing dualism of Zoroastrianism. Nor did it reach to the Zoroastrian conclusion that Satan and God were two coequal, but not coeternal, powers. Instead, Judaism explained the appearance of evil as a fall within God's creation, because God, being good, could not have created evil. Certain Jewish documents, mainly from the Greco-Roman period, present the explanation that the angel Satan exalted himself above the stars, refused to worship Adam as the likeness of God, and was consequently cast down from heaven. This story has some connection with the myth of the fallen day star mentioned in Isaiah 14:12ff. The Latin term for the day star is *Lucifer;* consequently, *Lucifer* came to mean Satan.

The admixture of Persian ideas are also to be recognized in the Jewish conception of demons, or evil spirits. The story of the "angels," or "sons of god" in Genesis 6:1ff., usually serves as a background explanation. These so-called angels were once created by God; but they fell from God's grace and were imprisoned. Their descendants, the demons or evil spirits, now inhabit the earth, and their primary function is to tempt individuals to commit sin. Later, there developed the conception of a structured realm of evil spirits, serving as Satan's ministers and hostile to God's sovereignty.

The Zoroastrian view of resurrection and life after death caused a sharp division among postexilic Jews. One group persisted in maintaining the old conviction that the dead led a shadowy existence in the underworld (called *sheol* in Hebrew, and *hades* in Greek); the other became attracted to the belief that "those who sleep in the dust of the earth shall awake, some to everlasting life, and some to shame and everlasting contempt" (Daniel 12:2). Unfortunately, nothing is known about the mechanism of resurrection to make any possible conclusions. And the same applies for the transition from preexilic prophetic ideas to postexilic *eschatological* ideas (ideas pertaining to the last things or final age), which depict the end of history and a new world in which God alone is sovereign. All that can be deduced is the tendency among Jews to regard the present age as evil, the order of nature disturbed, the heavenly bodies thrown into disorder, and terror reigning all over the earth. Toward the end of time, it was further thought, portents were to appear, God was to intervene in history, a great judgment was to follow, the righteous were to enter the new world (the kingdom of God), and the wicked were to be judged.

Details regarding the sequence of events leading to the end of time are lacking. What is known is that some time near the end of this present age, but prior to the ushering in of the new age, a Messiah (Anointed One) was to appear. This human, God-appointed ruler would be endowed with extraordinary qualities of righteousness, wisdom, and power. His mission would be to establish his kingdom in Zion (Israel) and destroy the hostile world power. These eschatological views, long central to the Zoroastrian religion, found their way into postexilic Judaism.

Jewish-Hellenistic Contact

In 332 BCE, the theocratic state centered in Palestine came under the powerful influence of Greek civilization through Alexander the Great and his successors. The Greek way of life—education, sports, theaters,

Judaism

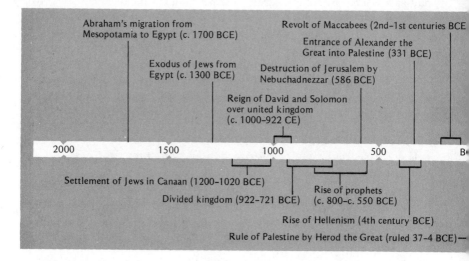

Abraham's migration from Mesopotamia to Egypt (c. 1700 BCE)

Revolt of Maccabees (2nd–1st centuries BCE

Entrance of Alexander the Great into Palestine (331 BCE)

Exodus of Jews from Egypt (c. 1300 BCE)

Destruction of Jerusalem by Nebuchadnezzar (586 BCE)

Reign of David and Solomon over united kingdom (c. 1000–922 CE)

2000   1500   1000   500   B

Settlement of Jews in Canaan (1200–1020 BCE)

Divided kingdom (922–721 BCE)

Rise of prophets (c. 800–c. 550 BCE)

Rise of Hellenism (4th century BCE)

Rule of Palestine by Herod the Great (ruled 37–4 BCE)—

libraries—quickly was adopted by educated as well as uneducated Jews, until King Antiochus IV (175–164 BCE) determined to hasten the process of Hellenization among Jews who stubbornly resisted change. He prohibited the Jews, on pain of death, to practice circumcision, to own any copies of the Torah, or to keep the Sabbath (holy day of rest and worship). In addition, he attempted to force them to worship Zeus by erecting an altar to that deity in the Temple at Jerusalem and by sacrificing pigs. The horror and indignation inspired by such sacrilege among Jewish believers led to open rebellion against the king and a call to all Jews to return to the "way of their fathers."

The revolt was led by an aged priest called Mattathias, who killed a commissioner who had ordered him to sacrifice to Zeus. Together with his five sons and a large following of supporters, Mattathias took to the desert. In 165 BCE, Judas Maccabeus, the son of Mattathias, recaptured most of Jerusalem and restored Jewish worship in the Temple. This period of Maccabean independence (celebrated today as Hanukkah) lasted till 63 BCE, when animosity between divergent Jewish parties led to violence and bloody massacres and, eventually, civil war. The Roman general Pompey, then stationed in Syria, was called upon to arbitrate: instead, he promptly occupied Palestine and declared it to be a Roman province.

During this period of Greco-Roman occupation the pervasive influence of Hellenistic culture on Judaism became quite obvious.[7] The biblical books of Ruth, Esther, Jonah, Job, and Ecclesiastes, among others, appeared at this time. In addition, the Septuagint (the transla-

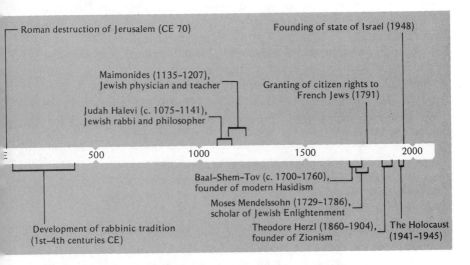

Roman destruction of Jerusalem (CE 70)

Founding of state of Israel (1948)

Maimonides (1135–1207),
Jewish physician and teacher

Judah Halevi (c. 1075–1141),
Jewish rabbi and philosopher

Granting of citizen rights to
French Jews (1791)

500   1000   1500   2000

Baal-Shem-Tov (c. 1700–1760),
founder of modern Hasidism

Moses Mendelssohn (1729–1786),
scholar of Jewish Enlightenment

Development of rabbinic tradition
(1st–4th centuries CE)

Theodore Herzl (1860–1904),
founder of Zionism

The Holocaust
(1941–1945)

tion of the Hebrew scripture into Greek) was completed by the second century BCE.

This era was also distinguished by the advent of various new Jewish groups and parties. A wealthy, aristocratic, and somewhat liberal group known as the Sadducees displayed a keen interest in disseminating Greek culture. Another group, the Pharisees, represented pious members of society whose main passion was the Jewish religion. They paid great attention to oral tradition, harnessed their aspirations to Messianic expectations, preached concepts related to resurrection, and struggled for liberation from worldly preoccupations.

Three other influential groups were founded during the Roman occupation of Palestine. One was the Herodians, who supported the Roman government, the house of Herod. Another, the Zealots, opposed the Roman government because in their view submission to the Romans meant forsaking God. Their recourse was to the sword, which they believed could hasten the Messiah's coming. The third group, called the Essenes, lived in a monastic commune, practiced nonviolence, and awaited the end of the world, at which time they as the "sons of light" would triumph over the "sons of darkness." The famous Dead Sea Scrolls, found near Qumran, have been attributed to this group.

In 66 CE, toward the end of Emperor Nero's reign, the discontent of the Jews against the Romans broke into open rebellion, which was suppressed with savagery and slaughter. In 70 CE Jerusalem was razed and the Temple set on fire. Three years later a band of Zealots at

Masada fought against the Romans until starvation led them to commit suicide rather than submit. A final attempt to liberate Palestine from Roman rule was made by Bar Kokhba, supported by Akiba, the greatest rabbi of the time. After three years of struggle (132–135) the Romans crushed the rebellion, and the Jewish population of Palestine was largely scattered throughout the Mediterranean basin.

For the Jewish people, historical events are far more than a mere sequence of names and incidents; to them historical events are acts of a god who is deliberately and purposefully guiding his people onward. Jewish people therefore see all historical events as crucial to the formation of their religion; in order to understand the character of Judaism, we have to examine the Bible.

The Bible

For many centuries the stories, ballads, laws, and religious activities of the Jews were transmitted orally from generation to generation. A few of these oral traditions may have been put into writing as early as 1000 BCE. During the period of the monarchy, Jews required codification of their oral traditions in response to the needs of an increasingly complex society. This process continued for several centuries, until their collection of sacred writings attained the status of Bible.

The term "Bible" is derived from a Greek word that means "books"; both Jews and Christians use the term Bible to mean their sacred books. Originally, these writings were written on skin or parchment and made up into individual rolls or scrolls.

Of course, there are many ancient copies of the Jewish Bible (called the Old Testament by Christians), and these are often referred to as "manuscripts." Until the discovery of the Dead Sea Scrolls in 1947, it was thought that the oldest manuscript dated from the ninth century CE. However, manuscripts discovered in caves beside the Dead Sea have been dated as far back as the second century BCE.

Because the common language in the early days of the Jews was Hebrew, the Jewish Bible was written in that language except for small portions of the books of Daniel and Ezra-Nehemiah, which were written in Aramaic (a Semitic dialect closely related to Hebrew).

The Jewish Bible, in its present form, contains twenty-four books (the same writings are presented as thirty-nine books in the Christian Bible, the Old Testament) and is divided into three main sections:

1. *Torah (Law or Instruction)*, consisting of the books of Genesis, Exodus, Leviticus, Numbers, and Deuteronomy
2. *Neviim (Prophets)*, consisting of the books of Joshua, Judges, Samuel, Kings (referred to as Former Prophets), Isaiah, Jeremiah,

Ezekiel, and the twelve "minor" prophets (referred to as Latter Prophets)

3. *Kethuviim (Writings)*, consisting of the books of Psalms, Proverbs, Job, Song of Solomon, Ruth, Lamentations, Ecclesiastes, Esther, Ezra-Nehemiah, Chronicles, and Daniel

Today, the Jewish people refer to their scriptures as *Tanak*, an acronym made up of the initial consonants of the three major divisions.

Torah

The most significant section is the Torah, the authorship of which is traditionally ascribed to Moses.[8] Scholars have traced some of the basic ideas in the Torah to Moses, but the collection of writings, as it appears today, came into existence over a period of six to seven hundred years. The Torah recounts the history of the Israelites from the days of their departure from Egypt, under the leadership of Moses, to the eve of their triumphant entry into the land of the Canaanites. Prefaced to this account are two other histories: the origin of the universe and of humankind, and the stories and sagas of the patriarchs. Scattered among these accounts are various legal, social, and religious instructions or codes.

An enormous amount of study has been devoted to the identification of the authors, dates, and the sequence of revisions of the Torah. The consensus is that there were at least four sets of editorial revisions,[9] the last of which was undertaken by the priests during the exile in Babylon in the sixth century BCE. By 400 BCE, the five books of the Torah as it appears today attained the status of scripture.

The importance of the Torah lies in the basic concepts and fundamental views that it conveys. Three interconnected central themes dominate the Torah: (1) God, (2) the universe, and (3) human beings.

"In the beginning God created the heavens and the earth," are the opening words of the Torah. There is no question in the Torah as to whether or not God exists—he *is*, and he is only One. Again, the Torah represents God as a personal God—not in the sense that he has a physical body, but in that he enters, instructs, and directs the life of every human being. He is, moreover, regarded as "merciful and gracious, slow to anger, and abounding in steadfast love and truthfulness" (Exodus 34:6–7). He is "God of gods and Lord of lords, the great, the mighty, and the terrible God" (Deuteronomy 10:17), who executes justice for the orphan and the widow. Nevertheless, he is a "jealous God, visiting the iniquity of the fathers upon the children to the third and fourth generation of those who hate him" (Exodus 20:5).

The Torah represents the nature and attributes of God in the following manner: those who love God and keep his commandments, or instructions, benefit from his love, mercy, and grace, whereas those who disobey his commandments reap only his anger and justice. Nowhere in the Torah is the paradox, or the apparent problem, between God's mercy and justice tackled, let alone resolved. Centuries later rabbinic commentary explained it in this way: if the world had been created on the basis of God's mercy alone, then the sins of the world would have been many; if, on the other hand, the world had been created strictly on the basis of God's justice, then the world would not have been able to exist; hence, to maintain a proper balance, God created the world with both His attributes—justice and mercy.

Of course, for centuries during the period of biblical Judaism, people worshiped other gods, practiced idolatry, and assumed polytheistic customs and rites (Deuteronomy 32:17). Nevertheless, God raised up courageous individuals—the prophets—who clearly protested and reminded the people of their covenant with God.

The opening statement in the Torah suggests that God is the only creative cause of the universe. Nowhere does the Torah suggest that

The Torah scroll, kept inside the Ark of the Covenant in the synagogue. The other two scrolls represent the Neviim and Kethuviim. The Jewish worshiper is wearing both tallit *and* tefillin.   From the private collection of Ray Kurkjian.

the universe is self-created. God is regarded as the creator of the heavens and earth: everything that is has come into being by his command. In fact, the Torah states (Genesis 1) that God's commanding word separated darkness from light, night from day, the heaven from the earth, and the seas from the dry land. At his word, the sun, the moon, all heavenly bodies, all water creatures, all vegetation, and all creatures and animals came into being. God's last act of creation was man and woman.

The Torah repeatedly insists that God is not a spirit in nature, nor part of nature, but above and distinctively apart from nature. Neither the stars nor the moon nor any other heavenly or earthly phenomenon is to be worshiped or thought to have godlike (i.e., divine) characteristics. God alone brought everything into existence and, as such, is the preserver and ruler of the universe. And, according to the Torah (Genesis 1), this created universe is "good."

Another viewpoint central to the Torah is that man and woman are created in the "image" of God (Genesis 1:26; 5:21). To be created in the image of God means, in the modern Jewish view, to be divinely ordained to demonstrate God's justice and mercy. Nowhere does the Torah instruct an individual to abandon the world (as do Christian, Hindu, and Buddhist ascetics or monastics) in order to please God. On the contrary, life is to be responded to with piety and reverence. In other words, a person ought to love the world and hallow life in such daily activities as eating, drinking, working, and pleasure, by raising them to their highest level so that every act is sacred and reflects the divine image. Hence, the Torah instructs how an individual's behavior must be governed from the cradle to the grave by moral codes. Naturally, a person is free to choose and is morally responsible for the choices made.

The Torah makes no attempt to offer philosophical explanations for these views; only the following assertions are made: that God exists, that he is the sole creator, that he is absolutely without a rival (or an incarnation), that he needs no representation of any sort, that the universe which he created is good, and that the purpose of human life is to serve God and fellow individuals. The importance of the Torah is illustrated in the following well-known Jewish story. A "heathen" once came to the Jewish scholar Shammai and said that he would become a proselyte (convert to Judaism) on condition that he be taught the entire Torah while standing on one foot. Shammai chased him away. So the man appealed next to Hillel, another Jewish scholar. "Whatever is hateful to you," said Hillel to the man, "do not do to your neighbor; that is the entire Torah. The rest is commentary—go and learn it."

Prophets

Many works and oracles believed to have been written by prophets gradually won an influential place in Jewish tradition. Although never attaining the same level of authority as the Torah, the writings of the prophets nevertheless came to be regarded as important works, and by 200 BCE they had attained the status of scripture.[10]

The books of Joshua, Judges, Samuel, and Kings constitute the category of the so-called Former Prophets, following immediately after the Torah. It is generally assumed that these books have had a very complex compositional history, but no consensus exists about the course of that history. Possibly, these books were not completely composed until shortly before, or even during, the Babylonian exile. Virtually nothing is known also about their authorship. Undoubtedly, the books from Joshua to Kings represent in their present form the final stage of a lengthy editorial process.

The basic theme in the book of Joshua is the fulfillment of God's promise first made to Abraham (Genesis 12:2–3) and regularly repeated afterward to his descendants: possession of the promised land (Canaan). The record in Joshua, however, lends little credence to the theory of a swift and conclusive conquest and occupation. Rather, the overall narrative suggests that the possession of the land was a slow, complex process involving periods of both bloodshed and relative calm.

The book of Judges describes the period between the settlement in the land of Canaan and the beginning of the monarchy. This portion of Jewish history is presented in the framework of a particular literary mold: apostasy of the Jewish people, oppression by enemies, crying to YHWH, raising up of judges (deliverers or leaders), a period of rest. This cyclic recurrence—apostasy, distress, conversion, and salvation—is repeated about fourteen times and markedly reflects the religious characteristic of the book of Judges.

The dominant theme in the books of Samuel and Kings is the rise and downfall of the monarchy. But this account of succession to the throne is governed by a religious standard: judgments on the character of the various kings. These judgments are usually confined to a single verse: "And he did that which was right [or evil] in the eyes of YHWH." Occasionally, however, they are longer and embrace fuller particulars. In any event, Jewish kings are judged not on "objective" criteria, but from the point of view of the so-called Deuteronomic Code (Deuteronomy 12–26).

This code prescribed, among other things, how the monarchy was to be established so as not to contravene the fundamental principles of the theocracy. Consequently, obedience to the code is the qualification for an approving verdict; deviation from it is the source of ill success brought about by God's condemnation.

This ethical and moral character is also found in the books of the Latter Prophets. These collections deal mainly with social systems, political activities, moral norms, and religious practices. Written and compiled some time between the eighth and fourth centuries BCE, they address the principles related to human conduct by condemning hypocritical attitudes and religious formalism. Over the years they gradually replaced the idea of a tribal and national god with one who was the God of the whole world. Obviously, it is impossible to analyze all the Latter Prophets in such a brief space. But a few of the more outstanding ones are worth mentioning.

The book of Amos pronounces in no uncertain terms the judgment coming upon both the surrounding nations and the Jewish people. The reason for such condemnation is social injustice. Here are the words in Amos:

> They sell the righteous for silver and the needy for a pair of shoes. They trample the head of the poor into the dust of the earth and turn aside the way of the afflicted. (Amos 2:6–7)

According to Amos, no amount of religious performance can ever salve the moral conscience of a society if cruelty, oppression, and injustice are tolerated:

> Thus says YHWH. . . . I hate, I despise your feasts, and I take no delight in your solemn assemblies. Even though you offer me your burnt offerings and cereal offerings, I will not accept them. . . . Take away from me the noise of your songs; to the melody of your harps I will not listen. But let justice roll down like waters, and righteousness like an ever-flowing stream. (Amos 5:21–24)

This strong rebuke for unrighteous attitudes and unjust activities stems from Amos's view of a just God who demands that his people reflect the divine image of justice and righteousness in their daily activities.

The message in the book of Hosea is, like the message of Amos, one of judgment—but judgment supplemented by a remarkable new picture of God. The Jewish people seemed to Hosea much like his own unfaithful wife Gomer, who had deserted him in pursuit of "foreign" lovers. Just as Hosea later restored Gomer to his home, so God would restore the wayward, unfaithful Israel. Hosea believed that despite Israel's infidelity to the covenant, God loved Israel.

If the book of Amos portrays a righteous and just God and the book of Hosea a loving and merciful God, it was left for Isaiah to capture another aspect of God: his holiness (Isaiah 1:11–17; 6:3). But the narrow, nationalistic concept of God is finally shattered in the book of Jeremiah. Here, it is insisted that God is supremely an ethical God and the Lord of the whole world. Hence, nothing short of a "change of heart" would be acceptable to God. More important than ceremonial religiosity is the "inwardness" of religion; and true piety consists of the personal relationship of an individual to God (Jeremiah 31:31–34).

Writings

If the Torah represents the most powerful influence in Judaism and the Prophets shaped its ethical and moral character, then its inspirational genius lies in the Writings. These important collections of poetic, proverbial, and philosophical material, which were written by unknown sages over several centuries, were finally recognized as scripture by 100 CE. The striking feature of the Writings is a shift in outlook. The writers were chiefly interested not in Judaism or in national concerns, but in humanity. They address their listeners with common, human problems arising from family relations, personal affairs, social and business matters, public interests, manners, and morals.

The book of Proverbs, for example, includes a collection of maxims, humor and sarcasm, epigrams, and pithy sayings. The great motive for living is to acquire wisdom. In other words, wisdom and knowledge are the secret source of a happy and prosperous life. In fact, wisdom, in the view of these sages, existed prior to creation, and at creation "she" was the pervading principle, a "master workman" (Proverbs 8:22–31). True living, then, consists in being in harmony with this universal principle (wisdom), which reveals itself to the minds of human beings (Proverbs 8:34–35).

Another book that voices the need of all generations and appeals at all times is Psalms—the hymnal and prayer book used in Jewish and Christian worship. Some Psalms can be dated from the Babylonian Exile and some after the return to Jerusalem, whereas others belong to the period of the monarchy and possibly were used in the liturgical worship of the Temple. The principal types, distinguished by their subjects, are hymns of praise, trust, and thanksgiving (e.g., Psalms 66; 100; 116; 135; 145); prayers, personal or collective, penitential (confessional), or otherwise (e.g., Psalms 3; 4; 5; 25; 55; 85; 106); enthronement psalms, addressed to kings during coronations (e.g., Psalms 93; 96; 97; 98; 99); rehearsals of national history (e.g., Psalms 78; 105; 106; 135; 136); and praises of the Torah (e.g., Psalms 1; 27; 119). The present final form of the collection of Psalms is governed by liturgical considerations for public worship. Yet these collections for common worship reveal deep human feelings and desires, both at the national and individual level, with all life's joys and woes, its hopes and fears, its longings and despair.

The books of Job and Ecclesiastes are two immortal classics, although virtually nothing is known regarding their authorship or date of composition. Each book views life from a different dimension. The book of Job challenges and denies the validity of the traditional view that the righteous are favored by God and therefore prosper, whereas the wicked are overtaken by misfortune and calamity sent by God. The book of Job proves conclusively that the facts of life contradict this theory and show that the wicked may prosper and lead a happy life, while the righteous may suffer and be overtaken by tragedy.

The story clearly indicates Job's stance on this matter. All the time that he suffers, his three friends doubt his righteousness; but Job knows that he is innocent. His friends try to explain his suffering by examining his moral conduct; Job seeks an answer for his suffering by examining God's intervention in human affairs. His friends declare that he is a sinner; Job declares that God is unjust (Job 16:18–21; 31:1–40). The story then concludes without explaining the cause of Job's suffering. The facts that clearly stand out, however, are that true piety needs no outward proof of success or prosperity and that God's rule is incomprehensible to the human mind.

The sweeping statement in the book of Ecclesiastes is quite arresting: "Vanity of vanities, everything is vanity" (Ecclesiastes 1:2; 12:8). The Hebrew word for vanity means breath or vapor, and therefore figuratively implies "impermanence," "transitoriness," and possibly "aimlessness." The basic theme of the book is to illustrate, by a series of wide-ranging examples drawn from the social world of human beings, in what sense everything is subject to this cosmic fact of vanity.

The value of work, pleasure, wisdom, and wealth are all explored; but the conclusion arrived at is that all such pursuits are vanity because the riddle of life is bounded by the riddle of death—the common fate of all (Ecclesiastes 2:4–21; 4:4–8; 9:11). But is this cosmic fact of vanity equally true of moral activities? The text of Ecclesiastes challenges the long-established orthodox doctrine that God made, ruled, and controlled all things. It states that God seems unconcerned with moral distinctions, because both the wicked and the righteous are somehow treated alike, and rewards are not necessarily bestowed in harmony with ability or merit (Ecclesiastes 9:1–3, 11). Also, "good" and "evil" are so divinely mixed up that nothing can be found out concerning the future (Ecclesiastes 1:15; 6:12; 7:13–14; 8:7). Consequently, to follow piety is absolutely vain or useless, especially since the destiny of human beings and of beasts is similar—death. And if death robs life of meaning and purpose, then life itself, according to Ecclesiastes, is "vanity of vanities."

Talmud and Midrash

By the time the Bible had been completed and assembled, great changes had taken place within Judaism. These changes gave rise to oral interpretations and traditions concerning many of the written laws; and though Judaism affirmed the binding character of the Torah, it also sanctioned and endorsed these "traditions," which came to be known as Talmud and Midrash.

The *Talmud* is a collection of commentaries, traditions, and precedents that supplements the Bible as a source of authority. The *Midrash* is a collection of literary works containing scriptural expositions and interpretations of both legal and nonlegal matters. Next to the Bible, the Talmud and the Midrash are the most sacred Jewish books. Schoolchildren use them as textbooks; rabbis—particularly Conservative and Orthodox ones—study them as sources of precepts and teachings; and pious Jews read them as guidebooks for day-to-day living. Biographical sketches, humorous anecdotes, parables, epigrams, treatises, and

Orthodox Jewish boys studying in the town of Gehula, Jerusalem, Israel. Abraham Menashe/Photo Researchers, Inc.

scholarly commentaries in the Talmud and Midrash provide not only an intimate glimpse into ancient Jewish life but also moral insights and spiritual values that have universal application.

The Talmud and Midrash are often thought of as "oral" Torah, in contrast to the "written" or "revealed" Torah. Jewish tradition maintains that from the very moment that Moses accepted the written Torah on Mount Sinai there existed an oral Torah that was handed on according to tradition from generation to generation. It is more probable that oral traditions developed over hundreds of years, until the volume of accumulated tradition taxed the capacity of each succeeding generation to sustain it. As a result, these traditions were written down and codified in legal form.

The product of two distinct Jewish centers of learning, the Talmud exists in two versions: the Palestinian and the Babylonian. The differences between the two versions in subject matter, method, presentation, and language may reflect the differing life-styles of the Jews who lived in Palestine and those who lived in Babylonia. Biblical commandments had to be applied differently in different circumstances. Today, decisions in matters of religious law are rendered on the basis of the Babylonian Talmud. Here are some Talmud excerpts:

"Then Moses said to God 'If I come to the people of Israel and say to them "The God of your fathers has sent me to you" and they ask "What is His name?" what shall I say to them?' " (Exodus 3:13) Moses asked the Holy One, praised be He, to tell him His great name, "And God said to Moses 'I am what I am.' " (Exodus 3:14) Rabbi Abba bar Mamal said: The Holy One, praised be He, said to Moses "You want to know My name. I am called according to My deeds. At various times I am called Almighty Lord of hosts, God, and Lord. When I judge My creatures, I am called God. When I wage war against the wicked, I am called Lord of hosts. When I suspend the punishment of man's sins, I am called Almighty. And when I have compassion upon My world, I am called Lord. Thus Scripture states 'I am what I am; I am called according to My deeds.' " (Exodus Rabbah 3:6)

Rabbi Huna and Rabbi Jeremiah said in the name of the Rabbi Hiyya-bar Aba: It is written, "They have forsaken Me and have not kept My law." (Jeremiah 16:11) This is to say: "If only they had forsaken Me but kept My law! Since they then would have been occupied with it, the light which is in it would have restored them to the right path." (Lamentations Rabbah II)

Resh Lakish said: "The commandment of the Lord is pure." (Psalms 19:9) If one's intent is pure, the Torah for him becomes a life-giving medicine, purifying him to life. But if one's intent is not pure, it becomes a death-giving drug, purifying him to death. (Yoma 72b)

Rabbi Eliezer said: the nations (i.e., non-Jews) will have no share in the world to come, as it is written "The wicked shall depart to Sheol, and all the nations that forget God" (Psalms 9:17). The first part of the verse refers to the wicked among Israel. However, Rabbi Joshua said to him: If the verse had stated "The wicked shall depart to Sheol, and all the nations," I would agree with you. But the verse goes on to say "that forget God." Therefore it means to say that there are righteous men among the other nations of the world who do have a share in the world to come. (Tosefta Sanhedrin 13:2)

Noncanonical Material

A large selection of noncanonical materials enjoyed great popularity and were widely circulated among the Jews during the Greco-Roman period. Written in Hebrew, Aramaic, and Greek sometime between 200 BCE and 100 CE, this mass of Jewish literature included legendary histories, collections of psalms, wisdom works, *esoteric* (secret) doctrines, and apocalyptic pronouncements. The word *apocalyptic* derives from a Greek root meaning to uncover; hence, apocalyptic literature deals with visions heretofore unknown and describes events or things to come.

The fall of Jerusalem in 70 CE, along with the rapid growth of Christian literature, forced the rabbis to take drastic action regarding noncanonical material. At the Council of Jamnia in 90 CE, the rabbis set up a canon of approved texts and strongly condemned all noncanonical material. Consequently, many noncanonical texts either dropped out of circulation or were systematically destroyed. Fortunately, for one reason or another, some of these manuscripts survived the vicissitudes of time.

No special order for the surviving noncanonical books is recognized by tradition, but they are identified in two broad categories:

1. *Palestinian books* (originally written in Hebrew or Aramaic): Testament of the Twelve Patriarchs, Psalms of Solomon, Lives of the Prophets, Jubilees, Testament of Job, Enoch, Martyrdom of Isaiah, Assumption of Moses, Apocalypse of Baruch, Life of Adam and Eve, and Paralipomena of Jeremiah.

2. *Alexandrian books* (originally written in Greek): Ariskas, Sibylline Oracles (a group of fifteen books), III and IV Maccabees, II Enoch, and III Baruch.

Many of these books contain esoteric and apocalyptic teachings, possibly originating from the Jewish-Persian period. The dominant themes in the apocalyptic literature are of symbolic signs and events that surround the "end" of time, cosmic wars, the Messianic Age, the resurrection of the dead, and the final judgment of all human beings. These noncanonical works were as popular among early Christians as they were among the Jews. Gradually, however, they lost their popularity among both groups.

Jewish Teachings

Affirmation of the existence of one supreme deity is the first fundamental tenet of Judaism. God is one, omnipotent, omniscient, and without limitations or form. He is not only the creator and master of the universe, but also an active participant in human affairs. He is holy and the embodiment of moral perfection. He is the God of mercy, love, and justice.

> There is a story that an emperor who wanted to prove God's existence once asked a prominent rabbi to show him God.
> "But you cannot see him," replied the rabbi.
> "Nevertheless, I want to see him," insisted the emperor.
> Leading him out to the open courtyard, the rabbi asked the emperor to look straight up at the sun.
> "But I cannot," replied the emperor.
> "If you cannot look at the sun," retorted the rabbi, "which is but one of the servants who stand in the presence of the Holy One, praised be He, then how can you see God?"
> Thus, God, for Judaism, is the only creative cause of existence. Everything has come into existence by His will.

Adherents of Judaism seek continually to know God's will and to implement it in everyday life. One of the responsibilities of a devout Jew is to recite twice a day the basic prayer called *Shema* ("Hear!"), recorded in Deuteronomy 6:4–9:

> Hear, O Israel: the Lord our God is one Lord; and you shall love the Lord your God with all your heart and with all your soul and with all your might. And these words which I command you this day shall be upon your heart; and you shall teach them diligently to your children, and shall talk of them when you sit in your house, and when you walk by the way, and when you lie down and when you rise; and you shall bind them as a sign upon your hand, and they shall be as frontlets between your eyes. And you shall write them on the doorposts of your house and on your gates.

The injunction that the words affirming the oneness of God and man's response to love God be engraved on the heart, between the eyes, and on the doors of every home is taken quite literally by Jews. *Tefillin*, little boxes containing the *Shema*, are strapped on the left arm (which is close to the heart) and the forehead (which is close to the mind and eyes). Similarly, *mezuzah*, small receptacles containing the *Shema*, are permanently fastened to the doorposts of Jewish homes, offices, and schools.

The second basic tenet of Judaism is that a Jewish person is free to accept or reject the *mitzvot* (commandments) of God, which traditionally were offered to, and accepted by, his people during the revelation at Mount Sinai. Judaism views human beings as autonomous agents neither wholly evil nor wholly good in nature, who can suppress their potential for evil by following God's commandments.

The essence of this obligation is perhaps best expressed in the Jewish legend telling of how God, having completed the requirements he demanded of humankind, offered them in the form of a scroll (the Torah) to various nations. All except the Jewish people refused, on the grounds that the Torah placed too many restrictions upon their lives. Only the Jewish people were willing to accept God's mandate without reservation.

Modern Judaism, therefore, represents Jews as a choosing, not as a chosen, people. God's acceptance of Israel can be explained in terms not of divine preference, but of human choice. There is no question of favoritism; on the contrary, Jews consider themselves committed to maintain a special sense of responsibility toward God and his commandments.

Jews also believe that Judaism has a particular role to play in the task of "world redemption." Since ancient times, Jewish tradition has asserted that a Messiah, endowed with strong leadership and great wisdom, will come to redeem humankind and establish God's kingdom on earth by ushering in an era of perfect peace. This Messiah is expected to be a human rather than a divine being—a descendant of the house of David.

Many Jews today still pray for the arrival of such a Messianic Age when they gather to worship in the synagogue. Others have reinterpreted this traditional belief. Instead of pinning their faith on an individual who will usher in the Messianic Age, they consider that some day humanity collectively will reach a level of transcendent enlightenment, justice, and kindness that will create the climate for God's kingdom on earth. Regardless of the interpretation placed on the Messianic tradition, Judaism is more concerned with this world than the next in striving toward the ideal.

Thus, the story of God's continual activity in history, and particularly in the history of the Jewish people, is the underlying concept of all Jewish teachings. Judaism cannot be defined in terms of Christian theological categories or Christian catechism. Yet, there is a logic immanent in Judaism that sooner or later becomes evident to the careful investigator. What is quite striking in Judaism is that faith is grounded on divine-human actions for a specific divine purpose: the establishment of peace and well-being in this world among humanity. But this divine-human action is understood in a twofold way. On the one hand, Judaism makes the claim that God "chose" the Jewish people from among the nations for the task of applying the strictest obedience to the Torah as an instrument for enhancing the well-being of all humanity. On the other hand, Judaism asserts that God's universal love and care will lead humanity to the day when all shall know that God is the only one. Consequently, Jews believe that their absolute loyalty and obedience to God's ordinances will result in the redemption of the entire human race.

Attempts to defend or reject this religious concept of singularity have been made through the ages, and today it is increasingly subject to attack. Several modern Jewish thinkers, and some forms of Zionism, have sought to abandon this problematic view. Other leading Jewish thinkers, however, continue to affirm this notion, reassuring the Jewish people of their divine election. To such individuals, the sanctity of Jewish life and faith, the modern land of Israel, and the very existence of the Jews—in one word, Judaism itself—is inconceivable without the concept of chosenness. This special covenantal relationship between God and his people does not in any way negate the universal rule of God. On the contrary, it is precisely this particular relation (God-Jews) that underscores the universalistic position (God-humanity). Humanity is neither expected nor obligated, as Jews are, to live within the jurisdiction of the Torah. The responsibility of non-Jews is only that they accept seven basic obligations: (1) not to profane God's name, (2) not to worship idols, (3) not to commit murder, (4) not to steal, (5) not to commit adultery, (6) not to be unjust, and (7) not to cut limbs from living animals (Genesis Rabbah 34:8). From the perspective of Jewish faith, the two sovereign aspects of God (the particular and the universal) are not two sets of contradictory assertions; rather, both are true as a description of Judaism, since neither is true without the other. God's purpose, it is argued, lies beyond the limits of mere human logic and reason.

Jewish Groups

One of the distinguishing characteristics of Judaism is its division into groups that vary widely in terms of practices and beliefs. As we have seen, the Greco-Roman period was marked by the rise of the Pharisees, the Sadducees, the Herodians, the Essenes, and the Zealots. During the Middle Ages, three new groups evolved: the Kassites, the Kabbalists, and the Hasidics.

The Karaites flourished in the Near East, especially in Babylonia (modern Iraq) from the ninth to the twelfth centuries. The name *Karaite* literally means "readers of scriptures." They were so called because of the exclusive adherence to the Bible as the only source of religious authority in Judaism. They repudiated the Talmud as a spurious invention of the rabbis.

Although the Kabbalistic movement may have originated in Palestine, its systematic development took place in Babylonia. The term *kabel* means "to receive" and the name Kabbalist at first described any Jewish mystic who was a teacher of secret or inward revelation. Hence Kabbalist became the name associated with those Jews who were particularly concerned with the philosophical mystic lore of Judaism based upon an occult interpretation of the Bible handed down as secret doctrine to the initiated. During the ninth and tenth centuries the Kabbalistic movement spread to Europe, especially to Italy, Spain, and Germany.

The two most important books of the movement composed and edited in Babylonia were the Sefer Yitzirah (The Book of Formation) and the Shiur Komah (The Measure of the Height). The former chiefly concerned the creative powers of letters and numbers, while the latter described in human terms the dimensions of the Deity. However, the book that came to be regarded as the most sacred of all Kabbalistic writings, and the very epitome of Jewish mysticism, is the Zohar.

The word *zohar* means "splendor" or "brightness" and is derived from Daniel 12:3. The book records the revelations said to have been received in the second century CE by Rabbi Simeon ben Yochai, during the thirteen years he was hiding in a cave, and transmitted by him to his disciples. Compiled and made public in 1300 by Moses de Leon of Granada, Spain, the Zohar come to be regarded as the Bible of medieval mysticism. The Zohar is a compendium of Jewish mystic lore on the nature of God, the mysteries of the Divine name, God's attributes and dimensions, the evolution of the universe, a person's place in the universe and the nature of the human soul, the characteristics of heaven and hell, the order of the angels and demons, magic, astrology, as well as expositions on many ethical themes and ceremonies.

The Hasidics (the term *Hasid* means "pious") are a mystical group still represented in modern Judaism; their origins go back to the Kabbalist Israel Baal-Shem-Tov (1700–1760). Famed as a miracle worker and healer, he was regarded as a true saint and mystic. By the efforts of a number of his disciples, the movement attracted a large following, especially among the Jews of the Polish Ukraine. In contrast to Kabbalistic mysticism, which was difficult to understand and appealed particularly to intellectuals, Hasidic mysticism became a

*A young Ethiopian Jewish girl
inside a synagogue in the village of Ambober, Ethiopia.*
Ilene Perlman/Impact Visuals.

vital, singing faith of the masses. Its appeal lay less in visions of
speedy Messianic deliverance than in relieving the gloom and depression of an impoverished people. Without suppressing the natural
impulses within humans Hasidic mysticism promoted contentment
coupled with meekness and modesty.[11]

Today, four modern variations of Judaism predominate in North
America: Orthodox, Reform, Conservative, and Reconstructionist.

The Orthodox, the largest group in contemporary Judaism, are
committed to remain as true as possible to biblical and Talmudic
regulations. Strict observance of the Sabbath is stressed, as is firm
compliance with regulations governing food. (Orthodox Jews eat only
kosher food—food that is ritually sanctioned.) In general, men and
women sit in separate areas of the synagogue, and both sexes cover
their heads once they step inside.

Reform Judaism reflects the spirit of the modern age by omitting
many traditional practices. Talmudic restrictions on the Sabbath and
on diet have been modified to make them less rigorous. Synagogue
services, which are conducted in the vernacular as well as in Hebrew,
are usually held on Friday nights. Men and women sit together and
are not obliged to cover their heads.

The followers of Conservative Judaism depart from a number of ancient practices but attempt to abide by biblical and Talmudic regulations regarding diet and Sabbath observance. Unlike Reform Judaism, Conservative Judaism has retained Saturday morning services and the requirement that men cover their heads. As in Reform Judaism, however, synagogue services are conducted in the vernacular and Hebrew. Conservative Judaism can also be distinguished from Orthodox Judaism by a general concern with the scientific study of biblical and Talmudic material.

Reconstructionist Judaism is a recent American movement founded by Mordecai M. Kaplan. In this new context, Judaism is understood not only as a religion but as an ongoing tradition with a unique culture comprising aspects such as its history, law, art, and music. Proponents of this point of view are chiefly concerned at present to persuade the Jewish community that Judaism is more than a religion. They hold that culture and tradition in their entirety have to be experienced rather than studied in isolation.

In addition to these groups, numerous smaller sects have spread throughout the world. The Falashas of Ethiopia practice a form of Judaism that seems to be rooted partly in ancient observances and partly in traditions that lie beyond the mainstream of Judaism. This is also true of Jewish sects in Yemen, India, China, and various other parts of the world.

Jewish Observances

Judaism has always defined itself in terms of rites or religious acts.[12] These observances either mark stages in individual life cycles or are related to the cycle of the religious calendar.

The most important and distinctive of all Jewish rites is the circumcision of all male children eight days after birth as an external symbol of commitment to Judaism. Another religious obligation is the *Bar Mitzvah* for boys reaching the age of thirteen. Recently, a *Bat Mitzvah* has been introduced by some groups, although not all, as a parallel ceremony for girls. In this rite, the young are recognized as responsible adults, members of the Jewish community and faith.

The marriage ceremony is largely a matter of local practice, but certain religious observances are common to most Jewish communities. The marriage vow is taken under a canopy that symbolizes the couple's home. At the end of the ceremony the bride and groom share a cup of wine, which symbolizes their common destiny. They also sign the marriage document as a legal contract. Jewish tradition makes provision for divorce in case a marriage breaks down. Divorced persons are encouraged to remarry and may wed another partner in the synagogue.

Jewish children celebrate both Bat Mitzvah and Bar Mitzvah in moving ceremonies at the Wailing Wall in Jerusalem.
Courtesy of Israel Government Tourist Office, Ministry of Tourism, Toronto.

Death is attended by an extremely detailed ceremonial pattern governed primarily by an overriding concern to comfort the bereaved. Burial takes place within twenty-four hours, except when a Sabbath or a holy day intervenes. (Some groups have relaxed this rule somewhat, although no group allows the body to "lie in state" for any length of time.) The burial is followed by a seven-day period of mourning, usually called *shiva* (meaning seven), limited to the immediate next-of-kin. The bereaved remain at home, except for Sabbath worship, and services are held there each evening. A general period of mourning continues for the next eleven months, after which a memorial stone is placed at the graveside.

The most important of all Jewish observances is the Sabbath (the Hebrew word *Shabbat* means rest), which starts every Friday evening at dusk and continues until dusk on Saturday. To proclaim the Sabbath, the woman of the house lights the candles while the man of the house recites a special benediction over the wine and bread. This ritual is followed by a festive meal.

Orthodox Jews usher in the Sabbath by attending synagogue services on Friday, before dinner. Some Conservative and Reform Jews attend a late evening service. For all three groups, however, Saturday is a day of synagogue worship. On this day, Orthodox Jews refrain from any type of work—a term that includes such activities as lighting or extinguishing a light or riding in an automobile. A symbolic ceremony in the home concludes the Sabbath. A lighted candle is extinguished in wine, and a spice box is passed around from hand to hand for the family to taste or smell, as it were, the sweetness of the Sabbath as it closes.

Holy Days

Rosh Hashanah (New Year), one of the two most sacred holy days in the Jewish calendar, is celebrated in the autumn (September or October) and ushers in a ten-day period of penitence. Orthodox and Conservative Jews, following ancient tradition, celebrate the occasion for two days; the Reform group, for one day only. The most important symbol of the festival is the *shofar* (ram's horn), which is blown in the synagogue during the service on New Year's Day and on each of the following ten days.

The second sacred Jewish holy day is Yom Kippur (Day of Atonement) celebrated at the end of the ten-day period of penitence following Rosh Hashanah. A day-long ritual of solemn prayers and fasting in the synagogue, including the confession of a catalog of shortcomings, transgressions, and sins, marks this important event. Just before sunset the entire congregation in the synagogue chants the Kol Nidré—a prayer of forgiveness for unfulfilled vows made to God. Candles are lit and members of the family ask forgiveness of each other. Fasting ends at sunset the next day, and the entire family gathers for a festive meal at home.

Festivals

The celebration of Sukkot (the Feast of Tabernacles) follows five days after Yom Kippur and continues for eight days (seven for Reform Jews). This is a joyous festival that marks the harvest festival of thanksgiving. A *sukkot* (a booth or tabernacle) is improvised by many families as a reminder of the temporary shelters that housed the ancient Jewish people during their wanderings in the desert. A table, chairs, and fruits furnish this improvised *sukkot,* and during the week of the festival the family meal is served there. Nowadays, many choose to celebrate Sukkot as a community or synagogue gathering. Special services are held in the synagogue on the first two and last two days of the festival, except among Reform Jews, who observe only the first and last day of the ritual.

The festival of Sukkot ends with another festival—that of Simhat Torah, which is dedicated to the glorification of the Torah. This marks the end of one annual cycle of readings from the Torah in the synagogue and the beginning of another cycle. On this occasion, worshipers read from the last chapters of the book of Deuteronomy and the

A cantor lighting the candelabrum for the annual celebration of Hanukkah, the Festival of Lights.
Courtesy of Ray Kurkjian.

first chapter of the book of Genesis in the Torah symbolizing the eternal continuity of the Torah.

Hanukkah (Festival of Lights), observed in the month of December, commemorates the Jewish battle for religious liberty led by Judas Maccabaeus against their Syrian-Greek overlords in 165 BCE. The event is marked at home by the lighting of a candle on a nine-branched *menorah* (candelabrum) every evening for eight successive evenings. Religious schools maintained by synagogues put on pageants and plays, all based on the Maccabean victory theme, and young and old exchange gifts.

The Purim festival, celebrated in February or March, commemorates the rescue of Persian Jews from destruction at the hands of Haman the oppressor through the boldness of Esther, who though a Jew was the Persian queen, and her uncle Mordecai. Because the Persians cast lots to determine the appropriate day for the Jewish massacre, the festival is known as Purim (Lots). On this day, the scroll of Esther is read and gifts are exchanged.

Pesach or Passover is the most important family festival in Judaism. This feast, sometimes referred to as the Feast of Freedom, is celebrated in March or April and lasts for eight days (seven among Reform Jews). It commemorates the deliverance of the Jews from Egypt. At special synagogue services held to mark the occasion, the Torah is read, the story of the Exodus recounted, and psalms of praise chanted.

Fifty days after Pesach is the festival of Shavuot (Weeks). Celebrated for two days (one day by Reform Jews), in May or June, this festival originally marked the wheat harvest. It now commemorates the anniversary of the giving of the Torah by God to Moses on Mount Sinai. Homes and synagogues are decorated with fresh fruits, plants, and flowers. Readings from the Torah include the books of Exodus and Ruth (a Moabite girl who adopted the Jewish faith).

In addition to these festivals, a number of Jews observe other traditional celebrations, depending on local customs and the country in which they live. The various groups within Judaism follow different styles of observances. Members of certain groups do not feel necessarily bound by traditional restrictions imposed on activities defined as work. Moreover, various popular forms of celebration have emerged in modern Israel, sometimes replacing traditional ones. All of these variations reflect different expressions of Jewish faith.

Modern Judaism

The Diaspora

The center of Jewish life and thought remained in the eastern Mediterranean until the Muslim conquest of Spain in the eighth century CE. Under the relatively tolerant Muslim administration, Spanish Jews flourished and became the leaders of worldwide Judaism. Entering the fields of government, science, medicine, philosophy, and literature, they made outstanding contributions in every field.

The restoration of Christian rule in Spain in the fourteenth century disrupted Jewish life. For almost a century Spanish Jews lived under the threat of persecution. Ultimately they were expelled from Spain, and thousands fled to Portugal, Italy, Turkey, Morocco, and other parts of Europe where Jews had taken refuge ever since the time of the Roman Empire. (By the end of the tenth century, for instance, there were already large Jewish colonies in Italy, Germany, France, and England.) By the end of the fifteenth century, however, almost every European nation had maltreated and expelled their Jewish populations. Jews fled once more, this time to eastern Europe and to the Muslim states of the Ottoman Empire.

Jewish refugees from Spain and Portugal who settled in the Ottoman world came to be known as Sephardim. They also developed their own language—mainly Spanish mixed with Hebrew. Jewish refugees in eastern Europe, on the other hand, came to be known as Ashkenazim. They, too, developed a language, known as Yiddish—a combination of German and Hebrew.

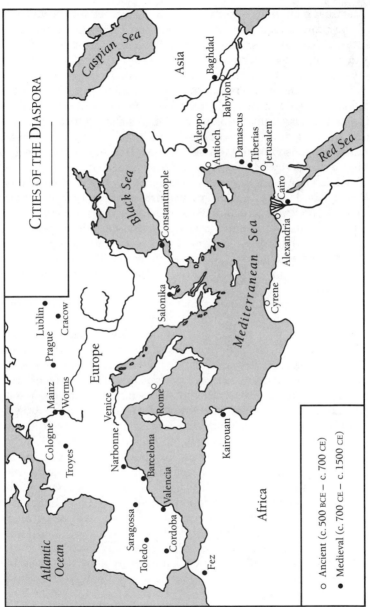

CITIES OF THE DIASPORA

○ Ancient (c. 500 BCE – c. 700 CE)
● Medieval (c. 700 CE – c. 1500 CE)

The treatment of Jews in sixteenth- and seventeenth-century Europe was no more tolerant or enlightened than it had been in preceding centuries. The establishment of the Inquisition by the Roman Catholic church (see p. 394) affected not only dissident Christians, but the Jews as well. A papal decree, issued in 1555, authorized the containment of Jews within special quarters, known as ghettos, and the restrictions imposed by a daily curfew forced the Jews to live in miserable conditions. Such irrational intolerance also was characteristic of the treatment of Jews during the uprising of Ukrainian (Cossack) peasants against the Polish nobility in 1648. The Jews became part of the general slaughter in an event known as a Jewish pogrom.

The late eighteenth and early nineteenth centuries saw the emancipation of the Jews in Europe, particularly after the French Revolution in 1789. Soon Jews were allowed to mix freely in social circles that had been closed to them in the past, to pursue various trades and professions that had denied them entry, to attend centers of higher learning, and to follow the religious life bequeathed to them by their ancestors. The more favorable atmosphere also affected Jewish life in other ways.

Disillusioned by movements that offered the hope of Messianic redemption and dissatisfied with the arid legalism of the rabbinical schools, the masses responded to a mystical movement known as Hasidism. Founded by Israel Baal-Shem-Tov (1700–1760), who was born in the Ukraine but later settled in Poland, the Hasidic movement, with its emphasis on mysticism and ecstasy, transformed the face of east European Jewry in the eighteenth and nineteenth centuries. Despite bitter persecution by members of the Orthodox rabbinical school, who viewed Hasidism as a threat to Jewry, the movement spread rapidly, until it included almost half of traditional rabbinism in its ranks.

Imbued with nineteenth-century European idealism, another group of Jews determined to reform Jewish belief and practice by placing more emphasis on ethics. The so-called Reform movement spread rapidly throughout Europe and later, the United States. The upsurge of nationalism in nineteenth-century Europe also affected the Jewish people. Theodore Herzl and other Jewish leaders came to the conclusion that despite the liberty accorded to Jews by European countries, the Jewish people would never be treated as equals except in their own homeland.

State of Israel

During the present century, this aspiration for status as a nation coalesced with the development of Zionism, a movement dedicated to the formation of a national homeland in the former ancient territory of the Jewish people in Palestine. In the meantime, a catastrophic event reduced the total population of the Jews by as much as one-third. That terrible incident was the Holocaust of 1941–1945, in which the German Nazis under Adolf Hitler applied the most effective method of exterminating the Jews that they could devise: asphyxiation by gas.

The Holocaust and World War II confirmed Zionists in their determination to establish a homeland in Palestine. Consequently, in 1948 the independent state of Israel came into being, thus ending the long centuries of exile and accelerating the "in-gathering" of the exiles. The chain of events that led to the startling reality of an established Jewish state are too recent and too well documented to need recount-

The western wall (Wailing Wall) of the Temple in Jerusalem. Jewish tradition requires separation of the sexes during prayer. Courtesy of Israel Government Tourist Office, Ministry of Tourism, Toronto.

ing. However one wishes to interpret the sequence of events that led to this consummation, one cannot deny that Judaism provides a graphic illustration of the long arm of history reaching into the present to influence the future. The modern state of Israel and the effect it has had, and continues to exert, on its neighbors are manifestations of the Jewish faith and 3500 years of Jewish history.

A number of specific historical events have a particular significance to those Jews who see Israel as their birthright and their homeland. One is, of course, the Exodus from Egypt. Others are associated with the Temple in Jerusalem: the dedication of the first Temple during the reign of King Solomon in the tenth century BCE; the total destruction of the Temple by the neo-Babylonians in August 587 BCE and its rededication under Persian sovereignty in March 516 BCE; and Judas Maccabaeus's reclamation of the Temple from the Seleucids (descendants of Seleucus, a general and successor of Alexander the Great) in 135 BCE and its rededication.

These events in Temple history are eclipsed by the final catastrophe in 70 CE, when the Romans leveled the Temple once and for all. Even to this day, Jews gather at the ruined western wall in Jerusalem to pray for the reconstruction and rededication of their ancient center of worship, whose site is now occupied by an Islamic mosque.

The indescribable horrors suffered by the Jewish people during the twenty centuries of exile that followed the Roman sack of the Temple are well documented. Those long, bloody centuries of hardship underline the significance of the proclamation of May 14, 1948, confirming the establishment of the modern state of Israel. It represents, perhaps, the most decisive event in the entire history of Judaism. The long Jewish struggle for national and religious independence was finally crowned with success on this date, which marked the end of two thousand years of exilic survival.

Hundreds of thousands of Jewish people, scattered throughout central and eastern Europe and western Asia, converged on Israel, which they saw as their homeland restored. The four wars of 1948, 1956, 1967, and 1973 did more than demonstrate their capacity to survive in a hostile environment. They resulted in territorial gains, the recovery of the Temple wall, and the confirmation of a "Messianic vision" eloquently expressed by David Ben Gurion, the first prime minister of Israel:

> The suffering of the Jewish people in the Diaspora, whether economic, political, or cultural, has been a powerful factor in bringing about the immigrations to the Land of Israel. But it was only the Messianic vision which made that factor fruitful and guided it towards the creation of the State. Suffering alone is degrading, oppression destructive; and if we

had not inherited from the prophets the Messianic vision of redemption, the suffering of the Jewish people in the Diaspora would have led to their extinction. The ingathering of the exiles, that is, the return of the Jewish people to its land, is the beginning of the realization of the Messianic vision.[13]

Two decisive moments, then, remain ineradicable in the memory of all Jews: the year 70, symbolizing national dispersement and religious oppression; and the year 1948, symbolizing national revivification and the beginning of the realization of the Messianic vision.

Status of Women

The status of Jewish women has changed in the course of Jewish history. Historically, men dominated public life as leaders, teachers, and priests; women tended the home and the children. Throughout the centuries Jewish women accepted this role as a dignified responsibility with many rights and in no sense inferior, or unequal, to the role played by men. However, males began to assert their dominance as time went on, particularly because men were not burdened by pregnancies or the nursing of babies. Soon strictures became generalized. Women were not allowed to perform certain religious duties, such as reading and studying the Torah or wearing the *tallit* and *tefillin* (see figure on p. 366). Males excluded women from being counted among the *minyan* (a quorum of ten, for purposes of public worship or for constituting a congregation) and segregated them (often by a curtain) during synagogue services. In addition, women came to be regarded (though not by all) as temptresses who threatened the purity of men. Worse still, the traditional Jewish prayerbook contained the following benediction for men: "Blessed are You, God . . . who has not made me a woman."

Male superiority and dominance was never so absolute in the Torah, in which women took leadership positions when the need arose. For instance, Miriam, the sister of Moses, was an organizer and leader (Exodus 15:20); Deborah served both as a judge and a general (Judges 4–5); Huldah was a prophetess (II Kings 22:14–20); Esther was a skilled diplomat (Book of Esther); and the Torah granted women many legal rights, including a share in real estate (Numbers 27:1–11). However, Talmudic injunctions barred women from becoming judges, leaders, rabbis, or cantors; instead, they were assigned undisputed power in ruling the home and raising children. The statement in the Torah that "he shall write her a bill of divorce" (Deuteronomy 24:1) was interpreted to mean that a woman could not divorce her husband against his will, whereas a man had the power to divorce his wife at

Jewish adult males use special objects in worship: a prayer shawl (tallit) *woven of wool or silk, with fringes attached to the four corners as ordained in Numbers 15:37–39; two small boxes of black leather* (tefillin), *containing parchment slips on which are inscribed four texts (Exodus 13:1–10, 13:11–16; Deuteronomy 6:4–9, 11:13–21), which are bound to the forehead and the left arm by straps; and a skullcap.*   From the private collection of Ray Kurkjian.

any time. Moreover, a woman was in no legal position to remarry if her husband had disappeared or if his death was not properly certified by witnesses, whereas a man could remarry under similar circumstances.

Today, however, Jewish women (except in conservative groups) are quite active in business, the professions, politics, and the military. In matters of religious responsibilities, Jewish women are gaining ground in their demand for equal rights to study the Torah and Talmud, to wear the *tallit* and *tefillin,* to be cantors, to be ordained as rabbis (a measure that has been strongly attacked by Orthodox Jewry), and to be counted among the *minyan.* These are bold decisions based on the interpretation of Jewish *halakah* (the guiding law of Jewish life) in a new spirit of gender equality.

Relinquishing or alloting to women a share in roles traditionally performed by or reserved for men is still not an easy matter for most males and many females with conservative views. But it is generally conceded that the inferior role of women in traditional Judaism is no longer tenable in modern society.

Notes

1. The Greek historian Herodotus was the first in the fifth century BCE to call the region "that part of Syria called Palestine." Since then, the term *Palestine* displaced the biblical one, *Canaan*. Today, the term *Israel* has largely displaced both ancient terms.

2. *El* is a generic term for god that occurs frequently in the writings of Semitic peoples. It is used throughout the Hebrew scripture (Old Testament). The term *Allah* in Islam is considered to be a derivative of *El*.

3. The traditional view was first challenged in 1878 by J. Wellhausen, whose skeptical view has been revived in modern times by, among others, J. Van Seters, in *Abraham in History and Tradition* (New Haven, Conn.: Yale University Press, 1975). See also J. Holt, *The Patriarchs of Israel* (Nashville, Tenn.: Vanderbilt University Press, 1964); and W. McKane, *Studies in the Patriarchal Narratives* (Edinburgh, Scotland: Handsel Press, 1979).

4. For a bibliographical list on the religion of biblical Judaism, see C. J. Adams, *A Reader's Guide to the Great Religions*, 2nd ed. (New York: Free Press, 1977), pp. 295–300.

5. The traditional account of Moses is recorded in Exodus 1–15. Scholars generally consider this account to be colored with elements of legend and folklore that show striking parallels to elements in the literature of ancient Near Eastern civilizations. See J. Pritchard, ed., *Ancient Near Eastern Texts Relating to the Old Testament*, 3rd ed., with supplement (Princeton, N.J.: Princeton University Press, 1969).

6. There is wide disagreement among scholars over the concept of Covenant-Election. It is usually assumed that the Jewish religion was from the first based on a "unique and exclusive" relationship between the Jews and YHWH, but investigations of the problem have resulted in radically differing conclusions. Three lines of thought dominate scholarly opinion: (1) that the concept of the "chosen people" was a relatively late religious expression, since early Jewish religion was nationalistic and God was the symbol of national unity; (2) that the conviction that God "chose" the Jews arose in the time of Moses during the formation of a religious community that had not previously existed; and (3) that the concept of God's "choice" of the Jews was the product of the merging of two traditions, the patriarchal and the Mosaic, implemented by the Deuteronomistic school in the seventh to sixth century BCE.

7. Hellenistic influence is particularly discernible in Jewish writers who wrote in Greek, including Josephus and Philo. Their writings are widely available in English.

8. For the standard English translation of the Torah, see *The Torah* (Philadelphia: Jewish Publication Society, 1962).

9. The body of literature analyzing the Torah (also called Pentateuch) is vast; see the bibliographical listing in B. W. Anderson, *Understanding the Old Testament*, 4th ed. (Englewood Cliffs, N.J.: Prentice-Hall, 1986), pp. 655–57.

10. For an English translation of the Prophets *(Nevi'im)*, see *The Prophets, Nevi'im, A New Translation* (Philadelphia: Jewish Publication Society, 1978).

11. For a good bibliographical list on mysticism, Messianism, and Hasidism, see Adams, *A Reader's Guide*, pp. 332–36.

12. There is an enormous literature on Jewish rites, customs, and observances. A good bibliographical listing can be found in Adams, *A Reader's Guide*, pp. 325–27.

13. Cited in I. Epstein, *Judaism: A Historical Presentation* (Harmondsworth Eng.: Penguin Books, 1959), p. 321.

13

Christianity

Historical Background

Christianity emerged in ancient Palestine in the shadow of the Roman Empire, which was at its zenith. The Romans had conquered Palestine in 63 BCE, and by the time of the birth of Jesus, their empire had imposed a political unity on the lands bordering the Mediterranean that greatly facilitated the spread of various religions.

Religiously, the Roman Empire was pluralistic. Greek and Roman religions were tolerated from the earliest times, and in the first century BCE emperor worship was encouraged, as a means chiefly of promoting loyalty to the empire. Mystery cults, largely of Middle Eastern origin, were also popular and widespread. Because the temper of the age was syncretistic, the mystery religions borrowed extensively from one another, and over time they came to share a number of common attributes. Central to every cult was a "savior god" who had died and been resurrected. Adherents attained immortality by sharing symbolically in the death and resurrection of the savior god, whether he was called Mithras or Osiris, Adonis or Attis, Orpheus or Dionysus (see Chapter 10).

Ultimately the religion of the savior god Jesus triumphed over all the others, unlikely an outcome as that must have seemed in the early days of Roman tolerance. Not only were many religions tolerated, but so were many sectarian or nonconforming groups within religions. Within Judaism, for instance, the Pharisees, who acted as the representatives of Jewish beliefs and practices, were mainly concerned with preserving the Jewish faith from compromises with Hellenism. The Sadducees, heavily represented in the wealthy elements of the population, controlled the central Temple in Jerusalem. The Zealots were fanatic patriots who refused any compromise with Rome and opposed all attempts to make Palestine subservient to Roman powers. Their revolt in 66–70 CE, which was ruthlessly crushed by the Romans, resulted in the burning of the Temple in Jerusalem and the dispersion of the Jews (see Chapter 12). The Essenes, a small communal group who lived in the vicinity of Qumran by the Dead Sea, opposed violence, lived by strict monastic rules, and patiently awaited the coming of the Messiah (Anointed One of God; see p. 337), who would deliver the Jews from foreign oppression. Jesus is thought to have belonged to this group.[1]

Hope of the coming of a Messiah (as an ideal king and savior) had been current in Egypt long before its appearance in Israel. Saul and David, the first two kings of Israel, were initiated into their royal office by anointing. Later generations that faced misfortune and destruction looked back to David as the ideal king and longed for a scion (son) of David who would deliver them from their oppressors and restore their ancient glory. During the exilic period, this longing took the form of a Messianic hope—that God would send his Anointed One (Messiah) to deliver his people from their enemies. Under Greco-Roman rule, particularly in the first and second centuries CE, Messianic hope became so strong among the Jews that many self-proclaimed Messiahs appeared. Jesus, among others, was recognized by his immediate followers as a Messiah.

Little did the early Christians realize that their message was to affect humankind so deeply. Based on the few years of association with Jesus, the disciples went about spreading the stories of Jesus—what he did and what he taught. As the number of believers increased, churches were established and it became necessary to record the sayings and doings of Jesus for circulation among believers. Eventually, a number of writings were selected and assembled to form the New Testament. The New Testament is then the primary source of information concerning Jesus and his teachings, as well as of the religious outlook of the early Christian community.

Christian Scriptures

Of all the major living religions, Christianity is the only one that reveres and includes in its sacred writings the whole scripture of the Jewish Bible—called the Old Testament by Christians, suggesting the "Old Covenant" made with God by Moses at Mount Sinai. Added to the Old Testament in Christian scripture is a collection of writings known as the New Testament—the "New Covenant" made by Jesus with his disciples at the Last Supper. Together, the Old Testament and the New Testament books constitute the sacred writings of Christianity and are commonly referred to as the Bible.

Sandwiched between the Old and New Testaments is a group of fourteen disputed books called the *Apocrypha*—a Greek term meaning "hidden." Written by Jews some time between the second century BCE and the first century CE, the Apocrypha has been a source of controversy among both Jews and Christians, neither of whom have ever been able to determine whether or not the books should be held as sacred as the other books of the Bible. At first the Apocrypha simply was restricted to a narrow circle of readers because of its esoteric nature. Later, it was condemned as heretical, but the question has remained unresolved. Some segments of the Christian community retain the Apocrypha in their Bible.

Since the Old Testament books are dealt with in Chapter 12, it is only fitting here to describe the contents of the New Testament. Naturally, many writings and collections of stories circulated widely during the first four hundred years of Christian history. Eventually, twenty-seven writings were assembled to form the New Testament, and they were accepted as *canonical* (divinely inspired works). First in order are the four Gospels (Matthew, Mark, Luke, and John), which record the life and teachings of Jesus. These are followed by the book known as the Acts of Apostles, which chronicles the history of the early Christian missionaries. Succeeding the Acts are a number of Epistles—letters written by various disciples (most notably Paul) either to individuals or to Christian communities. The last book is a visionary account of the final triumph of God called Revelation.

In its earliest form, Christian literature consisted of letters, or epistles. The epistles of Paul are probably the earliest writings in the New Testament. Some time during the first century a number of Paul's letters circulated among Christians. The four Gospels of the New Testament also appeared in the same century. However, there seemed to be no attempt on the part of the early Christian community to regard these writings as scripture. For the earliest Christians the scriptures of Judaism, particularly the Torah and the Prophets, were accounted as sacred texts. During the second century a flood of gospels and other literature forced the Christians to make selections in their estimation of an authoritative Christian literature. The earliest exact reference to the present collection of books in the New Testament appeared in 367 in a letter of Athanasius, bishop of Alexandria. A complete listing of the books of the Old and New Testaments was provided at a council held in Rome in 382. Thus, the Christian bible took its final shape by the late fourth century.

Jesus Christ

Primary Sources

Jesus left no writing of his own, so scholars have had to rely on three other sources of information about his life and teachings. The most important source comprises the four Gospels—those of Matthew, Mark, Luke, and John.[2] Next are the writings of Paul, although he had no close relationship with Jesus. Finally, there are a few references to Jesus by classical writers of the first and second centuries CE; what they say about Jesus, however, does little more than establish his historical existence.

The four Gospels and the writings of Paul are not merely accumulations of historical facts. Rather, they are documents of faith, and as

This Russian icon of the 16th century depicting Madonna and child is known as Our Lady of Yevsemanisk. The Granger Collection.

such are primarily concerned with the theological implications of the life and death of Jesus. Historians generally assume that after the death of Jesus some of his disciples recorded his sayings before they were forgotten. These writings, or group of documents, are called Q (from the German word *Quelle*, meaning source). It is further assumed that the Q documents, although on the whole authentic, were colored by presuppositions and included sayings mistakenly ascribed to Jesus. Furthermore, the gospel writers—particularly Matthew and Luke—are assumed to have used a great deal of material from the Q documents.[3] Whether or not this hypothesis is correct, two conclusions remain undisputed: that Jesus himself wrote nothing and that the content of the Gospels suggests or implies two sources. One is a record of sayings ascribed to Jesus, and the other is contemporary opinion reflecting the understanding of early Christians.

Early Life of Jesus

The date and place of Jesus' birth cannot be determined with certainty. According to the Gospel of Matthew, Jesus was born in Bethlehem in the days of King Herod, who died in 4 BCE. However, the Gospel of Luke seems to suggest two other dates: first, that Jesus was born in Bethlehem when Quirinius was governor of Syria, which was 6–9 CE; second, that Jesus was baptized at age thirty in the fifteenth year of the reign of Emperor Tiberius (26/27 CE), suggesting a date for the birth of Jesus of 4–3 BCE.

It was not until the sixth century CE that a Christian monk divided history into BC (before Christ) and AD (*Anno Domini*, year of our Lord), in order to relate the birth of Jesus to the ancient Roman calendar. Whether or not his calculation was correct, the beginning of the Christian era is assumed to date from the birth of Jesus. This reckoning has been accepted by the church and hallowed by long use.

As to the place of Jesus' birth, the Gospel writers vacillate between Bethlehem in Judea and Nazareth in Galilee, locations some 320 kilometers (200 miles) apart. The early Christian (and hence the Gospel writers) may have been influenced by a desire to make Jesus a descendant of King David from Bethlehem and thus link him with Old Testament prophecies concerning the Messiah. But because all the Gospel writers agree that the family of Jesus lived in Nazareth, scholars have been inclined to attach greater credibility to the theory that the latter was Jesus' birthplace.

Little is known about the childhood and youth of Jesus. Mark and John make no mention at all of Jesus' virgin birth, childhood, or youth. On the other hand, Matthew and Luke declare that Jesus was born from the virgin Mary and that supernatural events occurred at the time

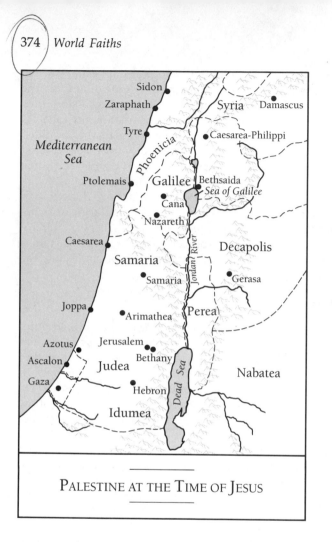

PALESTINE AT THE TIME OF JESUS

of his birth. Luke goes on to describe Jesus' circumcision rite when he was eight days old and his learned conversation with the Jewish rabbis in the Temple at Jerusalem when he was twelve (Luke 2:42–50). Mark and Matthew imply that Jesus' trade, like that of his father, Joseph, was carpentry, and that he had four brothers and a number of sisters (Mark 3:31; 6:3; Matthew 12:46; 13:55–56). Almost nothing else is known of his early years.

Baptism and Temptation

The Gospels relate that when Jesus was about thirty years old, a stern Jewish ascetic called John the Baptist appeared in Galilee and announced the coming judgment of God in the person of a Messiah, who would deliver the Jews from Roman rule. Standing by the River Jordan he proclaimed, "Repent, for the kingdom of heaven is coming!" Jesus was among those who were baptized in the river by John the Baptist.

This incident may have marked the turning point in Jesus' life. He at once withdrew to the wilderness beyond the Jordan, before finally deciding on his future career. What actually happened during his forty days in the wilderness is a mystery. Mark states that Jesus lived there with the wild beasts and that angels ministered to him (Mark 1:13). Matthew and Luke say that Satan appeared in person and challenged Jesus with three temptations. First, to prove his divinity, Jesus was challenged to convert the stones to bread. He declined, saying, "Man shall not live by bread alone." Second, Satan invited Jesus to throw himself from the top of the Temple in Jerusalem to land unharmed. Again he declined, saying, "You shall not tempt the Lord your God." Finally, he was offered control of the entire world if he would bow down and worship Satan. Jesus replied, "Begone Satan!"—an injunction that Satan followed without further urging (Matthew 4:3–11; Luke 3:1–13).

As soon as Jesus came out of the wilderness he returned to Galilee to find that John the Baptist had been arrested and imprisoned. Jesus felt that the time had arrived to assume his role. He now repeated John's message: "Repent, for the kingdom of heaven is coming!"

Mission and Crucifixion

Jesus gradually attracted a group of twelve disciples, who constantly traveled with him from place to place proclaiming the "good news." Some of his disciples were fishermen, others were artisans, and one was a tax collector—a profession widely despised because it was identified with graft and subservience to Rome. At first, Jesus spoke in Jewish synagogues, but when the crowds grew too large, he resorted to open places.

The events recorded in the Gospels establish Jesus' authoritative personality, his keen interest in and compassion for people, and his reputation for healing. His forceful speeches and imaginative use of parables attracted large crowds. Relating easily with people of all types, including prostitutes and social outcasts, he apparently disdained social barriers and prejudices.

He also made enemies, chiefly by challenging time-honored assumptions. He ignored a number of Jewish traditions, such as Sabbath restrictions and ritual cleanliness, and scorned those who in his view had substituted social and ceremonial practices for inward morality. Sternly rebuking those who professed to be religious but were insincere and hypocritical, he offended Jewish scribes and leaders by openly attacking them for their views and behavior regarding authority, the Torah, divorce, taxes, and resurrection. His aim, according to Matthew (10:34–36), was to resist peace, create disturbance, and plant the seeds of hate, envy, and contention. His reputation varied according to the viewpoints of three disparate groups: to the scribes, he was an imposter and a deceiver; to much of the public, he was a prophet; to his disciples, he was the Son of God (Matthew 14:33).

The mission of Jesus lasted only a year or two before he, like John the Baptist, was arrested. The reasons for his trial and execution, as implied in the Gospels, are puzzling and contradictory. The only fact that is clearly and unambiguously recorded is that Jesus met his death on the cross, just like any other convicted rebel or criminal under the Roman administration.

Resurrection and Ascension

The events that followed the death of Jesus were of greater importance to early Christians than were the events that preceded it. The Bible records three phenomenal incidents. First, Jesus was resurrected three

A procession of worshipers, led by priests, carry the cross along the Via Dolorosa (Latin, sad road) to the Church of the Holy Sepulchre in Jerusalem during Easter week. Courtesy of Israel Government Tourist Office, Ministry of Tourism, Toronto, Canada.

days after his crucifixion, and he subsequently appeared to many of his followers on numerous occasions. Second, forty days after his resurrection he was lifted up to heaven in the presence of a group of people who heard a voice saying, "Men of Galilee, why do you stand looking into heaven? This Jesus, who was taken up from you into heaven, will come in the same way as you saw him go into heaven" (Acts 1:10–11). Third, ten days after the ascent of Jesus—that is, on the day of the Jewish festival of Shavuot—a group of Jesus' followers spoke in "strange" languages and claimed to have been filled with the Holy Spirit.

All these events laid the groundwork for various new insights among the followers of Jesus—in particular, the attribution of "godhood" to him and the proclaiming of him as the "Son of God." This Christian insight steadily spread to various parts of the Roman and Persian empires.

Teachings

In his Gospel, John states that if everything Jesus did and taught were to be recorded, "the world itself could not contain the books that would be written" (John 21:25). This suggests that Jesus said much more than was recorded in the Gospels. Consequently, identifying precisely what Jesus taught is as difficult as establishing his identity exactly. As has been pointed out, Jesus left no written records. Sources of information that have survived are restricted primarily to the four Gospels, which do not read like verbatim reports of Jesus' words. Rather, the contents of the Gospels suggest that each writer used the material according to his own purposes and prejudices. This is not to imply that the Gospel writers distorted the message of Jesus—merely that what they wrote is likely to have been affected by their own perspectives as members of a community of early Christian believers.

Nonetheless, biblical scholars have carefully examined the Gospels as primary material in an attempt to discover the basic message of Jesus. Hundreds of books have been written, each asserting that the most fundamental teaching of Jesus encompasses one or more of the following concepts: the Fatherhood of God, the Kingdom of God, God's love of humankind, and God's universal plan of salvation. However, the crucial question underlying these concepts is whether Jesus considered himself to be God incarnate, or whether, instead, his followers endowed him with the status of Son of God after his death. The question remains unresolved because the Gospels present clear evidence justifying both views. Although it is impossible to examine in a few pages all these views, an attempt is made here to consider the basic concepts and teachings of Jesus, as recorded in the Gospels by some of his followers.

From the time of his baptism by John the Baptist to the end of his short life, the reality of God occupied the central place in the thoughts of Jesus. His own intimate relationship with God deeply impressed his disciples, as he strongly emphasized the Fatherhood of God. He regarded every human being as more than just a creature or servant of God—each individual was a child of God. With profound assurance he stressed the paternal character of God and taught his followers to address God not in the traditional form of "O God, Our Lord," but as "Our Father."

> Our Father who are in heaven,
> Hallowed be your name.
> Your kingdom come,
> Your will be done
> On earth as it is in heaven. (Matthew 6:9–11)

Of course, the Fatherhood concept of God did not originate with Jesus. Prophets in Judaism had spoken of God's paternal nature. "For you . . . O Lord, are our Father," says Isaiah, "our redeemer from of old is your name" (Isaiah 63:16). Jesus' concept of God is illustrated by the personal and intimate relationship with God implied by the terms Jesus used to address him. Jesus spoke of "my Father" and "your Father."

In reading the Gospels, one can immediately sense the remarkable closeness and intimate association that Jesus had with God. When the seventy disciples returned from their mission and related their successful ministry, Jesus rejoiced and on the spot proclaimed:

> I thank you Father, Lord of heaven and earth, that you have hidden these things from the wise and understanding and revealed them to babes: Yes, Father, for such was your gracious will. (Luke 10:21)

When his final hours of life on this earth were approaching, Jesus celebrated the Jewish annual Passover feast with his disciples for the last time and spoke to them after this Last Supper. The Gospel of John (chapters 14 to 17) gives us a vivid account of what Jesus spoke about. It is here (John 14–17) that Jesus reveals not only his deep relationship and intimacy with the Father, but how this relationship signifies to him complete union or oneness with the Father:

> If you had known me, you would have known my Father . . .
> He who has seen me has seen the Father . . .
> I am in the Father and the Father in me. (John 14:7, 9, 11)

Nevertheless, "the Father is greater than I," said Jesus, and "I do as the Father has commanded me" (John 14:28–31). Then suddenly he stopped and prayed:

> Father the hour has come;
> glorify your Son that the Son may glorify thee . . .
> Holy Father, keep them [disciples] in your name
> which you have given me, that they may be one,
> even as we are one . . .
> Now I am coming to you . . .
> O righteous Father, the world has not known you,
> but I have known you. (John 17:1)

Touched by Jesus' insight and prayer, the disciples followed him to the garden of Gethsemane. Deeply distressed and full of sorrow, Jesus fell to the ground and earnestly prayed once again:

> Abba, Father, all things are possible to you; remove this cup from me; yet not what I will, but what you will. (Mark 14:32–36)

When finally Jesus was crucified situated between two criminals, his close relationship with God is once again revealed by his words:

> Father, forgive them; for they know not what they do. (Luke 23:34)

His last words on the cross were,

> Father, into thy hands I commit my spirit! (Luke 23:46)

This personal closeness with the Father was the characteristic feature of Jesus' teaching. In fact, he taught that God was *everyone's* Father and that every person could communicate directly and intimately with him, regardless of place or time. "Beware of practicing your piety before men in order to be seen by them," said Jesus, "For then you will have no reward from *your* Father who is in heaven" (Matthew 6:1).

Jesus not only made all who heard him distinctly aware of their relationship with God, but directed their attention to the coming Kingdom of God which he referred to as the "Kingdom of Heaven." (See Matthew, chapters 13, 18–21 for parables of the Kingdom.) "The Kingdom of heaven may be compared to . . ." was the way Jesus began much of his teaching about God's Kingdom. His analogies regarding the Kingdom covered a wide range of everyday activities that everyone could understand.

> The Kingdom of heaven is like a grain of mustard seed
> which a man took and sowed in his field; it is the
> smallest of all seeds, but when it has grown, it is the

greatest of shrubs and becomes a tree, so that the birds
of the air come and make nests in its branches.
The Kingdom of heaven is like leaven which a woman
took and hid in three measures of meal, till it was all
leavened.
The Kingdom of heaven is like a treasure hidden in a
field, which a man found and covered up; then in his
joy he goes and sells all that he has and buys that field.
Again, the Kingdom of heaven is like a. . . . (Matthew 13:31–49)

Whatever else Jesus may have implied by teaching about the Kingdom of heaven this much is certain; he urged all men to seek primarily the Kingdom of God and His righteousness.

Therefore do not be anxious, saying "What shall we eat?" or "What shall we drink?" or "What shall we wear?" . . . Your heavenly Father knows that you need them all. But seek first his kingdom and his righteousness, and all these things shall be yours as well. (Matthew 6:31–33)

Jesus assured his hearers that God as a Father cared for every individual; no person was unworthy of receiving the Father's grace. Moreover, no person was to be excluded from the Kingdom of heaven, for it was accessible to all who asked.

Ask, and it will be given to you;
seek, and you will find;
knock, and it will be opened to you.
For every one who asks receives,
and he who seeks finds
and to him who knocks it will be opened. (Matthew 7:7–8)

A person's relationship with God is reasonably clear from the teachings of Jesus. What is less clear is how Jesus saw himself in relationship to God. Did he think of himself as a "child" or "son of God" in the same sense as he taught that everyone was a "child" or "son" of God? Or did he consider himself to be "The Son of God" in a very special sense? Did he regard himself as the Messiah (the Lord's anointed) or was it his disciples who later thought of him as the Messiah?

Obviously these questions have represented, and still represent, the knottiest issues of interpretation in the history of Christianity. And perhaps such crucial problems can never be finally answered. Nevertheless, one thing is beyond doubt: Jesus knew that he was "commissioned" or "sent" to proclaim the Kingdom and the Fatherhood of God (Luke 4:16–21, 43). Hence, he proclaimed that the Father's love for a person is so great and boundless that it is not governed by a person's goodness or wickedness. God manifests his love and mercy to all human beings—both good and bad—without regard to need or merit.

Jesus taught that the two concepts, the Fatherhood of God and the union of humankind, are inseparable. An individual who experiences an intimate fellowship with God the Father, must of necessity love humankind. Since it is the nature and character of the Father to love and be compassionate to all, then it follows that the "son" should reflect the nature of the Father (Luke 18:23–25). In fact, anyone who does not love mankind can know nothing about God, let alone be associated with him. To love the individual who is unjust, cruel, deceitful, ugly, and unlovable; to love the murderer, the social outcast, and one's enemy as much as the good and the lovable, is to love God. To feed the hungry, to clothe the naked, to welcome the stranger, to cheer the sick, to visit the imprisoned—in short, to love and serve humanity is to love and serve the Father (Matthew 25:24–46).

This teaching of Jesus so impressed the minds of many that an expert in Judaic Law (the Torah) once asked Jesus to explain what he meant by "loving one's neighbor as oneself" (Luke 10:29–37). Jesus replied by telling the story of a man who was robbed, beaten, stripped and left to die on the road. A priest and a teacher, who happened to pass that way, saw the man but ignored him and traveled on. A Samaritan (one of the Jewish group regarded as enemies by traditional Jews at that time) who was the next traveler to pass, pitied the man, stopped, helped him and took care of all his needs.

"Which of these three," said Jesus, "do you think, proved neighbor to the man who fell among the robbers?"

"The one who showed mercy to him."

"Then go and do likewise," said Jesus.

For Jesus the principles of love and mercy far outweighed any others. There was no question in his mind that the highest goal in life, the most valuable element in living, was to demonstrate God's nature: love, mercy, and compassion to one and all. However, one question still eludes us. What was Jesus' own view about human nature? Did he agree that one was "born in sin" and inherently evil? Is evil part of one's makeup, like one's lungs or the hair on one's head?

Two of the Gospel writers (Luke and John) have nothing to say about this problem of original sin. The other two Gospel writers (Matthew 15:1–20 and Mark 7:1–23), however, record a discussion among Jesus and certain Jewish religious authorities who questioned him regarding the Tradition of the Elders.

> "Why do your disciples transgress the Tradition of the Elders, and eat with hands defiled [ritually unwashed]?" they asked.

"And why do you transgress the commandment of God for the sake of your Tradition?" Jesus asked.

Then Jesus turned to all who were present there and said, "Hear me, all of you, and understand: not what goes into the mouth defiles a man, but what comes out of the mouth, this defiles a man." When his disciples showed by their questions that they did not understand what he was talking about, Jesus went on to say, "Do you not see that whatever goes into a man from outside cannot defile him, since it enters not in his heart but his stomach, and so passes on? What comes out of a man is what defiles a man. For from within, out of the heart of man, come evil thoughts, fornication, theft, murder, adultery, coveting, wickedness, deceit, licentiousness, envy, slander, pride, foolishness. All these evil things come from within, and they defile a man." (Matthew 15:1–20)

Thus, Jesus declared that sin lies deep in the heart of a human being. It is what lies in the heart—the hidden attitudes and motives—rather than outward actions that should be judged. But his statement offers no explanation of the nature of sin. Nor does he mention anything about original sin. It may be that his idea of the nature of sin was similar to one of the then current Judaic concepts, but certainly he shows no interest in defining sin or its origin in the abstract sense.

Nevertheless, the presence and problem of sin has been—and remains—a cause of dispute, schism, counterclaims of heresy, and even war among Christians. And no other person had more impact on this question of sin than Paul.

Paul

Paul has been frequently called the real founder of Christianity, because his views came to shape and dominate subsequent Christian thinking. Paul's unique philosophy is particularly apparent in his writings collected in the New Testament, in which he applies terms such as *sin, redemption, justification,* and *reconciliation* to create the vocabulary of Christian theology.[4] According to Paul, the human race sinned through Adam's disobedience and consequently lost its freedom and was condemned to death. The death of Jesus Christ, then, was the payment or atonement that redeemed humanity, or won for it freedom and eternal life. Here is how he described it:

As one man's trespass led to the condemnation for all men, so one man's act of righteousness leads to acquittal and life for all men. For as by one man's disobedience many were made sinners, so by one man's obedience many will be made righteous. (Romans 5:18–19)

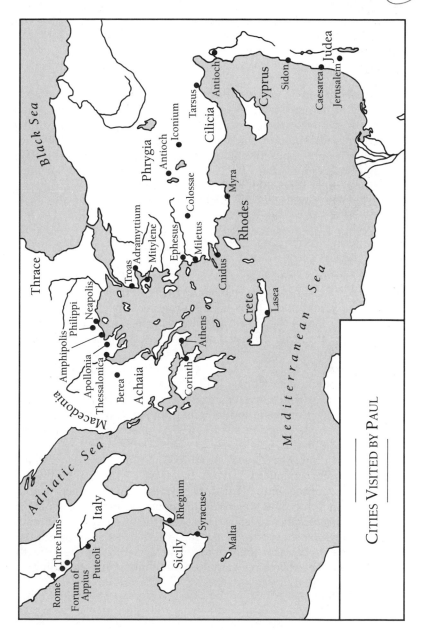

CITIES VISITED BY PAUL

In fact, Christ has been raised from the dead, the first fruits of those who have fallen asleep. For as by a man came death, by a man has come also the resurrection of the dead. For as in Adam all die, so also in Christ shall all be made alive. (I Corinthians 15:20–22)

Paul was a non-Palestinian Jew. Born at about the same time as Jesus, in the famous town of Tarsus in Cilicia (Turkey), he was a fanatically devoted Pharisee. He presumably purchased Roman citizenship and therefore enjoyed the legal status of a free-born Roman. He strongly opposed religious ideas that accommodated Hellenism or were compromised by Hellenistic influences, and he knew something about the adherents of the mystery cults, who claimed to have attained immortality by identification with a dying and rising savior god. To Paul, the Jew, these cults were anathema—and that included the cult of Jesus Christ. He was one of the spectators at the stoning of the Christian Stephen and joined in the persecution of the early Christian group.

On a journey to Damascus to arrest Christian believers, however, he experienced a traumatic event that convinced him that the dead and resurrected Jesus of the Christians had appeared to him as he had appeared to others. His fierce opposition to the Christian movement gave way, in the instant revelation, to unquestioning support of it. Over the following three years, he developed a number of basic Christian theological concepts, the effects of which have dominated Christian thinking ever since.

At the heart of Paul's teaching was the concept of the Lordship of Christ. In order to redeem individuals from sin and death, Christ, a divine being possessing the nature of God, assumed a human form and humbled himself to die on the cross. His subsequent resurrection and ascension into heaven was proof of his triumph over death and sin—a triumph that could be shared by all who bound themselves to him by faith. Consequently, Paul declared, it was unnecessary to abide by the Jewish Torah (Law) to attain righteousness in the sight of God. Belief in and acceptance of Jesus Christ was the true path to righteousness. Those who believed in Christ, regardless of whether or not they followed the precepts of the Torah, were declared righteous in the sight of God. The following quotations illustrate Paul's teaching:

Now we know that whatever the Law [Torah] says it speaks to those who are under the Law. No human being will be justified in His sight by works of the Law, since through the Law comes knowledge of sin. But now the righteousness of God has been manifested apart from the Law . . . the righteousness of God through faith in Jesus Christ for all who believe. (Romans 3:19–22)

But now we are discharged from the Law, dead to that which held us captive, so that we serve not under the old written code but in the new life of the Spirit. (Romans 7:6)

For the wages of sin is death, but the free gift of God is eternal life in Christ Jesus our Lord. (Romans 6:23)

We rejoice in God through our Lord Jesus Christ, through whom we have now received our reconciliation. (Romans 5:11)

Paul then set out on his famous missionary journeys, during which he established Christian churches in many of the principal cities of the Roman Empire. His teachings—and especially his criticism of the Jewish Torah—brought him into conflict with Jewish religious leaders, who were instrumental in his arrest in Jerusalem and indirectly responsible for the distrust in which Paul was held by the Roman authorities. Ultimately, he was taken into custody in Rome, where according to tradition, he was executed by the Romans for the crime of disturbing the peace.

Early Christianity

The Christian religion absorbed and adopted many elements and practices from Jewish, Greek, Roman, and other religious sources.[5] At least three basic Jewish traditional elements were carried over to Christianity in altered form. First, the Jewish rite of circumcision as the sign of the Covenant with God was replaced by the Christian rite of baptism as the sign of the New Covenant with God. Second, the Jewish weekly assemblies for regular Sabbath services that marked the seventh day, on which God rested from creation, were modified as regular weekly services on Sundays, commemorating the day of Jesus' resurrection. At these services, scriptures were read and instructions delivered in the Jewish tradition but in the presence of the Divine *Eucharist* (Communion) a Christian concept, rather than the *shekinah*, or Divine Presence, the Jewish equivalent. Third, the importance of the Jewish scriptures was recognized and accepted by Christians but colored and modified by Christian interpretations.

Greek culture and religion also played a role in the development of the Christian religion. Christian scholars soon learned the art of logical argument and the expression of philosophical ideas. From Roman culture Christians borrowed the model of a centralized authority of law and order and adapted it to fit an organized, self-governing religious body—the church.

Persecution and Triumph. The first few centuries were critical times for Christianity. To begin with, a series of persecutions threatened its survival. Accused of holding secret orgies and charged with infanticide, incest, and cannibalism, Christians were tortured. Emperor Nero (57–68 CE) used Christian victims for the bloody Roman arenas. Other emperors, such as Decius (249–251) and Diocletian (284–305), used ruthless measures in an attempt to stamp out Christianity. Christians not only survived these early trials, but by the middle of the fifth century, Christianity had emerged as the sole state religion of Rome.

The two emperors most instrumental in this development were Constantine (with his coemperor Licinius*) and Theodosius II. The so-called Edict of Milan, issued in 313 by the coemperors Constantine and Licinius, stated that "concerning the Christians . . . all who choose that religion are to be permitted to continue therein, without any difficulty or hindrance, and are not to be in any way troubled or molested."[6] But the Edict of Theodosius, issued around 395, went further in prohibiting, on pain of death, the existence of any religion except Christianity:

> We interdict all persons of criminal pagan mind from the accursed immolation of victims, from damnable sacrifices, and from all other such practices that are prohibited by the authority of the more ancient sanctions. We command that all their fanes, temples, and shrines, if even now any remain entire, shall be destroyed by the command of the magistrates, and shall be purified by the erection of the sign of the venerable Christian religion. All men shall know that if it should appear, by suitable proof before a competent judge, that any person has mocked this law, he shall be punished with death.[7]

Manicheism. The final triumph of Christianity over state persecution thus was accompanied by an ironic role reversal, as the persecuted, in league with the state, now became persecutors. And no religious group was persecuted as ruthlessly or ferociously as were the followers of Manicheism, a religion founded by Mani (216–276) in Mesopotamia. If the exact reasons for such universal opprobrium remain difficult to isolate, it is clear that Mani's teachings and practices were perceived as a major threat to Christianity.

In his teachings Mani made a deliberate effort to combine various Zoroastrian, Mesopotamian, Buddhist, and Christian elements, adapting or discarding whatever he felt was appropriate from other creeds. He was quite prepared to concede to his predecessors, such as Buddha, Zoroaster, and Jesus, the credit they deserved. But he considered himself the promised "Paraclete" of Jesus—the seal (end of the line of

---

*Under Diocletian, the empire had been divided, for administrative purposes, into eastern and western parts, which eventually were ruled by coemperors.

succession) of all previous prophets. He claimed to have ascended to heaven and there to have received the divine revelation in the form of a book. As recipient of the divine revelation, he regarded himself as the sole possessor of absolute truth.

At the center of Mani's system stood the doctrine of two eternal elements: God and Matter (or alternatively, Good and Evil, Light and Darkness, or Truth and Falsehood). Mani taught that these should not be recognized as two gods but rather as two primary elements, one called God and the other Matter, of which God is superior.

Mani's concept of the future life subsumed humanity under three classes: the Elect, the Hearers, and the Wicked. Immediately after death, according to Mani, the Elect ascend to the moon and are then conveyed to paradise; the Hearers pass through a long process of wandering and purification before they may join the Elect; and the Wicked roam around the universe in hopeless misery until they are consigned forever to the realm of darkness (much like followers of evil in Zoroastrianism).

At the time of Mani's death his religion had evolved into a highly organized system that had spread beyond the borders of the Roman Empire into Arabia, Iran, India, and China. Nothing is known for certain about the introduction and spread of Manicheism within the Roman Empire except for the evidence that it reached beyond Iran to Egypt, northern Africa, and Spain, and from Syria to Turkey, Greece, Italy, and France. Its prevalence is attested to by the determined opposition of the Christian emperors who showed as much intolerance toward Manicheism as Iranian rulers. Emperor Diocletian, for instance, drew up an edict against the Manicheans in 297. His prescriptions were draconian: all written materials and their authors, together with all ringleaders, were to be burned; all adherents were to be put to death and their properties confiscated; and anyone who held a position of high rank or status in society and was found to follow the Manichean religion was to be condemned to a fate far worse than death—compulsory labor in the mines.

Opposition against Manicheans was no less vigorous from Christian leaders. Christian writers from Syria, Iraq, and Armenia allude to the Manichean religion as a "dangerous, wicked" faith. Greek and Latin authors considered the Manichean religion to be an "insane *heresy*"[8]— that is, opposed to established dogma. By far the most celebrated of Western authorities on Manicheism was the Catholic saint Augustine, who for nine years (373–382) before his conversion to Christianity had been a professed Manichean. After his conversion, Augustine wrote several works arguing against Manicheans. Pope Leo I (440–461) played an especially prominent part in the persecution of the Manicheans. Little is known about the history of Manicheism in Europe after the sixth century, because by that time the term *Manichean* had come to be used in a very loose sense to designate any heretical group.

Internal Disputes and Divisions. This early period of Christianity was also characterized by the first signs of differentiation and schism within the Christian movement. In order to protect the message of Christianity, many men withdrew from worldly contact and lived as hermits in deserts and other lonely places around the Mediterranean; later, this movement led to the establishment of *monasticism* (organized asceticism practiced by orders of monks and nuns). At the same time, internal disputes began to threaten the survival of Christianity as the persecutions of the Roman emperors had never done. As these disputes gave rise to numerous "heretical" movements, the Christian church was compelled to formulate an official creed (or statement of belief) and to canonize certain writings as sacred scriptures. Also, the political and linguistic division of the Roman Empire into eastern and western parts in the fourth century created a basic rivalry for the

A Coptic Christian monastery, Cairo, Egypt.   Donna DeCesare/ Impact Visuals.

leadership of Christianity. Rome was the center of the west, where Latin was the dominant language; Constantinople was the center of the east, where Greek predominated. Inevitably, the Christian establishments in the two centers competed for leadership. The issue was temporarily resolved at an ecumenical council that convened in Constantinople in 381 and established five important ecclesiastical provinces, better known as Patriarchates: Rome, Constantinople, Alexandria, Antioch, and Jerusalem.

However, various decisions, formulated at subsequent councils,

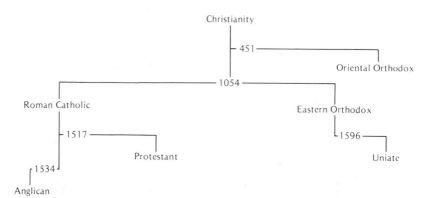

Anglican	Protestant	Eastern Orthodox	Oriental Orthodox
Church of England	Adventist	**Ancient Patriarchates**	Syrian
Church of Wales	Baptist		Coptic
Church of Ireland	Brethren	Constantinople	Armenian
Church of Scotland	Christian Scientist	Alexandria	Syro-Indian
Church of Canada	Church of God	Antioch	Ethiopian
Episcopal Church U.S.A.	Swedenborgian	Jerusalem	
Archbishopric of Jerusalem	Congregationalist		
Church of Australia/Tasmania	Disciples of Christ	**Autocephalous**	*Uniate*
Church of New Zealand	Evangelical	Russia	
Church of South Africa	Friends	Romania	Poland
Church of East Africa	Jehovah's Witnesses	Serbia	Ukraine
Church of West Africa	Mormon	Greece	Antioch
Church of Central Africa	Lutheran	Bulgaria	and so on
Church of West Indies	Mennonite	Georgia	
Nippon Sei Ko Kwai	Methodist	Cyprus	
Chung Hua Sheng Kung Hui	Moravian	Czechoslovakia	
Church of Uganda-Ruanda-Urandi	Nazarene	Poland	
Church of India, Pakistan,	Old Catholic	Albania	
Burma, Ceylon	Pentecostal	Sinai	
	Presbyterian		
	Reformed	**Autonomous**	
	Salvation Army	Finland	
	Spiritualist	China	
	Unitarian	Japan	
	Universalist		
	United Church		
	and so on		

hastened the fragmentation of Christianity. The first major rift came in the fifth and sixth centuries, when, discontented with certain issues and unwilling to be dominated by Constantinople, the Christian groups of Persia (also known as the Nestorian Church), Armenia, Syria (the so-called Jacobite Church), Ethiopia, Egypt (the Coptic Church), and India broke away from the rest of Christendom. To date, all have maintained an autonomous existence. An even larger schism, that between east and west, is conventionally dated to the year 1054 but will be dealt with here because its roots lay in the east-west division of the Roman Empire. From 1054, the churches in what had been the western part of the Roman Empire came to be known as the Roman Catholic churches, a strong, centralized organization headed by the pope (originally, merely the bishop of Rome). The churches in the eastern part of the Roman Empire, known as the Byzantine Empire, came to be called the Eastern Orthodox churches, each division of which was administratively independent and headed by its own patriarch. The four eastern patriarchs of Constantinople, Alexandria, Antioch, and Jerusalem loosely acknowledged the Roman pope as a "primary among equals," but the extent and the exact nature of the pope's authority could never be clearly defined and agreed upon. The result was the gradual and painful separation of the eastern and western parts of the Christian church.

Today, the Eastern Orthodox churches comprise the four ancient Patriarchates of Constantinople, Alexandria, Antioch, and Jerusalem; four more recent Patriarchates of Moscow, Serbia, Romania, and Bulgaria; the independent churches of Greece, Cyprus, Georgia, Albania, Finland, and Poland; and a number of national bodies (see figure on p. 389). This federation of churches has no central authority; each church is self-governing.

Further movements within Eastern Orthodox churches in the sixteenth century led to the separation of the Uniates, or Eastern Catholic churches. These Eastern Orthodox churches reestablished communion with the Roman Catholic church while retaining their ancient rites of worship and liturgy.

Christianity and Medieval Society

Spread of Christianity

In addition to unresolved disputes and internal disharmony, Christianity suffered severe setbacks after the rise of Islam in the seventh century. Within a century, the Arabs, inspired and united by Islam, conquered Syria, Palestine, Egypt, Sicily, Sardinia, Corsica, and Crete, as well as the entire Persian Empire. Despite this challenge to its monopoly on faith around the Mediterranean, Christianity slowly spread to the far corners of Europe, Africa, and Asia.

Between the fifth and eighth centuries, Christianity penetrated France, Britain, Ireland, and Scotland. Mainly through the efforts of Charlemagne, the Frankish ruler, the conversion of Germany was accomplished late in the eighth century. Between the tenth and eleventh centuries Christianity spread to Norway, Sweden, and Denmark. About the middle of the tenth century the Germans extended their political power and their Christian faith over Poland and the Baltic lands; by the thirteenth century, Estonia and Latvia were converted, mainly through German conquest. Similarly, Christianity prevailed in Finland through Swedish conquest around the thirteenth century.

In contrast to most of western Europe, where Christianity looked to Rome, the Christianity of eastern and central Europe looked to Constantinople. The Byzantine form of Christianity spread to the north and west of Constantinople. In the ninth century, two Greek brothers from Thessalonica, Cyril and Methodius, were sent by Photius, the patriarch of Constantinople, as missionaries to the Slavic peoples, the Bulgars and Serbs. Partly due to the efforts of these two men, Christianity gained a foothold also in Moravia (approximately the present location of Czechoslovakia). Around the tenth century, Byzan-

Saint Basil's Cathedral in Red Square, Moscow, the most famous of all Russian Orthodox churches. Built in the sixteenth century, it is now a tourist attraction. The Bettman Archive.

tine Christianity penetrated into Kiev and later to various parts of Russia. Nestorians and some contingents of other Eastern Christianity also spread the faith to central and eastern Asia, but the numerical gains in these areas represented distinct minorities in continents dominated by Hinduism, Buddhism, Islam, and other religions.

Rivalries and Persecutions

Coinciding with the spread of Christianity were several important and interesting, though perhaps paradoxical, developments. Particularly significant in the history of western Europe was a contest for supremacy between the papacy and various temporal states, in which each side asserted its authority and consequently denounced the other. Repeated attempts to resolve this tension came to nothing until changing times and circumstances reduced armed conflict to the level of an academic debate. Modern politics and society have largely relegated the concept of ecclesiastical power to limbo in the Western world.

Another significant development was a series of attempts to reform the standards of faith in Western Christianity. To this end a number of popes sought to improve the credibility of the clergy and struggled to eradicate simony (the selling of indulgences), clerical marriage, and concubinage. At the same time, various monarchs who were either deeply concerned for the survival of Christianity or desirous of territorial gain (or more likely, both) dreamed of a reinvigorated Christianity reconquering the lands that had fallen to Islam. Apparently with no thought of inconsistency and as a phase of the reform movement, Pope Urban II appealed to Christians in 1095 to fight a "holy war" in order to regain the places held sacred by the Christians. The result was a crusading movement, more popularly called the Crusades, that continued until nearly 1300 and gave rise to many acts of violence and barbarism. The net effect of these crusades was to embitter relations between Christians and Muslims permanently.

Although most religions engage in varying degrees of conflict and persecution, only two religions have attempted to exterminate all rivals and dominate the globe—Christianity and Islam. From the first time they collided, both Christianity and Islam displayed an exclusive, uncompromising, intolerant, and aggressive attitude. Both proclaiming a monopoly on absolute truth, each regarded all other religious values and spiritual qualities to be false and invalid. Both felt a pressing need to convert the whole world to the truth they each upheld. And to this end, both used military force unhesitatingly. The record on both sides is stained with acts of violence, barbarism, and atrociousness.

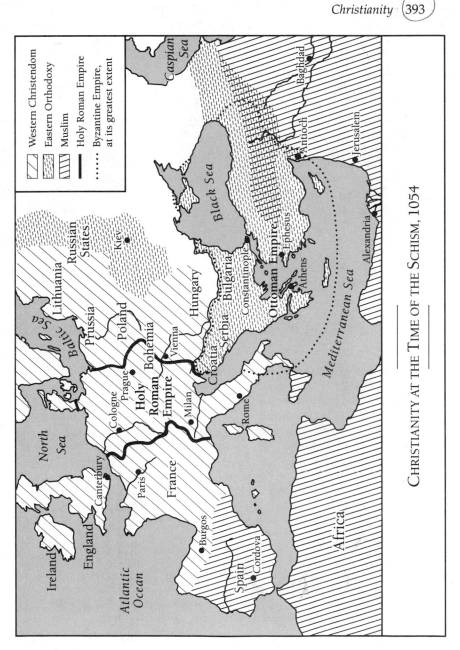

CHRISTIANITY AT THE TIME OF THE SCHISM, 1054

The Inquisition. Another aspect of reform was the attempt of the Christian leadership to stamp out all forms of heresy. In 1179 the Third Lateran Council invoked the aid of secular powers to prosecute deviants from the Christian faith. Consequently, the papacy established a tribunal to identify individuals or groups whose views did not correspond to the teachings of the Roman Catholic church. In 1233, under the special direction of the Dominican order of priests, the Inquisition was established as a general court with almost unlimited powers. Imprisonment, exile, physical torture, public burning, and a host of other horrors were inflicted upon all those whose religious views differed from papal orthodoxy.

The measures seem barbarous now, but by thirteenth-century standards they were not. They were simply the concomitants of power. Centuries later, Protestantism, which criticized the intolerance and interference of the Roman Catholic church, adopted the same brutal methods in imposing its own views upon those who refused to conform. Apart from Protestantism (see the following section), the Inquisition managed to suppress all groups or movements branded by the Roman Catholic church as heretical, as it was used as a weapon against the Jews and the Muslims as well before finally being abolished in 1834.

Persecution of the Jews. The era 500–1800 was the darkest and most unfortunate period in the history of Christianity, not least because of continual and relentless persecution of the followers of Judaism. The story of Christian attempts to forcibly convert Jews, by methods paralleling in ferocity those leveled against the Manicheans, makes sad reading. The centuries of cruelty suffered by the Jews at the hands of Christians demonstrates the wickedness (and futility) of attempting to spread Christianity (or any other religion) by the employment of sheer force. The fact that many Christian leaders once looked upon the persecution of Jews as a religious duty is revealed in the words of a ninth-century Christian preacher at Beziers, France:

> You have around you those who crucified the Messiah, who deny Mary the Mother of God. Now is the time when you should feel most deeply the iniquity of which Christ was the victim. This is the day on which our Prince has graciously given us permission to avenge this crime. Like your pious ancestors, hurl stones at the Jews, and show your sense of His wrongs by the vigour with which you resent them.[9]

Attempts to convert Jews by force or persecution were carried out in all areas of Europe, but with particular cruelty in Spain, where they were linked in the public mind with the bitter, centuries-long struggle to reconquer the country from the Arabs. In 1296, the passions of the

Spanish Christian populace of Toledo were so aroused against the Jews that synagogues were pillaged or utterly destroyed and thousands of Jews were butchered. In 1391 similar massacres were perpetrated in Cordova, Valencia, and Burgos, and in 1460 in Andalusia and Castile. Needless to say, many Jews converted to Christianity in order to save their lives or the lives of their families.

During their conquest of Central and South America in the sixteenth century, the Spanish also attempted the last forced mass conversion to Christianity. Cortés and his Spanish troops entered Tenochtitlán (near modern Mexico City), the capital of the Aztec Empire, in 1519 (see p. 60). Two years later, aided by thousands of American Indians, they completely leveled the ceremonial center, thus accelerating the forced conversion of the native people. But the Spanish conquest and widespread conversion to Christianity did not prevent the Aztec descendants from retaining some of their magical rites and religious beliefs, which have survived to the present day.[10] In fact, many descendants of the Aztecs still live in small villages around Mexico City, speak their ancestral language, and, in many cases, combine their Christian religion with the ancient religion to form a peculiar style of Mexican Catholicism.

Reformation and Counter-Reformation

The tides of reform that surged and ebbed through Western Christianity in the Middle Ages failed to eradicate abuses in church practices, such as simony, or to reverse what many saw as the increasing worldliness, venality, and power hunger of the church clergy and hierarchy—up to and including many popes. At the same time, the medieval ideal of a unified Christendom was fast losing whatever hold it had exerted on the popular imagination, as emerging nation-states came to realize that Rome's agenda was not their own. These trends, along with others, led to the religious movement commonly known as the Reformation.

Throughout the Middle Ages, religious movements branded as heresies by Rome had flared up in various parts of Europe. None were so threatening to Rome, however, as the Hussite movement—so-called after Jan Hus (1369?–1415), a Czech priest who attacked clerical privileges and abuses, denied papal infallibility, and espoused state supervision of the church. Jan Hus presented a serious problem to the church authorities, for his calls for reform struck a responsive chord in the laity while infuriating the clergy, and his denial of Rome's authority became a rallying point for Czech nationalists (including King Wenceslaus IV). Hus was burned at the stake in 1415, but the religious and historical forces behind his views proved too powerful for the church to eradicate.

On October 31, 1517, the German monk Martin Luther, following a common practice in university circles, affixed to the chapel door at the University of Wittenberg ninety-five theses challenging various church practices and doctrines. This date is generally regarded as marking the beginning of Protestantism, a religious movement whose numerous independent churches (see figure on p. 389) were united chiefly by a rejection of the religious authority of the papacy and an emphasis on the individual's responsibility for his or her own salvation through faith. Both of these doctrines appealed mightily not only to the many Christians disgusted with the corruption rampant among the clergy, but also to princes and kings eager to be rid of Rome's authority over their subjects. Royal patronage ensured the survival of the nascent Protestant churches. It also ensured that what had begun as a reform movement within the church would become inextricably intertwined with political disputes. Religious warfare, attended by persecution and civil strife, plagued Europe for the next 150 years. By the end of this period, Catholicism (as the church of Rome was now known) had succeeded in checking the advance of the Protestant churches, whereas the latter had succeeded in establishing their independence from Rome.

A concerted effort to halt the spread of Protestantism was launched by the Council of Trent in 1545. The chief accomplishments of the Counter-Reformation, as it became known, were the abolition of simony, the reform and reinvigoration of the clergy, and the encourage-

The elaborate outer gate and facade of the Church of San Francisco in Puebla de Acatepec, Mexico, covered with glazed tile and red brick. Carolyn Brown/Peter Arnold, Inc.

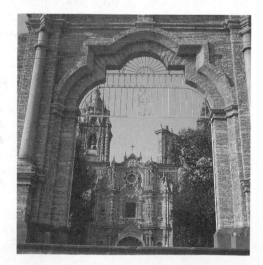

ment of education and proselytization as the most effective means of fighting Protestantism and advancing Catholicism. Spearheading the latter effort was the Society of Jesus (Jesuits), founded by Ignatius of Loyola in 1534. A militant, highly disciplined, and well-educated religious order, the Jesuits not only helped check the advance of Protestantism, but also established Roman Catholic missions in India, China, Japan, and the Americas. Protestant reformers, in contrast, were late in introducing their form of Christianity to non-European peoples. Not until the nineteenth and twentieth centuries were they able to compete with Roman Catholic missionaries on anything like equal footing outside Europe. That they finally were able to do so was largely due to the spread of imperialism and colonialism. In the meantime, various forces were changing, with increasing rapidity, the shape of Western civilization.

The Enlightenment

While various groups were developing Protestant principles in different directions and forming a multitude of churches, a succession of philosophers such as René Descartes, David Hume, Immanuel Kant, and G. W. Leibniz were turning away from theology to mount a rationalistic investigation of human nature. Similarly, scientists such as Galileo and Isaac Newton pursued their experiments on and investigations into natural phenomena independent of theological dogma. In art, history, and literature, theological issues and themes also were gradually superseded by an interest in human activity and behavior. These trends coalesced into the most influential intellectual movement in Western civilization prior to the twentieth century: the Enlightenment.

The Enlightenment began in the mid-seventeenth century in England and the Netherlands, but it was nowhere more eloquently articulated than in Germany and France. In Germany, Leibniz, G. E. Lessing, and Kant, and in France, Voltaire (the pen name of François Marie Arouet), Claude Adrien Helvétius, and Auguste Comte were its foremost philosophical offspring. Immanuel Kant (1724–1804), one of the most influential of all Enlightenment thinkers, rejected biblical, conciliar, or any other nonrational account of human nature and the universe. Kant, followed by G. W. F. Hegel, believed that human beings possessed a reasoning faculty that was capable of unraveling truth from tradition and reality from myth. Consequently, he and his successor dismissed the domain of the transcendent as irrelevant and defined religion as a manifestation of human self-expression.

Widespread disenchantment with religion after over a century of religious wars and distaste for and indignation against church dogma-

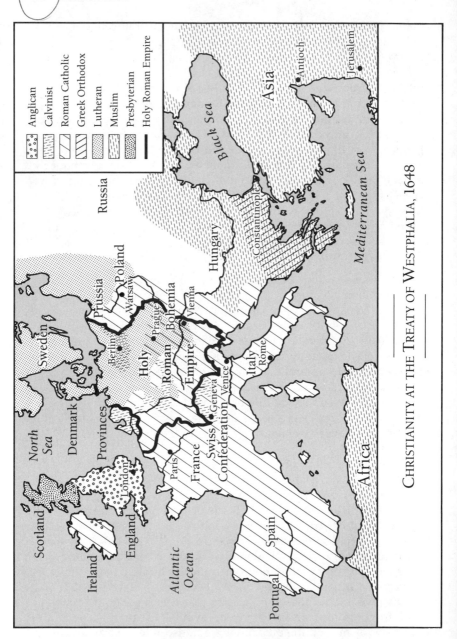

CHRISTIANITY AT THE TREATY OF WESTPHALIA, 1648

tism were two of the most important factors that shaped the Enlightenment's optimistic perception of human, mortal, temporal potential. In the field of sciences, the evidence of empirical discoveries led to conclusions that seemed to oppose theological judgments and affirmations of faith. The rubric of religion represented such a ponderous mass of absolute authority, superstition, and anti-intellectualism that many thinkers found themselves forced to choose between Christian principles and love of humanity. The social thinker Auguste Comte (1798–1857), for instance, advanced the idea that humans pass through three evolutionary stages in their quest for understanding of natural phenomena: (1) a search for a theological or supernatural explanation; (2) a search for a metaphysical or abstract explanation; and (3) a search for a social explanation. In Comte's view, humanity by the nineteenth century had reached the third stage—having graduated, as it were, from theology and philosophy.

Comte's sociological views led other thinkers, such as Hegel and Karl Marx, to amplify his emphasis on human autonomy and consciousness in different ways. The response of Christian churches was predictable. They branded anyone that had the temerity to reject ecclesiastical authority and to discard Christian doctrines and ethics as a godless sinner doomed to eternal damnation without hope of redemption. Such prospects, however, did not in any way arrest the intellectual and political aspirations of enthusiastic exponents of the spirit of the Enlightenment and their followers. On the contrary, secular rulers increasingly relegated religion to the private sector and demonstrated their reluctance to sanction state approval of one religious group at the expense of others. Similarly, with the authority of theology diminished, scientific data increasingly challenged the credibility of biblical accounts. Scientists grew increasingly confident that they would soon unlock all the mysteries and secrets of nature, including human nature.

Understandably, church leaders reacted strongly (as some still do) to the primacy of empirical reasoning and human rationality, arguing that denial of the transcending power of Christian revelation would only lead to an extension of human evil, an increase in the dehumanization of society, and total perdition. The evidence has not been conclusive or particularly reassuring on either account. In view of the horrors and bloodbaths of the French Revolution in 1789, and of the increasing degree and scale of horror culminating in the threat of a nuclear apocalypse, the application of Enlightenment beliefs has not proved an unqualified boon to humanity. Though the Age of Enlightenment was distinguished as much by its benefits as by its excesses—particularly in terms of human freedom, growth, and development, and in the recognition of women in their own right—the legacy it bequeathed to the twentieth century has not diminished the debate among Christians over the issue of faith versus reason. Events have a habit of overtaking debates. In the interval, various forces paved the way for drastic changes.

Modern Christianity

Religious Movements

To meet the challenges of these changes, provoked especially by the Industrial Revolution and the growth of cities, a variety of religious movements emerged in the nineteenth century. In 1844 the Young Men's Christian Association (YMCA) was founded by George Williams, an Englishman whose aim was to improve the physical, social, intellectual, and religious level of the young men in lower- and middle-income groups. The International Red Cross was organized in

Christianity

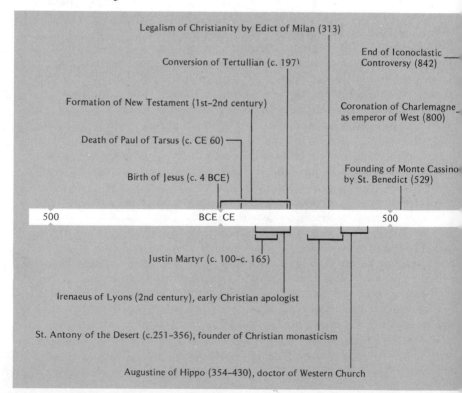

Legalism of Christianity by Edict of Milan (313)

End of Iconoclastic Controversy (842)

Conversion of Tertullian (c. 197)

Formation of New Testament (1st–2nd century)

Coronation of Charlemagne as emperor of West (800)

Death of Paul of Tarsus (c. CE 60)

Birth of Jesus (c. 4 BCE)

Founding of Monte Cassino by St. Benedict (529)

500   BCE CE   500

Justin Martyr (c. 100–c. 165)

Irenaeus of Lyons (2nd century), early Christian apologist

St. Antony of the Desert (c.251–356), founder of Christian monasticism

Augustine of Hippo (354–430), doctor of Western Church

1863, mainly through the efforts of the Swiss Henri Dunant, to take care of the sick and wounded in war. In 1878 the Salvation Army was begun by another Englishman, William Booth, in an effort to uplift, both physically and spiritually, the poor and downtrodden. In 1889 the Christian Social Union (CSU) was founded in England, mainly to resolve management-labor disputes by applying Christian principles.

Ecumenism

The outstanding movement among Christians in the twentieth century has been ecumenism—the trend toward worldwide unity or cooperation among churches. Paradoxically, Protestant reform that resulted in fragmentation in earlier centuries is now being countered by reform aimed at reunion, two types of which in particular are distinguishable.

The first consists of mergers of two or more religious groups to form one new institution. The United Church of Canada, for example, was formed in 1925 from groups of Methodists, Congregationalists, and Presbyterians. The Reformed Church of France was created in 1938 by

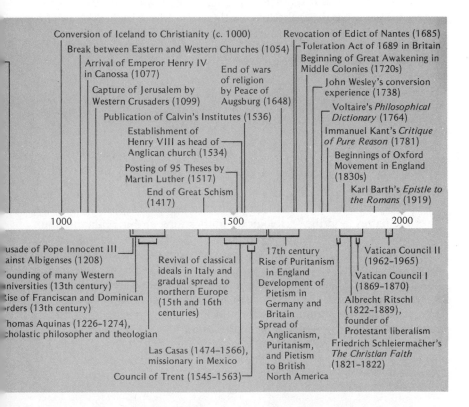

Conversion of Iceland to Christianity (c. 1000)
Break between Eastern and Western Churches (1054)
Arrival of Emperor Henry IV in Canossa (1077)
End of wars of religion by Peace of Augsburg (1648)
Capture of Jerusalem by Western Crusaders (1099)
Publication of Calvin's Institutes (1536)
Establishment of Henry VIII as head of Anglican church (1534)
Posting of 95 Theses by Martin Luther (1517)
End of Great Schism (1417)

Revocation of Edict of Nantes (1685)
Toleration Act of 1689 in Britain
Beginning of Great Awakening in Middle Colonies (1720s)
John Wesley's conversion experience (1738)
Voltaire's *Philosophical Dictionary* (1764)
Immanuel Kant's *Critique of Pure Reason* (1781)
Beginnings of Oxford Movement in England (1830s)
Karl Barth's *Epistle to the Romans* (1919)

1000   1500   2000

Crusade of Pope Innocent III against Albigenses (1208)
Founding of many Western universities (13th century)
Rise of Franciscan and Dominican orders (13th century)
Thomas Aquinas (1226–1274), scholastic philosopher and theologian

Revival of classical ideals in Italy and gradual spread to northern Europe (15th and 16th centuries)
Las Casas (1474–1566), missionary in Mexico
Council of Trent (1545–1563)

17th century Rise of Puritanism in England
Development of Pietism in Germany and Britain
Spread of Anglicanism, Puritanism, and Pietism to British North America

Vatican Council II (1962–1965)
Vatican Council I (1869–1870)
Albrecht Ritschl (1822–1889), founder of Protestant liberalism
Friedrich Schleiermacher's *The Christian Faith* (1821–1822)

the union of the Evangelical Methodist Church of France, the Reformed Evangelical Church of France, the Reformed Church of France, and a union of Evangelical Free Churches. The Church of Christ in Japan grew in 1941 from a union of fifteen religious bodies. The Church of South India resulted in 1947 from the union of four denominations. Twenty-seven independent regional churches joined in 1948 to form the Evangelical Church in Germany. Finally, the United Church of Christ in the United States was formed in 1961 by the amalgamation of the Congregational Christian churches with the Evangelical and Reformed church, both of which were the products of prior mergers.

Ecumenism has also taken the form of the convocation of international and independent Christian denominations for cooperation and federated action. The most visible manifestation of such a reunion was the organization of the World Council of Churches (WCC), which first met in 1948 in Amsterdam. Initially, only several Protestant denominations and a few representatives of Eastern Orthodoxy supported this organization. Since then, the World Council of Churches has convened several more times. Many Protestant denominations and various Eastern Orthodox contingents, including the Russian Orthodox church, have now joined the organization and regularly send delegates to the conferences. Since 1961, the Roman Catholic church has sent official observers.

Although it is too soon to predict the long-term effects of the ecumenical movement, one benefit seems evident: it has forced Christians with similar allegiances but differing convictions to examine the paradox of a single church divided against itself—a parody of Christian ideals.

Religious Pluralism

Thus, the age of cultural isolation and religious imperialism finally has given way to one of cultural diversity and religious pluralism. The decisive nature and the sociological ramifications of this phenomenon are, undeniably, quite momentous. At no other time in history— except, perhaps, during the Greco-Roman period—has Christianity been more attracted to the fusion of East-West religious ideas and practices.[11] And, experimentation with alternative religions is a burgeoning phenomenon in modern society. The responses of various Christian thinkers, Roman Catholic and Protestant, to religious pluralism have led to the development of five important perspectives:

1. Exclusive
2. Teleological

3. Relative

4. Single-world-religion

5. Dialogic

Exclusive Perspective. To exclusivists, only one religion is true or valid; all other religious traditions are dismissed as false. From this perspective, the imperative role of the true religion is to replace all other religions by confronting their adherents with an uncompromising alternative. In the classic statement of this position, J. N. D. Anderson said:

> These other religions, then, like so much else in the world of men, are made up of elements whose ultimate origins are diverse. But in so far as these diverse elements have been welded into systems which serve only to divert and keep men from that way of salvation and life which cost God Himself the incarnation and the cross, the Christian must regard them as Satanic substitutes, however good they may be in parts.[12]

Teleological Perspective. Those who take the teleological perspective view one particular religion as the pinnacle and completion of all other religions: in other words, one religion is seen to be the fulfillment of what is best and true in the others. The difference between this and the previous position is one of degree only. Whereas the former view idealizes a particular religious tradition and consequently considers all other religions to be false and invalid, the teleological view affirms the superiority of one religious tradition and the inferiority of all the rest. In the words of E. O. James:

> In [Christianity], the highest insights of Judaism, Islam, Zoroastrianism, Hinduism, and Buddhism have been realized, fulfilling alike the prophetic revelations and mystical knowledge of God, and of sacramental union with Him in its transcendental and immanental aspects. . . . To discover the reality of Christ in all the religions of the world is the essence of the ecumenical approach.[13]

A somewhat similar position is held by those who see all other faiths as a *praeparatio evangelica*—preparation for the Gospel. Their argument is that in Christianity reposes the divine initiative; in all other religions, the human initiative reigns. In Christianity, God through Christ moves authentically to people, whereas in other religions people move toward God. Christianity is indubitable and inclusive, whereas other religions are dubious and partial.

Relative Perspective. Those who take a relative perspective argue that all religions have an identical goal and, therefore, represent different ways of reaching ultimate truth. No religion possesses absolute truth—only relative truth. As a result, all religious traditions are considered to be simply different paths to the same goal. According to Arnold Toynbee:

> What, then, should be the attitude of contrite Christians toward the other higher religions and their followers? I think that it is possible for us, while holding that our own convictions are true and right, to recognize that, in some measure, all the higher religions are also revelations of what is true and right. They also come from God and each presents some facet of God's truth.[14]

Another advocate of this stance, Sri Ramakrishna (1836–1886), a follower of Hinduism, set out to try all other religious paths to experience the divine. In a twelve-year period he practiced Shaktism, Jainism, Buddhism, Islam, and Christianity. His conclusion was that the diverse religions, including the several traditions of Hinduism, were different paths to the same spiritual goal.

The subsequent establishment of Ramakrishna Mission centers in various parts of Europe and America and the influence of the Hindu philosopher-statesman S. Radhakrishnan have greatly contributed to this all-inclusive view of religion. An articulate spokesman of modern Hinduism, Radhakrishnan proclaimed that the essential truth of all religions is the same: "The different religious traditions are governed by the same spirit, and work for the redemption of both man and universe. Cosmic salvation is the aim of all religions. The different names we give to the Supreme apply to the one Supreme."[15]

Such assertions are, without doubt, worthy of consideration, but they leave unresolved a number of problematic issues. Recently, several scholars have explored these questions and expressed misgivings. There is a growing awareness that underlying the apparent similarities among various religious traditions are some very deep-rooted differences. In fact, the basic problem confronting students of religion is the supposition that differing religions offer different answers to the *same* questions. The truth of the matter, however, is that different religions offer different answers because they raise *different* questions. And this is precisely why each religion is essentially distinct.

Single-World-Religion Perspective. Advocates of this view maintain that the same forces that will inevitably transform the present world into a world community will also give rise to one world religion. In the words of A. C. Bouquet, "The whole trend of global life today is in the direction of a single world-religion."[16]

At least three ways of achieving this one religion have been postulated. The most simplistic is that one of the living religious traditions will eventually become the world religion by displacing all the rest. Another is that the best insights from all the religious traditions will be selected and adapted to produce one new religion. And the third, which lies somewhere between the first two, theorizes that the more each religion is forced (by the impact of religious pluralism and the emergence of a world culture) to go through the process of reconception—that is to say, the rediscovery of what is essential in its own particular religion—the nearer all will come to constituting one world religion.

Dialogic Perspective. From a purely practical point of view, "dialogic" simply means communication: open and frank discussion among persons who seek mutual understanding or harmony. To supporters of this view, one must seek to put aside all preconceptions about religions other than one's own and be prepared to listen and understand other religionists, even when their utterances or behavior seems unintelligible. The act of dialogue is really a means whereby members of each religion learn how to communicate with each other honestly and openly.

The value of dialogue, or of personal, sympathetic communication among persons of differing religious standpoints, need scarcely be stressed. It is usually argued that it is good for adherents of different religions to meet, seriously and sympathetically—to find out both in what they agree and in what they differ. Some people have insisted, in fact, that the *only* mode of interreligious relationship appropriate to this age is the act of dialogue; and further, that through this method, future relationships among adherents of various religious persuasions will develop differently from those anticipated now.

The dialogic perspective has become exceedingly popular, not least because it seems to offer the most promising and valid tool whereby people of different religious traditions can find a common ground to serve humanity in cooperation with one with another. The following statement illustrates the adopted position of Roman Catholic Christians vis-à-vis members of other faiths:

> The Catholic Church rejects nothing which is true and holy in these religions. She looks with sincere respect upon those ways of conduct and of life, those rules and teachings which, though differing in many particulars from what she holds and sets forth, nevertheless often reflect a ray of that Truth which enlightens all men. . . . The Church therefore has this exhortation for her sons: prudently and lovingly, through dialogue and collaboration with the followers of other religions, and in witness of Christian faith and life, acknowledge, preserve, and promote the spiritual and moral goods found among these men, as well as the values of their society and culture.[17]

The importance of entering into dialogue with people of differing faiths and ideologies also is explicitly stated in the statement and guidelines on dialogue offered by the World Council of Churches to its member churches:

> Thus, to the member churches of WCC we feel able with integrity to commend the way of dialogue as one in which Jesus Christ can be confessed in the world today; at the same time we feel able with integrity to assure our partners in dialogue that we come not as manipulators but as genuine fellow-pilgrims, to speak with them of what we believe God to have done in Jesus Christ.[18]

Thus, the process of global dependence has forced individuals all over the world to meet and dialogue in order to face the challenge that lies ahead: living together harmoniously in a world of cultural and religious differences.

Emancipation of Women

Until very recently Christian churches of all types generally supported the cultural conventions that conferred on women, in legal terms, a status of subservience and incompetence. The courage and determination of pioneering leaders of women's rights to fight against longstanding customs of the church and society have brought about important breakthroughs in different ways and in varying degrees. Emma Hart Willard (1787–1870), regarded as the first American woman publicly to support higher education for women, founded a girl's seminary in Watertown, New York, which was later moved to Troy, New York. In 1824, Catharine Beecher led the establishment of a seminary for women in Hartford, Connecticut. Soon thereafter, women started to pray aloud in mixed church assemblies; and after a long period of resistance, they formed their own voluntary missionary societies.

Several prominent Christian advocates of women's rights identified themselves with the struggle for the abolition of slavery—notably, Sarah and Angelina Grimke, Lydia Child, Elizabeth Stanton, and Harriet Beecher Stowe. The latter's novel, *Uncle Tom's Cabin,* published in 1851, made a vivid and unforgettable impression and touched many consciences.

Most Christian churches have not moved much beyond that point, however. Many do not reflect the cultural conventions of the present but preserve those of the past. In general, women have been kept out of power in church life, in home or foreign missions, in leadership, in administrative positions, and in policy making. William Augustus Muhlenberg (1796–1877), an Episcopalian clergyman, aroused strong opposition among his fellow religionists when he established an order of deaconesses in 1857 in New York. Not until the beginning of this century did other Christian churches follow suit.

If the emergence of feminist and women's liberation movements in church and society in modern times has posed a challenge to the old, familiar Christian patterns, it has also originated fresh sources of energy and insight. Women have been elected to executive positions in churches of many denominations, and several churches have pioneered in ordaining women to the Christian ministry and, occasionally, electing them to the highest church rank (e.g., several Protestant churches have elected women as moderators of their general assemblies).

The Roman Catholic church also has made some progress in women's rights, particularly after Vatican II, the Ecumenical Council

Saint Peter's Basilica in Vatican City, the mother church of Catholicism. The area occupied by the basilica, including the square, is believed to have been the site of the circus of Emperor Nero (54–68 CE), where hundreds of Christians suffered martyrdom. Tradition holds that the apostle Peter died here on a cross about 64 CE. The present structure dates from 1506. From the private collection of C. LaVigna.

of 1962–1965. No such transformation had taken place since the Council of Trent. Since Vatican II, however, many familiar features of church life, such as ecclesiastical administration, devotional practices, form and language of worship, ecumenical relationships, attitudes to non-Christians, and the role of nuns and women, have changed. Female laity have been given active roles in church life and in educational institutions, and they may now be appointed to advisory school boards, parish councils, and diocesan senates. As a result, many Catholic women, including several nuns, have become prominent in social service and civil rights activities. Since the 1970s, the National Coalition of American Nuns has sought from the Roman curia (the papal court of the Roman Catholic church) full equality with priests, challenging the church's justification of an all-male priesthood. That they have failed says much about the inherent conservatism of the church hierarchy.

The extent of the injustices and inequalities suffered by all women throughout the world can never be fully estimated. To this day, women in the arts, the sciences, business, politics, education, and religious institutions have remained "the second sex," in the words of the French philosopher Simone de Beauvoir. Feminists and women's liberation advocates are seeking to remedy this situation on several fronts. Some women, such as Sally Cunneen and Rosemary Reuther, are striving to change the masculine image projected in the Godhead, in Christian theology, and in religious symbols. Others, such as Angela Davis and Michelle Wallace, are attempting to change the lamentable status and condition of black women. Issues related to the role of women in Christian churches undoubtedly are very complex, but the combined efforts and courageous accomplishments of female leaders are bound, in the long run, to remedy the inequalities that still remain.

Christian Teachings

Several principles that throughout the ages have been accepted as fundamental tenets of Christianity are explicitly summarized in the professions of faith known as creeds (from the Latin *credo,* "I believe"). Of the various creeds promulgated through the centuries, two have emerged as predominant in contemporary Christian churches:

The Apostles' Creed
I believe in God the Father Almighty, Maker of heaven and earth, and in Jesus Christ, His only Son, our Lord, Who was conceived by the Holy Ghost, born of the Virgin Mary, suffered under Pontius Pilate, was crucified, died, and was buried; He descended into hell; the third day He rose again from the dead. He ascended into heaven. And sitteth on the right hand of God the Father Almighty; from thence He shall come

to judge the quick and the dead. I believe in the Holy Ghost, the holy Catholic Church; the Communion of saints; the forgiveness of sins; the resurrection of the body; and the life everlasting.

The Nicene Creed
I believe in one God, the Father almighty, maker of heaven and earth, and of all things visible and invisible. And in one Lord Jesus Christ, the only-begotten Son of God. Born of the Father before all ages. God of God, light of Light, true God of the True God. Begotten not made; being of one substance with the Father; by whom all things were made. Who for us men, and for our salvation, came down from heaven. And was incarnate by the Holy Ghost of the Virgin Mary and was made man. He was crucified also for us, suffered under Pontius Pilate, and was buried. And the third day He rose again according to the Scriptures. And ascended into heaven. He sitteth at the right hand of the Father. And He shall come again with glory to judge both the living and the dead; of whose kingdom there shall be no end. And I believe in the Holy Ghost, the Lord and giver of life; Who proceedeth from the Father (and the Son); Who together with the Father and the Son is adored and glorified; Who spake by the Prophets. And in one, holy, catholic and apostolic Church. I confess one baptism for the remission of sins. And I look for the resurrection of the dead. And the life of the world to come.*

At least three fundamental beliefs can be distinguished in these creeds. First, Christians affirm the existence of one God in the form of Three Persons, or Trinity: the Father, Son, and Holy Spirit (Holy Ghost). This concept of Unity in Trinity, or Trinity in Unity, is considered to lie beyond the limits of human comprehension and therefore to be a divine mystery. The idea is not entirely foreign to human experience, however; water, for instance, retains its chemical identity regardless of whether it takes the form of ice, liquid, or steam. To a Christian, the idea of the Trinity is *not* analogous to three roles played by a single person (e.g., a man who simultaneously assumes the roles of son, husband, and father); rather, it signifies three distinct beings that are yet fully one God.

The second basic Christian doctrine is that of the Incarnation: the belief that in Jesus, God assumed a human body. To Christians Jesus was not merely a prophet or teacher, but "the only-begotten Son of God" who was at the same time genuinely human and genuinely divine. Thus, Jesus is identified with God as well as with humanity— he is God-man, both truly God and truly human simultaneously. Further, Christianity claims that even though Jesus was put to death,

---

*From George Brantl, ed., *Catholicism* (New York: Washington Square Press, Inc., 1967) pp. 175–176.

he was resurrected three days later, ascended into heaven, and is presently with God the Father, awaiting the time of his return to judge every person, dead or alive, and to establish his eternal kingdom.

Finally, Christianity firmly holds to the doctrine of reconciliation, or Atonement. In the view of Christians, Adam, the father of humankind, estranged humanity from God by his disobedience, as a consequence of which all humans are sinners. But if Adam represents humankind, so does Jesus, whose death is viewed as a self-sacrifice that atoned for the original sin of Adam. Jesus' resurrection is interpreted as proof of this universal Atonement and a triumph over death. All those who believe in Jesus thus are no longer alienated from God, but are his children.

Christian Sacraments

Christians also express themselves in several religious acts considered as sacraments. A *sacrament* is an outward sign, or the performance of a rite, through which divine grace is sought and conferred. Both Roman Catholics and Eastern Orthodox adherents regard seven rites as sacraments: Baptism, Confirmation/Chrismation, Penance/Confession, Eucharist/Holy Communion, Matrimony, Holy Orders (ordination), and Holy Unction/*Euchelaion* (last rites). Many Protestant groups consider only two of these to be sacraments: Baptism and Holy Communion. A brief description of these seven sacraments will serve to indicate their correspondence to the different stages of life.

Baptism is recognized as the first stage of initiation into the Christian faith. Most Christian churches baptize the candidate in infancy, although a few Protestant subgroups wait until adolescence or adulthood. The next stage comes with the sacrament of Confirmation or Chrismation, performed by Eastern Orthodox churches immediately after the infant's baptism but by Roman Catholics on children between the ages of seven and fourteen. The third sacrament is the Confession of sins followed by the granting of absolution, or formal forgiveness. The fourth sacrament to be conferred is the Eucharist, or Holy Communion, in which the believer partakes of bread and wine, representing, respectively, the body and blood of Jesus. Matrimony, the fifth sacrament, differs in form from one church to another, according to local customs; in all cases, however, its purpose is to confer divine sanctification upon the union of male and female. Holy Orders, the sixth sacrament, is the rite in which clergy are ordained. The seventh sacrament, known as Holy Unction or *Euchelaion*, is administered to Roman Catholics whose death seems imminent. Among Eastern Orthodox, *Euchelaion* (the offering of prayer and anointing with oil) is administered as often as may be necessary to comfort and heal the sick.

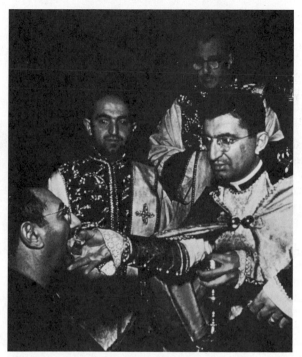

The sacrament of the Holy Eucharist (Holy Communion) as observed by the Armenian Orthodox churches.   Courtesy of the Armenian Church Diocese of North America.

Protestants differ among themselves on questions of theology and church policy, but most insist that there are only two sacraments, Baptism and Communion, because in their view Christ instituted only these two sacraments. Moreover, Protestants not only reject the doctrinal authority of the Roman Catholic and Eastern Orthodox churches, but they also maintain that the Bible is the only source of authority and that the Holy Spirit, rather than the Roman Catholic or Eastern Orthodox church, illuminates the minds of individuals who read and study the Bible.

The distinctions among Eastern Orthodox, Roman Catholic, and Protestant churches are very complex. Suffice it to say that many Protestants repudiate the following fundamental elements upheld by both Eastern Orthodox and Roman Catholics: apostolic succession (the line of succession from Jesus, through the apostles, to the popes and patriarchs), hierarchical structure, an *episcopate* (office of bishop), a system of priesthood, prayers offered to saints, intercession for the departed, and various other minor issues. By the same token, Eastern Orthodox groups reject the supremacy of the pope and papal infallibility (the doctrine that formal papal decrees on matters of faith must be accepted as true). Instead, Eastern Orthodox churches assert the supremacy of the College of Bishops among their own ranks, stressing the infallibility of the church as a whole.

Christian Observances

Thus, all three branches of Christianity—Eastern Orthodox, Roman Catholic, and Protestant—have developed a variety of teachings and practices based upon the same fundamental Christian principles. The differences between the groups are even more pronounced in the observances of Christian festivals, which are divided into two distinct series. One comprises the veneration of saints. The other is associated with the *liturgical* year (the annual calendar of public prayer and worship) and commemorates the sacred events of the Christian religion—in particular, the cycle of events connected with the life of Jesus Christ. A brief comment on these two series will indicate the sharp difference in practices among Eastern Orthodox, Roman Catholic, and Protestant churches.

Veneration of Saints

Eastern Orthodox, Roman Catholic, and Anglican churches observe the feasts of saints concurrently with the liturgical festivals. The feasts celebrated include those of Mary, the mother of Jesus (the Blessed Virgin Mary)[19]; Joseph, the husband of Mary; the archangels; and the apostles. In addition, there are the feasts of numerous "patron saints," who intercede with God on behalf of those who pray to them for help. The lists of saints and martyrs recognized by Eastern Orthodox, Roman Catholic, and Anglican churches differ quite widely. The importance of the saints and martyrs in popular devotion is incalculable, however.

Many Protestant churches renounce on theological grounds any sort of veneration of saints. Instead, they observe Reformation Sunday (the Sunday nearest to October 31), representing the day when Martin Luther nailed his ninety-five statements to the door of the church.

Liturgical Calendar

The liturgical festivals gravitate around two great events: Christmas and Easter. Christmas is a fixed festival commemorating the birth of Jesus Christ and is celebrated by most Christians annually on December 25. Preceding Christmas is Advent, a solemn period of expectation and preparation. Advent marks the beginning of the ecclesiastical year

A Russian Orthodox wedding in Moscow, Russia. Jerry Cooke/Photo Researchers, Inc.

and starts four Sundays before Christmas. Following Christmas is the celebration of the Epiphany (manifestation of Jesus Christ), observed on January 6. Two incidents are commemorated in order to recall this manifestation: the baptism of Jesus and the visit of the Wise Men (Magi) to Bethlehem.

Not all Christians mark all these days. Eastern Orthodox churches, for example, do not celebrate Christmas on December 25; rather, they celebrate the Epiphany, on January 6. Also, Roman Catholics, Anglicans, and Protestant groups differ as to the length of Advent (from twenty-two to twenty-eight days). Roman Catholics, Eastern Orthodox, and Anglicans, but not Protestants, observe the Epiphany of January 6. Roman Catholics, however, disassociate the incident of the baptism of Jesus from the visit of the Wise Men. They observe the former on January 13.

Differences exist also in the observances associated with the Easter cycle of events. The date of Easter is movable and is calculated on the basis of both the Gregorian calendar and the Julian calendar. Roman Catholics, Anglicans, and Protestants follow the Gregorian calendar. Thus, Easter is observed on the first Sunday after the first full moon following the vernal equinox (March 21), usually rotating between March and April. Eastern Orthodox churches follow the Julian calendar and consequently celebrate Easter on a different date, usually several weeks after the Gregorian date.

Again, variations exist in the observances that precede Easter. Roman Catholic, Eastern Orthodox, and Anglican churches observe the solemn period of fasting and prayer known as Lent, including Holy Week, although the method and duration of observance differ among them. In recent years some Protestant groups have introduced the observance of Lent in their churches. As to the two feasts that follow Easter, Ascension Day and Pentecost Sunday, all Christian churches except the Unitarians and a few Protestant groups observe them, although their role and significance vary from church to church.

Notes

1. The Essene-Christian and Essene-Jesus relationships have long fascinated New Testament scholars, several of whom have maintained that the Essenes trained or controlled Jesus and (with or without the cooperation of the Romans) revived him after his ordeal, thus creating the myth that Jesus had risen from the dead. Other critics have modified this theory in various ways. According to M. A. Larson, for example:

   Jesus . . . had for some years been a member of the Essene community, but had developed serious doubts concerning the validity of its Judaic discipline, and, even more significantly, had become convinced that He, instead of the long overdue Teacher, was the true incarnate Messiah in his human manifestation. . . . We believe that He consciously re-created the career of the Teacher of Righteousness and pursued by design a course of action which would lead inevitably to His sacrificial and spectacular death as an atonement for the sins of mankind, persuaded that in this way but in no other could He establish the kingdom of heaven.

   The Religion of the Occident (Patterson, N.J.: Littlefield, Adams, 1961), pp. 291–292.

2. Any study on the nature of Christianity must take into account the striking resemblances or parallels in the Synoptic Gospels (those of Matthew, Mark, and Luke). See, for instance, R. Bultmann, *The History of the Synoptic Tradition* (New York: Harper & Row, 1963); W. R. Farmer, *The Synoptic Problem* (New York: Macmillan, 1964); and F. C. Grant, *The Gospels: Their Origin and Growth* (New York: Harper & Row, 1957).

3. One of the most recent studies on the literary formation of the Gospels is K. Koch, *The Growth of the Biblical Tradition* (New York: Scribner's, 1969).

4. For a definition of the terms applied by Paul, see G. Kittel, *Theological*

Dictionary of the New Testament (Grand Rapids, Mich.: Eerdmans, 1964).

5. For a fundamental study on the heritage of early Christianity, see J. B. Tyson, *A Study of Early Christianity* (New York: Macmillan, 1973), pp. 31–121; and A. D. Nock, *Early Gentile Christianity and Its Hellenistic Background* (New York: Harper & Row, 1964).

6. Cited in H. Bettenson, ed., *Documents of the Christian Church*, 2nd ed. (London: Oxford University Press, 1963), p. 16.

7. Theodosian Code XVI.10.25 (435), in *The Theodosian Code and Novels and Sirmondian Constitutions* (Princeton: Princeton University Press, 1952), p. 476.

8. According to Bishop Titus, in his *Treatise Against the Manichaeans*.

9. Cited in C. H. Robinson, *The Conversion of Europe* (London: Longmans, Green, 1917), p. 547.

10. For an annotated bibliography on the religions of Mexico and of Central and South America, see J. A. Vázquez in C. J. Adams, *A Reader's Guide to the Great Religions*, 2nd ed. (New York: Free Press, 1977), pp. 78–89.

11. The encounter of East-West religious faiths has produced a serious question among Christians: What ought to be the attitude of the Christian (and hence, churches) toward other faiths, including polytheistic ones? The discussion or debate has produced a large library of lively literature. Among others, see A. J. Toynbee, *Christianity Among the Religions of the World* (New York: Scribner's, 1957); W. E. Hocking, *The Coming World Civilization* (New York: Harper & Row, 1956); O. C. Thomas, *Attitudes Toward Other Religions: Some Christian Interpretation* (London: SCM Press, 1969); H. Kraemer, *The Christian Message in a non-Christian World*, 3rd ed. (Grand Rapids, Mich.: Eerdmans, 1963); P. Tillich, *Christianity and the Encounter of World Religions* (New York: Columbia University Press, 1964); H. R. Schlette, *Towards a Theology of Religions* (London: Herder & Herder, 1966); R. E. Whitson, *The Coming Convergence of World Religions* (London: Newman, 1971); F. Schuon, *The Transcendent Unity of Religions* (New York: Harper & Row, 1975); J. B. Cobb, *Christ in a Pluralistic Age* (Philadelphia: Westminster Press, 1975); and W. C. Smith, *Towards a World Theology (New York: Macmillan, 1981)*.

12. J. N. D. Anderson, *The World's Religion*, 3rd ed. (Grand Rapids, Mich.: Eerdmans, 1968), p. 192.

13. E. O. James, *Christianity and Other Religions* (London: Hodder & Stoughton, 1968), p. 173.

14. A. J. Toynbee, *Christianity Among the Religions of the World* (New York: Scribner's, 1957), pp. 99–100.

15. S. Radhakrishnan, *Religion in a Changing World* (London: Allen & Unwin, 1967), p. 129.

16. A. C. Bouquet, *The Christian Faith and Non-Christian Religions* (New York: Pelican Books, 1958), p. 365.

17. W. M. Abbott and J. Gallagher, eds., *The Documents of Vatican II* (New York: America Press/Guild Press, 1966), pp. 662–63. Contrast this statement with the statement issued by Theodosius (see p. 386). The Roman Catholic church has certainly come a long way in this regard.

18. *Guidelines on Dialogue with People of Living Faiths and Ideologies* (Geneva: World Council of Churches, 1979), p. 11.

19. For the Catholic position on the Virgin Mary, see M. P. Carroll, *The Cult of the Virgin Mary* (Princeton, N.J.: Princeton University Press, 1986). For the Eastern Orthodox position, see E. L. Mascall, ed., *The Mother of God: A Symposium* (Westminster, Eng.: Dacre Press, 1959).

14

Islam

Misrepresentations of Islam

Few religions, if any, have been so badly represented and widely misunderstood by Westerners as Islam, which was established in Arabia in the seventh century as a result of the preaching and teaching of the Prophet Muhammad. In spite of the geographic proximity of the Islamic world to Western cultures, and the many ways in which Islam resembles Christianity and Judaism, misunderstandings have persisted on several levels.

To begin with, many Western scholars, as well as the public at large, still use inaccurate terminology in referring to the religion as Muhammadanism and the followers of Islam as Muhammadans. Those terms imply a generic relationship with Muhammad—a view refuted by Muslims. The correct name for the religion is Islam, and the proper term for identifying its adherents is Muslims.[1] The word *Islam* has two meanings: "submission" and "peace"—that is, submission to the will and guidance of God and living in peace with one's self and with one's surroundings. The essence of Islam, therefore, lies in submission to God, which results in peace of mind and soul.

Further, Western historians, until very recently, have portrayed a distorted image of Muhammad, the historic founder of Islam. Although recent biographies are less polemic and more objective, accounts written in the past tended to characterize Muhammad as a cruel, shrewd, and lustful imposter who propagated a faith in which the chief dramatic feature was that males were permitted to marry several wives (polygamy). Muslims, naturally, repudiate such misconceptions. To them, Muhammad is *the* Prophet (or Messenger) of God and the highest exemplar of humanity; and polygamy is the exception rather than the rule among adherents of Islam, although limited polygamy (up to four wives) is permitted, provided that all wives are treated equally.

Third, many Westerners, even when they seem to acknowledge the political importance of Muslim nations, fail to understand the religious significance of Islam.[2] Many Jews and Christians regard Islam as a corruption of their respective religious traditions, whereas Muslims consider Islam to be a purification and fulfillment of Judaism and Christianity.

Fourth, the common impression in the West is that Islam is entirely an Arab religion, when in fact Islam is one of the world's most widely diffused religions. More than half of the total world Muslim population is found in the East: China, southeastern Asia, and the Indian peninsula, including Burma and Sri Lanka. The remaining Muslims are dispersed across eastern Europe, including Turkey, the Balkan nations, Russia, the Middle East (including the Arab world), and Africa. Small groups are also found in various Western countries.

Finally, Westerners persist in drawing a distinction between religion and politics (church and state) to explain the reactions, at times quite violent, of Muslims against Western political, social, and intellectual policies. What Westerners fail to understand is that the Islamic community is at once a political and religious community. From its very beginnings, Islam has viewed religion and politics (church and state) as necessarily and rightfully inseparable. To Muslims, then, the notion of religion as separable from the totality of the human context is unimaginable, even detestable. All of life is sacred and must conform to the larger whole—the identity of the Islamic faith. All who belong to this great Islamic faith share a sense of identity, a sense of global community. To believe otherwise would be to deny the validity of one of the core concepts of Islam—that of the *umma,* or community of the faithful governed by the dictates of *shari'ah* (divine law). Indeed, the very concept of a "religion" in the sense of a religious organization separate from other political and social structures is completely foreign to Islam.

Historical Background

For thousands of years, Arab nomads lived in settlements in and around the Arabian peninsula. Well before the birth of Christ, they had organized a lucrative caravan trade that supplied the incense of Arabia and the spices of India to the Mediterranean world. Above all else, the highest loyalty of an Arab was to the tribe or clan, which claimed descent from a common ancestor.

Among the sedentary people who inhabited the city of Mecca, the Arab tribe of the Qurayish enjoyed a special favored position in the early centuries of the Common Era. They controlled the caravan trade route and so were relatively prosperous, and they were respected for their managerial abilities and religious affiliations. Arab tribes came to Mecca not only to trade but to worship in its temple, called *Ka'ba*, where the Qurayish worshiped their venerated deity *Allah* (al-Ilah), as well as other deities.

In spite of Mecca's remote location and favored status, it was not immune from attack by foreign powers and rival factions. Tradition states that in the year in which Muhammad was born (probably 570 CE), the Christian ruler of Abyssinia led a punitive force mounted on elephants against Mecca in order to destroy the temple, only to be forced to retreat after an outbreak of smallpox among his troops. This incident is commemorated as "the year of the elephant."

Mecca was also the scene of incessant quarreling among Qurayish chiefs in the interests of religion. Senseless bloodshed and intertribal anarchy plagued the city sporadically. Open conflict was common, especially during the annual period of pilgrimage. Throughout Arabia, drinking, gambling, and dancing were customary features of most religious convocations and festivals. Polytheism, animism, and the practice of burying unwanted female infants alive were commonplace.

Muhammad the Prophet

The origin of Islam lies either at the beginning of time, at creation, or in the sixth century CE in Arabia, depending upon the point of view one wishes to take. From the orthodox Muslim perspective, the story of Islam starts not with Muhammad, but shares a common tradition with Judaism and a common Biblical origin when God (in Arabic, Allah) created the world and the first man, Adam. The descendants of Adam are traced to Noah, who had a son named Shem. This is where the word *Semite*—descendants of Shem—comes from, and like the Jews, Arabs regard themselves as a Semitic people. Shem's descendants are then traced to Abraham and to his wives Sarah and Hagar. At this point, two familiar stories about Abraham provide the cornerstones of the Islamic religion. The first, Abraham's attempted sacrifice of his son Isaac, demonstrates the submission of Abraham in the supreme test: hence the word "Islam." The second, concerning Ishmael's banishment, gave rise to the belief that Ishmael (the son of Abraham and Hagar) went to Mecca and that eventually from his descendants the prophet Muhammad emerged in the sixth century CE.

Little is known of the early life of Muhammad. Tradition states that he was born in the city of Mecca around 570, to parents who belonged to the Qurayish clan. His father, Abdullah ibn Muttalib, died before his birth and his mother, Aminah bint Wahb, died when he was six, leaving him an orphan. Muhammad then went to live with his grandfather, who was the custodian of the *Ka'ba*. But this arrangement lasted for only two years, until the death of the grandfather. Muhammad was then left in the care of his paternal uncle Abu Talib.

As a child, Muhammad traveled by caravan with his uncle to Syria, where a Christian monk one day drew the uncle's attention to the fact that the child bore the marks of prophethood. Like all other boys of his day, Muhammad also spent time as a shepherd, leading his flock to the caves and rocks near his home.

Later, as a young man, Muhammad joined the merchant caravans, and at the age of twenty-five entered the service of a wealthy widow named Khadijah. Soon, his relationship with her deepened into love, and although she was fifteen years older, he married her.

Divine Call and Revelation

According to tradition, Muhammad experienced his first unexpected divine communication with the angel Gabriel at the age of forty. Like Abraham, Moses, Samuel, and Jesus, Muhammad heard a divine voice, which said, "Recite!" Overwhelmed by this voice and the appearance of the archangel Gabriel, Muhammad fell prostrate to the ground. The voice repeated, "Recite!" "What shall I recite?" asked Muhammad in terror. And the answer came:

> Recite—in the name of thy Lord who created!
> Created man from clots of blood!
> Recite—for thy Lord is most beneficent,
> who has taught the use of the pen;
> has taught man that which he knew not! (Qur'an 96:1–4)*

---

*Throughout this chapter, numbers in parentheses are chapter and verse citations of the *Qur'an*, the Islamic scripture, unless otherwise stated.

Terrified by the overwhelming divine presence, Muhammad rushed home and told Khadijah that he had either become "possessed" (mad), or a prophet. On hearing the full story, his wife encouraged him: "Rejoice and be of good cheer, you will be the Prophet of this people!" Such experiences recurred throughout his life, giving him spiritual inspiration and guidance.

Some modern scholars have sought to explain these divine experiences as epileptic seizures, because they involved intense physical trembling, sweating, and auditory hallucinations. Other critics, however, have maintained that Muhammad's behavior differed very little from that of other prophets. Muhammad himself was sincerely convinced that he was *rasulullah*—the messenger or prophet of God (Qur'an 33.40).

Muhammad, it is further stated, was ridiculed and accused of being a sorcerer. The greatest opposition came from the leaders of the Qurayish tribe, who saw his teachings as a threat to Meccan social and economic life. Muhammad's preaching on social justice was essentially directed against the privileged, and they resented it. Consequently, the leaders of the Qurayish decided that each group within the tribe must take the necessary steps to suppress this "heretical" faith.

Muhammad was fairly safe so long as he lived under the protection of his uncle, who, although he did not accept Muhammad's religion, used all his prestige and power within the community to save his nephew's life. But in 620 both Muhammad's wife, Khadijah, and his uncle, Abu Talib, died. These deaths stripped Muhammad of his comparative immunity from local animosity and presaged his forced departure from Mecca.

Establishment of Islamic Community

The opportunity to leave Mecca arrived when a delegation from Yathrib (later renamed Medina* in honor of Muhammad) invited Muhammad to mediate their tribal feuds in return for protection of himself and his followers. After completing preliminary negotiations, Muhammad and his followers arrived secretly at Medina on September 24, 622. This migration is known in Arabic as *Hijrah* (Latin, *hegira*, for "flight"), and the year during which it occurred marks the beginning of all Muslim calendars.

Muhammad soon settled the tribal feuds that he had been invited to mediate and won over to his faith the inhabitants of Medina. He devoted his attention not only to social and political issues, but also to

*Presumably short for *Medinat al-nabi*, meaning "the city of the Prophet."

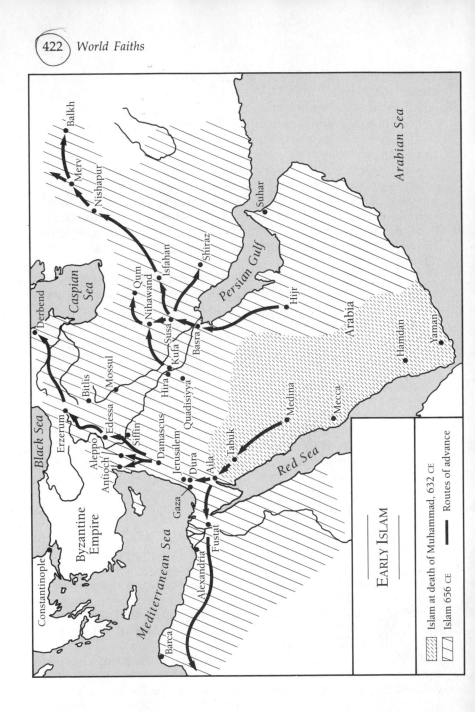

EARLY ISLAM

Islam at death of Muhammad, 632 CE

Islam 656 CE

— Routes of advance

moral and educational concerns, initiating ordinances governing marriage, divorce, fasting, almsgiving, and the treatment of slaves, prisoners of war, and enemies. He also married a number of women, possibly in order to cement political alliances. Under his direction civil and religious authority was fused, and within ten years he had succeeded in organizing his society into a Muslim state.

During this period Muhammad's religious interests were governed by his relationship with neighboring Jewish and Christian communities. He had hoped that they would convert to his faith, especially since he borrowed freely from both religious traditions.[3] Instead, however, he embroiled himself in so many disputes with the Jews and Christians that he was led to conclude that they had fallen away from the true faith and falsified the scriptures.

Later, he persuaded his followers to attack several wealthy Jewish and Christian communities in the neighborhood of Medina. Some Jews and Christians abandoned their possessions and fled for their lives. Others submitted to conditional treaties: freedom of worship in return for a substantial tribute. Still others surrendered their religion and submitted to his political and religious authority.

The moral effect of victory over local Jewish and Christian communities led Muhammad to declare war against unbelievers—even his own countrymen—and to divide their spoils among his followers. He recruited volunteers who were prepared to raid the caravans of rival and unassimilated traders.

Subsequent and repeated attacks on unbelieving merchants yielded successes that were interpreted as divine victories. Further, Muhammad was convinced that if his religious mission was to succeed, it was necessary to create an ordered community—and eventually a state. In the absence of any stable "national" institution, the powerful administration and firm social structure of Muhammad's community made him a "super chieftain." Gradually, various tribes sent delegations to offer their allegiance and submission to Muhammad and his new monotheistic faith. In testimony to their sincerity, they often sealed their allegiance by giving their women in marriage to Muhammad.

Finally, the time came to strike at the hostile Meccans by intercepting and raiding their caravans. The first raid was spectacularly successful, both militarily and economically. A second attempt, however, ended in failure, with Muhammad being slightly wounded. In retaliation, the Meccans prepared for a grand assault. With some ten thousand men they advanced on Medina, but Muhammad had ordered several trenches dug around the town, and the battle (known as the Battle of the Trench) ended with the retreat of the Meccans. After a skillful exercise of diplomacy and military pressure, Muhammad and ten thousand of his followers marched into Mecca in January 630. His former fellow townsmen, who had once conspired against him, put up no resistance.

One of Muhammad's first acts was to go to the holy temple, the Ka'ba, and reverently *circumambulate*, or walk around it, seven times. Next, he ordered the destruction of all the idols within the temple, including the paintings of Abraham and the angels. Then he walked over to the nearby *Zamzam* well, which tradition associates with the biblical story of Hagar and her son Ishmael, and sanctioned its use. And finally, he restored the boundary pillars that defined the sacred territory of Mecca. Henceforth, all followers of his faith, called Muslims (Arabic for "those who have submitted"), would be free to travel securely on a pilgrimage to Mecca.

For the next two years, Muhammad's power came to be acknowledged by all in Arabia. He unified the Arab tribes under a *theocracy*, governed by the will of God. Former tribal loyalties were now transferred to the *umma*. This religious commitment was to unite them more closely than tribal ties of blood ever had.

Tradition states that in his last sermon, Muhammad proclaimed this fundamental shift in age-old loyalties in the following words: "O believers, listen to my words and take them to heart. Know that every Muslim is a brother unto every other Muslim; for you are now one brotherhood" (Qur'an 49.10). Muhammad died suddenly in 632, following a few days' illness.

Islamic Empires

Establishment of the Caliphate

Muhammad's death left the Muslim community with a leadership crisis. What happened subsequently has been vigorously disputed by his followers. According to the Sunni group (the "traditionalists," who make up the majority of Muslims), Muhammad left no successor. According to the Shi'ites (the "partisans"), Muhammad designated his cousin 'Ali (who was also his son-in-law) as his successor. The Prophet's preference may have been general knowledge, but two of his fathers-in-law met with the leaders of Medina to select a single leader. The choice fell on the aging Abu Bakr. 'Ali and his kinsmen agreed for the sake of unity, but they were deeply offended. Abu Bakr (ruled 632–634) was now the *caliph* (from Arabic *Khalifah*, meaning "successor"), who was to assume only the administrative responsibilities, not the office of prophethood.

This decision immediately provoked divisions among various Arab groups. Some decided to cut their ties with Medina and the newly elected caliph. Others began to follow leaders who claimed to have prophetic powers like Muhammad's. Abu Bakr dealt swiftly and firmly with the disaffected, then announced a program of expansion, mainly into Syria, which was at that time under Byzantine control. His age and health, however, did not allow him to undertake major military expeditions. Abu Bakr's plans for conquest were to be carried out by 'Umar, who was appointed caliph by Abu Bakr before the latter's death in 634.

Conquest and Settlement

'Umar and Successors. The amazingly rapid expansion of Islam began under the skillful leadership of 'Umar (ruled 634–644). His military campaigns were waged on two fronts: against the Byzantine Empire to the north and west and the Persian Empire to the east. From the former, he conquered Syria in 636, Palestine in 638, and Egypt in 642. For Christianity, this meant that three of the four Patriarchates (Jerusalem, Antioch, and Alexandria) were now under the jurisdiction of Muslim overlords. To the east, 'Umar's forces overran Iraq and the Iranian plateau in 642. In all the conquered lands, the indigenous inhabitants were required to live in peace, accept 'Umar's protection, and pay taxes, but they were allowed to keep their own religions and customs. Muslim Arabs were accommodated in newly constructed towns that were supported by taxes paid by the conquered. Thus, by conquest and settlement, 'Umar laid the foundation of an empire that would incorporate both Arab culture and Islamic features.

'Umar's plans were interrupted when he was stabbed to death by an Iranian slave. The leading companions of the Prophet then met to elect a new caliph. Despite 'Ali's pleas and claims, they selected 'Uthman, another son-in-law of Muhammad, and a prominent member of the Umayyad family in Mecca. 'Uthman (ruled 644–656) immediately strengthened the control of the Muslim Empire by placing members of his clan in key positions. This policy antagonized many devout Arab Muslims, including 'Ali, who on several occasions opposed 'Uthman's policies.

After 'Uthman was assassinated in 656 by one of his opponents, the deeply shocked people of Medina hailed 'Ali as caliph (ruled 656–661). But Meccans and a number of other leading Muslims rejected 'Ali, accusing him of collusion in the assassination plot. The fragile unity of the Muslim community finally fractured on this issue of succession, never to be reestablished. 'Ali and his partisans were challenged by Mu'awiyah I, the Muslim governor of Syria, who had the support of the Meccans and other leading tribesmen. In the ensuing flux of changing loyalties a third group emerged, called the Khariji ("seceders"), who opposed both 'Ali and Mu'awiyah. One of the Khariji assassinated 'Ali in 661, and Mu'awiyah was installed as caliph.

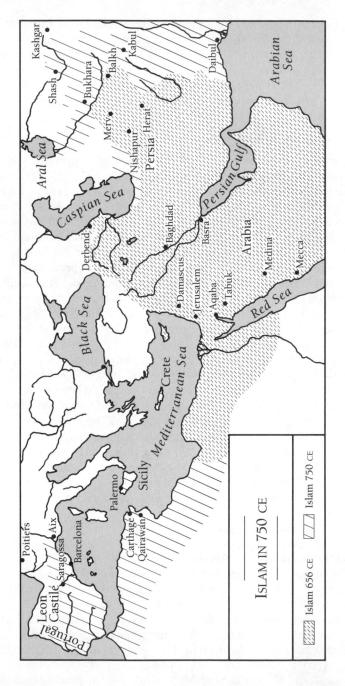

ISLAM IN 750 CE

Islam 656 CE

Islam 750 CE

Umayyad Dynasty (661–750). Mu'awiyah (ruled 661–680) was a superb statesman who moved the caliphate to Damascus, where he established the Umayyad dynasty. Under Mu'awiyah's leadership, Islamic expansion was resumed, internal feuds and revolts were stamped out, administration was centralized, and an attempt was made to systematize the legal and ethical teachings of Muhammad that affected Islamic society at large. Thus, a distinctive Islamic civilization emerged under the Umayyad caliphate.

The momentum of Islamic conquest and settlement carried the Umayyads eastward to India as far as the borders of China, and westward to the Atlantic Ocean, through Libya, Tunisia, Algeria, Morocco, and across the Strait of Gibraltar into Spain, Portugal, and France. Only in 733, a century after the Prophet's death, was the Muslim advance westward halted by the Franks, at the decisive battle of Tours.

The Dome of the Rock (Mosque of Omar), built in 690 CE *over the traditional site of Solomon's Temple, in Jerusalem, Israel. One of the most beautiful examples of Islamic architecture in the world, the mosque is covered with blue, green, and white tile mosaics that offer quotes from the Qur'an in praise of Muhammad, and is topped by a dome of gold leaf.* UPI/Bettmann.

'Abbasid Dynasty (750–1258). The Umayyad dynasty was overthrown seventeen years after the battle of Tours by the 'Abbasid dynasty. Because the new dynasty represented the interests of the Islamicized Iraqi aristocracy, the caliphate was moved from Syria to Baghdad. Six years later, a rival caliphate was established by the Umayyads in Cordova, Spain. Under this caliphate (756–1236) and its successor, the Moorish caliphate at Granada, the Muslims of Spain built a rich and influential culture that lasted until 1492.

Although the 'Abbasid dynasty enjoyed one of the longest reigns of any in Islam, its influence gradually waned after the ninth century, as rival caliphs and independent rulers established themselves in Tunisia, Egypt, Syria, and Iran. The eighth to ninth centuries, especially the reign of Harun al-Rashid (786–809), marked the pinnacle of Islamic wealth and culture. Medicine, science, mathematics, fine arts, and philosophy flourished throughout the Muslim Empire.

By the end of the ninth century, Turkish officers had made themselves masters of the 'Abbasid caliphs, dethroning them at will, appropriating the imperial revenues, and plundering the royal palaces. Local governors asserted authority over the provinces they ruled, and social and religious revolts became endemic in the empire.

Seljuk Turkish marauders swept over Syria and Palestine, capturing Jerusalem in 1070. Tales of horror and desecration perpetrated by Turks were spread by Western pilgrims to the courts of the Frankish kingdoms. The result was the launching of the Crusades. At first, common hatred of the Turks united western and eastern Christians in the capture of Jerusalem in 1099; the final outcome, however, was not only unsuccessful but disastrous for the Christians. In 1187 the Muslims recaptured Jerusalem, and over the next hundred years they reconquered the entire area.

Meanwhile, great movements of tribal peoples after the eleventh century were resulting in political and social dislocations throughout the Muslim Empire. First, the Ghaznavids, who originated in Afghanistan, and then the Seljuk Turks, from central Asia, raided and invaded the territories of Iran and Iraq. The Mongols, another Asiatic group, sacked Baghdad in 1258 and overthrew the 'Abbasid dynasty. Four decades later they embraced Islam.

Mongol Empire (c. 1200–1368)

Originally Mongols consisted of loosely organized nomadic tribes in Mongolia, Manchuria, and Siberia. Sometime around 1200, a chieftain later known as Genghis Khan (his real name was Temjun) unified and organized the scattered Mongol tribes of Mongolia, Manchuria, and

Siberia into a superior fighting force. As the undisputed master of Mongolia, he and his successors set out on a spectacular career of world conquest.

The Mongols are popularly viewed as the most savage conquerors of history. They spread terror and destruction everywhere, and whenever they met resistance, they systematically slaughtered the local population. But their vast empire also contributed to increased contacts between peoples. At its greatest extent, during the reign of Kublai Khan (1279–1294), one of the grandsons of Genghis Khan, the Mongol Empire extended from the Pacific Ocean westward to the Danube River—the largest area ever controlled by one state in world history.

In 1256, Hulagu Khan, brother of Kublai Khan, marched with his Mongol army into Iran, destroying several cities. Two years later he entered Iraq and devastated Baghdad, putting the Caliph al-Musta'ism to death and sparing only some Shi'ites and Christians. Less than forty years later, his descendants, under the leadership of Ghazan Khan (1295–1304) embraced Islam and became patrons of Muslim culture and civilization. Yet it was not the Mongols of Iraq who restored Islam's military glory. That task was left to the Ottoman Turks, who became the last Islamic dynasty to hold on to the caliphate.

Ottoman Empire (c. 1300–1922)

The empire of the Ottoman Turks was founded in present-day Turkey by Osman (Arabic, 'Uthman) in 1300 and spanned a period of more than six centuries, ending only in 1922. Constantly varying in extent, it included in different epochs Turkey, Syria, Palestine, Jordan, Egypt, Iraq, parts of Arabia and North Africa, Cyprus, Crete, Greece, the Balkan states, and parts of Hungary, Austria, and southern Russia.

In their initial stages of expansion, the Ottomans were leaders of the Turkish *gazis*—warriors for the faith of Islam. Osman and his immediate successors concentrated their attacks on Byzantine territories (modern Turkey), southern and central Europe, and southwestern Asia. The Ottomans' reputation as champions of militant Islam was cemented by Sultan Mehmet II's capture in 1453 of Constantinople (modern Istanbul), the last remnant of the once mighty Christian Byzantine Empire.

Sultan Mehmet accorded the patriarch of the Greek Orthodox church certain prerogatives, safeguarding his security, recognizing his jurisdiction over his prelates, and granting him some administrative authority. Nevertheless, all Christians remained outside the *umma*. In the world of Islam, Christians living within an Islamic sphere of influence belonged to the *dhimmi*—people held under or protected by the dictates of the conscience of Islam. They could retain their own religious and social customs but were subject to certain restrictions or bans (e.g., they were forbidden to convert Muslims to Christianity, to marry Muslim women, or to hold high governmental office) and were required to pay a special tribute. In sum, the *dhimmi* represented an alien and unassimilable element in the body politic of the *umma*.

Although conquered Christians were treated as a separate group within the Ottoman Empire, under the leadership of their own patriarchs and bishops, Muslim breakaway groups or revolutionary movements met with severe and summary punishment. The Ottoman Sultan Selim I (ruled 1512–1520), for instance, massacred most of the Shi'ite Muslims of Turkey and forced the survivors underground.

Selim's successor, Suleiman the Magnificent (1520–1566), spearheaded a renewed Islamic advance into Europe, invading Serbia, Hungary, and Austria. He incited the newly converted Protestant princes of Germany against the pope and the Holy Roman emperor, and he made Ottoman Hungary a stronghold for Protestant groups, particularly Calvinists. For almost two centuries, support of Protestantism remained a basic Ottoman policy.

Mughal Empire (1526–1857)

Meanwhile, Islam in India was deeply affected by the Mughals. The term *Mughal* is the Persian version of the Indian word *Mogul*, meaning Mongol. In 1526, Babar, a descendant of the great Mongol conquerors Timur (or Tamerlane) and Genghis Khan, established the Islamic Mughal Empire in India. His grandson, Akbar the Great (1542–1605) conquered northern India and Afghanistan and extended his rule as far north as Hyderabad, West Pakistan. In time, great numbers of Hindus, especially from the lower classes, converted to Islam.

Mughal civilization in India fused indigenous Indian traditions with Mongolian, Iranian, and Arab elements. Under the early Mughal emperors, India flourished, but then trouble developed during the reign of Emperor Aurangzeb (1658–1707), a harsh and narrow-minded ruler who tried to force Hindus and other Indians to convert to Islam. He also imposed a special tax on Hindus and destroyed many of their temples. Large numbers of Hindus were alienated by Aurangzeb's policies, and many rebelled. His long and disastrous wars sapped the economy and morale of both the army and the ruling class. Finally, he was defeated by guerrilla tactics employed by Hindus from southern India. His disastrous defeat left to his descendants a troubled inheritance.

The Daratagaha Mosque in Colombo, Sri Lanka. Mosques can be erected on large grounds or squeezed, as here, between commercial buildings. In the background is the Town Hall.　Courtesy of British Airways (BOAC).

Persecution and Decline

Throughout the Islamic world, conquered "pagan" peoples had to choose between conversion to Islam, or death by the sword. Jews and Christians had an alternative to conversion: they could adhere to their respective religions in return for payment of heavy taxes.

The conquest of Iran, Iraq, and the eastern littoral of the Mediterranean by Muslim Arabs in the seventh century brought comparative respite to the Manicheans in their homeland. When the 'Abbasid caliphs succeeded the Umayyads, however, they renewed the persecution that had been the common lot of Manicheans under Persian kings. The 'Abbasid Caliph al-Mahdi (775–785) determined to extirpate all heretics, including Manicheans, and for this purpose he instituted a court of inquisition, under the direction of a chief in-

Islam

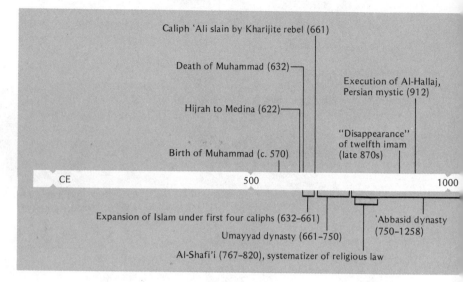

Caliph 'Ali slain by Kharijite rebel (661)

Death of Muhammad (632)

Execution of Al-Hallaj, Persian mystic (912)

Hijrah to Medina (622)

"Disappearance" of twelfth imam (late 870s)

Birth of Muhammad (c. 570)

CE   500   1000

Expansion of Islam under first four caliphs (632–661)

'Abbasid dynasty (750–1258)

Umayyad dynasty (661–750)

Al-Shafi'i (767–820), systematizer of religious law

quisitor. This individual had full plenary powers, and the ruthless measures taken, records of which survive, make blood-chilling reading. The religious policy of al-Mahdi was generally followed by his successors, especially by the Caliph al-Muqtadir (ruled 908–932), but in spite of the worst that the 'Abbasids could do, the Manichean religion survived within the Muslim Empire, possibly until the Mongol invasion of the thirteenth century.

Under the early Mughal emperors, India flourished as a result of the fusion of indigenous traditions with Mongolian elements. But in the seventeenth and eighteenth centuries trouble developed. The emperors Jahangir and Aurangzeb, in particular, tried to force Hindus, Sikhs, and other Indians to convert to Islam—a situation that led to ever-escalating violence.

The atrocities perpetrated in the name of Islam during the centuries between 600 and 1800 were as terrible as those committed elsewhere during the same period in the name of religious hegemony. Many pious Muslims accepted (and still accept) the principle that military success is closely linked to divine favor—a belief that inevitably led to bloody and violent confrontation. But by 1800 the once-proud realms of the Muslim Ottoman and Mughal empires were being humiliated by the European powers, whose military units outclassed the Muslim troops and decisively defeated them. To Muslims, this shattering reversal of the normal historical course of events remains inexplicable.

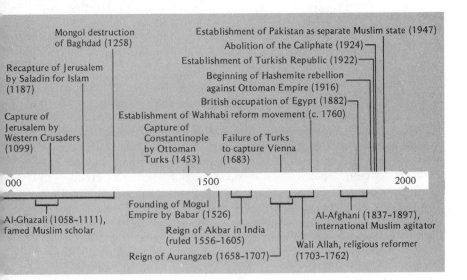

Abolishment of the Caliphate

The situation of Muslim communities in the eighteenth and nineteenth centuries was deplorable. On the one hand, European powers were gradually expanding and partitioning among themselves territory in Africa, western Asia, and India that for centuries had known only Muslim dominion. On the other hand, many Muslims dismissed the Ottoman religious establishment as an un-Islamic development and questioned whether the authority of the Ottoman sultan was truly derived from God, or from the consensus of the Muslim community.

While various Muslim political organizations rose and fell according to the vicissitudes of time, the institution of the caliphate—or rather, the head of state, who in theory represented the Prophet's "successor"—survived. The caliphate justified the claim of succeeding heads of state to the allegiance of all their subjects, both those who accepted the Islamic religion and those who paid tribute. All through Islamic history, rival dynasties ruled vast territories in the name of the caliphate, claiming thus to be the successors of Muhammad and the defenders of Islam—until March 3, 1924, when one of the most decisive moments in the history of Islam arrived.

On that date the Turkish National Assembly abolished the institution of the caliphate, thus ending almost 1300 years of unbroken historical tradition. In the course of its turbulent history, the caliphate underwent numerous modifications, was battled over by rival caliphs, and, at times, was the focus of powerful popular resentment. Nevertheless, for 1300 years it was recognized both as a moral link among Muslims and a symbol of Islamic solidarity. In 1924, however, Mustafa Kemal Ataturk, the first president of the Republic of Turkey and the champion of modern Turkish nationalists, dealt the mortal blow to the institution in the following statement: "The idea of a single caliph, exercising supreme religious authority over all the peoples of Islam, is an idea taken from fiction, not from reality." Soon after, the Turkish National Assembly decreed the abolition of the caliphate and the last Ottoman holder of the title, Caliph 'Abdul Majid, was sent into exile.

The abolition of the caliphate offended Sunni Muslims everywhere, and various attempts were made to restore this fundamental institution. Three congresses were held—in Cairo in March 1926, in Mecca in July 1926, and in Jerusalem in 1931—but the fate of the caliphate remained unchanged. Similarly, the attempt of King Faruk of Egypt in 1939 to revive the caliphate met with vigorous opposition, especially from the Turkish government.

To date, nothing has replaced this institution in the Muslim world. Whether or not Muslim opinion is finally resigned to its loss is difficult to say. Clearly, though, the excision of the ancient title represents a self-inflicted wound that has left an indelible mark on the Muslim consciousness.

Modern Trends

Role of Women

According to Islamic theology and law, men and women are equal before God, but this ideal is seldom realized in practice. In ancient times, it is more than probable that with isolated exceptions, the status of women in society did not vary appreciably from culture to culture. In the past, discrimination against women paled into insignificance beside the savage and focused brutality directed against minorities and dissenters everywhere.

It is only by modern, largely Western standards that women in Islamic communities seem to suffer discrimination today. The status of women in Islam is only one of many Islamic characteristics that distinguish the world of Islam from the rest of the Western world. Islamic tradition and Western liberalism offer radically opposite solutions to an issue that persists in creating tension and disruption, even in Western societies. Obviously, whatever changes are to be made must be introduced carefully within the framework of the Islamic tradition, not as models cut from Western patterns. Disenchantment about the status of women in Islamic communities is likely to be resolved in terms of how Muslim women can take their rightful place in Islamic society and carry out their obligations so that they contribute fully to the development of their communities.

Muslim women, like men, are obliged to fulfill the Five Pillars of Islam: profession of faith, prayer, almsgiving, fasting, and pilgrimage (see pp. 445–448). But unlike men, they enjoy certain exemptions from these duties when they are menstruating, pregnant, or ill.

To undertake a pilgrimage to Mecca at least once in a lifetime is incumbent upon every adult Muslim who is physically, mentally, and financially capable of doing so. Women who wish to perform the pilgrimage must be accompanied by a husband or a male relative. To

Two Muslim women descend the steps of the Dome of the Rock (Mosque of Omar) in Jerusalem after worshiping. Courtesy of Israel Government Tourist Office, Ministry of Tourism, Toronto, Canada.

enter the state of sanctity, men are required to don a special garment consisting of two large pieces of white seamless cloth. Women, however, are permitted to wear any clothing that covers the entire body except the face and the hands, although some women prefer to veil their faces too. If menstruation occurs during the period of sanctity, women are excused from performing some rites.

The Qur'an also embodies some important legal proscriptions. Polygamy is strictly regulated to a maximum of four wives, provided that husbands can do justice to all; if they cannot, they may only marry one woman. However, polyandry, the practice of a woman marrying several men, is not allowed under any circumstances. In general, Muslims tend to live monogamous lives.

Marriage has no sacramental status in Islam; it is simply a contractual relationship or agreement. The rights of the bride require due status, contract, and provision before any sexual relations are legitimately sanctioned. Sexual relations outside marriage are prohibited, and fornicators and adulterers are punished. Divorce is possible, but only after certain requirements are met. Inheritance laws require that females receive half as much as male inheritors.

Modesty among females is emphasized by regulations governing their appearance and conduct in society. A woman may in no way compromise the integrity of her reputation or stir the passions of males by immodest dress or conduct.

Conflict of Values

The respective roles women and men are to assume as members of Islamic society thus are clearly delineated. Threatening this legal and creedal unity, however, is a conflict of values between traditionalists and modernists. The vast majority of Muslims oppose modernity and accuse its champions of unfaithfulness to Islam in favor of Western ideologies. But the ruling elites in almost all Islamic countries are educated and trained according to modern Western concepts. In the eyes of the reactionaries—or rather, of antimodernists and anti-Westerners—such rulers are both unrepresentative of the Muslim masses and, more seriously, absolutely unfaithful to Islamic ideals. The goal of reactionaries is to bring their social order and political aspirations in line with the *shari'ah*, which provides guidelines for every sphere of life.

This conflict between the two sectors of Muslim society constitutes a grave problem for all Islamic societies. The struggle for freedom from Westernization and modernity has generated revolutions (such as in Iran) and ideas of nationalism that promote a "holy war" against all foreign domination. In virtually every area of the globe, with the exception of Russia and China, Muslims have obtained independence from "foreign" domination. Yet rapid population growth, industrialization, and political rivalries have created severe problems. Ironically, Islam has not lost adherents; on the contrary, it is making significant numbers of converts in recently industrialized societies, particularly in Africa.

The old longing for strong, one-man leadership that will bring religious unity and social justice still haunts popular Islamic imagination. In fact, the aspiration of such Muslims is to unify the world—by waging a holy war against unbelievers, if necessary—under the one government of God and in a culture that is Muslim in character and expression.

Qur'an

Muhammad, like Jesus Christ, wrote nothing. But, the utterances of the revelations he received were recorded by his supporters and organized by editors working under Caliph 'Uthman into the scriptural Qur'an (Koran).[4] The Arabic word *Qur'an* means "recitation," and professional Muslim reciters evoke the beauty of the Arabic language when they read with specific intonations. Besides being revered for its religious significance, the Qur'an represents a perfect model of Arabic literature and is therefore used as a text to study the Arabic language. Muslims regard the Qur'an as revelations of God transmitted to Muhammad through the angel Gabriel, and they believe that all of its 114 chapters, or *sura*, mirror an original text preserved in heaven.

The arrangement of the chapters seems to be determined by length, with the longest chapters placed at the beginning and the shortest ones toward the end. The only exception to this ordering is the first chapter, a short one usually considered by Westerners as the "Lord's Prayer" of Islam:

> In the name of God, the merciful, the compassionate.
> Praise be to God, Lord of the worlds,
> The merciful, the compassionate,
> Master of the day of judgement.
> You alone we serve; to You alone we cry for help.
> Guide us in the straight path,
> The path of those You have blessed;
> Not of those who have incurred Your anger,
> Nor of those who go astray.[5]

The contents of the Qur'an are varied. Some sections deal with ceremonial and civil law, whereas others offer theological views and moral exhortations. Various chapters refer to biblical characters such

A Qur'anic inscription (in Arabic) that reads: "In the name of God, the merciful, the compassionate." This statement, which is found in the opening line of every chapter in the Qur'an, is inscribed in many mosques. Courtesy of MSA Services in Canada.

as Adam, Moses, Abraham, Mary, Joseph, and Jesus. For instance, Adam is described as the first prophet, while Satan's fall from his position in heaven among the angels is explained by his refusal to worship Adam on God's command. Moses is acknowledged as having "talked with God" and having given the Torah to the Jews. Jesus is regarded not only as a prophet, but also as the son of Mary, a servant of God, and a "messiah," committed to "redeeming" the Jews from the bondage of the Torah, with its accretion of irrelevant rites and practices. Not only are the miracles of Jesus mentioned, but the Annunciation to Mary of the birth of Jesus, which resembles the account in Luke's Gospel, is recounted twice in the Qur'an. Moreover, there is a reference to the Last Supper and the Ascension. However, the Christian doctrine of the divinity of Jesus, in particular the dogmas of sonship, intercessor, crucifixion, and resurrection are categorically denied in the Qur'an. Here are a few instances:

Praise belongs to God, who has not taken to Him a son. (Sura 17.110)

They are unbelievers who say: "The messiah, Mary's son, is God." The messiah, son of Mary, was only a messenger. (Qur'an 5.76–79)

They did not slay him, [i.e., Jesus] neither crucified him . . . No indeed! God raised him up to Him. (Qur'an 4.155–156)

The Qur'an's teaching about God is expressed in the form of adjectives, such as all-seeking, all-powerful, all-knowing, all-hearing, from which are derived the ninety-nine "beautiful names" of God. Occasionally, however, there are longer passages that attempt to describe the glory and power of God.

> God, there is no god but He, the living, the everlasting!
> Slumber seizes Him not, neither sleep; to Him belongs all
>   that are in the heavens and the earth.
> Who is there that shall intercede with Him except by His
>   permission?
> He knows what lies before them and what is after them;
>   and they comprehend not anything of His knowledge
>   except such as He wills.
> His throne comprises the heavens and the earth;
> the preserving of them oppresses Him not;
> He is the all-high, the all-glorious. (Qur'an 2.255–256)

The Qur'an makes a fundamental distinction between God and all else, including human beings who are finite creatures. God alone is infinite as well as absolute. To point to an individual such as Jesus with delineations of birthplace and birthdate and then to say simply that he is God, or the second person in the Godhead, is, according to the Qur'an, impossible and unpardonable. The Qur'anic judgment against those who uphold the Christian doctrine of the Trinity is similar to its judgment against infidels.

> Those who say: "the Messiah, son of Mary, is God," are infidels . . .
> Those who say: "God is the third of three," are infidels, for there is no
> God but One . . .
> Those who associate anything with God, God will prohibit them from
> entering paradise, and their refuge shall be hell. (Qur'an 5.76–77)

The Qur'an is, first and foremost, a scripture to be confessed by rehearsing its contents. Muslim piety and even scholarship demand memorization and recitation of the Qur'an in Arabic. Indeed, the chanting of the Qur'an is the primary music of Islam and is reflected in the speech of all faithful Muslims. The divine command to Muhammad was to "recite." Since then, Muslims have obeyed this divine command by reciting the contents of the Qur'an. The following is a popular proverbial saying:

> If any man recites the Qur'an and memorizes it, God will cause him to
> enter paradise and will grant him the right to intercede successfully for
> ten people of his household, all of whom deserve hell fire.

Besides providing a rich, varied, and abiding source for strict memorization and recitation, the Qur'an is warning, guidance, criterion, and

A young Turkish student illuminating a page from the Qur'an.   Courtesy of
Turkish Tourism and Information Office.

mercy. Its subject is human beings; its theme is the exposition of
reality; its aim is an invitation to humankind to accept God's guidance
in the 'right' path (Qur'an 1.5). Unlike the multiple authorship of most
other scriptures, the Qur'an is the product of one man's revelations.
Though references to topics such as theology, jurisprudence, science,
and history are scattered throughout the Qur'an and appear to be
somewhat incoherent, the sense of divine claim and authority, the
dignity of human existence, the folly of human perversity, the im-
pending day of judgment and destiny, the eternal condition of bliss or
doom, and the reality of God's mercy are all dominant themes in the
Qur'an.

While the followers of Islam respect the scriptures of Judaism and
Christianity, they regard the Qur'an as the pure and final essence of
divine revelation, superseding the other scriptures. Its inspiration and
authority are thought to extend to every letter and title (of which there
are 323,621) so that every faithful Muslim must memorize and recite
the Qur'an in Arabic. Although the Qur'an has been translated into
some forty languages, it is believed to lose much of its inspiration in

translation; no translation has ever fully conveyed the eloquence or flavor of the original Arabic. Its religious and social influence over millions of believers can hardly be overestimated.

Next to the Qur'an, the most important piece of Islamic literature is the *Hadith* (Tradition), which provides the basis of Islamic law, theology, and custom. The Hadith is based on the actions and sayings of the Prophet Muhammad, who is regarded as the most competent and the most appropriate authority for interpreting the Qur'an. Since Muhammad never recorded his sayings, it was left to a succession of reliable narrators to record them in what gradually evolved into the Hadith. By the ninth century, the Hadith was established as the norm by which the beliefs and practices of the Muslim community were governed.

Hadith

As one might suppose, there are a vast number of versions or editions of the Hadith, but no single collection has won the full acceptance of all Muslims. Certain compilers are trusted more than others, but what has been accepted by one school or group has been rejected by another. One of the main reasons for this disagreement is that each version of the Hadith is a unique collection of events and sayings transmitted with the authority of a particular chain of narrators. To be acceptable, the Hadith must include the name of each human link in the chain between the Prophet and the person who recorded the Prophet's life and words. Here for example, is the opening statement of a typical Hadith:

> Al-Bukhari writes: "Abdallah ibn-al-Aswad told me: Al-Fadl ibn-al-Ata told us: Isma'il ibn-Umayya told us on the authority of Yahya ibn-Abdallah ibn-Sayfi that he heard Abu Ma'bad, the freedman of Ibn-Abbas, say, 'I heard Ibn-Abbas say:' 'When the Prophet,' the blessings of Allah be upon him, and peace, 'sent Mu'adh to the Yemen, he said to him . . .' "

The obvious question that bothers scholars is: what faith can be placed on the authority or reliability of each transmitter? To be sure, many Muslim scholars admit that many Hadiths are spurious, but no way has yet been devised to check or confirm the authenticity of the names mentioned in the chain or of the tradition transmitted by a particular version of the Hadith. Nevertheless, a great deal of precious information, which would otherwise have gone unrecorded, is preserved in the Hadith; for example, the moral precepts of the Prophet. True, the general principles by which all moral issues must be regulated are in the Qur'an, but not all the issues are clearly elaborated there. In addition, almost all of the early history of Islam and the religious opinions of the first generations of pious Muslims can be deduced from various versions of the Hadith. Therefore, even though the authenticity of certain versions of the Hadith may be questioned, their historical and moral value should not be underestimated.

Islamic Teachings

Articles of Faith

Muhammad's teachings, as recorded in the Qur'an, constitute the wellspring of Islamic faith and practice. The following selection from the Qur'an summarizes the Islamic articles of faith:

> True piety is this: to believe in God, and the Last Day, the Angels, the Book, and the Prophets. (Qur'an 2.176)

Of the five tenets central to Islam, the foremost is the oneness of God. "There is no other god but God" is an assertion on which Muhammad laid great stress, and he rejected the Christian concept of the Trinity as polytheistic (Qur'an 4.168–69; 5.78; 112.1). He was unequivocal on this point. For Muhammad and all Muslims there is but one God, who exists from eternity to all eternity. He is all-seeing, all-hearing, all-speaking, all-knowing, all-willing, all-powerful—and above all, an absolute unity.[6] Everything comes into being through his divine will and creative word. He is the creator, provider, and protector of humanity and the universe.

A second fundamental tenet of Islam is belief in intermediary beings called angels, two of whom play especially prominent roles: Gabriel, who appeared before Muhammad to reveal to him that he had been called by God; and *Iblis*, or *Shaitan* (Satan), who along with the *jinn* (rebellious angels) are destined to be judged and condemned to hell. Other angels record men's actions, receive their souls at death, and bear witness for or against them on the Day of Judgment.

The third important teaching Muslims profess is belief in the prophets. Islam maintains that God has communicated his divine message and guidance to humanity throughout the ages through the medium of selected members of the human race—the prophets or messengers of God. Muslims honor a total of twenty-eight prophets of God, including Muhammad. Eighteen of these prophets are well-known biblical figures, beginning with Adam and continuing with, among others, Abraham, Noah, Isaac, Ishmael, Moses, Zechariah, John, and Jesus. According to Islamic doctrine, these men were selected to convey the divine messages in order to keep humanity on the right track. At a particular point in history, which happened to be the seventh century, Muhammad was selected as the last messenger and commanded to convey God's complete design to the entire human race.

Thus, Muhammad is thought of as the seal of the prophets, through whom God revealed his eternal message in its definitive form.

The fourth principal teaching of Islam is the sacredness of the Qur'an. Although Muslims respect the scriptures of Judaism and Christianity, they regard the Qur'an as God's final revelation, super-seding all previous revelations.[7] Its message is addressed to all humanity, including Jews and Christians, who are considered to belong to a community defined as the "people of the book."

The fifth doctrine that occupies a very important place in the minds of Muslims is that of the day of judgment. Heaven, hell, and the final day of judgment are described elaborately and powerfully. Every individual will be called to account. There will be a resurrection of the body, a final judgment, and a final destiny in heaven or hell depending on one's record on earth.

The vivid descriptions of heaven and hell and the elaborate portrayal of the final judgment are very similar to the Book of Revelation in the New Testament and yet more powerful. The events of the last day are described as cataclysmic; that is, as appearing suddenly with great cosmic changes and at a time known only to God. On that day, when the trumpet sounds, the sun shall be darkened, the stars shall fall, the heavens shall be split asunder, the mountains shall turn to dust, and the earth shall be crushed.

> When the sun shall be darkened,
> When the stars shall be thrown down,
> When the mountains shall be set moving,
> When the pregnant camels shall be neglected,
> When the savage beasts shall be mustered,
> When the seas shall be set boiling . . .
> When the heavens shall be stripped off,
> When hell shall be set blazing,
> When paradise shall be brought nigh,
> Then shall a soul know what it has produced! (Qur'an 81.1–14)

> When the trumpet is blown with a single blast,
> and the earth and the mountains are lifted up
> and crushed with a single blow, then, on that day, the
>   terror shall come to pass . . .
> And the angels shall stand upon its borders . . .
> On that day you shall be exposed, not one secret of
>   yours concealed. (Qur'an 69.14–30)

On that last day, according to the Qur'an, the graves will open and humanity will be called to account. The guardian angel of each individual will bear witness to that person's record on earth. Each person's deeds will be weighed in the divine balance, and a "book" (containing one's record of life) will be placed in one's hand. If the "book" is placed in one's right hand, then the individual will be among the blessed; but if the "book" is placed in one's left hand, then the individual will be among the damned.

> Then as for him who is given his book in his right hand . . .
>   he shall be in a pleasing life, in a lofty garden . . .
> But as for him who is given his book in his left hand,
>   he shall say, "Would that I had not been given my book
>   and not known my reckoning! Would it had been the
>   end!"
> Take him and fetter him, and then roast him in Hell!
>   (Qur'an 69.13–37)

The terror of the Qur'anic portrayal of hell defies description. All worshipers of gods other than God, all the proud and the evildoers, are to be cast into the fires of hell. They will abide there forever, with no release from its torments. On the other hand, all the blessed and God-fearing individuals, all the humble and charitable, all those who suffered for God's sake, all those, especially, who fought in the name of, and for, God, are to be provided with fine garments, music, feasting, beautiful maidens, and inexpressible bliss in the garden of paradise.

Two important concepts emerge out of these descriptions. First, the picture of life after death depicted in the Qur'an justifies the notion of *al-jihad* ("the Holy War"), since death in battle fought on behalf of God guarantees a believer's entrance into paradise. To put it differently, the Qur'an sanctions retaliation as a religious practice and supports it with powerful incentives:

> O believers, prescribed for you is retaliation . . .
> In retaliation there is life for you . . .
> Holy things demand retaliation. (Qur'an 2.172–196)

The second concept is less well defined; it is the concept of free will. If God is all-powerful, all-present and all-knowing, then is everything predestined by him, or do individuals have a free will? Can they make a choice? The Qur'an seems to sway between these two viewpoints. While God is regarded as the source of good and evil, and while Muslims are content to explain all events (whether joyful or disastrous) as the decree of God, the Qur'an often speaks of one's moral choice. Of course, all religions that predicate an omnipotent (all-powerful), omniscient (all-knowing) and omnipresent (all-present) God, sooner or later face this dilemma. Suffice it to say that complete "submission" to the will of God is still a dominant feature of Islam.

The Five Pillars of Islam

Just as five fundamental tenets must be accepted by every faithful Muslim, so must five important religious duties be performed by every devout follower. These requirements are usually known as the Five Pillars of Islam.

The first duty of a Muslim is to recite the *shahada*, or confession of faith: "There is no other god but God, and Muhammad is the Prophet of God." This, the shortest and most incisive creed of any religion, is repeated many times a day by countless devout Muslims.

The second duty of a Muslim is to pray five times a day: at daybreak, at noon, in midafternoon, after sunset, and in the late evening. Generally, Muslims go to a *mosque*, a building or place for prayer. If that is not possible, it does not matter where they pray, so long as the obligation is met. Forehead, hands, and feet must be washed as a prelude to prayer, and the courtyards of mosques are equipped with washing facilities for this purpose (see photo below). If no water is available, the hands and

A Muslim man doing ablutions (washing of the head, hands, and feet) before prayer. The courtyards of mosques are equipped with washing facilities. Ingeborg Lippman/Peter Arnold, Inc.

face may be wiped with fine, clean sand. Muslims pray on a mat or carpet, and all recite their prayers in Arabic, no matter what the linguistic and cultural background of the worshiper may be. Friday noon is set aside as a time of public prayer, and Muslims observe this religious duty collectively in their different communities.

The third duty is to give alms to the poor as an outward sign of true piety. Sharing the abundance bestowed by God is thought of as a privilege.

The fourth duty is to fast during the month of *Ramadan* (the ninth month in the Islamic calendar). What distinguishes this observance from other fasts is that during the day Muslims must abstain from drink, food, and sexual relations; these proscriptions are lifted between sunset and sunrise, however. Only invalids, travelers, soldiers at war, and pregnant or menstruating women are excused from fasting, though they must make up some other time for any days missed.

The fifth duty is to make a pilgrimage to the holy city of Mecca at least once in a lifetime. Only poverty, illness, or bondage can excuse a believer from this duty. The importance of this annual gathering of Muslims from many countries would be difficult to overestimate. Muslims from all walks of life and of varying colors, races, and nationalities realize their equality before God as they meet on common ground. Since all Muslims cannot hope to make the costly journey to Mecca, they may make the trip by proxy through another pilgrim. In such cases, the custom is for the would-be pilgrim to contribute as much as he or she can afford so that a substitute can go in his or her place. Such substitutes bring merit upon all those who make their pilgrimage possible.

Long before the days of Muhammad, Mecca had been a sacred center to which Arabian people came yearly, on a pilgrimage to the sacred cube-shaped shrine known as the *Ka'ba* (cube). In the shrine was a black stone about the size of a pomegranate and oval in shape. It was traditionally believed to have been brought down to Abraham by the angel Gabriel. Moreover, legend said that the holy stone had once been so brilliantly white that pilgrims could be guided to the city by its radiance. Because of humanity's wickedness the stone had turned black.

Only a few steps away from the *Ka'ba* was the sacred well of Zamzam, believed to contain miraculous healing powers, though later tradition connected it with Hagar, who, when she left Abraham's tent, wandered with her son Ishmael through the barren desert in search of water. In desperation, she left Ishmael, who was too exhausted to travel any further, lying on the hot earth, while she ran back and forth in search of water. In the meantime, Ishmael, tossing restlessly, kicked his heels and accidentally uncovered the opening to the well. Hagar and her son decided to remain there, and in the years to come the children and grandchildren of Ishmael multiplied to become the Arab race. (Arabs consider themselves sons of Abraham through Ishmael.)

The black stone in the *Ka'ba* and the well of Zamzam are not the only factors that made Mecca a holy city. Eight years after Muhammad had fled from Mecca to Medina, a delegation from Mecca negotiated a peaceful settlement with Muhammad. In 630 Muhammad and some 10,000 followers peacefully entered Mecca, the city of his birth. Walking first seven times around the outside of the *Ka'ba*, Muhammad entered the shrine and destroyed all of its 360 idols and images. Then he dedicated the *Ka'ba* to God and proclaimed Mecca to be the holiest city of Islam.

Each year following this incident, Muhammad came to Mecca from Medina to lead a large group of people in a pilgrimage to the holy *Ka'ba*. His first pilgrimage was in 632, when it is said that 100,000 faithful followers walked and performed many solemn rites. The pilgrimage to the holy city then became a popular means of securing God's favor.

No religious ritual has done more to unite the Muslims than the rite of pilgrimage. Every devout Muslim must make a pilgrimage to the sacred city of Mecca at least once in his or her lifetime. During the same period each year, hundreds of thousands of Muslims from all walks of life and of varying race and nationality (for example, Arabs, Turks, Persians, Indians, Chinese) meet on common ground and realize their equality before God. Before entering the holy precincts, all pilgrims wear a white seamless garment and abstain from shaving or cutting their hair. However, simply visiting Mecca is not enough. Three main rituals and various other duties are prescribed:

1. Before entering the most sacred precincts of the very large open-air center where the *Ka'ba* is located, pilgrims stop to perform their ablutions, put on the white seamless garment, remove their sandals or shoes, and approach the *Ka'ba* barefoot. Then, like their prophet Muhammad, they walk around it seven times; three times quickly and four times slowly. On each circuit they pause to kiss or—if the crowd is too great—to touch with the hand or a stick the southeast corner of the *Ka'ba*, where the black stone is located.

2. The next observance commemorates Hagar's frantic search for water for her son Ishmael. Pilgrims walk quickly seven times across the valley between the two mounds of Safa and Marwa, some five hundred yards apart.

3. The climactic ritual is a march to the Mount of Mercy, on the plain of Arafat, some fifteen miles east of Mecca. This ceremony is a day's journey on foot but many stop to rest at the sanctuary of Mina, the halfway point. All pilgrims must, however, arrive at Mount Mercy on the following morning. Once there, pilgrims "stand before God" from noon to sunset, absorbed in pious meditation. The night is then spent in the open. The following morning, pilgrims return to Mina, where animal sacrifices and three days of feasting follow. A final trip around the *Ka'ba* in Mecca, and the discarding of the seamless garment completes the pilgrimage. The pilgrim is now permitted to assume the special title of *Hajj*—one who has made the pilgrimage to the holy city.

Jihad (Holy War)

In addition to these obligations, the Qur'an enjoins Muslim believers to "strive in the way of God." What this means is spelled out in the following passages:

> O believers, fear God. Fight in the path of God against those who fight against you; but do not commit aggression. . . . Slay them wheresoever you find them, and expel them from where they have expelled you. . . . Fight against them until sedition is no more and allegiance is rendered to God alone. (Qur'an 2.186)

> Fight against those who believe not in God, nor in the last day; who prohibit not what God and his Prophet have prohibited; and who refuse allegiance to the true faith. (Qur'an 9.29)

This quality of combativeness—or rather, of being actively engaged in combat against "pagans" or opponents—is called *jihad,* meaning "holy war." It entails an active struggle using armed force wherever necessary. The object of jihad is not so much the conversion of individuals to Islam as the gaining of political control over societies, in order to govern them in accordance with the principles of Islam.

Classical Islamic teaching held that the world was divisible into three spheres: *dar al-Islam,* the zone of Islam; *dar as-sulh,* the zone of peace (areas defined in terms of peace pacts that the Muslims had concluded with neighbors); and *dar al-harb,* the zone of war. In modern times, the Muslim position on the zone of war has been modified in the sense that no nation or territory is regarded as hostile unless it is actively so. Thus, jihad is no longer thought of as an offensive engagement for expansion, but as a defensive reaction against liberalism, modernism, and Westernization.

Shari'ah (Divine Law)

The word *shari'ah* is derived etymologically from a root meaning way, road, or path. Hence, *shari'ah* is the path that leads to God, the embodiment or codification of divine law. In Islamic thought, only one who accepts the injunctions of the *shari'ah* as binding is, properly speaking, a Muslim, although it may not be possible to realize its teachings or follow its commands fully.

In Islam, *shari'ah* is not simply a set of teachings, but a guide to human action that encompasses every facet of human life. In fact,

A Muslim prays in a mosque. Mosques are open daily for worshipers, who are enjoined to pray five times a day. Various formal positions are assumed during prayer: standing, bowing, kneeling, and prostrating by touching the ground with the forehead. Courtesy of Turkish Tourism and Information Offices, Ottawa, Canada.

religion to a Muslim is fundamentally *shari'ah*, the universal moral principles that must be applied to all daily actions and details—eating, sleeping, marriage, procreation, divorce, trade, and prayer. In one sense, then, *shari'ah* is for Islam the means of integrating human society—the way by which one gives religious significance to one's daily life.

All Muslims consider themselves to be part of the *umma*, or community of the faithful. There is no priesthood and there are no holy orders in Islam, but men trained in the *shari'ah*, known as *'ulama*, guide the affairs of the community. Every Muslim is under the authority, directly or indirectly, of various religious leaders.

Some time between the eighth and ninth centuries, four important schools of *shari'ah*, representing different interpretations of the Qur'an and the Hadith, developed. These four schools of law are: the Malaki, the Hanafi, the Shafi'i, and the Hanbali. The last two are quite conservative in their interpretation of the Qur'an and the Hadith, whereas the Malaki depend upon the consensus of the community and the Hanafi extend orthodox teaching by analogy. Of the four, the one with the fewest followers today is the Hanbali, spread between Syria and Egypt. The Malaki school is dominant in northern Africa, the Hanafi school in Turkey. The strength of the Shafi'i school has always been in Syria and Egypt.

The *shari'ah* provides for Muslims the knowledge of right and wrong in matters of politics, economics, society, and religion. In the Islamic view, the *shari'ah* contains definitive teachings that should form the basis of Islamic political theory. In the domain of economics, the *shari'ah* contains both general principles and specific instructions on matters such as poverty, taxes, and inheritance. The social teachings of the *shari'ah* constitute a vast body of prescriptions dealing with issues such as education, status, the family unit, and the functions and roles of the sexes.[8] And in matters of religion, the *shari'ah* prescribes the details of the religious duties related to the Five Pillars.

To live according to the *shari'ah* is, for Muslims, to live according to divine law—according to the norm that God has provided and willed for humans. This norm is considered to be the blueprint for a perfect human and social life.

Islamic Groups

Khariji

Despite the ideal of a unified, consolidated community taught by Muhammad, sectarian differences arose among Muslim believers immediately after his death. These differences arose principally out of disputes over leadership and dynastic succession. In the seventh century, a group of active dissenters, the Khariji (from the Arabic word *khuruj*, meaning rebel), accused the elected caliphs, especially 'Uthman, of nepotism and misrule. Their discontentment led to the assassination of 'Uthman. Later, they also denounced 'Ali for submitting his claim to the caliphate.

The Khariji stressed three fundamental principles: (1) any person who committed a grave sin and did not sincerely repent ceased to be a Muslim; (2) Islamic idealism meant aggressive militancy, or jihad, which in the view of the Khariji was equal in importance to the Five Pillars of Islam; and (3) the leadership should be open not just to those who belonged to the Qurayish tribe (the Sunni position), or just to those who belonged to the Prophet's family (the Shi'ite position), but to any individual, whatever his race or color, who had a righteous character.

The Khariji did not last long in history, but they left a permanent mark on the development of Islam. Today, a group known as the Ibadi, found in parts of Africa, is considered to have inherited the Khariji legacy, although the group applies less aggressive methods.

Sunni and Shi'ite

Although there are numerous groups within Islam, the major division is between the Sunni and the Shi'ite groups.[9] The Sunni are in the majority; the Shi'ite comprise not more than 15 percent of the total Muslim population. The Shi'ite and their various subsects are found mainly in Iran, and to some extent in India. In the ninth century a Shi'ite subsect, known as the Ismaili, appeared in India. This group, which is headed by the Agha Khan, maintains that there is always an *imam*, or religious leader, directly representing God on earth. Another subsect originating in India in the latter half of the nineteenth century, the Ahmadiya, has been particularly active in propagating the Islamic faith, especially among westerners.

The Sunni and the Shi'ite differ on two fundamental points: line of succession and religious authority. The Sunni follow a line of succession originated among the friends of Muhammad, beginning with Abu Bakr. The Shi'ite hold that succession in the leadership of Islam follows through the family of Muhammad, and consequently they consider that 'Ali, the son-in-law of Muhammad, was the Prophet's rightful successor. In the matter of religious authority, the Sunni maintain that the Qur'an, as interpreted by *sunna* (tradition) and the *ijma'* (agreements, among scholars), is the only authoritative basis of Islam, whereas the Shi'ite insist that Islamic religious authority is vested in an *imam*, who is infallible in all pronouncements regarding matters of doctrine and practice. All members of the Shi'ite group must recognize and submit to the authority of the *imam*. Further, most Shi'ite assert that there have been twelve *imams* since the death of Muhammad, and that one more, who will herald the end of this world, is still to come.

Sufi

The mystical movement in Islam goes by the name of Sufism. The origin of the term *Sufi* is complex, but the word is generally connected with the wearing of an undyed garment made of wool (Arabic *suf*). Initially, Muslims wore such garments as a mark of personal penitence. Later, however, wool garments became the regular uniform of Sufis.

The Sufi movement emerged out of early ascetic reactions by certain Muslims against the legalistic and ritualistic expression of Islam. Groups of ascetics began to meet for the purpose of reciting the Qur'an aloud, and these recitations gradually assumed a liturgical character that evolved in the direction of mystical love. When the Sufis sought to express their views in bolder terms, however, they were charged with heresy by the "orthodox" Muslims. As usual, all repressive tactics proved futile, and the Sufi movement grew in strength and popularity.

Three important views are shared by most Sufi groups: (1) that truth or reality may be found not by rational knowledge, but by direct and personal experience, culminating in absorption or union with the godhood; (2) that Sufi *shaikhs* (masters, in the sense of Zen masters) are to be venerated in their lifetime and, after death, elevated to the rank of saints; and (3) that *celibacy* (abstinence from sexual intercourse) is preferable to marriage, provided the Sufi's heart is unstained and his or her mind free from sin and lust.

The name with which the Sufi movement is most often associated is that of al-Ghazali (d. 1111),[10] who combined personal experiences with philosophical ideas and mystical systems in such a way as to win an honorable place among orthodox Muslims. What al-Ghazali did not foresee was that his attempted synthesis of the philosophical and the mystical would open the door to all sorts of popular religious practices and "heterodox" intellectual ideas that would gravely debase his ideals.

The pursuit of the mystical or ecstatic state of Sufism led to the introduction of alien practices and ideas. Within the ranks of the Sufis were wide gradations, which ultimately led to the development of several Sufi orders spread throughout the Muslim world. Today, some Sufi orders are local and regional, whereas others are global. These orders are centered around their founders, whose shrines serve as pilgrimage sites. The Sufi monastery, called *tékké* or *zawiyah*, has become the center of public religiosity, often overshadowing the mosque. Techniques of inducing autohypnotic states through certain practices, such as chanting formulas or frenzied dancing, have become *the* expression of religiosity. *Shaikhs* initiate novices into the practice of *dhikr* (or *zikr*, meaning remembrance of God), provided the disciples demonstrate an unquestioning faith in their masters.

The spread of Islam outside the Muslim world was largely due to Sufi orders, because the Sufi could easily make compromises with local customs and beliefs. By the same token, many "primitive" elements were absorbed into Sufi practices, and superstitious cults, occultism, various kinds of miracles, saint worship, and several unorthodox practices crept into the Sufi orders. Since the nineteenth century the Sufi orders have been in decline, largely because of reform movements aimed at purifying their accretions and superstitions, the advent of modern education, and rapid industrialization.

Islamic Observances

As we noted above, although there is no priesthood in Islam, men trained in Muslim law, the *'ulama,* guide the affairs of the community. Every Muslim is, therefore, under the authority of an *'ulama.* Of the several solemn observances that are as binding upon a Muslim as are religious duties, four of the most important are birth, circumcision, marriage, and death.

Seven days after birth, the parents name the child, cut its hair, and offer a sacrifice. The meat of the sacrificial animal is given to the poor, and monetary gifts corresponding to the weight of the hair are distributed in alms. Circumcision of male children is usually performed at the age of four or later. Both occasions usually are marked by family gatherings and festivities.

The general rule for marriage is that a Muslim male may marry a non-Muslim (a Christian or a Jew, but not a polytheist), whereas a Muslim female may marry only a Muslim. Essential to the marriage ceremony are the presence of witnesses and a contract specifying the bride-price. The bride-price of goods is given by the groom (or his father) to the father of the bride. As a rule, only part of the bride-price is paid on marriage; the remainder is paid if and when the marriage is dissolved.

When a Muslim dies, the body is washed with water, usually by someone of the same sex, and burial follows promptly after the recitation of short prayers. All Muslims are laid to rest on their right side facing Mecca. Males and females are never buried in the same grave unless joint interment is unavoidable, in which case a partition is raised to separate the corpses.

Friday Prayer

All faithful Muslims assemble every Friday noon for solemn community prayer. This is not necessarily a day of rest but rather a day on which all business activities are temporarily suspended for an interval of communal prayer in the mosque. Behavior appropriate to the occasion includes the rite of ablution, or purification; the removal of shoes or sandals; and the performance of the prayer ritual. Facing toward Mecca, the faithful place themselves in rows behind an *imam* to perform the prayer ritual. Following this public prayer is an address, or sermon, given by the *imam*, which is composed of praises of God, blessings on the Prophet, prayer from the Muslim community, a recitation from the Qur'an, and extemporaneous admonitions to piety. Also, God's blessing is invoked on the leaders of the Muslim states.

Festivals

Properly speaking, Muslims acknowledge only two festivals: the pilgrimage, or, more precisely, the feast celebrating its successful conclusion; and the feast marking the end of Ramadan, the period of fasting and abstention.

The *'id-al-azha* (Festival of Sacrifices), also known as *'id-al-kabir* (Great Festival) or *Qurban Bairam* (Turkish, for Festival of Sacrifice), lasts for four days and is connected with the pilgrimage. Pilgrims celebrate it in the month of pilgrimage, in the valley of Mina (where Mecca is located), and nonpilgrims celebrate it at home. Every Muslim is expected to sacrifice an animal—although this is not a legal duty except in fulfillment of a vow—just as Abraham sacrificed a sheep instead of his son. After the feasting is over, most families visit the tombs of their relatives, where palm branches are laid on the graves and food is distributed to the poor at the cemetery. Professional reciters are hired to pray at the graveside, after which the men leave the cemetery. The women, however, maintain a vigil throughout the day, and in many Muslim countries it is customary for them to spend the night in a tent at the cemetery.

The second Muslim festival celebrated with great joy and feasting takes place at the end of Ramadan, as soon as the new moon appears. The first three days are celebrated as the *'id-al-fitir* (Festival of Fast Breaking) or *Ramazan Bairam* (Turkish for Festival of Ramadan), or as *'id-al-saghir* (Little Festival) or *Kuchuk Bairam* (Turkish for Little Festival). Soon after sunrise, everyone dresses in new or clean clothes, and the men assemble in the mosques for prayers. On this occasion families and friends visit each other and presents are exchanged, especially cakes and candies. Many Muslims also visit family graves to recite prayers and to offer food to the less fortunate.

Bedouins in Sinai, Egypt wearing white kaffiyehs (an Arab headdress) share a meal during Ramadan, the sacred month during which Muslims fast from dawn until sunset.   Jeff Rotman/Peter Arnold, Inc.

Muharram

Muharram, the first month of the Islamic year, begins with a ten-day mourning observance among the Shi'ites. The occasion marks the martyrdom of 'Ali, son-in-law of the Prophet Muhammad, and his sons Hassan and Hussain. The incident that sets the mood for this commemorative day is the tragedy of Karbala rather than the assassination of 'Ali. On the tenth of Muharram (October 10, 680), Hussain, who came to be considered the third *imam*, was killed in a revolt in Karbala, Iraq. His grave on the battlefield became, almost immediately, a shrine for pilgrims. To this day, many Shi'ites go to Karbala to die or ask that their bodies be transported to this "holy city" for burial, because tradition asserts that those who are buried by the shrine will certainly enter paradise.

Shi'ite Muslims often commemorate this martyrdom by reenacting the suffering and burial of Hussain. The observance culminates with a reenactment of the "passion," or "vicarious suffering," and death of Hussain. A big procession, designed as a funeral parade, dramatizes the burial of Hussain.

The Sunni Muslims also observe Muharram, but only for one day and with a different emphasis. They believe the creation of Adam and Eve, heaven and hell, and life and death took place on this day.

Other Memorials

There are various other Islamic observances, but the dates and even the events that they commemorate vary depending on the history and racial background of the people. For instance, Indian Muslims observe the anniversary of the death of Hassan, the brother of Hussain. Other Muslims observe the birthday of Hussain. The Shi'ite Muslims commemorate the birthday and death of 'Ali, whereas Indian Muslims commemorate the death of 'Ali on the twenty-first day of Ramadan. Another purely Shi'ite festival is the *'id-al-ghadir* (Festival of the Lake of Humm). This place is thought to be where the Prophet Muhammad nominated 'Ali as his successor. One more very important observance is the *lailat al-bara'a* (Night of Privilege). For some Muslims (mainly from India and Indonesia), this day is set aside for the commemoration of the dead. Others (mainly from Egypt) believe that a little after sunset on that night, the "Heavenly Tree" is shaken and the leaves that fall from the tree identify the human beings who will die in the following year.

There are also a number of memorial days connected with the Prophet Muhammad that are celebrated by almost all Muslim people. These observances include the birthday and death of the Prophet; the Night of Fulfilled Desires, commemorating the night on which the Prophet Muhammad was conceived; and the Night of the Ascension of the Prophet.

Notes

1. For the history of the term *Islam* and its meaning, see W. C. Smith, *The Meaning and End of Religion* (New York: Macmillan, 1963), Chap. 4.
2. For an attempt to capture the spirit of Islam, see S. A. Nigosian, *Islam: The Way of Submission* (Northants, Eng.: Thorsons, 1987), Chap. 1.
3. On the Jewish influence on Muhammad and Islam, see A. I. Katsh, *Judaism in Islam* (New York: Bloch, 1954). On the Christian influence, see R. Bell, *The Origin of Islam in Its Christian Environment* (London: Macmillan, 1926).
4. For English translations of the Qur'an, see A. J. Arberry, *The Koran Interpreted*, 2 vols. (London: Allen & Unwin, 1955); and M. Pickthall, *The Meaning of the Glorious Koran* (New York: Mentor, 1953). For a bibliographical listing of commentaries, critical works, and analyses of the contents of the Qur'an, see C. J. Adams, *A Reader's Guide to the Great Religions*, 2nd ed. (New York: Free Press, 1977), pp. 423–28.

5. Author's translation from Arabic.

6. Islamic theology provides one of the most comprehensive lists of devotional expressions about God, consisting of ninety-nine "most beautiful names" of God. For the list of names, see Nigosian, *Islam*, pp. 143ff.

7. Mentioned in the Qur'an as earlier books of scripture are the Torah of Moses, the Zabur (Psalms) of David, and the *Injil* (Gospel) of Jesus. On the doctrine of scripture, see A. Jeffery, *The Qur'an as Scripture* (New York: R. F. Moore, 1952).

8. On the traditional role of the sexes, the family unit, education, and the like, see D. May, "Women in Islam: Yesterday and Today," in C. K. Pullapilly, ed., *Islam in the Contemporary World* (Notre Dame, Ill: Cross Roads Books, 1980), pp. 370–401.

9. The term *Sunni* (derived from *sunna*, meaning tradition, community, or consensus) refers to the followers of the traditional way. The term *Shi'ite* (or *Shi'ah*) means "partisan."

10. The work of al-Ghazali was translated by W. H. T. Gairdner, *Qur'an, Mishkat al-Anwar* (London: Royal Asiatic Society, 1924). Some scholars are of the opinion that al-Ghazali stands on the same level as Saint Augustine and Luther in terms of religious vigor and intellectual insight; see W. M. Watt, *The Faith and Practice of al-Ghazali* (London: Allen & Unwin, 1953).

15

Baha'i

Beginnings

The Baha'i religion originated in Iran in 1844. Abdul Baha, the eldest son of Baha'u'llah, from whom the religion gets its name, explained what it is to be a Baha'i in these terms: "To be a Baha'i simply means to love all the world; to love humanity and try to serve it; to work for universal peace and universal brotherhood."[1]

The word *Baha'i* derives from the title by which the founder of the faith is known: Baha'u'llah, meaning Glory of God. A Baha'i is one who accepts Baha'u'llah as his Lord, knows his teachings, and obeys his precepts. A Baha'i's sole object in life is to love God—and to love God means to love everything and everybody, for all are of God. This love transcends sect, nation, class, or race.

Although the Baha'is are not a large group, they are found throughout the world. The World Center, the international headquarters of the faith, is situated in Haifa, Israel. Unlike in other religious organizations, Baha'i institutions are social rather than ecclesiastical. Their Spiritual Assemblies, both local and national, are responsible for upholding the teachings, conducting the meetings, stimulating active service, and promoting the welfare of the Baha'i cause.

The Bab (1819–1850)

Shi'ite Muslims, particularly in Iran, have always claimed that there are twelve legitimate descendants, or *imams*, of 'Ali, the son-in-law and successor of the Prophet Muhammad (see Chapter 14). These twelve *imams* are often referred to as *babs* (gates), since they are believed to function as the gates by which believers gain access to the true faith. Shi'ites have always believed that one day the twelfth *imam*, who disappeared in mysterious and unexplained circumstances during the ninth century, would reappear as the Messiah.

In 1844 a Persian Shi'ite Muslim named 'Ali Muhammad declared that he was the long-awaited twelfth *imam* and assumed the title of *bab*. Gathering around him a group of disciples, who called themselves Bab'is, The Bab launched a movement for religious and social reform. Within a short time this movement had gained so much momentum that both religious and political forces within Iran took drastic counteraction. The Bab was publicly executed on July 9, 1850, and many of his followers were eliminated through either imprisonment or execution. Before The Bab died, however, he foretold the appearance of a leader greater than he to carry on the work of establishing a universal religion, so that his remaining disciples were sustained by the hope that all was not lost.

Baha'u'llah (1817–1892)

Among this group of survivors was a man called Mirza Hussain Ali, the eldest son of the minister of state, who, by virtue of his family connections, was spared the fate of many of his companions. He had abandoned his family name and assumed the title *Baha'u'llah* (Glory of God).

In 1852 an event occurred that affected the future course of the movement. One of The Bab's followers attempted to assassinate the Iranian shah, an act that provoked further persecution against the Bab'is. Baha'u'llah was first imprisoned and later exiled to Baghdad, then under the jurisdiction of the Turkish government. During this period, which lasted approximately ten years, a number of significant developments occurred.

First, Baha'u'llah made his place of residence in Baghdad a center of learning to which students from near and far were attracted, and many Bab'is gradually formed a community in exile. Second, Baha'u'llah wrote several books, including *Hidden Words, Seven Valleys,* and *The Book of Certitude*—all aimed at encouraging and guiding his followers. Third, it was revealed to Baha'u'llah that he was the long-awaited leader predicted by The Bab. Fourth, when the authorities in Baghdad

Baha'i

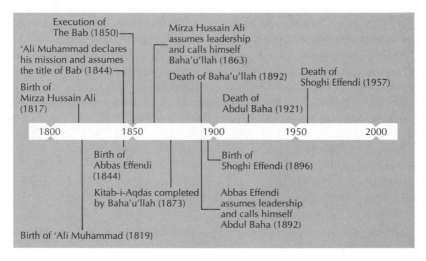

sought to suppress The Bab's movement, Baha'u'llah was ordered into even more distant exile. His destination was to be Istanbul.

While the caravan was being prepared for the long journey, Baha'u'llah and his dedicated followers encamped for twelve days (April 21–May 2, 1863) in the garden of Ridvan, just outside Baghdad. When all had assembled, Baha'u'llah made an unexpected announcement: the one whose coming had been foretold by their master, The Bab, was none other than he, Baha'u'llah. All those who recognized him as the Chosen of God, the Promised One of all the prophets, were to follow him. Except for a few who remained unconvinced, the company of Bab'is recognized him as the fulfillment of the prophecy and from that day called themselves Baha'is.

The caravan of displaced Baha'is paused in Istanbul for only a few months before being forced to move on to Adrianople, in European Turkey. During his four and a half years in Adrianople, Baha'u'llah resumed his teaching and gathered a large following. He also wrote letters to numerous religious leaders, rulers, and kings, including the pope and the president of the United States. To all, he announced his mission and called upon them to promote the unity of humankind and the establishment of the true, universal religion.

His energetic proselytizing, however, stimulated further opposition, which resulted in the banishment of Baha'u'llah and his followers to Acre, in Palestine—then a Turkish enclave to which criminals were exiled. A few years later the restrictions that had at first been imposed on the small religious colony were relaxed, and shortly afterward Baha'u'llah and his group moved to Bahji, on the slopes of Mount Carmel. His mission, however, terminated with his death on May 29, 1892, at the age of seventy-five. Today, a shrine dedicated to his memory stands on Mount Carmel in Israel.

Abdul Baha (1844–1921)

Baha'u'llah left a will in which he appointed his eldest son, Abbas Effendi, as his successor. In assuming the leadership of the movement, Abbas Effendi changed his name to Abdul Baha (Servant of Baha, or Servant of Glory). He had shared the persecutions, exiles, and imprisonment of his father and now as leader he carried on his father's program of writing. In 1908, when he was freed by the Turkish authorities, he undertook extensive teaching tours in Europe, the United States, and Canada. He preached and taught the faith of the Baha'i and established numerous Assemblies in various nations. On his return to Palestine he wrote *The Divine Plan*, a work that invoked all Baha'is to spread Baha'u'llah's message—the unification of humankind through the medium of Baha'i, to the four corners of the world. He died on November 28, 1921, at the age of seventy-seven, leaving a will that directed his grandson, Shoghi Effendi, to assume leadership of the Baha'i faith.

The Shrine of The Bab on Mount Carmel in Haifa, Israel. The site was selected by Baha'u'llah before his death in 1892, and his remains were placed there in 1909.   Courtesy of Israel Government Tourist Office, Ministry of Tourism, Toronto, Canada.

Shoghi Effendi (1896–1957)

Shoghi Effendi ("the Guardian") was the last in a direct line of succession from Baha'u'llah. He continued the work of establishing local and national Assemblies in various parts of the world until his death on November 2, 1957. Two important innovations were made under his guidance: the structure that governs matters of administration and the Universal House of Justice, which is the supreme legislative body governing the affairs of the Baha'i faith at the international level.

Baha'i Scriptures

The written works of The Bab, Baha'u'llah, Abdul Baha, and Shoghi Effendi, which make up the sacred literature of the Baha'is, are considered to be inspired but human, poetic but practical. The writings of The Bab consist mainly of commentaries, expositions, exhortations, and prayers. Those of Baha'u'llah are more comprehensive in range and deal with every phase of human life: individual and social, material and spiritual. His work also includes interpretations of ancient and modern scriptures of other religions, as well as prophetic pronouncements, all written either in Persian or in Arabic.

One of the unique features of the Baha'i faith is the *Book of the Covenant*, in which Baha'u'llah provides, in clear and unambiguous terms, an authorized interpretation of what he is saying. In this book, Baha'u'llah vested full powers over the interpretation of his writings and over the direction of the Baha'i faith in his eldest son, Abdul Baha. In the same way, when Abdul Baha appointed his eldest grandson, Shoghi Effendi, as his successor, he stipulated in his will that Shoghi Effendi should be the sole interpreter of the writings and the guardian of the faith. Since his death, no individual can claim special authority for interpreting the sacred writings of the Baha'i.

Among the hundreds of writings of Baha'u'llah, two books are regarded as especially important by Baha'is: the Kitab-i-Aqdas (Most Holy Book) and the Kitab-i-Iqan (Book of Certitude). The former deals with Baha'i laws and institutions, and the latter consists of revelatory concepts. Baha'is consider both books to be no less divinely inspired than the sacred writings of other religions.

Baha'i Teachings

The basic teaching of the Baha'i faith may be summed up in nine words: the oneness of God and the unity of humanity. God is one, even though people call him by different names. In essence, God is unknowable, but he has made known his truth according to the requirements of an advancing civilization through his chosen prophets or messengers in nearly every era. These prophets or messengers are considered by the Baha'is to be "manifestations of God." Included in this group are Abraham, Moses, Zoroaster, Krishna, Buddha, Jesus, Muhammad, and Baha'u'llah. The religions that evolved out of these manifestations of God were the product of two factors: interpretations influenced by human limitations and varying degrees of revealed truth.

On the basis of these assumptions, Baha'is affirm that Baha'u'llah, for the first time in religious history, took the necessary step to assure the unity of his followers for all time: he appointed his eldest son, Abdul Baha, as his successor and decreed that Abdul Baha was divinely authorized to interpret his teachings. In a thousand or more years, another manifestation of God may appear; but until then, the words of Baha'u'llah, Abdul Baha, and "the Guardian" Shoghi Effendi, along with the decisions of the Universal House of Justice, constitute the authorities to which all believers must turn. No Baha'i may found a sect based on any supposed divine revelation or particular interpretation.

Abdul Baha, as the authorized interpreter of the Baha'i faith, summarized its teachings in a set of principles. Twelve of the most important of them are as follows:[2]

1. *Humanity.* All the people of the world are created by God and are therefore members of one human family. Since God is just, kind, and merciful to all members of the human race, each individual should follow God's example in dealing with others.

2. *Truth.* Truth is one and does not admit of multiple divisions. Each individual must seek this truth independently, forsaking imitations and traditions.

3. *Religions.* The universal message of all religions is the same: peace and good will. It is in the interest of humanity that all religious systems dispel animosity, bigotry, and hatred and promote love, accord, and spiritual brotherhood.

4. *Religion and science.* Humanity is endowed with intelligence and reason in order to test the validity of ideas. If religious beliefs and opinions fly in the face of scientific evidence, they are little more than superstitions and unfounded assumptions.

5. *Sex.* Differences that distinguish one sex from another are not peculiar to humans; these differences are common to all living things and do not favor one sex over another. Therefore, the equality of men and women must be universally acknowledged.

6. *Prejudice.* Prejudice destroys human well-being and happiness; therefore, humanity must actively work to abolish all forms of prejudice—religious, racial, class, and national.

7. *Peace.* The establishment of a permanent and universal peace through world government will be achieved in this century.

8. *Education.* Since education is essential to humanity, there should be one universal standard of training and teaching. This universal curriculum should also establish a global code of ethics.

9. *Economy.* Happiness, prosperity, and the stability of humanity depend on economic equality. Society must, therefore, adjust the balance of the global economy in favor of the majority instead of the few.

10. *Human rights.* God's dominion is characterized by justice and equity without distinction or preference, so that a uniform standard of human rights must be universally recognized and adopted.

11. *Language.* One of the great factors in the unification of human beings is language. Therefore, a specially appointed committee should select an auxiliary language that will be universally adopted as a medium of international communication.

12. *Work.* Any work performed in a spirit of service is considered to be an act of worship.

Aside from these fundamental teachings, Baha'is believe that the Day of Judgment is determined as much by events in the present as in the future. In this sense, every day is a Day of Judgment. Every individual is being tested or judged now by the advent of the revelation of God. In addition, each individual is called to account for his or her actions after death. By rejecting the oneness or unity of humankind, civilization is destroying itself—in itself the Day of Judgment. However, Baha'is affirm, on the basis of Baha'u'llah's sayings, that humanity and the physical earth will survive as a new, universal civilization eventually emerges.

After death, the soul continues to evolve into different states and conditions. The so-called spiritual body that a soul inhabits when the physical body dies is thought of as comprising the moral qualities and spiritual perceptions developed during one's lifetime. Heaven and hell are not places but conditions of the soul, which is in a continual and eternal state of evolution. When the soul is near God and his purposes, that is heaven. When the soul is distant from God, that is hell.

To put it differently: according to the Baha'i faith, heaven represents a state of perfection, and hell of imperfection; heaven is the fulfillment of harmony with God's will and one's fellow beings, and hell is the absence of such harmony. The joys of heaven are spiritual, and the sorrows of hell consist of the absence of these joys. Baha'is reject any belief in the objective existence of the forces of evil. Just as darkness is simply the absence of light, so evil is explained as the absence of divine qualities at any particular level of existence.

Baha'i Worship

The Baha'i faith has no rituals, no professional priesthood, and no monastic orders. A respected individual in the community who is well educated in the Baha'i faith conducts the regular meetings for united worship. These meetings consist of prayers, selected readings from the writings of Baha'u'llah and Abdul Baha and from the scriptures of the other world religions, and, occasionally, questions and answers. Mutual service and spiritual fellowship are the factors that bring adherents together for worship.

The basic unit of worship is the local spiritual Assembly. In every city, town, or district where there are nine or more adult Baha'is, a nine-member administrative body is elected annually on April 21 to govern the affairs of the particular community. The second level of Baha'i administration is the national spiritual Assembly. This, too, is a nine-member body elected annually by delegates attending a national convention. The third and highest level of Baha'i administration is the Universal House of Justice, made up of nine members elected once every five years at a convention.

Baha'is meet in the homes of members or in some other buildings, as they do not have local houses of worship. They have constructed several magnificent temples around the world, however. Two of these temples have been designed and built by Canadian architects: the shrine of The Bab on Mount Carmel in Haifa is the work of Sutherland Maxwell of Montreal, Quebec; and the temple at Wilmette, Illinois, is the work of Louis Bourgeois of Nicolet, Quebec. All the temples are constructed according to Baha'u'llah's instructions. They are located in a large garden adorned with fountains, trees, and flowers, and they are surrounded by a number of accessory buildings devoted to educational, charitable, and social purposes. All of these temples are nine-sided, and all are covered with domes. The number nine is very significant to Baha'is, because, as the largest single-digit numeral, it represents the universal unity that Baha'is seek.

Baha'i house of worship in Sydney, Australia. While each house of worship differs from the others in general design, they all have the unifying architectural feature of nine sides—nine being the largest single digit, symbolizing oneness and unity.   Courtesy of Baha'i Community of Canada.

Baha'i Obligations

Very few obligations regulate the lives of the Baha'is. One duty is to pray. Although the recitation (or chanting) of prayer is enjoined upon every Baha'i, prayer is not confined to the use of prescribed forms, important as those are. Baha'is believe that one's whole life can be a prayer—that work devoted to the glory of God and the good of one's neighbor is also prayer.

Another obligation is to fast. The month of 'Ala (the nineteenth month in the Baha'i calendar*) is appointed for fasting, and during the entire nineteen days of the month, both food and drink are forbidden from sunrise to sunset. All Baha'is, except children, invalids, travelers, pregnant women, and the sick, are enjoined to keep the fast.

A third obligation relates to marriage. Monogamy is the rule, and a couple may marry only after the consent of their parents. In the matter of divorce, a couple is bound not only by Baha'i teaching, but also by the laws of the country of residence. According to Baha'i teaching, divorce is permitted after a year's separation and only if, during that period, the couple is not able to restore a harmonious relationship.

Finally, Baha'i parents are under a religious obligation to educate their children. The use of narcotics and intoxicants of any kind, except for medicinal purposes, is strictly prohibited.

Spread of Baha'i Faith

There are neither paid missionaries nor professional clergy in the Baha'i religion. All the work of teaching and spreading the faith is done by volunteer teachers known as pioneers. Normally, application for membership is made to the local spiritual Assembly and is open to all who accept the tenets of the Baha'i faith, recognize the five "stations" of prophethood (The Bab, Baha'u'llah, Abdul Baha, Shoghi Effendi, and the Universal House of Justice), and accept the Baha'i scriptures (known as the Tablets of God) and the administrative order. In matters of financial support, contributions are accepted only from Baha'is and are wholly voluntary; personal solicitation is strictly forbidden.

The Baha'i faith has followers on every continent in the world. Much of the work demands sacrifices from individual believers, who leave their homes, their careers, and their comforts in order to spread the Baha'i faith.

*The Baha'is use a calendar that was established by The Bab and confirmed by Baha'u'llah. The year begins on March 21 and is divided into nineteen months of nineteen days each, with four (five in leap years) additional intercalary days.

Baha'i Festivals

Baha'i followers observe a number of festivals based primarily on important historical events and religious anniversaries. The following are some of the more important ceremonies.

The birth of The Bab is celebrated annually on October 20, the day The Bab was born in Shiraz, Iran, in 1819. Baha'is honor him as the forerunner of Baha'u'llah and the herald of a new era.

The Bab revealed his mission to his first disciple, Mulla Husayn, in 1844. The anniversary of this declaration is commemorated annually on May 23. It was The Bab who also inaugurated the Baha'i calendar, which dates from the year of his declaration (1844).

The anniversary of The Bab's martyrdom is commemorated on July 9 at noon, with readings and prayers from Baha'i scriptures, because The Bab was martyred by a firing squad in the barracks square of Tabriz, Iran, at noon on that date in 1850.

The birth of Baha'u'llah (Mirza Hussain Ali) is celebrated annually on November 12, to commemorate the day he was born in Teheran, Iran, in 1817.

The most important festival in the Baha'i faith is the Feast of Ridvan (known as the Lord of Feasts), which extends over a period of twelve days, from April 21 to May 2. It commemorates the period in 1863 during which Baha'u'llah declared his mission in the garden of Ridvan, just outside Baghdad. The first of Ridvan (April 21) is also the day on which every town, district, or village elects nine representatives to the local Assemblies.

The ascension of Baha'u'llah is commemorated on May 29, the day that Baha'u'llah died in 1892, in Akko, Palestine, where he had lived in exile. His burial place in Bahji, just outside Akko, is considered the holiest shrine of the Baha'i world.

The Covenant of Baha'u'llah, in which he declared the appointment of his eldest son, Abdul Baha, as the authorized interpreter of his teachings, is celebrated annually on November 26.

The ascension of Abdul Baha (Abbas Effendi) is commemorated annually on November 28, the day he died in 1921 at the age of seventy-seven.

The Nineteen-Day Feast assumed a special importance after the death of Abdul Baha. It is observed on the first day of each of the nineteen Baha'i months.

The Feast of Naw Ruz (New Year) is celebrated on March 21 and follows immediately after nineteen days of fasting. It is celebrated by picnics or festal gatherings at which music, the chanting of verses, and short addresses suitable to the occasion are contributed by those present.

Notes

1. *Baha'i World Faith, Selected Writings of Baha'u'llah and 'Abdu'l-Baha* (Wilmette, Ill.: Baha'i Publishing Trust, 1976), p. 240.

2. See G. Faizi, *The Baha'i Faith* (Wilmette, Ill.: Baha'i Books, 1975), pp. 45–85; and J. E. Esslemont, *Baha'u'llah and the New Era* (Wilmette, Ill.: Baha'i Books, 1976), pp. 83–180.

16

Religion in Global Perspective

Global Awareness

Human society is witnessing the beginning of the end of the age of cultural and religious isolation. People previously isolated one from another by distance, culture, and language are becoming increasingly aware of each other's customs and ways of thinking. A constant stream of journals, books, films, documentaries, and conferences keeps the human race abreast of news and events from around the world. Similarly, the scientific and technological achievements of this century, as much as they have altered the pattern of everyday living, have had no effect more profound or far-reaching than the development of global awareness.

This global awareness, resulting from factors such as the development of extensive trade, economic interdependence, efficient transportation, and rapid means of communication, is inevitably creating a climate conducive to a full understanding of what is meant by "human solidarity." The words of Socrates, "I am neither an Athenian nor a Greek, but a citizen of the world," are echoed today with increasing conviction by a growing number of enlightened citizens of a true world community.

The independent histories and religious traditions of nations and civilizations, past and present, are being forged into something new: an integrated world history. Consequently, ancient views and traditional beliefs are being seriously questioned. All over the world, many people are discarding the traditional answers proposed by religions to the questions centered on the meaning of existence, because they feel that the answers no longer address the increasing complexities of modern society.

The scientific and technological achievements that have radically altered the patterns of human life are also affecting moral and religious values. Human beings have been so successful in breaking the bonds of gravity—not merely yearning for the moon but grasping it—that they can look at the universe and their position in it from a new perspective. Progress in explaining "natural" causes and effects has modified the fear and awe of "supernatural" phenomena. Medical achievements have advanced to the point at which healing can be explained without reference to taboos and magical rites. Hence, religious beliefs are being questioned or actually discarded as inadequate and obsolete. In addition, people are examining their own, personal faith and comparing it with various religions as alternative ways of interpreting life.

New Religious Movements

At no time since the Greco-Roman period have ordinary people been more attracted to the fusion of religious ideas and practices from East and West than they are now. Manifestations of a departure from traditional religious hegemonies are fourfold:

1. The sheer volume of literature relating to interreligious encounters

2. The active participation in dialogue of both lay and clerical members of different and sometimes divergent religious faiths and persuasions

3. A worldwide phenomenon of experimentation with alternative religions by people raised in traditional faiths that were usually confirmed and affirmed by a particular culture

4. Of most significance, the proliferation of modern religious groups

These religious groups have been profoundly affected by the vaulting achievements of science and technology and their concomitant— global integration. These modern religious groups have assimilated beliefs and practices from other faiths—Eastern and Western, extant and extinct. In addition, they adumbrate elements of modern science.

Never before has humanity witnessed, both quantitatively and quali-
tatively, the integration of religious ideas and practices on such a
global scale.

To be sure, all religious movements appropriate elements from other
cultures. Judaism, for instance, reflects the influences of ancient Mesopotamian, Egyptian, Canaanite, and Persian religions. Similarly,
Christianity retains, in addition to Judaic characteristics, vestiges of
ancient Greek, Roman, and native Mediterranean religions. So also do
other religions, such as Islam, Buddhism, Jainism, mirror their ancient
and primordial roots. But these represent relatively ancient accretions.
The sixteenth century, the Age of Discovery, marked a watershed of
sorts between geographic isolation and the global village.

Prior to the sixteenth century, characteristics assimilated or incorporated by neophyte religious systems in particular could be attributed to the influence exerted by local or contiguous cultures. Geographic isolation confirmed, reinforced, and perpetuated the natural
proclivity of people to think of themselves as rather special.

The Age of Discovery did not change this mode of thinking, but it
initiated a process of challenge that worked gradually like yeast in a
stodgy leaven of hardened misconceptions. In the most recent decades
of this century there has been an unprecedented acceleration of this
process: an explosive fermentation, as people rise from cultural isolation to global integration. One consequence has been the proliferation
of modern religious movements that draw inspiration for their interpretations from many disparate religious, political, social, philosophical, psychological, and scientific systems.

A global awareness animates most, if not all, modern religious
groups, which tend to be highly syncretistic. They have been able to
reconcile, within the framework of their individual systems, modern
scientific knowledge and ideas and practices from religions around the
world. Their emergence since the nineteenth century has provoked
the interest of sociologists, historians, and comparative historians of
religion, among others.

Comparison of Religions

This recent fusion of religious ideas and practices from around the
world has contributed to the supposition that the ends or goals of all
religions are similar and that they all have a common essence. In other
words, all religions are simply considered different paths to the same
ultimate goal or destination. Is this assumption correct or unfounded?

It is often stated that no matter when or how human beings developed, from the time they became human their irresistible urge to
worship has created, and still creates, endless forms of religious be-

havior. Indeed, so powerful is this force within human beings that it has produced a mosaic of beliefs, attitudes, and practices. Yet there is a unity within this rich diversity.

Surrounded and often threatened by forces that are seldom understood, people have always sought to penetrate the mystery of life. No matter when or where one has lived, one's religious needs have not changed: to bear the sorrows of life one needs strength; to face the daily battle for survival one needs protection; in the hour of conflict one needs assurance; in the hour of grief one needs comfort. To soothe the pangs of conscience one needs a faith; to face the dangers of life one needs a conviction; to break the grip of fear and loneliness one needs sustaining courage.

To find a way to live peacefully in spite of forces which tend toward destructive conflict is only one aspect of the search. Another aspect is the eternal quest for a purpose in one's existence. Both are legitimate goals for a person: to look for ways of avoiding or escaping dangers that threaten one's life, on the one hand; and to look for inspiration, or a profound motivation to justify one's existence, on the other. These two goals are inseparable and together they represent the ultimate goal of all religions; they will remain so to the end of time.

But recently a number of scholars have explored these assumptions and expressed their misgivings.[1] R. C. Zaehner, for instance, states:

> the basic principles of Eastern and Western, which in practice means Indian and Semitic, thought are, I will not say irreconcilably opposed; they are simply not starting from the same premise.[2]

Similarly, G. Rupp writes:

> the frequently advanced if somewhat facile assertion that the various religious perspectives and correlative practices are simply different paths or ways to the same ultimate destination . . . is, I think, inadequate because it does not do justice to the situation of pluralism even within a single tradition. . . . Hence a more accurate aphorism would be: each of the various religious traditions includes different approaches leading to different goals.[3]

As was highlighted in the discussion of religious pluralism in Chapter 13 (see pp. 402–406), a basic problem that confronts comparative historians of religion is the supposition that differing religions give different answers to the same questions. Hopefully, it is clear to a student of the histories of religion included in this text, however, that differing religions give different answers because they ask different questions. And this is precisely why each religion is essentially a distinct religion, because each religion emphasizes a different path and a different goal. A few general remarks may be in order to illustrate significant differences in the ultimate goals and the paths that lead to these goals in the different religions.

Obedience, Belief, or Submission?

Obeying the Torah is the path of Judaism that leads to blessings in this life and a favorable portion in the world to come. *Believing* in the plan of redemption in Christ as provided by God is the path of Christianity that leads to salvation and eternal life. *Submitting* to the will of God is the path of Islam that leads to eternal pleasures in paradise.

A cursory comparison of these so-called "Western" religions will indicate the immense gulf that separates them from each other. Not only does each religion have a distinctive ultimate path and a distinctive ultimate destination but also a distinctive conception of God and humanity. Let us analyze this.

The Torah means the "whole Torah," which consists of a dual divine revelation: the written part that was handed down at Mount Sinai, and the oral part that was "preserved by the scriptural heroes, passed on by prophets in the obscure past, finally and most openly handed down to the rabbis who created the Palestinian and Babylonian Talmuds."[4] Rabbinic Judaism holds that just as rabbis on earth study and live by the Torah so do God and the angels in heaven. As a matter of fact, God prays in the rabbinic mode, dons phylacteries, carries out his acts of compassion according to Judaic ethics and governs the world according to the rules of the Torah.[5] One rabbinic exegesis of the creation story is that God was guided by the Torah in creating the world.[6] Hence he who embodies the teachings of the Torah not only conforms to God's will but to God's way.

In this sense, humanity is divided into two groups: those who are bound to live by the Torah and those who are not bound by the Covenant. It is expected, therefore, of every pious Jew to discharge as many of the six hundred and thirteen commandments of the Torah as is applicable to an individual, while for the non-Jew the requirement is that one at least conform to the "seven commandments ordained upon the sons of Noah."[7] Thus, the values that shape Judaism—in fact its organizing principle of reality—is the divine covenant, the Torah.

To speak of the divine covenant, however, brings up in Islam the question of living according to the divine will, the will of God. In fact, the term *Islam* is closely associated with this cardinal idea. The Arabic term *salama*, from which *Islam* is derived, has two meanings: peace and submission. They, therefore, who through free choice submit themselves to God's will, gain peace. The order and regularity of the world of nature indicates its subservience to God's will. But the difference between the regularity of the natural order and humanity is *choice*. A stone has no choice but to fall. A tree has no choice but to grow. Only a person can accept or refuse to submit to God's will. Moreover, a person's choice is conscious and active, whereas that of nature is passive or servile. Hence, humanity may be divided into two groups: those who have surrendered to God's will (i.e., Muslims) and those who have rejected conformity to the Divine will (i.e., non-Muslims).

To speak of surrendering to divine will brings up in Christianity the issue of faith in God. "Faith is the assurance of things hoped for, the conviction of things not seen."[8] Faith is the assent to whatever God reveals as true, simply because God has revealed it. In other words, the act of faith is based on the absolute reliability of the revealing authority. The experience of "being a Christian" begins in the very commitment of faith. One believes, because God says so. It is by faith, then, that a person accepts God's revelation. The content of divine revelation may be seen in nature, in Christ, and in the Church that is the mystical Body of Christ. The Incarnation—that is to say, God becoming man by the union of a divine and a human nature in the person of Christ—is the mystery which lies at the heart of Christian faith. Christ is, therefore, in every sense, God as well as man. This is the mystery of the Incarnation: the unity of a dual nature in one person, Christ.

Similarly, the Trinity is the mystery of the unity in three persons: God, Christ, and the Holy Spirit. Christ, the second person, is God's Son incarnate, while the Holy Spirit, the third person of the Trinity, is the Spirit of Love. One God, three persons. A mystery infinitely unfathomable to the human mind.

The Incarnation, furthermore, reveals the supreme condescension of God in the redemption of mankind. Because Adam, the first man, sinned, all humanity is tainted with what is known in Christianity as "original sin." Thus, Adam's disobedience merited for the human race the miseries that accompany a "fallen" nature as well as eternal punishment. Consequently, the human race is incapable of redeeming itself from this state. It stands in need of a "new Adam." And here is where God's condescension to act on behalf of humanity is seen. In the dispensation of divine providence, Christ, the God-man, comes to buy humanity back from sin and to restore it to its destiny. Faith in Christ, therefore, means faith in the plan of redemption in Christ as provided by God. Hence, humanity is divided into two groups: those who have accepted by faith God's salvation in Christ and those who have not.

As one can see, the differences of these three religions in their view of God, humanity, and of the required path for the acquisition of happiness are quite striking. Moreover, the view of a triune God in Christianity is considered by Judaism and Islam to be highly offensive and scandalous.[9] Muslims usually interpret Christ's "sonship" in the physical sense and look upon it with a feeling akin to horror.[10] Judaism, too, does not accept the divinity of Jesus as the "only-begotten son" of God.

Again, the doctrine of original sin is absolutely repudiated in Islam. Hereditary depravity and "natural sinfulness" are emphatically denied. The Muslim cannot conceive how the Almighty Creator of the universe, the All-good, the All-wise, could create a world to be tainted by humanity's sin. Similarly, Judaism differs from Christianity on the doctrine of original sin. Judaism does not interpret the story of Adam and Eve as reflecting humanity's fall from grace. Unlike Christianity, Judaism makes no attempt to derive from the Garden of Eden allegory any lessons or rules about the nature of human beings.

Similarities and Differences in Ultimate Goals

Thus, while Judaism, Christianity, and Islam share a broad common heritage, there are, nevertheless, some deep-rooted sensitive areas that need to be explored. Furthermore, there is the question of the ultimate goals. A "portion in the world to come," "salvation and eternal life," and "eternal pleasure in paradise," are the respective goals of Judaism, Christianity, and Islam. An extraordinary similarity seems to leap out at first glance. But, sooner or later, one realizes that the similarity is simply in terminology. Just as the words "God," "Messiah," "humanity," "sin," and so on, are common terms which denote different suppositions in different religious traditions, so also do the words "salvation," "eternal life," or "world to come."

Judaism has always been more concerned with this world than the next and has always concentrated its religious efforts toward building an ideal world for the living. One rabbinic conception is that had Israel not sinned (by disobeying the Torah), the end would have come at the time of the conquest of Palestine and "the sacred community would have lived in eternal peace under divine law."[11] Another view is that "the rule of the pagans depends upon the sin of Israel. If Israel would constitute a full and complete replication of 'Torah' . . . then pagan rule would come to an end."[12] If all Israel, says another rabbinic theory, would properly keep a single Sabbath, the Messianic age would be ushered in.[13] Thus, the Judaic notion of the "world to come" is inextricably bound up with the restoration of Israel to the land, the reconstruction of the Temple and of the holy city of Jerusalem, and the inauguration of the Messianic age that would end the rule of pagans over the "people of God" and restore peace and justice.

This Judaic anticipation of the future is quite different from Christianity's anticipation of "the last things" and the Islamic concept of the "Day of Judgment." For Christianity, Christ will come again triumphant at the end of the world as judge of all human beings and all angels. This second coming and general judgment will manifest the mercy and the justice of God. In fact, Christ's second coming will be preceded by the universal preaching of the Gospel, the conversion of the Jews, the great apostasy with the coming of the anti-Christ, and cataclysmic events and extraordinary disturbances of nature.[14] Moreover, there will be a general resurrection of the dead, followed by the Last Judgment that will determine the eternal destiny of each person in heaven or hell. Finally, the eternal "kingdom of God" will be established by the creation of a new heaven and a new earth.

In Islam, the so-called "end of the world" *(al-akhirah)*, which will come suddenly and cataclysmically, is not the beginning of the establishment of the "kingdom of God," but a "Day of Judgment." Islam regards that realization of Judgment as taking place in this world. The final objective of Islam, therefore, is not extrinsic to this world but *in* it and *of* it. Paradise and hell are not "places and/or regimes beyond space-time but moral principles whose reality is so vividly grasped by the Islamic consciousness as to give them the appearance of a space-time beyond space-time."[15]

Comparing Eastern Religions

Our inquiry thus far has been restricted to the so-called "Western" religions. An attempt to compare the "Eastern" religions, either one with another or "Eastern with Western," will yield the same result. For instance, a person's ultimate destination in Hinduism is the realization of the identity of Brahman-Atman, the One and the All. The highest bliss, says Hinduism, is the realization that the individual self (Atman) is the Universal Self (Brahman). To put it differently, the Ultimate— the One, Brahman—is all that exists, including human beings. There is no hierarchy of God, humans, and universe; there is no Creator above and creatures below; no duality; only One. To attain this ultimate goal of bliss, Hinduism, unlike the "Western" religions, does not prescribe an exclusive path. Through the centuries it developed numerous paths and various systems, all designed to capitalize on the nature, temperament, interests, and aptitudes of the individual. Hinduism, therefore, recommends different paths for different people. To speak of people, however, is to speak of human beings, and here there is a radical difference between Hinduism and the "Western" religions in the concept of the nature of human beings.

The doctrine of *karma-samsara* is one of the distinctive features of Hinduism. This *karma-samsara* operates like a law of nature. There is no judge to whom one must account for one's actions on earth. There is no judgment to be pronounced, as in Christianity or Islam, that justifies a person's eternal damnation or bliss. According to Hinduism, one's destiny is not determined by God, as in most "Western" religions, but by the eternal twin law of *karma-samsara*. Seen from a Hindu perspective, the theory of eternal retribution, so common in Judaism, Zoroastrianism, Christianity, and Islam, reveals not only a total disproportion between cause and effect but also an inconsistency with God's love for his created beings. One's life on earth, therefore, is not terminated by one existence but is an inevitable consequence of *karma-samsara*. As such, a person's suffering, pain, sickness, and all sorts of ill fortune are not regarded as originating from God or Satan, as in some "Western" religions, but as the result of one's evil *karma* in past existences. Hence, the eternal law of *karma-samsara* and the theory of Brahman-Atman is certainly foreign to Judaism, Zoroastrianism, Christianity, and Islam.

Similarly, various distinctive elements, related to the concept of God and human beings, may be pointed out not only between Buddhism and the "Western" religions but also between Buddhism and Hinduism. It is unnecessary, however, to belabor the point, except to indicate, as an instance, the doctrine of *anatta* (no self), which, although it is a fundamental feature in Buddhism, is nevertheless diametrically opposed to the central concept of "self" (or "soul") in Hinduism and in most of the "Western" religions. Hinduism affirms that the self *(atman)* is eternal and immortal (also maintained by Christianity and Islam) and moving from one perishable form to another (not maintained by "Western" religions), while Buddhism flatly denies the idea of a self separate from the body, let alone the immortality of the self.

These few general remarks clearly illustrate an important factor: the profound differences in the paths and the ultimate goals in the various religious traditions. Captivated by the ideal of relativity of all religious traditions, many have either glossed over the characteristic features that distinguish religions from each other or have simply sought to emphasize the presence of "common" elements in all the various religious traditions. To adopt the view that the diverse religious traditions are simply different ways to the same ultimate destination is highly objectionable. In the first place, such a view is based on an unfounded supposition. In the second place, it paves the way for compromising the fundamental and valuable differences among various religious traditions. And in the third place, that view prohibits the exploration of deep-rooted differences and how these differences may be negotiated and resolved to meet the challenge of religious pluralism in an emerging world culture.

Notes

1. For the following discussion, see S. A. Nigosian, "Dialoguing for Differences," *Al-Mushir* 21/1 (1979): 4–10.
2. See, for instance, R. C. Zaehner, *Foolishness to the Greeks: An Inaugural Lecture delivered before the University of Oxford on 2 November 1953*, (Oxford, Eng.: Oxford University Press, 1953), p. 17; cf. also R. C. Zaehner, *Concordant Discord: The Interdependence of Faiths* (Oxford, Eng.: Oxford University Press, 1970), pp. 7–9, 19–24.
3. G. Rupp, "Religious Pluralism in the Context of an Emerging World Culture," *Harvard Theological Review* 2 (Apr. 1974): 217.
4. J. Neusner, *Between Time and Eternity: The Essentials of Judaism* (Belmont, Calif.: Dickenson, 1975), p. 36.
5. Ibid., p. 37.
6. *Genesis Rabbah* 1:1.
7. These seven commandments, which the ancient rabbis conceived as binding on all humanity, are: to refrain from idolatry, incest and adultery, bloodshed, the profanation of God's name, injustice and lawlessness, robbery, and inhumane conduct.
8. Hebrews 11:1.
9. On this, see for instance, A. Ali, "Islam and Christianity," in R. Eastman, ed., *The Ways of Religion* (San Francisco: Canfield Press, 1975), pp. 467–475; K. Cragg, *The Call of the Minaret* (New York: Oxford University Press, 1956), pp. 304–318; W. Herberg, "Judaism and Christianity: Their Unity and Difference," *The Journal of Bible and Religion* 21/2 (1953): 67–78; M. N. Kertzer, *What is a Jew?* (New York: Macmillan, 1972), pp. 172–179.
10. Qur'an 19.91–94
11. J. Neusner, *Between Time and Eternity*, p. 38.
12. Ibid., p. 38.
13. Ibid., p. 38.
14. See Matt. 24:14; Rom. 11:25; 2 Thess. 2:3–4; Matt. 24:29.
15. I. R. al Faruqi, "Islam," in Wing-tsit Chan, et al., *The Great Asian Religions* (New York: Macmillan, 1969), p. 312.

Glossary

acolyte One who waits on a person; an attendant.

agni Fire, the household hearth, or ritual fire; written with a capital *A*, it refers to the Vedic god of fire.

agnostic A person who believes that the existence of a God or of a spiritual world is unknown or unknowable.

ahimsa Indian term meaning *noninjury* or *nonviolence.*

ajiva One of the two eternal realities in Jain dualism, identified with matter.

Allah Arabic term meaning *God.*

Amitabha The Buddha of Infinite Light, regarded as the incarnation of infinite compassion and the object of worship in the Buddhist Pure Land school. The Chinese term is *O-mi-to,* while the Japanese term is *Amida.*

anatta Buddhist term for *no self*—that is, no permanent ego or soul that makes a person.

anicca Impermanence, change, transformation; a characteristic of existence, according to Buddhists.

animism The belief that every object, like every human being, harbors an individual spirit, or soul.

anthropomorphic Personifying; treating someone or something as though it were human.

apocalyptic Pertaining to a supposed revelation or vision about events or things to come.

Apocrypha The "hidden" books; a collection of fourteen books, the authority of which is disputed for inclusion in the Christian Bible.

Aranyakas Forest Books, which are Vedic speculations about sacrifice.

arhat The ideal person in Theravada Buddhism who has attained the goal of no-rebirth, or liberation.

ascetic One who lives a life of contemplation and rigorous self-denial for religious purposes.

asha-vant A follower of Asha, or Truth, in Zoroastrianism.

ashrama The four stages of Hindu life—(1) student, (2) householder, (3) forest-dweller, and (4) renouncer or wanderer.

Atash Zoroastrian word for fire.

atheist A person who disbelieves in the existence of God.

atman The individual self, soul, essence, or nature of a person. Written with a capital *A*, it refers to the Hindu Supreme Self.

aum Expanded form of *om*, a mystic syllable.

avatar Hindu term for incarnation of a deity in human or animal form.

avidya Indian term for ignorance, especially about the self and the universe.

bab Arabic term meaning *gate*, and by implication, *forerunner*. The title The Bab is used by the Baha'i in reference to their founder, 'Ali Muhammad.

Bar Mitzvah Jewish religious ceremony for boys who are ready to assume religious duties.

Bat Mitzvah Jewish religious ceremony for girls who are ready to assume religious duties.

bhakti Devotion to a deity; in Hinduism, one of the paths to liberation (*bhakti-marga*).

bodhi Knowledge, enlightenment.

bodhisattva The ideal person in Mahayana Buddhism who has attained enlightenment but, moved by compassion to aid humanity, delays indefinitely the final step to *nirvana* or Buddhahood; such a person is regarded as a savior.

Brahman The nondual, self-existent, supreme soul; the Ultimate or Absolute Reality of Hinduism.

brahmin The priestly caste, the highest ranked of the four Hindu castes.

Buddha A title meaning *awakened one* or *enlightened one*; there have been past Buddhas and there will be others in the future. The historical figure Siddhartha Gautama is one of the Buddhas, though he is often referred to simply as Buddha.

butsudan A Buddhist shelf, altar, or shrine.

caliph Arabic term meaning *successor;* a title given to the successors of Muhammad.

canonical Officially accredited group of writings accepted as scripture or of divine authority.

caste The stratification of Indian society into a hierarchy of distinct groups.

celibacy Unmarried or single state, marked by abstinence from sexual intercourse.

centaurs Demonic spirits inhabiting bodies that are half-human and half-horse, representing the nature spirit of wood and wilderness.

Ch'an Chinese term meaning *meditation;* introduced by Bodhidharma in the sixth century, the Ch'an sect developed into a school that emphasizes meditation as a means of liberation. The Japanese equivalent is Zen.

chandala An "outcast" in Hindu society.

charismatic Gifted; possessed of divine powers or talents.

chiao Taoist term meaning *relativity;* everything that is relative to time and place.

chrismation Eastern Orthodox sacrament, involving the rite of applying consecrated oil or chrism.

chun-tzu The superior man; the ideal or noble man in Confucianism.

circumambulate To walk around in a circular fashion.

clan A social unit smaller than the tribe but larger than the family, usually claiming descent from a common ancestor.

clitoridectomy Incision of the clitoris; practiced among various African and Asian societies.

cosmogony A theory or account of the origin of the universe.

cosmology A theory or body of doctrines concerning the origin and structure of the natural order or universe.

Covenant A contract or bond made between God and his people, pledging mutual rights and duties.

daevas Demons, evil spirits, or malevolent gods.

dakhma Zoroastrian Tower of Silence where corpses are exposed to the sun and the vultures.

dar-al-harb Arabic term meaning *zone of war.*

dar-al-Islam Arabic term meaning *zone of Islam.*

dar-as-sulh Arabic term meaning *zone of peace.*

deva Vedic divine being; a god.

dhikr (zikr) Arabic term meaning *remembrance*.

dhimmi Non-Muslims living under Islam and protected by it.

diaspora Greek term meaning *dispersion throughout the world*, applied to the Jewish people after the downfall of the kingdom of Judah.

divination The art of interpreting dreams, revealing future events, discovering the past, or obtaining any required information.

dreg-vant A Zoroastrian follower of evil or falsehood.

dukkha Buddhist term for human suffering, dissatisfaction, anxiety, frustration, and misery.

episcopate Position or office of bishop.

eschatological Pertaining to the last things or final age.

esoteric Secret, private, select.

Eucharist Holy Communion; the Lord's Supper. One of the sacraments performed by all Christian churches.

exorcism The process of trying to cast out evil spirits thought to have possession of a person.

fetishism The belief in or worship of an object regarded, with a feeling of awe, as having mysterious powers residing in it.

flamen Roman priest whose duty is to light the altar fires.

fu Taoist term meaning *return* or *reversal;* the invariable law of nature; the process by which all things are ordained to return to their original state.

gahambar Zoroastrian seasonal festivals or celebrations.

geisha A woman trained in the Japanese art of hospitality, entertainment, and friendship.

genius The guardian deity, or ancestral spirit of a person or family.

ghee Melted or liquid butter.

gurdwara The name for a Sikh temple.

guru A Hindu or Sikh spiritual teacher, or instructor.

Hadith The title given to the collection of Islamic traditions, especially the sayings and actions of the Prophet Muhammad.

Hajj Title of a Muslim pilgrim who has traveled to Mecca, which every Muslim is obliged to do at least once in a lifetime.

halakah The guiding law of Jewish life; a collection of legal materials in the Midrash.

hamestagna An intermediate place between heaven and hell in Zoroastrianism.

haoma A plant whose juice is used in Zoroastrian ritual. The Hindu equivalent is *soma*.

hara-kiri In Shinto, the act of honorable self-execution or ritual suicide by ripping open the abdomen with a knife.

haruspex Roman diviner, consulted for important matters.

heresy Religious opinion contrary to established dogma.

hierophant A revealer of sacred mysteries and esoteric principles.

Hijrah (hegira) Arabic term meaning *flight;* the flight of Muhammad and his disciples from Mecca to Medina on September 24, 622.

honden Main altar, sanctuary, or hall in Shinto shrine.

hua Taoist term meaning *transformation;* an eternal or infinite process of change involving ceaseless mutations with no absolute end.

Iblis Distortion of the Greek word *diabolos,* meaning *devil* or *Satan.*

ijma' Consensus of scholars reflecting their unanimous opinion.

imam The title for a religious leader in Islam who directly represents God on earth.

Injil Arabic term meaning *gospel.*

Jataka Pali term meaning *Birth Tales;* a collection of 550 stories about Buddha.

jati Hindu term meaning *birth* and used in reference to the caste system.

jen Virtue, compassion, human-heartedness, love; a cardinal virtue in Confucianism.

jihad Arabic term meaning *holy war.*

jinn The rebellious angels in Islam; genies, evil spirits.

jiva One of the two eternal realities in Jain dualism, identified with soul.

jnana Knowledge; in Hinduism, one of the paths to liberation *(jnana-marga).*

Jok In Dinka belief, the invisible, superhuman forces in the world that transcend ordinary human ability and affect human lives for good or evil.

Ka'ba The rectangular or cube-like temple in Mecca; the center of Islamic pilgrimage.

kachina A masked dancer; one of the most important features of Hopi ritual.

kami In Shinto, any being, object, or natural phenomenon believed to possess a mysterious power or spirit.

karma Action; moral law of cause and effect; in Hinduism, one of the paths to liberation *(karma-marga).*

koan The technical term in Ch'an or Zen Buddhism for a riddle, a phrase, or a word of nonsensical language that cannot be understood by reason or by intellect; it is used as an exercise for breaking the limitations of reason and thought.

kshatriya The second caste in Hindu society which protects and promotes the material welfare of society.

kuei Malevolent spirits in early Chinese religion.

kusti The Zoroastrian sacred thread given at the time of initiation.

Lamaism A term or title used for some members of the Tibetan Order of Buddhism.

li Proper conduct exemplified by the criterion of reciprocity; a code of behavior followed by Confucians.

lingam A representation of the erect penis among Hindus as the male creative force of the universe.

mandala Symbolic diagrams, charts, or circles, used especially as aids in mystical and magical rites by Buddhist esoteric sects.

mantra A magical formula based on the power of sound; used by Hindu and Buddhist esoteric sects.

Mara In Buddhism, the personification of evil who tempted Siddhartha.

marga Hindu term meaning *way* or *path*.

menorah A candelabrum used in Jewish worship. The nine-branched *menorah* is used during Hanukkah; the seven-branched one is used in synagogue services.

Midrash The collection of literary works containing scriptural expositions and interpretations of both legal and nonlegal matters.

moksha In Hinduism, release or liberation from the cycle of existence.

monasticism Organized asceticism as practiced by orders of monks and nuns.

monist A person who accepts the view that one single principle or reality exists.

monotheist A person who accepts the view that one God exists.

mosque The Muslim place or building of prayer.

mudra Ritual gestures of the hands and fingers used symbolically and magically, especially in Buddhist esoteric sects.

mystae Initiates, particularly in mystery religions.

Nhialic In Dinka belief, the unseen, powerful forces that affect human lives for good or evil.

nirvana Extinction; the state achieved by Buddhists, releasing the individual from the cycle of existence; the state of perfect bliss.

numen In Roman religion, a supernatural quality or presiding spirit.

occultism the art of manipulating or counteracting against malevolent spirits, forces, or powers.

Olorun The supreme deity (Lord/Owner) of the sky in Yoruba religion.

on In Shinto, the obligation individuals have to their benefactors and the gratitude that expresses it.

orenda Algonquin high god or holy force, who holds all things together.

orisha Divinities in Yoruba religion, believed to control the relation between heaven and earth.

pantheist A person who believes that all laws, forces, and existing phenomena in the universe are the manifestations of God; one who believes that God is everything and everything is God.

Parsee (Parsi) Name given to followers of the Zoroastrian faith.

pavi In Zoroastrianism, a flat space marked as sacred precinct for the performance of rituals or ceremonies.

polytheist A person who believes that numerous supernatural beings, usually endowed with anthropomorphic (humanlike) characteristics, govern various aspects of the natural world.

powwow Gathering of native American Indians to perform the old ceremonies and participate in tribal traditions.

proselyte A convert to some group, party, or religion.

puja In Hinduism, actions prescribed for the worship of a deity by offering food, flowers, music, lights, and adoration.

Purusha Hindu term meaning *cosmic Man.*

Qur'an The name of the Islamic scripture.

rabbi A teacher or spiritual leader of a Jewish congregation.

rajah Indian term for a prince, chieftain, or tribal head.

Ramadan The Muslim rite of fasting during the ninth month in the lunar calendar, commemorating the revelation that came to Muhammad.

rasulullah Arabic term meaning *messenger* or *prophet of God;* title applied to Muhammad.

rishi Hindu term for a seer or holy sage.

sacerdos Roman priest officiating at sacrificial rites.

sacrament Any rite, ordained or accepted by the Christian church, through which divine grace is sought and conferred.

saisei-itchi In Shinto, the principle by which religious and political dimensions of life are integrated, or essentially one.

sake Japanese alcoholic beverage made from rice.

samadhi The deepest state of trance or yoga self-possession.

samsara Rebirth; reincarnation; the cycle of successive existences.

samurai A member of the military class or leading family in Japan.

sangha The name given to the monastic order founded by Buddha; Buddhist community of monks and nuns.

sati (suttee) Hindu practice of burning alive a widow on her husband's funeral pyre.

satori Enlightenment; a technical term to describe a state of consciousness beyond the realm of differentiation.

seilenoi Demonic spirits distinguished by the body of a man with the hindquarters (legs, tails, and testicles) of a horse. Roman counterpart: satyrs.

shahada The Muslim proclamation or recitation of witness: "There is no other god but God and Muhammad is the Prophet of God."

shaikh A Sufi master who initiates novices into the practice of *dhikr*.

Shaitan Arabic term for Satan.

shakti Hindu term for active, creative feminine power extrapolated into a cosmic principle.

shari'ah Islamic divine law or regulations.

shekinah In Judaism, divine presence; the manifestation of God's presence.

Shema The Jewish prayer or proclamation of God's unity, based on Deuteronomy 6:4–9.

shen Beneficient spirits in early Chinese religion.

shu The Confucian virtue of reciprocity.

skandhas In Buddhism, the five impermanent elements that form a person: body, feelings, perceptions, dispositions, and consciousness.

smriti The body of "remembered" sacred tradition in Hinduism as distinguished from *sruti*, or revelation.

sopherim Jewish scribes and expounders of Jewish laws.

spear-master A Dinka prayer-leader, often with spear in hand, sometimes thrusting towards the sacrificial offering; the most important person in the Dinka tribe who presides over all affairs of life.

sruti The eternal, sacred knowledge of Hindus, revealed to the *rishis* and transmitted orally by *brahmins* from generation to generation.

sudra The fourth caste in Hindu society, the only duty of which is to serve the three upper castes.

sudreh A sacred shirt worn by Zoroastrians from the time of their initiation.

sunna Arabic term meaning *tradition*. Written with a capital *S*, it refers to Muslim law based, according to tradition, on the teachings and practices of Muhammad, and observed by orthodox Muslims; it is supplementary to the Qur'an.

sunyata Emptiness; the true nature of all things, according to Buddhist theory.

sura Arabic term for chapter.

synagogue A building used by a Jewish congregation as a house of worship and religious instruction.

tablet In Chinese religion, a piece of wood, stone, or metal, with an inscription, used as a memorial wall panel.

taboo Originally, a Polynesian word used to designate something forbidden; one should avoid what is proscribed because of its dangerous or sacred character.

Tad Ekam Hindu term for *That One;* the First Principle, which is indescribable, uncharacterizable, and without qualities or attributes.

Talmud The collection of commentaries, traditions, and precedents that supplements Jewish scriptures.

tanha Selfish craving for sentient existence from which Buddhists seek release.

Tantrism (Tantricism) The belief in the search for spiritual power and ultimate release from the cycle of rebirth by the repetition of *mantras* and other esoteric rites.

Tao The metaphysical cosmic force behind all phenomena; a code of behavior (way or path of moral rightness).

Tathagata A title of the Buddha, translated as "he who has discovered the truth," used by himself and later by his followers.

tat tvam asi A Hindu expression or formula that means "That art Thou." It refers to humans and the universe as being part of and one with the Absolute.

taurobolium Roman baptismal font in the form of a pit into which initiates of the Cybele mystery cult stood to undergo their initiatory rites.

te A general term for Confucian virtue, truth, or power.

theism A belief in the existence of God (or gods) and in a spiritual world.

theocracy Government or state in which God is considered to rule.

T'ien The ancient Chinese deity whose name meant the sky or heaven; in Confucianism, the Mandate of Heaven.

tiep In Dinka belief, an individual's ghost, shadow, or spirit.

Tirthankara In Jainism, the line of succession pre- and post-Mahavira.

Tripitaka The Triple Canon or Three Baskets, referring to the Pali canon of Buddha's discourses as accepted by the Theravada schools.

'ulama Divines; theologians; teachers of Islam.

umma A term applied to the Islamic community.

Upanishads A class of philosophical treaties (108 in number) attached to the Brahmana portion of Hindu scriptures.

vaisya The third caste in Hindu society, the duty of which is contributing to the economic well-being of society.

varna Hindu term for caste or social-class system.

Vedas The name of the four works which constitute the Hindu scriptures. The four works are: Atharva-Veda, Sama-Veda, Yajur-Veda, and the Rig-Veda. Attached to the Vedas are the Brahmanas and the Upanishads.

wakan The Sioux high god or holy force, that holds all things together.

wu-wei Taoist term meaning *nonaction;* the natural course of things.

yang In Chinese religion, the male, bright, positive force in the universe.

yi Righteousness; a cardinal virtue of Confucianism.

yin In Chinese religion, the female, dark, negative force in the universe.

yoga A system of disciplinary exercises and meditation directed toward identification or union with Brahman.

yoni A representation of the vagina among Hindus as the female creative force of the universe.

Zamzam The name of the well next to the Ka'ba temple in Mecca, where Hagar and Ishmael are said to have stopped for water.

zazen Sitting in meditation; a part of Ch'an or Zen Buddhist training.

Zen See Ch'an.

Bibliography

References

Adams, C. J. (ed.). *A Reader's Guide to the Great Religions*. 2nd ed. New York: Free Press, 1977.
Brandon, S. G. F. (ed.). *Dictionary of Comparative Religion*. New York: Scribner's, 1970.
Crim, K. (ed.). *Abingdon Dictionary of Living Religions*. Nashville, Tenn.: Abingdon Press, 1981.
Eliade, M. (ed.). *The Encyclopedia of Religion*. 16 vols. New York: Macmillan, 1987.

Chapter 1 Understanding Religion

Argyle, M. *Religious Behaviour*. London: Routledge & Kegan Paul, 1958.
Baird, R. D. *Category Formation and the History of Religion*. The Hague, Netherlands: Mouton, 1971.
Bellah, R. *Beyond Belief*. New York: Harper & Row, 1970.
Berger, P. L. *The Sacred Canopy: Elements of a Sociological Theory of Religion*. Garden City, N.Y.: Doubleday, 1967.
Bowker, J. W. *The Sense of God: Sociological, Anthropological and Psychological Approaches to the Origin of the Sense of God*. Oxford, Eng.: Clarendon Press, 1973.

De Vries, J. *The Study of Religion: A Historical Approach.* New York: Harcourt Brace Jovanovich, 1967.

De Waal Malefijt, A. *Religion and Culture: An Introduction to Anthropology of Religion.* New York: Macmillan, 1968.

Dewey, J. *A Common Faith.* New Haven, Conn.: Yale University Press, 1969.

Eliade, M. *A History of Religious Ideas.* 2 vols. Chicago: University of Chicago Press, 1978, 1982.

———. *The Quest: History and Meaning in Religion.* Chicago: University of Chicago Press, 1969.

———. *The Sacred and the Profane: The Nature of Religion.* New York: Harper & Row, 1961.

Frazer, J. G. *The New Golden Bough.* T. H. Gaster (ed.). New York: Criterion Books, 1959.

Freud, S. *Civilization and Its Discontents.* New York: Norton, 1961.

———. *The Future of an Illusion.* Edinburgh, Scotland: Horace Liveright and the Institute of Psycho-analysis, 1938.

Fromm, E. *The Forgotten Language.* New York: Grove Press, 1951.

Hick, J. *Philosophy of Religion.* 2nd ed. Englewood Cliffs, N.J.: Prentice-Hall, 1973.

Holm, J. *The Study of Religions.* New York: Seabury Press, 1977.

Hume, D. *Dialogues Concerning Natural Religion.* New York: Bobbs-Merrill, 1947.

Huxley, J. S. *Religion Without Revelation.* New York: Harper & Row, 1957.

James, W. *The Varieties of Religious Experience.* New York: Collier Books, 1970.

Jung, C. G. *Psychology and Religion.* New Haven, Conn.: Yale University Press, 1938.

King, W. L. *Introduction to Religion: A Phenomenological Approach.* 2nd ed. New York: Harper & Row, 1968.

Kristensen, W. B. *The Meaning of Religion: Lectures in the Phenomenology of Religion.* The Hague, Netherlands: Martinus Nijhoff, 1960.

Ling, T. *Karl Marx and Religion.* New York: Barnes & Noble, 1980.

Müller, F. M. *Natural Religion.* London: Longmans, 1881.

———. *Introduction to the Science of Religion.* London: Longmans, 1873.

Novak, K. *Ascent of the Mountain, Flight of the Dove.* New York: Harper & Row, 1971.

Parrish, F. L. *The Classification of Religions: Its Relation to the History of Religions.* Scottsdale, Ariz.: Herald Press, 1941.

Schmidt, W. *The Origin and Growth of Religion: Facts and Theories.* New York: Lincoln MacVeagh, 1931.

Schuon, F. *The Transcendent Unity of Religions.* New York: Harper & Row, 1975.

Sharpe, E. J. *Comparative Religion: A History.* New York: Scribner's, 1975.

Smart, N. *The Phenomenon of Religion.* New York: Herder & Herder, 1973.

Smith, W. C. *The Meaning and End of Religion.* New York: Mentor Books, 1962.

Tart, C. *States of Consciousness.* New York: Dutton, 1975.

Van der Leeuw, G. *Religion in Essence and Manifestation.* 2 vols. New York: Harper & Row, 1963.

Vernon, G. *Sociology of Religion.* New York: McGraw-Hill, 1962.

Waardenburg, J. *Classical Approaches to the Study of Religion.* 2 vols. The Hague, Netherlands: Mouton, 1974.

Wallace, A. F. C. *Religion: An Anthropological View.* New York: Random House, 1966.

Ward, D. J. *The Classification of Religions: Different Methods, Their Advantages and Disadvantages.* Chicago: Open Court, 1909.

Weber, M. *Sociology of Religion.* Boston: Beacon Press, 1964.

Yinger, J. M. *The Scientific Study of Religion.* New York: Macmillan, 1970.

Chapter 2 Religion in Prehistory

Albright, W. F. *From The Stone Age to Christianity.* New York: Doubleday, 1957.

Atkinson, R. J. C. *Stonehenge.* Harmondsworth, Eng.: Penguin Books, 1960.

Gill, S. D. *Beyond "The Primitive": The Religions of Nonliterate Peoples.* Englewood Cliffs, N.J.: Prentice-Hall, 1981.

Gimbutas, M. *The Goddesses and Gods of Old Europe, 6500–3500 B.C.: Myths and Cult Images.* Berkeley, Calif.: University of California Press, 1982.

Graziosi, P. *Paleolithic Art.* New York: McGraw-Hill, 1960.

Hays, H. R. *In the Beginnings: Early Man and His Gods.* New York: G. P. Putman's Sons, 1963.

James, E. O. *The Beginning of Religion.* London: Hutchinson's Library, 1949.

———. *Prehistoric Religion.* New York: Barnes & Noble, 1962.

Levy, G. R. *Religious Conceptions of the Stone Age.* New York: Harper Torchbooks, 1963.

Luquet, G. H. *The Art and Religion of Fossil Man.* Oxford, Eng.: Oxford University Press, 1930.

Maringer, J. *The Gods of Prehistoric Man.* New York: Alfred A. Knopf, 1960.

Thom, A. *Megalithic Sites in Britain.* Oxford, Eng.: Clarendon Press, 1967.

Chapter 3 African Religion

Abrahamsson, H. *The Origin of Death: Studies in African Mythology.* Uppsala, Sweden: Almqvist, 1951.

Baeta, C. G. *Prophetism in Ghana: A Study of Some "Spiritual" Churches.* London: SCM Press, 1962.

Barrett, D. B. *Schism and Renewal: An Analysis of Six Thousand Contemporary Religious Movements.* London: Oxford University Press, 1968.

Bascom, W. *African Art in Cultural Perspective.* New York: W. W. Norton, 1973.

Bohannan, P., & P. Curtin. *Africa and Africans,* 2nd ed. New York: Natural History Press, 1971.

Courtlander, H. *Tales of Yoruba Gods and Heroes.* New York: Crown, 1973.

Deng, F. M. *The Dinka of the Sudan.* New York: Holt, Rinehart & Winston, 1972.

Forde, D. (ed.). *African Worlds.* London: Oxford University Press, 1954.

Guggenheim, H. *Dogon World.* New York: The Wunderman Foundation, 1975.

Hastings, A. *A History of African Christianity, 1950–1975.* New York: Cambridge University Press, 1979.

Idowu, E. B. *African Traditional Religion: A Definition.* London: SCM Press, 1973.

King, N. Q. *Christian and Muslim in Africa.* New York: Harper & Row, 1971.

―――. *Religions of Africa.* New York: Harper & Row, 1970.

Lawson, E. T. *Religions of Africa: Traditions in Transformation.* San Francisco: Harper & Row, 1984.

Lienhardt, G. *Divinity and Experience—The Religion of the Dinka.* Oxford: Oxford University Press, 1961.

Mbiti, J. S. *African Religions and Philosophy.* New York: Anchor Books, 1970.

―――. *Concepts of God in Africa.* New York: Praeger, 1966.

Murdock, G. P. *Africa, Its People and Their Culture History.* New York: McGraw-Hill, 1959.

Parrinder, E. G. *African Traditional Religion,* 3rd ed. London: Penguin Books, 1979.

―――. *West African Religion,* 2nd ed. New York: Barnes & Noble, 1970.

―――. *African Mythology.* London: Paul A. Hamlyn, 1967.

P'Bitek, O. *African Religions in Western Scholarship.* Nairobi, Kenya: East African Publishing House, 1970.

Peel, J. D. Y. *Aladura: A Religious Movement among the Yoruba.* London: Oxford University Press, 1968.

Ranger, T. O., & I. Kimambo (eds.). *The Historical Study of African Religion.* Berkeley, Calif.: University of California Press, 1972.

Ray, B. C. *African Religions.* Englewood Cliffs, N.J.: Prentice-Hall, 1976.

Soyinka, W. *The Interpreters.* New York: Macmillan, 1970.

Sundkler, B. G. M. *Bantu Prophets in South Africa,* 2nd ed. London: Oxford University Press, 1961.

Trimingham, J. S. *The Influence of Islam in Africa.* London: Longmans, Green, 1968.

Turner, H. W. *Religious Innovations in Africa.* Boston: G. K. Hall, 1980.

―――. *African Independent Church.* 2 vols. Oxford: Clarendon Press, 1967.

Turner, V. W. *Revelation and Divination in Ndembu Ritual.* Ithaca, N.Y.: Cornell University Press, 1975.

Zahn, D. *The Religion, Spirituality and Thought of Traditional Africa.* Chicago: University of Chicago Press, 1979.

Zuesse, E. M. *Ritual Cosmos: The Sanctification of Life in African Religions.* Athens, Ohio: Ohio University Press, 1979.

Chapter 4 American Indian Traditions

Mayan

Benson, E. P. *The Maya World.* New York: Crowell, 1977.
Coe, W. R. *Tikal: A Handbook of the Ancient Maya Ruins.* 3rd ed. Philadelphia: University Museum, University of Pennsylvania, 1970.
Morley, S. G. *The Ancient Maya.* 3rd ed. Stanford, Calif.: Stanford University Press, 1956.
Thompson, J. E. S. *Maya History and Religion.* Norman, Okla.: University of Oklahoma Press, 1972.
————. *The Rise and Fall of Maya Civilization.* 2nd ed. Norman, Okla.: University of Oklahoma Press, 1966.

Aztec

Burland, C. A. *The Gods of Mexico.* London: Eyre & Spottiswoode, 1967.
Caso, A. *The Aztecs: People of the Sun.* Norman, Okla: University of Oklahoma Press, 1970.
Krickeberg, W., H. Trimborn, W. Müller, and O. Zerrics. *Pre-Columbian American Religions.* New York: Holt, Rinehart & Winston, 1969.
Soustelle, J. *The Daily Life of the Aztecs.* London: Weidenfeld & Nicolson, 1961.
Vaillant, G. C. *The Aztecs of Mexico.* Harmondsworth, Eng.: Penguin Books, 1952.

American Indian

Alexander, H. B. *The World's Rim: Great Mysteries of the North American Indians.* Lincoln, Neb.: University of Nebraska Press, 1969.
Atkinson, W. *Indians of the Southwest.* San Antonio, Tex.: Naylor, 1935.
Black, E. with J. E. Brown. *The Sacred Pipe.* Norman, Okla.: University of Oklahoma Press, 1953.
Catlin, G. *O-Kee-Pa: A Religious Ceremony and Other Customs of the Mandans.* Lincoln, Neb.: University of Nebraska Press, 1976.
Coffer, W. E. *Spirits of the Sacred Mountain: Creation Stories of the American Indians.* New York: Van Nostrand Reinhold, 1978.
Coles, R. *Children of Crisis.* Vol. 4. *Eskimos, Chicanos, Indians.* Boston: Little, Brown, 1977.
Deloria, V. *God Is Red.* New York: Grosset & Dunlap, 1973.
Driver, H. E. *Indians of North America.* Chicago: University of Chicago Press, 1961.
Farb, P. *Man's Rise to Civilization as Shown by the Indians of North America.* New York: Dutton, 1968.
Hultkrantz, A. *The Religion of the American Indians.* Berkeley, Calif.: University of California Press, 1979.
————. *Conceptions of the Soul Among North American Indians.* Stockholm: Ethnographical Museum of Sweden, 1953.

LaBarre, W. *The Ghost Dance: Origins of Religion.* New York: Doubleday, 1970.

―――. *The Peyote Cult.* Hamden, Conn.: Shoe String Press, 1947.

LaPointe, J. *Legends of the Lakota.* San Francisco: Indian Historical Press, 1976.

Marriott, A. & C. K. Rachlin. *Plains Indian Mythology.* New York: Mentor, 1977.

Morriseau, N. with S. Dewdney. *Legends of My People: The Great Ojibway.* Toronto: McGraw-Hill, 1965.

Paper, J. *Offering Smoke, The Sacred Pipe and Native American Religion.* Moscow, Idaho: University of Idaho Press, 1988.

Radin, P. *The Trickster: A Study in American Indian Mythology.* New York: Schocken Books, 1972.

Slotkin, J. S. *The Peyote Religion.* Glencoe, Ill.: Free Press, 1956.

Starkoff, C. *The People of the Center.* New York: Seabury Press, 1967.

Underhill, R. *Red Man's Religion.* Chicago: University of Chicago Press, 1972.

―――. *Red Man's America.* Chicago: University of Chicago Press, 1971.

Waters, F. *Book of the Hopi.* New York: Ballantine Press, 1963.

Chapter 5 Hinduism

Allchin, R. *The Birth of Indian Civilization.* Middlesex, Eng.: Pelican Books, 1968.

Ashby, P. H. *Modern Trends in Hinduism.* New York: Columbia University Press, 1974.

Ashe, G. *Gandhi: A Study in Revolution.* London: Heinemann, 1968.

Baig, T. A. (ed.). *Women of India.* New Delhi: Publications Division, Ministry of Information and Broadcast, 1958.

Banerjee, P. *Early Indian Religions.* New York: Wiley, 1973.

Banerji, S. C. *Dharma-Sutras: A Study of Their Origin and Development.* Calcutta: Punthi Pustak, 1962.

Beane, W. C. *Myth, Cult and Symbols in Sakta Hinduism: A Study of the Indian Mother Goddess.* Leiden, Netherlands: Brill, 1977.

Bhandarkar, R. G. *Vaisnavism, Saivism and Minor Religious Systems.* Varanasi, India: Indological Book House, 1965.

Bharati, A. *The Tantric Tradition.* London: Rider, 1970.

Bhattacharji, S. *The Indian Theogony.* Cambridge, Eng.: Cambridge University Press, 1970.

Bragdon, C. *An Introduction to Yoga.* New York: Knopf, 1963.

Coomaraswamy, A. K. *The Dance of Siva.* New York: Farrar, Straus and Giroux, 1957.

Cox, O. C. *Caste, Class and Race: A Study in Social Dynamics.* Garden City, N.Y.: Doubleday, 1948.

Danielou, A. *Hindu Polytheism.* New York: Pantheon Books, 1964.

Das, R. K. *Temples of Tamiland.* Bombay: Bharatiya Vidya Bhavan, 1964.

Derrett, J. D. M. *Religion, Law and the State of India.* New York: Free Press, 1968.

Deutsch, E. *A Source Book of Advaita Vedanta.* Honolulu: University Press of Hawaii, 1971.

Dhavamony, M. *Love of God According to Saiva Siddhanta.* Oxford, Eng.: Clarendon Press, 1971.

Edgerton, F. *The Beginnings of Indian Philosophy.* Cambridge, Mass.: Harvard University Press, 1965.

Edwards, E. M. & H. L. O. Garrett. *Mughal Rule in India.* Delhi, India: S. Chand & Co., 1956.

Eliade, M. *Yoga: Immortality and Freedom.* New York: Pantheon Books, 1958.

Embree, A. T. *The Hindu Tradition.* New York: Vintage Paperbacks, 1972.

Fairservis, W. A. *The Roots of Ancient India: The Archaeology of Early Indian Civilization.* New York: Macmillan, 1971.

Farquhar, J. N. *Modern Religious Movements in India.* Delhi, India: Munshiram Manoharlal, 1967.

Fišer, I. *Indian Erotics of the Oldest Period.* Praha Yugoslavia, Universita Karlova, 1966.

Ghurye, G. S. *Caste and Class in India.* 4th ed. Bombay: Popular Book Depot, 1957.

Gonda, J. *Visnuism and Sivaism: A Comparison.* London: Athlone Press, 1970.

———. *The Vision of the Vedic Poets.* The Hague, Netherlands: Mouton, 1965.

Hopkins, E. W. *The Great Epic of India.* Calcutta: Punthi Pustak, 1969.

Hutton, J. H. *Caste in India: Its Nature, Function and Origin.* 4th ed. London: Oxford University Press, 1969.

Ions, V. *Indian Mythology.* London: Hamlyn, 1967.

Isherwood, C. *Ramakrishna and His Disciples.* New York: Simon & Schuster, 1959.

Iyer, M. K. V. *Advaita Vedanta According to Samkara.* Bombay: Asia Publishing House, 1964.

Keith, A. B. *The Aitareya Aranyaka.* Oxford, Eng.: Oxford University Press, 1969.

Koelman, G. M. *Patanjala Yoga: From Related Ego to Absolute Self.* Poona, India: Papal Athenaeum, 1970.

Kramisch, S. *The Hindu Temple.* 2 vols. Calcutta: University of Calcutta, 1946.

Lewis, O. *Village Life in North India.* Urbana, Ill.: University of Illinois Press, 1958.

Lingat, R. *The Classical Law of India.* Berkeley, Calif.: University of California Press, 1973.

Majumdar, B. *Krsna in History and Legend.* Calcutta: University of Calcutta, 1969.

Mate, M. S. *Temples and Legends of Maharachtra.* Bombay: Bharatiya Vidya Bhavan, 1962.

Maury, C. *Folk Origins of Indian Art*. New York: Columbia University Press, 1969.

Narayan, R. K. *Gods, Demons and Others*. London: Heinemann, 1965.

O'Flaherty, W. D. *Asceticism and Eroticism in the Mythology of Siva*. London: Oxford University Press, 1973.

Pothacamury, T. *The Church in Independent India*. New York: Maryknoll, 1958.

Radhakrishnan, S. *The Hindu View of Life*. London: Allen & Unwin, 1960.

———. *The Principal Upanishads*. New York: Harper & Row, 1953.

Rai, L. L. *A History of the Arya Samaj*. Bombay: Orient Longmans, 1967.

Shils, E. *The Intellectual Between Tradition and Modernity*. The Hague, Netherlands: Mouton, 1961.

Singer, M. *When a Great Tradition Modernizes*. New York: Praeger, 1972.

——— (ed.). *Krishna: Myths, Rites and Attitudes*. Chicago: University of Chicago Press, 1968.

Singh, I. *Rammohun Roy*. Bombay: Asia Publishing House, 1958.

Smith, B. (ed.). *Hinduism: New Essays in the History of Religions*. Leiden, Netherlands: Brill, 1979.

Thomas, P. *Hindu Religion, Customs and Manners*. Bombay: Taraporevala, 1972.

van Buitenen, J. A. B. *The Bhagavadgita in the Mahabarata*. Chicago: University of Chicago Press, 1981.

Walker, B. *Hindu World: An Encyclopaedic Survey of Hinduism*. London: Allen & Unwin, 1968.

Wasson, R. G. *Soma: Divine Mushroom of Immortality*. New York: Harcourt Brace Jovanovich, 1968.

Williams, M. M. *Indian Epic Poetry*. London: Williams & Norgate, 1963.

Younger, P. *Introduction to Indian Religious Thought*. Philadelphia: Westminster Press, 1972.

Zaehner, R. C. *The Bhagavadgita*. London: Oxford University Press, 1969.

Zimmer, H. *Myths and Symbols in Indian Art and Civilization*. New York: Harper Torchbooks, 1962.

———. *Philosophies of India*. New York: Meridian Books, 1956.

Chapter 6 Buddhism

Akiyama, Z., and S. Matsubara. *Arts of China: Buddhist Cave Temples*. Tokyo: Kobansha, 1969.

Ambedkar, B. H. *The Buddha and His Dhamma*. Bombay: People's Education Society, 1957.

Appleton, G. *On the Eightfold Path*. London: SCM Press, 1961.

Bell, C. *Religions of Tibet*. Oxford, Eng.: Clarendon Press, 1931.

Benz, E. *Buddhism or Communism: Which Holds the Future of Asia?* Garden City, N.Y.: Doubleday, 1965.

Boyd, J. W. *Satan and Mara: Christian and Buddhist Symbols of Evil*. Leiden, The Netherlands: Brill, 1975.

Brannen, N. S. *Soka Gakkai: Japan's Militant Buddhists.* Richmond, Va.: Knox Press, 1968.

Bunnag, J. *Buddhist Monks, Buddhist Laymen.* Cambridge, Eng.: Cambridge University Press, 1973.

Burtt, E. A. (ed.). *The Teachings of the Compassionate Buddha.* New York: Mentor Books, 1955.

Bush, R. *Religion in Communist China.* Nashville, Tenn.: Abingdon Press, 1970.

Chang, G. C. C. *The Buddhist Teaching of Totality.* University Park, Pa.: Pennsylvania State University Press, 1971.

Chapin, H. *A Long Roll of Buddha Images.* Revised by A. Sopher. Ascona, Switzerland: Artibus Asiae, 1972.

Ch'en, K. K. S. *Buddhism in China.* Princeton, N.J.: Princeton University Press, 1972.

Conze, E. *Buddhist Texts Through the Ages.* New York: Philosophical Library, 1969.

———. *Buddhist Thought in India.* London: Allen & Unwin, 1962.

———. *Buddhism: Its Essence and Development.* New York: Harper Torchbooks, 1959.

Coomaraswamy, A. K. *Buddha and the Gospel of Buddhism.* New York: Harper Torchbooks, 1964.

Dasgupta, S. *An Introduction to Tantric Buddhism.* Berkeley, Calif.: Shambhala, 1974.

Dator, J. A. *Soka Gakkai: Builders of the Third Civilization.* Seattle: University of Washington Press, 1969.

Dayal, H. *The Bodhisattva Doctrine in Sanskrit Literature.* Delhi, India: Motilal Banarsidass, 1970.

Drummond, R. H. *Gautama the Buddha: An Essay in Religious Understanding.* Grand Rapids, Mich.: Eerdmans, 1974.

Dumoulin, H. *A History of Zen Buddhism.* Boston: Beacon Press, 1969.

Dutt, N. *Buddhist Sects in India.* Calcutta: Firma KLM, 1977.

Dutt, S. *Buddhist Monks and Monasteries of India.* London: Allen & Unwin, 1962.

Foucher, A. *The Life of the Buddha: According to the Ancient Texts and Monuments of India.* Middleton, Conn.: Wesleyan University Press, 1963.

Grimm, G. *The Doctrine of the Buddha.* Delhi, India: Motilal Banarsidass, 1958.

Grousset, R. *In the Footsteps of the Buddha.* New York: Grossman, 1971.

Herold, A. F. *The Life of Buddha, According to Legends of Ancient India.* Tokyo: Tuttle, 1974.

Hoffman, H. *The Religions of Tibet.* London: Allen & Unwin, 1961.

Humphreys, C. *Sixty Years of Buddhism in England.* London: Buddhist Society, 1968.

Hunter, L. *Buddhism in Hawaii.* Honolulu: University of Hawaii Press, 1971.

Jacobson, N. P. *Buddhism: The Religion of Analysis.* Carbondale, Ill.: Southern Illinois University Press, 1970.

Kamstra, J. H. *Encounter or Syncretism: The Initial Growth of Japanese Buddhism.* Leiden, Netherlands: Brill, 1967.

Kapleau, P. (ed.). *The Three Pillars of Zen.* Boston: Beacon Press, 1967.

Kelen, B. *Gautama Buddha in Life and Legend.* New York: Lothrop, Lee & Shepard, 1967.

Lama, D. *My Land and My People.* Ed. D. Howarth. New York: Weidenfeld & Nicholson, 1962.

Lillie, A. *The Life of Buddha.* Delhi, India: Seema Publications, 1974.

Ling, T. O. *Buddhism and the Mythology of Evil.* London: Allen & Unwin, 1962.

Marshall, G. N. *Buddha: The Quest for Serenity.* Boston: Beacon Press, 1978.

Matsunaga, A. *The Buddhist Philosophy of Assimilation.* Tokyo: Sophia University, 1969.

Matsunaga, A. & D. Matsunaga. *The Buddhist Concept of Hell.* New York: Philosophical Library, 1972.

Mookerji, R. K. *Asoka.* Delhi, India: Motilal Banarsidass, 1962.

Morgan, K. W. (ed.). *The Path of Buddha: Buddhism Interpreted by Buddhists.* New York: Ronald Press, 1956.

Munsterberg, H. *Chinese Buddhist Bronzes.* Tokyo: Charles Tuttle, 1967.

Murti, T. R. V. *The Central Philosophy of Buddhism.* London: Allen & Unwin, 1961.

Nakamura, H. *Gotama Buddha.* Kyoto, Japan: Hozokan, 1965.

Nyanaponika, T. *The Heart of Buddhist Meditation.* London: Rider, 1962.

Pardue, P. A. *Buddhism.* New York: Macmillan, 1971.

Paul, D. Y. *Women in Buddhism.* Berkeley, Calif.: Asian Humanities Press, 1979.

Percheron, M. *Buddha and Buddhism.* New York: Harper & Row, 1957.

Perry, E. and S. Ratnayaka. *The Sangha of the Tri-ratana.* Evanston, Ill.: Religion and Ethics Institute, 1974.

Prebisch, C. S. *American Buddhism.* North Scituate, Mass.: Duxbury Press, 1979.

———— (ed.). *Buddhism: A Modern Perspective.* University Park, Pa.: Pennsylvania State University Press, 1975.

Przyluski, J. *The Legend of Emperor Asoka.* Calcutta: K. L. Mukhopadhyaya, 1967.

Pye, M. *The Buddha.* London: Duckworth, 1979.

Rahula, W. *What the Buddha Taught.* New York: Grove Press, 1962.

Robinson, R. H. *Early Madhyamika in India and China.* Madison, Wis.: University of Wisconsin Press, 1967.

Saha, K. *Buddhism and Buddhist Literature in Central Asia.* Calcutta: K. L. Mukhopadhyaya, 1970.

Saunders, E. D. *Buddhism in Japan, With an Outline of Its Origins in India.* Philadelphia, Pa.: University of Pennsylvania Press, 1964.

Schechter, J. *The New Face of Buddha.* New York: Coward-McCann, 1967.

Shangharakshita, B. *The Three Jewels: An Introduction to Buddhism.* London: Hutchinson, 1968.

Streik, L. (ed.). *World of Buddha: A Reader.* Garden City, N.Y.: Doubleday, 1969.

Streng, F. J. *Emptiness: A Study in Religious Meaning.* Nashville, Tenn.: Abingdon Press, 1967.

Sullivan, M. *The Cave Temples of Maichisan.* Berkeley, Calif.: University of California Press, 1969.

Suzuki, B. L. *Mahayana Buddhism.* New York: Macmillan, 1965.

Suzuki, D. T. *Zen and Japanese Culture.* Princeton, N.J.: Princeton University Press, 1970.

Swearer, D. *The Sangha in Transition.* Philadelphia, Pa.: Westminster Press, 1970.

Thomas, E. J. *The Life of Buddha as Legend and History.* 3rd ed. New York: Barnes & Noble, 1952.

Tin, P. M. *Buddhist Devotion and Meditation.* London: SPCK, 1964.

Vajiranana, P. *Buddhist Meditation in Theory and Practice.* Colombo, Sri Lanka: Gunasena, 1962.

Waddell, L. A. *Tibetan Buddhism.* New York: Dover, 1972.

Welbon, G. R. *The Buddhist Nirvana and Its Western Interpreters.* Chicago: University of Chicago Press, 1968.

Welch, H. *Buddhism Under Mao.* Cambridge, Mass.: Harvard University Press, 1972.

Wright, A. F. *Buddhism in Chinese History.* New York: Atheneum Press, 1967.

Chapter 7 Jainism and Sikhism

Jainism

Bhargava, D. *Jaina Ethics.* Delhi, India: Motilal Banarsidass, 1968.

Deo, S. B. *History of Jaina Monasticism, From Inscriptions and Literature.* Poona, India: Deccan College Postgraduate & Research Institute, 1956.

Gopalan, S. *Outlines of Jainism.* New York: Halsted Press, 1973.

Jain, H. *Mahavira: His Times and His Philosophy of Life.* New Delhi: Bharatiya Jnanpith, 1974.

Jain, K. C. *Jainism in Rajasthan.* Sholapur, India: Doshi, 1963.

Jain, S. A. *Reality.* Calcutta: Vira Sasana Snagha, 1960.

Jaini, P. S. *Jaina Path of Purification.* Berkeley, Calif.: University of California Press, 1979.

Law, B. C. *Mahavira: His Life and Teachings.* London: Luzac, 1937.

Mehta, M. L. *Jaina Philosophy.* Varanasi, India: P. V. Research Institute, 1971.

———. *Jaina Culture.* Varanasi, India: P. V. Research Institute, 1969.

Mookerjee, S. *The Jaina Philosophy of Non-Absolutism.* Calcutta: Bharati Mahavidyala, 1944.

Schubring, W. *The Religion of the Jainas.* Calcutta: Calcutta Sanskrit College Research Series 52, 1966.

———. *The Doctrine of the Jainas.* Delhi, India: Motilal Banarsidass, 1962.

Sharma, S. R. *Jainism in South India.* Dharwar, India: Kamalapur, 1940.

Sogani, K. C. *Ethical Doctrines in Jainism.* Sholapur, India: Jaina Sainskrti Sainrakshaka Sangha, 1967.
Tatia, N. *Studies in Jaina Philosophy.* Varanasi, India: Jain Cultural Research Society, 1951.

Sikhism

Archer, J. C. *The Sikhs.* Princeton, N.J.: Princeton University Press, 1946.
Bannerjee, A. C. *Guru Nanak and His Times.* Patiala, India: Punjabi University, 1971.
Cole, W. O. *Sikhs: Their Religious Beliefs and Practices.* New York: Oxford University Press, 1978.
Cole, W. O. & P. Singh Sambhi. *The Sikhs.* London: Routledge & Kegan Paul, 1978.
Duggal, K. S. *The Sikh Gurus: Their Lives and Teachings.* New York: Vikas, 1980.
Grewal, J. S. *From Guru Nanak to Maharaja Ranjit Singh.* Amritsar, India: Guru Nanak University, 1972.
———. *Guru Nanak in History.* Chandigarh, India: Punjab University, 1969.
Grewal, J. S. & S. S. Bal. *Guru Gobind Singh: A Biographical Study.* Chandigarh, India: Punjab University, 1967.
Gupta, H. R. *History of the Sikh Gurus.* New Delhi: Kapur, 1973.
James, A. G. *Sikh Children in Britain.* Clarendon, Eng.: Oxford University Press, 1974.
Kohli, S. S. *Outlines of Sikh Thought.* New Delhi: Punjabi Prakashak, 1966.
———. *A Critical Study of the Adi Granth.* New Delhi: Punjabi Writers' Cooperative, 1961.
Loehlin, C. H. *The Sikhs and Their Scriptures.* 2nd ed. Lucknow, India: Lucknow Publishing House, 1964.
Macauliffe, M. A. *The Sikh Religion.* 6 vols. New Delhi: Chand, 1963.
McLeod, W. H. *The Evolution of the Sikh Community.* Oxford, Eng.: Oxford University Press, 1976.
———. *Guru Nanak and the Sikh Religion.* London: Oxford University Press, 1968.
Narang, G. C. *Transformation of Sikhism.* New Delhi: New Book Society of India, 1960.
Singh, D. *Guru Nanak's Message in Japji.* Amritsar, India: Singh, 1970.
Singh, G. N. (ed.). *Guru Nanak, His Life, Times and Teachings.* New Delhi: National Publishing House, 1969.
Singh, H. *Guru Nanak and Origins of the Sikh Faith.* Bombay: Asia Publishing House, 1969.
Singh, H. (ed.). *Perspectives on Guru Nanak.* Patiala, India: Punjabi University, 1971.
Singh, J. *Sikh Ceremonies.* Chandigarh, India: Religious Book Society, 1968.
Singh, K. *Hymns of Guru Nanak.* Bombay: Orient Longmans, 1972.
———. *A History of the Sikhs.* 2 vols. Princeton, N.J.: Princeton University Press, 1963–1966.

————. *The Sikhs Today*. Bombay: Orient Longmans, 1964.

————. *Guru Gobind Singh*. Ludhiana, India: Lahore Bookshop, 1951.

Singh, M. *Adi Granth*. 6 vols. Amritsar, India: SGPC, 1969.

Singh, P. *The Sikh Gurus and the Temple of Bread*. 2nd ed. Amritsar, India: SGPC, 1971.

Singh, S. *Philosophy of Sikhism*. 2nd ed. Delhi, India: Sterling, 1966.

Singh, T. *Guru Nanak, Founder of Sikhism*. Delhi, India: Gurdwara Parbandhak Committee, 1969.

————. *Guru Tegh Bahadur*. Delhi, India: Gurdwara Parbandhak Committee, 1967.

————. *Sikh Religion: An Outline of Its Doctrines*. Amritsar, India: SGPC, 1963.

————. *Sikhism: Its Ideals and Institutions*. Bombay: Orient Longmans, 1951.

Talib, G. S. *Guru Nanak, His Personality and Vision*. Delhi, India: Kapur, 1969.

Chapter 8 Taoism and Confucianism

Religion in Chinese Society

Ahern, E. M. *The Cult of the Dead in a Chinese Village*. Stanford, Calif.: Stanford University Press, 1973.

Bush, R. C. *Religion in Communist China*. Nashville, Tenn.: Abingdon Press, 1970.

Chan, W. T. *A Source Book in Chinese Philosophy*. Princeton, N.J.: Princeton University Press, 1967.

Croll, E. *The Women's Movement in China*. London: Anglo-Chinese Educational Institute, 1974.

Fairbank, J. K. (ed.). *Chinese Thought and Institutions*. Chicago: University of Chicago Press, 1957.

Fitzgerald, C. P. *China: A Short Cultural History*. 3rd ed. New York: Praeger, 1961.

Franke, W. *A Century of Chinese Revolution, 1851–1949*. New York: Harper Torchbooks, 1970.

Freedman, M. (ed.). *Family and Kinship in Chinese Society*. Stanford, Calif.: Stanford University Press, 1970.

Howard, S. D. *Chinese Religions*. New York: Holt, Rinehart & Winston, 1968.

Jordan, D. K. *Gods, Ghosts and Ancestors: The Folk Religion of a Taiwanese Village*. Berkeley, Calif.: University of California Press, 1972.

Lessa, W. A. *Chinese Body Divination*. Los Angeles: United World Academy & Fellowship, 1968.

MacInnis, D. E. *Religious Policy and Practice in Communist China*. New York: Macmillan, 1972.

Moore, C. E. (ed.). *The Chinese Mind*. Honolulu, Hawaii: East-West Center Press, 1969.

Rosaldo, M. Z. & L. Lamphere (eds.). *Woman, Culture and Society*. Stanford: Stanford University Press, 1974.

Smith, D. H. *Chinese Religions*. New York: Holt, Rinehart & Winston, 1968.
Thompson, L. G. *Chinese Religion*. 3rd ed. Belmont, Calif.: Wadsworth, 1979.
Waley, A. *The Nine Songs: A Study of Shamanism in Ancient China*. London: Allen & Unwin, 1955.
Watson, W. *Early Civilization in China*. London: Thames Hudson, 1966.
Weber, M. *The Religion of China*. London: Macmillan, 1968.
Wolf, A. P. (ed.). *Religion and Ritual in Chinese Society*. Stanford, Calif.: Stanford University Press, 1974.
Wolf, M. & R. Whitke (eds.). *Women in Chinese Society*. Stanford, Calif.: Stanford University Press, 1975.
Yang, C. K. *Religion in Chinese Society*. Berkeley, Calif.: University of California Press, 1961.
Yu-lan, F. *History of Chinese Philosophy*. 2 vols. Princeton, N.J.: Princeton University Press, 1952–1953.

Taoism

Blofeld, J. *Beyond the Gods. Buddhist and Taoist Mysticism*. New York: Dutton, 1974.
———. *The Secret and Sublime: Taoist Mysteries and Magic*. London: Allen & Unwin, 1973.
Chung-yuan, C. *Creativity and Taoism*. New York: Julian Press, 1963.
Cooper, J. *Taoism: The Way of the Mystic*. Northamptonshire, Eng.: Aquarian Press (Thorsons Group), 1972.
Creel, H. G. *What Is Taoism?* Chicago: University of Chicago Press, 1970.
Gia-Fu, F. & J. English. *Tao Te Ching*. New York: Vintage Books, 1972.
Hoff, B. *The Tao of Pooh*. New York: Penguin Books, 1983.
Kaltenmark, M. *Lao Tzu and Taoism*. Stanford, Calif.: Stanford University Press, 1969.
Liu, D. *The Tao and Chinese Culture*. New York: Schocken Books, 1978.
———. *The Tao of Health and Longevity*. New York: Schocken Books, 1978.
Rawson, P. & L. Legeza. *Tao: The Eastern Philosophy of Time and Change*. New York: Avon Books, 1973.
Saso, M. *Taoism and the Rite of Cosmic Renewal*. Pullman, Wash.: Washington State University Press, 1972.
Saso, M. & D. W. Chappell (eds.). *Buddhist and Taoist Studies I*. Honolulu, Hawaii: University of Hawaii Press, 1977.
Smullyan, R. M. *The Tao Is Silent*. New York: Harper & Row, 1977.
Watson, B. *The Complete Works of Chuang Tzu*. New York: Columbia University Press, 1968.
Welch, H. *Taoism: The Parting of the Way*. Boston: Beacon Press, 1966.
Wing-tsit, C. *The Way of Lao Tzu*. Indianapolis, Ind.: Bobbs-Merrill, 1963.

Confucianism

Chai, C. & W. Chai. *Confucianism*. New York: Barron's Educational Series, Woodbury, N.Y., 1973.

Chang, C. *The Development of Neo-Confucian Thought.* New York: Twayne, 1957.

Creel, H. G. *Confucius and the Chinese Way.* New York: Harper & Row, 1960.

————. *Chinese Thought: From Confucius to Mao Tse Tung.* Chicago: University of Chicago Press, 1953.

————. *Confucius: The Man and the Myth.* New York: Day, 1949.

Fingarette, H. *Confucius: The Secular as Sacred.* New York: Harper Torchbooks, 1972.

Giles, L. *The Book of Mencius.* London: Murray, 1942.

Liu, W. *Confucius, His Life and Time.* New York: Philosophical Library, 1955.

Smith, D. H. *Confucius.* New York: Scribner's, 1973.

Waley, A. *The Analects of Confucius.* London: Macmillan, 1938.

Ware, J. R. *The Sayings of Mencius.* New York: New American Library, 1960.

Watson, B. *Hsun Tzu: Basic Writings.* New York: Columbia University Press, 1963.

Wilhelm, R. *Confucius and Confucianism.* Port Washington, Wis.: Kennikat Press, 1970.

Wright, A. F. *The Confucian Persuasion.* Stanford, Calif.: Stanford University Press, 1960.

Chapter 9 Shinto

Anesaki, M. *History of Japanese Religion.* Tokyo: Charles Tuttle, 1963.

Aoki, M. Y. *Ancient Myths and Early History of Japan: A Cultural Foundation.* New York: Exposition Press, 1974.

Ashton, W. G. *Nihongi: Chronicles of Japan from the Earliest Times to A.D. 697.* New York: Paragon, 1969.

Blacker, C. *The Catalpa Bow: A Study of Shamanistic Practices in Japan.* New York: Macmillan, 1967.

Bloom, Q. A. *The Life of Shinran Shonin: The Journey to Self-Acceptance.* Leiden, Netherlands: Brill, 1968.

Bock, F. G. *Engi-Shiki: Procedures of the Engi Era.* Tokyo: Sophia University, Books I–V, 1970; Books VI–X, 1972.

Brown, D. M. *Nationalism in Japan: An Introductory Historical Analysis.* Berkeley, Calif.: University of California Press, 1971.

Cary, O. *A History of Christianity in Japan.* 2 vols. New York: F. H. Revell, 1909; reprint: Mich.: Scholarly Press, 1971.

Creemers, W. *Shrine Shinto After World War II.* Leiden, Netherlands: Brill, 1968.

Drummond, R. H. *A History of Christianity in Japan.* Grand Rapids, Michigan: Eerdmans, 1971.

Earhart, H. B. *A Religious Study of the Mount Haguro Sect of Shugendo: An Example of Japanese Mountain Religion.* Tokyo: Sophia University, 1970.

Elison, G. *Deus Destroyed: The Image of Christianity in Early Modern Japan.* Cambridge, Mass.: Harvard University Press, 1973.

Fridell, W. M. *Japanese Shrine Mergers, 1906–12: State Shinto Moves to the Grassroots.* Tokyo: Sophia University, 1973.

Hall, J. W. *Japan: from Prehistory to Modern Times.* New York: Delacorte Press, 1970.

Herbert, J. *Shinto: Fountainhead of Japan.* New York: Stein & Day, 1967.

Holtom, D. C. *The National Faith of Japan.* New York, Paragon, 1965.

Hori, I. *Folk Religion in Japan: Continuity and Change.* Ed. by J. M. Kitagawa and A. L. Miller, Chicago: University of Chicago Press, 1968.

Iglehart, C. W. *A Century of Protestant Christianity in Japan.* Rutland, Vt.: Tuttle, 1959.

Kato, G. *A Study of Shinto: The Religion of the Japanese Nation.* New York: Barnes & Noble, 1971.

Kato, G. & H. Hoshino. *Kogoshui: Gleanings from Ancient Stories.* 3rd ed. New York: Barnes & Noble, 1972.

Kidder, E. *Early Buddhist Japan.* New York: Praeger, 1975.

———. *Japan Before Buddhism.* New York: Praeger, 1966.

Kishimoto, H. (ed.). *Japanese Religion in the Meiji Era.* Tokyo: Obunsha, 1956.

Kitagawa, J. M. *Religion in Japanese History.* New York: Columbia University Press, 1966.

Laures, J. *The Catholic Church in Japan: A Short History.* Notre Dame, Ind.: University of Notre Dame Press, 1962.

Mason, J. W. T. *The Meaning of Shinto: The Primaeval Foundations of Creative Spirit in Modern Japan.* Port Washington, Wis.: Kennikat Press, 1967.

Matsumoto, S. *Motoori Norinaga, 1730–1801.* Cambridge, Mass.: Harvard University Press, 1970.

Matsunaga, D. & A. Matsunaga. *Foundation of Japanese Buddhism.* 2 vols. Los Angeles: Buddhist Books International, 1974.

McFarland, H. N. *The Rush Hour of the Gods: A Study of New Religious Movements in Japan.* New York: Macmillan, 1967.

Morioka, K. *Religion in Changing Japanese Society.* Tokyo: University of Tokyo Press, 1975.

Morris, I. I. *The World of the Shining Prince: Court Life in Ancient Japan.* New York: Knopf, 1964.

Munsterberg, H. *The Arts of Japan: An Illustrated History.* Rutland, Vt.: Tuttle, 1957.

Murakami, S. *Japanese Religion in the Modern Century.* Tokyo: University of Tokyo Press, 1980.

Muraoka, T. *Studies in Shinto Thought.* Tokyo: Ministry of Education, 1964.

Naofusa, H. *Understanding Japan: Japanese Shinto.* Tokyo: International Society for Educational Information, 1966.

Norbeck, E. *Religion and Society in Modern Japan: Continuity and Change.* Houston, Tex.: Tourmaline Press, 1970.

Offner, C. B. & H. Van Straelen. *Modern Japanese Religions with Special Emphasis Upon Their Doctrines of Healing.* Leiden, Netherlands: Brill, 1963.

Ono, S. *Shinto: The Kami Way.* Rutland, Vt.: Tuttle, 1962.

Philippi, D. L. R. *Kojiki.* Tokyo: University of Tokyo Press, 1968.

Phillips, J. M. *From the Rising of the Sun: Christians and Society in Contemporary Japan.* Maryknoll, N.Y.: Orbis Books, 1981.

Ross, F. H. *Shinto: The Way of Japan.* Boston: Beacon Press, 1965.

Schneider, D. B. *Konko-kyo: A Japanese Religion.* Tokyo: International Institute for the Study of Religion, 1962.

Smith, R. J. *Ancestor Worship in Contemporary Japan.* Stanford, Calif.: Stanford University Press, 1974.

Smith, W. W. *Confucianism in Modern Japan: A Study of Conservatism in Japanese Intellectual History.* 2nd ed. Tokyo: Hokuseido Press, 1973.

Suzuki, D. T. *Shin Buddhism.* New York: Harper & Row, 1970.

———. *Zen and Japanese Culture.* New York: Pantheon, 1959.

Thomsen, H. *The New Religions of Japan.* Rutland, Vt.: Tuttle, 1963.

Van Staelen, H. *The Religion of Divine Wisdom.* Kyoto, Japan: Veritas Shion, 1957.

Varley, H. P., I. Varley, & N. Morris. *Samurai.* New York: Delacorte Press, 1971.

Woodward, W. P. *The Allied Occupation of Japan, 1945–1952, and Japanese Religions.* Leiden, Netherlands: Brill, 1972.

Chapter 10 Roots of Western Religions

Mesopotamian

Chiera, E. *They Wrote on Clay.* Chicago: University of Chicago Press, 1962.

Contenau, G. *Everyday Life in Babylon and Assyria.* New York: Norton, 1966.

Gaster, Th. H. *The Oldest Stories in the World.* Boston: Beacon Press, 1958.

Hallo, W. H. & W. K. Simpson. *The Ancient Near East: A History.* New York: Harcourt Brace Jovanovich, 1971.

Heidel, A. *The Babylonian Genesis.* 2nd ed. Chicago: University of Chicago Press, 1951.

———. *The Gilgamesh Epic and Old Testament Parallels.* Chicago: University of Chicago Press, 1951.

Hooke, S. H. *Assyrian and Babylonian Religion.* Oxford, Eng.: Oxford University Press, 1962.

Jacobsen, T. *The Treasures of Darkness: A History of Mesopotamian Religion.* New Haven, Conn.: Yale University Press, 1976.

Kramer, S. N. *The Sumerians: Their History, Culture and Character.* Chicago: University of Chicago Press, 1963.

———. *Sumerian Mythology.* New York: Harper & Row, 1961.

———. *History Begins at Sumer.* New York: Doubleday, 1959.

Oppenheim, A. L. *Ancient Mesopotamia.* Chicago: University of Chicago Press, 1977.

Ringgren, H. *Religions of the Ancient Near East.* London: SPCK, 1976.

Roux, G. *Ancient Iraq.* London: Allen & Unwin, 1964.

Saggs, H. W. F. *The Greatness That Was Babylon.* Toronto, Can.: New American Library of Canada, 1968.

Sollberger, E. *The Babylonian Legend of the Flood.* London: Trustees of the British Museum, 1962.

Egyptian

Aldred, C. *Akhenaten, Pharaoh of Egypt; A New Study.* London: Thames & Hudson, 1968.

Allen, T. C., trans., *The Book of the Dead.* Chicago: University of Chicago Press, 1974.

Bleeker, C. J. *Egyptian Festivals: Enactments of Religious Renewal.* Leiden, Netherlands: Brill, 1967.

Breasted, J. H. *The Development of Religion and Thought in Ancient Egypt.* New York: Harper & Row, 1959.

Çerny, J. *Ancient Egyptian Religion.* New York: Holt, Rinehart & Winston, 1952.

Edwards, I. E. S. *The Pyramids of Egypt,* rev. ed. London: Penguin Books, 1961.

Emery, W. B. *Archaic Egypt.* Baltimore: Penguin Books, 1963.

Faulkner, R. O. *The Ancient Egyptian Coffin Texts.* Warminster, Eng.: Aris & Phillips, 1973.

———. *The Ancient Egyptian Pyramid Texts.* Oxford, Eng.: Clarendon Press, 1969.

Frankfort, H. *Ancient Egyptian Religion.* New York: Harper & Row, 1961.

———. *Kingship and the Gods.* New York: Harper & Row, 1961.

Gardiner, A. *Egypt of the Pharaohs.* Oxford, Eng.: Oxford University Press, 1966.

Griffiths, J. G. *The Origins of Osiris.* Berlin: Hessling, 1966.

———. *The Conflict of Horus and Seth: From Egyptian and Classical Sources.* Liverpool, Eng.: Liverpool University Press, 1960.

Hallo, W. H. & W. K. Simpson. *The Ancient Near East: A History.* New York: Harcourt Brace Jovanovich, 1971.

Hayes, W. C. *Most Ancient Egypt.* Chicago: University of Chicago Press, 1964.

———. *The Sceptre of Egypt.* New York: Metropolitan Museum of Art, Vol. 1, *From the Earliest Times to the End of the Middle Kingdom,* 1953; Vol. 2, *The Hyksos Period and the New Kingdom,* 1959.

Ions, V. *Egyptian Mythology.* London: Hamlyn, 1965.

Mercer, S. A. B. *The Religion of Ancient Egypt.* London: Luzac, 1949.

Morenz, S. *Egyptian Religion.* London: Methuen, 1973.

Redford, D. *Akhenaten: The Heretic King.* Princeton, N.J.: Princeton University Press, 1987.

Sauneron, S. *The Priests of Ancient Egypt.* New York: Grove Press, 1960.

Wilson, J. A. *The Culture of Ancient Egypt.* 5th ed. Chicago: University of Chicago Press, 1958.

Greek

Berve, H. *Greek Temples, Theatres and Shrines.* New York: Abrams, 1963.

Burkert, W. *Greek Religion.* Cambridge, Mass.: Harvard University Press, 1985.

Bury, J. B. *A History of Greece.* 4th ed. London: Macmillan, 1975.

Chadwick, J. *The Mycenaean World*. Cambridge, Eng.: Cambridge University Press, 1976.

Dietrich, B. C. *The Origins of Greek Religion*. New York: De Gruyter, 1974.

Drees, L. *Olympia: Gods, Artists and Athletes*. London: Pall Mall Press, 1968.

Ferguson, J. *The Heritage of Hellenism*. London: Thames & Hudson, 1973.

Festugiere, A. J. *Personal Religion Among the Greeks*. Berkeley, Calif.: University of California Press, 1954.

Grant, F. C. (ed.). *Hellenistic Religions: The Age of Syncretism*. New York: Liberal Arts Press, 1954.

Grant, M. *Myths of the Greeks and Romans*. London: Weidenfeld & Nicolson, 1962.

Guthrie, W. K. C. *The Religion and Mythology of the Greeks*. Cambridge, Eng.: Cambridge University Press, 1964.

———. *The Greeks and Their Gods*. London: Methuen, 1962.

———. *Orpheus and Greek Religion: A Study of the Orphic Movement*. London: Methuen, 1952.

Hadas, M. *Hellenistic Culture: Fusion and Diffusion*. New York: Columbia University Press, 1959.

Halliday, W. R. *Greek Divination: A Study of Its Methods and Principles*. London: Macmillan, 1913.

Kerényi, K. *Eleusis: Archetypal Image of Mother and Daughter*. New York: Pantheon Books, 1967.

———. *The Religion of the Greeks and Romans*. London: Thames & Hudson, 1962.

Martin, L. H. *Hellenistic Religions*. New York: Oxford University Press, 1987.

Murray, G. *Five Stages of Greek Religion*. Boston: Beacon Press, 1951.

Mylonas, G. E. *Eleusis and the Eleusinian Mysteries*. Princeton, N.J.: Princeton University Press, 1961.

Nilsson, M. P. *A History of Greek Religion*. New York: Norton, 1964.

———. *Greek Folk Religion*. New York: Harper & Row, 1961.

Otto, W. F. *The Homeric Gods*. London: Thames & Hudson, 1979.

———. *Dionysus: Myth and Cult*. Bloomington, Ind.: Indiana University Press, 1965.

Parke, H. W. *Greek Oracles*. London: Hutchinson's University Library, 1967.

Persson, A. W. *The Religion of Greece in Prehistoric Times*. Berkeley, Calif.: University of California Press, 1942.

Rose, H. J. *Religion in Greece and Rome*. New York: Harper & Row, 1959.

———. *Ancient Greek Religion*. London: Hutchinson, 1946.

Roman

Barrow, R. H. *The Romans*. New York: Penguin Books, 1949.

Bell, H. I. *Cults and Creeds in Graeco-Roman Egypt*. New York: Oxford University Press, 1953.

Bloch, R. *The Origins of Rome*. London: Thames & Hudson, 1966.

Brown, P. *The World of Late Antiquity from Marcus Aurelius to Muhammad.* London: Thames & Hudson, 1971.

Cary, M. & H. H. Scullard. *A History of Rome Down to the Reign of Constantine.* 3rd ed. New York: St. Martin's Press, 1976.

Cumont, F. *The Oriental Religions in Roman Paganism.* New York: Dover, 1956.

Dumezil, G. *Archaic Roman Religion with an Appendix on the Religion of the Etruscans.* 2 vols. Chicago: University of Chicago Press, 1970.

Ferguson, J. *The Religions of the Roman Empire.* London: Thames & Hudson, 1970.

Grant, F. C. (ed.). *Ancient Roman Religion.* New York: Liberal Arts Press, 1957.

Grant, M. *Roman Myths.* London: Weidenfeld & Nicolson, 1971.

Harris, J. R. *The Oriental Cults in Roman Britain.* Leiden, Netherlands: Brill, 1965.

Heyob, S. K. *The Cult of Isis Among Women in the Graeco-Roman World.* Leiden, Netherlands: Brill, 1975.

Hyde, W. W. *Paganism to Christianity in the Roman Empire.* New York: Octagon Books, 1970.

Michels, A. K. *The Calendar of the Roman Republic.* Princeton, N.J.: Princeton University Press, 1967.

Rahner, H. *Greek Myths and Christian Mystery.* London: Burns & Oates, 1963.

Rose, H. J. *Ancient Roman Religion.* London: Hutchinson's University Library, 1948.

Taylor, L. R. *The Divinity of the Roman Emperor.* Middletown, Conn.: American Philological Association, 1931.

Vermaseren, M. J. *Cybele and Attis: The Myth and the Cult.* London: Thames & Hudson, 1977.

———. *Mithras, The Secret God.* London: Chatto & Windus, 1963.

Walters, V. J. *The Cult of Mithras in the Roman Provinces of Gaul.* Leiden, Netherlands: Brill, 1974.

Witt, R. E. *Isis in the Graeco-Roman World.* London: Thames & Hudson, 1971.

Chapter 11 Zoroastrianism

Boyce, M. *Zoroastrians: Their Religious Beliefs and Practices.* London: Routledge & Kegan Paul, 1979.

———. *A Persian Stronghold of Zoroastrianism.* Oxford, Eng.: Oxford University Press, 1977.

———. *A History of Zoroastrianism.* 2 vols. Leiden, Netherlands: Brill, 1975, 1982.

Dhalla, M. N. *History of Zoroastrianism.* New York: Oxford University Press, 1963.

Duchesne-Guillemin, J. *Religion of Ancient Iran.* Bombay: Tata Press, 1973.

———. *The Western Response to Zoroaster.* Westport, Conn.: Greenwood Press, 1973.

————. *Symbols and Values in Zoroastrianism.* New York: Harper & Row, 1970.

————. *The Hymns of Zoroaster.* Boston: Beacon Press, 1963.

Frye, R. N. *The Heritage of Persia.* London: Weidenfeld & Nicolson, 1963.

Ghirshman, R. *Iran: From the Earliest Times to the Islamic Conquest.* Harmondsworth, Eng.: Penguin Books, 1954.

Gnoli, G. *Zoroaster's Time and Homeland.* Naples, Italy: Instituto Universitario Orientale, 1980.

Henning, W. B. *Zoroaster: Politician or Witch Doctor?* Oxford, Eng.: Oxford University Press, 1950.

Herzfeld, E. E. *Zoroaster and His World.* New York: Octagon Books, 1974.

Hinnells, J. R. *Zoroastrianism and the Parsis.* London: Ward Lock Educ., 1981.

————. *Persian Mythology.* London: Hamlyn House, 1973.

Insler, S. *The Gathas of Zarathustra.* Leiden, Netherlands: Brill, 1975.

Jackson, A. V. W. *Zoroaster: The Prophet of Ancient Iran.* New York: Columbia University Press, 1965.

Kulke, E. *The Parsees in India.* Munich, W. Ger.: Weltforum Verlag, 1974.

Masani, R. P. *Zoroastrianism: The Religion of the Good Life.* New York: Collier Books, 1962.

Mirza, H. D. K. *Outlines of Parsi History.* Bombay: Industrial Press, 1974.

Modi, J. J. *Religious Ceremonies and Customs of the Parsis.* 2nd ed. London: Luzac, 1954.

Moulton, J. H. *The Teachings of Zarathustra.* 2nd ed. Bombay: Meherji Byramji Mithaiwala, 1917.

————. *The Treasure of the Magi: A Study of Modern Zoroastrianism.* London: Oxford University Press, 1917.

Nanavutty, P. *The Parsis.* New Delhi: National Book Trust, 1977.

Nigosian, S. A. *The Zoroastrian Faith: Tradition and Modern Research.* Montreal, Canada: McGill-Queen's University Press, 1993.

Olmstead, A. T. *History of the Persian Empire.* Chicago: University of Chicago Press, 1948.

Pangborn, C. R. *Zoroastrianism: A Beleaguered Faith.* New York: Advent Books, 1983.

Pavry, J. C. *The Zoroastrian Doctrine of a Future Life.* New York: AMS Press, 1965.

Zaehner, R. C. *The Teachings of the Magi.* London: Sheldon Press, 1975.

————. *The Dawn and Twilight of Zoroastrianism.* London: Weidenfeld & Nicolson, 1961.

————. *Zurvan: A Zoroastrian Dilemma.* Oxford, Eng.: Oxford University Press, 1955.

Chapter 12 Judaism

Adler, M. *The World of the Talmud.* 2nd ed. New York: Schocken Books, 1970.

Albright, W. F. *Yahweh and the Gods of Canaan.* Garden City, N.Y.: Doubleday, 1968.

Anderson, G. W. *The History and Religion of Israel.* London: Oxford University Press, 1966.

Bamberger, B. J. *The Search for Jewish Theology.* New York: Behrman, 1978.

Ben-zvi, I. *The Exiled and the Redeemed.* Philadelphia: Jewish Publication Society, 1961.

Berkovits, E. *Faith After the Holocaust.* New York: Ktav, 1973.

Blau, J. L. *Modern Varieties of Judaism.* New York: Columbia University Press, 1966.

Buber, M. *Israel and the World.* 2nd ed. New York: Schocken Books, 1963.

———. *Moses, the Revelation, and the Covenant.* New York: Harper & Row, 1958.

Davis, M. *The Emergence of Conservative Judaism.* Philadelphia: Jewish Publication Society of America, 1963.

de Vaux, R. *Early History of Israel.* Philadelphia: Westminster Press, 1978.

Dimont, M. *Jews, God and History.* New York: New American Library, 1964.

Donin, H. H. *To Be a Jew.* New York: Basic Books, 1972.

Finkelstein, L. *The Jews: Their History, Culture and Religion.* 2 vols. New York: Harper & Row, 1960.

Freud, S. *Moses and Monotheism.* New York: Random House, 1967.

Gaster, T. H. *Festivals of the Jewish Year.* London: Apollo, 1961.

Glazer, N. *American Judaism.* 2nd ed. Chicago: University of Chicago Press, 1972.

Guttman, J. *Philosophies of Judaism.* New York: Schocken Books, 1973.

Herberg, W. *Judaism and Modern Man.* New York: Atheneum, 1970.

Hertzberg, A. *The Zionist Idea.* New York: Atheneum, 1970.

Jacobs, L. *Principles of the Jewish Faith: An Analytical Study.* London: Vallentine, Mitchell, 1964.

Joseph, D. *Faithful City: The Siege of Jerusalem.* New York: Simon & Schuster, 1964.

Kaplan, M. M. *The Meaning of God in Modern Jewish Religion.* New York: Jewish Reconstructionist Press, 1962.

Kaufmann, Y. *The Religion of Israel.* Chicago: University of Chicago Press, 1960.

Klausner, J. *The Messianic Idea in Israel.* New York: Macmillan, 1955.

Klein, I. *Guide to Jewish Religious Practice.* New York: Jewish Theological Society of America, 1979.

Koltun, E. (ed.). *The Jewish Woman.* New York: Schocken Books, 1976.

Lacks, R. *Women and Judaism.* New York: Doubleday, 1980.

Martin, B. *Great Twentieth Century Jewish Philosophers.* New York: Macmillan, 1970.

Meiselman, M. *Jewish Woman in Jewish Law.* New York: Ktav, 1978.

Neusner, J. *Between Time and Eternity: The Essentials of Judaism.* Belmont, Calif.: Dickenson, 1975.

Nigosian, S. A. *Judaism: The Way of Holiness.* Wellingborough, Eng.: Thorsons, 1986.

———. *Occultism in the Old Testament.* Philadelphia: Dorrance, 1978.

Philipson, D. *The Reform Movement in Judaism.* New York: Ktav, 1967.

Ringgren, H. *Israelite Religion*. Philadelphia: Fortress Press, 1966.
Rosenzweig, F. *Star of Redemption*. Boston: Beacon Press, 1972.
Sachar, A. L. *A History of the Jews*. New York: Knopf, 1973.
———. *Israel: The Establishment of a State*. London: Weidenfeld & Nicolson, 1952.
Sandmel, S. *The Hebrew Sciptures: An Introduction*. New York: Knopf, 1962.
Schauss, H. *Guide to Jewish Holy Days*. New York: Schocken Books, 1970.
Scholem, G. G. *The Messianic Idea in Judaism*. New York: Schocken Books, 1971.
———. *Major Trends in Jewish Mysticism*. New York: Schocken Books, 1941.
Singer, S. A. *Medieval Jewish Mysticism: The Book of the Pious*. Wheeling, Ill.: Whitehall, 1971.
Trepp, L. *Complete Book of Jewish Observance*. New York: Summit Books, 1980.
Zimmels, H. J. *Ashkenazim and Sephardim*. Oxford, Eng.: Oxford University Press, 1958.

Chapter 13 Christianity

Atiya, A. S. *A History of Eastern Christianity*. London: Methuen, 1968.
Aulen, G. E. H. *Jesus in Contemporary Historical Research*. Philadelphia: Fortress Press, 1976.
Bainton, R. H. *The Reformation of the Sixteenth Century*. Boston: Beacon Press, 1962.
———. *Early Christianity*. Princeton, N.J.: Van Nostrand, 1960.
Baur, W. *Orthodoxy and Heresy in Earliest Christianity*. Philadelphia: Fortress Press, 1971.
Bornkamm, G. *Paul*. New York: Harper & Row, 1971.
———. *Jesus of Nazareth*. New York: Harper & Row, 1960.
Carpenter, H. *Jesus*. Oxford, Eng.: Oxford University Press, 1980.
Carroll, M. P. *The Cult of the Virgin Mary*. Princeton, N.J.: Princeton University Press, 1986.
Chadwick, H. *The Early Church*. Harmondsworth, Eng.: Penguin Books, 1967.
Chadwick, O. *The Reformation*. Harmondsworth, Eng.: Penguin Books, 1964.
Clark, E. T. *The Small Sects in America*. Nashville, Tenn.: Abingdon Press, 1949.
Cobb, J. B. *Christ in a Pluralistic Age*. Philadelphia: Westminster Press, 1975.
Cohn, N. *The Pursuit of the Millennium*. New York: Oxford University Press, 1970.
Conzelmann, H. *Jesus*. Philadelphia: Fortress Press, 1975.
Cunliffe-Jones, H. (ed.). *A History of Christian Doctrine*. Philadelphia: Fortress Press, 1980.
Daniel-Rops, H. *Jesus and His Times*. Garden City, N.Y.: Doubleday, 1958.
Diehl, C. *Byzantium: Greatness and Decline*. New Brunswick, N.J.: Rutgers University Press, 1957.

Dolan, J. P. *History of The Reformation.* New York: Desclee, 1965.

Dunstan, J. L. *Protestantism.* Englewood Cliffs: N.J.: Prentice-Hall, 1961.

Dvornik, F. *Byzantium and the Roman Primacy.* New York: Fordham University Press, 1966.

Enslin, M. S. *Christian Beginnings.* New York: Harper & Row, 1956.

Glover, R. H. *The Progress of World-Wide Missions.* Rev. & enl. ed. by J. H. Kane. New York: Harper & Row, 1960.

Goppelt, L. *Apostolic and Post-Apostolic Times.* New York: Harper & Row, 1970.

Grollenberg, L. *Jesus.* Philadelphia: Westminster Press, 1978.

Gustafson, J. M. *Can Ethics Be Christian?* Chicago: University of Chicago Press, 1975.

Hackel, S. *The Orthodox Church.* London: Ward Lock Educational, 1971.

Herrin, J. *The Formation of Christendom.* Princeton, N.J.: Princeton University Press, 1987.

Hillerbrand, H. *The Reformation.* New York: Harper & Row, 1964.

Hopkins, C. H. *History of the Y.M.C.A. in North America.* New York: Association Press, 1951.

Hudson, W. S. *Religion in America.* 2nd ed. New York: Scribner's, 1973.

Hughes, P. *A Short History of the Catholic Church.* 8th ed. London: Burns & Oates, 1978.

Hussey, J. M. *The Byzantine World.* New York: Harper Torchbooks, 1961.

Kee, H. C. *The Origins of Christianity.* Englewood Cliffs, N.J.: Prentice-Hall, 1973.

Kelly, J. N. D. *Early Christian Doctrines.* London: Adam & Charles Black, 1958.

Latourette, K. S. *A History of Christianity.* 2 vols. New York: Harper & Row, 1975.

Leeming, B. *Principles of Sacramental Theology.* Westminster, Eng.: Newman Press, 1956.

Lieu, S. N. C. *Manichaeism in the Latter Roman Empire and Medieval China: A Historical Survey.* Manchester, Eng.: Manchester University Press, 1985.

Littell, F. *The Origins of Sectarian Protestantism.* New York: Macmillan, 1968.

Marty, M. E. *Protestantism.* New York: Doubleday, 1974.

McGrath, A. M. *What a Modern Catholic Believes About Women.* Chicago: Thomas More Association, 1972.

McKenzie, J. L. *The Roman Catholic Church.* New York: Doubleday, 1969.

Neill, S. *A History of Christian Missions.* Harmondsworth, Eng.: Penguin Books, 1975.

Ostrogorsky, G. *History of the Byzantine State.* Oxford, Eng.: Basil Blackwell, 1956.

Powers, J. M. *Eucharistic Theology.* New York: Herder & Herder, 1967.

Rahner, K. *Foundations of Christian Faith.* New York: Seabury Press, 1978.

Reuther, R. R. (ed.). *Religion and Sexism: Images of Women in the Jewish and Christian Traditions.* New York: Simon & Schuster, 1974.

Robinson, J. M. *A New Quest for the Historical Jesus.* London: SCM Press, 1961.

Runciman, S. *The Fall of Constantinople, 1453.* Cambridge, Eng.: Cambridge University Press, 1969.

——. *A History of the Crusades.* 3 vols. Cambridge, Eng.: Cambridge University Press, 1951–1954.

Sanders, E. P. *Paul and Palestinian Judaism.* Philadelphia: Fortress Press, 1977.

Schlette, H. R. *Towards a Theology of Religions.* London: Herder & Herder, 1966.

Schweitzer, A. *The Quest of the Historical Jesus.* New York: Macmillan, 1968.

Smith, W. C. *Towards a World Theology.* New York: Macmillan, 1981.

Song, R. H. *The Sacred Congregation for the Propagation of the Faith.* Washington, D.C.: Catholic University of America, 1961.

Southern, R. W. *Western Society and the Church in the Middle Ages.* Harmondsworth, Eng.: Penguin Books, 1970.

Spitz, L. W. *The Protestant Reformation.* Englewood Cliffs, N.J.: Prentice-Hall, 1966.

Stendhall, K. *Paul Among Jews and Gentiles.* Philadelphia: Fortress Press, 1976.

Todd, J. M. *Catholicism and the Ecumenical Movement.* New York: Longmans, Green, 1956.

Vasiliev, A. A. *History of the Byzantine Empire 324–1453.* Madison, Wis.: University of Wisconsin Press, 1952.

Vermes, G. *Jesus the Jew.* London: Fontana Press, 1976.

von Campenhausen, H. *The Formation of the Christian Bible.* Philadelphia: Fortress Press, 1972.

Ware, T. *The Orthodox Church.* Harmondsworth, Eng.: Penguin Books, 1963.

Widengren, G. *Mani and Manichaeism.* New York: Holt, Rinehart & Winston, 1965.

Zernov, N. *The Russians and Their Church.* 3rd ed. London: SPCK, 1978.

Chapter 14 Islam

Abdal-Ati, H. *The Family Structure in Islam.* Plainfield, N.J.: American Trust, 1977.

Abdul-Rauf, M. *The Islamic View of Women and the Family.* New York: Speller, 1977.

Alderson, A. D. *The Structure of the Ottoman Dynasty.* Oxford, Eng.: Clarendon Press, 1956.

Andrae, T. *Mohammed: The Man and His Faith.* New York: Harper & Row, 1960.

Arberry, A. J. *Sufism.* London: Allen & Unwin, 1950.

—— (ed.). *Religion in the Middle East: Three Religions in Concord and Conflict.* 2 vols. London: Cambridge University Press, 1969.

Arnold, T. *The Caliphate.* Oxford, Eng.: Clarendon Press, 1924.

Ayoub, M. M. *Redemptive Suffering in Islam.* The Hague, Netherlands: Mouton, 1978.

Azizullah, M. *Glimpses of the Hadith.* Takoma Park, Md.: Crescent Public, 1973.

Bakhtiar, L. *Sufi Expressions of the Mystic Quest.* New York: Avon Books, 1976.

Beck, L. & N. Keddie (eds.). *Women in the Muslim World.* Cambridge, Mass.: Harvard University Press, 1978.

Bell, R. *The Origin of Islam in Its Christian Environment.* London: Macmillan, 1926.

Blunt, W. *Splendors of Islam.* New York: Viking Press, 1976.

Bosworth, C. E. *The Islamic Dynasties.* Edinburgh, Scot.: Edinburgh University Press, 1967.

Bravmann, M. M. *The Spiritual Background of Early Islam.* Leiden, Netherlands: Brill, 1972.

Brockelmann, C. *History of the Islamic Peoples.* New York: Capricorn Books, 1973.

Coulson, N. *A History of Islamic Law.* Edinburgh, Scot.: Edinburgh University Press, 1964.

Daniel, N. *Islam and the West.* Edinburgh, Scot.: Edinburgh University Press, 1966.

Dawood, N. J. *The Koran.* Middlesex, Eng.: Penguin Books, 1959.

Doe, B. *Southern Arabia.* London: Thames & Hudson, 1971.

Donaldson, D. M. *The Shi'ite Religion.* London: Luzac, 1933.

Edwards, E. M. & H. L. O. Garrett. *Mughal Rule in India.* Delhi, India: S. Chand, 1956.

Ezzati, A. F. *An Introduction to the History of the Spread of Islam.* London: Ludo Press, 1976.

Friedlander, I. *The Whirling Dervishes.* New York: Collier Books, 1975.

Gibb, H. A. R. *Modern Trends in Islam.* New York: Octagon Press, 1972.

Glubb, J. B. *The Life and Times of Muhammed.* London: Hodder & Stoughton, 1970.

Goldziher, I. *Muslim Studies.* 2 vols. London: Allen & Unwin, 1967–1971.

Grube, E. J. *The World of Islam.* London, Eng.: Hamlyn, 1967.

Guillaume, A. *The Life of Muhammed.* London: Oxford University Press, 1955.

Hitti, P. K. *History of the Arabs.* London: Macmillan, 1964.

Hodgson, M. G. S. *The Venture of Islam.* 3 vols. Chicago: University of Chicago Press, 1974.

Hollister, J. N. *The Shi'a of India.* London: Luzac, 1953.

Hourani, A. *Western Attitudes Towards Islam.* Southampton, Eng.: Southampton University Press, 1974.

Ikram, S. M. *Muslim Civilization in India.* New York: Columbia University Press, 1964.

Ivanov, W. *Brief Survey of Evolution of Ismailism.* Leiden, Netherlands: Brill, 1952.

Jameelah, M. *Islam Versus the West.* Lahore, Pakistan: Kazi Publications, 1968.

Jomier, J. *The Bible and the Koran.* Chicago: Regnery, 1967.

Juynboll, G. H. A. *The Authenticity of the Tradition Literature.* Leiden, Netherlands: Brill, 1969.

Katsh, A. I. *Judaism in Islam.* New York: Bloch, 1954.

Kelen, B. *Muhammed: The Messenger of God.* Nashville, Tenn.: Nelson, 1975.

Lammens, H. *Islam, Beliefs and Institutions.* London: Methuen, 1929.

Lewis, B. (ed.). *The World of Islam: Faith, People, Culture.* London: Thames & Hudson, 1976.

Mahmasani, S. *The Philosophy of Jurisprudence in Islam.* Leiden, Netherlands: Brill, 1962.

Miller, W. *The Ottoman Empire and Its Successors, 1801–1927.* Cambridge, Eng.: Cambridge University Press, 1936.

Nasr, S. H. *Shi'ite Islam.* Albany, N.Y.: SUNY Press, 1974.

———. *Ideals and Realities of Islam.* Boston: Beacon Press, 1972.

Nigosian, S. A. *Islam: The Way of Submission.* Northants, Eng.: Thorsons, 1987.

Padwick, C. E. *Muslim Devotions.* London: SPCK, 1961.

Peters, F. E. *Allah's Commonwealth.* New York: Simon & Schuster, 1973.

Pickthall, M. *The Meaning of the Glorious Koran.* New York: Mentor, 1953.

Pullapilly, C. K. (ed.). *Islam in the Contemporary World.* Notre Dame, Ill.: Cross Roads Books, 1980.

Rahman, F. *Islam.* New York: Holt, Rinehart & Winston, 1966.

Rodinson, M. *Mohammed.* Harmondsworth, Eng.: Penguin Books, 1973.

Rosenthal, E. I. J. *Islam in the Modern National State.* Cambridge, Eng.: Cambridge University Press, 1965.

Schacht, J. & C. E. Bosworth. *The Legacy of Islam.* 2nd ed. Oxford, Eng.: Oxford University Press, 1974.

Schimmel, A. *Mystical Dimensions of Islam.* Chapel Hill, N.C.: University of North Carolina Press, 1975.

Schuon, F. *Understanding Islam.* London: Allen & Unwin, 1963.

Shah, I. *The Sufis.* Garden City, N.Y.: Doubleday, 1971.

Smith, J. I. *The Islamic Understanding of Death and Resurrection.* Albany, N.Y.: SUNY, 1981.

———. *Women in Contemporary Muslim Societies.* Lewisburg, Pa.: Bucknell University Press, 1979.

Smith, M. *The Sufi Path of Love.* London: Luzac, 1954.

Smith, W. C. *Islam in Modern History.* New York: New American Library, 1957.

Spear, P. *Twilight of the Mughals.* London: Cambridge University Press, 1951.

Spuler, B. *The Muslim World.* Leiden, Netherlands: Brill, 1960.

Sugana, G. M. *The Life and Times of Muhammed.* London: Hamlyn, 1969.

Sweetman, J. W. *Islam and Christian Theology.* 2 vols. London: Lutterworth Press, 1945–1955.

Trimingham, J. S. *The Sufi Orders in Islam.* London: Oxford University Press, 1970.

Tritton, A. S. *Islam: Belief and Practices.* London: Hutchinson's University Library, 1951.

von Grunebaum, G. E. *Modern Islam: The Search for Cultural Identity*. Berkeley, Calif.: University of California Press, 1962.

————. *Unity and Variety in Muslim Civilization*. Chicago: University of Chicago Press, 1955.

————. *Muhammadan Festivals*. New York: Schuman, 1951.

Watt, W. M. *Islamic Philosophy and Theology*. Edinburgh, Scot.: Edinburgh University Press, 1962.

————. *Muhammad: Prophet and Statesman*. London: Oxford University Press, 1961.

Wolfson, H. A. *The Philosophy of the Kalams*. 2 vols. Cambridge, Mass.: Cambridge University Press, 1970.

Chapter 15 Baha'i

Afnan, R. M. *The Revelation of Bahaullah and the Bab*. New York: Philosophical Library, 1970.

Esslemont, J. E. *Baha'u'llah and the New Era*. Wilmette, Ill.: Baha'i Books, 1976.

Faizi, G. *The Baha'i Faith*. Wilmette, Ill.: Baha'i Books, 1975.

Gaver, J. *Baha'i Faith*. New York: Award Books, 1968.

Martin, J. D. & W. S. Hatcher. *The Baha'i Faith: The Emerging Global Religion*. New York: Harper & Row, 1985.

Miller, W. M. *Baha'ism: Its History and Teachings*. Pasadena, Calif.: Carey Library, 1974.

Townshend, G. *The Promise of All Ages*. Oxford, Eng.: Ronald Press, 1972.

Chapter 16 Religion in Global Perspective

New Religious Movements

Burrell, M. C. *The Challenge of the Cults*. Grand Rapids, Iowa: Baker Book House, 1985.

Ellwood, R. S. *Religious and Spiritual Groups in Modern America*. Englewood Cliffs, N.J.: Prentice-Hall, 1973.

Glock, C. Y. & R. N. Bellah (eds.). *The New Religious Consciousness*. Berkeley, Calif.: University of California Press, 1976.

Harper, M. H. *Gurus, Swamis and Avataras*. Philadelphia: Westminster Press, 1972.

Needleman, J. *The New Religions*. Garden City, N.Y.: Doubleday, 1970.

Zaretsky, I. I. & M. P. Leone (eds.). *Religious Movements in Contemporary America*. Princeton, N.J.: Princeton University Press, 1974.

Comparative Religion

Anderson, J. N. D. *Christianity and Comparative Religion*. Downers Grove, Ill.: Inter-Varsity Press, 1970.

Bowman, J. (ed). *Comparative Religion*. Leiden, Netherlands: E. J. Brill, 1972.

Burch, G. B. *Alternative Goals in Religion: Love, Freedom, Truth*. Montreal, Canada: McGill-Queen's University Press, 1972.

Cave, S. *Christianity and Some Religions of the East*. London: Duckworth, 1949.

De Silva, L. A. *Problem of the Self in Buddhism and Christianity*. New York: Barnes & Noble, 1979.

Eliade, M. *Patterns in Comparative Religion*. New York: Meridian, 1963.

Eliade, M. and J. Kitagawa. *The History of Religions: Essays in Methodology*. Chicago: University of Chicago Press, 1959.

James, E. O. *Comparative Religion*. 2nd ed. London: Methuen, 1961.

———. *Christianity and other Religions*. London: Hodder & Stoughton, 1968.

James, W. *The Varieties of Religious Experience*. New York: Collier Books, 1970.

King, W. *Buddhism and Christianity: Some Bridges of Understanding*. Philadelphia: Westminster, 1962.

Mountcastle, W. M. *Religion in Planetary Perspective*. Nashville, Tenn.: Abingdon, 1978.

Paden, W. E. *Religious Worlds. The Comparative Study of Religion*. Boston, Mass.: Beacon, 1988.

Parrinder, G. *Comparative Religion*. Westport, Conn.: Greenwood Press, 1975.

Samartha, S. J. (ed). *Living Faiths and Ultimate Goals. Salvation in World Religions*. Maryknoll, N.Y.: Orbis Books, 1974.

Schlette, H. R. *Towards a Theology of Religions*. London: Burns & Oates, 1966.

Schuon, F. *The Transcendent Unity of Religions*. New York: Harper & Row, 1975.

Smith, W. C. *Towards a World Theology*. Philadelphia: Westminster, 1981.

Wach, J. *Types of Religious Experience. Christian and Non-Christian*. Chicago: University of Chicago Press, 1951.

———. *The Comparative Study of Religions*. Columbia: Columbia University Press, 1958.

Watt, W. M. *Truth in the Religions*. Edinburgh: Edinburgh University Press, 1963.

Whitson, R. E. *The Coming Convergence of World Religions*. New York: Newman Press, 1971.

Zaehner, R. C. *The Comparison of Religions*. Boston, Mass.: Beacon, 1958.

Index

Abdul Baha, 462, 466, 468, 469
Abraham, 323, 326, 344, 419–20, 424, 438, 442, 446, 447, 454, 464
Adi Granth. *See* Scriptures, Sikhism
Ahmadiya. *See* Groups, Islam
Ahriman, 306, 309–13, 318
Ahura Mazda. *See* God, Zoroastrian
Analects. *See* Scriptures, Confucian
Ancestors, 3, 21, 39–48, 57, 92, 104, 153, 178, 179, 180, 183–84, 196, 199, 205, 212, 213, 217, 218, 221, 225, 228, 231, 234, 238, 239, 328, 419
Angels, 297, 301, 303, 336, 337, 354, 420, 424, 437, 438, 442, 443, 446, 475, 478
Anglican. *See* Groups, in Christianity
Apocalyptic literature, 350–51
Apocrypha, 371

Ascetics, 75, 91, 109, 111, 117, 119, 121, 126, 129, 153, 158–60, 164, 237, 277, 343, 374, 388, 452
Ashkenazim. *See* Groups, in Judaism
Ashrama, 90–91
Asoka, 109, 120, 134–35, 153
Augustine, 1, 387
Avatar. *See* Incarnation
Avesta. *See* Scriptures, Zoroastrian
Awareness, 4, 147, 471–73

Bab, 460, 468, 469
Baha'u'llah, 459, 460–62, 464, 465, 466, 468, 469
Bhagavad Gita. *See* Scriptures, Hindu
Bhakti Marga, 96–98
Bible. *See* Scriptures
Bodhidharma, 147
Bodhisattva, 144, 148, 152
Brahman-Atman. *See* God, Hindu

Brahmin. *See* Priests, priestesses, Hindu
Buddha, 386, 464
  childhood, 120–21, 143, 152, 154nn. 3, 4
  deified, 144
  enlightened, 119, 123–24, 143
  founder of Buddhism, 109, 119, 124–26
  mission, 121–24
  quest, 121–24, 143
  reincarnated, 143
  teachings, 124–32, 151
  temptations, 123
  worshiped, 143, 144, 147, 150–51

Caliph
  Abu Bakr, 424–25, 451
  'Ali, 425, 451, 454, 456, 460
  Mu'awiyah, 425
  'Umar, 425
  'Uthman, 425, 437
Caliphate
  'Abbasid, 428
  abolishment of, 433–34
  Mongol, 112, 428–29
  Mughal, 112, 166, 167, 169, 170, 175, 430
  Ottoman, 429–30
  rival Caliphates, 428, 433
  Umayyad, 427
Canaanites, 324–25, 326, 328, 341
Caste, 76, 88–89, 101, 104, 115–17, 120, 127, 158, 159, 165, 176
Ch'an (Zen). *See* Groups, in Buddhism
Christ. *See* Jesus Christ
Chuang Tzu, 186–87, 190, 191
Circumcision, 47, 338, 356, 374, 385, 453
Comparison of religions, 473–80
Confucius
  author, 180
  biography, 185, 186, 194–99
  founder of Confucianism, 185

honored, 206
mission, 198
teachings, 199–202
Consciousness, 4, 123, 127, 132, 159, 163, 218
Conservative Judaism. *See* Groups, in Judaism
Constantine, 386
Covenant, 192, 325, 329–30, 342, 353, 371, 385, 463, 469, 475
Creed, 388
  Buddhism, 151
  Christianity, 406–9
Crusades, 392, 428

Dalai Lama, 138–40
Deities. *See* God (gods, goddesses, deities)
Demons, 75, 123, 151, 152, 153, 181, 187, 250, 271–72, 297, 303, 332, 336, 337, 354
Dharma, 124, 127
Dialogue, 136, 405–6, 472
Divination, 29, 34, 42, 48–50, 56, 58, 68, 180, 182, 221, 224, 231, 234, 250, 293, 325, 332
Doctrine. *See* Teachings
Dreams, 3, 35, 49, 120, 136, 182, 190
Dualism, 64, 94, 145, 159, 163, 189–90, 292, 299, 303–4, 310, 318, 336

Eastern Orthodox. *See* Groups, in Christianity
Ecumenism, 401–2
Emancipation, 91–98
Emperor Worship, 182–83, 228, 229, 232, 234, 291–92, 369
Enlightenment, 119, 123–24, 147, 148, 150, 352, 397–400
Essene. *See* Groups, Judaism
Ethics, 2, 4, 7, 45, 159, 163, 219, 223, 230, 233, 336, 345, 354, 399, 475
Exile, 333–37, 344, 346, 370

Festivals
Baha'i, 469
Buddhist, 152–53
Christian, 412–14
Egyptian, 262–63
Greek, 274–75
Hindu, 106–9
Islamic, 454–56
Judaic, 358–60, 377, 378
Mesopotamian, 250–51
Roman, 283–85
Shinto, 240–41
Sikh, 175
Taoist and Confucian, 212–14
Yoruban, 38
Zoroastrian, 317
Five Pillars of Islam, 445–48
Freud, Sigmund, 3, 259

Gandhi, Mahatma, 104, 113–15, 170
Gautama, Siddhartha. *See* Buddha
Ghosts, 3, 35, 72–73, 184, 212
Gilgamesh, 252–53
God (gods, goddesses, deities)
African, 39–44
Baha'i, 459, 461, 463–66, 468
Canaanite, 324–25, 330–32
Christian, 377–85, 403, 408–10,
476–77
Dinka, 35–37
Egyptian, 255–59
Greek, 265–72
Hindu, 75, 79–88, 93–109, 115,
127, 478
Islamic, 417–18, 439, 442–50,
451, 454, 475–76, 477
Jain, 165
Judaic, 326–39, 341–53, 475
Mayan, 57–58
Mesopotamian, 248–53
Philistine, 325
Roman, 280–82, 285–91, 338
Shinto, 218, 220, 221, 222, 223,
224, 228, 231, 232, 234, 236,
237, 238
Sikh, 171–72

Taoist and Confucian, 180–81,
211–14
Yoruban, 37–38
Zoroastrian, 297, 298, 301, 302,
303, 304, 306, 309–13, 318
Groups
in Buddhism, 132–33, 135, 139,
143–49, 152–53, 225
in Christianity, 388–90, 394,
396–97, 401–2, 410–14
in Hinduism, 99–101, 111–13
in Islam, 424, 425, 436, 450–53,
460
in Jainism, 160–62
in Judaism, 339–40, 348, 353–56,
357, 358, 360, 362, 366, 370,
381
in Shinto, 227–29, 231–39
in Sikhism, 172–73
in Taoism, 192–94
in Zoroastrianism, 318
Gurdwara, 166, 171, 173, 175
Guru, 4, 90, 166, 168–75

Hadith, 441–42
Hasidic. *See* Groups, in Judaism
Heaven, 42–44, 144, 146, 183, 192,
196, 201, 220, 260–61, 297,
301, 311–13, 318, 329, 343,
354, 376, 379, 380, 387, 409,
410, 438, 443, 456, 465, 466,
475, 478
Heavenly Masters, 192–94
Hell, 144, 146, 260–61, 297, 311–
13, 318, 354, 408, 443, 444,
456, 465, 466, 478
Heroes, 271–72, 308
Hijrah, 421
History of religions
African, 28–34
American Indian, 53–55, 72–
73
Aztec, 59–60
Baha'i, 459–63
Buddhism, 119, 132–42
Chinese, 178–79, 184–85

History of religions *(continued)*
  Christianity, 32–34, 385–406
  Confucianism, 194–96, 203–10
  Egyptian, 253–54
  Greek, 264–65
  Hinduism, 75–76, 109–15
  Islam, 32–34, 419, 421–37
  Jainism, 157
  Judaism, 360–65
  Mayan, 55–56
  Mesopotamian, 246–48
  Roman, 278–80
  Shinto, 220–31
  Sikhism, 166–67, 170–71, 175–76
  Taoism, 191–94
  Zoroastrianism, 298–99, 304–8,
    318–19
Holy Spirit, 336, 377, 408, 409,
    411, 476
Holy War, 392, 436, 444, 448
Homer, 267–69

Imam, 4, 451, 452, 454, 455, 460
Incarnation
  Jesus Christ, 377, 409
  Krishna, 80, 96–97, 106, 108–9
  Mahavira, 159
  Vishnu, 99
Inquisition, 394
Ismaili. *See* Groups, in Islam

Jesus Christ, 113, 369, 370, 382,
    386, 403, 411, 412, 413, 438,
    464, 475
  biography, 373–77
  incarnation, 377, 476
  in Islam, 420, 438, 442, 477
  mission, 375–76, 414 n.1
  resurrection and ascension, 287,
    376–77, 384, 385, 409, 410,
    438
  Son of God, 376, 377, 380, 408,
    409, 476, 477
  sources, 372–73
  teachings, 377–82
Jihad. *See* Holy War

Jnana Marga, 93–96
Judgment
  Baha'i, 465
  Christianity, 374, 399
  Islam, 439, 442, 443, 478
  Judaism, 333, 337, 345, 351
  Sikhism, 172
  Taoism, 189
  Zoroastrianism, 297, 310–11

Ka'ba, 419, 420, 446, 447, 448
Kabir, 112, 167
Kami, 218, 220, 221–22, 225, 231,
    232, 233, 234, 236, 238, 240,
    241
Karma, 86–89, 117, 127, 158, 159,
    163–64, 479
Karma Marga, 92–93
Khalsa, 170, 173, 174
Kharijii. *See* Groups, in Islam
Koan, 148
Krishna, 80, 96–97, 106, 108–9

Lao Tzu, 185–86, 192
Law, 4, 5, 45, 78, 86, 116, 190,
    200, 236, 247, 255, 314, 334,
    349, 418
Luther, Martin, 396, 412

Madhva, 95–96
Madhyamika. *See* Groups, in
    Buddhism
Magi, 302, 413
Magic, 18, 20–23, 34, 49, 58–59,
    62, 68, 75, 77, 100, 150,
    188, 217, 221, 238, 239, 250,
    263, 271, 282–83, 293, 332,
    354, 472
Mahavira, 109, 157–59
Mahayana. *See* Groups, in Buddh-
    ism
Mani, 307, 386–88
Mantra, 82, 106, 108, 148
Marx, Karl, 3, 399

Mary, the Virgin, 373, 408, 409, 412
Mencius, 203–4
Messiah, 192, 297, 337, 352, 370, 373, 374, 380, 438, 439, 460, 477
See also Savior
Messianic (concept), 192, 194, 336, 350, 352, 355, 362, 364–65, 370, 477
Midrash, 348–50
Missionary, 31, 60, 113, 134–40, 225, 226, 227, 236, 371, 385, 397, 468
Monastics, 133, 141, 143, 144, 178, 343, 370, 388
Monotheism, 75, 259, 292, 293, 318, 326, 327, 423
Morals, 2, 4, 5, 7, 44–45, 69, 72, 75, 160, 165, 167, 189, 190, 196, 200, 201, 207, 223, 234, 333, 343, 345, 349, 423, 441, 444, 472, 478
Moses, 247, 259, 279, 349, 420, 438, 442, 464
author, 341
biography, 327–30
law-giver, 329–30, 360, 371
leader, 323, 326, 341
liberator, 328
Mosque, 4, 27, 445, 454
Muhammad, 425, 437, 441, 442, 443, 445, 446, 447, 450, 455, 456, 460, 464
characterization, 417–18
childhood, 419–20
establishment of community, 421–24
family, 34, 451
in Hadith, 441
mission, 420–21, 447
revelation, 420–21
Muharram, 455–56
Müller, Friedrich Max, 3
Mystery religions, 275–77, 286–91, 293, 369

Mystics, 4, 75, 100, 112, 121, 148, 149, 191, 194, 207, 275, 276, 354, 355, 362, 452
Mythology
African, 42–44
American Indian, 64–65
definition of, 293
Dinka, 35–37
Egyptian, 264
Greek, 277–78
Hindu, 79
Mesopotamian, 251–53
Shinto, 220
Yoruban, 37–38

Nagarjuna, 145
Nanak, 112, 167–68, 171
New Year
Baha'i, 469
Hindu, 107–8
Judaic, 358
Mesopotamian, 250–51
Shinto, 240–41
Taoist and Confucian, 211, 212–13
Zoroastrian, 317, 318
Nirvana, 128, 131–32, 143–44, 152–53
Numina, 280–81
Nuns, 137, 141, 151, 164, 388, 408

Observances
African, 45–50
American Indian, 65–69
Aztec, 61–62
Baha'i, 466, 468–69
Buddhist, 149–53
Christian, 410–14
Hindu, 104–9
Islamic, 445–50, 453–54
Jain, 164–66
Judaic, 356–60
Mayan, 58–59
Shinto, 239–42
Sikh, 173–75

Observances *(continued)*
Taoist and Confucian, 210–14
Zoroastrian, 313–17
Occultism
African, 48–50
Aztec, 62
Buddhist, 148
Dinka, 35
Egyptian, 263
Hindu, 100–101
Islamic, 453
Judaic, 332, 333, 354
Mayan, 58
Mesopotamian, 250
Shinto, 221, 236, 237, 238
Taoist, 194
Oracles, 239, 250, 267, 272–74,
293, 332, 344
Oriental Orthodox. *See* Groups, in
Christianity
Orthodox Judaism. *See* Groups, in
Judaism

Patanjali, 94
Patriarchates, 389, 390, 425
Paul, 371, 372, 382–85
Persecution
of American Indians, 73, 395
of Aztecs, 60, 395
of Baha'i, 460–61
of Buddhism, 137–38, 227, 306–
7
of Christianity, 226–27, 306–7,
384, 385–86, 387, 388, 396
of Confucianism, 204–6
of heretics, 394, 395, 431
of Hinduism, 112, 306–7
of Islam, 394, 430
of Judaism, 306–7, 338–40, 360–
62, 394–95
of Manicheism, 306–7, 386–88,
394, 431–32
of Mayans, 53
of Mazdakism, 306–7
of pagans, 431
of Sikhism, 169–71

of Taoism, 192
of Zoroastrianism, 307–8
Pharaoh, 253–55, 259, 262, 263,
323, 328
Pharisee. *See* Groups, in Judaism
Philistines, 324, 325
Pilgrimage
Buddhist, 151
Hindu, 106
Islamic, 424, 435, 446–48, 452,
454
Shinto, 234–239
Plato, 270–71
Pope, 390, 392, 395, 411, 412
Leo I, 387
Urban II, 392
Powwow, 73
Prehistoric
artwork, 22–24
bear skulls, 19–20
civilization, 26
corpses, 20–22, 24
human skulls, 17–18, 20, 23
monuments, 24–26
religion, 17–26
tombs, 24–26
Priests, priestesses
African, 45
American Indian, 68–69
Aztec, 62
Buddhist, 224, 239
Christian, 391, 394, 408
Egyptian, 257, 262
Greek, 273
Hindu, 77, 88–89, 91, 106,
109, 111, 120, 121, 127,
157
Judaic, 334–35, 341, 365, 381
(*See also* Rabbi)
Mayan, 58
Mesopotamian, 250, 251
Roman, 282–83
Shinto, 224, 228, 230, 239
Sikh, 176
Taoist, 191, 194
Yoruban, 37

Zoroastrian, 299, 300, 302, 303, 305, 314, 315, 316, 317, 319
Prophet
  African, 45
  Baha'i, 461, 464, 468
  Islamic, 417, 418, 419–20, 421, 425, 438, 441, 442, 443, 445, 447, 454, 455, 456, 460
  Judaic, 332–33, 340, 341, 342, 344–46, 378
  Protestant. *See* Groups, in Christianity
Pure Land. *See* Groups, in Buddhism
Pyramid, 55–57, 251, 255, 258, 260, 261–62

Qur'an. *See* Scriptures, Islamic

Rabbi, 334, 335, 348, 349, 350, 351, 354, 365, 366, 374, 475
Radhakrishnan, 113, 404
Ramadan, 446, 454
Ramakrishna, 109, 113, 404
Ramanuja, 95–96
Reality, 4, 5, 83–85, 95–96, 99, 109, 115, 145, 157, 159, 163, 190–91
  See also Truth
Rebirth
  African, 37
  American Indian, 72
  Buddhist, 126–32, 144, 146, 150
  Greek, 277
  Hindu, 85–88, 100, 109, 126, 479
  Jain, 159, 163–64
  Sikh, 172
  Taoist, 192
  See also Incarnation
Reconstructionist. *See* Groups, in Judaism
Reformation, 395–97, 412
Reform Judaism. *See* Groups, in Judaism
Reincarnation. *See* Rebirth

Religion
  approaches and goals of, 7–14, 473–80
  comparison of, 473–80
  definitions of, 1–6
  etymology of, 1–2
  history of, 7
  origin of, 3, 17, 28
  phenomenology of, 8
  philosophy of, 7
  psychology of, 8
  sociology of, 7–8
  study of, 6–15
Religious encounters, 32–34, 112–15, 223–28, 472–73
Religious pluralism, 402–6, 480
Remus, 278–79
Resurrection, 5, 369, 478
  of Attis, 287
  in Islam, 443
  of Christ, 287, 376–77, 384, 385, 409, 410, 438
  in Judaism, 336, 337, 351, 376
  of Marduk, 251
  of Osiris, 258–59, 288
  in Zoroastrianism, 297, 310–11
Revelation, 4, 7, 34, 166, 168, 192, 239, 301, 336, 352, 354, 387, 399, 437, 443, 476
Roman Catholic. *See* Groups, in Christianity
Romulus, 278–79

Sacraments, 410–12
Sacred pipe, 65, 68
Sacrifice
  African, 45–46
  Aztec, 61–62
  Buddhist, 149
  Canaanite, 325
  Dinka, 36
  Greek, 274
  Hindu, 77, 78, 81–82, 89, 92, 119, 127, 157
  Islamic, 453, 454
  Judaic, 331, 332

Sacrifice *(continued)*
  Mayan, 58
  Mesopotamian, 250
  Prehistoric, 20, 21
  Taoist and Confucian, 182, 183,
    184, 196, 202
  Yoruban, 38
  Zoroastrian, 299
Sadducee. *See* Groups, in Judaism
Sages, 4, 120, 201
Saints, 272, 354, 411, 412
Salvation, 72, 290, 310, 377, 396,
    404, 409, 476, 477
Samsara. *See* Rebirth, Hindu
Sangha, 124–26
Sankara, 95–96
Sargon (King), 247
Satan, 123, 297, 336, 337, 375,
    438, 442, 479
Sati (Satee), 111, 117
Savior, 312, 369, 370, 384
  See also Messiah
Scriptures
  Baha'i, 463, 468, 469
  Buddhist, 119, 132, 137, 139,
    142–44, 147, 155n. 14
  Chinese, 179–80, 197, 202–3
  Christian, 33, 76, 340, 370, 371–
    73, 381, 388, 411, 443
  Confucian, 199, 202–3, 206
  Hindu, 76–79, 96–98, 127, 159,
    167, 309
  Islamic, 33, 76, 167, 436, 437–
    41, 452, 454
  Jain, 162
  Judaic, 335, 338, 339, 340–48,
    352, 353, 354, 358, 359, 360,
    365, 366, 371, 376, 381, 384,
    385, 438, 443, 475, 477
  Shinto, 219–20, 233, 234
  Sikh, 171, 172, 173, 174, 175
  Taoist, 186–88
  Zoroastrian, 308–9
Sectarian Shinto. *See* Groups, in
    Shinto
Sects. *See* Groups

Sephardim. *See* Groups, in Juda-
    ism
Shari'ah, 418, 436, 449–50
Shi'ite. *See* Groups, in Islam
Shoghi Effendi, 463, 464, 468
Shrine, 4, 29, 36, 37, 46, 48, 101,
    106, 137, 150, 152, 162, 183,
    211, 212, 221, 224, 227, 229,
    231–33, 234, 236, 237, 238,
    239, 240, 241, 452, 455, 462,
    466, 469
Shrine Shinto. *See* Groups, in
    Shinto
Sin, 381–85, 409, 410, 476, 477
Skandhas, 127
Soul, 3, 57, 72, 84, 163–64, 172,
    184, 212, 234, 241, 301, 304,
    310, 312, 354, 442, 465, 479
Spirits, 3, 35–50, 63–65, 101, 153,
    180–81, 182, 183, 184, 201,
    212, 217, 218, 223, 231, 236,
    238, 250, 271, 292, 303, 304,
    337
  See also Holy Spirit
State Shinto. *See* Groups, in
    Shinto
Sufi. *See* Groups, in Islam
Sunni. *See* Groups, in Islam
Synagogue, 334, 352, 355, 356,
    358, 360, 365, 375, 395

Talmud, 348–50, 355, 356, 365,
    366, 475
Tantrism
  in Buddhism, 148–49
  in Hinduism, 100, 111
Tao, 2, 188–91, 194
Tao Te Ching. *See* Scriptures,
    Taoist
Teachings
  African, 39–45
  Aztec, 60–61
  Baha'i, 463–66
  Buddhist, 126–32, 143–49, 479
  Christian, 382–85, 396, 399,
    408–12

Confucian, 204–10
Dinka, 35–37
Hindu, 79–98, 100, 102, 319
Islamic, 442–44
Jain, 162–64
Judaic, 351–53
Manichee, 387
Mayan, 56–58
Sikh, 171–72
Taoist, 188–91
Yoruban, 37–38
Zoroastrian, 309–13
Theravada. *See* Groups, in Buddhism
Tibetan Buddhism, 138–40
T'ien-t'ai (Tendai). *See* Groups, in Buddhism
Tirthankara, 157–58, 162, 164, 165
Torah. *See* Scriptures, Judaic
Trickster, 63
Trinity, 409, 439, 442, 476
Truth, 4, 5, 83–85, 121–23, 124, 127–29, 145, 387, 392, 403, 404, 464
  See also Reality; Dharma

Umma, 34, 418, 424, 429, 430, 449
Uniate. *See* Groups, in Christianity

Universal House of Justice, 463, 464, 466, 468

Varna. *See* Caste
Vedas. *See* Scriptures, Hindu
Vision quest, 69
Vivekananda, 109, 113

Women
  in Buddhism, 140–41
  in Christianity, 406–8
  in Hinduism, 92, 115–17
  in Islam, 423, 430, 434–36, 453
  in Jainism, 160
  in Judaism, 355, 357, 365–67
  in Shinto, 230–31
  in Taoism and Confucianism, 208–10, 211

Yin-Yang, 181–82
Yoga, 94, 100, 104, 111, 120, 148, 157

Zealots. *See* Groups, in Judaism
Zen, 147–48, 225, 452
Zionism. *See* Groups, in Judaism
Zoroaster, 299–304, 318, 386, 464